"Mohlman, Deckersbach, and Weissman provide a splendid introduction to the neurocognitive perspective. They have selected top scholars to write thorough, thought-provoking overviews that are highly accessible and informative. Importantly, although this volume is organized around traditional diagnostic categories, it gently forces the reader to think in a transdisciplinary fashion. The resulting book brings us many steps closer to understanding fundamental processes that underlie individual differences in mental health symptoms and their effective treatment."

—*J. Gayle Beck*, *PhD, Lillian and Morrie Moss Chair of Excellence,*
Department of Psychology, University of Memphis

"This remarkable volume is a bold and much-needed step toward integrating and bridging neuroscience and clinical psychology. Drs. Mohlman, Deckersbach, and Weissman assembled an outstanding group of experts to pave the way for the next generation of a neuroscience-informed clinical psychology. A prime example for a cross-disciplinary approach, this excellent book is a must-read for any scientifically based mental health care professional."

—*Stefan G. Hofmann*, *PhD, Professor of Psychology, Department of Psychological*
and Brain Sciences, Boston University; Author of An Introduction to Modern CBT

"This book provides a fascinating look into how discoveries in basic science can be used to inform and improve psychological treatments for a wide range of mental health issues. The research reported in this book is at the forefront of the most exciting work in clinical psychology and provides fresh new ideas about how to develop state-of-the-art psychological treatments."

—*Christopher G. Beevers*, *PhD, Professor of Psychology and Director of the*
Institute for Mental Health Research, University of Texas at Austin

"This book bridges the gap between basic and clinical science and provides an important perspective for understanding the nature and treatment of psychiatric problems. The integrative neurocognitive viewpoint of this volume expertly examines theory and data in a way that offers an invaluable approach to mental health problems. From professional researchers and psychotherapists to students alike, the authors have done a superb job producing a text that will be indispensable for all students of mental health."

—*Rick Ingram*, *PhD, Director of Clinical Training,*
Department of Psychology, University of Kansas

D1519280

FROM SYMPTOM TO SYNAPSE

This edited volume bridges the gap between basic and applied science in understanding the nature and treatment of psychiatric disorders and mental health problems. The book discusses using brain imaging, physiological indices of emotion, cognitive enhancement strategies, neuropsychological and cognitive training, and related techniques as tools for increasing our understanding of anxiety, depression, addictions, schizophrenia, ADHD, and other disorders. Mental health professionals will learn how to integrate a neurocognitive perspective into their clinical research and practice of psychotherapy.

Jan Mohlman, PhD, is Associate Professor at William Paterson University.

Thilo Deckersbach, PhD, is Associate Professor of Psychology at Harvard Medical School.

Adam S. Weissman, PhD, is the Founder and Executive Director of Child & Family Cognitive Behavioral Psychology, PLLC in Scarsdale and Manhattan and is on the clinical faculty at Columbia University.

FROM SYMPTOM TO SYNAPSE

A Neurocognitive Perspective
on Clinical Psychology

*Edited by Jan Mohlman, Thilo Deckersbach,
and Adam S. Weissman*

NEW YORK AND LONDON

First published 2015
by Routledge
711 Third Avenue, New York, NY 10017

and by Routledge
27 Church Road, Hove, East Sussex BN3 2FA

Routledge is an imprint of the Taylor & Francis Group, an informa business

© 2015 Taylor & Francis

The right of the editors to be identified as the authors of the
editorial material, and of the authors for their individual chapters,
has been asserted in accordance with sections 77 and 78 of the
Copyright, Designs and Patents Act 1988.

All rights reserved. No part of this book may be reprinted
or reproduced or utilised in any form or by any electronic,
mechanical, or other means, now known or hereafter invented,
including photocopying and recording, or in any information
storage or retrieval system, without permission in writing from the
publishers.

Trademark notice: Product or corporate names may be trademarks
or registered trademarks, and are used only for identification and
explanation without intent to infringe.

Library of Congress Cataloging in Publication Data
From symptom to synapse : a neurocognitive perspective on
clinical psychology / [edited by] Jan Mohlman, Thilo Deckersbach,
Adam S. Weissman.
      p. ; cm.
  Includes bibliographical references and index.
  I. Mohlman, Jan, editor. II. Deckersbach, Thilo, 1969– , editor.
  III. Weissman, Adam S. (Adam Scott), 1980– , editor.
  [DNLM: 1. Mental Disorders—therapy. 2. Brain—
  physiopathology. 3. Cognition. 4. Neurobiology—methods.
  5. Psychology, Clinical—methods. 6. Psychotherapy. WM 400]
  RC467
  616.89-dc23   2014028099

ISBN: 978-0-415-83586-2 (hbk)
ISBN: 978-0-415-83587-9 (pbk)
ISBN: 978-0-203-50713-1 (ebk)

Typeset in Bembo
by HWA Text and Data Management, London

Printed and bound in the United States of America by Publishers Graphics,
LLC on sustainably sourced paper.

For David, Carol, and Kay.
J. M.

For my parents, Ina and Klaus Deckersbach, in memoriam.
T. D.

To my wonderful fiancée, Annie Denenberg.
To my loving sisters, Ilan and Jennifer Weissman.
In loving memory of Jonas and Marion Freeman, and Allen Salomon.
A. S. W.

CONTENTS

FIGURES

TABLES

ABOUT THE EDITORS

Jan Mohlman, PhD, is Associate Professor at William Paterson University. Dr. Mohlman's research seeks to explain how processes of aging (e.g., hearing loss, progressive brain disease, deficits in cognitive skills) impact the presentation and treatment of anxiety and other mood problems in later life. Dr. Mohlman's work also extends to treatment outcome research, applying methodology from affective and cognitive neuroscience to inform studies of cognitive behavior therapy. Dr. Mohlman has published peer-reviewed journal articles and book chapters and has won several research grants and teaching and mentoring awards.

Thilo Deckersbach, PhD, is Associate Professor of Psychology at Harvard Medical School. He serves as the Director of Psychology in the Bipolar Clinic and Research Program and as the Director of Research in the Division of Neurotherapeutics at the Massachusetts General Hospital in Boston. Dr. Deckersbach's research has been supported by the National Institute of Mental Health, NARSAD, TSA, OCF, and DBDAT. He has published peer-reviewed papers and book chapters. His neuroimaging research (fMRI and PET) focuses on the interaction of cognitive and emotional processes in bipolar disorder.

Adam S. Weissman, PhD, is the Founder and Executive Director of Child & Family Cognitive Behavioral Psychology, PLLC in Scarsdale and Manhattan. Formerly Senior Clinical Consultant at Harvard Medical School, Dr. Weissman is currently on the Clinical Faculty at Columbia University, where he trains and supervises advanced doctoral students in cognitive behavior therapy with children and adolescents. He is a nationally recognized expert in the treatment of a wide range of youth anxiety and mood disorders, ADHD, disruptive behavior problems, tic/habit disorders, and related conditions, and has published peer-reviewed articles, book chapters, and edited books, the majority focusing on cognitive-behavioral therapy and neuropsychological assessment for children and adolescents.

CONTRIBUTORS

Sherry A. Beaudreau
Department of Psychiatry and Behavioral Sciences, Palo Alto VA,
Stanford University of Medicine

Jennifer C. Britton
Department of Psychology, University of Miami

Amanda W. Calkins
Department of Psychiatry, Massachusetts General Hospital,
Harvard Medical School

Susanna W. Chang
Department of Psychiatry,
UCLA Semel Institute for Neuroscience and Human Behavior

Yun Chen
Department of Psychology, University of North Carolina-Chapel Hill

Allison P. Danzig
Child and Family Cognitive Behavioral Psychology, Stony Brook University

Stacey B. Daughters
Department of Psychology, University of North Carolina-Chapel Hill

Thilo Deckersbach
Department of Psychiatry, Massachusetts General Hospital,
Harvard Medical School

Rudi De Raedt
Department of Experimental Clinical and Health Psychology,
Ghent University

Christen M. Deveney
Department of Psychology, Wellesley College

Jill Ehrenreich-May
Department of Psychology, University of Miami

Stephanie M. Gorka
Department of Psychology, University of Illinois-Chicago

Natasha S. Hansen
University of Boulder, Colorado

Michael V. Hernandez
Department of Psychology, University of Miami

Navneet Kaur
Massachusetts General Hospital, Harvard Medical School, Tufts University

Sarah M. Kennedy
Department of Psychology, University of Miami

Maria Alexandra Kredlow
Department of Psychology, Boston University

Matthew M. Kurtz
Department of Psychology and Program in Neuroscience and Behavior,
Wesleyan University

Jocelyn Lichtin
Mount Sinai School of Medicine

John R. McQuaid
San Francisco VA Medical Center, UCSF

Jan Mohlman
Department of Psychology, William Paterson University

Samantha J. Moshier
Department of Psychological and Brain Sciences, Boston University

Michael W. Otto
Department of Psychological and Brain Sciences, Boston University

Rebecca B. Price
Department of Psychiatry, University of Pittsburgh School of Medicine

Alexander H. Queen
Department of Psychology, University of Miami

Ilana Seager
Department of Psychology, University of Miami

Greg Siegle
University of Pittsburgh School of Medicine

Carolyn N. Spiro
Department of Psychology, Rutgers University

Alexandra Sturm
Department of Education, Department of Psychiatry, UCLA

Adam S. Weissman
Child and Family Cognitive Behavioral Psychology, Columbia University

ACKNOWLEDGMENTS

We acknowledge the contributions of several individuals with deep gratitude. First, we would like to thank the talented authors and researchers who contributed to this book. They are at the forefront of clinical psychology and are steering the field in exciting new directions. We are profoundly inspired by their work and look forward to their next wave of research.

We would also like to thank the members of the Neurocognitive Therapies/ Translational Research Special Interest Group of the Association of Behavioral and Cognitive Therapies for motivating us to embark on this project. We are fortunate to have such innovative, engaged colleagues who helped us preserve this moment in the evolution of clinical psychology.

Every book goes through multiple stages of writing and editing. We extend special thanks to George Zimmar, Elizabeth Lotto, Dana Bliss, and the editorial staff at Routledge for their ongoing guidance in the completion of this volume. We are grateful for their knowledge and expertise.

Last, we thank the family members and friends who supported and encouraged us throughout the preparation of this book.

1

INTRODUCTION

Integrating Brain and Body Measures with the Study of Psychological Disorders

Jan Mohlman, Thilo Deckersbach, and Adam S. Weissman

The scientifically informed practice of clinical psychology has taken an innovative new direction and is gaining momentum. This progress is largely attributable to the integration of research in affective, cognitive, and behavioral neuroscience with traditional clinical psychology. The decade from 1990 until 2000, known as "the Decade of the Brain" (Library of Congress; www.loc.gov/loc/brain/), produced the first wave of empirical studies on the neural bases of psychopathology. This research was made possible by technical advances in methodology and tools such as functional magnetic resonance imaging (fMRI), neural tract tracing methods, and behavioral paradigms that correct cognitive deficits or protect against further decline. The knowledge gained during and subsequent to this period is now being applied for the first time to enhance the recognition and treatment of emotional disorders. As a result, the focus on integrating biological and psychological perspectives has never been stronger. This new approach has been termed the *neurocognitive perspective*.

The neurocognitive approach has opened fresh avenues for research and innovation in clinical practice. In the past, the typical clinical trial utilized self-report and clinician-rated measures of symptom severity as primary indices of outcome. However, more recently, strategies for assessing and treating disorders have been expanded to include cognitive and biological variables (e.g., executive functions, indices of neurobiology, aspects of brain function). For example, scholars have begun to examine symptom- and diagnosis-specific brain-behavior relations, linking distinct neurocognitive profiles to cognitive (e.g., worry, cognitive distortions), emotional (e.g., fear, rumination, depressed mood), and behavioral dysfunction (e.g., inattention, impulsivity, compulsive behaviors), as well as symptom severity, comorbidity, and treatment response. These connections have been found across a number of common clinical populations including anxiety disorders (e.g., Legerstee, Tulen, Dierckx, Treffers, Verhulst, & Utens, 2010; Matthews, Mogg, Kentish, & Eysenck, 1995; McClure et al., 2007; Mohlman & Gorman, 2005; Roy et al., 2008, Weissman, Chu, Reddy, & Mohlman, 2012); mood disorders (e.g., Deckersbach et al., 2010; Siegle, Carter, & Thase, 2006; Weissman & Bates, 2010); attention-deficit/hyperactivity disorder (ADHD; e.g., Barkley, 1997; Hale et al., 2009; Reddy & Hale, 2007); and disruptive behavior disorders (e.g., Clark, Prior, & Kinsella; 2002; Turgay, 2005). Recent studies have extended these findings, demonstrating the clinical utility of neurocognitive assessment in differential diagnosis and case formulation (Hale et al., 2011; Weissman et al., 2012) as well as the efficacy of cognitive-behavioral (e.g., Kuelz et al., 2006; Legerstee et al., 2010; Matthews et al., 1995; Mohlman & Gorman, 2005; Siegle et al., 2006); pharmacological (Hale, Fiorello, & Brown, 2005; Hale et al., 2011); and neurocognitive therapies (e.g., Kerns, Eso, & Thomson, 1999; Koster, Fox, & MacLeod, 2009; Vassilopoulos, Banerjee, & Prantzalou, 2009) in treating both affective and cognitive impairments in individuals with comorbid neuropsychological, emotional, and behavioral difficulties.

History, Evolution, and Professional Impact of the Neurocognitive Perspective

It is difficult to pinpoint exactly how and when the neurocognitive perspective on clinical psychology first emerged; however, there were harbingers of this trend in the late 1980s and early 1990s. These ideas emerged as occasional speculation by researchers working in cognitive and affective neuroscience and just beginning to consider the bridge to practice.

One early example of the neurocognitive perspective was the proposition that executive functions (skills governed by the frontal lobes of the brain) facilitate the successful use of cognitive behavioral techniques (e.g., Hariri, Bookheimer, & Mazziotta, 2000; Martin, Oren, & Boone, 1991; Posner & Rothbart, 1998). Executive skills and the prefrontal cortex are known to contribute to the regulation and management of emotion (Posner & Rothbart, 1998) through processes such as reappraisal and verbal rehearsal (Koenigsberg et al., 2009: Ochsner et al., 2002; Ochsner & Gross, 2008). Recent fMRI data and other methods of neuroimaging have indeed implicated these neural areas in the effortful regulation of emotion (Beauregard, Levesque, & Bourgouin, 2000; Hariri, Bookheimer, & Mazziotta, 2000).

Other signs of the emergence of the neurocognitive perspective can be found in the domains of scholarly publication, the research priorities of funding agencies, the focus of professional groups, and as a presence in graduate training curricula. For instance, a 2009 *Journal of Abnormal Psychology* special issue on cognitive bias modification provided initial evidence that cognitive training techniques such as attentional bias modification may be effective in (1) reducing selective attentional processing of threat and (2) mitigating associated real-world anxiety vulnerability and state, trait, and clinical anxiety symptom severity. Results reported in this special issue further suggested that attentional selectivity may not only play a causal role in the pathogenesis of anxiety disorders but may serve as an important mechanism of therapeutic change. Another example is the 2011 issue of *Clinical Psychology: Science and Practice*, which features a trio of articles discussing the process-based approach to research, diagnosis, and treatment of depression. Each article highlights the use of brain and body measures as new tools for facilitating mental health through the investigation of learned helplessness, which is mechanistically related to mood disorders.

The growing interest in clinical applications of neurocognitive measures has also permeated the clinical, education, and public health sectors (Reddy, Weissman, & Hale, 2013). Increased demands from third-party payers for efficient, cost-effective, and evidence-based assessments and interventions, along with heightened public awareness of the value of neuropsychological assessment for diagnosis and treatment planning, have increased the implementation and promotion of these techniques among mental health service providers and policy makers. Additionally, the proliferation of books on the use of neuropsychological assessment in clinical practice (e.g., Hale & Fiorello, 2004; Reddy et al., 2013) has contributed in part to changes in doctoral and postdoctoral education across the nation. Neuropsychology postdoctoral fellowships and institutes (e.g., Fielding Institute) have shown significant growth and are in high demand for advanced professional training. For example, a number of clinical, counseling, and school psychology doctoral and pre-doctoral internship programs are placing greater emphasis on didactic curricula and clinical training in neuropsychological assessment and neuroscience.

The research agenda promoted by the U.S. government has also shifted to emphasize clinical application and an interdisciplinary approach. For example, the Research Domain Criteria Project (RDoC), launched by the National Institute of Mental Health, is an ambitious call for researchers to develop, in essence, a transdiagnostic and neurocognitive system for classifying psychopathology. This new system would hinge upon basic mechanisms and dimensions of functioning that can be studied at different levels of analysis (e.g., neural, behavioral). Thus, rather than developing interventions that are disorder specific, the RDoC targets processes such as fear circuitry and attentional bias, which cut across disorders. On a global scale, the federal government (e.g., National Institutes of Mental Health, U.S. Department of Education Institute of Education Sciences) has begun to regard clinical-translation research as a priority area for empirical investigation and grant funding.

Recently, the first graduate training programs offering formal training in neurocognitive approaches have emerged. Teachers College Graduate Program in Neuroscience and Education focuses on the educational and clinical implications of recent advances in understanding brain-behavior relationships. One objective of the multidisciplinary program is to prepare a new kind of specialist: a professional with dual preparation able to bridge the gap between research on underlying brain, cognition, and behavior, and the problems encountered in clinical settings. A second objective is to provide rigorous training and relevant experiences that would allow students to further their knowledge and make links between neuroscience, cognition, and clinical practice.

Additionally, there are a number of professional meetings that focus on various topics of particular interest to those working from the neurocognitive framework, including the annual Wisconsin Symposium on Emotion and the Cognitive Remediation in Psychiatry conference held in New York. Efforts to formalize and advance the neurocognitive approach can also be seen in various professional groups. One of the first organized groups of clinical psychologists in the United States was likely to have been the Neurocognitive Therapies/ Translational Research Special Interest Group (Mohlman & Deckersbach, 2009) of the Association for the Behavioral and Cognitive Therapies. This cadre of approximately sixty-five researchers and clinicians has attempted to formalize the neurocognitive perspective and promote the use of brain and body measures through research symposia, clinical training workshops, published articles, and other means. Many of these individuals have authored chapters in this volume. Likewise, national organizations such as the American Psychological Association, National Academy of Neuropsychology, and Society for Neuroscience are recognizing the important influence of neuroscience and neuropsychological assessment in modifying interventions and developing innovative treatments.

Over the past few years, a number of books have been published that showcase the clinical use of neuropsychological assessment, neuroscience, and intervention (e.g., Borod, 2000; Castillo, 2008; Gross, 2007; Hunter & Donders, 2007; Riccio, Sullivan, & Cohen, 2010). These noteworthy texts have focused primarily on neuropsychological interventions with individuals with complex medical conditions (Castillo, 2008) and/or developmental and neurological disorders (Hunter & Donders, 2007; Noggle, Davis, & Barisa, 2008; Riccio et al., 2010). What is missing, however, is a comprehensive text that presents models integrating neuropsychological assessment, brain and body measures, and intervention for individuals with common emotional and behavioral disorders and related conditions across the life span. This volume serves to fill this critical void in the literature.

Benefits of the Neurocognitive Perspective: Conceptualizing and Assessing Emotional Disorders

There are many compelling reasons for developing a neurocognitive perspective of emotions and disorders. As noted by Rottenberg and Johnson (2007), emotion is a multidimensional construct, often conceptualized as a constellation of interacting behaviors, thoughts, and patterns of neural and physiological arousal. This structure begs for collaboration across psychological disciplines. With collaboration, researchers are exposed to new tools and the new ways of thinking to accompany those tools, and the opportunity to merge innovative ideas. A neurocognitive approach could aid in more refined definitions and characterizations of disparate and associated emotion states. Thus, bridging interdisciplinary gaps enhances knowledge of basic mechanisms of emotion and mood states. Such mechanisms might be prone to manipulation, which could benefit patients efficiently and effectively.

Another compelling reason for adopting a neurocognitive perspective is to better recognize and measure severity of symptoms, syndromes, and disorders. Many disorders in the *Diagnostic and Statistical Manual* (DSM5; American Psychiatric Association, 2013) are characterized by deficits in cognitive abilities and aberrant patterns of neural activation (Table 1.1); however, such variables have taken a distant backseat to mood symptoms in the diagnosis and measurement of clinical outcome.

One relevant example of how the neurocognitive perspective has contributed to our understanding of specific disorders can be found throughout the literature on obsessive compulsive disorder (OCD). In recent functional neuroimaging studies, distinct patterns of brain activation show an association with disparate OCD symptom dimensions (e.g., checking versus contamination; Deckersbach, Savage, & Rauch, 2009). In addition, in the child literature, research suggests that the use of neurocognitive methods may be appropriate to assess more general ADHD-related attention deficits versus more emotion-based, threat-related automatic biases in attention found in children with anxiety disorders (e.g., Puliafico & Kendall, 2006; Weissman et al., 2012). Consistent with this position, Weissman et al. (2012) found that ADHD youth demonstrated poorer performance on selective, sustained, and shifting attention relative to anxious youth, who exhibited greater attentional biases toward threatening facial cues, which could have implications for effective treatment, treatment matching, and the use of adjunctive neurocognitive techniques. For instance, executive attention training may be preferred for children with ADHD (Kerns et al., 1999), while attentional bias modification may be effective for children with anxiety disorders (Riemann, Amir, & Lake, 2010). In addition, pharmacological treatments may vary for these children based on whether the anxiety or ADHD symptoms predominate (e.g., Hale et al., 2005).

TABLE 1.1 Cognitive and neurobiological symptoms and associated DSM-IV disorders

Neurocognitive Symptom	Disorders Associated with Symptom
Trouble concentrating/paying attention	Generalized Anxiety Disorder
	Posttraumatic Stress Disorder
	Math and Test Anxiety
	Major Depressive Disorder
	Bipolar Disorder
	Attention Deficit Hyperactive Disorder
	Borderline Personality Disorder
	Psychotic Disorders
	Substance Intoxication and Withdrawal Syndromes
	Delirium
	Brain Fog and "Chemo Fog"
Difficulty making decisions	Major Depressive Disorder
	Dysthymic Disorder
	Bipolar Disorder
	Dependent Personality Disorder
Memory impairment	Posttraumatic Stress Disorder
	Dissociative Disorders
	Substance Intoxication, Withdrawal Syndromes
	Amnestic Disorders
	Dementias
Amygdalar overactivity	Major Depressive Disorder
	Anxiety Disorders
	Borderline Personality Disorder
Frontal lobe overactivity	Schizophrenia
	Obsessive Compulsive Disorder
	Generalized Anxiety Disorder
	Frontotemporal Dementia
Hippocampal atrophy	Posttraumatic Stress Disorder
	Major Depressive Disorder
	Schizophrenia
	Dementias

Benefits of the Neurocognitive Perspective: Optimizing Treatment

The neurocognitive perspective also affords benefits for treatment. Current interventions, while more effective than ever, still fall short of optimal effectiveness (Lazar, 2010). Given that pharmacotherapy and psychological interventions appear to act on different brain circuits (Goldapple et al., 2004), it was originally hoped that the combination of psychosocial and pharmacological strategies would lead to enhanced therapies for frequently occurring disorders such as anxiety and depression. However, especially for anxiety disorders, the majority of studies indicate minimal benefits of combining medication and therapy over the use of one strategy on its own (Simpson & Liebowitz, 2005).

Similarly, for bipolar disorder, antidepressant medication does not appear to offer any benefits for treating a depressive episode, whereas intensive psychotherapy (e.g., cognitive behavior therapy, family-focused therapy, or interpersonal and social rhythm therapy) has been shown to shorten the length of depressive episodes (Miklowitz et al., 2007). Overall, it has been recognized that for many diagnostic groups, neurocognitive impairments contribute substantially to patients' inability to function in daily life. For example, difficulties in declarative memory (the ability to learn and remember new information), attention, and executive functioning in schizophrenia have been linked with patients' difficulties to work or function in general (McGurk & Mueser, 2004).

Consequently, cognitive impairments have become a central target in psychosocial interventions for schizophrenia (adjunctive to medication). A meta-analysis of twenty-six randomized, controlled trials of cognitive remediation in schizophrenia including 1,151 patients found that cognitive remediation was associated with significant improvements in cognitive performance (effect size = 0.41), psychosocial functioning (effect size = 0.36), and a small effect on symptoms (0.28). Cognitive remediation for schizophrenia appears to work best when it is provided in the context of adjunctive comprehensive psychiatric rehabilitation (McGurk et al., 2007) or when it is combined with vocation rehabilitation (Bell et al., 2008).

For other disorders, such as bipolar disorder, the link between functioning difficulties and cognitive impairment is increasingly recognized. At work, employed individuals with bipolar disorders have increased rates of absenteeism (days missed at work) and presenteeism (decreased work performance when at work) corresponding to missing the equivalent of a full week of lost work every month (Kessler et al., 2005, 2006). Both depressive symptoms and cognitive impairment contribute to lower work functioning (Altshuler et al., 2008; Bauer et al., 2001; Brissos et al., 2008; Gildengers et al., 2007; Judd et al., 2008), but work functioning does not return to normal even if patients are asymptomatic (Judd et al., 2005, 2008). Neuropsychological studies in bipolar disorder have shown that approximately 30 percent to 40 percent of individuals with bipolar disorder exhibit cognitive impairments even when they are not in an acute mood episode (Altshuler et al., 2008; Bauer et al., 2001; Brissos et al., 2008; Cavanagh et al., 2002; Clark, Iversen, & Goodwin, 2002; Gildengers et al., 2007). As in schizophrenia, this involves difficulties in attention, declarative memory, and executive functioning. Multiple studies have now linked these cognitive impairments with work-functioning difficulties such that patients with more cognitive impairments have lower work functioning, and a recent pilot study in employed patients with bipolar disorder employing cognitive remediation techniques found improved work functioning both at the end of treatment and at the 3-month follow-up (Altshuler et al., 2008; Gildengers et al., 2007; Harvey et al., 2010; Jaeger et al., 2007).

The addition of brain imaging to conventional clinical psychology has in some respects leveled the playing field between psychopharmacological and psychological interventions. We now know that in some cases, psychotherapy leads to corrective changes in brain function that rival or compete with those of medications. Contemporary psychotherapies may be as likely as medication to lead to alterations in brain function, and these alterations may have enhanced durability when compared against those resulting from pharmacological approaches (Cozolino, 2010; Farb, Anderson, Mayberg, Bean, McKeon, & Segal, 2010).

Finally, an additional benefit of the neurocognitive approach to treatment is the prediction of nonresponders even before an intervention has begun (Mayberg, 2006; Siegle, Steinhauer, Friedman, Thompson, & Thase, 2011). This application can drastically reduce the public health burden associated with emotional disorders and allow for a data-driven approach to treatment.

The Field's Response to the Neurocognitive Perspective

Clinical psychologists have largely embraced the shift to a neurocognitive perspective and have called this momentum "...a time of unprecedented advancements in the methods and technologies that are available to study the neural basis of psychological disorders" (p. 121, Richards, Lee, & Daughters, 2011). Others welcome the "...new generation of therapies" (p. 235, Siegle et al., 2007) and "...clinics of tomorrow" that will be likely to follow such advancements (p. 305, Siegle, Ghinassi, & Thase, 2011). This area is not without controversy, however. It can be daunting to identify and fully understand an entirely new discipline (Rottenberg & Johnson, 2007), particularly for those who have spent their time in the more traditional clinical domain. Creativity and resourcefulness are required to find ways to translate neurocognitive aspects into practice. It is also difficult to ascertain when it is cost-effective to integrate sophisticated methodologies into clinical settings. Some have argued, therefore, that basic neurocognitive research has yet to be effectively translated into significantly improved interventions (Richards et al., 2011).

Other reasons for the lag in application include the lack of interdisciplinary collaboration and replication of clinical findings to date. Sorenson notes that, "...until we better understand brain dysfunction...fMRI will not provide the information needed to choose between therapies (p. 942, 2006)," and Mitterschifthaler et al. argue, "fMRI is still a long way from being used in the diagnosis and treatment of individual patients (p. 859, 2006)." Siegle (2011), a proponent of the move toward a neurocognitive approach, has identified some challenges that must soon be met before we integrate neuroscience into the clinics of the future. These include adherence to basic standards of measurement in the use of neuroimaging and targeting identified mechanisms in treatment. Development of standardized databases, increasing ease of interpretation of data, and making techniques affordable are imminent priorities. Reshaping cognitive processes (e.g., attentional bias, learned helplessness) could result in treatments that appear dramatically different from those currently being used. Despite these words of caution, however, many researchers are in agreement that now is the time to make the leap from basic research to practice (Rottenberg & Johnson, 2007).

The Neurocognitive Perspective and the Field of Clinical Psychology

The emergence of a neurocognitive perspective necessitates that clinical psychologists keep pace with the field of neuroscience to be an active part of this progressive new framework. To this end, the current volume is meant to give clinical researchers, practitioners, students, and other interested parties an introduction to the integration of brain and body measures and clinical psychology. The chapters included in this book provide nascent evidence that basic and applied research can be successfully integrated toward the development and testing of new interventions. Each chapter in this book fills a void in the treatment of at least one psychiatric disorder (e.g., mood, anxiety, psychotic, substance use disorders) and provides a literature review and critique, followed by suggestions for future studies. Clinical application is highlighted in each chapter.

Deveney provides readers with a background in the methods used to identify the neural and physiological mechanisms associated with psychopathology and treatment. This methodology chapter describes the application of neuropsychological testing, measures of peripheral nervous system activity (e.g., heart rate, skin conductance), electroencephalography, functional magnetic resonance imaging, positron emission tomography, genetics, and hormones. The relative strengths and weaknesses of each technique, focusing on the promises and pitfalls of moving them into the clinic, are discussed. Each methodological section concludes with an example of how each measure has contributed important insight into the field's understanding of psychopathology and its treatment.

Next, moving into content areas, neurocognitive aspects of anxiety disorders have been extensively studied and are covered in three chapters representing the broad human lifespan. According to Sturm and Chang, translational research in pediatric anxiety disorders is evolving within an integrative framework that synthesizes findings from developmental psychopathology and neuroscience. Within this emerging translational context, the authors provide a comprehensive overview and update on differential diagnosis, neurocognition, and evidence-based treatments of childhood anxiety disorders. Discussion of differential diagnosis covers common comorbidities and associated problems in cognitive, emotional, and social functioning. Descriptions of the disorders' etiology and course highlight the neuropathological mechanisms implicated in disease course.

Cognitive models of anxiety disorders have focused on specific components, including biases in attention allocation, automatic thoughts, interpretations, rumination, and dysfunctional attitudes and schemas, all of which are implicated in both the onset and maintenance of anxiety. Based on the numerous studies that have used neuroimaging tools to examine the neural mechanisms of anxiety disorders, Moshier, Calkins, Kredlow, and Otto identify the functional and structural neurobiological architecture of cognitive models of anxiety. Elucidating the neural basis of how different clinical treatment modalities impact clinical features and brain mechanisms will facilitate in the clinician a richer understanding of the impact of cognitive models of anxiety disorders.

Although relatively under-studied, anxiety disorders in later life have recently moved into the clinical and research spotlight. Mohlman, Beaudreau, and Price argue that a neurocognitive approach to understanding anxiety is particularly relevant to older adults, given the effects of normal aging on cognitive abilities and the brain. Older adults are known to experience declines in several specific cognitive domains (e.g., processing speed, memory recall, selective attention) and brain areas (e.g., the prefrontal cortex), and these deficits can affect the presentation and treatment of anxiety states. They can also be exacerbated when anxiety is present. This chapter discusses innovative approaches to anxiety treatment in the context of an older patient's psychiatric and cognitive comorbidities and discusses upcoming trends in neurocognitive aspects of mental health in later life.

ADHD is one of the most prevalent neurodevelopmental disorders of childhood. ADHD encompasses a complex mix of neurocognitive deficits that contribute to developmentally inappropriate symptoms of inattention, impulsivity, and hyperactivity as well as deficits in executive functioning that result in poor planning, organization, mental flexibility, self-monitoring, and social problem-solving skills. Symptoms typically present across multiple settings, contributing to behavioral, academic, and/or social impairments, which are often exacerbated by the presence of co-occurring symptomatology or comorbid disorders. The chapter by Weissman, Reddy, and Hale provides a broad overview of the clinical, biological, neurocognitive, and psychosocial factors that contribute to the etiology, development, and presentation of ADHD children.

In addition, the chapter discusses diagnostic challenges including symptom overlap with other psychiatric disorders, useful, pragmatic neuropsychological assessment techniques to aid in differential diagnosis and treatment planning, and concludes with a brief review of novel "neurotherapeutic" interventions which have shown initial promise in the treatment of ADHD children and adults.

Kurtz critically summarizes contemporary research showing that neurocognitive deficits in attention, memory, problem solving, and other cognitive capacities are core features of schizophrenia that are not artifacts of symptoms, are evident before formal diagnosis, and are persistent throughout the course of the disorder. The relationship of these deficits to structural and functional neuroimaging findings on the one hand and functional outcome in the disorder on the other are discussed. The chapter concludes with a review of the current status of a group of behavioral interventions, labeled cognitive remediation, that are designed to address these neurocognitive deficits directly in schizophrenia.

The chapter by Britton, Kennedy, Seager, Queen, Hernandez, Spiro, and Eherenreich-May highlights the unique aspects of major depressive disorder in children and adolescents. The authors elaborate on the physiological, social, and cognitive changes that occur in these early phases of life and how the neurocognitive approach can enhance outcome for this vulnerable patient group. Contemporary findings from face processing, emotion regulation, self referential processing, and reward processing tasks are discussed and integrated with the treatment outcome literature.

De Raedt conceptualizes vulnerability for depression as a process reactive to stress and residing in genetic, biological, and cognitive characteristics. The intriguing observations that after each episode people become more vulnerable for relapse or recurrence because successive depressive episodes are triggered by progressively milder stressors and that the number of previous episodes revealed to be among the strongest predictors of relapse or recurrence in several studies suggest that depressive episodes leave a scar that increases vulnerability to new episodes. In this way, depressive disorder is framed within a life-span perspective, focusing on information processing from childhood to old age. Despite well-established cognitive, behavioral and pharmacological treatment options for depression, relapse or recurrence rates after remission or recovery remain elevated. This highlights the importance of investigating underlying working mechanisms of this scar, focusing on the interaction between biological factors and information processing.

Cognitive problems in bipolar disorder have long been thought to remit once depression or mania is effectively treated. As noted in the chapter by Deckersbach, Kaur, and Hansen, however, neuropsychological research over the past fifteen years has documented that 30 to 40 percent of patients with bipolar disorder continue to have cognitive difficulties even when they are not depressed or manic. The chapter summarizes the current status of neuropsychological research in bipolar disorder (affected and preserved cognitive domains), reviews factors that contribute to cognitive impairment (e.g., medication), and also reviews the impact neuropsychological impairments have on daily functioning in individuals with bipolar disorder, concluding with a review of implications and shortcomings of existing behavioral or cognitive behavioral treatments in addressing cognitive and functioning difficulties. Additionally, a new approach on how to treat cognitive and functioning problems in bipolar disorder is described with particular relevance to bipolar patients.

Behavioral health research has also recently taken a neurocognitive focus. Phantom limb is a common perceptual experience in which individuals report experiencing the sensation of having a limb even after it has been amputated. In a majority of people reporting phantom limb, the sensations include pain. Phantom limb pain (PLP) is associated not only with distress but with decreased life satisfaction and functioning. PLP is hypothesized to arise from neural reorganization occurring after limb loss. Areas of the somatosensory cortex previously associated with the removed limb become associated with other body areas that are adjacently mapped in the brain. Several theorists have suggested that visual feedback (e.g., the illusion of an intact limb produced using a mirror) can correct this problematic remapping. The chapter by McQuaid describes the etiology of phantom limb pain and the hypothesized model of neuroplasticity contributing to the pain experience, in addition to recent clinical interventions developed based on this understanding, including pharmacologic, psychosocial and visual feedback approaches. The chapter concludes with findings on efficacy and effectiveness of interventions and provides future directions for better understanding and treating PLP.

As noted in the chapter by Gorka, Chen, and Daughters, the clinical picture of substance use disorders can include compulsive drug taking, decreased sensitivity to reward, and decrements in the control of emotion and cognition. These and other aspects make them difficult to treat and elevate the chances of relapse. The chapter covers neurobiology, established (pharmacological, psychosocial), and novel (cognitive remediation, mindfulness, anti-addiction vaccines) approaches to treatment of substance use disorders. Primitive and higher-order brain circuits (e.g., dorsolateral prefrontal cortex) are discussed from a transdiagnostic viewpoint that cuts across all drug classes.

Finally, Siegle and Hansen summarize commonalities in shared processes across disorders (novel perspectives on common features) and commonalities in interventions (novel perspectives on common change processes) from a mechanistic point of view. In addition to discussing similarities and differences in strategies and outcomes, the authors embed discussion of new neurocognitive perspectives in other recent advances in the literature. Additionally, they provide concrete standards useful for improving psychiatry clinic intake procedures, with the ultimate goal of providing patients with personalized treatment.

Although this volume is organized in DSM-based disorder categories, it is our hope that the neurocognitive perspective will contribute to the push toward a transdiagnostic disorder scheme in which underlying mechanisms shared by numerous disorders are included in the main focus of treatment. This book provides an introduction to the first empirically based neurocognitive models of emotional disorders and corresponding treatments developed by researchers in clinical psychology. The current models will likely be modified, refined, and even challenged with time as research continues to accumulate on each topic. However, the current series of chapters clearly demonstrates that researchers in the mental health field are ready and able to cross disciplines with the ultimate goal of developing a neurocognitive perspective on clinical problems.

References

Altshuler, L. L., Bearden, C. E., Green, M. F., van Gorp, W., & Mintz, J. (2008). A relationship between neurocognitive impairment and functional impairment in bipolar disorder: a pilot study. *Psychiatry Research, 157,* 289–293.

American Psychiatric Association. (2013). *Diagnostic and statistical manual of mental disorders* (5th ed.). Arlington, VA: American Psychiatric Publishing.

Barkley, R. A. (1997). Behavioral inhibition, sustained attention, and executive functions: constructing a unifying theory of ADHD. *Psychological Bulletin, 121,* 65–94.

Bauer, M. S., Kirk, G. F., Gavin, C., & Williford, W. O. (2001). Determinants of functional outcome and healthcare costs in bipolar disorder: a high-intensity follow-up study. *Journal of Affective Disorders, 65,* 231–241.

Beauregard, M., Levesque, J., & Bourgouin, P. (2000). Neural correlates of conscious self-regulation of emotion. *Journal of Neuroscience, 21,* 1–6.

Bell, M. D., Zito, W., Greig, T., & Wexler, B. E. (2008). Neurocognitive enhancement therapy with vocational services: work outcomes at two-year follow-up. *Schizophrenia Research, 105,* 18–29.

Borod, J. C. (2000). *The neuropsychology of emotion.* New York: Oxford University Press.

Brissos, S., Dias, V. V., Carita, A. I., & Martinez-Aran, A. (2008). Quality of life in bipolar type I disorder and schizophrenia in remission: clinical and neurocognitive correlates. *Psychiatry Research, 160,* 55–62.

Castillo, C. (2008). *Children with complex medical issues in schools: Neuropsychological descriptions and interventions.* New York: Springer Publishing Company.

Cavanagh, J. T., Van Beck, M., Muir, W., & Blackwood, D. H. (2002). Case-control study of neurocognitive function in euthymic patients with bipolar disorder: an association with mania. *British Journal of Psychiatry, 180,* 320–326.

Clark, C. C., Prior, M. M., & Kinsella, G. G. (2002). The relationship between executive function abilities, adaptive behaviour, and academic achievement in children with externalising behaviour problems. *Journal of Child Psychology & Psychiatry & Allied Disciplines, 43*(6), 785–796.

Clark, L., Iversen, S. D., & Goodwin, G. M. (2002). Sustained attention deficit in bipolar disorder. *British Journal of Psychiatry, 180,* 313–319.

Cozolino, L. (2010). *The neuroscience of psychotherapy: Healing the social brain.* New York: W. W. Norton & Co.

Deckersbach, T., Savage, C. R., & Rauch, S. L. (2009). Neuropsychology of obsessive-compulsive disorder. In S. J. Wood, N. B. Allen, & C. Pantelis (eds), *Neuropsychology of mental illness* (pp. 342–352). New York: Cambridge University Press.

Deckersbach, T., Nierenberg, A. A., Kessler, R., Lund, H. G., Ametrano, R. M., Sachs, G. ... & Dougherty, D. (2010). Cognitive rehabilitation for bipolar disorder: an open trial for employed patients with residual depressive symptoms. *CNS Neuroscience and Therapeutics, 16,* 298–307.

Farb, N. A. S., Anderson, A. K., Mayberg, H., Bean, J., McKeon, D., & Segal, Z. V. (2010). Minding one's emotions: mindfulness training alters the neural expression of sadness. *Emotion, 10,* 25–33.

Gildengers, A. G., Butters, M. A., Chisholm, D., Rogers, J. C., Holm, M. B., Bhalla, R. K. ... & Mulsant, B. H (2007). Cognitive functioning and instrumental activities of daily living in late-life bipolar disorder. *American Journal of Geriatric Psychiatry, 15,* 174–179.

Goldapple, K., Segal, Z., Garson, C., Lau, M., Bieling, P., Kennedy, S. ... & Mayberg, H. (2004). Modulation of cortical-limbic pathways in major depression. *Archives of General Psychiatry, 61,* 34–41

Gross, J. J. (2007). *Handbook of emotion regulation.* New York: Guilford.

Hale, J. B., & Fiorello, C. A. (2004). *School neuropsychology: A practitioner's handbook.* New York, NY: Guilford Press.

Hale, J. B., Fiorello, C. A., & Brown, L. (2005). Determining medication treatment effects using teacher ratings and classroom observations of children with ADHD: does neuropsychological impairment matter? *Educational and Child Psychology, 22,* 39–61.

Hale, J. B., Reddy, L. A., Decker, S. L., Thompson, R., Henzel, J., Teodori, A. ... &Denckla, M. B. (2009). Development and validation of an executive function and behavior rating screening battery sensitive to ADHD. *Journal of Clinical and Experimental Neuropsychology, 31,* 897–912.

Hale, J. B., Reddy, L. A., Semrud-Clikeman, M., Hain, L., Whitaker, J., Morley, J. ... & Jones, N. (2011). Executive impairment determines ADHD medication response: implications for academic achievement. *Journal of Learning Disabilities, 44,* 196–212.

Hariri, A.R., Bookheimer, S.Y., & Mazziotta, J.C. (2000). Modulating emotional responses: effects of a neocortical network on the limbic system. *NeuroReport, 11,* 43–48.

Harvey, P. D., Twamley, E. W., Vella, L., Patterson, T., & Heaton, R. K. (2010). Results of the Validation of Everyday Real World Outcomes (VALERO) study: validation of 6 real world rating scales for their relationship with neurocognitive and functional ability. 49th Annual Meeting of the American College of Neuropsychopharmacology. Miami, FL, December 5–9.

Hunter, S. J., & Donders, J. (eds) (2007). *Pediatric neuropsychological intervention.* New York, NY: Cambridge University Press.

Jaeger, J., Berns, S., Loftus, S., Gonzalez, C., & Czobor, P. (2007). Neurocognitive test performance predicts functional recovery from acute exacerbation leading to hospitalization in bipolar disorder. *Bipolar Disorder, 9,* 93–102.

Judd, L. L., Akiskal, H. S., Schettler, P. J., Endicott, J., Leon, A. C., Solomon, D. A. ... & Keller, M. (2005). Psychosocial disability in the course of bipolar I and II disorders: a prospective, comparative, longitudinal study. *Archives of General Psychiatry, 62,* 1322–1330.

Judd, L. L., Schettler, P. J., Solomon, D. A., Maser, J. D., Coryell, W., Endicott, J., & Akiskal, H. S. (2008). Psychosocial disability and work role function compared across the long-term course of bipolar I, bipolar II and unipolar major depressive disorders. *Journal of Affective Disorders, 108,* 49–58.

Kerns, K., Eso, K., & Thomson, J. (1999). Investigation of a direct intervention for improving attention in young children with ADHD. *Developmental Neuropsychology, 16,* 273–295.

Kessler, R. C., Chiu, W. T., Demler, O., Merikangas, K. R., & Walters, E. E. (2005). Prevalence, severity, and comorbidity of 12-month DSM-IV disorders in the National Comorbidity Survey Replication. *Archives of General Psychiatry, 62,* 617–627.

Kessler, R. C., Akiskal, H. S., Ames, M., Birnbaum, H., Greenberg, P., Hirschfeld, R. M. A. ... & Wang, P. S. (2006). Prevalence and effects of mood disorders on work performance in a nationally representative sample of U.S. workers. *American Journal of Psychiatry, 163,* 1561–1568.

Koenigsberg, H. W., Fan, J., Ochsner, K. N., Liu, X., Guise, K., Pizzarello, S. ... & Siever, L. J. (2009). Neural correlates of the use of psychological distancing to regulate responses to negative social cues. *Neuropsychologia, 48,* 854–863.

Koster, E. H. W., Fox, E., & MacLeod, C. (2009). Introduction to the special section on cognitive bias modification in emotional disorders. *Journal of Abnormal Psychology, 118,* 1–4.

Kuelz, A. K., Riemann, D., Halsband, U., Vielhaber, K., Unterrainer, J., Kordon, A., & Voderholzer, U. (2006). Neuropsychological impairment in obsessive-compulsive disorder—improvement over the course of cognitive behavioral treatment. *Journal of Clinical and Experimental Neuropsychology, 28,* 1273–1287.

Lazar, S. G. (2010). *Psychotherapy is worth it: A comprehensive review of its cost-effectiveness.* Arlington, VA: American Psychiatric Publishing.

Legerstee, J. S., Tulen, J. H. M., Dierckx, B., Treffers, P. D. A., Verhulst, F. C., & Utens, E. M. W. J. (2010). CBT for childhood anxiety disorders: differential changes in selective attention between treatment responders and non-responders. *Journal of Child Psychology and Psychiatry, 51,* 162–172.

Martin, D.J., Oren, Z., & Boone, K. (1991). Major depressives' and dysthymics' performance on the Wisconsin Card Sorting Test. *Journal of Clinical Psychology, 47,* 684–690.

Matthews, A., Mogg, K., Kentish, J., & Eysenck, M. (1995). Effect of psychological treatment on cognitive bias in generalized anxiety disorder. *Behaviour Research and Therapy, 33,* 293–303.

Mayberg, H. S. (2006) Defining neurocircuits in depression: strategies toward treatment selection based on neuroimaging phenotypes. *Psychiatric Annals, 36,* 259–268.

McClure, E. B., Adler, A., Monk, C. S., Cameron, J., Smith, S., Nelson, E. E. ... & Pine, D. S. (2007). fMRI predictors of treatment outcome in pediatric anxiety disorders. *Psychopharmacology, 191,* 97–105.

McGurk, S. R., Twamley, E. W., Sitzer, D. I., McHugo, G. J., & Mueser, K. T. (2007). A meta-analysis of cognitive remediation in schizophrenia. *American Journal of Psychiatry, 164,* 1791–1802.

McGurk, S. R., & Mueser, K. T. (2004). Cognitive functioning, symptoms, and work in supported employment: a review and heuristic model. *Schizophrenia Research, 70,* 147–173.

Miklowitz, D. J., Otto, M. W., Frank, E., Reilly-Harrington, N. A., Kogan, J. N., ... & Sachs, G. S. (2007). Intensive psychosocial intervention enhances functioning in patients with bipolar depression: results from a 9-month randomized controlled trial. *American Journal of Psychiatry, 164,* 1340–1347.

Mitterschiffthaler, M. T., Ettinger, U., Mehta, M. A., Mataix-Cols, D., & Williams, S. C. R. (2006). Applications of functional magnetic resonance imaging in psychiatry. *Journal of Magnetic Resonance Imaging, 23,* 851–861.

Mohlman, J., & Deckersbach, T. (2009). Expanding the scope of clinical psychology: the neurocognitive therapies/translational research SIG. *The Behavior Therapist, 32,* 127.

Mohlman, J., & Gorman, J. M. (2005). The role of executive functioning in CBT: a pilot study with anxious older adults. *Behaviour Research and Therapy, 43,* 447–465.

Noggle, C. A., Davis, A. S., & Barisa, M. (2008). *Neuropsychology and neuroimaging: Integrating and understanding structure and function in clinical practice.* New York: Springer.

Ochsner, K. N., & Gross, J. J. (2008). Cognitive emotion regulation: insights from social cognitive and affective neuroscience. *Current Directions in Psychological Science, 17,* 153–158.

Ochsner, K. N., Bunge, S. A., Gross, J. L., & Gabrieli, J. D. E. (2002). Rethinking feelings: an fMRI study of the cognitive regulation of emotion. *Journal of Cognitive Neuroscience, 14,* 1215–1229.

Posner, M. I., & Rothbart, M. K. (1998). Attention, self-regulation, and consciousness. *Philosophical Transcripts of the Royal Society of London, B353,* 1915–1927.

Puliafico, A. C., & Kendall, P. C. (2006). Threat-related attentional bias in anxious youth: A review. *Clinical Child and Family Psychology Review, 9,* 162–180.

Reddy, L. A., & Hale, J. B. (2007). Inattentiveness. In A. R. Eisen (ed.), *Clinical handbook of childhood behavioral problems* (pp. 156–211). New York: Guilford Press.

Reddy, L. A., Weissman, A. S., & Hale, J. B. (2013). *Neuropsychological assessment and intervention for emotional and behavior disordered youth: An integrated step-by-step evidence-based approach.* Washington, DC: APA Press.

Riccio, C. A., Sullivan, J. R., & Cohen. M. J. (2010). *Neuropsychological assessment and intervention for childhood and adolescent disorders.* Hoboken, NJ: Wiley.

Richards, J. M., Lee, M. R., & Daughters, S. B. (2011). Why should clinical researchers care about cognitive affective neuroscience? *The Behavior Therapist, 34,* 121–132.

Riemann, B. C., Amir, N., & Lake, P. M. (2010). Clinical application of attention training for adolescent anxiety. Paper presented at the Annual Meeting of the Association for Behavioral and Cognitive Therapies, San Francisco, CA, November 18–20.

Rottenberg, J., & Johnson, S. (2007). Introduction: bridging affective and clinical science. In J. Rottenberg & S. Johnson (eds), *Emotion and psychopathology* (pp. 3–10). Washington DC: American Psychological Association Press.

Roy, A. K., Vasa, R. A., Bruck, M., Mogg, K., Bradley, B. P., Sweeney, M. ... & Pine, D. S. (2008). Attention bias toward threat in pediatric anxiety disorders. *Journal of the American Academy of Child and Adolescent Psychiatry, 47,* 1189–1196.

Siegle, G. J. (2011). Beyond depression commentary: wherefore art thou, depression clinic of tomorrow? *Clinical Psychology: Science and Practice, 18,* 305–310.

Siegle, G. J., Carter, C. S., & Thase, M. E. (2006). Use of fMRI to predict recovery from unipolar depression with cognitive behavior therapy. *The American Journal of Psychiatry, 163,* 735–738.

Siegle, G. J., Ghinassi, F., & Thase, M. E. (2007). Neurobehavioral therapies in the 21st century: summary of an emerging field and an extended example of cognitive control training for depression. *Cognitive Therapy and Research, 31*, 235–262.

Siegle, G. J., Steinhauer, S. R., Friedman, E. S., Thompson, W. S., & Thase, M. E. (2011). Remission prognosis for cognitive therapy for recurrent depression using the pupil: utility and neural correlates. *Biological Psychiatry, 69*, 726–733.

Simpson, H. B., & Liebowitz, M. R. (2005). Combining pharmacotherapy and cognitive behavior therapy in the treatment of OCD. In J. S. Abramowitz & A. C. Houts (eds), *Concepts and controversies in obsessive-compulsive disorder* (pp. 359–376). New York: Springer.

Sorenson, A. G. (2006). The use of fMRI in the clinic. *Journal of Magnetic Resonance Imaging, 23*, 941–944.

Turgay, A. (2005). Treatment of comorbidity in conduct disorder with attention-deficit hyperactivity disorder (ADHD). *Essential Psychopharmacology, 6, 277–290.*

Vassilopoulos, S. P., Banerjee, R., & Prantzalou, C. (2009). Experimental modification of interpretation bias in socially anxious children: changes in interpretation, anticipated interpersonal anxiety, and social anxiety symptoms. *Behaviour Research and Therapy, 47*, 1085–1089.

Weissman, A. S., & Bates, M. E. (2010). Increased clinical and neurocognitive impairment in children with autism spectrum disorders and comorbid bipolar disorder. *Research in Autism Spectrum Disorders, 4*, 670–680.

Weissman, A. S., Chu, B. C., Reddy, L. R., & Mohlman, J. (2012). Attention problems in anxious and inattentive-impulsive youth: implications for diagnosis and treatment. *Journal of Clinical Child and Adolescent Psychology, 41*, 117–127.

2

TOOLS OF THE NEUROCOGNITIVE PSYCHOLOGIST

Christen M. Deveney

Introduction

Some have argued that psychiatric disorders should be considered brain disorders (Insel, 2011). Even if one disagrees with this sentiment and prefers to consider mental illnesses as disorders of behavior, the fact remains that all behaviors involve the brain. As such, studies of the brain are uniquely poised to specify core features of the disorders clinical psychologists observe and treat in the clinic. For example, neural and genetic measures have identified risk factors for psychiatric disorders (Gilbertson et al., 2002; Kong et al., in press) and are paving the way toward improved diagnostic systems by identifying both overlapping and distinct neural patterns across disorders (Brotman et al., 2010; Weissman, Chu, Reddy, & Mohlman, 2012). These measures also set the stage for more efficacious treatments by identifying neural changes following psychosocial treatments (Paquette et al., 2003), predictors of response to psychosocial and pharmacological interventions (Maslowsky et al., 2010; McClure et al., 2007; Pizzagalli, 2010; Siegle, Carter, & Thase, 2006), and even direct manipulations of brain activity to ameliorate the symptoms of the most severe and treatment-refractory patients (Kennedy et al., 2011; Mayberg et al., 2005).

Understanding the neurocognitive approach (i.e., the merging of psychological and biological perspectives) to clinical psychology research requires greater literacy about these measures and is important for clinicians and researchers alike. For example, being able to conceptualize how the brain changes after cognitive behavioral therapy can help clinicians explain how treatment can mitigate disorders of the brain. Increasing awareness of cognitive training methods (Amir, Beard, Burns, & Bomyea, 2009) may allow clinicians to expand the types of treatments available for patients in and out of the clinic. Neurocognitive tools facilitate the study of processes occurring outside of conscious awareness or in populations unable to report their experience using traditional measures (e.g., self-report, behavioral). Finally, a better understanding of existing paradigms and techniques will facilitate collaborations between clinician-researchers and experts in these biological measures. In particular, clinicians can help basic researchers design clinically relevant experiments, identify clinical issues that may be related to the biological findings, or suggest behavioral and clinical avenues for identifying likely biological differences.

The goal of this chapter is to provide an accessible explanation of lesion studies, neuropsychological testing, electroencephalography, event-related brain potentials, magnetic resonance imaging (MRI), functional MRI, peripheral measures such as electromyography and electrocardiography, and hormones and behavioral endocrinology—some of the tools used by researchers adopting a neurocognitive perspective and referenced in the subsequent chapters.

This review begins with some general background about brain organization followed by a brief description of each methodology. Each methodological description includes examples of how studies using this technique are relevant to clinical psychology. They also include a discussion of the relative advantages and disadvantages of each method to help clinician-researchers critically evaluate the literature and identify the best tools to pursue their research questions. Readers are not intended to come away from this chapter as experts ready to move these technologies into their clinics or laboratories. Indeed, this is a rapidly changing field, and new technologies emerge frequently, resulting in rapid updating of standard practices. Instead, the goal of this chapter is for the reader to walk away with the sense of how neurocognitive methods address clinically relevant questions and to become familiar with some of the major findings that have already been described in the literature. For readers who are interested in gaining a more advanced understanding of these methods, a list of recommended readings can be found at the end of the chapter. In addition, readers should refer to Chapter 13 on innovative strategies by Hansen and Siegle in this book.

Brief Background on the Body-Brain Organization

A brief foray into the general organization of the brain will help set the stage for the specific measures discussed in the remainder of the chapter. Even without the labels on Figure 2.1, it is clear that the brain consists of several distinct parts including blood vessels, fluid-filled spaces (ventricles), and different types of tissue (gray and white matter; Martin, 2001). Like any organ, the brain requires nourishment in the form of oxygen and glucose, which is supplied by blood vessels that innervate the brain. This is why illnesses or events that block blood flow to the brain (i.e., heart attacks or strokes) destroy brain cells and impair

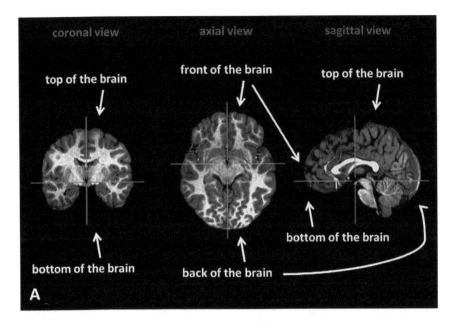

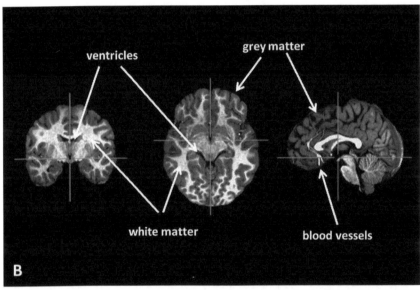

FIGURE 2.1 Basic views of brain structure. Images from a magnetic resonance imaging (MRI) scan. Panel A: Three different ways of viewing the brain in three-dimensional space (coronal, axial, sagittal). Panel B identifies some key general structures in the brain.

cognition. The brain itself is surrounded by cerebral spinal fluid that cushions the brain by filling in the various spaces within the brain including the ventricles and the spaces (i.e., sulci) between the folds of the brain (i.e., gyri). When the brain is damaged in any way—as from the progression of a neurogenerative disease like Alzheimer's—the amount of cerebral spinal fluid increases to fill the gaps left from lost brain matter (Martin, 2001).

The brain can be divided into cortical (or cortex: loosely defined, the outer parts of the brain) and subcortical regions (loosely defined, the inside of the brain; Breedlove & Watson, 2013; Gazzaniga, Ivry, & Mangun, 2013). The cortex is often divided into subsections (lobes) based on the presence of larger sulci (spaces between the folds, or gyri). Although the divisions are anatomical, they map on to some general differences in function between the lobes (Breedlove & Watson, 2013; Gazzaniga et al., 2013). The frontal lobe is the last to mature and is typically associated with complex cognitive processes like executive functioning, planning, and inhibitory control (Breedlove & Watson, 2013; Gazzaniga et al., 2013). The parietal lobe is associated with visuospatial processes and the integration of sensory information from various parts of the body (Breedlove & Watson, 2013; Gazzaniga et al., 2013). The temporal lobe is associated with memory and also with language (comprehension and production; Breedlove & Watson, 2013; Gazzaniga et al., 2013). Finally, the occipital lobe is involved primarily with visual processing (Martin, 2001).

Subcortical regions are those deeper inside the brain, and many of these are involved in emotional processes of interest to clinical psychologists. For example, clinical psychologists have likely heard of the amygdala, a subcortical structure that has been linked with emotional responses (LeDoux, 1996) and is often over-reactive in populations with psychiatric disorders (more on that later). Other subcortical regions include the hippocampus (closely tied to memory processes), the striatum (linked with reward and motor responses), the hypothalamus (which coordinates the endocrine/hormone system with the nervous system), and the thalamus (a coordination site between regions). Other structures of interest include the brainstem, which controls basic bodily functions like respiration and cardiac function, and the cerebellum, which is associated with motor control and balance (Martin, 2001).

References to brain structures typically involve a description of (1) whether it is on the left or right side of the brain (hemisphere) or present at the midline (middle of the brain); (2) the lobe involved (frontal, parietal, temporal, occipital); (3) Brodmann area (based on a map of the brain created in the early twentieth century that divided brain tissue up into regions with similar cellular structure); and (4) coordinates that identify a specific location within the three-dimensional structure (if you are facing the brain, the x coordinate reflects the distance to the left or right of the brain; the y coordinate to the front or back of the brain; and the z coordinate from the bottom to the top of the brain).

Within each of these lobes are neurons—approximately 100 billion in the entire brain (Huettel, Song, & McCarthy, 2009; Martin, 2001). For the purposes of this chapter, only a basic understanding of neurons is necessary, but interested readers should refer to the recommended reading list at the end of the chapter for additional information on these amazing cells. Each neuron consists of a region that receives signals (dendrites), a cell body containing the nucleus for the cell, a long axon with a white coating (myelin) that the neural signal travels down, and a region that transmits that signal to other neurons (axon terminals). The brain communicates via electrical signals that travel down one neuron and trigger a second neuron via chemicals called neurotransmitters. Neurotransmitters can either facilitate or hinder the triggering of that second neuron. Psychotropic medications typically manipulate the quantity of neurotransmitters available to trigger or inhibit neuronal transmission in an effort to restore a balance to the neural system. These effects can be direct (e.g., the medication mimics the action of the neurotransmitter at the synapse) or indirect (e.g., the medication increases the action of enzymes that decompose neurotransmitters at the synapse).

Connections between neurons are the basis for many of our most basic thoughts, emotions, and behaviors. For example, neuronal transmission explains why touching a hot stove causes an individual to remove the hand from the heat source (Breedlove & Watson, 2013). Sensory neurons in the palm transmit a signal to motor neurons in the spinal cord, which, in turn, feed back to motor fibers to withdraw the hand. However, neuronal communication is also at the root of many complex cognitive and emotional processes of interest to clinical psychologists including emotion regulation, rumination, and worry.

Brain Activity and Psychopathology

There are a number of ways to understand how abnormalities in the brain may contribute to symptoms of psychiatric disorders. First, specific regions of the brain may be over- or underdeveloped. Second, brain functioning may be atypical in populations with psychiatric disorders, even if the structures themselves are not abnormal. For example, many psychiatric disorders are characterized by excessive cognitive and behavioral reactions to emotional stimuli. Such reactions could stem from heightened responses to emotional stimuli, suggesting that they feel the stimulus more intensely. Alternatively, their emotional experience may be normal, but due to less activity in regions associated with emotion regulation, patients cannot modulate their emotional experience, causing it to appear excessive. Of course, both types of processes and a number of brain regions could be faulty at the same time (e.g., the emotional reaction is excessive and the individual lacks the means to regulate). A related possibility is that the areas of the brain may not "speak" to each other correctly in psychiatric populations. Keeping with the example above, it is possible that the individual's emotional reactions are normal, and the regions supporting emotion regulation processes are also normal, but the connection between the two regions is broken, resulting in the inability to use the appropriate brain regions to dampen their emotional experience. These different ways that neural abnormalities can translate into abnormal behavior are not mutually exclusive and are often interrelated.

The tools used to study the healthy brain are also useful in understanding potential biological contributors to emotional and behavioral dysfunction. Therefore, the following paragraphs provide an overview of several techniques that are used frequently by researchers adopting a neurocognitive approach and referenced in later chapters in this book. We begin with a brief review of lesion studies and neuropsychological testing before turning to various measures of brain activity and brain structure. Next, we discuss how the use of peripheral psychophysiological measures like heart rate, skin sweating, and hormones can provide useful information about psychological processes.

Lesion Studies and Neuropsychological Testing

Before *in vivo* imaging (i.e., on a living person) was possible, knowledge about what brain regions were responsible for various cognitive, motor, and sensory functions was based on studies of patients with brain injuries or lesions. These individuals would be asked to complete a variety of tasks, and their ability to perform each task was compared with postmortem and, later, neuroimaging assessments of the location of the brain damage. Such studies began to clarify what regions were important for various cognitive, emotional, memory, and sensory processes. Anyone who has taken an introductory psychology course is familiar with the classic case example of Phineas Gage, whose brain injury altered his behavior and personality in dramatic ways and highlighted the role of the brain in personality and emotion (Gleitman, Gross, & Reisberg, 2010). Henry Molaison (H. M.) is another famous example (Scoville & Milner, 1957). During surgery for severe epilepsy in the 1950s, several structures essential for memory formation were removed. Not surprisingly, after surgery, H. M. appeared unable to form new memories, and initially researchers believed he would never be able to learn any new information. However, creative paradigms revealed that H. M. could learn new motor skills despite having no conscious memory of prior experiences with those stimuli (Corkin, 2002). As a result of H. M.'s performance, the field's understanding of memory processes was dramatically changed.

The more recent advent of *in vivo* imaging techniques has not eliminated enthusiasm for studying patients with brain lesions. Indeed, neuroimaging techniques allow us to better identify the nature of the brain damage for associations with psychological functioning. For example, work by researchers at the University of Iowa involves patient S. M., a woman with a genetic condition that destroys the amygdala. The amygdala, an almond-shaped structure in the temporal lobe of the brain, is commonly thought to be essential for the experience of fear (LeDoux, 1996), and it is more active in populations characterized by excessive levels of fear (Shin & Liberzon, 2010). When early studies revealed that S. M. could not experience fear, the researchers concluded that the amygdala was essential for this emotional experience (Adolphs, Tranel, Damasio, & Damasio, 1995). However, a more recent realization was that S. M. could experience fear under circumstances not tested in the early studies (Feinstein et al., 2013). As a result, it was concluded that the amygdala is an important, but not essential, brain structure for the emotional experience of fear.

One of the most interesting aspects of this case is that S. M. was not able to experience fear, and she was not able to recognize fearful expressions in others, although she was able to label other emotional facial displays. Researchers hypothesized that her difficulties labeling fear stemmed from the fact that S. M. did not look at the eye regions of the faces and was, therefore, missing the key signs of fear (Adolphs et al., 2005). Simply instructing S. M. to look at the eye region when making an emotion judgment eliminated her fear-labeling deficit (Adolphs et al., 2005). These examples demonstrate how studies of patients with brain damage contribute to a basic understanding of how the brain works in healthy populations and suggest ways that behavioral deficits in other populations could be remedied.

The field of neuropsychology builds on these initial studies of patients with brain abnormalities and is also used to study the cognitive deficits experienced by relatively healthy individuals. A number of standardized cognitive tasks exist to probe specific areas of cognitive functioning. For example, the Continuous Performance Task (Beck, Bransome, Mirsky, Rosvold, & Sarason, 1956) is frequently used to identify impulse/inhibition deficits in populations with attention deficit hyperactivity disorder (ADHD; Losier, McGrath, & Klein, 1996); and the Wechsler Memory Scale (Wechsler, 1945) has been used to quantify memory deficits in various populations (Frangou, Donaldson, Hadjulis, Landau, & Goldstein, 2005; Sternberg & Jarvik, 1976). Such studies are useful ways of studying whether similar symptom profiles are subserved by the same, or distinct, neurocognitive substrates. A recent example by two editors of this book used neuropsychological tests to reveal that the inattention symptoms common to children with ADHD and those with anxiety are likely to be subserved by different cognitive mechanisms (Weissman et al., 2012).

Indeed, sometimes these standard neurocognitive measures can be adapted to study clinical phenomena closely tied to symptoms of psychiatric disorders. For example, continuous performance tasks have been adapted to include different stimulus types (faces, words) and emotional qualities (positive, negative, neutral, frustrating, non-frustrating) to probe issues surrounding inhibition difficulties in socioemotional contexts (Lewis, Lamm, Segalowitz, Stieben, & Zelazo, 2006).

Advantages

A clear strength of lesion and neuropsychological studies of individuals with various cognitive impairments/neuropsychological deficits is that they reveal—in dramatic ways—the impact of brain damage on cognitive functioning. However, neuropsychological measures are also ideal tools for someone taking the first steps toward adopting a neurocognitive approach to the study of psychiatric illness. Such measures are inexpensive, do not require complicated equipment to administer, are noninvasive, and are easy for patients to complete. In addition, most standardized neurocognitive measures have performance norms that allow a researcher to compare the performance of study participants with a larger and well-established dataset. As mentioned above, neuropsychological tests can be easily adapted for use with clinical populations and can provide information about cognitive functioning even without expensive neuroimaging equipment. The National Institute of Health (NIH) recently launched the NIH Toolbox (NIH, 2013)—a standardized set of computerized measures that can be used to measure various cognitive and emotional processes of interest to many clinical researchers. Many of these are freely available (http://www.nihtoolbox.org/Pages/default.aspx) and are appropriate for use across many different ages.

Disadvantages

As with the methods discussed later in the chapter, lesions and neuropsychological measures have certain limitations. The primary disadvantage is that these techniques typically involve studying individuals whose brains are, by definition, atypical. In addition, because brain damage does not occur neatly in discrete regions, it can be difficult to link the impairments these patients exhibit on cognitive tasks to specific regions.

One way of addressing this issue is to selectively damage or block specific regions of the brain; however, this is only possible with animals or with procedures like transcranial magnetic stimulation (TMS). While much important information has been gathered from studies with animals, these too have limitations. First, important anatomical differences exist between humans and other animals, limiting the ability to link findings from animals to human behavior. In addition, some human behaviors, including those highly relevant to psychiatric disorders, are impossible to model in animals because they are not believed to exist outside of humans (e.g., rumination). Finally, poor performance on a single neuropsychological task can be the result of more than one cognitive process. For example, a failure to remember something might be the result of attention abnormalities, so the information was never encoded into memory; intact ability to encode the memory but an inability to retrieve the memory; or an inability to communicate the information retrieved from memory. Often researchers and neuropsychologists will employ a battery of tests meant to isolate the relevant cognitive process, but this is not always possible due to limitations in individual tests and difficulties isolating specific subcomponent processes.

Electroencephalography and Event-Related Brain Potentials

As mentioned above, neurons are the building blocks of the brain, and connections between neurons make the brain work. When a single neuron fires, a small electrical signal is released. When millions of neurons fire in synchrony, the signal can be detected by electrodes placed on the scalp. These summed electrical signals, sometimes called "brain waves," can be measured by sensors placed directly on the brain (typically during neurosurgery) but also on the scalp (Breedlove & Watson, 2013; Gazzaniga et al., 2013). These measurements are called *electroencephalography* or EEG (Luck, 2005). Today, some EEG studies with healthy individuals use cloth caps with electrodes sewn into the appropriate locations, while others utilize net-like devices with embedded electrodes. Either type of device is positioned over the person's head, and recordings are made relatively easily and without any discomfort to the participant (Luck, 2005).

To the unfamiliar, an EEG can seem like a series of random squiggly lines. However, those seemingly random "squiggles" actually reflect differentiable patterns related to psychological states. For example, human sleep is divided into several stages (e.g., stage 1, slow wave, rapid-eye movement), and each of these stages is associated with EEG patterns that differ in the size (i.e., amplitude) and number of cycles (i.e., frequency) of the signal (Research Institute, 2006). Deep sleep is characterized by large and slow signals, while active wakefulness and thinking are associated with small fast signals. It is every EEG researcher's nightmare to watch a study participant's brain activity get slower and larger during the experiment, as it usually indicates that the participant is falling asleep!

Researchers have examined whether certain EEG profiles (e.g., the amount of activity in specific frequency bands) are associated with phenomena related to clinical psychology. Classic studies of depression linked less alpha activity (8–14 Hz) recorded from sensors placed over the right versus the left frontal cortex with depression (Henriques & Davidson, 1991). More recently, research revealed that some of the memory deficits observed in older populations may be due to decreases in slow wave sleep (0.8–4.6Hz; Mander et al., 2013).

EEG recordings can also reveal how the brain responds to specific stimuli (Luck, 2005). When EEG patterns are recorded while a participant does a task (e.g., viewing pictures or words on a computer screen), extracting the EEG activity associated with each event can identify the various cognitive and sensory processes that occur in response to the stimuli. Typically, researchers extract the EEG signals from a time period around each stimulus and then create separate averages for each stimulus type (e.g., positive, negative, and neutral images, or words versus faces). When enough stimuli are averaged together, noise in the EEG signal drops out, leaving only the EEG pattern present every time a stimulus is elicited. This average EEG signal associated with specific events is called the *event-related brain potential* or ERP (Luck, 2005).

As mentioned above, ERPs help to index the cognitive processes engaged during a task, and comparisons of ERPs elicited by different task conditions or by different patient groups can identify important clinical differences. For example, individuals interested in whether populations with psychosocial deficits exhibit abnormal brain responses to faces have capitalized on an ERP component sensitive to face processing to highlight a face-specific deficit in populations with autism (McPartland, Dawson, Webb, Panagiotides, & Carver, 2004). In the figure below, the ERP describes brain activity to words presented after participants had regulated their emotions using cognitive reappraisal strategies similar to those used in cognitive behavioral therapy (Deveney, unpublished data). The black, gray, and dashed lines reflect brain activity to words viewed after participants had up-regulated, maintained, or down-regulated unpleasant emotions, respectively. Starting at 200 ms and continuing throughout the entire 900-ms period, the black line clearly deviates from the gray and gray dashed lines, indicating that making oneself feel worse altered how the brain processed other stimuli that it encountered.

ERP components are typically labeled according to their polarity and the approximate time at which the component peaks (e.g., the P300 component is

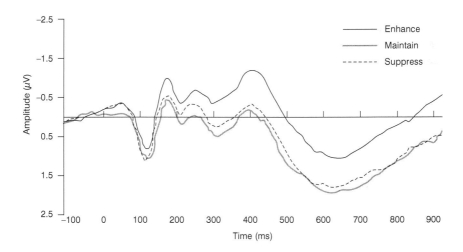

FIGURE 2.2 Example of ERPs elicited by a word after participants increased (enhanced), maintained, or decreased (suppressed) their negative emotion. Note: by convention, negative values on the y-axis are plotted upwards (Deveney, unpublished data).

a positive going EEG deflection peaking approximately 300 ms after a stimulus begins, whereas the N100 component is a negative going deflection peaking approximately 100 ms after a stimulus begins). For a review of major ERP components, see Luck, 2005.

Advantages

Relative to behavioral measures like response time and accuracy, ERPs permit researchers to identify the subprocesses associated with a particular behavior. For example, a simple memory task might suggest that stimulus A is better remembered than stimulus B but not how this was accomplished. Maybe A received more initial attention and, therefore, encoding was stronger than B. Alternatively, maybe A received later and more elaborative rehearsal than B, and it was this later memory process that facilitated the preferential recall of A versus B. ERPs are ideal tools to parse apart these different explanations. They can also examine which cognitive processes are abnormal in particular patient populations. This may ultimately contribute to the development of interventions that target those specific processes.

Unlike many other neuroimaging methods, EEGs measure neural activity directly and within milliseconds of neuronal firing. For researchers, EEG has the additional advantage of being significantly less expensive than many other techniques in terms of start up costs (e.g., MRI scanners are vastly more expensive than EEG systems), and ongoing use (e.g., use of an MRI scanner requires ongoing payment for hours used and often trained technologists to run the equipment). Finally, EEG can be recorded safely from individuals who cannot participate in other imaging techniques (e.g., pregnant women, individuals with metal in their bodies, and individuals who might be too claustrophobic).

Disadvantages

The primary disadvantage of EEG as a neuroimaging method is its poor spatial resolution: that is, its limited ability to identify where in the brain something is happening. In fact, signals recorded by one electrode can stem from neural activity on the other side of the brain! Although increasingly sophisticated methods, including simultaneous EEG and functional MRI (fMRI) recordings, have improved the ability of researchers to identify the source of EEG signals, EEG remains a poor choice for researchers wishing to localize functions/activity in the brain. Second, scalp EEG recordings cannot be made from subcortical structures, which are often abnormal and therefore of research interest, in psychiatric disorders. Third, relative to behavioral and questionnaire/interview methodologies, EEG recordings require sophisticated equipment that is expensive and not always easily transportable. Recent developments are making the ability to record EEG in more naturalistic settings increasingly viable (see Chapter 13 by Hansen and Siegle in this book), rendering this concern less significant. Fourth, like other neuroimaging methods, ERPs are only reliable if averaged across a number of events. This can require participants to sit through long and often boring experimental sessions, and it can also make it impossible to study rare or single events.

MRI and fMRI

As of April 2013, approximately 142,500 articles listed in the PubMed database had the term *MRI, fMRI*, or *functional MRI* in the title or abstract. The first human MRI image was generated in 1973, and the first fMRI paper was published in 1992 (Huettel et al., 2009). The explosion in MRI/fMRI research speaks volumes about the contribution this technique has made to the field and its potential for the future. Prior to MRI, images of the brain required exposure to radiation—as with computerized axial tomography or position emission tomography. Such aspects limited the number of scans any single individual could complete, made it extremely difficult to study many populations, and may have reduced the representativeness of the individuals volunteering to do such studies for research purposes. MRI has no known deleterious effects either during or after scans (Huettel et al., 2009) and, as such, allows researchers to study the brain with no risk to the participant. MRI is increasingly being used to study populations of interest to clinical psychologists—including individuals with various mental illnesses and neurological problems. As such, it is important for clinical psychologists to understand this technique and its limitations. However, the physics of MRI and fMRI are complex, and entire textbooks are devoted to the intricacies of these techniques (see Huettel et al., 2009, and the list of recommended readings at the end of this chapter). Therefore, the goal of this section is to provide readers with a very basic understanding of how MRI and fMRI inform us about brain structure and function. Individuals interested in a more in-depth discussion of MRI physics and issues surrounding the correct acquisition and analysis of the data should refer to the list of recommended readings at the end of this chapter.

At its heart, MRI involves the application of strong magnetic fields and a measurement of how these fields influence atoms. Before delving into the physics, consider what happens during a conference presentation. Before the presentation begins, individual audience members are seated throughout the room and face different directions. Some look forward awaiting the speaker, others are turned to speak to colleagues to their right or left, and still others look toward the back of the room and all possible angles between. However, when the speaker begins, audience members turn and look toward the front of the room. Their head positions are suddenly aligned. Now imagine a cell phone goes off on one side of the room. Every audience member turns to look at the source of the noise. Head positions remained aligned, albeit facing a different direction than before the phone rang. If the phone is quickly silenced and the speaker resumes, audience members will gradually turn back to face the speaker at various rates, perhaps reflecting their interest in the presentation or their feelings toward the individual who forgot to turn off his or her cell phone before the symposium. However, after a short period of time, the entire audience will once again face forward until another disturbance causes the audience to turn again.

I use this example because some basic concepts of MRI can be represented by the speaker, the audience members, and the cell phone. The speaker represents the stable magnet present in the scanner. Audience members represent the protons present in hydrogen atoms that are plentiful in the brain and body. Like the audience members facing forward when a presentation starts, protons align with the magnetic field once a participant enters the stable magnetic field of the scanner. Next, a brief radiofrequency pulse is added to the system (e.g., the cell phone ring) and shifts the protons out of alignment with the magnet's magnetic field (as when the audience turned to look for the cell phone source). Because the pulse is brief, the protons are pulled back into alignment by the stable magnetic field of the scanner (as when the audience resumes attention to the speaker). The protons emit energy as they move back into alignment, and this energy is measured by special detectors that surround the patient's head; it is this energy that is measured by MRI. The process of aligning protons, knocking them over, and measuring the energy that is released as they return to alignment with the stable magnetic field when done repeatedly forms the basis of MRI (Figure 2.3).

Just as individual audience members will disengage their attention from the cell phone back to the speaker at varying speeds, the rate at which individual protons realign with the magnetic field differs depending on properties of the tissue being scanned. This difference allows us to generate images of different tissue types. In the brain, this is primarily a difference between gray matter (made of up cell bodies) and white matter (made up of the myelinated axons). When this process is

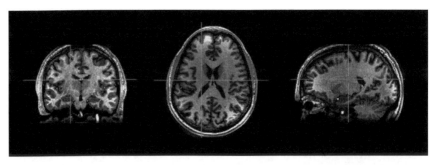

FIGURE 2.3 Example of MRI image of the brain. The image provides information about the structure of the brain but no information about its function (Deveney, unpublished data).

repeated for different portions of the brain, the end result is a three-dimensional image of brain structure like the one in Figure 2.3. Note that this image is actually a compilation of thousands of small three-dimensional boxes called voxels.

Thus far, we have discussed how MRI scanners create pictures of tissue, with the brain being of most interest to the clinical psychologist. Such studies have tremendous value. For example, studies of the normal trajectories of brain development in children (Giedd et al., 1999; Giedd & Rapoport, 2010) laid the groundwork for studies of abnormal brain development in children with psychiatric disorders including ADHD (Shaw et al., 2007) and schizophrenia (Rapoport et al., 1999). Studies of brain structure have contributed to debates over the diagnostic presentation of pediatric bipolar disorder (Adleman et al., 2012) and have helped to clarify that reduced hippocampal volume in adults with posttraumatic stress disorder (PTSD) represents a vulnerability to, rather than the product of, stressful life events associated with PTSD (Gilbertson et al., 2002).

Notably, much of the brain dysfunction observed in populations with psychopathology is related to *function* rather than structure. Consequently, fMRI is a valuable tool with which to study the function of the human brain in healthy and clinical populations. To the patient, fMRI is fairly indistinguishable from an MRI scan. The primary difference is that she or he is asked to complete a task while in the scanner instead of just lying quietly. From a physics perspective, fMRI and MRI both involve measurements of magnetic properties; however, fMRI measures the magnetic properties of oxygenated versus deoxygenated blood that result from changes in blood flow to different brain regions (Huettel et al., 2009). The basic idea is that completing a task involves neural activity that requires energy. This energy is provided by an increase in oxygenated blood flow into regions of the brain recruited for the task, pushing out deoxygenated blood from those regions. Because deoxygenated blood interferes with MR signals, reducing the amount of deoxygenated blood in the tissue increases the MR signal and indexes brain function. When fMRI articles refer to blood-oxygenation-level dependent (BOLD) signals, it is this basic process that is being measured. Specifically, fMRI involves the measurement of the ratio of oxygenated-to-deoxygenated blood present in a specific region of brain tissue over time (Huettel et al., 2009). Changes in BOLD signal in specific regions due to different tasks or different stimuli have provided the basis for understanding what regions of the brain are associated with various cognitive processes and how psychiatric populations exhibit different patterns of activation.

It is important to clarify that fMRI does not measure neural activity directly. Rather, fMRI measures are based on the assumption that blood flow changes reliably estimate neural activity. While evidence suggests that this is a reasonable assumption, the exact relationship between BOLD fMRI signals and neural activity in the brain is not fully understood (Huettel et al., 2009). Until recently, it was extremely difficult to simultaneously record fMRI BOLD signal along with a direct measure of neural activity (e.g., EEG). However, recent technical advances are helping to make this possible and may help answer this question (Huster, Debener, Eichele, & Herrmann, 2012).

fMRI experiments typically present different types of stimuli (e.g., happy or angry faces) and compare how the BOLD signal changes differ between tasks (e.g., high and low cognitive load), stimulus types (e.g., faces versus objects), and participant groups (e.g., developing children or those with an autism spectrum disorder). Unlike behavioral analyses that might involve a single statistical test on response time or accuracy, fMRI statistical tests are conducted at each voxel. The result of a group analysis consists of a single statistical value for each voxel for each statistical test.

Most fMRI analysis programs allow you to change what voxels are displayed depending on the level of statistical significance. If you set this level to be very high (statistically lenient, e.g. $p = .10$), the entire brain will appear to be significant (Figure 2.4). This is clearly not what the figures in most fMRI papers look like, so how do researchers select appropriate significance levels to identify which statistical effects are reliable and which are spurious?

In fMRI analyses, statistical tests are being conducted at each and every voxel in the brain—which equals thousands of statistical tests. This is what individuals refer to when they say fMRI has a multiple comparison problem. So where should one set the criteria for determining that a brain region is significant? Traditional significance levels ($p < .05$) would result in hundreds of spurious and meaningless findings, but applying a strict Bonferroni correction based on the number of statistical tests would eliminate the vast majority of meaningful findings. This is an important issue, and there are no clear answers in the literature as yet (Lieberman & Cunningham, 2009). In each fMRI article, the authors will describe how they attempted to correct for the number of statistical

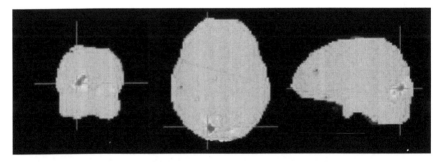

FIGURE 2.4   Example of a fMRI contrast from a single subject with excessively lenient statistical levels ($p=.90$). Note that every voxel from the fMRI image is displayed in a grey tone and no structural details from the underlying MRI image are visible. Slight differences in the grey tones of the image reflect voxels with different significance levels (Deveney, unpublished data).

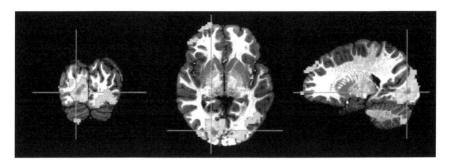

FIGURE 2.5 The same fMRI image as in Figure 2.4 when statistical levels are more stringent ($p<.001$) and only clusters with at least 20 voxels are displayed. Note that most of the MRI structural details are now visible. The cluster identified by the cross hairs reflect the most significant cluster in the data (Deveney, unpublished data).

tests they conducted. Typically, this involves setting a minimum threshold for each voxel (height threshold, e.g., $p < .001$) and requiring a certain number of adjacent voxels to be significant at that threshold (called a cluster threshold). As shown in Figure 2.5, different significance thresholds identify different clusters of activation that would be interpreted in a discussion. Note that the results of the fMRI task are overlaid on a typical MRI of the brain to help identify what anatomical structures are involved in the significant effects.

Advantages

MRI and fMRI allow researchers to identify where in the brain something is happening—whether that something is a difference in the size of a specific brain structure between patient populations or a difference in how a specific brain region is recruited by patients and non-patients during a task. The non-invasive nature of MRI and fMRI studies has made them ideal tools with which to study healthy and clinical populations relative to techniques that require exposure to radioactive substances. In addition, fMRI techniques examine the entire brain rather than being limited to neurons on the cortical surface as in EEG methods. The most significant contributions of fMRI are likely still in the future. It is important to remember what a new technology this is, and given the complexity of the brain, many studies are still trying to identify how the healthy brain functions before addressing how these processes go awry in populations with psychiatric disorders.

Disadvantages

The primary disadvantage of fMRI is the slow speed and responsivity of the BOLD signal. The BOLD response typically begins 2 seconds after a stimulus appears and peaks approximately 4 to 6 seconds later, fully resolving a number of seconds later, depending on the stimulus duration. Consequently, fMRI is a poor estimate of *when* neural events occur, and other methods such as EEG and ERP are far superior to address these questions (Huettel et al., 2009). This slow response requires experimental designs to be longer than would be required for behavioral and EEG/ERP tasks.

Although there are no known adverse effects of MRI/fMRI on most individuals (Huettel et al., 2009), the scanning environment is not always advisable or tolerated by participants (Mohlman et al., 2012). First, the scanner is a strong magnet, and people who have metal in their body should not undergo scans. Second, an abundance of caution has excluded pregnant women from being involved in fMRI scans for research purposes. Third, the scanning environment is loud, and patients can feel confined by the narrow space within the MRI scanner and the head coil that records MRI signals. As a result, scanning can be difficult for many individuals, and extensive training and habituation efforts are often required to make these scans tolerable. Fourth, motion is a significant problem for MRI/fMRI scans, and data are frequently lost because participants have difficulty staying still for the periods of time required to collect good images.

Finally, conducting MRI/fMRI research is expensive. As mentioned above, purchasing and maintaining a magnet is a formidable cost typically born only by major medical research institutions. In addition, there are expenses associated with hiring individuals trained to operate and maintain the equipment, and there are relatively large costs associated with managing the large data files produced by each study participant. Finally, translating data collected at the scanner into meaningful data to be described in a research paper requires a substantial amount of work, training, specialized software, and an appreciation for the complexity of these analyses.

Peripheral Psychophysiological Measures: Electromyography, Electrocardiography, and Skin Conductance

Direct measures of brain activity are not always necessary to study aspects of psychological functioning. Indeed, there are a number of times when measuring brain activity directly is impossible or even undesirable, as when studying populations unlikely to tolerate having electrodes on their heads or confinement in an MRI scanner. There are also instances when the research question being asked lends itself to measurement by another technique. The following is a review of physiological measures from around the body that are useful for individuals conducting research on psychiatric populations (Andreassi, 1995).

Electromyography

Take a moment to furrow your brows and think briefly about the muscles you moved when doing so. Do the same when you smile. Each of those muscle movements generated small electrical signals. Like EEG recordings of neuronal activity, the electrical activity from the muscle fibers can be measured via electrodes placed on the skin surface. This measure is called electromyography or EMG (Fridlund & Cacioppo, 1986). Importantly, visible movement of the muscles is not necessary in order to detect electrical changes in these muscles.

Over the past several decades, EMG recorded from facial muscles has provided insight into the emotional experience of healthy and psychiatric populations. When you furrowed your brows earlier, you moved the *corrugator supercillii* muscles that lie on the upper edge of the eyebrows near the innermost corner of the eye. Greater activity in these muscles has been associated with greater negative affect and the viewing of negative images (Bradley, Cuthbert, & Lang, 1990; Cuthbert, Schupp, Bradley, McManis, & Lang, 1998). Participants asked to contract these muscles without any suggestion of emotions typically report greater negative emotion than individuals asked to contract other muscles (Levenson, Ekman, & Friesen, 1990). On the opposite emotional spectrum are the zygomatic muscles located above the corners of the mouth near the cheekbones, which you moved when you smiled (Levenson et al., 1990). As you might imagine, activity in these muscles corresponds with positive emotions and emotional stimuli.

EMG has been useful to clinical psychologists in a variety of ways from basic questions about whether females are more emotionally expressive than males (Dimberg & Lundquist, 1990) to studies revealing that the flat affect displayed by individuals with schizophrenia belies intact emotional experiences in this population (Kring & Elis, 2013; Kring, Kerr, Smith, & Neale, 1993).

Electrocardiography

No television or movie depiction of a hospital is complete without an electrocardiogram (ECG or EKG) trace on the monitor adjacent to the fictional patient. Great drama ensues whenever the signal on the monitor goes flat, reflecting the cessation of a heart beat. What few viewers understand is that this signal represents the electrical currents produced when the heart contracts. The characteristic shape of an ECG recording relates to the different stages that make up a heartbeat from blood flowing into the atria to blood being pushed out of each ventricle, to the resetting of the heart muscles in anticipation of the next heartbeat (Andreassi, 1995). In addition to insight about cardiovascular functioning, ECG measures also tap into emotional processes of interest to clinical psychologists. For example, changes in heart rate—the number of heart beats per minute—can differ between task conditions and for different clinical populations (Shalev et al., 1998). Heart rate variability, or respiratory sinus arrhythmia, is also a measure of interest for clinical psychologists. In short, the degree to which the heart rate varies versus rigidly beats in the same exact pattern over a period of time has been linked with cardiac health and emotion regulation ability (Porges, 2001).

Skin Conductance or Galvanic Skin Response

Most people have experienced an increase in sweating during periods of stress or marked emotion. However, it is the rare individual who might connect this sweating response to increased electrical conductance properties in their skin due to the presence of salt (Boucsein et al., 2012). However, in the 1800s, researchers observed that the electrical conductance properties of the skin changed as a result of emotional and cognitive stimuli and, since that time, skin conductance (SC) responses have been of interest to psychologists (Andreassi, 1995). For example, theories that aggressive and psychopathic behavior stemmed from abnormally low physiological arousal or reactivity to the pain of other individuals has been investigated in a number of studies with modest associations (Lorber, 2004).

Advantages

Studies of peripheral measures of nervous system functioning have provided important information about emotional functioning and, even relative to EEG, are less invasive, easy to apply, and lend themselves to more naturalistic studies with greater ecological validity. Technological advances are allowing these measures to be used in combination with neuroimaging techniques that will help the field associate peripheral measures of emotion with neural markers of this same process (Heller, Greischar, Honor, Anderle, & Davidson, 2011).

Disadvantages

Like EEG and fMRI, these measures still require electrodes and wires to participants, which may disrupt typical emotional responses. In addition, while individual psychophysiological measures are consistently associated with emotional responses, groups of physiological measures do not always cohere in synchrony (Kreibig, 2010). Specific measures may also have unique limitations. For example, SC recordings can be easily altered by the amount of conducting gel used in the electrode (Boucsein et al., 2012). The failure to maintain a consistent amount of gel across participants could artificially induce SC differences between participants. Similarly, caffeine can alter heart rate, and differences in propensity to drink coffee before an experimental session can alter the likelihood of detecting reliable differences between groups

(Jennings et al., 1981). In addition, SC responses are slow and can habituate easily. Therefore, they may not be appropriate for certain types of research questions and experimental designs.

Hormones or Behavioral Endocrinology

Perhaps because the primary treatment for psychiatric disorders involves medications that alter neurotransmitter functioning, clinical psychologists often overlook the impact of hormones on mood and cognition. Hormones, chemicals in the body secreted by endocrine glands (e.g., hypothalamus, pituitary gland, thyroid, adrenal glands, and pancreas), have long been linked to psychological functioning of interest to clinical psychologists. For example, changes in thyroid levels are known to influence mood and energy levels, at times dramatically (Breedlove & Watson, 2013).

A large amount of research about hormones has been conducted with animals, in large part because of the experimental control permitted to evaluate the relationship between specific hormones and specific behaviors (Breedlove & Watson, 2013). Let us take the example of a researcher interested in whether hormone X influences an animal's appetite. The researcher has a number of different techniques at her/his disposal. The researcher could identify animals that display appetite extremes (i.e., those that eat a lot and those that eat very little) and compare the average amount of hormone X in the bloodstream of the low- versus high-appetite group. The researcher could also inject a group of animals with a synthetic form of hormone X, another group with a placebo, and then measure how much each group ate. Another strategy is to create "knock out" animals—those animals that have had their genetic profile altered so hormone X can no longer function. The researcher would then look to see whether the knock out animals ate amounts of food different from animals whose genes had not been tampered with. Convincing evidence for a relationship between hormone X and appetite would exist if (1) the natural big eaters had higher levels of hormone X in their bloodstream; (2) animals receiving injections of hormone X ate more; and (3) the knock out animals ate less than control animals (Breedlove & Watson, 2013).

Increasingly, these basic animal studies have been translated into the human domain and into areas of interest to clinical psychologists. For example, interpersonal deficits are key symptoms of many psychiatric disorders, including autism spectrum disorders (Baron-Cohen, 1988; Volkmar et al., 1987). In addition to studies using neuroimaging methods like EEG and fMRI (Baron-Cohen et al., 1999; McPartland et al., 2004), researchers have examined the role of hormones in the interpersonal difficulties experienced by these populations. For example, if the hormone oxytocin plays a key role in social behaviors like breastfeeding and bonding, and oxytocin deficiencies have been tied to poorer affiliative behaviors

(Donaldson & Young, 2008; Insel, 2010), might individuals with autism spectrum disorders have deficient levels of this hormone? Some evidence suggests that this is the case (Green et al., 2001; Insel, 2010). Perhaps most excitingly, basic studies suggesting that oxytocin administration can improve social behaviors in animals led to studies evaluating whether oxytocin inhalation can improve social behaviors in both healthy and autistic populations (Domes et al., 2013; Guastella et al., 2010). Although the human translational research is in its infancy and many questions about efficacy and safety remain, this example demonstrates the power of the neurocognitive approach in an elegant manner.

Advantages

A wealth of animal research exists to guide human research in behavioral endocrinology and often provides very clear associations between specific hormones and specific behaviors. In addition, a number of naturally occurring endocrine disorders can be used to examine the relationship between hormones and certain psychiatric symptoms in humans.

Disadvantages

Many of the disadvantages of lesion studies also apply to behavioral endocrinology. For example, many of the techniques employed in animal research are unethical to conduct in humans. The complexity and interrelatedness of many hormones can make it difficult to pinpoint a hormone's specific relationship with human behavior—especially use of the techniques available in animal research. Also similar to lesion studies, some human behaviors cannot be adequately modeled in animals and are, therefore, challenging to study using these techniques. Finally, many hormones of interest to clinical psychologists have natural increases and decreases according to time of day or in relation to other biological processes like the menstrual cycle. Consequently, researchers must be aware of these confounds and standardize data collection across participant groups.

Conclusions and Additional Resources

The goal of this chapter was to introduce readers to some of the techniques employed by researchers adopting a neurocognitive approach toward the study of psychiatric disorders. While complex and technical at times and not comprehensive (e.g., there are a number of additional fascinating measures including transcranial magnetic stimulation, near infrared spectroscopy, and position emission tomography, to name a few), hopefully the reader walked away with increased awareness and understanding of the tools that exist to probe questions relevant for clinical psychologists. After reading this chapter, the reader can consider the clinical problems that have been most vexing and least amenable to behavioral or self-report measure inquiry and muse about whether a biological approach may provide valuable insight.

As mentioned in the introduction, the goal of the chapter was not to make the reader an expert in each methodology. Instead, a list of recommended readings is provided that can serve as a starting point for individuals interested in learning more about various measures. Along with this list of readings are a few helpful online resources that cover some basic background on the brain and links to some of the most cutting-edge research on neuroscience and psychiatric illness.

Should you decide to embark upon the use of neurocognitive methods for the first time, know that you are not alone! There are a number of resources available to help. These programs and events are typically staffed by individuals who know, use, and recommend these methods and are willing to share their enthusiasm and expertise with individuals looking to learn. These additional resources come in three main forms. First, many professional associations have pre-conference workshops designed for attendees to receive introductory and advanced training from experts. For example, the Association for the Advancement of Behavioral and Cognitive Therapies, the Society for Psychophysiological Research, and the Society for Neuroscience all offer such workshops. Second, more intensive workshops that involve hands-on data collection and analyses are offered by a number of academic institutions. Interested individuals can start by looking at programs offered by the University of California, Los Angeles (http://www.brainmapping.org/NITP/Summer2012.php), Massachusetts General Hospital, Athinoula A. Martinos Center for Biomedical Imaging (http://www.nmr.mgh.harvard.edu/martinos/training/fMRIVisitFellowProg.php), and the ERP boot camp at the University of California, Davis (http://erpinfo.org/the-erp-bootcamp). Third, training opportunities exist for the software used to analyze these data. For example, the Analysis of Functional Neuroimaging program was created and supported by individuals at the National Institute of Health. This team of experts hosts a boot camp open to the public that describes appropriate use of the software and reviews some of the issues around accurately analyzing fMRI data (http://afni.nimh.nih.gov/bootcamp/.). Similar training programs exist for other software programs, and there is often a considerable amount of online support from users and program support staff.

Finally, technology is advancing at a rapid pace, allowing innovative ways to probe clinical questions using ecologically valid methods. For example, new technologies permit ambulatory monitoring of physiological measures so researchers can study individuals in their daily lives or simultaneously record physiological activity from people in a social interaction. Hansen and Siegle's chapter later in this book reviews a number of recent innovations that should encourage the adoption of neurocognitive strategies for the study of psychiatric illness.

Recommended Readings

Bandettini, P. A. (2012). Twenty years of functional MRI: the Science and the stories. *NeuroImage, 62*, 575–588.

Cacioppo, J., Tassinary, L. G., & Berntson, G. G. (2007). *Handbook of psychophysiology.* Cambridge: Cambridge University Press.

Davidson, R. J., Scherer, K. R., & Goldsmith, H. (2009). *Handbook of affective sciences.* Oxford: Oxford University Press.

Hashemi, R. H., Bradley, W. G., Jr. (2010). *MRI: The basics.* 3rd edn. Baltimore, MD: Wolters Kluwer Lippincott Williams and Wilkins.

Huettel, S. A., Wong, A. W., & McCarthy, G. (2009). *Functional magnetic resonance imaging.* Sunderland, MA: Sinauer Associations, Inc.

Luck, S.J. (2005). *An introduction to the event-related potential technique.* Cambridge, MA: The MIT Press.

Online Resources

Allen Institute for Brain Science - http://www.alleninstitute.org/

CalTech Tedx series on the Brain - http://tedxcaltech.caltech.edu/

Experts in Emotion series - http://www.yalepeplab.com/teaching/psych131_summer2013/expertseries.php

National Institute of Mental Health—brain basics - http://www.nimh.nih.gov/brainbasics/index.html

NIH Brain Initiative http://www.nih.gov/science/brain/

References

Adleman, N. E., Fromm, S. J., Razdan, V., Kayser, R., Dickstein, D. P., Brotman, M. A., ... & Leibenluft, E. (2012). Cross-sectional and longitudinal abnormalities in brain structure in children with severe mood dysregulation or bipolar disorder. *Journal of Child Psychology and Pyschiatry, 53*(11), 1149–1156. doi: 10.1111/j.1469-7610.2012.02568.x

Adolphs, R., Tranel, D., Damasio, H., & Damasio, A. R. (1995). Fear and the human amygdala. *Journal of Neuroscience, 15*(9), 5879-5891.

Adolphs, R., Gosselin, F., Buchanan, T. W., Tranel, D., Schyns, P., & Damasio, A. R. (2005). A mechanism for impaired fear recognition after amygdala damage. *Nature, 433*(7021), 68–72. doi: 10.1038/nature03086

Amir, N., Beard, C., Burns, M., & Bomyea, J. (2009). Attention modification program in individuals with generalized anxiety disorder. *Journal of Abnormal Psychology, 118*(1), 28–33. doi: 10.1037/a0012589

Andreassi, J. L. (1995). *Psychophysiology: Human behavior and psychophysiological response* (3rd edn). Hillsdale, NJ: Erlbaum.

Baron-Cohen, S. (1988). Social and pragmatic deficits in autism: cognitive or affective? *Journal of Autism and Development Disorders, 18*(3), 379–402.

Baron-Cohen, S., Ring, H. A., Wheelwright, S., Bullmore, E. T., Brammer, M. J., Simmons, A., & Williams, S. C. (1999). Social intelligence in the normal and autistic brain: an fMRI study. *European Journal of Neuroscience, 11*(6), 1891–1898.

Beck, L. H., Bransome, E. D., Jr., Mirsky, A. F., Rosvold, H. E., & Sarason, I. (1956). A continuous performance test of brain damage. *Journal of Consulting Psychology, 20*(5), 343–350.

Boucsein, W., Fowles, D. C., Grimnes, S., Ben-Shakhar, G., Roth, W. T., Dawson, M. E., & Filion, D. L. (2012). Publication recommendations for electrodermal measurements. *Psychophysiology, 49*(8), 1017–1034. doi: 10.1111/j.1469-8986.2012.01384.x

Bradley, M. M., Cuthbert, B. N., & Lang, P. J. (1990). Startle reflex modification: emotion or attention? *Psychophysiology, 27*(5), 513–522.

Breedlove, S.M., & Watson, N.V. (2013). *Biological psychology: An introduction to behavioral, cognitive, and clinical neuroscience* (7th edn). Sunderland, MA: Sinauer Associates Inc.

Brotman, M. A., Rich, B. A., Guyer, A. E., Lunsford, J. R., Horsey, S. E., Reising, M. M., … & Leibenluft, E. (2010). Amygdala activation during emotion processing of neutral faces in children with severe mood dysregulation versus ADHD or bipolar disorder. *American Journal of Psychiatry, 167*(1), 61–69. doi: 10.1176/appi.ajp.2009.09010043

Corkin, S. (2002). What's new with the amnesic patient H. M.? *Nature Reviews Neuroscience, 3*(2), 153–160. doi: 10.1038/nrn726

Cuthbert, B. N., Schupp, H. T., Bradley, M., McManis, M., & Lang, P. J. (1998). Probing affective pictures: attended startle and tone probes. *Psychophysiology, 35*(3), 344–347.

Dimberg, U., & Lundquist, L. O. (1990). Gender differences in facial reactions to facial expressions. *Biological Psychology, 30*(2), 151–159.

Domes, G., Heinrichs, M., Kumbier, E., Grossmann, A., Hauenstein, K., & Herpertz, S. C. (2013). Effects of intranasal oxytocin on the neural basis of face processing in autism spectrum disorder. *Biological Psychiatry, 74*(3), 164–71. doi: 10.1016/j.biopsych.2013.02.007

Donaldson, Z. R., & Young, L. J. (2008). Oxytocin, vasopressin, and the neurogenetics of sociality. *Science, 322*(5903), 900–904. doi: 10.1126/science.1158668

Feinstein, J. S., Buzza, C., Hurlemann, R., Follmer, R. L., Dahdaleh, N. S., Coryell, W. H., … & Wemmie, J. A. (2013). Fear and panic in humans with bilateral amygdala damage. *Nature Neuroscience, 16*(3), 270–272. doi: 10.1038/nn.3323

Frangou, S., Donaldson, S., Hadjulis, M., Landau, S., & Goldstein, L. H. (2005). The Maudsley Bipolar Disorder Project: executive dysfunction in bipolar disorder I and its clinical correlates. *Biological Psychiatry, 58*(11), 859–864. doi: 10.1016/j.biopsych.2005.04.056

Fridlund, A. J., & Cacioppo, J. T. (1986). Guidelines for human electromyographic research. *Psychophysiology, 23*(5), 567–589.

Gazzaniga, M., Ivry, R. B., & Mangun, G. R. (2013). *Cognitive neuroscience: The biology of the mind* (4th edn). New York: W.W. Norton & Company.

Giedd, J. N., & Rapoport, J. L. (2010). Structural MRI of pediatric brain development: what have we learned and where are we going? *Neuron, 67*(5), 728–734. doi: 10.1016/j.neuron.2010.08.040

Giedd, J. N., Blumenthal, J., Jeffries, N. O., Castellanos, F. X., Liu, H., Zijdenbos, A., … & Rapoport, J. L. (1999). Brain development during childhood and adolescence: a longitudinal MRI study. *Nature Neuroscience, 2*(10), 861–863. doi: 10.1038/13158

Gilbertson, M. W., Shenton, M. E., Ciszewski, A., Kasai, K., Lasko, N. B., Orr, S. P., & Pitman, R. K. (2002). Smaller hippocampal volume predicts pathologic vulnerability to psychological trauma. *Nature Neuroscience, 5*(11), 1242–1247. doi: 10.1038/nn958

Gleitman, H., Gross, J. J., & Reisberg, D. (2010). *Psychology* (8th edn). New York: W.W. Norton & Company.

Green, L., Fein, D., Modahl, C., Feinstein, C., Waterhouse, L., & Morris, M. (2001). Oxytocin and autistic disorder: alterations in peptide forms. *Biological Psychiatry, 50*(8), 609–613.

Guastella, A. J., Einfeld, S. L., Gray, K. M., Rinehart, N. J., Tonge, B. J., Lambert, T. J., & Hickie, I. B. (2010). Intranasal oxytocin improves emotion recognition for youth with autism spectrum disorders. *Biological Psychiatry, 67*(7), 692–694. doi: 10.1016/j.biopsych.2009.09.020

Heller, A. S., Greischar, L. L., Honor, A., Anderle, M. J., & Davidson, R. J. (2011). Simultaneous acquisition of corrugator electromyography and functional magnetic resonance imaging: a new method for objectively measuring affect and neural activity concurrently. *Neuroimage, 58*(3), 930–934. doi: 10.1016/j.neuroimage.2011.06.057

Henriques, J. B., & Davidson, R. J. (1991). Left frontal hypoactivation in depression. *Journal of Abnormal Psychology, 100*(4), 535–545.

Huettel, S. A., Song, A. W., & McCarthy, G. (2009). *Functional magnetic resonance imaging* (2nd edn). Sunderland, MA: Sinauer Associates, Inc.

Huster, R. J., Debener, S., Eichele, T., & Herrmann, C. S. (2012). Methods for simultaneous EEG-fMRI: an introductory review. *Journal of Neuroscience, 32*(18), 6053–6060. doi: 10.1523/jneurosci.0447–12.2012

Insel, T. R. (2010). The challenge of translation in social neuroscience: a review of oxytocin, vasopressin, and affiliative behavior. *Neuron, 65*(6), 768–779. doi: 10.1016/j.neuron.2010.03.005

Insel, T. R. (2011). Mental illness defined as disruption in neural circuits. Retrieved 7/2/2014 from http://www.nimh.nih.gov/about/director/2011/mental-illness-defined-as-disruption-in-neural-circuits.shtml

Institute of Medicine Committee on Sleep Medicine and Research. (2006). H. R. Colten & B. M. Altevogt (eds.), *Sleep disorders and sleep deprivation: An unmet public health problem*. Washington, DC: National Academies Press.

Jennings, J. R., Berg, W. K., Hutcheson, J. S., Obrist, P., Porges, S., & Turpin, G. (1981). Committee report. Publication guidelines for heart rate studies in man. *Psychophysiology, 18*(3), 226–231.

Kennedy, S. H., Giacobbe, P., Rizvi, S. J., Placenza, F. M., Nishikawa, Y., Mayberg, H. S., & Lozano, A. M. (2011). Deep brain stimulation for treatment-resistant depression: follow-up after 3 to 6 years. *American Journal of Psychiatry, 168*(5), 502–510. doi: 10.1176/appi.ajp.2010.10081187

Kong, A., Frigge, M. L., Masson, G., Besenbacher, S., Sulem, P., Magnusson, G., ... & Stefansson, K. (2012). Rate of de novo mutations and the importance of father's age to disease risk. *Nature, 488*(7412), 471–475. doi:10.1038/nature11396

Kreibig, S. D. (2010). Autonomic nervous system activity in emotion: a review. *Biological Psychology, 84*(3), 394–421. doi: 10.1016/j.biopsycho.2010.03.010

Kring, A. M., & Elis, O. (2013). Emotion deficits in people with schizophrenia. *Annual Review of Clinical Psychology, 9*, 409–33. doi: 10.1146/annurev-clinpsy-050212-185538

Kring, A. M., Kerr, S. L., Smith, D. A., & Neale, J. M. (1993). Flat affect in schizophrenia does not reflect diminished subjective experience of emotion. *Journal of Abnormal Psychology, 102*(4), 507–517.

LeDoux, J. E. (1996). *The emotional brain*. New York: Simon and Shuster.

Levenson, R. W., Ekman, P., & Friesen, W. V. (1990). Voluntary facial action generates emotion-specific autonomic nervous system activity. *Psychophysiology, 27*(4), 363–384.

Lewis, M. D., Lamm, C., Segalowitz, S. J., Stieben, J., & Zelazo, P. D. (2006). Neurophysiological correlates of emotion regulation in children and adolescents. *Journal of Cognitive Neuroscience, 18*(3), 430–443. doi: 10.1162/089892906775990633

Lieberman, M. D., & Cunningham, W. A. (2009). Type I and Type II error concerns in fMRI research: re-balancing the scale. *Social Cognitive and Affective Neuroscience, 4*(4), 423–428. doi: 10.1093/scan/nsp052

Lorber, M. F. (2004). Psychophysiology of aggression, psychopathy, and conduct problems: a meta-analysis. *Psychological Bulletin, 130*(4), 531–552. doi: 10.1037/0033-2909.130.4.531

Losier, B. J., McGrath, P. J., & Klein, R. M. (1996). Error patterns on the continuous performance test in non-medicated and medicated samples of children with and without ADHD: a meta-analytic review. *Journal of Child Psychology and Pyschiatry, 37*(8), 971–987.

Luck, S. J. (2005). *An introduction to the event-related potential technique.* Cambridge, MA: MIT Press.

Mander, B. A., Rao, V., Lu, B., Saletin, J. M., Lindquist, J. R., Ancoli-Israel, S., ... & Walker, M. P. (2013). Prefrontal atrophy, disrupted NREM slow waves and impaired hippocampal-dependent memory in aging. *Nature Neuroscience, 16*(3), 357–364. doi: 10.1038/nn.3324

Martin, J. H. (2001). *Neuroanatomy: Text and atlas* (2nd edn). New York: McGraw-Hill Publishing Company.

Maslowsky, J., Mogg, K., Bradley, B. P., McClure-Tone, E., Ernst, M., Pine, D. S., & Monk, C. S. (2010). A preliminary investigation of neural correlates of treatment in adolescents with generalized anxiety disorder. *Journal of Child and Adolescent Psychopharmacology, 20*(2), 105–111. doi: 10.1089/cap.2009.0049

Mayberg, H. S., Lozano, A. M., Voon, V., McNeely, H. E., Seminowicz, D., Hamani, C., ... & Kennedy, S. H. (2005). Deep brain stimulation for treatment-resistant depression. *Neuron, 45*(5), 651–660. doi: 10.1016/j.neuron.2005.02.014

McClure, E. B., Adler, A., Monk, C. S., Cameron, J., Smith, S., Nelson, E. E., ... & Pine, D. S. (2007). fMRI predictors of treatment outcome in pediatric anxiety disorders. *Psychopharmacology, 191*(1), 97–105. doi: 10.1007/s00213-006-0542-9

McPartland, J., Dawson, G., Webb, S. J., Panagiotides, H., & Carver, L. J. (2004). Event-related brain potentials reveal anomalies in temporal processing of faces in autism spectrum disorder. *Journal of Child Psychology and Pyschiatry, 45*(7), 1235–1245. doi: 10.1111/j.1469-7610.2004.00318.x

Mohlman, J., Eldreth, D. A., Price, R. B., & Chazin, D. (2012). Predictors of unsuccessful magnetic resonance imaging scanning in older generalized anxiety disorder patients and nonanxious controls. *Journal of Behavioral Medicine*, 35, 19–26.

NIH. (2013). NIT Toolbox: Assessment of neurological and behavioral function. Retrieved 5/15/2013 from http://www.nihtoolbox.org/Pages/default.aspx

Paquette, V., Levesque, J., Mensour, B., Leroux, J. M., Beaudoin, G., Bourgouin, P., & Beauregard, M. (2003). "Change the mind and you change the brain": effects of cognitive-behavioral therapy on the neural correlates of spider phobia. *Neuroimage, 18*(2), 401–409. doi: S1053811902000307 [pii]

Pizzagalli, D. A. (2010). Frontocingulate dysfunction in depression: toward biomarkers of treatment response. *Neuropsychopharmacology, 36*(1), 183–206. doi: npp2010166 [pii] 10.1038/npp.2010.166

Porges, S. W. (2001). The polyvagal theory: phylogenetic substrates of a social nervous system. *International Journal of Psychophysiology, 42*(2), 123–146.

Rapoport, J. L., Giedd, J. N., Blumenthal, J., Hamburger, S., Jeffries, N., Fernandez, T., … & Evans, A. (1999). Progressive cortical change during adolescence in childhood-onset schizophrenia. A longitudinal magnetic resonance imaging study. *Archives of General Psychiatry, 56*(7), 649–654.

Scoville, W. B., & Milner, B. (1957). Loss of recent memory after bilateral hippocampal lesions. *Journal of Neurology, Neurosurgery and Psychiatry, 20*(1), 11–21.

Shalev, A. Y., Sahar, T., Freedman, S., Peri, T., Glick, N., Brandes, D., … & Pitman, R. K. (1998). A prospective study of heart rate response following trauma and the subsequent development of posttraumatic stress disorder. *Archives of General Psychiatry, 55*(6), 553–559.

Shaw, P., Eckstrand, K., Sharp, W., Blumenthal, J., Lerch, J. P., Greenstein, D., … & Rapoport, J. L. (2007). Attention-deficit/hyperactivity disorder is characterized by a delay in cortical maturation. *PNAS, 104*(49), 19649–19654. doi: 10.1073/pnas.0707741104

Shin, L. M., & Liberzon, I. (2010). The neurocircuitry of fear, stress, and anxiety disorders. *Neuropsychopharmacology, 35*(1), 169–191. doi: 10.1038/npp.2009.83

Siegle, G. J., Carter, C. S., & Thase, M. E. (2006). Use of FMRI to predict recovery from unipolar depression with cognitive behavior therapy. *American Journal of Psychiatry, 163*(4), 735–738. doi: 163/4/735 [pii]10.1176/appi.ajp.163.4.735

Sternberg, D. E., & Jarvik, M. E. (1976). Memory functions in depression. *Archives of General Psychiatry, 33*(2), 219–224.

Volkmar, F. R., Sparrow, S. S., Goudreau, D., Cicchetti, D. V., Paul, R., & Cohen, D. J. (1987). Social deficits in autism: an operational approach using the Vineland Adaptive Behavior Scales. *Journal of American Academy of Child and Adolescent Psychiatry, 26*(2), 156–161. doi: 10.1097/00004583-198703000-00005

Wechsler, D. (1945). A standardized memory scale for clinical use. *Journal of Psychology, 19*, 87–95.

Weissman, A. S., Chu, B. C., Reddy, L. A., & Mohlman, J. (2012). Attention mechanisms in children with anxiety disorders and in children with attention deficit hyperactivity disorder: implications for research and practice. *Journal of Clinical Child and Adolescent Psychology, 41*(2), 117–126. doi: 10.1080/15374416.2012.651993

3

PEDIATRIC ANXIETY

A Neurocognitive Review

Alexandra Sturm and Susanna W. Chang

Anxiety disorders are one of the most common psychiatric conditions of childhood with estimated prevalence rates ranging from 3 percent to 25 percent (Bernstein, Borchardt, & Perwien, 1996; Cartwright-Hatton, McNicol, & Doubleday, 2006; Kessler et al., 1994). They confer substantial clinical impairment and increased risk for persistent negative long-term outcomes for affected youth. Studies indicate that anxiety disorders in childhood are associated with psychosocial impairment in multiple domains of functioning including school, home, and peer relationships (Langley, Bergman, McCracken, & Piacentini, 2004). Children with anxiety disorders have fewer close friendships, experience more peer victimization, and have greater perceptions of parental over-control, attachment, and rejection than their healthy peers (Crawford & Manassis, 2011; Hale, Klimstra, Branje, Wijsbroek, & Meeus, 2013; Scharfstein, Alfano, Beidel, & Wong, 2011; Storch et al., 2006). Moreover, anxiety disorders often persist into adulthood and are predictive of later psychopathology, including adult substance use disorders and depression (Cole, Peeke, Martin, Truglio, & Seroczynski, 1998; Costello, Mustillo, Erkanli, Keeler, & Angold, 2003).

Although current treatment approaches are effective for many, 20 percent to 35 percent of children do not experience optimal symptom improvement, suggesting the need for further research into etiology and treatment development (Rynn et al., 2011). Advances in research methodology including neuroimaging, neuropsychology, and behavioral genetics have worked synergistically to create a clearer picture of the neurobiological factors underlying anxiety. Integration of these biological processes with clinical phenomenology will inform a translational neurocognitive approach, which has the potential to advance existing theoretical models of anxiety as well as the development of novel treatment modalities. In this chapter, following a brief review of the symptom dimensions of anxiety disorders, we explore the current literature on genetics, neuroimaging, and neuropsychological domains, collectively termed neurocognition. We conclude with a discussion of how existing neurocognitive perspectives can advance our understanding of the underlying etiology of anxiety disorders as well as inform future directions for novel therapeutics.

Symptom Dimensions

Anxiety disorders all share the core feature of threat relevant response, which manifest in cognitive, physiological, and behavioral domains. Clinical symptoms may include somatic complaints, hypervigilance to threat, worry, intrusive thoughts, repetitive rituals, and behavioral avoidance (Craske & Waters, 2005). Anxiety disorders can be distinguished from one another primarily based on the nature and focus of the threat. In youth, the most commonly diagnosed anxiety disorders include social anxiety disorder, generalized anxiety disorder, and separation anxiety disorder (SAD; Costello, Egger, & Angold, 2004). SAD is defined as the unrealistic worry upon separation or anticipated separation from a major attachment figure (APA, 2000) and is the only anxiety disorder with a specific childhood onset. Separation-anxious symptoms often show a waxing and waning course; however, chronic symptoms are not uncommon (Eisen et al., 2011). Social anxiety disorder (SoAD) is the most common anxiety disorder (13.3 percent lifetime; Kessler et al., 1994) and is defined by a "marked fear or anxiety about one or more social situations in which the individual is exposed to possible scrutiny by others" (APA, 2013, p. 202). Generalized anxiety disorder (GAD) is characterized by the broadest range of threat response and is marked by excessive, uncontrollable, and persistent worry about a wide range of life events along with accompanying physical symptoms of tension.

Obsessive-compulsive disorder (OCD) traditionally has been classified as an anxiety disorder (APA, 2000). However, the reorganized *Diagnostic and Statistical Manual of Mental Disorders* (5th ed.) places OCD in the umbrella category of "Obsessive-Compulsive and related disorders," which includes conditions such as body dysmorphic disorder, hoarding disorder, and trichotillomania (APA, 2013). Although the classification of OCD has shifted most recently to bring primary focus to obsessive preoccupation and repetitive behaviors, OCD continues to share many features and treatment approaches with other anxiety disorders. Therefore, we include OCD under subheadings in relevant sections of this chapter to mark it as a distinct diagnostic category, while maintaining the historical understanding of it as a clinical disorder characterized by areas of overlap in phenomenology and neurobiology with anxiety disorders.

OCD is often distinguished from anxiety disorders based on clinical characteristics and etiology. The essential features of OCD are obsessions and/

or compulsions that are distressing or time-consuming or cause significant interference in normal functioning. Obsessions are recurrent, persistent, intrusive, and distressing thoughts, images, or impulses, whereas compulsions are defined as repetitive behaviors or mental acts performed in response to an obsession and designed to reduce distress or avoid some perceived harm. Although OCD manifests as a relatively heterogeneous disorder in childhood, some symptoms are seen more commonly than others. Research has shown that OCD symptoms consistently load onto four factors: *forbidden thoughts* (aggression, sexual, religious, and checking compulsions); *symmetry* (repeating, ordering, and counting compulsions and symmetry obsessions); *cleaning* (cleaning and contamination); and *hoarding* (Leckman, Bloch, & King, 2009).

For the purposes of this chapter, we will focus our remaining discussion on the anxiety disorders of social, separation, generalized anxiety in addition to OCD. Although specific phobia is a commonly diagnosed anxiety disorder in childhood (Essau, Conradt, & Petermann, 2000), it has not been the focus of many neurocognitive investigations, and we have chosen to omit it from this chapter's consideration. Research suggests that specific phobias relative to other anxiety disorders are not associated with a clear pattern of neuropsychological impairment, although it is unclear whether this is due to the absence of deficit or the presence of other confounding anxiety disorders (Costello, Egger, & Angold, 2004; Larson, South, & Merkley, 2011). Moreover, isolated specific phobias are characterized by low continuity across development, and lower rates of impairment compared to other anxiety disorders (Costello et al., 2003; Pine, Wasserman, & Leibenluft, 1999).

Comorbidity and Differential Diagnosis

Comorbidity in anxiety disorders "is the rule rather than the exception" (Gotlieb & Hammen, 1992). As many as 75 percent of youth with an anxiety disorder are diagnosed with a comorbid psychiatric condition, including depression, bipolar disorder, autism spectrum disorders, oppositional-defiant disorder, substance use, and ADHD (Dickstein et al., 2005; Essau, 2003; Harpold et al., 2005; Jarrett & Ollendick, 2008; Lewinsohn, Zinbarg, Seeley, Lewinsohn, & Sack, 1997; White, Oswald, Ollendick, & Scahill, 2009). However, anxiety disorders most frequently co-occur with other anxiety disorders (Costello et al., 2003). Between 14 percent and 19 percent of youth with any primary anxiety disorder have been diagnosed with a secondary anxiety disorder (Lewinsohn et al., 1997; Essau, 2003), with certain anxiety conditions such as GAD (53 percent) and OCD (33 percent; Masi, Mucci, Favilla, Romano, & Poli, 1999; Langley, Lewin, Bergman, Lee, & Piacentini, 2010) most likely to be comorbid.

OCD

OCD shows a unique pattern of comorbidity with tic disorders and ADHD not shared by non-OCD anxiety disorders. Reported comorbidity of tics and OCD is relatively high, ranging from 10 percent to 40 percent (Leckman et al., 2009) such that "tic-related OCD" has become one clinically informative categorical distinction. Children with tic-related OCD also have higher rates of disruptive behavior disorders (i.e., ADHD), culminating in a trio of OCD, comorbid tics, and ADHD frequently observed in clinical cases and community samples (Peterson, Pine, Cohen, & Brook, 2001). Indeed, the presence of ADHD and other disruptive behavior disorders has been found to be associated with lower response to CBT in children with OCD. However, tic and anxiety comorbidity did not appear to impact treatment response in the same study (Storch et al., 2008).

With such high rates of diagnostic comorbidity, accurate diagnoses of anxiety disorders are essential to treatment planning and research clarity. Anxiety can be normative within certain developmental contexts and crosses a diagnostic threshold only when associated persistence, pervasiveness, avoidance, and distress are related to functional impairment (Albano, Causey, & Carter, 2001). Clinicians can differentiate between anxiety disorders by examining the nature of the feared stimulus (Ollendick, Grills, & Alexander, 2013). The persistent and excessive worry about general events of daily life in GAD differs from the specific fear of social evaluation in social phobia. GAD is the anxiety disorder most phenomenologically similar to OCD, as both are characterized by intrusive and recurrent thoughts. However, the content of anxious cognitions in GAD involves everyday matters while the obsessions of OCD are typically more irrational in nature (APA, 2013).

Clearly, the presentation of anxiety disorders in youth is heterogeneous and characterized by high rates of comorbidity. Specific symptom profiles in conjunction with underlying genetic, neurobiological, and neuropsychological correlates of each disorder will ultimately help to differentiate among the various diagnoses and guide treatment approaches.

Biological Factors

Genetics

Behavioral genetics studies have examined the independent contributions of genetic heritability, shared, and non-shared environmental factors in anxiety disorders and OCD. Transmission models of anxiety disorders highlight the interplay between genetic and environmental factors. However, genetic influences still account for approximately 50 percent of the variance in both anxiety and OCD, supporting a familial aggregation of anxiety disorders (Eley, Rijsdijk, Perrin, O'Connor, & Bolton, 2008; Ogliari et al., 2010; Scaini, Ogliari, Eley, Zavos, & Battaglia, 2012; Taylor, Jang, & Asmundson, 2010).

High comorbidity rates between anxiety disorders in youth can also be attributed primarily to genetic factors, which explain between 58 percent and 77 percent of the covariation between GAD, SAD, and social phobia (Ogliari et al., 2010). Genetic factors also predict stability of anxiety symptoms and disorders over time, with novel genetic influences emerging during adolescence (van Grootheest, Bartels, Cath, Beekman, & Boomsma, 2007; Zavos, Gregory, & Eley, 2012).

Research has also targeted the identification of specific candidate genes implicated in anxiety development. Much of this work has focused on the promoter region (5-HTTPLR) of the serotonin transporter gene (SLC6A4), a sequence of DNA that regulates brain serotonin levels. The short form of 5-HTTPLR is associated with a number of anxious traits. Carriers of the short form (allele) of 5-HTTLPR show greater negative emotionality and elevated activation in emotion-related brain regions (amygdala), which is consistent with the anxiety phenotype (Canli & Lesch, 2007; Murphy et al., 2012). Furthermore, child carriers of the short allele had a significantly greater attentional bias toward fearful faces compared to their long allele peers (Thomason et al., 2010). Continued study of the serotonin transporter gene shows promise in explaining many of the features specific to anxiety disorders.

OCD

Family studies thus far suggest a mixed transmission model for OCD (i.e., a gene of major effect superimposed on a combination of multiple minor genes), with glutamate and serotonin system genes being most replicated (Arnold, Sicard, Burroughs, Richter, & Kennedy, 2006; Stewart et al., 2007). Given the heterogeneity of anxiety disorders including OCD and the likelihood of multiple genes being implicated in disease etiology, research is moving toward the examination of gene by environment interactions for a variety of anxiety disorders (Fox et al., 2005).

Neuroimaging

Anxiety and OCD both exhibit dysregulation in the neural circuitry involving prefrontal cortical and subcortical areas with differences in the particular structure and function of implicated brain regions. Neuroimaging studies have examined the "fear circuit" implicated in anxiety, namely the amygdala and ventrolateral (vlPFC) and ventromedial (vmPFC) prefrontal cortices. The amygdala is necessary for establishing conditioned fear, new stimulus-threat contingencies, and the expression of cue-specific fear in a rapid automatic detection and response process (LeDoux, 1993; Davidson, 2002). The medial prefrontal cortical (mPFC) areas (dorsomedial and ventromedial) are essential to the regulation of amygdala activity and resulting behavior (Blackford & Pine, 2012). Traditionally, the vmPFC is thought to regulate emotion, motivation, and other amygdala-based processes including attention bias to threat through a more gradual process. One implication of such a model is that clinical symptoms of anxiety may result when amygdala hypersensitivity is not appropriately modulated by adequate engagement of the ventral PFC (vPFC).

The most consistent findings in youth with anxiety include increased activation of the amygdala, vlPFC, and dmPFC when viewing negative emotional expressions (Blackford & Pine, 2012). While viewing happy or fearful faces, amygdala activity was positively correlated with social dimensions of anxiety including humiliation, peer rejection, and public performance in anxious youth (Killgore & Yurgelun-Todd, 2005). Another study indicated that adolescents with social anxiety experienced greater amygdala activation in addition to increased activity between the vlPFC and amygdala during a peer evaluation task (Guyer et al., 2008). Such findings confirm the presence of a fear circuit involving the vPFC and amygdala in anxiety disorders, but it remains to be determined whether circuit abnormalities precede (and thus a risk factor) or are a consequence of the anxiety process.

OCD

OCD along with ADHD and Tourette's syndrome is also characterized by dysregulation of the fronto-striatal system. It is postulated that insufficient modulation of the ventral (affective) cortico-striatal loop through the dorsal (cognitive) circuit results in neural abnormalities in OCD (Brem et al., 2012). Functional imaging has consistently revealed hyperactivity in the orbitofrontal cortex (OFC), anterior cingulate cortex (ACC), and caudate nucleus in youth with OCD (Maia, Cooney, & Peterson, 2008). These are areas implicated in the suppression of inappropriate cognitions and behaviors (Bradshaw & Sheppard, 2000), emotional processing, and error and conflict monitoring (Simmons et al., 2008). Moreover, OCD symptom severity is positively correlated with hyperactivity of these brain regions (Abramovitch, Mittelman, Henin, & Geller, 2011). However, it is unclear whether the hyperactivity is a cause or a consequence of OCD symptoms (Maia et al., 2008). In fact, increased activation in OFC may be indicative of compensatory strategies attempting to reduce obsessive or compulsive behaviors (Radua & Mataix-Cols, 2009).

The regions of hyperactivity in pediatric OCD also reflect areas of increased structural volume. Structural differences between youth with OCD and healthy controls include predominantly increased volumes of frontal (ACC and OFC) and striatal (putamen and caudate) regions, with increased volume in other associated areas including the thalamus and cerebellum (Abramovitch et al., 2011; Blackford & Pine, 2012).

Neuroimaging findings also correspond to neuropsychological impairment in OCD. During successful response inhibition, adolescents with OCD show decreased activation in the OFC, thalamus, and basal ganglia (Woolley et al., 2008). In addition, caudate activation was negatively correlated with a behavioral measure of cognitive flexibility in OCD while positively correlated in healthy controls (Britton et al., 2010).

A complicating factor in the identification of brain regions implicated in anxiety disorders and OCD is that the very regions and networks that show abnormality also continue to develop and change through adolescence. Cortical gray matter reaches a peak in pre-adolescence (ages 10 to 12), followed by pruning to increase efficiency that can be graphically depicted as an inverted U of cortical brain development (Geidd, 2004; Geidd et al., 1999). Interestingly, the subcortical structures implicated in child OCD are phylogenetically older than the brain regions associated with adult OCD and mature earlier in the course of neurodevelopment than frontal areas, which continue to develop into early adulthood (Marsh, Maia, & Peterson, 2009). The evidence from child OCD imaging studies supports fronto-striatal abnormality and suggests the possibility of developmentally based neural dysplasia, where abnormal rates of synaptic pruning and myelination within fronto-striatal networks may result in lower volumes in striatal structures and higher volumes in vPFC and thalamus (Rosenberg & Keshavan, 1998; Szeszko et al., 2004).

Improving functional connectivity between frontal and limbic regions as well as normalizing activity in distinct brain areas have been shown to be a possibility with effective interventions in OCD. Children with OCD showed reduced gray matter in the right and left parietal lobes and reduced right parietal white matter, which normalized with successful treatment relative to healthy controls (Lázaro et al., 2008). Given the developmental dysplasia hypothesis, the timing of early interventions may be critical to the amelioration of potential neural abnormalities in pediatric OCD.

Neuropsychology

Anxiety

Examining neuropsychology (NP) in the context of developing neural networks, comorbidity, and behavioral genetics has implications for not only how studies are interpreted but mechanisms of treatment response. NP studies are limited methodologically by samples that are heterogeneous for age, comorbidity, and diagnosis. With these limitations in mind, research in anxiety has focused on impairment in attention, learning, and working memory with equivocal results (Visu-Petra et al., 2009). Toren et al. (2000) found significant differences on verbal but not nonverbal processing in children with any anxiety disorder compared to controls. Anxious youth also made significantly more total errors and perseverative responses on the Wisconsin Card Sorting Task (WCST; Grant & Berg, 1948), revealing a possible deficit in cognitive flexibility. However, other studies have found no differences between groups on attention and verbal working memory (Günther et al., 2004).

Researchers have also recently explored aspects of learning in anxious youth as assessed by a reversal learning task and failed to identify significant impairment (Dickstein et al., 2010). Learning has also been examined using the Morris Water Maze (Morris, 1984) task of spatial navigation (Mueller et al., 2009). Although anxious youth were not impaired in the learning aspect of the task, they did show impaired spatial navigation ability. Spatial navigation is proposed to elicit a spatial working memory demand (Chrastil, 2013), but it is difficult to disentangle the separate component skills that comprise spatial navigation, making interpretation of findings difficult.

Overall there is little evidence of consistent NP impairment in youth with anxiety disorders in the realms of attention, working memory, and learning. NP tasks that tap emotion-driven centers of the brain have had more success in revealing NP deficits related to anxiety, specifically, using tasks of risk and reward.

Risk taking is defined as engagement in behaviors that simultaneously involve a high potential for punishment and opportunity for reward (Leigh, 1999). Anxiety is specifically associated with risk-avoidant decision making (Maner et al., 2007). Although much of the research in this realm is with adults, there are likely parallels that can be drawn to pediatric populations. In a non-clinical sample of university students, trait anxiety was associated with highly risk-avoidant decision making relative to controls. In addition, high trait anxiety was predictive of more pessimistic risk appraisals such as heightened perceptions of the likelihood and severity of negative outcomes (Maner & Schmidt, 2006). Adults with high trait anxiety also show impaired decision making and greater physiological response in anticipation of advantageous trials on the Iowa Gambling Task, a decision-making task of monetary risk and reward with an uncertain premise and outcome (Bechara, Damasio, Damasio, & Anderson, 1994; Miu, Heilman, & Houser, 2008).

Recent work has also differentiated independent neural pathways for risk and reward. The dmPFC is linked to aversion to uncertainty, with greater activation present in individuals with a low preference for risk. In contrast, the vmPFC is linked to the approach of rewards, where a higher risk preference is linked to greater activation (Xue et al., 2009). Greater activation in dmPFC regions in concert with attenuated activation of the vmPFC observed in anxiety disorders may reflect an anxious individual's desire to avoid risk despite possible reward. Adolescents with social phobia also showed greater caudate and putamen activation with increased incentives compared to typical controls and adolescents with GAD (Guyer et al., 2012). These findings reveal that adolescents with social anxiety disorder who are typically characterized by greater concern for social evaluation and performance may be more sensitive to cues indicative of reward and punishment on a neural level. Adolescents with GAD also showed a unique pattern of activation, specifically greater putamen activation in response to gain versus loss, demonstrating a greater sensitivity to anticipated loss compared to typical controls.

OCD

Studies of pediatric OCD reveal a profile of NP deficits, which supports a fronto-striatal model of dysfunction. The most consistent impairments in pediatric OCD are in areas of executive function, specifically set-shifting. Shin et al. (2008) found that children with OCD performed significantly worse than controls on the WCST (Grant & Berg, 1948), a measure of set-shifting and nonverbal abstract concept formation. Similarly, Ornstein and colleagues (2010) found that OCD youths made more errors on tasks measuring set-shifting and cognitive flexibility (CVLT and D-KEFS trail making; Delis, Kramer, Kaplan, & Ober, 1987; Delis, Kaplan, & Kramer, 2001). Poor performance on measures of set shifting has been shown to negatively correlate with symmetry and ordering symptoms of OCD in adults (Lawrence et al., 2006). Clinically, it is reasonable to postulate that the presence and severity of perseverative behaviors seen in many youth with OCD might be a result of executive dysfunction involving difficulty in set shifting and cognitive flexibility.

There is also some evidence of attention, working memory, planning, and organization difficulties, although task-specific differences make definitive conclusions hard to reach. Impairment on Finger Windows (Sheslow & Adams, 1990), a task of visual attention and spatial working memory, has been noted (Chang, McCracken, & Piacentini, 2007) along with deficits in attention and concentration as measured by the Conner's Continuous Performance Test (Shin et al., 2008; Shin, Cho, Chun, & Hong, 2000). Attention and working memory are inextricably linked; one must be able to attend to stimuli to be able to encode events to memory. Absence of consistent visual and spatial working memory findings in several samples (Beers et al., 1999; Chang et al., 2007; Ornstein et al., 2010; Shin et al., 2008) suggest that youth with OCD may have selective impairment on attention rather than encoding. Deficits in planning and organization in youth with OCD have also received some support in the literature. Children with OCD performed significantly worse than controls on measures of perceptual organization (Shin et al., 2008), planning, and procedural learning (Behar et al., 1984; Ornstein et al., 2010), and mental rotation (Behar et al., 1984).

Impairment in aspects of motor control is also consistent across studies of pediatric OCD. Flessner et al. (2010) found that WISC-IV Coding scores (Wechsler, 2003), which involve psychomotor processing, negatively predicted OCD symptom severity in a sample of 63 OCD youths. The same study sample showed significant impairment on the Rey Complex Figure Test (RCFT; Rey, 1964) Copy accuracy. In some cases, accuracy on executive tasks in OCD may be intact, but performance is characterized by a general pattern of slowed processing, suggesting that more complex behavioral sequencing is difficult, leading to an overall inefficient response style (Andres et al., 2007).

Research into risk and reward processes in OCD has primarily been in adults and indicate that risk aversion in adult OCD is mediated by aberrant limbic responses to reward and loss contingencies. During a risky choice game, OCD adults showed increased amygdala activation to loss and less nucleus accumbens (Nacc) activation to reward. Functional connectivity between the amygdala, Nacc and frontal regions including the OFC and dACC also showed decreased activity. The fronto-limbic differences in OCD patients were also associated with symptom severity (Admon et al., 2012). These findings have also been extended to a monetary incentive delay task in adults with OCD who were slower to respond to reward and had reduced activation of the Nacc in response to reward (Figee et al., 2011). It appears, however, that brain response to risk and reward is malleable. When treated with medication (serotonin reuptake inhibitors), reward and punishment learning in adults with OCD normalized (Palminteri, Clair, Mallet, & Pessiglione, 2012). Research into the influence of reward/punishment processes in OCD and other anxiety disorders has significant implications for treatment, particularly for behavioral interventions that rely heavily on exposures that may create acute initial distress with rewards being achieved more gradually as treatment milestones are progressively met.

Attentional Bias to Threat

In everyday life, there are infinite environmental demands for attention that are in direct conflict with independent purposeful goals. The ability to attend to important environmental cues and ignore information irrelevant to goals is an important skill that is impaired in a range of psychopathology including anxiety disorders. Attentional biases in processing threat-related information have been theorized to have a prominent role in the etiology and maintenance of anxiety disorders (Mathews & MacLeod, 1985; Mathews & MacLeod, 2002; Mogg, Mathews, & Eysenck, 1992). A growing body of research has indicated that the attentional system of anxious individuals, both adults and children, may be distinctively sensitive to and biased in favor of threat-related stimuli in the environment. As a consequence, threat-related information may be favored at various stages of processing including the early stages of attention and encoding and the later ones of memory and interpretation (Bar-Haim, Lamy, Pergamin, Bakermans-Kranenbrug, & van IJzendoorn, 2007).

This attentional bias to threat has been observed across a wide range of anxiety disorders as well as in high trait anxious individuals using different methodologies including visual dot-probe, emotional Stroop, and emotional n-back paradigms. Most studies investigating the effect of AMP on anxiety disorders have used a variation of the now classic probe detection task (MacLeod, Matthews, & Tata, 1986), which has been modified to create an attention bias either toward or away from threatening cues. In the basic probe detection paradigm, two stimuli, one neutral and the other threat-related, are presented simultaneously on a computer screen. The stimuli disappear, and one is replaced by a neutral probe (either a letter or symbol), and participants are asked to identify the probe as quickly and accurately as possible. Faster response latency to probes replacing threat versus neutral stimuli is thought to reflect an attention bias toward threat. This paradigm has been modified for use in attention training protocols to systematically increase the proportion of probes appearing at the location of the neutral stimuli, thereby inducing a bias away from threat over a systematic repetition of hundreds of trials. A recent meta-analytic report indicated threat-related bias was significant in both clinically diagnosed samples as well as those with high self-reported anxiety, with the magnitude of bias not differing between these populations (Bar-Haim et al., 2007). This finding appears to generally hold true for both adult and child groups. Although fewer in number than adult studies, child research examining threat bias in clinically anxious youth is growing. In the majority of these studies, anxious youth are diagnostically assessed using the Anxiety Disorders Interview Schedule: Child/Parent Versions (ADIS-IV-C/P; Silverman & Albano, 1996). The inclusion diagnoses most often consisted of separation anxiety, social phobia, specific phobia, and generalized anxiety disorder, while OCD and PTSD were often excluded from the study eligibility (Britton et al., 2013; Eldar et al., 2012; Rozenman, Weersing, & Amir, 2011).

Theoretical models of threat bias suggest that it is not a unitary construct but may be composed of subcomponents including facilitated attention to threat (i.e., early attention orienting), difficulty disengaging attention away from threat (the degree to which a threat stimulus captures attention and impairs attention switching to another stimulus), and attention avoidance of threat. Both difficulty in threat disengagement and attention avoidance of threat have been shown to be present at late (more conscious, strategic) stages of processing of attention bias, although difficulty in disengagement may occur during both early (automatic) and later (strategic) stages of information processing (Cisler & Koster, 2010). Research utilizing a variety of task paradigms including a modified dot-probe methodology developed to disentangle the various components of attention bias, has most consistently implicated difficulty in threat disengagement in anxious individuals as a component of attention bias (Cisler & Olatunji, 2010; Koster, Crombez, Verschuere, & De Houwer, 2004). Despite these emerging data, there is little theoretical agreement on what components comprise attention bias and furthermore what potential mechanisms may mediate these components, suggesting the need for greater research.

The underlying neural basis of threat bias in anxiety is consistent with the fear circuitry involving the vPFC and amygdala previously mentioned. The amygdala, the emotional processing center of the brain, is characterized by enhanced sensitivity to threat, driving a bottom-up process of anxiety generation. The vPFC's role, in part, is to modulate emotional responding; however, the vPFC fails to adequately engage in top-down regulatory processes to counteract amygdala hypersensitivity. The result is an automatic, often unconscious, attentional bias to threat, which subsequently fuels anxious cognitions and behaviors (Bishop, 2008).

Adolescents with GAD have shown greater amygdala, vPFC, and ACC activation relative to controls when viewing fearful versus happy faces. Significant positive correlation between the top-down (vPFC and ACC) and bottom-up (amygdala) regions using functional connectivity analyses supported the proposed fear circuitry between PFC and amygdala (McClure, Monk, et al., 2007). Attentional bias to threat was also examined in a large sample ($N = 101$) of youth with GAD, social anxiety, and/or separation anxiety using an emotional dot-probe task (Roy et al., 2008). In an emotional dot-probe task, attentional bias toward threat is operationalized by a faster reaction time when a target probe is presented where a threatening face appeared compared to a neutral or happy face. Anxious children in this sample showed a greater attentional bias toward threat, specifically angry faces, compared to controls. Similarly, Telzer et al. (2008) also used an emotional dot-probe task to assess attentional bias in sixteen healthy children and found that higher trait anxiety was associated with attentional bias toward threat (angry faces). Consistent with other results, there was no relationship found between trait anxiety and happy faces.

OCD

Research into threat bias in OCD is less studied in general and entirely absent in children. Findings to date in adult OCD are equivocal. Some research suggests that adult OCD patients with contamination concerns demonstrate a content-specific (i.e., contamination and checking content) attentional bias toward threatening information (Moritz, Von Mühlenen, Randjbar, Fricke, & Jelinek, 2009; Summerfeldt & Endler, 1998; Tata, Leibowitz, Prunty, Cameron, & Pickering, 1996). Based on such studies, one proposal has been that OCD is characterized by specific versus global attention biases, with particular difficulty in disengaging attention from personally salient stimuli (da Victoria, Nascimento, & Fontenelle, 2012). Such an interpretation is broadly consistent with cognitive models of OCD, which propose that negative interpretation of intrusive thoughts triggers anxiety and maladaptive strategies that interfere with a person's ability to attend to competing stimuli, further skewing attention and maintaining OCD cognitive distortions. However, other studies have indicated no difference in threat bias despite content-specific stimuli between OCD adults and healthy controls (Harkness, Harris, Jones, & Vaccaro, 2009). Other studies have suggested that OCD is more associated with an early attention bias to threat. An evoked potential study recently indicated larger P1 amplitudes and longer N1 latency in OCD, suggesting early attentional biases to threat in both OCD and panic disorder (Thomas, Gonsalvez, & Johnstone, 2013). Such findings support the idea of preferential processing of threat stimuli in both OCD and panic disorder and may represent attentional processes that contribute to the automatic and uncontrollable nature of symptoms in these conditions. Collectively, these inconsistent findings underscore the need for greater research into attention biases in OCD, particularly with pediatric populations, based on differentiating variables such as symptom severity and OCD subtype.

Models of Etiology

Symptom heterogeneity across anxiety disorders has hampered our ability to develop clear etiological models and effectively target and treat psychopathology. However, biological markers of anxiety disorders including genetic, neurobiological, and NP indices have growing potential to aid in determining relevant endophenotypes for a range of anxiety conditions. Endophenotypes, the intermediate biological processes between clinical symptoms and underlying genetic etiology, present more specific and tangible targets for treatment development (Chamberlain, Blackwell, Fineburg, Robbins, & Sahakian, 2005). Integrating established theoretical models, specifically those based in information processing and neuroimaging research, can help us to advance our understanding of potential endophenotypes of anxiety.

Information processing theory of anxiety is centered on the idea that interpretation of internal or external stimuli is negatively biased, resulting in distorted perception and interpretation of personal experiences. Dysfunctional beliefs may persist over time and develop into cognitive schemas, which can be defined as a cognitive framework or concept that helps organize and interpret information (Beck, 2005). Specifically in anxiety disorders, attention bias toward threat ultimately results in entrenched cognitive schemas focused on maladaptive beliefs. For example, a child with social phobia who preferentially attends to what are perceived as negative social cues and interpretations may ultimately engage in systematic avoidance of various social situations (e.g., activities with peers, public performances), which leads to maintenance of the initial fears (belief that social actions will result in rejection, criticism, etc.) given no disconfirming evidence. These beliefs often concern impending danger at every stage of information processing including perception, interpretation, and recall (Beck & Clark, 1997). The maladaptive beliefs are automatic, or effortless, rapid, and require little awareness (Logan, 1997). Although information processing theory has slightly different applications for each disorder, the general preoccupation with and misinterpretation of threatening information is central to generalized anxiety disorder, social anxiety disorder, separation anxiety, and obsessive-compulsive disorder. Processing biases to threat have their roots in dedicated brain circuitry, and the control or the responsiveness of this circuitry is posited to differ in anxious and non-anxious people (Mogg & Bradley, 1998). Neurobiological studies can help to elucidate the neural circuitry implicated, which may lead to a better understanding of how to shape and implement the most effective interventions.

OCD

Neuroimaging findings highlight the importance of context in the attentional bias signature of anxiety. Greater association between the vlPFC and vmPFC, regulatory regions of the brain and amygdala, suggests that increased amygdala activation demands greater energy be directed toward top-down regulatory control functions to extinguish an overactive fear response (Kim, Gee, Loucks, Davis, & Whalen, 2011; Phelps, Delgado, Nearing, & LeDoux, 2004). Neurobiological models of OCD are also consistent with an imbalance between emotion-based intrusive thoughts and repetitive behaviors and the executive ability to inhibit. Youth with OCD possess a lower threshold for fear activation than their healthy peers, and intrusive thoughts that are easily and unconsciously inhibited in typical children may result in consistent activation of a "worry" circuit in children with OCD (Abramovitch et al., 2011). This circuit likely involves the thalamus, caudate, and OFC. The ability to flexibly shift behavioral responses following feedback is an important function of the OFC and is impaired in pediatric OCD. Interestingly, reduced bilateral OFC activation during a task of reversal learning has been suggested as a potential endophenotype for OCD. Adults with OCD and their unaffected relatives showed the same underactivation of the OFC, which may serve as possible biomarker of vulnerability for OCD (Chamberlain et al., 2008).

Evidence-based Treatments

Standard Treatments

Cognitive behavioral therapy (CBT) is considered the optimal first-line treatment for anxiety disorders and OCD, particularly for younger children with mild-to-moderate symptom severity. Several controlled multi-site trials with youth have demonstrated the efficacy and tolerability of CBT and serotonergic agents for anxiety disorders alone and in combination (Kendall, 1994; March et al., 2004; Walkup et al., 2008). In the largest clinical trial of its kind to date for pediatric anxiety, both sertraline (55 percent response rate) and CBT (60 percent response rate) individually were found to be effective for the treatment of child anxiety (Walkup et al., 2008). However, the combination of CBT plus medication was found to be superior to either intervention alone (81 percent). CBT was based on Kendall's Coping Cat treatment manual, a developmental adaptation of adult CBT protocols for children, which was skills and exposure-based. CBT proposes in part to directly target negative automatic cognitive processes and to strengthen strategic top-down processes through behavioral exposures and the development of explicit and conscious coping strategies. It appears that CBT may enable anxious patients to think and act more flexibly, which in turn allows the development of more effective cognitive strategies and the potential remediation of anxiety symptoms and related cognitive deficits (Katrin Kuelz et al., 2006). It is important to note, however, that behavioral interventions are more cognitively demanding, requiring higher levels of motivation, effort, and behavioral compliance than medication. A child laboring under the multiple burdens of academic failure, high comorbidity, and cognitive deficits may experience greater benefit from a multi-modal treatment approach that incorporates pharmacology, CBT, as well as family and school interventions (Barrett, Dadds, & Rapee, 1996; Peris et al., 2008).

Treatment with either CBT or SRIs (fluoxetine) has been associated with increases in right vlPFC activity in anxious participants relative to healthy controls (Maslowsky et al., 2010). For example, in a study of fourteen adolescents with GAD, half treated with CBT and half with fluoxetine, performance on a functional MRI probe detection task was used to assess neural response to angry faces before and after treatment. Regardless of treatment type, findings indicated significant increase in right vlPFC activation in response to angry faces. Results are consistent with previous research indicating that the vlPFC region is involved in the effective modulation of negative emotions (Maslowsky et al., 2010). The same study found a trend indicating a greater decrease in attentional bias toward threat stimuli in the medication versus CBT group from pre to post-treatment. Such provocative findings warrant greater investigation into the neural and cognitive correlates of treatment outcome in anxiety.

Novel Treatments

Although many children benefit greatly from standard treatments of CBT and pharmacotherapy, a sizable proportion of youth (20 percent to 35 percent) either do not improve or derive only partial benefit, emphasizing the need for broader treatment options (Walkup et al., 2008; Rynn et al., 2011). In a recent review, Rynn et al. (2011) highlighted six possible new pharmacotherapy treatment approaches explored in recent randomized controlled trials. These include D-Cycloserine (DCS), Riluzole, Memantine, anti-convulsant medications, and propanalol. Storch et al. (2010) augmented CBT with DCS, a relatively novel medication treatment for anxiety disorders that enhances extinction of learned fear. Findings indicated that DCS was well tolerated, and DCS + CBT treatment resulted in greater symptoms reduction (72 percent) than CBT alone (58 percent).

A growing body of research also supports attention bias modification (ABM) training as a novel treatment approach for youth with anxiety. ABM is a novel theory-driven treatment derived from established experimental data on threat-related attention biases in anxiety (Bar-Haim et al., 2007) and utilizes computer-based attention training protocols to directly target and implicitly modify biased attention patterns in anxiety-disordered individuals. Most studies investigating the effect of ABM on anxiety disorders have used a variation of the now classic probe detection task (MacLeod et al., 1986), which has been modified to create an attention bias either toward or away from threatening cues. In a recent meta-analysis of ABM treatment outcomes (Hakamata et al., 2010) from ten published randomized controlled trials, ABM was shown to produce a significant medium effect for anxiety ($d = .61$). Moreover, when studies were limited to clinically diagnosed samples (three studies), the effect size was medium to large and comparable to those observed for CBT and SSRIs ($d = .78$), suggesting that overall ABM is a promising new intervention for anxiety management.

Despite such promising outcomes, ABM protocols have not been widely tested with patients with anxiety disorders, with only a handful of studies thus far published in clinical adult populations with GAD (Amir, Beard, Burns, & Bomyea, 2009), and Social Anxiety Disorder (Amir, Beard, Taylor, et al., 2009; Schmidt, Richey, Buckner, & Timpano, 2009). Although child work in the area is scant, a growing number of studies indicate positive findings. A small open ABM trial with clinically anxious youth recently showed positive results (Rozenman et al., 2011) along with a randomized controlled trial (RCT) in anxious youth indicating decreased threat bias after training was related to reduced vulnerability to stress (Bar-Haim, Morag, & Glickman, 2011). A more recent RCT suggested that ABM compared to two control conditions reduced pediatric anxiety symptoms and severity in clinically diagnosed youth (Eldar et al., 2012).

From a mechanism perspective, it is not entirely clear which attention component is being trained with existing ABM protocols; that is, whether facilitated attention to or difficulty disengaging from threat stimuli is most implicated in ABM. However, one recent evoked potential study revealed that attention training away from threat modulated anxious adults' top-down processes of attention control rather than early attention orienting processes (Eldar & Bar-Haim, 2010). Moreover, evidence supports the idea that threat bias in anxiety may rely to a larger degree on more top-down and elaborative/ strategic processing of threat than on automatic pre-attentive processes (Bar-Haim et al., 2007; McNally, 1995). In one of the few imaging studies to examine the effects of ABM, lateral frontal regions in healthy adults were altered by attention training toward and away from threat (Browning, Holmes, Murphy, Goodwin, & Harmer, 2010). Accordingly, higher-order attention control ability appears to play a role in the degree to which an individual can disengage attention from threat, serving as a possible predictor of treatment response and potentially modifiable by ABM.

Predictors of Treatment Response

Anxiety

Fifteen years ago, March and Curry (1998) emphasized personalized treatment for children with anxiety disorders so as to maximize symptom reduction and long-term remittance. In the past few years, researchers have just started to answer the call for neurocognitive predictors of treatment response in youth with anxiety. McClure, Adler, et al. (2007) explored fMRI predictors of CBT and fluoxetine treatment response in a sample of fifteen children with GAD. Youth with the greatest activation in the left amygdala showed the strongest response to both treatments. According to the current neurobiological understanding of anxiety, a child who shows stronger prefrontal cortical activity may be better able to regulate anxiety. In support, Maslowsky et al. (2010) reported increases in vlPFC activation after treatment with CBT or Sertraline, lending credence to the exploration of specific patterns of vlPFC activation as a pre-treatment correlate of treatment response.

Demographic and clinical predictors of treatment response have also been examined in youth with anxiety disorders. As part of a multi-site 8-week clinical trial of fluvoxamine in non-OCD anxiety, potential moderators (age, gender, race/ethnicity, anxiety disorder, severity, comorbidity, intellectual level, family socioeconomic status), and mediators (treatment adherence, dosage, treatment-emergent adverse events and study blindness; The Research Units on Pediatric Psychopharmacology Anxiety Study Group, 2003) were explored. Among the potential moderators, lower parent-reported depression symptoms and higher overall symptom severity were associated with fluvoxamine efficacy. In addition, a diagnosis of social phobia was associated with less improvement on the primary anxiety outcome measure.

OCD

Although standardized predictors of treatment response to CBT or medication in child OCD have yet to be clearly established, a recent review of predictors of treatment response in pediatric OCD reported that children with comorbid tic disorders as well as externalizing disorders such as ADHD and oppositional defiant disorder had a poorer response to medication (March et al., 2007; Masi et al., 2006). In contrast, baseline severity of OCD symptoms and family dysfunction were associated with poorer response to CBT (Ginsburg, Kingery, Drake, & Grados, 2008).

Neurocognitive factors are just beginning to be examined as predictors of treatment response. A recent study indicated that poor visual memory before treatment predicted worse response to CBT (Flessner et al., 2010). Moreover, memory problems were related to organizational deficits, suggesting that such executive function difficulties may preclude children with OCD from deriving maximum benefit from treatments such as CBT where organized goal setting is emphasized. Studies of adult OCD also lend support to memory as a significant predictor of treatment response. D'Alcante et al. (2012) found that better cognitive and executive abilities (higher verbal IQ, higher CVLT learning score, fewer Stroop errors) were associated with greater response to CBT or fluoxetine in adult OCD. However, mental flexibility, as measured by perseverations on the CVLT, predicted better response to CBT and worse response to fluoxetine. In contrast, Moritz and colleagues (2005) found that overall neurocognitive impairment on executive tasks did not function as a reliable early indicator of non-response to CBT in adult OCD patients.

Family history of OCD has also proven to be a predictor of poor treatment response. In the POTS study, Garcia et al. (2010) found that participants with a family history of OCD had an effect size six times lower than youth without a family genetic loading. Strong evidence of genetic transmission of OCD symptoms suggests that family-focused CBT may be a particularly helpful treatment option for families with high rates of OCD and greater likelihood of family conflict and accommodation.

In the growing age of personalized medicine, predictors of treatment response in children with OCD and anxiety may help to advance translational research and therapies. Identification of relative weakness on key predictors of treatment response may guide intervention researchers in their development of treatment strategies to strengthen or compensate for these limitations.

Future Directions

The past 20 years of research in treatments for pediatric anxiety have largely focused on comparative randomized controlled trials that have established general best practice guidelines (March, 2011). However, recent advances in translational research have primed the field for the development of more personalized, preventative and curative treatment approaches. With current treatment rates hovering at 60 percent to 70 percent for pharmacological and CBT treatments, there remains significant room for improvement of existing treatment as well as the development of novel interventions for pediatric anxiety disorders.

From a neurocognitive perspective, current standard treatments such as CBT may benefit from the incorporation of strategies to help address potential executive function deficits such as impaired organization, which may prove to be an obstacle for optimal CBT implementation. Toward this end, organizational strategies such as outlining a succinct number of treatment goals for each session and highlighting simple "take home messages" may be helpful in maximizing CBT treatment outcomes for youth struggling with cognitive limitations.

Research based in translational neuroscience has also opened avenues for the integration of novel interventions such as ABM with standard treatments such as CBT and pharmacotherapy. Increasingly, translations from basic experimental psychology and cognitive neuroscience are yielding innovative approaches to treatment focused on cognitive remediation or training in a variety of psychiatric disorders including schizophrenia, dyslexia, attention deficit hyperactivity disorder as well as anxiety (Fisher, Holland, Merzenich, & Vinogradov, 2009; Gabrieli, 2009; Klingberg et al., 2006). Such translational paradigms based on attention bias modification have already begun to be applied to the treatment of anxiety disorders. Continuing research into the efficacy and mechanisms underlying ABM should help to elucidate whether it is best utilized as an independent or augmentative treatment for pediatric anxiety disorders. Moreover, exploring potential mechanisms such as baseline threat bias as well as higher-order attention control capacities will serve to clarify etiology and predictors of treatment response and, ultimately, refine available treatments.

Research into NP dimensions of pediatric anxiety also needs to be conducted within a developmental context in which sensitivity to age-related changes associated with anxiety phenomenology, brain maturation, and gene by environment interactions are carefully considered. For instance, it has been shown that the developmental course of anxiety symptoms during adolescence is such that an initial decrease in anxiety during early adolescence is followed by a subsequent increase from middle to late adolescence (Van Oort, Greaves-Lord, Verhulst, Ormel, & Huizink, 2009). Such information on anxiety trajectory along with research elucidating critical neural windows of brain maturation may help investigators better hone and target interventions to increase efficacy.

Moreover, cognitive processes such as attention bias to threat and sensitivity to risk/reward may further clarify the etiology and maintenance of anxiety from a mechanistic perspective.

A broad neurocognitive perspective to the clinical study of pediatric anxiety is valuable. Within this perspective, information from varied domains of investigation including genetics, neuroimaging, and neuropsychology can be integrated into a translational framework that can inform our understanding of not only phenomenology but predictors of treatment response as well as novel interventions with the potential to increase our ability to help the greatest number of youth affected with anxiety disorders.

References

Abramovitch, A., Mittelman, A., Henin, A., & Geller, D. (2011). Neuroimaging and neuropsychological findings in pediatric obsessive-compulsive disorder: A review and developmental considerations. *Neuropsychiatry, 2*(4), 313–329.

Admon, R., Bleich-Cohen, M., Weizmant, R., Poyurovsky, M., Faragian, S., & Hendler, T. (2012). Functional and structural neural indices of risk aversion in obsessive-compulsive disorder (OCD). *Psychiatry Research, 203*(2–3), 207–213.

Albano, A. M., Causey, D., & Carter, B. (2001). Fear and anxiety in children. In C. E. Waler & M. C. Roberts (Eds.), *Handbook of clinical and child psychology* (3rd edn, pp. 291–316). New York: Wiley.

American Psychiatric Association. (2000). Diagnostic and statistical manual of mental disorders (4th edn, text rev.). Washington, DC: American Psychiatric Association.

American Psychiatric Association. (2013). *Diagnostic and statistical manual of mental disorders* (5th edn). Arlington, VA: American Psychiatric Publishing.

Amir, N., Beard, C., Burns, M., & Bomyea, J. (2009). Attention modification program in individuals with generalized anxiety disorder. *Journal of Abnormal Psychology, 118*(1), 28–33.

Amir, N., Beard, C., Taylor, C. T., Klumpp, H., Elias, J., Burns, M., & Chen, X. (2009). Attention training in individuals with generalized social phobia: A randomized controlled trial. *Journal of Consulting and Clinical Psychology*, 77(5), 961–973.

Andres, S., Boget, T., Lazaro, L., Penades, R., Morer, A., Salamero, M., & Castro-Fornieles, J. (2007). Neuropsychological performance in children and adolescents with obsessive-compulsive disorder and influence of clinical variables. *Biological Psychiatry, 61*(8), 946–951.

Arnold, P. D., Sicard, T., Burroughs, E., Richter, M. A., & Kennedy, J. L. (2006). Glutamate transporter gene SLC1A1 associated with obsessive-compulsive disorder. *Archives of General Psychiatry, 63*(7), 769–776.

Bar-Haim, Y., Morag, I., & Glickman, S. (2011). Training anxious children to disengage attention from threat: A randomized controlled trial. *The Journal of Child Psychology and Psychiatry, 52*(8), 861–869.

Bar-Haim, Y., Lamy, D., Pergamin, L., Bakermans-Kranenburg, M. J., & van IJzendoorn, M. H. (2007). Threat-related attentional bias in anxious and nonanxious individuals: A meta-analytic study. *Psychological Bulletin, 133*(1), 1–24.

Barrett, P. M., Dadds, M. R., & Rapee, R. M. (1996). Family treatment of childhood anxiety: A controlled trial. *Journal of Consulting and Clinical Psychology, 64*(2), 333–342.

Bechara, A., Damasio, A. R., Damasio, H., & Anderson, S. W. (1994). Insensitivity to future consequences following damage to human prefrontal cortex. *Cognition, 50*(1–3), 7–15.

Beck, A. T. (2005). The current state of cognitive therapy: A 40-year retrospective. *Archives of General Psychiatry, 62*(9), 953–959.

Beck, A. T., & Clark, D. A. (1997). An information processing model of anxiety: Automatic and strategic processes. *Behavioral Research and Therapy, 35*(1), 49–58.

Beers, S. R., Rosenberg, D. R., Dick, E. L., Williams, T., O'Hearn, K. M., Birmaher, B., & Ryan, C. M. (1999). Neuropsychological study of frontal lobe function in psychotropic-naïve children with obsessive-compulsive disorder. *American Journal of Psychiatry, 156*(5), 777–779.

Behar, D., Rapoport, J. L., Berg, C. J., Denckla, M. B., Mann, L., Cox, C., ... & Wolfman, M. G. (1984). Computerized tomography and neuropsychological test measures in adolescents with obsessive-compulsive disorder. *American Journal of Psychiatry, 141*(3), 363–369.

Bernstein, G. A., Borchardt, C. M., & Perwien, A. R. (1996). Anxiety disorders in children and adolescent: A review of the past 10 years. *Journal of the American Academy of Child and Adolescent Psychiatry, 35*(9), 1110–1119.

Bishop, S. J. (2008). Neural mechanism underlying selective attention to threat. *Annals of the New York Academy of Sciences, 1129*, 141–152.

Blackford, J. U., & Pine, D. S. (2012). Neural substrates of childhood anxiety disorders: A review of neuroimaging findings. *Child and Adolescent Psychiatric Clinics of North America, 21*(3), 501–525.

Bradshaw, J. L., & Sheppard, D. M. (2000). The neurodevelopmental frontostriatal disorders: Evolutionary adaptiveness and anomalous lateralization. *Brain and Language, 73*(2), 297–320.

Brem, S., Hauser, T. U., Iannoccone, R., Brandeis, D., Drechsler, R., & Walitza, S. (2012). Neuroimaging of cognitive brain function in paediatric obsessive compulsive disorder: A review of literature and preliminary meta-analysis. *Journal of Neural Transmission, 119*(11), 1425–1448.

Britton, J. C., Bar-Haim, Y., Clementi, M. A., Sankin, L. S., Chen, G., Shechner, T., ... & Pine, D. S. (2013). Training-associated changes and stability of attention bias in youth: Implications for attention bias modification treatment for pediatric anxiety. *Developmental Cognitive Neuroscience, 4*, 52–64.

Britton, J. C., Rauch, S. L., Rosso, I. M., Killgore, W. D. S., Price, L. M., Ragan, J., ... & Stewart, S. E. (2010). Cognitive inflexibility and frontal-cortical activation in pediatric obsessive-compulsive disorder. *Journal of the American Academy of Child and Adolescent Psychiatry, 49*(9), 944–953.

Browning, M., Holmes, E. A., Murphy, S. E., Goodwin, G. M., & Harmer, C. J. (2010). Lateral prefrontal cortex mediates the cognitive modification of attentional bias. *Biological Psychiatry, 67*(10), 919–925.

Canli, T., & Lesch, K. (2007). Long story short: The serotonin transporter in emotion regulation and social cognition. *Nature Neuroscience, 10*(9), 1103–1109.

Cartwright-Hatton, S., McNicol, K., & Doubleday, E. (2006). Anxiety in a neglected population: Prevalence of anxiety disorders in pre-adolescent children. *Clinical Psychology Review, 26*(7), 817–833.

Chamberlain, S. R., Blackwell, A. D., Fineburg, N. A., Robbins, T. W., & Sahakian, B. J. (2005). The neuropsychology of obsessive compulsive disorder: The importance of failures in cognitive and behavioural inhibition as candidate endophenotypic markers. *Neuroscience and Biobehavioral Reviews, 29*(3), 1–21.

Chamberlain, S. R., Menzies, L., Hampshire, A., Suckling, J., Fineberg, N. A., del Campo, N., ... & Sahakian, B. J. (2008). Orbitofrontal dysfunction in patients with obsessive-compulsive disorder and their unaffected relatives. *Science, 321*(5887), 421–422.

Chang, S. W., McCracken, J. T., & Piacentini, J. C. (2007). Neurocognitive correlates of child obsessive compulsive disorder and Tourette syndrome. *Journal of Clinical and Experimental Neuropsychology, 29*(7), 724–733.

Chrastil, E. R. (2013). Neural evidence supports a novel framework for spatial navigation. *Psychonomic Bulletin and Review, 20*(2), 208–227.

Cisler, J. M., & Koster, E. H. W. (2010). Mechanisms of attentional bias towards threat in anxiety disorders: An integrative review. *Clinical Psychology Review, 30*, 203–216.

Cisler, J. M., & Olatunji, B. O. (2010). Components of attentional biases in contamination fear: Evidence for difficulty in disengagement. *Behaviour Research and Therapy, 48*(1), 74–78.

Cole, D. A., Peeke, L. G., Martin, J. M., Truglio, R., & Seroczynski, A. D. (1998). A longitudinal look at the relation between depression and anxiety in children and adolescents. *Journal of Counseling and Clinical Psychology, 66*(3), 451–460.

Costello, E. J., Egger, H. L., & Angold, A. (2004). The developmental epidemiology of anxiety disorders. In T. Ollendick & J. March (Eds.), *Phobic and anxiety disorders in children and adolescents: A clinician's guide to effective psychosocial and pharmacological interventions* (pp. 61–91). New York: Oxford University Press.

Costello, E. J., Mustillo, S., Erkanli, A., Keeler, G., & Angold, A. (2003). Prevalence and development of psychiatric disorders in childhood and adolescence. *Archives of General Psychiatry, 60*(8), 837–844.

Craske, M. G., & Waters, A. M. (2005). Panic disorder, phobias, and generalized anxiety disorder. *Annual Review of Clinical Psychology, 1*, 197–225.

Crawford, A. M., & Manassis, K. (2011). Anxiety, social skills, friendship quality, and peer victimization: An integrated model. *Journal of Anxiety Disorders, 25*(7), 924–931.

D'Alcante, C. C., Diniz, J. B., Fossaluza, V., Batistuzzo, M. C., Lopes, A. C., Shavitt, R. G., ... & Hoexter, M. Q. (2012). Neuropsychological predictors of response to randomized treatment in obsessive-compulsive disorder. *Progress in Neuro-Psychopharmacology and Biological Psychiatry, 39*(2), 310–317.

da Victoria, M. S., Nascimento, A. L., & Fontenelle, L. F. (2012). Symptom-specific attentional bias to threatening stimuli in obsessive-compulsive disorder. *Comprehensive Psychiatry, 53*, 783–788.

Davidson, R. J. (2002). Anxiety and affective style: Role of prefrontal cortex and amygdala. *Biological Psychiatry, 51*(1), 68–80.

Delis, D. C., Kaplan, E., & Kramer, J. H. (2001). *Delis-Kaplan Executive Function System (D-KEFS)*. San Antonio, TX: The Psychological Corporation.

Delis, D. C., Kramer, J. H., Kaplan, E., & Ober, B. A. (1987). *The California Verbal Learning Test.* New York: The Psychological Corporation.

Dickstein, D. P., Finger, E. C., Brotman, M. A., Rich, B. A., Pine, D. S., Blair, J. R., & Leibenluft, E. (2010). Impaired probabilistic reversal learning in youths with mood and anxiety disorders. *Psychological Medicine, 40*(7), 1089–1100.

Dickstein, D. P., Rich, B. A., Binstock, A. B., Pradella, A. G., Towbin, K. E., Pine, D. S., & Leibenluft, E. (2005). Comorbid anxiety in phenotypes of pediatric bipolar disorder. *Journal of Child and Adolescent Psychopharmacology, 15*(4), 534–548.

Eisen, A. R., Sussman, J. M., Schmidt, T., Mason, L., Hausler, L. A., & Hashim, R. (2011). Separation anxiety disorder. In D. McKay & E. A. Storch (Eds.), *Handbook of child and adolescent anxiety disorders* (pp. 245–259). New York, NY: Springer.

Eldar, S., & Bar-Haim, Y. (2010). Neural plasticity in response to attention training in anxiety. *Psychological Medicine, 40*(4), 667–677.

Eldar, S., Apter, A., Lotan, D., Perez-Edgar, K., Naim, R., Fox, N. A., ... & Bar-Haim, Y. (2012). Attention bias modification treatment for pediatric anxiety disorders: A randomized controlled trial. *American Journal of Psychiatry, 169*(2), 213–220.

Eley, T. C., Rijsdijk, F. V., Perrin, S., O'Connor, T. G., & Bolton, D. (2008). A multivariate genetic analysis of specific phobia, separation anxiety and social phobia in early childhood. *Journal of Abnormal Child Psychology, 36*(6), 839–848.

Essau, C. A. (2003). Comorbidity of anxiety disorders in adolescents. *Depression and Anxiety, 18*(1), 1–6.

Essau, C. A., Conradt, J., & Petermann, F. (2000). Frequency, comorbidity, and psychosocial impairment of anxiety disorders in German adolescents. *Journal of Anxiety Disorders, 14*(3), 263–279.

Figee, M., Vink, M., de Geus, F., Vulink, N., Veltman, D. J., Westenberg, H., & Denys, D. (2011). Dysfunctional reward circuitry in obsessive-compulsive disorder. *Biological Psychiatry, 69*(9), 867–874.

Fisher, M., Holland, C., Merzenich, M. M., & Vinogradov, S. (2009). Using neuroplasticity-based auditory training to improve verbal memory in schizophrenia. *American Journal of Psychiatry, 166*(7), 805–811.

Flessner, C. A., Allgair, A., Garcia, A., Freeman, J., Sapyta, J., Franklin, M. E., ... & March, J. (2010). The impact of neuropsychological functioning on treatment outcome in pediatric obsessive-compulsive disorder. *Depression and Anxiety, 27*(4), 365–371.

Fox, N. A., Nichols, K. E., Henderson, H. A., Rubin, K., Schmidt, L., Hame, D., ...& Pine, D. S. (2005). Evidence for a gene-environment interaction in predicting behavioral inhibition in middle childhood. *Psychological Science, 16*(12), 921–926.

Gabrieli, J. D. E. (2009). Dyslexia: A new synergy between education and cognitive neuroscience. *Science, 325*(5938), 280–283.

Garcia, A. M., Sapyta, J. J., Moore, P. S., Freeman, J. B., Franklin, M. E., March, J. S., & Foa, E. B. (2010). Predictors and moderators of treatment outcome in the pediatric obsessive compulsive treatment study (POTS I). *Journal of the American Academy of Child and Adolescent Psychiatry, 49*(10), 1024–1033.

Geidd, J. N. (2004). Structural magnetic resonance imaging of the adolescent brain. *Annals of the New York Academy of Science, 1021*, 77–85.

Geidd, J. N., Blumenthal, J., Jeffries, N. O., Castellanos, F. X., Liu, H., Zijbenbos, A., … & Rapoport, J. L. (1999). Brain development during childhood and adolescence: A longitudinal MRI study. *Nature, 2*(10), 861–863.

Ginsburg, G. S., Kingery, J. N., Drake, K. L., & Grados, M. A. (2008). Predictors of treatment response in pediatric obsessive-compulsive disorder. *Journal of the American Academy of Child and Adolescent Psychiatry, 47*(8), 868–878.

Gotlieb, I. H., & Hammen, C. L. (1992). *Psychological aspects of depression: Toward a cognitive-interpersonal integration.* New York: Wiley.

Grant, D. A., & Berg, E. (1948). A behavioral analysis of degree of reinforcement and ease of shifting to new responses in Weigl-type card-sorting problem. *Journal of Experimental Psychology, 38*(4), 404–411.

Günther, T, Holtkamp, K., Jolles, J., Herpertz-Dahlmann, B., & Konrad, K. (2004). Verbal memory and aspects of attentional control in children and adolescents with anxiety disorders or depressive disorders. *Journal of Affective Disorders, 82*(2), 265–269.

Guyer, A. E., Choate, V. R., Detloff, A., Benson, B., Nelson, E. E., Perez-Edgar, K., … & Ernst, M. (2012). Striatal functional alteration during incentive anticipation in pediatric anxiety disorders. *American Journal of Psychiatry, 169*(2), 205–212.

Guyer, A. E., Lau, J. Y., McClure-Tone, E. B., Parrish, J., Shiffrin, N. D., Reynolds, R. C., … & Nelson, E. E. (2008). Amygdala and ventrolateral prefrontal cortex function during anticipated peer evaluation in pediatric social anxiety. *Archives of General Psychiatry, 65*(11), 1303–1312.

Hakamata, Y., Lissek, S., Bar-Haim, Y., Britton, J. C., Fox, N., Leibenluft, E., … & Pine, D. S. (2010). Attention bias modification treatment: A meta-analysis towards the establishment of novel treatment for anxiety. *Biological Psychiatry, 68*(11), 982–990.

Hale, W. W., Klimstra, T. A., Branje, S. J. T., Wijsbroek, S. A. M., & Meeus, W. H. J. (2013). Is adolescent generalized anxiety disorder a magnet for negative parental interpersonal behaviors? *Depression and Anxiety, 30*(9), 849–856.

Harkness, E. L., Harris, L. M., Jones, M. K., & Vaccaro, L. (2009). No evidence of attentional bias in obsessive compulsive checking on the dot probe paradigm. *Behaviour Research and Therapy, 47*(5), 437–443.

Harpold, T. L., Wozniak, J., Kwon, A., Gilbert, J., Wood, J., Smith, L., & Biederman, J. (2005). Examining the association between pediatric bipolar disorder and anxiety disorders in psychiatrically referred children and adolescents. *Journal of Affective Disorders, 88*(1), 19–26.

Jarrett, M. A., & Ollendick, T. H. (2008). A conceptual review of the comorbidity of attention-deficit/hyperactivity disorder and anxiety: Implications for future research and practice. *Clinical Psychology Review, 28*(7), 1266–1280.

Katrin Kuelz, A., Riemann, D., Halsband, U., Vielhaber, K., Unterrainer, J., Kordon, A., & Voderholzer, U. (2006). Neuropsychological impairment in obsessive-compulsive disorder – Improvement over the course of cognitive behavioral treatment. *Journal of Clinical and Experimental Neuropsychology, 28*(8), 1273–1287.

Kendall, P. C. (1994). Treating anxiety disorders in children: Results of a randomized clinical trial. *Journal of Consulting and Clinical Psychology, 62*(1), 100–110.

Kessler, R. C., McGonagle, K. A., Zhao, S., Nelson, C. B., Hughes, M., Eshleman, S., ... & Kendler, K. S. (1994). Lifetime and 12-month prevalence of DSM-III-R psychiatric disorders in the United States. *Archives of General Psychiatry, 51*(1), 8–19.

Killgore, W. D. S., & Yurgelun-Todd, D. A. (2005). Social anxiety predicts amygdala activation in adolescents viewing fearful faces. *Developmental Neuroscience, 16*(15), 1671–1675.

Kim, M. J., Gee, D. G., Loucks, R. A., Davis, F. C., & Whalen, P. J. (2011). Anxiety dissociates dorsal and ventral medial prefrontal cortex functional connectivity with the amygdala at rest. *Cerebral Cortex, 21*(7), 1667–1673.

Klingberg, T., Fernell, E., Olesen, P. J., Johnson, M., Gustafsson, P., Dahlström, K., ... & Westerberg, H. (2006). Computerized training of working memory in children with ADHD – A randomized controlled trial. *Journal of the American Academy of Child and Adolescent Psychiatry, 44*, 177–186.

Koster, E. H., Crombez, G., Verschuere, B., & De Houwer, J. (2004). Selective attention to threat in the dot probe paradigm: Differentiating vigilance and difficulty to disengage. *Behaviour Research and Therapy, 42*(10), 1183–1192.

Langley, A. K., Bergman, L., McCracken, J., & Piacentini, J. C. (2004). Impairment in childhood anxiety disorders: Preliminary examination of the child anxiety impact rating scale parent version. *Journal of Child and Adolescent Psychopharmacology, 14*(10), 105–114.

Langley, A. K., Lewin, A. B., Bergman, R. L., Lee, J. C., & Piacentini, J. (2010). Correlates of comorbid anxiety and externalizing disorders in childhood obsessive compulsive disorder. *European Child and Adolescent Psychiatry, 19*(8), 637–645.

Larson, M. J., South, M., & Merkley, T. (2011). Neuropsychological considerations in child and adolescent anxiety. In D. McKay & E. A. Storch (Eds.), *Handbook of child and adolescent anxiety disorders* (pp. 75–89). New York: Springer.

Lawrence, N. S., Wooderson, S., Mataix-Cols, D., David, R., Speckens, A., & Phillips, M. L. (2006). Decision making and set shifting impairments are associated with distinct symptoms dimensions in obsessive-compulsive disorder. *Neuropsychology, 20*(4), 409–419.

Lázaro, L., Bargalló, N., Castro-Fornieles, J., Falcón, C., Andrés, S., Calvo, R., & Junqué, C. (2008). Brain changes in children and adolescents with obsessive-compulsive disorder before and after treatment: A voxel-based morphometric MRI study. *Psychiatry Research: Neuroimaging, 172*(2), 140–146.

Leckman, J. F., Bloch, M. H., & King, R. A. (2009). Symptom dimensions and subtypes of obsessive-compulsive disorder: A developmental perspective. *Dialogues in Clinical Neuroscience, 11*(1), 21–33.

LeDoux, J. E. (1993). Emotional memory systems in the brain. *Behavioral Brain Research, 58*(1–2), 69–79.

Leigh, B. C. (1999). Peril, chance, and adventure: Concepts of risk, alcohol use, and risky behavior in young adults. *Addiction, 94*(3), 371–383.

Lewinsohn, P. M., Zinbarg, R., Seeley, J. R., Lewinsohn, M., & Sack, W. H. (1997). Lifetime comorbidity among anxiety disorders and between anxiety disorders and other mental disorders in adolescents. *Journal of Anxiety Disorders, 11*(4), 377–394.

Logan, G. (1997). Automaticity and reading: Perspectives from the instance theory of automatization. *Reading and Writing Quarterly, 13*(2), 123–146.

MacLeod, C., Matthews, A., & Tata, P. (1986). Attentional bias in emotional disorders. *Journal of Abnormal Psychology, 95*(1), 15–20.

Maia, T. V., Cooney, R. E., & Peterson, B. S. (2008). The neural bases of obsessive-compulsive disorder in children and adults. *Developmental Psychopathology, 20*(4), 1251–1283.

Maner, J. K., & Schmidt, N. B. (2006). The role of risk avoidance in anxiety. *Behavior Therapy, 37*(2), 181–189.

Maner, J. K., Richey, J. A., Cromer, K., Mallott, M., Lejuez, C. W., Joiner, T. E., & Schmidt, N. B. (2007). Dispositional anxiety and risk-avoidant decision-making. *Personality and Individual Differences, 42*(4), 665–675.

March, J. S. (2011). Looking to the future of research in pediatric anxiety disorders. *Depression and Anxiety, 28*(1), 88–98.

March, J. S., & Curry, J. F. (1998). Predicting the outcome of treatment. *Journal of Abnormal Child Psychology, 26*(1), 39–51.

March, J. S., Foa, E., Gammon, P., Chrisman, A., Curry, J., Fitzgerald, D., … & Tu, X. (2004). Cognitive-behavior therapy, sertraline, and their combination for children and adolescents with obsessive-compulsive disorder – The Pediatric OCD Treatment Study (POTS) randomized controlled trial. *Journal of the American Medical Association, 292*(16), 1969–1976.

March, J. S., Franklin, M. E., Leonard, H., Garcia, A., Moore, P., Freeman, J., & Foa, E. (2007). Tics moderate treatment outcome with sertraline but not cognitive-behavior therapy in pediatric obsessive-compulsive disorder. *Biological Psychiatry, 61*(3), 344–347.

Marsh, R., Maia, T. V., & Peterson, B. S. (2009). Functional disturbances within frontostriatal circuits across multiple childhood psychopathologies. *American Journal of Psychiatry, 166*(6), 664–674.

Masi, G., Mucci, M., Favilla, L., Romano, R., & Poli, P. (1999). Symptomatology and comorbidity of generalized anxiety disorder in children and adolescents. *Comprehensive Psychiatry, 40*(3), 210–215.

Masi, G., Millepiedi, S., Mucci, M., Bertini, N., Pfanner, C., & Arcangeli, F. (2006). Comorbidity of obsessive-compulsive disorder and attention-deficit/hyperactivity disorder in referred children and adolescents. *Comprehensive Psychiatry, 47*(1), 42–47.

Maslowsky, J., Mogg, K., Bradley, B. P., McClure-Tone, E., Ernst, M., Pine, D. S., & Monk, C. S. (2010). A preliminary investigation of neural correlates of treatment in adolescents with generalized anxiety disorder. *Journal of Child and Adolescent Psychpharmacology, 20*(2), 105–111.

Mathews, A., & MacLeod, C. (1985). Selective processing of threat cues in anxiety states. *Behaviour Research and Therapy, 23*(5), 563–569.

Mathews, A., & MacLeod, C. (2002). Induced processing biases have causal effects on anxiety. *Cognition & Emotion, 16*(3), 331–354.

McClure, E. B., Adler, A., Monk, C. S., Cameron, J., Smith, S., Nelson, E. E., … & Pine, D. S. (2007). fMRI predictors of treatment outcome in pediatric anxiety disorders. *Psychopharmacology, 191*(1), 97–105.

McClure, E. B., Monk, C. S., Nelson, E. E., Parrish, J. M., Adler, A., Blair, R. J. R., … & Pine, D. S. (2007). Abnormal attention modulation of fear circuit function in pediatric generalized anxiety disorder. *Archives of General Psychiatry, 64*(1), 97–106.

McNally, R. J. (1995). Automaticity and the anxiety disorders. *Behaviour Research and Therapy, 33*(7), 747–754.

Miu, A. C., Heilman, R. M., & Houser, D. (2008). Anxiety impairs decision-making: Psychophysiological evidence from an Iowa Gambling Task. *Biological Psychiatry, 77*(3), 353–358.

Mogg, K., & Bradley, B. P. (1998). A cognitive-motivational analysis of anxiety. *Behaviour Research and Therapy, 36*(9), 809–838.

Mogg, K., Mathews, A., & Eysenck, M. (1992). Attentional bias to threat in clinical anxiety states. *Cognition & Emotion, 6*(2), 149–159.

Moritz, S., Von Mühlenen, A., Randjbar, S., Fricke, S., & Jelinek, L. (2009). Evidence for an attentional bias for washing- and checking-relevant stimuli in obsessive-compulsive disorder. *Journal of the International Neuropsychological Society, 15*(3), 365–371.

Moritz, S., Kloss, M., Jacobsen, D., Fricke, S., Cutler, C., Brassen, S., & Hand, I. (2005). Neurocognitive impairment does not predict treatment outcome in obsessive-compulsive disorder. *Behavior Research and Therapy, 43*(6), 811–819.

Morris, R. (1984). Developments of a water-maze procedure for studying spatial learning in the rat. *Journal of Neuroscience Methods, 11*(1), 47–60.

Mueller, S.C., Temple, V., Cornwell, B., Grillon, C., Pine, D.S., & Ernst, M. (2009). Impaired spatial navigation in pediatric anxiety. *Journal of Child Psychology & Psychiatry, 50(10)*, 1227–1234.

Murphy, S. E., Norbury, R., Godlewska, B. R., Cowen, P. J., Mannie, Z. M., Harmer, C. J., & Munafò, M. R. (2012). The effect of the serotonin transporter polymorphism (5-HTTLPR) on amygdala function: A meta-analysis. *Molecular Psychiatry, 18*(4), 1–9.

Ogliari, A., Spatola, C. A., Pesenti-Gritti, P., Medda, E., Penna, L., Stazi, M. A., … & Fagnani, C. (2010). The role of genes and environment in shaping co-occurrence of DSM-IV defined anxiety dimensions among Italian twins aged 8–17. *Journal of Anxiety Disorders, 24*(4), 433–439.

Ollendick, T. H., Grills, A. E., & Alexander, K. L. (2013). Fears, worries, and anxiety in children and adolescents. In C. A. Essau & F. Peterman (Eds.), *Anxiety disorders in children and adolescents: Epidemiology, risk factors and treatment* (pp. 1–31). New York: Brunner-Routledge.

Ornstein, T. J., Arnold, P., Manassis, K., Mendlowitz, S., & Schachar, R. (2010). Neuropsychological performance in childhood OCD: A preliminary study. *Depression and Anxiety, 27*(4), 372–380.

Palminteri, S., Clair, A., Mallet, L., & Pessiglione, M. (2012). Similar improvement of reward and punishment learning by serotonin reuptake inhibitors in obsessive-compulsive disorder. *Biological Psychiatry, 72*(3), 244–250.

Peris, T. S., Bergman, L., Langley, A., Chang, S., McCracken, J. T., & Piacentini, J. (2008). Correlates of accommodation of pediatric obsessive-compulsive disorder: Parent, child, and family characteristics. *Journal of the American Academy of Child and Adolescent Psychiatry, 47*(10), 1173–1181.

Peterson, B. S., Pine, D. S., Cohen, P., & Brook, J. S. (2001). Prospective, longitudinal study of tic, obsessive-compulsive, and attention-deficit/hyperactivity disorders in an epidemiological sample. *Journal of the American Academy of Child and Adolescent Psychiatry, 40*(6), 685–689.

Phelps, E. A., Delgado, M. R., Nearing, K. I., & LeDoux, J. E. (2004). Extinction learning in humans: Role of the amygdala and vmPFC. *Neuron, 43*(6), 897–905.

Pine, D. S., Wasserman, G. A., & Leibenluft, E. (1999). Memory and anxiety in prepubertal boys at risk for delinquency. *Journal of the American Academy of Child and Adolescent Psychiatry, 38*(8), 1024–1031.

Radua, J., & Mataix-Cols, D. (2009). Voxel-wise meta-analysis of grey matter changes in obsessive-compulsive disorder. *British Journal of Psychiatry, 195*(5), 393–402.

Research Units on Pediatric Psychopharmacology Anxiety Study Group. (2003). Searching for moderators and mediators of pharmacological treatment effects in children and adolescents with anxiety disorders. *Journal of the American Academy of Child and Adolescent Psychiatry, 42*(1), 13–21.

Rey, A. (1964). *L'Examen clinique en psychologie*. Paris: Presses Universitaires de France.

Rosenberg, D. R., & Keshavan, M. S. (1998). Toward neurodevelopmental model of obsessive-compulsive disorder. *Biological Psychiatry, 43*(9), 623–640.

Roy, A. K., Vasa, R. A., Bruck, M., Mogg, K., Bradley, B. P., Sweeney, M., ... & The CAMS Team. (2008). Attention bias toward threat in pediatric anxiety disorders. *Journal of the American Academy of Child and Adolescent Psychiatry, 47*(10), 1189–1196.

Rozenman, M., Weersing, R., & Amir, N. (2011). A case series of attention modification in clinically anxious youths. *Behavior Research and Therapy, 49*(5), 324–330.

Rynn, M., Puliafico, A., Heleniak, C., Rikhi, P., Ghalib, K., & Vidair, H. (2011). Advances in pharmacotherapy for pediatric anxiety disorders. *Depression and Anxiety, 28*(1), 76–87.

Scaini, S., Ogliari, A., Eley, T. C., Zavos, H., & Battaglia, M. (2012). Genetic and environmental contributions to separation anxiety: A meta-analytic approach to twin data. *Depression and Anxiety, 29*(9), 754–761.

Scharfstein, L., Alfano, C., Beidel, D., & Wong, N. (2011). Children with generalized anxiety disorder do not have peer problems, just fewer friends. *Child Psychiatry and Human Development, 42*(6), 712–723.

Schmidt, N. B., Richey, J. A., Buckner, J. D., & Timpano, K. R. (2009). Attention training for generalized social anxiety disorder. *Journal of Abnormal Psychology, 118*(1), 5–14.

Sheslow, D., & Adams, W. (1990). *Wide range assessment of memory and learning*. Wilmington, DE: Jastak Associates.

Shin, M. S., Cho, S. Z., Chun, S. Y., & Hong, K. E. M. (2000). A study of the development and standardization of ADHD diagnostic system. *Korean Journal of Child and Adolescent Psychiatry, 11*, 91–99.

Shin, M., Choi, H., Kim, H., Hwang, J., Kim, B., & Cho, S. (2008). A study of neuropsychological deficit in children with obsessive-compulsive disorder. *European Psychiatry, 23*(7), 512–520.

Silverman, W. K., & Albano, A. M. (1996). *The Anxiety Disorders Interview Schedule for DSM-IV—Child and Parent Versions*. San Antonio, TX: Physiological Corporation.

Simmons, A., Matthews, S. C., Feinstein, J. S., Hitchcock, C., Paulus, M. P., & Stein, M. B. (2008). Anxiety vulnerability is associated with altered anterior cingulate response to an affective appraisal task. *Neuroreport, 19*(10), 1033–1037.

Stewart, S. E., Rosario, M. C., Brown, T. A., Carter, A. S., Leckman, J. F., Sukhodolsky, D., ...& Pauls, D. L. (2007). Principal components analysis of obsessive-compulsive disorder symptoms on children and adolescents. *Biological Psychiatry, 61*(3), 285–291.

Storch, E. A., Merlo, L. J., Larson, M. J., Geffken, G. R., Lehmkuhl, H. D., & Jacob, M. L. (2008). Impact of comorbidity on cognitive-behavioral therapy response in pediatric obsessive-compulsive disorder. *Journal of the American Academy of Child and Adolescent Psychiatry, 47*(5), 583–592.

Storch, E. A., Ledley, D. R., Lewin, A. B., Murphy, T. K., Johns, N. B., Goodman, W. K., & Geffken, G. R. (2006). Peer victimization in children with obsessive-compulsive disorder: Relations with symptoms and psychopathology. *Journal of Clinical Child and Adolescent Psychology, 35*(3), 446–455.

Storch, E. A., Murphy, T. K., Goodman, W. K., Geffken, G. R., Lewin, A. B., Henin, A., … & Geller, D. A. (2010). A preliminary study of D-Cycloserine augmentation of cognitive-behavioral therapy in pediatric obsessive-compulsive disorder. *Biological Psychiatry, 68*(11), 1073–1076.

Summerfeldt, L. J., & Endler, N. S. (1998). Examining the evidence for anxiety-related cognitive biases in obsessive-compulsive disorder. *Journal of Anxiety Disorder, 12*(6), 579–598.

Szeszko, P. R., MacMillan, S., McMeniman, M., Chen, S., Baribault, K., Lim, K. O., … & Rosenberg, D. R. (2004). Brain structural abnormalities in psychotropic drug-naïve pediatric patients with obsessive-compulsive disorder. *American Journal of Psychiatry, 161*(6), 1049–1056.

Tata, P. R., Leibowitz, J. A., Prunty, M. J., Cameron, M., & Pickering, A. D. (1996). Attentional bias in obsessional compulsive disorder. *Behavioural Research and Therapy, 34*(1), 53–60.

Taylor, S., Jang, K. L., & Asmundson, G. J. G. (2010). Etiology of obsessions and compulsions: A behavioral-genetics analysis. *Journal of Abnormal Psychology, 119*(4), 672–682.

Telzer, E. H., Mogg, K., Bradley, B. P., Mai, X., Ernst, M., Pine, D. S., & Monk, C. S. (2008). Relationship between trait anxiety, prefrontal cortex, and attention bias to angry faces in children and adolescents. *Biological Psychiatry, 79*(2), 216–222.

Thomas, S. J., Gonsalvez, C. J., & Johnstone, S. J. (2013). Neural time course of threat-related attentional bias and interference in panic and obsessive-compulsive disorders. *Biological Psychiatry, 94*, 116–129.

Thomason, M. E., Henry, M. L., Hamilton, J. P., Joormann, J., Pine, D. S., Ernst, M., … & Gotlieb, I. H. (2010). Neural and behavioral responses to threatening emotion faces in children as a function of the short allele of the serotonin transporter gene. *Biological Psychiatry, 85*(1), 38–44.

Toren, P., Sadeh, M., Wolmer, L., Eldar, S., Koren, S., Weizman, R., & Laor, N. (2000). Neurocognitive correlates of anxiety disorders in children: A preliminary report. *Journal of Anxiety Disorders, 14*(3), 239–247.

van Grootheest, D. S., Bartels, M., Cath, D. C., Beekman, J. J., & Boomsma, D. I. (2007). Genetic and environmental contributions underlying stability in childhood obsessive-compulsive behavior. *Biological Psychiatry, 61*(3), 308–315.

Van Oort, F. V., Greaves-Lord, K., Verhulst, F. C., Ormel, J., & Huizink, A. C. (2009). The developmental course of anxiety symptoms during adolescence: The TRAILS study. *Journal of Child Psychology and Psychiatry, 50*(10), 1209–1217.

Visu-Petra, L, Miclea, M., Cheie, L., & Benga, O. (2009). Processing efficiency in preschoolers' memory span: Individual differences related to age and anxiety. *Journal of Experimental Child Psychology, 103*(1), 30–48.

Walkup, J. T., Albano, A. M., Piacentini, J., Birmaher, B., Compton, S. N., Sherrill, J. T., ... & Kendall, P. C. (2008). Cognitive behavioral therapy, sertraline, or a combination in childhood anxiety. *New England Journal of Medicine, 359,* 2753–2766.

Wechsler, D. (2003). *Wechsler Intelligence Scale for Children—4th Edition (WISC-IV®).* San Antonio, TX: Harcourt Assessment.

White, S. W., Oswald, D., Ollendick, T., & Scahill, L. (2009). Anxiety in children and adolescents with autism spectrum disorders. *Clinical Psychology Review, 29*(3), 216–229.

Woolley, J., Heyman, I., Brammer, M., Frampton, I., McGuire, P. K., & Rubia, K. (2008). Brain activation in paediatric obsessive-compulsive disorder during tasks of inhibitory control. *British Journal of Psychiatry, 192*(1), 25–31.

Xue, G., Lu, Z., Levin, I. P., Weller, J. A., Li, X., & Bechara, A. (2009). Functional dissociations of risk and reward processing in the medial prefrontal cortex. *Cerebral Cortex, 19*(5), 1019–1027.

Zavos, H. M. S., Gregory, A. M., & Eley, T. C. (2012). Longitudinal genetic analysis of anxiety sensitivity. *Developmental Psychology, 48*(1), 204–212.

4

NEUROCOGNITIVE PERSPECTIVES ON ANXIETY AND RELATED DISORDERS

Samantha J. Moshier, Amanda W. Calkins,
Maria Alexandra Kredlow, and Michael W. Otto

Anxiety disorders are the most prevalent class of psychiatric disorders, with prevalence estimates of approximately 18% of the population (approximately 43 million U.S. adults) affected in a given year (Kessler et al., 2005). These disorders are associated with disability, lost productivity, and increased health care utilization. It is estimated that anxiety disorders cost the United States $42.3 billion annually (Greenberg et al., 1999). Although effective treatments for anxiety disorders exist, many individuals do not receive treatment. Among those who do, many do not respond to, relapse after, or prematurely drop out of treatment (Pollack et al., 2008). Thus, there is much room for the consideration of novel and more efficient treatment approaches for these disorders.

Given the successes of cognitive-behavioral therapy (CBT) for anxiety disorders to date (Butler, Chapman, Forman, & Beck, 2006; Hofmann & Smits, 2008), this chapter elucidates how a neurocognitive perspective could inform further advances in CBT. In particular, we evaluate evidence for the neurocognitive mechanisms involved in both the pathophysiology and treatment of anxiety and related disorders and consider how these processes might be targeted to enhance or complement CBT. Novel strategies may directly ameliorate neurocognitive changes associated with anxiety disorders and better support and enhance the uptake and retention of the therapeutic learning provided by CBT. We start this discussion with evidence for brain region and deficits involved with perhaps the most basic processes behind fear acquisition and amelioration—fear conditioning and extinction.

The DSM describes the anxiety disorders as those that "share features of excessive fear and anxiety and related behavioral disturbances" (American Psychiatric Association, 2013). In DSM-5, these include social anxiety disorder

(SAD), panic disorder (PD), agoraphobia, generalized anxiety disorder (GAD), specific phobia, and the recent additions of selective mutism and separation anxiety disorder. Although classified as anxiety disorders in DSM-IV, obsessive-compulsive disorder (OCD) and posttraumatic stress disorder (PTSD) have been classified in the DSM-5 within the obsessive-compulsive and related disorders and the trauma- and stressor-related disorders, respectively. However, given the shared features of these disorders (e.g., elevated sensitivity to threat; Craske et al., 2009) and the central role of learning and extinction processes across anxiety disorders and OCD and PTSD (Foa & Kozak, 1986; Rauch, Shin, & Phelps, 2006), we will include discussion of OCD and PTSD in the current chapter.

Fear Learning and Extinction: Evidence from the Conditioning Laboratories

The acquisition and extinction of conditioned fear has been implicated in numerous theories of clinical anxiety, and the neurobiology of these processes has been studied in animal and human models. Briefly, a conditioned fear response (CR) is acquired when a neutral stimulus (the conditioned stimulus or CS) is repeatedly paired with an intrinsically aversive unconditioned stimulus (UCS). With repeated presentation of this pairing, subjects learn that the CS predicts the UCS, causing the CS alone to elicit a fear response. The CR can be extinguished by repeatedly presenting the CS without any UCS, leading to a decline in fear response (for review, see Hermans, Craske, Mineka, & Lovibond, 2006). Although most experimental studies focus on models in which fear is acquired through direct experience with an aversive stimulus, fear may also be learned through vicarious (observational) or informational transmission (Rachman, 1977). These pathways to fear learning are proposed to operate similarly to direct fear conditioning; however, several potential differences should be noted. In models of social fear learning, expressions of distress from others (e.g., fearful facial expression, arm movement in response to shock) can serve as the aversive US (Olsson & Phelps, 2007). In addition, "instructed" or informational transmission of fear is unique to humans and is likely more dependent on representations in higher cortical areas (for review, see Olsson & Phelps, 2007).

The amygdala is at the center of the fear-conditioning network in the brain, with studies showing that the acquisition of fear is disrupted when the amygdala is lesioned or pharmacologically blocked (Maren & Quirk, 2004). In addition, stronger amygdala reactivity has been associated with a stronger conditioned fear response (Phelps, Delgado, Nearing, & LeDoux, 2004). Importantly, fear extinction does not consist of the "unlearning" of the CS-UCS association, but instead, creates a new association with safety that inhibits the original association (Quirk, Garcia, & Gonzalez-Lima, 2006). Numerous animal and human studies show that this process involves interaction between the prefrontal cortex (PFC), basolateral amygdale (BLA), and hippocampus (for review, see Quirk et al., 2006). The ventromedial PFC (vmPFC) plays a crucial role, with studies suggesting that consolidation of extinction learning leads to potentiation of vmPFC activity, which inhibits fear response (Milad & Quirk, 2002). The hippocampus encodes context during both fear acquisition and extinction and is essential to consolidation of extinction (Herry et al., 2010). At the neurotransmitter level, GABA and N-methyl-D-aspartate (NMDA) have been implicated in fear conditioning and extinction, with the inhibitory neurotransmitter GABA thought to be involved in the inhibition of the amygdala during extinction retrieval (i.e., the expression of the inhibitory memory upon presentation of the extinguished CS), and NMDA receptors in the BLA in the acquisition of both conditioned fear and extinction (for review, see Quirk & Mueller, 2008).

Several theories propose specific mechanisms by which aberrant fear conditioning may lead to clinical anxiety. Both the acquisition and extinction of fear responses play a role, because the development and persistence of anxiety disorders may be influenced by aberrations in the ease by which new fear associations are acquired, the difficulty by which safety is (re)learned as a result of fear extinction, or the degree to which safe versus unsafe conditions are discriminated, thereby influencing the predictability of perceived danger (Orr et al., 2000). To date, studies of fear conditioning have examined aspects of each of these processes, with better support for the notions of impaired extinction of fears in anxiety patients as well as impairments in the ability to discriminate safety from danger (Grillon, Lissek, McDowell, Levenson, & Pine, 2007; Grillon & Morgan, 1999; Grillon et al., 2009; Jovanovic et al., 2010; Lissek et al., 2010; Milad et al., 2008, 2013; Orr et al., 2000). In terms of differential acquisition of fears, results have been surprisingly complex. In a meta-analysis of forty-six comparisons between anxiety patients and controls on the ease of fear acquisition (with positive scores representing greater acquisition of conditioned fear responses among anxiety patients), Lissek et al. (2005) found that twenty-five (55%) studies were positive (reflecting better acquisition among anxious samples), eight (17%) were negative, and thirteen (28%) reported near zero effect sizes. In part to understand this variability in findings, Grillon (2009) has emphasized a dual-model theory of fear conditioning in humans, with fear conditioning potentially engaging a lower-order defensive process that is outside conscious awareness as well as a higher order cognitive system linked to conscious awareness of anticipation and danger. Each component is relevant to the cognitive and exposure interventions applied in CBT for anxiety disorders and relevant to both the anticipation of threat as well as fear responses upon exposure to feared stimuli. Grillon (2009) posited that human fear conditioning may preferentially rely on higher-order cognitive processes that are more dependent on hippocampal rather than amygdala function, unless the stimuli are particularly fear relevant or an intense UCS is used, thereby ensuring amygdala involvement. Initial work has mapped extinction deficits on brain activity, with findings of reduced activity in the vmPFC and the hippocampus and increased activity in the dorsal anterior cingulate cortex (ACC) occurring in PTSD patients during extinction (Milad et al., 2009). Hence, it is possible that these patterns of activation may contribute to deficient extinction learning (Milad et al., 2009).

Given this evidence from the conditioning laboratory, neurocognitive investigations of the correlates of anxiety disorders themselves should see activations in limbic and pre-frontal structures, reflecting both the salience of fear stimuli for anxiety patients and, perhaps, particular abnormalities and challenges in the cognitive processing of these stimuli. Also of relevance are any aberrations in information processing/cognitive ability that would affect the relearning of safety or the application of relevant emotional processing skills. In the sections below, neuroimaging findings for each disorder will be considered first, followed by findings from neuropsychological studies investigating cognitive deficits among individuals with anxiety disorders.

Neuroimaging Findings

Regarding neuroimaging findings, expectations for limbic and frontal circuit involvement in anxiety and related disorders have been confirmed. More specifically, there is convergent support for the involvement of limbic and paralimbic structures (amygdala, hippocampus, insula) as well as the prefrontal cortex in the experience and evaluation of threat (e.g., Etkin & Wager, 2007; Freitas-Ferrari et al., 2010; Graham & Milad, 2011; Klumpp, Angstadt, & Phan, 2012; Phan, Fitzgerald, Nathan, & Tancer, 2006). There is, however, variability in results, perhaps reflecting the variable stimuli, paradigms, and patient populations studied. Each diagnostic group will be considered individually.

Posttraumatic Stress Disorder

Patients with PTSD have repeatedly been shown to demonstrate amygdala hyperactivity in response to trauma-related stimuli and trauma-unrelated emotional facial expressions (Etkin & Wager, 2007; Rauch et al., 2000; Shin, Rauch, & Pitman, 2006). The strength of amygdala response to trauma-related cues has been positively associated with PTSD symptom severity across multiple studies (e.g., Rauch et al., 1996; Shin et al., 2004). Notably, a meta-analysis of neuroimaging studies of emotional processing across several anxiety disorders found that during exposure to emotional stimuli, hyperactivation of the amygdala was more frequently observed in social anxiety disorder (SAD) and specific phobia than PTSD (Etkin & Wager, 2007). However, it should be noted that significant heterogeneity existed within the types' negative emotional stimuli presented by individual studies in the analysis (e.g., trauma scripts, emotional faces).

PTSD has also been characterized by alterations in prefrontal cortex in both structural and functional neuroimaging studies, which have been conceptualized as reflecting deficits in reflexive emotion regulation processes and cognitive control (Etkin & Wager, 2007). Individuals with PTSD show reduced volume of vmPFC and dorsal ACC (Rauch et al., 2003; Woodward et al., 2006; Yamasue et al., 2003), and it has been suggested that the amygdala may have excessive influence over areas such as the ACC and visual cortex during presentation of personal trauma scripts (Gilboa et al., 2004). Results of fMRI studies show a failure to recruit medial prefrontal regions during exposure to both trauma-related and unrelated emotional stimuli (Etkin & Wager, 2007; Shin et al., 2006). Hypoactivation of mPFC during symptom provocation has been correlated with PTSD symptom severity in several studies (for review, see Shin et al., 2006). Similarly, PTSD patients have been characterized by reduced activation of mPFC during fear extinction recall, with activation strength being found to correlate positively with the magnitude of extinction learning (Milad et al., 2009). However, a few studies have found contrasting evidence indicative of hyperactivity in prefrontal regions across resting and symptom provocation paradigms (Sachinvala, Kling, Suffin, Lake, & Cohen, 2000; Zubieta et al., 1999), perhaps reflecting differences in imaging technique or the dissociative state of the patients (Shin et al., 2006).

The hippocampus has also been implicated in PTSD. Patients have shown reduced hippocampal activation during fear extinction recall testing, with results demonstrating a positive association between hippocampal activity and successful fear extinction recall (Milad et al., 2009). Quantitative meta-analysis also suggests that PTSD patients show reduced hippocampal activation in response to negative emotional stimuli (Etkin & Wager, 2007). Yet other studies have found increased hippocampal activity in PTSD patients both at rest and in response to cognitive tasks (Sachinvala et al., 2000; Semple et al., 2000; Shin et al., 2006). Additionally, a number of studies have reported reduced hippocampal volume in PTSD patients compared to trauma-exposed or non-trauma-exposed controls (Bremner et al., 1995; Lindauer et al., 2004). It is still unclear whether reduced hippocampal volume is acquired as a result of trauma exposure or PTSD or whether it is a preexisting risk factor for PTSD. Twin studies provide evidence that it is a preexisting vulnerability factor for the development of PTSD upon exposure to trauma (Gilbertson et al., 2002). However, a recent meta-analysis (Woon, Sood, & Hedges, 2010) reported that hippocampal volume is reduced in trauma-exposed controls compared to non-exposed controls (although not to the extent found in PTSD patients), indicating that it may be a consequence of trauma exposure.

Studies comparing PTSD patients and controls show that these patterns of alterations in amygdala, prefrontal, and hippocampal regions are also present at rest. For instance, Chung and colleagues (2006) found increased blood perfusion in limbic regions and decreased activation of cortical regions (superior frontal gyrus and temporal and parietal regions) during resting state. Consistent with symptom provocation or cognitive task studies, Kim and colleagues (2012) found that PTSD patients at rest also showed reduced perfusion and glucose metabolism in the left hippocampus. These and other studies of PTSD patients at rest have also found evidence for other alterations in neural activity, including increased activation of cerebellum, fusiform, and occipital gyri (Bonne et al., 2003; Kim et al., 2012; True et al., 1993), and decreased activation of caudate nucleus (Lucey et al., 1997).

In summary, PTSD is characterized by increased amygdala reactivity and failure to recruit medial and prefrontal regions in response to trauma and emotionally valenced cues. Neuroimaging studies of PTSD patients at rest generally support these patterns but also show alterations in cerebellum and other brain regions. Studies also provide consistent evidence for alterations in hippocampal structure (decreased volume) and function (typically hypoactivation) within PTSD. However, evidence exists that findings of reduced hippocampal volume may be a consequence of trauma exposure.

Social Anxiety Disorder

Several functional neuroimaging studies of SAD patients have examined the neural response to facial emotional processing paradigms, which have strong conceptual relevance to the core symptoms of SAD. Results suggest amygdala hyperactivity in SAD relative to controls in response to neutral (Birbaumer et al., 1998), angry (Stein, Goldin, Sareen, Zorrilla, & Brown, 2002), disgusted (Phan et al., 2006), and fearful (Phan et al., 2006) faces. Inconsistencies have been found with regard to amygdala reactivity to happy faces (Phan et al., 2006; Straube, Mentzel, & Miltner, 2005). Moreover, amygdala responsivity may be modulated by the intensity of the emotional expression (Evans et al., 2008; Yoon, Fitzgerald, Angstadt, McCarron, & Phan, 2007) and has been demonstrated to be exaggerated in response to symptom provocations such as a public-speaking task (Lorberbaum et al., 2004) and social comments (Blair et al., 2008).

Additional regions of the "fear circuit" have also been implicated in SAD. Compared with controls, SAD patients have demonstrated increased activity in the insula (Shah, Klumpp, Angstadt, Nathan, & Phan, 2009; Straube et al., 2005) and the hippocampus (Furmark et al., 2005; Lorberbaum et al., 2004; Stein, Goldin, et al., 2002) in response to emotional stimuli and symptom provocation.

More recently, abnormalities throughout these areas have been demonstrated in response to anticipation (Brühl et al., 2011) and presentation (Shah et al., 2009) of non-social negative emotional stimuli. This suggests that SAD patients may have more general alterations in emotional processing circuits (Brühl et al., 2011).

SAD patients also demonstrate decreased activation in prefrontal regions compared with controls during exposure to emotional or cognitive tasks. For example, Gentili and colleagues (2009) found that SAD patients had reduced left dorsolateral prefrontal cortex (dlPFC) activation in response to emotional and neutral faces compared to scrambled images. Similarly, SAD patients undergoing a public-speaking challenge task demonstrated reduced activity in dlPFC and dorsal anterior cingulate (Lorberbaum et al., 2004). In a study by Goldin and colleagues (2009), SAD patients showed reduced dorsomedial and dorsolateral PFC activation during a cognitive regulation task, suggesting a reduced ability to utilize emotion regulation strategies under socially threatening conditions. However, contrasting reports of hyperactivity in the dlPFC during anticipatory anxiety exist (e.g., Guyer et al., 2008), potentially indicating that prefrontal activation is increased during anticipatory anxiety but decreased during symptom provocation/emotional processing (Ferreri, Lapp, & Peretti, 2011).

Recent studies are looking beyond region-specific neural activity and studying functional connectivity. Resting-state functional connectivity MRI was used during a facial emotion processing task, showing that SAD patients had reduced functional coupling of the left amygdala and the medial orbitofrontal cortex (OFC) and posterior cingulate cortex (Hahn et al., 2011). Moreover, strength of connectivity was negatively associated with social anxiety severity. Klumpp and colleagues (2012) reported that SAD patients showed reduced connectivity between the insula and anterior cingulate cortex when processing fearful faces, which they suggest indicates deficient subcortical-PFC connectivity. These studies provide evidence for network-wide rather than region-specific alterations in neural functioning in SAD.

Although very few studies have examined brain function at rest, there are some data to suggest the presence of alterations in the resting state in SAD. Warwick and colleagues (2008) used single-photon emission computed tomography (SPECT) to examine resting state perfusion in SAD patients and controls, finding evidence of increased perfusion of right cerebellum and bilateral prefrontal cortex and decreased perfusion in the left cerebellum, pons, and precuneus. Interestingly, SAD severity was positively correlated with left frontal cortex perfusion and negatively correlated with right fusiform and right lingual perfusion. The authors suggest that the hyperactivation of prefrontal regions may be representative of modulation of excessive amygdala activation thought to characterize SAD (Warwick et al., 2008). Although these results are at odds with findings of reduced prefrontal activity during emotion regulation and symptom provocation tasks (see above), they are consistent with the finding of hyperactivity in frontal cortex found during anticipatory anxiety by Guyer and colleagues (2008).

Although the literature is not entirely consistent, several core patterns emerge to characterize patterns of neural function in SAD. One of the primary features appears to be amygdala hyperactivity in response to symptom provocation; however, findings of fear circuit hyperactivity in response to general negative emotional stimuli suggest that SAD may also be characterized by more general alterations in emotional processing. Furthermore, SAD patients show reduced activation in frontal areas, possibly reflecting difficulties regulating negative emotional or anxious states. Disparate findings of prefrontal activation suggest that SAD patients may be characterized by hypoactivation of frontal regions during symptom provocation or emotional processing and by hyperactivation of these regions during anticipatory anxiety.

Panic Disorder

Under conditions of panic provocation (e.g., CO_2 inhalation, lactate infusion), patients with PD show functional differences in insular, cingular, frontal, and brain stem areas (Dresler et al., 2012; Pfleiderer et al., 2007). Of particular relevance to panic disorder are findings that the anterior cingulate cortex (ACC) and insula play a role in interoceptive awareness; thus the alterations in these regions may reflect interoceptive sensitivity in PD (Graeff & Del-Ben, 2008), consistent with cognitive-behavioral models emphasizing the role of fear of anxiety symptoms (anxiety sensitivity) in the etiology and maintenance of this disorder (McNally, 2002; Reiss, Peterson, Gursky, & McNally, 1986; Schmidt, Lerew, & Jackson, 1997; Smits, Berry, Tart, & Powers, 2008; Smits, Powers, Cho, & Telch, 2004).

As with SAD and PTSD, PD patients have demonstrated amygdala hyperactivity in response to emotional stimuli (van den Heuvel et al., 2005), and during spontaneous panic attack (Garakani et al., 2007). Yet this pattern of activation has not been completely consistent. Boshuisen and colleagues. (2002) reported decreased blood flow to the right amygdala during anticipation of a panic challenge. Tuescher and colleagues (2011) reported that compared to PTSD patients, PD patients demonstrated reduced amygdala activation in response to a threat association and increased activation in response to a safety cue. Such contrasting findings likely reflect the small sample sizes, diverse methodology, and heterogeneous samples frequently characteristic of these studies (Kim, Dager, & Lyoo, 2013).

It has also been suggested that PD patients also show deficiencies in prefrontal areas associated with emotion regulation. Ball and colleagues (2012) reported reduced dorsomedial PFC and dlPFC in both panic disorder and generalized anxiety disorder patients during an emotion regulation task. Similarly, Akiyoshi and colleagues (2003) found evidence of hypoactivity of left frontal cortex in panic patients viewing anxiety-relevant or emotional stimuli but not neutrally valenced images. These results are also consistent with patterns of frontal hypoactivity described in PTSD and SAD, possibly indicating a more general deficit in emotion regulation across the anxiety disorders (Ball et al., 2012).

Resting-state studies of panic disorder patients also have found evidence of alterations in brain function. Wiedemann and colleagues (1999) found frontal asymmetry in panic patients compared to controls during both rest and exposure to emotional stimuli. Several other studies of panic disorder patients in resting state have found reduced hippocampal activation (Bisaga et al., 1998; De Cristofaro, Sessarego, Pupi, Biondi, & Faravelli, 1993), with Bisaga and colleagues (1998) also finding reduced blood glucose metabolism in right inferior parietal and right superior temporal regions. Additionally, consistent with some findings of hyperactive amygdala response to emotional or panic-related stimuli, panic patients at rest have demonstrated increased amygdala activity (Sakai et al., 2005). However, it should be noted that conditions considered "at rest" may be significantly more anxiety-provoking for panic disorder patients given the confined nature of the scanner environment.

Overall, although there is evidence of amygdala hyperactivity at rest and in response to panic-related and emotional stimuli in PD patients, the literature is less consistent regarding this pattern than for disorders such as PTSD and SAD. However, the finding of reduced prefrontal activation across PD, PTSD, and SAD, occurring in response to symptom-irrelevant but emotional stimuli has led researchers to propose that these patterns reflect a more general emotion regulation dysfunction across anxiety and related disorders. Finally, more specific to PD, the insula and ACC may play a role in interoceptive sensitivity.

Generalized Anxiety Disorder

In contrast to the other anxiety disorders, there are fewer data demonstrating an increased amygdala response to emotional stimuli in GAD. This finding concords with theoretical models emphasizing the ability of worry to suppress or inhibit amygdalar activation via frontal recruitment (e.g., Borkovec, 1994). In fact, several studies have found evidence of reduced amygdala response (Blair et al., 2008; McClure et al., 2007) in response to threatening faces. Comparison of GAD and SAD patients during a facial emotion processing task has led Blair and colleagues (2008) to suggest that GAD is more strongly characterized by alterations in prefrontal regions instead of amygdala. Several studies support the possibility of hyperactivity in frontal areas in GAD when viewing emotional facial expressions, completing a passive viewing task, or at rest (Blair et al., 2008, 2012;

Mathew et al., 2004; Wu et al., 1991). Such results have been interpreted as indicating the presence of an over-engaged cognitive control system in GAD (Etkin & Wager, 2007). This pattern is in contrast to the report of hypoactivity in PFC regions in PTSD and SAD, which has been conceptualized as contributing to failure to appropriately regulate emotional responding. However, the pattern of prefrontal hyperactivity in GAD is consistent with findings that worry, the core feature of GAD, is associated with prefrontal engagement (specifically, mPFC and ACC regions) in both GAD patients and controls (Paulesu et al., 2010).

Yet, the literature is not completely consistent regarding patterns of prefrontal activation associated with GAD. Ball and colleagues (2012) found reduced activation of dmPFC and dlPFC in GAD patients compared to controls during an emotion regulation task. Similarly, Monk and colleagues (2008) studied adolescents with GAD, finding increased amygdala responding to masked faces and noting that the negative coupling of amygdala response and vmPFC activation was weaker in GAD patients than controls. Further study is needed to clarify the subject, task, or measurement-related characteristics that might contribute to these inconsistencies.

In summary, GAD appears to be characterized by prefrontal hyperactivity and reduced amygdala response to emotional stimuli, which is consistent with theoretical models of worry. However, findings are not completely consistent, and additional neuroimaging studies of GAD are needed to clarify disparate findings.

Obsessive-Compulsive Disorder

OCD is characterized by dysfunction in cortico-striatal circuitry (e.g., Baxter et al., 1987; Harrison et al., 2009; Rauch et al., 1994; Schwartz, Stoessel, Baxter, Martin, & Phelps, 1996), representing a pattern that is not found in PTSD, SAD, GAD, or specific phobia (Stein et al., 2010). It is hypothesized that an imbalance of activity between "direct" and "indirect" pathways within the orbitofrontal-subcortical pathway leads to excess activation of the OFC, which manifests as obsessive-compulsive behavior (Saxena & Rauch, 2000). Imaging studies have supported this proposition, with PET and fMRI studies showing a relatively consistent pattern of hyperactivity in the OFC at rest and during symptom provocation (Menzies et al., 2008). Research advancements have led to the refining and modification of this "cortico-striatal loop" model, leading to more specific hypotheses regarding the role of distinct OFC regions. Milad and Rauch (2012) suggest that the lOFC, found to be hyperactive in OCD patients, may mediate obsessions, while the mOFC, typically underactive in OCD patients, may be associated with deficits in extinction retrieval (i.e., recall of the extinction memory upon post-consolidation exposure to the extinguished CS).

Recent research also implicates brain regions outside this "cortico-striatal loop" in OCD. Elevations in dorsal ACC activity may contribute to obsessions (consistent with its role in error monitoring) or increased fear and anxiety (consistent with its role in the expression of fear conditioning; Milad & Rauch, 2012). The amygdala has also been implicated. Studies have consistently shown that patients demonstrate amygdala hyperactivation in response to symptom provocation. The literature is somewhat inconsistent with regard to amygdala activation in response to generally negative or aversive stimuli. Several studies have found no evidence of hyperactivation in response to such cues, (e.g., Menzies et al., 2008; Rauch et al., 2007); however, a more recent study utilizing a more sensitive experimental paradigm found that amygdala hyperactivation was present in OCD patients viewing generally aversive stimuli (Simon, Kaufmann, Musch, Kischkel, & Kathmann, 2010). A separate study found amygdala hyperresponsivity in response to emotional faces in OCD patients (Cardoner et al., 2011), suggesting the need for further clarification of amygdala responsivity in OCD. Finally, there is evidence of deficient extinction learning in OCD, with patients showing reduced activation of the vmPFC during conditioning and extinction, and enhanced activation of the caudate and hippocampus during conditioning only (Milad et al., 2013).

In sum, consistent evidence of cortico-striatal dysfunction exists in studies of OCD, with more recent research clarifying the specific roles of distinct orbitofrontal cortex regions. Like the anxiety disorders, OCD is also characterized by deficient extinction learning and amygdala hyperresponsivity upon symptom provocation. However, in contrast to findings of more general hyperactivity to emotional stimuli in disorders such as SAD or PTSD, the response in OCD appears to be symptom-specific.

Perspectives Provided by Neuropsychological Assessment

The most consistent picture of neuropsychological deficits emerges in studies of PTSD. Strong evidence of performance decrements in executive functioning (EF) in PTSD exists, particularly within the domains of inhibitory control and set-shifting (for review, see Aupperle, Melrose, Stein, & Paulus, 2012; Polak, Witteveen, Reitsma, & Olff, 2012). Interestingly, between-group differences in EF components such as selective attention, inhibitory control, working memory, planning, and cognitive flexibility are larger when comparing PTSD patients to trauma-exposed individuals than non-trauma exposed individuals (Polak et al., 2012). These results, which run counter to some individual studies (e.g., Stein, Jang, Taylor, Vernon, & Livesley, 2002), suggest that deficits in EF are associated with PTSD rather than trauma exposure more generally. Moreover, low cognitive function, and EF in particular, may be a marker of premorbid vulnerability for PTSD (Gilbertson et al., 2006).

Attentional control deficits have also been widely documented in PTSD, with the strongest effects occurring in combat veterans (Qureshi et al., 2011). Although some studies have suggested the presence of learning and memory deficits, the data appear to be less clear in these areas (Qureshi et al., 2011). Some data suggest that the variable findings in the literature may be due to differences in the sample characteristics or test scoring procedures. For example, being male, experiencing war-related trauma, or being of older age have been associated with increased deficits in EF in PTSD (Aupperle et al., 2012; Qureshi et al., 2011).

Despite a relative consistency of findings across studies and reviews with regard to neuropsychological performance in PTSD, a number of factors must be considered when interpreting the findings. Because the large majority of studies compare patients and controls on raw rather than normed scores, there is a greater likelihood of detecting differences that are statistically significant but are not necessarily clinically meaningful. In addition, many studies have not examined covariates that may account for the differences between patient and control groups, such as general intelligence, education level, or age. Many of the reviews described above do not describe or meaningfully distinguish between these study characteristics, potentially accounting for inconsistencies in results.

Results of neuropsychological assessment in patients with panic disorder and social anxiety disorder are more variable. EF deficits have been found in PD (Airaksinen, Larsson, & Forsell, 2005) but have not been demonstrated consistently (Purcell, Maruff, Kyrios, & Pantelis, 1998). Additional studies have found areas of weakness in verbal and spatial learning, visuoconstructive abilities, and episodic and visual memory in PD patients (Airaksinen et al., 2005; Asmundson, Stein, Larsen, & Walker, 1994; Deckersbach, Moshier, Tuschen-Caffier, & Otto, 2011; Kaplan et al., 2006; Lucas, Telch, & Bigler, 1991). However, other studies have found no significant differences in tests of memory between panic disorder patients and controls (e.g., Gladsjo et al., 1998). Notably, the study by Gladsjo and colleagues (1998) finding no evidence of memory deficits in panic disorder patients was the only study to covary full-scale IQ score, raising the possibility that specific neuropsychological deficits associated with panic disorder may be confounded by IQ.

Furthermore, few studies of panic disorder patients have examined the clinical meaning of decrements in neuropsychological performance. Lucas and colleagues (1991) found that panic disorder patients had greater rates of clinical-level impairment in visual recall. Asmundson and colleagues (1994) examined rates of clinically impaired verbal learning (defined as two standard deviations below the mean) in panic disorder patients, finding significant differences between panic patients and controls on only a single trial of a multi-trial test (i.e., the 5th trial of the California Verbal Learning Test). The authors interpreted these findings to suggest that clinical significance of the findings may be modest and that the differences may reflect mediators of test performance such as fatigue or loss of interest rather than an underlying neurocognitive deficit.

Similar inconsistencies are apparent in the social anxiety literature. A systematic review by O'Toole and Pedersen (2011) found indication of visual scanning and visuospatial deficits, with minimal evidence for verbal memory, visual recognition, or executive function weakness. However, results have been widely varied, and one recent study assessing nine areas of cognitive functioning found no differences between patients with SAD and controls, including visual spatial processing and visual working memory (Sutterby & Bedwell, 2012). Results may vary due to test scoring procedures; for instance, Sutterby and Bedwell (2012) transformed raw scores into z-scores according to the mean of the control group, while many others (e.g., Airaksinen et al., 2005; Asmundson et al., 1994; Cohen et al., 1996) compared only raw scores, which are more likely to detect significant between-group differences.

Data also indicate that the sample characteristics of neuropsychological evaluations of PD and SAD may influence the results. Kaplan and colleagues (2006) found that compared to controls or individuals with PD alone, those with comorbid PD and MDD demonstrated negative attentional bias and visual discrimination and working memory deficits. Such results highlight the importance of controlling for comorbid symptoms or, preferably, excluding individuals with conditions that may confound results.

Neuropsychological function in GAD has been relatively unstudied. Research to date provides little support for the presence of cognitive deficits, with the exception of a study by Wolski & Maj (1998), who found that anxious patients, most of whom were diagnosed with GAD, performed more poorly on a modified Sternberg memory task. However, there is evidence that worry, the core feature of GAD, is associated with reduced working memory capacity. More specifically, Hayes and colleagues (2008) found that worry-prone individuals (as compared to "low" worriers) demonstrated reduced working memory performance when instructed to think about a personal worry. These results suggest that worry may take up more working memory capacity in those who are frequent worriers and may thereby reduce attentional capacity for directing thoughts away from the worry (Hayes et al., 2008). Furthermore, there is growing evidence of problems with memory and EF specifically in individuals with late life GAD (Butters et al., 2011; Mohlman, 2013), a topic addressed in more depth elsewhere in this volume (Mohlman et al., Chapter 5).

Studies of neuropsychological performance in individuals with OCD have demonstrated consistent patterns of deficits in a number of areas. Recently, Abramovitch and colleagues (2013), conducted a meta-analysis of 115 studies comparing OCD patients and controls across domains of neuropsychology. A large effect was found supporting the presence of a nonverbal memory deficit in OCD patients, and a moderate effect was found for domains of executive function, sustained attention, and processing speed (with patients performing more poorly). A small effect was found for verbal memory and visuospatial ability. Interestingly, neither OCD symptom severity nor depressive symptom severity were moderators of these effects. The authors suggest that these results may not be clinically significant and emphasize that the role of these deficits in the development and maintenance of OCD is unknown. As with reviews of neuropsychological function in other psychiatric disorders, the characteristics of individual studies (e.g., use of raw versus normed data, inclusion of covariates, matching of samples) is not commented on, and individual examination of these studies reveals variation across these features. Moreover, these results may not be specific to OCD, as one major limitation to this literature is the lack of comparison of OCD to other psychiatric conditions. Recently, a comparison of inhibitory control abilities among patients with OCD and panic disorder did not support the hypotheses that such deficits are specific to OCD (Thomas, Gonsalvez, & Johnstone, 2014)

To summarize, a large body of research suggests that the anxiety disorders are characterized by the presence of neuropsychological deficits. However, results of such studies vary markedly and are limited by substantial heterogeneity in study inclusion/exclusion criteria, assessment and scoring methods, and sample characteristics such as medication use and comorbidity. There does not appear to be any clear neuropsychological signature for any of the anxiety disorders; however, PTSD is frequently characterized by EF impairment, and there is some evidence for performance decrements in memory across many of the anxiety disorders.

One implication of these findings is that in providing efficacious treatment, CBT must overcome cognitive deficits that may slow the uptake of therapeutic learning. Interestingly, there has been little investigation of the degree of these effects on CBT. The literature in this area has primarily focused on the effect of executive skills on the treatment of older adults, with some data suggesting that individuals with poorer executive functioning respond more poorly to treatment for mood and anxiety disorders (Mohlman, 2005).

Given the overall efficacy of CBT, there is reliable evidence that these learning-based interventions are resilient to the cognitive deficits found for some patients with anxiety disorders, yet the field is largely uninformed of the degree to which CBT outcomes are moderated by cognitive abilities. Clearly, additional research is needed on this topic.

Implications of Neuroimaging and Neuropsychological Findings for Treatment

Inconsistent results are common in the neuroimaging and neuropsychological investigations of anxiety disorders. Nonetheless, as reviewed above, there is evidence that the anxiety disorders are associated with alterations in neural activation and neuropsychological performance. However, it is not known whether these alterations are simply the resultant correlates of anxiety disorders (reflecting state-specific consequences of having an anxiety disorder), predisposing or maintaining factors for anxiety disorders, or both. In the next section, we consider these questions in relation to observed changes in neuropsychiatric profiles across treatment as well as additional treatment implications for these findings.

Traditional treatments for the anxiety disorders, OCD, and PTSD include both psychotherapy and pharmacologic agents. CBT, which targets the cognitive (e.g., exaggerated or erroneous thoughts about the fears) and behavioral patterns (e.g., avoidance) that maintain symptoms, has gained strong support in the research literature. Several meta-analyses show that CBT holds significant benefit over placebo in terms of both symptom reduction (Butler et al., 2006; Hofmann & Smits, 2008; Smits et al., 2008) and quality of life (Hofmann, Wu, & Boettcher, 2014). Although there is less evidence regarding comparative efficacy of CBT with active treatments, meta-analysis has found that CBT was superior to other psychotherapies, particularly for anxiety and mood disorders (Tolin, 2010). Principle medications used are selective serotonin reuptake inhibitors, given alone, or in combination with benzodiazepines; benzodiazepines alone; as well as some use of older antidepressants (monoamine oxidase inhibitors or tricyclic antidepressants), select agents such as beta-blockers, or for extreme anxiety, atypical antipsychotics (Cloos & Ferreira, 2009; Comer, Mojtabai, & Olfson, 2011; Ravindran & Stein, 2010; Vasile, Bruce, Goisman, Pagano, & Keller, 2005). Although similar effect sizes are found for pharmacotherapy and CBT treatment strategies (Eddy, Dutra, Bradley, & Westen, 2004; Mitte, 2005; Otto, Pollack, & Maki, 2000), CBT treatments have benefits of strong maintenance of treatment gains (Hollon, Stewart, & Strunk, 2006) as well as cost-effectiveness and acceptability (Issakidis, Sanderson, Corry, Andrews, & Lapsley, 2004; McHugh et al., 2007; Otto et al., 2000). One recent meta-analytic review determined that 75 percent of psychiatric patients report a preference for psychological treatment over pharmacotherapy (McHugh, Whitton, Peckham, Welge, & Otto, 2013).

Neuroimaging of Treatment Response

Research shows that effective treatment for the anxiety disorders is associated with increased prefrontal activation and decreased limbic activation; that is, normalization of the fear network (Quidé, Witteveen, El-Hage, Veltman, & Olff, 2012). This same effect occurs despite evidence for different modes and pathways of action for psychosocial and pharmacologic treatments. For example, one of the broadest characterizations is that psychosocial treatments lead to increased recruitment of frontal areas for subsequent dampening of limbic activity (a "top-down" effect), whereas pharmacologic treatments may first decrease over-activity of limbic structures (a "bottom-up" effect; Quidé et al., 2012). Yet, this proposition has only mixed support from the nine resting-state studies and eleven cognitive/challenge studies reviewed by Quidé (2012), with several studies showing decreased activation in PFC regions following treatment (Nakao et al., 2005; Paquette et al., 2003; Yamanishi et al., 2009). Nonetheless, CBT has been found to act on brain areas involved in processes such as EF, self-regulation, emotion regulation, and empathy (for review, see: Porto et al., 2009; Quidé et al., 2012). For example, using PET, patients with panic disorder have shown increased activation in the left inferior and right dlPFC (Prasko et al., 2004) and the right medial PFC (Sakai et al., 2006) after CBT. Patients with PTSD who complete CBT have demonstrated increased rostral ACC activation; moreover, reduction in amygdala activation from before to after treatment was significantly associated ($r = -.85$) with symptom improvement (Felmingham et al., 2007). A separate study of PTSD patients showed that CBT led to increased activation of temporal areas previously associated with empathy and forgivability judgments (Farrow et al., 2005). Patients with SAD undergoing CBT show normalized prefrontal EEG responses (Miskovic et al., 2011). Furthermore, patients who have received CBT for SAD demonstrate increased activation and earlier temporal onset of dmPFC and dlPFC activity during a cognitive reappraisal task, while amygdala activation during the task remained unchanged in response to treatment (Goldin, Ziv, Jazaieri, Hahn, Heimberg, et al., 2013). In addition, hyperactivation present in cortico-striatal regions (OFC and caudate) in OCD has been shown to normalize after CBT (Morgieve et al., 2013; Nakao et al., 2005).

Moreover, studies show a pattern of reduced limbic activation after CBT. Successful treatment of spider phobia was associated with reductions in insular and ACC activation during subsequent symptom provocation (Straube, Glauer, Dilger, Mentzel, & Miltner, 2006). Similar findings were documented in a PET study of patients receiving CBT or citalopram for treatment of social anxiety disorder (Furmark et al., 2002). Compared with those in a waitlist control group, both treatment groups demonstrated an association between symptom improvement and attenuated activation of the amygdala, hippocampus, and medial and anterior temporal cortex (Furmark et al., 2002). Hence, reduced amygdala activation may be a final common pathway of successful treatment, regardless of the pathway to that result. These findings within clinically anxious samples are consistent with results from neuroimaging studies of fear extinction in healthy adults. Several studies have shown that extinction learning leads to reduced amygdala response (Sehlmeyer et al., 2009) and that extinction retrieval results in increased vmPFC activation (Milad et al., 2009).

Mindfulness-based approaches have also been considered a viable strategy for aiding emotional processing and have been gaining increasing empirical support within the anxiety disorders (for review, see Hofmann, Sawyer, Witt, & Oh, 2010). These interventions aim to directly target attentional allocation (Segal, Williams, & Teasdale, 2002) and train patients to be aware of their experiences (thoughts, feelings, sensations, behavior) and to let them run their course rather than trying to modify or suppress them (Hayes, Luoma, Bond, Masuda, & Lillis, 2006). There is growing evidence that such strategies may be mediated by increased activation in frontal areas associated with attentional control and emotion regulation. For example, in a study comparing the effects of mindfulness-based stress reduction (MBSR) and a stress-management education course, Holzel and colleagues (2013) found that at baseline, GAD patients had greater amygdala reactivity to neutral faces but not angry faces. After treatment, both treatment groups demonstrated decreased amygdala activation to neutral faces. However, only the group that received MBSR demonstrated increased activation in the vlPFC and increased PFC-amygdala connectivity. Another study comparing MBSR to an aerobic exercise intervention for patients with social anxiety disorder found that MBSR led to greater increases in parietal cortical areas during presentation of ideographic negative self-beliefs (Goldin, Ziv, Jazaieri, Hahn, & Gross, 2013). Moreover, meditation practice was positively correlated with increases in activation of these brain regions and with decreases in negative emotion during the task, suggesting that MBSR may have effects via changes in attentional regulation (Goldin et al., 2013).

This pattern of findings within patients treated for anxiety disorders is also consistent with experimental studies documenting the neural correlates of cognitive reappraisal. Healthy participants, when asked to reinterpret their responses to negative emotional stimuli, demonstrate increased activation in PFC and ACC areas (consistent with the task demands of applying a reappraisal strategy) and reduced activation in amygdala and insular activation (Ochsner & Gross, 2005).

One interpretation of these data is that attentional and cognitive-control strategies, used in mindfulness and CBT approaches, naturally target executive functions mediated through PFC activity. Actively learning to re-interpret threat cues and respond differently to negative or catastrophic cognitions and resultant emotions should have appropriate reflections in both frontal activity and resultant limbic activation. These general interpretations of such interventions broadly fit some of the data from neuroimaging studies of the psychosocial treatment of anxiety disorders. Yet, it still remains unclear whether frontal and limbic findings are simply the reflection of effective treatment or whether frontal activation is independently important for the treatment of anxiety disorders. That is, aside from specific mindfulness or cognitive-restructuring interventions, is frontal activation useful for treatment outcome in the anxiety disorders? Relevant to this question are studies of interventions that directly target neural activation.

Novel Strategies to Influence Frontal Activation

Cognitive control training (CCT; Siegle, Ghinassi, & Thase, 2007), a computerized intervention designed to activate the dlPFC, represents one such strategy for changing brain activation independent of a focus on changing anxiety-related responses. CCT consists of two computerized training tasks. The first, the Wells training task, was designed to improve selective attention to specific information and perhaps thereby increase ability to selectively attend away from ruminative thoughts (Wells, 2000). The second task is a variant of the Paced Auditory Serial Addition Task (PASAT; Gronwall, 1977), which is known to specifically activate the prefrontal cortex (Lazeron, Rombouts, de Sonneville, Barkhof, & Scheltens, 2003). In this version of the PASAT, participants must continuously add serially presented digits, thereby requiring holding information in working memory. One session of CCT takes approximately thirty minutes to complete and includes both tasks.

To date, CCT has been investigated mainly as a treatment for depression and rumination symptoms, with two studies showing that three to six sessions of CCT lead to a reduction in depression and rumination (Calkins, McMorran, Siegle, & Otto, 2014; Siegle et al., 2007). However, given the evidence of deficient prefrontal control and emotion regulation ability in the anxiety disorders and related conditions such as OCD, there is impetus for examination of CCT in this area. Calkins and Otto (2013) examined the effect of three sessions of CCT on obsessive-compulsive (OC) symptoms in an analog sample of individuals with elevations in self-reported OC symptoms. CCT did not differ significantly from a control task, indicating that three sessions alone do not influence OC symptoms. This raises the possibility that the effects of CCT are more mood-related; however, it is possible that CCT might exert effects at a higher dose, when used as an adjunctive treatment, or when targeting other anxiety symptoms.

Preliminary results also suggest that there is potential for matching neurobehavioral treatments to specific neural profiles. Price and colleagues (2013) provided support for this concept by demonstrating that three interventions (cognitive restructuring, Tetris, and the PASAT, described above as part of CCT) differentially affected specific regulatory brain regions during sadness and guilt inductions in healthy individuals. These results raise the possibility that as neurobehavioral assessment strategies develop, treatments may be selected based on each patient's profile of neural activity. Further support for this was found by Siegle and colleagues (2014), who demonstrated that the efficacy of CCT for rumination in depressed patients was predicted by pupillary oscillations, a physiological measure of task engagement. Specifically, those who were more engaged in the task at the first visit demonstrated the greatest reductions in rumination.

This preliminary work is particularly relevant for differentiating the effects of targeted brain-region activation from the effects of anxiety treatments on the brain. The former assumes changes of brain activation are the causal force in ameliorating symptoms; the latter is consistent with brain changes correlated to the useful cognitive and behavioral skills used to treat anxiety. More research is needed to determine whether strategies to boost dlPFC activation, independent of or in interaction with other treatment strategies, can aid treatment outcome. Such strategies may be particularly useful in individuals with identified cognitive deficits. In a pilot study, Mohlman (2008) demonstrated that for older adults with GAD and low scores on executive skills tests, CBT combined with executive skills training led to greater improvement in worry and executive function than CBT alone.

In summary, research on brain activation patterns correlated with anxiety disorders and their treatment have led to both an interpretation of the potential effects of psychosocial interventions on top-down processing of anxiety and to preliminary studies directly targeting frontal activation as a potential treatment strategy. These strategies are directed at an intermediate stage of processing of threat cues, aiding the reinterpretation of, and potentially dampening the limbic response to, anxiety cues. An alternative approach is to decrease the degree to which threat cues are attended to and processed in the first place.

Threat-related Attentional Bias Modification

Cognitive models of anxiety disorders suggest that information-processing biases contribute to the etiology and maintenance of anxiety (Beck & Clark, 1997; Eysenck, 1992; Rapee & Heimberg, 1997). Consistent with this proposition, patients with anxiety disorders reliably demonstrate biased attention toward negative emotional information (Bar-Haim, Lamy, Pergamin, Bakermans-Kranenburg, & van IJzendoorn, 2007). Assessed with experimental tasks such as the emotional Stroop task and the dot probe, these attentional biases occur when using masked exposure to stimuli, indicating that they operate at an early, non-conscious level of processing. Because such bias is found across the anxiety disorders and in highly trait-anxious individuals, it is thought to be a feature of high trait anxiety rather than a disorder-specific characteristic (Cisler & Koster, 2010). However, a number of studies have found evidence of reduced attentional bias to threat after successful treatment of GAD and SAD (Lundh & Öst, 2001; Mathews, Mogg, Kentish, & Eysenck, 1995; Mogg, Mathews, & Eysenck, 1992), suggesting that the bias may be state-specific or primed in vulnerable individuals by factors such as mood state or stressful events (Mathews et al., 1995).

Anxiety-disordered patients also tend to assign negative interpretations to ambiguous cues. For instance, when asked to write out spoken homophones with both a threatening and a neutral meaning, patients (and those with high trait anxiety) are more likely to use the threatening spelling (e.g., Eysenck, MacLeod, & Mathews, 1987). It has been suggested that interpretive bias occurs through the same mechanisms of attentional bias, with a competition between threatening and non-threatening interpretations resulting in inhibition of the non-threatening interpretation (Bishop, 2007; Mathews & Mackintosh, 1998).

More recently, efforts have turned toward clarifying the potentially causal role of attentional biases in anxiety. More specifically, attentional bias modification (ABM) strategies use computer-based attention training protocols to target implicit or automatic attentional biases (MacLeod, Koster, & Fox, 2009; Mobini & Grant, 2007), seeking, from a neurocognitive perspective, to directly manipulate such biases and patterns of neural activation via repeated computer exercises (bottom-up intervention as opposed to the top-down approaches reviewed above).

Most ABM studies use variants of the dot-probe task, first developed by MacLeod and colleagues (1986). The dot-probe task can be used to both measure and to manipulate threat-related attentional biases. In the dot-probe task, two stimuli are presented for a very brief period of time, one threat-related and one neutral (typically words or images: e.g., the words "table" and "gun" or an image of a neutral face and an angry face); these stimuli are then removed, and a small target probe replaces one of the stimuli. These target probes are one of two variants as well (e.g., the letters E and F or arrow images ">" or "<"), and participants are asked to discriminate as quickly as possible between two variants of the probe. In versions of ABM designed to measure attentional biases (rather than train attention), the targets appear with equal probability at the location of threat and neutral stimuli. Participants' response latencies to the threat or neutral stimuli then provide information on their attentional bias (toward threat or neutral). Attentional bias toward threat is indicated when participants' mean reaction times are significantly faster to probes that replaced threat-related stimuli rather than neutral stimuli. The opposite pattern (significantly faster mean reaction times to probes replacing neutral stimuli) indicates avoidance of or disengagement from threat.

In attention-bias *modification* (as opposed to simply measuring the level of bias) variants of the dot-probe task, the target probe location is systematically manipulated to increase the proportion of targets appearing at the location of the intended training bias (e.g., to train attention away from threatening stimuli, the probe is placed more frequently at the location of the neutral stimuli). This implicitly learned bias away from threat is gradually induced with tens to hundreds of repeated trials. Other tasks, such as a visual search task (VST), may similarly train attention in anxiety disorders (Dandeneau, Baldwin, Baccus, Sakellaropoulo, & Pruessner, 2007). The VST trains participants to locate a single smiling face in a matrix of frowning faces, and the anxiolytic effects shown from this initial study are quite impressive and equal those obtained with the dot-probe task; however, these results await replication.

Over the past few years, ABM studies have shown significant effects of attention training on anxiety symptoms in anxious patients and in sub-clinical populations (Bar-Haim et al., 2007). These studies have focused mostly on generalized and social anxiety disorder employing dot-probe training protocols. Some of the most impressive evidence to date comes from a study of adults with SAD, who underwent eight sessions of ABM (160 trials each session) across four weeks and subsequently had significantly reduced levels of social anxiety with considerable retention at four-month follow-up (Amir, Beard, Taylor, et al., 2009). At post-treatment assessment, 50 percent of participants in the ABM condition no longer met criteria for SAD; similar rates of recovery were present in a trial comparing ABM to a computerized control condition in GAD patients (Amir, Beard, Burns, & Bomyea, 2009). Although these acute effects appear to be similar in magnitude to those reported by psychosocial or medication treatments, ABM interventions have yet to be compared to established treatments in large randomized trials.

In a meta-analysis of ABM on attention bias and subjective experiences in thirty-seven studies, with 2,135 participants ABM has a reliable effect on attentional bias (Beard, Sawyer, & Hofmann, 2012). Similar to other meta-analytic reviews (Hakamata et al., 2010), the authors found statistically significant and large effects of ABM on attention with large fail-safe calculations. It should be noted, however, that these large effect sizes are in contrast to small effects reported by Hallion and Ruscio (2011); this may be due to the fact that the meta-analysis by Beard and colleagues included only primary outcome data as opposed to a composite score across multiple outcomes. Results revealed that effect size estimates for the subjective experiences obtained directly after ABM were small and that comparisons with control conditions were non-significant, indicating that ABM is not an effective state emotional or motivational manipulation but rather addresses automatic processes.

ABM may also be used as a preventive measure for reducing anxiety and stress vulnerability in individuals who face stressful naturalistic circumstances, which could range from mild (e.g., upcoming midterm exams) to severe (e.g., military deployment to combat). This potential application was demonstrated by See and colleagues (2009) who followed students in Singapore who were preparing to immigrate to Australia for education experiences, which was an event rated as highly stressful by these students. The authors examined the use of ABM before migration, and half of the participants were randomly biased away from emotionally negative word stimuli, and half received a placebo control training not intended to change attention patterns. Training reduced anxiety responses to the upcoming naturalistic stressor of migration and reduced state anxiety scores after immigration (See et al., 2009).

In addition to ABM, recent research has focused on the use of an approach avoidance task (AAT; Rinck & Becker, 2007). The premise behind the AAT is that perceptions of stimuli from the environment trigger an automatic motivated orientation and behavioral response of approach and/or avoidance (Taylor & Amir, 2012). This behavioral response is measured through the AAT by using arm flexion/extension with a joystick apparatus (approach, pulling toward oneself; avoidance, pushing away from oneself). The AAT is thought to capture relatively automatic tendencies and, like ABM, may be able to be experimentally manipulated to address mechanisms underlying anxiety disorders. To date, this research has focused on SAD and has not been conducted in clinical samples; however, findings support the use of AAT to manipulate automatic approach tendencies (Heuer, Rinck, & Becker, 2007; Roelofs et al., 2010; Taylor & Amir, 2012).

In a recent AAT study, participants responded to pictures of faces conveying positive or neutral emotional expressions by pulling a joystick toward themselves (approach) or by moving it to the right (sideways control). Participants were randomly assigned to complete an AAT designed to increase approach tendencies for positive social cues by pulling these cues toward themselves on the majority of trials or to a control condition in which there was no contingency between the arm movement direction and picture type (Taylor & Amir, 2012). After the manipulation, participants took part in a relationship-building task with a trained confederate. The authors found that participants trained to approach positive stimuli displayed greater social approach behaviors during the social interaction and elicited more positive reactions from their partner compared to participants in the control group, which supports that modifying automatic approach tendencies may facilitate engagement in the types of social approach behaviors. AAT did not influence participant's subjective level of anxiety, a finding consistent with ABM, which indicated that perhaps AAT has a more direct impact on behavior rather than state anxiety, or changes are outside conscious awareness (Taylor & Amir, 2012).

In summary, attentional modification strategies targeting automatic processing occurring early in the chain of cognitive and behavioral responses to threat stimuli represent new and exciting methods that do not require a traditional therapeutic approach. Yet, further research is needed to reveal more about the reliability of ABM or the most relevant targets for ABM training. For example, in a recent review, Cisler and Koster (2010) describe three components of attention bias: facilitation of threat, impaired disengagement from threat, and avoidance of threat. Moreover, they propose that these three components of attentional bias are differentially mediated, with threat facilitation mediated by amygdala activity, threat disengagement mediated by attentional control (implicating prefrontal cortex), and threat avoidance mediated by emotion regulation (also implicating prefrontal cortex). To date, it remains unclear exactly how ABM strategies affect each of the three underlying components of attentional bias.

Neurocognitive Advances and the Extinction of Fears

An alternative strategy from changing the immediate processing of threat cues is to alter the ease by which learned fears may be extinguished. Advances brought by neurocognitive science have identified the fear circuits involved in extinction learning, resulting in the examination of pharmacologic strategies to speed extinction learning (Ressler et al., 2004). Likewise, advances in basic research on the consolidation of memories have also led to new strategies for aiding extinction of fear learning (Nader, Schafe, & Le Doux, 2000a). Each of these approaches will be considered in turn.

Animal research has shown that fear extinction is modulated by activity of the glutamatergic NMDA receptor in the amygdala; inhibitors of this activity appear to block the retention of extinction learning (Falls, Miserendino, & Davis, 1992) and, likewise, partial agonists enhance this learning (Walker, Ressler, Lu, & Davis, 2002). Most of the agonist research has been conducted on d-cycloserine (DCS), a partial agonist at the glycine site of the glutamatergic NMDA receptor, which has also been used as antibiotic treatment of tuberculosis (at higher, more sustained dosing). Fairly consistent evidence shows that single doses of DCS enhance the consolidation of the new learning that occurs during extinction (Davis, Ressler, Rothbaum, & Richardson, 2006), with augmentation effects remaining when DCS is administered within several hours after extinction learning (Richardson, Ledgerwood, & Cranney, 2004). Accordingly, DCS appears to act as a memory enhancer, aiding the consolidation of learning during extinction trials, thereby leading to reduced fear response to fear cues examined in later trials. These findings from animal laboratories have been translated successfully to human clinical studies, in what has been described as a particular success of translational research (Anderson & Insel, 2006).

The first study of DCS applied as an augmentation strategy for exposure therapy in the anxiety disorders was completed by Ressler and colleagues (2004) in a placebo-controlled trial examining responses to virtual-reality exposures for height phobics. One dose of DCS was taken two to four hours prior to each of two virtual-reality exposure sessions to heights. Outcome measures included measures of acrophobia within the virtual environment, measures of acrophobia in the real world, and general measures of an overall improvement. Electrodermal skin conductance was also measured during the virtual exposure sessions. Patients receiving DCS had significantly more improvement than patients receiving placebo and showed significantly greater decrease in post-treatment skin conductance fluctuations during the virtual exposure. Additionally, patients receiving DCS had greater improvement on general measures of the real-world acrophobia symptoms (avoidance, anxiety, attitudes toward heights, clinical global measures). These improvements were maintained at three-month follow-up (Ressler et al., 2004).

Subsequent studies of DCS in combination with exposure therapy have been promising, with positive effects more evident in those trials that offered only brief treatment. This can be explained by the fact that with a greater number of exposure sessions, the value of a memory enhancer should decline due to the repeated opportunities for sufficient learning. For example, two studies have shown that a five-session exposure-based treatment for social anxiety disorder is augmented by DCS versus placebo (Guastella et al., 2008; Hofmann et al., 2006). These positive findings have been extended to five-session treatment for panic disorder (Otto, Tolin, et al., 2010). Findings have been mixed for DCS augmentation of OCD (Kushner et al., 2007; Wilhelm et al., 2008) and PTSD (Litz et al., 2012), yet even when stronger overall results are not achieved by endpoint, DCS does appear to speed treatment results (Chasson et al., 2010; de Kleine, Hendriks, Kusters, Broekman, & van Minnen, 2012; Kushner et al., 2007; Siegmund et al., 2011). The reliability of the DCS augmentation effect also appears to be attenuated when full courses of CBT (e.g., twelve sessions) are offered (Hofmann et al., 2013).

Some of the variability in the effects of DCS may be explained by the success of exposure sessions. Smits and colleagues have shown that the success of the exposure session (defined as low fear at the conclusion of exposure) predicts the advantage of DCS over placebo augmentation (Smits, Rosenfield, Otto, Marques, et al., 2013; Smits, Rosenfield, Otto, Powers, et al., 2013). These findings also raise the possibility that DCS may have detrimental effects when administered after inadequate/unsuccessful exposure sessions.

As noted, DCS augmentation is directed at NMDA receptors in the amygdala. During extinction consolidation, there is also substantial crosstalk between the amygdalae and the frontal lobes (Kim et al., 2013). Enhancement of frontal lobe activity with the noradrenergic agent yohimbine has been an additional approach to enhancing exposure success. Like DCS, yohimbine is administered in single doses prior to exposure sessions. To date, two of three placebo-controlled investigations have shown this to be a successful augmentation strategy (Meyerbroeker, Powers, van Stegeren, & Emmelkamp, 2012; Powers, Smits, Otto, Sanders, & Emmelkamp, 2009; Smits et al., 2014). Also, like DCS, augmentation success appears to be dependent on the degree to which the exposure session itself is effective in helping patients achieve low fear by the end of the session (Smits et al., in press). That is, both DCS and yohimbine appear to help set into memory information on the final meaning of the exposure stimuli during a session of exposure.

In summary, there is a growing body of evidence for the efficacy of DCS as a means of augmenting memory consolidation of successful exposure sessions, thereby speeding recovery from anxiety disorders. Results to date provide evidence that DCS enhances CBT for panic disorder (Otto, Tolin, et al., 2010), social anxiety disorder (Hofmann et al., 2006, 2013), and specific phobia (Smits,

Rosenfield, Otto, Powers, et al., 2013); however, DCS may also speed the effect of exposure-based treatment for OCD (Chasson et al., 2010). There is also tentative support for yohimbine in SAD (Smits et al., in press) and specific phobia (Powers et al., 2009) when applied in a similar single-dose strategy prior to each exposure session. It is important to note that other strategies for enhancing memories of fear extinction are also under consideration, including the use of cortisol, methylene-blue, oxytocin, and modafinil to try to aid the consolidation of the safety learning from exposure (Hofmann, Smits, Asnaani, Gutner, & Otto, 2011). In the next few years, research is expected to elucidate which of these agents is most appropriate for transition to clinical practice.

Procedural Strategies for Boosting Exposure Efficacy: Memory Reconsolidation Blockade and Post-retrieval Extinction

As ongoing translational research seeks to extend the efficacy of pharmacologic augmentation strategies for exposure, there is also research investigating new procedural interventions to change core aspects of the extinction process (Bouton, 2002; Nader, Schafe, & Le Doux, 2000a; Schiller et al., 2010). These procedural interventions are aimed at attenuating one of the relative weaknesses of extinction—the degree to which the original fear learning remains in competition with the newer safety learning from extinction. This competition is reflected in the way that the original fear learning may again play a dominant role with the passage of time (spontaneous recovery) when the feared stimulus is reintroduced (reinstatement), when the subject returns to the context in which the feared stimuli was conditioned (renewal), and when the feared stimulus is reintroduced and feared negative consequence ensues (reacquisition; Bouton, 2002). Clinically, this could explain non-response to, partial response to, and relapse after exposure therapy for anxiety and traumatic stress disorders. It had long been assumed that once fear memories were consolidated, they were not susceptible to change (Glickman, 1961; McGaugh, 1966). Recent research, however, has revealed that when fear memories are reactivated, they reconsolidate and are once again malleable and susceptible to modification (Nader, Schafe, & LeDoux, 2000b).

The concept of interference with memory reconsolidation is not new (Sara, 2000), but recent animal research has revealed innovative methods to capitalize on this window of memory lability. The initial groundbreaking study by Nader and colleagues (2000a) investigated whether interfering with protein synthesis, which is thought to be necessary for memory consolidation, would disrupt the reconsolidation of fear memories in rats. Their results supported this hypothesis: Injecting the lateral and basal nuclei of the amygdala of a rat with a protein synthesis inhibitor (anisomnycin) during reconsolidation resulted in amnesia for a fear memory up to fourteen days after conditioning. Nader and colleagues (2000a) also found that the window of lability seemed to last within six hours of reactivation of the memory. Later research found similar results using the beta-adrenergic antagonist propranolol in animals and humans (Brunet et al., 2008; Debiec & Ledoux, 2004; Kindt, Soeter, & Vervliet, 2009). Although research has suggested that this paradigm is not simply enhancing extinction but interfering with memory reconsolidation (Dudai, 2006; Duvarci & Nader, 2004), others have questioned whether the effects of propranolol may reflect a more general fear-dampening effect (Schiller & Phelps, 2011). These reconsolidation blockade strategies are effective in animals but have limitations in their potential for human use. Although protein synthesis inhibitors have helped researchers understand the molecular mechanisms of consolidation and reconsolidation, they are unsafe for use in humans (Hartley & Phelps, 2010). Additionally, further research on the efficacy of beta-adrenergic antagonists in humans is needed, as results have led to questions regarding the duration and mechanisms of effects (Muravieva & Alberini, 2010) and have indicated the possibility of differential efficacy in males and females (Nugent et al., 2010).

In an attempt to find a less invasive strategy, researchers decided to capitalize on reconsolidation as a memory-updating mechanism and tested the use of extinction during the reconsolidation window. This led to the development of a paradigm called *post-retrieval extinction* (PRE), where a memory is retrieved, and this retrieval is followed by extinction during the reconsolidation window. Extensive research in animals (Clem & Huganir, 2010; Flavell, Barber, & Lee, 2011; Monfils, Cowansage, Klann, & LeDoux, 2009; Rao-Ruiz et al., 2011) provided support for this paradigm, showing that the reconsolidation of memories could be interrupted and the reinstatement of fear could be prevented using PRE. This has also been demonstrated in animal models of non-fear-based memories (Flavell et al., 2011; Xue et al., 2012). Schiller and colleagues (2010) were the first to translate these animal findings to humans, randomizing subjects to extinction training without retrieval, extinction training ten minutes after retrieval, and extinction training six hours after retrieval. In contrast to subjects in the extinction-only group and that of extinction six hours after retrieval, subjects in the group that received extinction training ten minutes after retrieval (inside the reconsolidation window) did not display reinstatement of fear one day later. Even more noteworthy, when tested one year later, reinstatement was significant in the extinction-only group and that of extinction six hours after retrieval but not in the group of extinction ten minutes after retrieval. They also demonstrated that the interference produced by PRE was specific to the retrieved memory, not associated memories. This study supports the efficacy and specificity of PRE in humans and also supports previous findings that the reconsolidation window occurs between ten minutes and six hours after retrieval of a memory. These findings have been replicated in other human samples

(Agren et al., 2012; Oyarzun et al., 2012) and with non-fear-based memories (Xue et al., 2012). In addition, Agren and colleagues (2012) also demonstrated that PRE during the reconsolidation window disrupted not only reinstatement but reacquisition of fear.

Notably, not all the aforementioned findings have been successfully replicated (Golkar, Bellander, Olsson, & Ohman, 2012; Kindt & Soeter, 2011; Soeter & Kindt, 2011), suggesting that further research is needed to understand this paradigm and how it can be most effectively applied. One possible explanation is that boundary conditions limit efficacy. Specifically, the age, strength, and hippocampal-dependence of a memory (Auber, Tedesco, Jones, Monfils, & Chiamulera, 2013) have been identified as potential boundary conditions. For example, there is some evidence that over time, memories generally become increasingly stable and less susceptible to disruption (Milekic & Alberini, 2002), and some researchers suggest that PRE does not have the potential to be effective for remote memories, such as those in PTSD (Costanzi, Cannas, Saraulli, Rossi-Arnaud, & Cestari, 2011). Others suggest that few memories are immune to modification and that the right application of PRE may be able to interfere with remote and more potent memories (Auber et al., 2013; Finnie & Nader, 2012; Suzuki et al., 2004). If we consider reconsolidation to be a memory-updating mechanism, as has been suggested (Sara, 2000; Tronson & Taylor, 2007), it is conceivable that more trials may be necessary to update a more potent memory. This is also consistent with the Debiec and colleagues (2002) findings that a higher dose may be necessary to disrupt the reconsolidation of hippocampal-dependent memories as well as the Xue and colleagues' (2012) effective use of PRE applied across two consecutive days. Given the potential application, further research into the multiple administrations of PRE for more potent memories is warranted.

Preventing Disorder Onset

Application of PRE to new fears potentially opens the door to prevention strategies for disorder onset in response to recent traumas, where interruption of the consolidation process may help prevent the formation of PTSD. For instance, Holmes and colleagues (2009), recognizing the limitations to PTSD treatments that must be administered weeks or months after trauma, proposed the development of a "cognitive vaccine" to prevent trauma-related flashbacks. Drawing from cognitive science demonstrating that the brain has limited resources and that memory consolidation may be disrupted within a six-hour window, the authors propose the use of a widely available visuospatial task (Tetris) as a method of disrupting the consolidation of trauma memories. In an experimental analog design, the authors found that playing Tetris for ten minutes one half-hour after viewing a trauma film reduced the frequency of flashbacks and PTSD symptoms during the next week when compared to a no-task condition. A second study comparing Tetris to both a no-task condition and a verbal knowledge computer game again demonstrated that different computer games may have differential effects on flashback symptoms; Tetris was again shown to reduce flashbacks while the comparison game actually increased flashbacks (Holmes, James, Kilford, & Deeprose, 2010). Moreover, the study showed that the effects of Tetris were maintained when played four hours after trauma exposure, suggesting that there might be promising maintenance of effects over time.

In summary, basic work on memory consolidation has led to new strategies to not only extinguish fear memories but to try to modify the original memory to provide greater protection from relapse. These strategies appear promising, although much more work is needed to translate basic findings into clinical procedures.

Chapter Summary and Future Directions

Neurocognitive perspectives are informing treatment of anxiety disorders in several substantial ways. First, basic research on the neural circuitry underlying fear extinction has led to pharmacologic strategies to modify these circuits to aid extinction learning. This strategy is most prominently represented by single-dose DCS augmentation of exposure-based CBT and represents an entirely new approach to combination treatment. Traditional combination treatment for anxiety disorders combines two anxiolytic strategies—CBT plus antidepressants or benzodiazepines, for example—in order to try to achieve better treatment outcome. The goal of significantly better treatment outcome is both infrequently achieved and surprisingly complex in terms of mode of action (Otto, McHugh, & Kantak, 2010). As an alternative approach, combination treatment with DCS is not targeted toward anxiolysis directly but to enhancing the retention of the therapeutic learning provided by the CBT. This is a truly novel approach for pharmacotherapy, an approach that now has overall support for speeding treatment response and has initial guidance on how to reduce variability in outcomes by judiciously using DCS with only the most successful exposure sessions. The end result may be the development of post-treatment dosing strategies, where DCS (or another memory-enhancing agent) will be given only *after* exposure sessions judged to be successful (Smits, Rosenfield, Otto, Powers, et al., 2013). Research is now directed at these post-session dosing strategies as well as at expanding the list of potential mood enhancers to be used with CBT. Research is also turning toward characterization of which patients may most need this combination treatment strategy (e.g., Smits et al., in press). For example, research indicates that neuropsychological deficits can pose an obstacle to benefits for CBT for generalized anxiety disorder in elderly patients

(Caudle et al., 2007), yet it is not known whether DCS augmentation effects will be more substantial in these patients. Hence, testing DCS augmentation in specialty populations and with attention to baseline cognitive impairments will be an important next step in this area of study.

Second, basic research on mechanisms of memory consolidation and reconsolidation is leading to novel strategies for both improving exposure-based interventions and trying to prevent the onset of PTSD or severe phobias after trauma. This research is in its earliest translational stages, with initial proof-of-concept studies showing important memory reconsolidation blockade effects in humans. Research next needs to test whether these effects reliably transfer to the older and more powerful memories that characterize clinical fears. If they do, cognitive-behavior therapists will have an expanded strategy for increasing the benefit and staying power of exposure-based interventions.

Third, neurocognitive research has helped change the focus on the stage of processing targeted in anxiety treatment. Traditional CBT has focused on changing the meaning and processing of fear stimuli with intentional cognitive strategies as well as exposure-based interventions. Attentional bias modification strategies have moved the intervention's mechanism to an earlier automatic stage of processing, changing the way threat stimuli are attended to in the first place. Ongoing research suggests that changing this first stage of threat-related processing can have powerful effects for the entire chain of subsequent cognitive and behavioral responses by helping to undo the patterns that maintain anxiety disorders. At this point, promising early findings are being subjected to replication, with attention to individual differences in ABM as well as attention to the parameters of training (number and type of trials) that lead to reliable effects.

Fourth, elucidation of the brain regions most activated in anxiety disorders and most altered by successful treatment has led to novel targets for interventions. Particularly innovative new treatment strategies use specific cognitive tasks to activate brain regions (e.g., CCT) or to provide interference (e.g., Tetris) of anxiety-related brain processes. Much more research is needed to document the potential benefits of these approaches and to elucidate the correct dose and application of these strategies.

As our understanding of the neurocognitive underpinnings of these disorders continues to increase, attention must be paid to comorbidity between disorders. Across the anxiety disorders (as they were defined by the DSM-IV-TR), approximately 30 pecent of patients have a comorbid disorder (Brown, Campbell, Lehman, Grisham, & Mancill, 2001), and these rates may be higher for specific disorders such as PTSD (Brady, Killeen, Brewerton, & Lucerini, 2000; Brown et al., 2001). For example, depression is associated with its own neurocognitive characteristics and interventions (see Chapter 9), and little is known about whether these characteristics add to or otherwise modify the neurocognitive patterns observed in the anxiety disorders.

Overall, neurocognitive perspectives provide the potential for enhanced understanding and treatment of the anxiety disorders. A variety of promising strategies are nearing the point where they will be ready for regular clinical application. Those engaged in all of these areas of study have the vision of and a promising roadmap to a future of reduced suffering for individuals with anxiety disorders.

References

Abramovitch, A., Abramowitz, J. S., & Mittelman, A. (2013). The neuropsychology of adult obsessive-compulsive disorder: A meta-analysis. *Clinical Psychology Review, 33,* 1163–1171.

Agren, T., Engman, J., Frick, A., Bjorkstrand, J., Larsson, E. M., Furmark, T., & Fredrikson, M. (2012). Disruption of reconsolidation erases a fear memory trace in the human amygdala. *Science, 337,* 1550–1552.

Airaksinen, E., Larsson, M., & Forsell, Y. (2005). Neuropsychological functions in anxiety disorders in population-based samples: Evidence of episodic memory dysfunction. *Journal of Psychiatric Research, 39,* 207–214.

Akiyoshi, J., Hieda, K., Aoki, Y., & Nagayama, H. (2003). Frontal brain hypoactivity as a biological substrate of anxiety in patients with panic disorders. *Neuropsychobiology, 47,* 165–170.

American Psychiatric Association (2013). *Diagnostic and statistical manual of mental disorders* (5th ed.). Arlington, VA: American Psychiatric Publishing.

Amir, N., Beard, C., Burns, M., & Bomyea, J. (2009). Attention modification program in individuals with generalized anxiety disorder. *Journal of Abnormal Psychology, 118,* 28–33.

Amir, N., Beard, C., Taylor, C. T., Klumpp, H., Elias, J., Burns, M., & Chen, X. (2009). Attention training in individuals with generalized social phobia: A randomized controlled trial. *Journal of Consulting and Clinical Psychology, 77,* 961–973.

Anderson, K. C., & Insel, T. R. (2006). The promise of extinction research for the prevention and treatment of anxiety disorders. *Biological Psychiatry, 60,* 319–321.

Asmundson, G. J., Stein, M. B., Larsen, D. K., & Walker, J. R. (1994). Neurocognitive function in panic disorder and social phobia patients. *Anxiety, 1,* 201–207.

Auber, A., Tedesco, V., Jones, C. E., Monfils, M. H., & Chiamulera, C. (2013). Post-retrieval extinction as reconsolidation interference: Methodological issues or boundary conditions? *Psychopharmacology, 226,* 631–647.

Aupperle, R. L., Melrose, A. J., Stein, M. B., & Paulus, M. P. (2012). Executive function and PTSD: Disengaging from trauma. *Neuropharmacology, 62,* 686–694.

Ball, T. M., Ramsawh, H. J., Campbell-Sills, L., Paulus, M. P., & Stein, M. B. (2012). Prefrontal dysfunction during emotion regulation in generalized anxiety and panic disorders. *Psychological Medicine, 43,* 1475–1486.

Bar-Haim, Y., Lamy, D., Pergamin, L., Bakermans-Kranenburg, M. J., & van IJzendoorn, M. H. (2007). Threat-related attentional bias in anxious and nonanxious individuals: A meta-analytic study. *Psychological Bulletin, 133,* 1–24.

Baxter, L. R., Jr., Phelps, M. E., Mazziotta, J. C., Guze, B. H., Schwartz, J. M., & Selin, C. E. (1987). Local cerebral glucose metabolic rates in obsessive-compulsive disorder.

A comparison with rates in unipolar depression and in normal controls. *Archives of General Psychiatry, 44*, 211–218.

Beard, C., Sawyer, A. T., & Hofmann, S. G. (2012). Efficacy of attention bias modification using threat and appetitive stimuli: A meta-analytic review. *Behavior Therapy, 43*, 724–740.

Beck, A. T., & Clark, D. A. (1997). An information processing model of anxiety: Automatic and strategic processes. *Behaviour Research and Therapy, 35*, 49–58.

Birbaumer, N., Grodd, W., Diedrich, O., Klose, U., Erb, M., Lotze, M., … & Flor, H. (1998). fMRI reveals amygdala activation to human faces in social phobics. *Neuroreport, 9*, 1223–1226.

Bisaga, A., Katz, J. L., Antonini, A., Wright, C. E., Margouleff, C., Gorman, J. M., & Eidelberg, D. (1998). Cerebral glucose metabolism in women with panic disorder. *American Journal of Psychiatry, 155*, 1178–1183.

Bishop, S. J. (2007). Neurocognitive mechanisms of anxiety: An integrative account. *Trends in Cognitive Sciences, 11*, 307–316.

Blair, K., Geraci, M., Devido, J., McCaffrey, D., Chen, G., Vythilingam, M., … & Pine, D. S. (2008). Neural response to self- and other referential praise and criticism in generalized social phobia. *Archives of General Psychiatry, 65*, 1176–1184.

Blair, K., Geraci, M., Smith, B. W., Hollon, N., DeVido, J., Otero, M., … & Pine, D. S. (2012). Reduced dorsal anterior cingulate cortical activity during emotional regulation and top-down attentional control in generalized social phobia, generalized anxiety disorder, and comorbid generalized social phobia/generalized anxiety disorder. *Biological Psychiatry, 72*, 476–482.

Bonne, O., Gilboa, A., Louzoun, Y., Brandes, D., Yona, I., Lester, H., … & Shalev, A. Y. (2003). Resting regional cerebral perfusion in recent posttraumatic stress disorder. *Biological Psychiatry, 54*, 1077–1086.

Borkovec, T. D. (1994). The nature, functions, and origins of worry. In G. C. L. Davey & F. Tallis (Eds.), *Worrying: Perspectives on theory, assessment and treatment.* Wiley Series in Clinical Psychology (Vol. xv, pp. 5–33). Oxford: John Wiley & Sons.

Boshuisen, M. L., Ter Horst, G. J., Paans, A. M., Reinders, A. A., & den Boer, J. A. (2002). rCBF differences between panic disorder patients and control subjects during anticipatory anxiety and rest. *Biological Psychiatry, 52*, 126–135.

Bouton, M. E. (2002). Context, ambiguity, and unlearning: Sources of relapse after behavioral extinction. *Biological Psychiatry, 52*, 976–986.

Brady, K. T., Killeen, T. K., Brewerton, T., & Lucerini, S. (2000). Comorbidity of psychiatric disorders and posttraumatic stress disorder. *Journal of Clinical Psychiatry, 61* (Suppl 7), 22–32.

Bremner, J. D., Randall, P., Scott, T. M., Bronen, R. A., Seibyl, J. P., Southwick, S. M., … & Innis, R. B. (1995). MRI-based measurement of hippocampal volume in patients with combat-related posttraumatic stress disorder. *American Journal of Psychiatry, 152*, 973–981.

Brown, T. A., Campbell, L. A., Lehman, C. L., Grisham, J. R., & Mancill, R. B. (2001). Current and lifetime comorbidity of the DSM-IV anxiety and mood disorders in a large clinical sample. *Journal of Abnormal Psychology, 110*, 585–599.

Brühl, A. B., Rufer, M., Delsignore, A., Kaffenberger, T., Jäncke, L., & Herwig, U. (2011). Neural correlates of altered general emotion processing in social anxiety disorder. *Brain Research, 1378*, 72–83.

Brunet, A., Orr, S. P., Tremblay, J., Robertson, K., Nader, K., & Pitman, R. K. (2008). Effect of post-retrieval propranolol on psychophysiologic responding during subsequent script-driven traumatic imagery in post-traumatic stress disorder. *Journal of Psychiatric Research, 42*, 503–506.

Butler, A. C., Chapman, J. E., Forman, E. M., & Beck, A. T. (2006). The empirical status of cognitive-behavioral therapy: A review of meta-analyses. *Clinical Psychology Review, 26*, 17–31.

Butters, M. A., Bhalla, R. K., Andreescu, C., Wetherell, J. L., Mantella, R., Begley, A. E., & Lenze, E. J. (2011). Changes in neuropsychological functioning following treatment for late-life generalised anxiety disorder. *The British Journal of Psychiatry, 199*, 211–218.

Calkins, A. W., & Otto, M. W. (2013). Testing the boundaries of computerized cognitive control training on symptoms of obsessive compulsive disorder. *Cognitive Therapy and Research, 37*, 587–594.

Calkins, A. W., McMorran, K., Siegle, G., & Otto, M. W. (2014). The effects of computerized cognitive control training on community adults with depressed mood. *Behavioural and cognitive psychotherapy.* doi: 10.1017/S1352465814000046

Cardoner, N., Harrison, B. J., Pujol, J., Soriano-Mas, C., Hernandez-Ribas, R., Lopez-Sola, M., ... & Menchon, J. M. (2011). Enhanced brain responsiveness during active emotional face processing in obsessive compulsive disorder. *World Journal of Biological Psychiatry, 12*, 349–363.

Caudle, D. D., Senior, A. C., Wetherell, J. L., Rhoades, H. M., Beck, J. G., Kunik, M. E., ... & Stanley, M. A. (2007). Cognitive errors, symptom severity, and response to cognitive behavior therapy in older adults with generalized anxiety disorder. *American Journal of Geriatric Psychiatry, 15*, 680–689.

Chasson, G. S., Buhlmann, U., Tolin, D. F., Rao, S. R., Reese, H. E., Rowley, T., ... & Wilhelm, S. (2010). Need for speed: Evaluating slopes of OCD recovery in behavior therapy enhanced with d-cycloserine. *Behaviour Research and Therapy, 48*, 675–679.

Chung, Y. A., Kim, S. H., Chung, S. K., Chae, J. H., Yang, D. W., Sohn, H. S., & Jeong, J. (2006). Alterations in cerebral perfusion in posttraumatic stress disorder patients without re-exposure to accident-related stimuli. *Clinical Neurophysiology, 117*, 637–642.

Cisler, J. M., & Koster, E. H. (2010). Mechanisms of attentional biases towards threat in anxiety disorders: An integrative review. *Clinical Psychology Review, 30*, 203–216.

Clem, R. L., & Huganir, R. L. (2010). Calcium-permeable AMPA receptor dynamics mediate fear memory erasure. *Science, 330*, 1108–1112.

Cloos, J. M., & Ferreira, V. (2009). Current use of benzodiazepines in anxiety disorders. *Current Opinion in Psychiatry, 22*, 90–95.

Cohen, L. J., Hollander, E., DeCaria, C. M., Stein, D. J., Simeon, D., Liebowitz, M. R., & Aronowitz, B. R. (1996). Specificity of neuropsychological impairment in obsessive-compulsive disorder: A comparison with social phobic and normal control subjects. *Journal of Neuropsychiatry and Clinical Neurosciences, 8*, 82–85.

Comer, J. S., Mojtabai, R., & Olfson, M. (2011). National trends in the antipsychotic treatment of psychiatric outpatients with anxiety disorders. *American Journal of Psychiatry, 168*, 1057–1065.

Costanzi, M., Cannas, S., Saraulli, D., Rossi-Arnaud, C., & Cestari, V. (2011). Extinction after retrieval: Effects on the associative and nonassociative components of remote contextual fear memory. *Learning and Memory, 18*, 508–518.

Craske, M. G., Rauch, S. L., Ursano, R., Prenoveau, J., Pine, D. S., & Zinbarg, R. E. (2009). What is an anxiety disorder? *Depression and Anxiety, 26*, 1066–1085.

Dandeneau, S. D., Baldwin, M. W., Baccus, J. R., Sakellaropoulo, M., & Pruessner, J. C. (2007). Cutting stress off at the pass: Reducing vigilance and responsiveness to social threat by manipulating attention. *Journal of Personality and Social Psychology, 93*, 651–666.

Davis, M., Ressler, K., Rothbaum, B. O., & Richardson, R. (2006). Effects of D-cycloserine on extinction: Translation from preclinical to clinical work. *Biological Psychiatry, 60*, 369–375.

Debiec, J., & Ledoux, J. E. (2004). Disruption of reconsolidation but not consolidation of auditory fear conditioning by noradrenergic blockade in the amygdala. *Neuroscience, 129*, 267–272.

Debiec, J., LeDoux, J. E., & Nader, K. (2002). Cellular and systems reconsolidation in the hippocampus. *Neuron, 36*, 527–538.

Deckersbach, T., Moshier, S. J., Tuschen-Caffier, B., & Otto, M. W. (2011). Memory dysfunction in panic disorder: An investigation of the role of chronic benzodiazepine use. *Depression and Anxiety, 28*, 999–1007.

De Cristofaro, M. T., Sessarego, A., Pupi, A., Biondi, F., & Faravelli, C. (1993). Brain perfusion abnormalities in drug-naive, lactate-sensitive panic patients: A SPECT study. *Biological Psychiatry, 33*, 505–512.

de Kleine, R. A., Hendriks, G. J., Kusters, W. J., Broekman, T. G., & van Minnen, A. (2012). A randomized placebo-controlled trial of D-cycloserine to enhance exposure therapy for posttraumatic stress disorder. *Biological Psychiatry, 71*, 962–968.

Dresler, T., Guhn, A., Tupak, S. V., Ehlis, A.-C., Herrmann, M. J., Fallgatter, A. J., ... & Domschke, K. (2012). Revise the revised? New dimensions of the neuroanatomical hypothesis of panic disorder. *Journal of Neural Transmission, 120*, 3–29.

Dudai, Y. (2006). Reconsolidation: The advantage of being refocused. *Current Opinion in Neurobiology, 16*, 174–178.

Duvarci, S., & Nader, K. (2004). Characterization of fear memory reconsolidation. *Journal of Neuroscience, 24*, 9269–9275.

Eddy, K. T., Dutra, L., Bradley, R., & Westen, D. (2004). A multidimensional meta-analysis of psychotherapy and pharmacotherapy for obsessive-compulsive disorder. *Clinical Psychology Review, 24*, 1011–1030.

Etkin, A., & Wager, T. D. (2007). Functional neuroimaging of anxiety: A meta-analysis of emotional processing in PTSD, social anxiety disorder, and specific phobia. *American Journal of Psychiatry, 164*, 1476–1488.

Evans, K. C., Wright, C. I., Wedig, M. M., Gold, A. L., Pollack, M. H., & Rauch, S. L. (2008). A functional MRI study of amygdala responses to angry schematic faces in social anxiety disorder. *Depression and Anxiety, 25*, 496–505.

Eysenck, M. W. (1992). *Anxiety: The cognitive perspective*. Psychology Press.

Eysenck, M. W., MacLeod, C., & Mathews, A. (1987). Cognitive functioning and anxiety. *Psychology Research, 49*, 189–195.

Falls, W. A., Miserendino, M. J., & Davis, M. (1992). Extinction of fear-potentiated startle: Blockade by infusion of an NMDA antagonist into the amygdala. *Journal of Neuroscience, 12*, 854–863.

Farrow, T. F., Hunter, M. D., Wilkinson, I. D., Gouneea, C., Fawbert, D., Smith, R., ... & Woodruff, P. W. (2005). Quantifiable change in functional brain response to empathic and forgivability judgments with resolution of posttraumatic stress disorder. *Psychiatry Research, 140,* 45–53.

Felmingham, K., Kemp, A., Williams, L., Das, P., Hughes, G., Peduto, A., & Bryant, R. (2007). Changes in anterior cingulate and amygdala after cognitive behavior therapy of posttraumatic stress disorder. *Psychological Science, 18,* 127–129.

Ferreri, F., Lapp, L. K., & Peretti, C.-S. (2011). Current research on cognitive aspects of anxiety disorders. *Current Opinion in Psychiatry, 24,* 49–54.

Finnie, P. S., & Nader, K. (2012). The role of metaplasticity mechanisms in regulating memory destabilization and reconsolidation. *Neuroscience and Biobehavioral Review, 36,* 1667–1707.

Flavell, C. R., Barber, D. J., & Lee, J. L. (2011). Behavioural memory reconsolidation of food and fear memories. *Nature Communications, 2,* 504.

Foa, E. B., & Kozak, M. J. (1986). Emotional processing of fear: Exposure to corrective information. *Psychological Bulletin, 99,* 20–35.

Freitas-Ferrari, M. C., Hallak, J. E. C., Trzesniak, C., Filho, A. S., Machado-de-Sousa, J. P., Chagas, M. H. N., … & Crippa, J. A. S. (2010). Neuroimaging in social anxiety disorder: A systematic review of the literature. *Progress in Neuro-Psychopharmacology and Biological Psychiatry, 34,* 565–580.

Furmark, T., Appel, L., Michelgard, A., Wahlstedt, K., Ahs, F., Zancan, S., … & Fredrikson, M. (2005). Cerebral blood flow changes after treatment of social phobia with the neurokinin-1 antagonist GR205171, citalopram, or placebo. *Biological Psychiatry, 58,* 132–142.

Furmark, T., Tillfors, M., Marteinsdottir, I., Fischer, H., Pissiota, A., Langstrom, B., & Fredrikson, M. (2002). Common changes in cerebral blood flow in patients with social phobia treated with citalopram or cognitive-behavioral therapy. *Archives of General Psychiatry, 59,* 425–433.

Garakani, A., Buchsbaum, M. S., Newmark, R. E., Goodman, C., Aaronson, C. J., Martinez, J. M., … & Gorman, J. M. (2007). The effect of doxapram on brain imaging in patients with panic disorder. *European Neuropsychopharmacology, 17,* 672–686.

Gentili, C., Ricciardi, E., Gobbini, M. I., Santarelli, M. F., Haxby, J. V., Pietrini, P., & Guazzelli, M. (2009). Beyond amygdala: Default mode network activity differs between patients with social phobia and healthy controls. *Brain Research Bulletin, 79,* 409–413.

Gilbertson, M. W., Paulus, L. A., Williston, S. K., Gurvits, T. V., Lasko, N. B., Pitman, R. K., & Orr, S. P. (2006). Neurocognitive function in monozygotic twins discordant for combat exposure: Relationship to posttraumatic stress disorder. *Journal of Abnormal Psychology, 115,* 484–495.

Gilbertson, M. W., Shenton, M. E., Ciszewski, A., Kasai, K., Lasko, N. B., Orr, S. P., & Pitman, R. K. (2002). Smaller hippocampal volume predicts pathologic vulnerability to psychological trauma. *Nature Neuroscience, 5,* 1242–1247.

Gilboa, A., Shalev, A. Y., Laor, L., Lester, H., Louzoun, Y., Chisin, R., & Bonne, O. (2004). Functional connectivity of the prefrontal cortex and the amygdala in posttraumatic stress disorder. *Biological Psychiatry, 55,* 263–272.

Gladsjo, J. A., Rapaport, M. H., McKinney, R., Lucas, J. A., Rabin, A., Oliver, T., … & Judd, L. L. (1998). A neuropsychological study of panic disorder: Negative findings. *Journal of Affective Disorders, 49,* 123–131.

Glickman, S. E. (1961). Perseverative neural processes and consolidation of the memory trace. *Psychological Bulletin, 58,* 218–233.

Goldin, P., Manber-Ball, T., Werner, K., Heimberg, R., & Gross, J. J. (2009). Neural mechanisms of cognitive reappraisal of negative self-beliefs in social anxiety disorder. *Biological Psychiatry, 66*, 1091–1099.

Goldin, P., Ziv, M., Jazaieri, H., Hahn, K., & Gross, J. J. (2013). MBSR vs aerobic exercise in social anxiety: fMRI of emotion regulation of negative self-beliefs. *Social Cognitive Affective Neuroscience, 8*, 65–72.

Goldin, P., Ziv, M., Jazaieri, H., Hahn, K., Heimberg, R., & Gross, J. J. (2013). Impact of cognitive behavioral therapy for social anxiety disorder on the neural dynamics of cognitive reappraisal of negative self-beliefs: Randomized clinical trial. *JAMA Psychiatry, 70*, 1048–1056.

Golkar, A., Bellander, M., Olsson, A., & Ohman, A. (2012). Are fear memories erasable?-reconsolidation of learned fear with fear-relevant and fear-irrelevant stimuli. *Frontiers Behavioral Neuroscience, 6*, 80.

Graeff, F. G., & Del-Ben, C. M. (2008). Neurobiology of panic disorder: From animal models to brain neuroimaging. *Neuroscience & Biobehavioral Reviews, 32*, 1326–1335.

Graham, B. M., & Milad, M. R. (2011). The study of fear extinction: Implications for anxiety disorders. *American Journal of Psychiatry, 168*, 1255–1265.

Greenberg, P. E., Sisitsky, T., Kessler, R. C., Finkelstein, S. N., Berndt, E. R., Davidson, J. R., ... & Fyer, A. J. (1999). The economic burden of anxiety disorders in the 1990s. *Journal of Clinical Psychiatry, 60*, 427–435.

Grillon, C. (2009). D-cycloserine facilitation of fear extinction and exposure-based therapy might rely on lower-level, automatic mechanisms. *Biological Psychiatry, 66*, 636–641.

Grillon, C., & Morgan III, C. A. (1999). Fear-potentiated startle conditioning to explicit and contextual cues in Gulf War veterans with posttraumatic stress disorder. *Journal of Abnormal Psychology, 108*, 134–142.

Grillon, C., Lissek, S., McDowell, D., Levenson, J., & Pine, D. S. (2007). Reduction of trace but not delay eyeblink conditioning in panic disorder. *American Journal of Psychiatry, 164*, 283–289.

Grillon, C., Pine, D. S., Lissek, S., Rabin, S., Bonne, O., & Vythilingam, M. (2009). Increased anxiety during anticipation of unpredictable aversive stimuli in posttraumatic stress disorder but not in generalized anxiety disorder. *Biological Psychiatry, 66*, 47–53.

Gronwall, D. (1977). Paced auditory serial-addition task: A measure of recovery from concussion. *Perceptual and Motor Skills, 44*, 367–373.

Guastella, A. J., Richardson, R., Lovibond, P. F., Rapee, R. M., Gaston, J. E., Mitchell, P., & Dadds, M. R. (2008). A randomized controlled trial of D-cycloserine enhancement of exposure therapy for social anxiety disorder. *Biological Psychiatry, 63*, 544–549.

Guyer, A. E., Lau, J. Y., McClure-Tone, E. B., Parrish, J., Shiffrin, N. D., Reynolds, R. C., ... & Nelson, E. E. (2008). Amygdala and ventrolateral prefrontal cortex function during anticipated peer evaluation in pediatric social anxiety. *Archives of General Psychiatry, 65*, 1303–1312.

Hahn, A., Stein, P., Windischberger, C., Weissenbacher, A., Spindelegger, C., Moser, E., ... & Lanzenberger, R. (2011). Reduced resting-state functional connectivity between amygdala and orbitofrontal cortex in social anxiety disorder. *NeuroImage, 56*, 881–889.

Hakamata, Y., Lissek, S., Bar-Haim, Y., Britton, J. C., Fox, N. A., Leibenluft, E., ... & Pine, D. S. (2010). Attention bias modification treatment: A meta-analysis toward the establishment of novel treatment for anxiety. *Biological Psychiatry, 68*, 982–990.

Hallion, L. S., & Ruscio, A. M. (2011). A meta-analysis of the effect of cognitive bias modification on anxiety and depression. *Psychological Bulletin, 137*, 940–958.

Harrison, B. J., Soriano-Mas, C., Pujol, J., Ortiz, H., Lopez-Sola, M., Hernandez-Ribas, R., ... & Cardoner, N. (2009). Altered corticostriatal functional connectivity in obsessive-compulsive disorder. *Archives of General Psychiatry, 66*, 1189–1200.

Hartley, C. A., & Phelps, E. A. (2010). Changing fear: The neurocircuitry of emotion regulation. *Neuropsychopharmacology, 35*, 136–146.

Hayes, S., Hirsch, C., & Mathews, A. (2008). Restriction of working memory capacity during worry. *Journal of Abnormal Psychology, 117*, 712–717.

Hayes, S. C., Luoma, J. B., Bond, F. W., Masuda, A., & Lillis, J. (2006). Acceptance and commitment therapy: Model, processes and outcomes. *Behaviour Research and Therapy, 44*, 1–25.

Hermans, D., Craske, M. G., Mineka, S., & Lovibond, P. F. (2006). Extinction in human fear conditioning. *Biological Psychiatry, 60*, 361–368.

Herry, C., Ferraguti, F., Singewald, N., Letzkus, J. J., Ehrlich, I., & Luthi, A. (2010). Neuronal circuits of fear extinction. *European Journal of Neuroscience, 31*, 599–612.

Heuer, K., Rinck, M., & Becker, E. S. (2007). Avoidance of emotional facial expressions in social anxiety: The Approach-Avoidance Task. *Behaviour Research and Therapy, 45*, 2990–3001.

Hofmann, S. G., & Smits, J. A. (2008). Cognitive-behavioral therapy for adult anxiety disorders: A meta-analysis of randomized placebo-controlled trials. *Journal of Clinical Psychiatry, 69*, 621–632.

Hofmann, S. G., Wu, J. Q., & Boettcher, H. (2014). Effect of cognitive-behavioral therapy for anxiety disorders on quality of life: A meta-analysis. *Journal of Consulting and Clinical Psychology, 82*, 375–391.

Hofmann, S. G., Sawyer, A. T., Witt, A. A., & Oh, D. (2010). The effect of mindfulness-based therapy on anxiety and depression: A meta-analytic review. *Journal of Consulting and Clinical Psychology, 78*, 169–183.

Hofmann, S. G., Smits, J. A., Asnaani, A., Gutner, C. A., & Otto, M. W. (2011). Cognitive enhancers for anxiety disorders. *Pharmacology Biochemistry and Behavior, 99*(2), 275–284.

Hofmann, S. G., Meuret, A. E., Smits, J. A., Simon, N. M., Pollack, M. H., Eisenmenger, K., ... & Otto, M. W. (2006). Augmentation of exposure therapy with D-cycloserine for social anxiety disorder. *Archives of General Psychiatry, 63*, 298–304.

Hofmann, S. G., Smits, J. A., Rosenfield, D., Simon, N., Otto, M. W., Meuret, A. E., ... & Pollack, M. H. (2013). D-Cycloserine as an augmentation strategy with cognitive-behavioral therapy for social anxiety disorder. *American Journal of Psychiatry, 170*, 751–758.

Hollon, S. D., Stewart, M. O., & Strunk, D. (2006). Enduring effects for cognitive behavior therapy in the treatment of depression and anxiety. *Annual Review Psychology, 57*, 285–315.

Holmes, E. A., James, E. L., Coode-Bate, T., & Deeprose, C. (2009). Can playing the computer game "Tetris" reduce the build-up of flashbacks for trauma? A proposal from cognitive science. *PLoS One, 4*, e4153.

Holmes, E. A., James, E. L., Kilford, E. J., & Deeprose, C. (2010). Key steps in developing a cognitive vaccine against traumatic flashbacks: Visuospatial Tetris versus verbal Pub Quiz. *PLoS One, 5*(11), e13706.

Holzel, B. K., Hoge, E. A., Greve, D. N., Gard, T., Creswell, J. D., Brown, K. W., … & Lazar, S. W. (2013). Neural mechanisms of symptom improvements in generalized anxiety disorder following mindfulness training. *NeuroImage: Clinical, 2*, 448–458.

Issakidis, C., Sanderson, K., Corry, J., Andrews, G., & Lapsley, H. (2004). Modelling the population cost-effectiveness of current and evidence-based optimal treatment for anxiety disorders. *Psychological Medicine, 34*, 19–35.

Jovanovic, T., Norrholm, S. D., Blanding, N. Q., Davis, M., Duncan, E., Bradley, B., & Ressler, K. J. (2010). Impaired fear inhibition is a biomarker of PTSD but not depression. *Depression and Anxiety, 27*, 244–251.

Kaplan, J. S., Erickson, K., Luckenbaugh, D. A., Weiland-Fiedler, P., Geraci, M., Sahakian, B. J., … & Neumeister, A. (2006). Differential performance on tasks of affective processing and decision-making in patients with panic disorder and panic disorder with comorbid major depressive disorder. *Journal of Affective Disorders, 95*, 165–171.

Kessler, R. C., Berglund, P., Demler, O., Jin, R., Merikangas, K. R., & Walters, E. E. (2005). Lifetime prevalence and age-of-onset distributions of DSM-IV disorders in the National Comorbidity Survey Replication. *Archives of General Psychiatry, 62*, 593–602.

Kim, J. E., Dager, S. R., & Lyoo, I. K. (2013). The role of the amygdala in the pathophysiology of panic disorder: Evidence from neuroimaging studies. *Biology of Mood & Anxiety Disorders, 2*(1), 20.

Kim, S. Y., Chung, Y. K., Kim, B. S., Lee, S. J., Yoon, J. K., & An, Y. S. (2012). Resting cerebral glucose metabolism and perfusion patterns in women with posttraumatic stress disorder related to sexual assault. *Psychiatry Research, 201*, 214–217.

Kindt, M., & Soeter, M. (2011). Reconsolidation in a human fear conditioning study: A test of extinction as updating mechanism. *Biological Psychology, 92*(1), 43–50.

Kindt, M., Soeter, M., & Vervliet, B. (2009). Beyond extinction: Erasing human fear responses and preventing the return of fear. *Nature Neuroscience, 12*, 256–258.

Klumpp, H., Angstadt, M., & Phan, K. L. (2012). Insula reactivity and connectivity to anterior cingulate cortex when processing threat in generalized social anxiety disorder. *Biological Psychology, 89*, 273–276.

Kushner, M. G., Kim, S. W., Donahue, C., Thuras, P., Adson, D., Kotlyar, M., … & Foa, E. B. (2007). D-cycloserine augmented exposure therapy for obsessive-compulsive disorder. *Biological Psychiatry, 62*, 835–838.

Lazeron, R. H., Rombouts, S. A., de Sonneville, L., Barkhof, F., & Scheltens, P. (2003). A paced visual serial addition test for fMRI. *Journal of the Neurological Sciences, 213*, 29–34.

Lindauer, R. J., Vlieger, E. J., Jalink, M., Olff, M., Carlier, I. V., Majoie, C. B., … & Gersons, B. P. (2004). Smaller hippocampal volume in Dutch police officers with posttraumatic stress disorder. *Biological Psychiatry, 56*, 356–363.

Lissek, S., Powers, A. S., McClure, E. B., Phelps, E. A., Woldehawariat, G., Grillon, C., & Pine, D. S. (2005). Classical fear conditioning in the anxiety disorders: A meta-analysis. *Behaviour Research and Therapy, 43*, 1391–1424.

Lissek, S., Rabin, S., Heller, R. E., Lukenbaugh, D., Geraci, M., Pine, D. S., & Grillon, C. (2010). Overgeneralization of conditioned fear as a pathogenic marker of panic disorder. *American Journal of Psychiatry, 167*, 47–55.

Litz, B. T., Salters-Pedneault, K., Steenkamp, M. M., Hermos, J. A., Bryant, R. A., Otto, M. W., & Hofmann, S. G. (2012). A randomized placebo-controlled trial of D-cycloserine and exposure therapy for posttraumatic stress disorder. *Journal of Psychiatric Research, 46*, 1184–1190.

Lorberbaum, J. P., Kose, S., Johnson, M. R., Arana, G. W., Sullivan, L. K., Hamner, M. B., ... & George, M. S. (2004). Neural correlates of speech anticipatory anxiety in generalized social phobia. *Neuroreport, 15*, 2701–2705.

Lucas, J. A., Telch, M. J., & Bigler, E. D. (1991). Memory functioning in panic disorder: A neuropsychological perspective. *Journal of Anxiety Disorders, 5*, 1–20.

Lucey, J. V., Costa, D. C., Adshead, G., Deahl, M., Busatto, G., Gacinovic, S., ... & Kerwin, R. W. (1997). Brain blood flow in anxiety disorders. OCD, panic disorder with agoraphobia, and post-traumatic stress disorder on 99mTcHMPAO single photon emission tomography (SPET). *The British Journal of Psychiatry, 171*, 346–350.

Lundh, L. G., & Öst, L. G. (2001). Attentional bias, self-consciousness and perfectionism in social phobia before and after cognitive-behaviour therapy. *Scandinavian Journal of Behaviour Therapy, 30* (1), 4–16.

MacLeod, C., Koster, E. H., & Fox, E. (2009). Whither cognitive bias modification research? Commentary on the special section articles. *Journal of Abnormal Psychology, 118*, 89.

MacLeod, C., Mathews, A., & Tata, P. (1986). Attentional bias in emotional disorders. *Journal of Abnormal Psychology, 95*, 15–20.

Maren, S., & Quirk, G. J. (2004). Neuronal signalling of fear memory. *Nature Reviews Neuroscience, 5*, 844–852.

Mathew, S. J., Mao, X., Coplan, J. D., Smith, E. L., Sackeim, H. A., Gorman, J. M., & Shungu, D. C. (2004). Dorsolateral prefrontal cortical pathology in generalized anxiety disorder: A proton magnetic resonance spectroscopic imaging study. *American Journal of Psychiatry, 161*, 1119–1121.

Mathews, A., & Mackintosh, B. (1998). A cognitive model of selective processing in anxiety. *Cognitive Therapy and Research, 22*, 539–560.

Mathews, A., Mogg, K., Kentish, J., & Eysenck, M. (1995). Effect of psychological treatment on cognitive bias in generalized anxiety disorder. *Behaviour Research and Therapy, 33*, 293–303.

McClure, E. B., Monk, C. S., Nelson, E. E., Parrish, J. M., Adler, A., Blair, R. J., ... & Pine, D. S. (2007). Abnormal attention modulation of fear circuit function in pediatric generalized anxiety disorder. *Archives of General Psychiatry, 64*, 97–106.

McGaugh, J. L. (1966). Time-dependent processes in memory storage. *Science, 153*, 1351–1358.

McHugh, R. K., Whitton, S. W., Peckham, A. D., Welge, J. A., & Otto, M. W. (2013). Patient preference for psychological vs pharmacologic treatment of psychiatric disorders: A meta-analytic review. *Journal of Clinical Psychiatry, 74*, 595–602.

McHugh, R. K., Otto, M. W., Barlow, D. H., Gorman, J. M., Shear, M. K., & Woods, S. W. (2007). Cost-efficacy of individual and combined treatments for panic disorder. *Journal of Clinical Psychiatry, 68*, 1038–1044.

McNally, R. J. (2002). Anxiety sensitivity and panic disorder. *Biological Psychiatry, 52*, 938–946.

Menzies, L., Chamberlain, S. R., Laird, A. R., Thelen, S. M., Sahakian, B. J., & Bullmore, E. T. (2008). Integrating evidence from neuroimaging and neuropsychological studies of obsessive-compulsive disorder: The orbitofronto-striatal model revisited. *Neuroscience & Biobehavioral Reviews, 32*, 525–549.

Meyerbroeker, K., Powers, M. B., van Stegeren, A., & Emmelkamp, P. M. (2012). Does yohimbine hydrochloride facilitate fear extinction in virtual reality treatment of fear of flying? A randomized placebo-controlled trial. *Psychotherapy and Psychosomatics, 81*, 29–37.

Milad, M. R., & Quirk, G. J. (2002). Neurons in medial prefrontal cortex signal memory for fear extinction. *Nature, 420*, 70–74.

Milad, M. R., & Rauch, S. L. (2012). Obsessive-compulsive disorder: Beyond segregated cortico-striatal pathways. *Trends in Cognitive Sciences, 16*, 43–51.

Milad, M. R., Orr, S. P., Lasko, N. B., Chang, Y., Rauch, S. L., & Pitman, R. K. (2008). Presence and acquired origin of reduced recall for fear extinction in PTSD: Results of a twin study. *Journal of Psychiatric Research, 42*, 515–520.

Milad, M. R., Furtak, S. C., Greenberg, J. L., Keshaviah, A., Im, J. J., Falkenstein, M. J., ... & Wilhelm, S. (2013). Deficits in conditioned fear extinction in obsessive-compulsive disorder and neurobiological changes in the fear circuit. *JAMA Psychiatry, 70*(6), 608–618.

Milad, M. R., Pitman, R. K., Ellis, C. B., Gold, A. L., Shin, L. M., Lasko, N. B., ... & Rauch, S. L. (2009). Neurobiological basis of failure to recall extinction memory in posttraumatic stress disorder. *Biological Psychiatry, 66*, 1075–1082.

Milekic, M. H., & Alberini, C. M. (2002). Temporally graded requirement for protein synthesis following memory reactivation. *Neuron, 36*, 521–525.

Miskovic, V., Moscovitch, D. A., Santesso, D. L., McCabe, R. E., Antony, M. M., & Schmidt, L. A. (2011). Changes in EEG cross-frequency coupling during cognitive behavioral therapy for social anxiety disorder. *Psychological Science, 22*, 507–516.

Mitte, K. (2005). Meta-analysis of cognitive-behavioral treatments for generalized anxiety disorder: A comparison with pharmacotherapy. *Psychological Bulletin, 131*, 785–795.

Mobini, S., & Grant, A. (2007). Clinical implications of attentional bias in anxiety disorders: An integrative literature review. *Psychotherapy: Theory, Research, Practice, Training, 44*, 450.

Mogg, K., Mathews, A., & Eysenck, M. W. (1992). Attentional bias to threat in clinical anxiety states. *Cognition & Emotion, 6*, 149–159.

Mohlman, J. (2005). Does executive dysfunction affect treatment outcome in late-life mood and anxiety disorders? *Journal of Geriatric Psychiatry and Neurology, 18*, 97–108.

Mohlman, J. (2008). More power to the executive? A preliminary test of CBT plus executive skills training for treatment of late-life GAD. *Cognitive and Behavioral Practice, 15*, 306–316.

Mohlman, J. (2013). Executive skills in older adults with GAD: Relations with clinical variables and CBT outcome. *Journal of Anxiety Disorders, 27*, 131–139.

Monfils, M. H., Cowansage, K. K., Klann, E., & LeDoux, J. E. (2009). Extinction-reconsolidation boundaries: Key to persistent attenuation of fear memories. *Science, 324*, 951–955.

Monk, C. S., Telzer, E. H., Mogg, K., Bradley, B. P., Mai, X., Louro, H. M., ... & Pine, D. S. (2008). Amygdala and ventrolateral prefrontal cortex activation to masked angry faces in children and adolescents with generalized anxiety disorder. *Archives of General Psychiatry, 65*, 568–576.

Morgieve, M., N'Diaye, K., Haynes, W. I., Granger, B., Clair, A. H., Pelissolo, A., & Mallet, L. (2013). Dynamics of psychotherapy-related cerebral haemodynamic changes in obsessive compulsive disorder using a personalized exposure task in functional magnetic resonance imaging. *Psychological Medicine*, 1–13.

Muravieva, E. V., & Alberini, C. M. (2010). Limited efficacy of propranolol on the reconsolidation of fear memories. *Learning and Memory, 17*, 306–313.

Nader, K., Schafe, G. E., & Le Doux, J. E. (2000a). Fear memories require protein synthesis in the amygdala for reconsolidation after retrieval. *Nature, 406,* 722–726.

Nader, K., Schafe, G. E., & LeDoux, J. E. (2000b). The labile nature of consolidation theory. *Nature Reviews Neuroscience, 1,* 216–219.

Nakao, T., Nakagawa, A., Yoshiura, T., Nakatani, E., Nabeyama, M., Yoshizato, C., … & Kanba, S. (2005). Brain activation of patients with obsessive-compulsive disorder during neuropsychological and symptom provocation tasks before and after symptom improvement: A functional magnetic resonance imaging study. *Biological Psychiatry, 57,* 901–910.

Nugent, N. R., Christopher, N. C., Crow, J. P., Browne, L., Ostrowski, S., & Delahanty, D. L. (2010). The efficacy of early propranolol administration at reducing PTSD symptoms in pediatric injury patients: A pilot study. *Journal of Traumatic Stress, 23,* 282–287.

Ochsner, K. N., & Gross, J. J. (2005). The cognitive control of emotion. *Trends in Cognitive Sciences, 9,* 242–249.

Olsson, A., & Phelps, E. A. (2007). Social learning of fear. *Nature Neuroscience, 10,* 1095–1102.

Orr, S. P., Metzger, L. J., Lasko, N. B., Macklin, M. L., Peri, T., & Pitman, R. K. (2000). De novo conditioning in trauma-exposed individuals with and without posttraumatic stress disorder. *Journal of Abnormal Psychology, 109,* 290–298.

O'Toole, M. S., & Pedersen, A. D. (2011). A systematic review of neuropsychological performance in social anxiety disorder. *Nordic Journal of Psychiatry, 65,* 147–161.

Otto, M. W., McHugh, R. K., & Kantak, K. M. (2010). Combined pharmacotherapy and cognitive-behavioral therapy for anxiety disorders: Medication effects, glucocorticoids, and attenuated treatment outcomes. *Clinical Psychology: Science and Practice, 17,* 91–103.

Otto, M. W., Pollack, M. H., & Maki, K. M. (2000). Empirically supported treatments for panic disorder: Costs, benefits, and stepped care. *Journal of Consulting and Clinical Psychology, 68,* 556–563.

Otto, M. W., Tolin, D. F., Simon, N. M., Pearlson, G. D., Basden, S., Meunier, S. A., … & Pollack, M. H. (2010). Efficacy of d-cycloserine for enhancing response to cognitive-behavior therapy for panic disorder. *Biological Psychiatry, 67,* 365–370.

Oyarzun, J. P., Lopez-Barroso, D., Fuentemilla, L., Cucurell, D., Pedraza, C., Rodriguez-Fornells, A., & de Diego-Balaguer, R. (2012). Updating fearful memories with extinction training during reconsolidation: A human study using auditory aversive stimuli. *PLoS One, 7*(6), e38849.

Paquette, V., Levesque, J., Mensour, B., Leroux, J. M., Beaudoin, G., Bourgouin, P., & Beauregard, M. (2003). "Change the mind and you change the brain": Effects of cognitive-behavioral therapy on the neural correlates of spider phobia. *NeuroImage, 18,* 401–409.

Paulesu, E., Sambugaro, E., Torti, T., Danelli, L., Ferri, F., Scialfa, G., … & Sassaroli, S. (2010). Neural correlates of worry in generalized anxiety disorder and in normal controls: A functional MRI study. *Psychological Medicine, 40,* 117–124.

Pfleiderer, B., Zinkirciran, S., Arolt, V., Heindel, W., Deckert, J., & Domschke, K. (2007). fMRI amygdala activation during a spontaneous panic attack in a patient with panic disorder. *World Journal of Biological Psychiatry, 8,* 269–272.

Phan, K. L., Fitzgerald, D. A., Nathan, P. J., & Tancer, M. E. (2006). Association between amygdala hyperactivity to harsh faces and severity of social anxiety in generalized social phobia. *Biological Psychiatry, 59,* 424–429.

Phelps, E. A., Delgado, M. R., Nearing, K. I., & LeDoux, J. E. (2004). Extinction learning in humans: Role of the amygdala and vmPFC. *Neuron, 43*, 897–905.

Polak, A. R., Witteveen, A. B., Reitsma, J. B., & Olff, M. (2012). The role of executive function in posttraumatic stress disorder: A systematic review. *Journal of Affective Disorders, 141*, 11–21.

Pollack, M. H., Otto, M. W., Roy-Byrne, P. P., Coplan, J. D., Rothbaum, B. O., Simon, N. M., & Gorman, J. M. (2008). Novel treatment approaches for refractory anxiety disorders. *Depression and Anxiety, 25*, 467–476.

Porto, P. R., Oliveira, L., Mari, J., Volchan, E., Figueira, I., & Ventura, P. (2009). Does cognitive behavioral therapy change the brain? A systematic review of neuroimaging in anxiety disorders. *Journal of Neuropsychiatry and Clinical Neuroscience, 21*, 114–125.

Powers, M. B., Smits, J. A., Otto, M. W., Sanders, C., & Emmelkamp, P. M. (2009). Facilitation of fear extinction in phobic participants with a novel cognitive enhancer: A randomized placebo controlled trial of yohimbine augmentation. *Journal of Anxiety Disorders, 23*, 350–356.

Prasko, J., Horacek, J., Zalesky, R., Kopecek, M., Novak, T., Paskova, B., … & Hoschl, C. (2004). The change of regional brain metabolism (18FDG PET) in panic disorder during the treatment with cognitive behavioral therapy or antidepressants. *Neuroendocrinology Letters, 25*, 340–348.

Price, R. B., Paul, B., Schneider, W., & Siegle, G. J. (2013). Neural correlates of three neurocognitive intervention strategies: A preliminary step towards personalized treatment for psychological disorders. *Cognitive Therapy and Research, 37*, 657–672.

Purcell, R., Maruff, P., Kyrios, M., & Pantelis, C. (1998). Neuropsychological deficits in obsessive-compulsive disorder: A comparison with unipolar depression, panic disorder, and normal controls. *Archives of General Psychiatry, 55*, 415–423.

Quidé, Y., Witteveen, A. B., El-Hage, W., Veltman, D. J., & Olff, M. (2012). Differences between effects of psychological versus pharmacological treatments on functional and morphological brain alterations in anxiety disorders and major depressive disorder: A systematic review. *Neuroscience & Biobehavioral Reviews, 36*, 626–644.

Quirk, G. J., & Mueller, D. (2008). Neural mechanisms of extinction learning and retrieval. *Neuropsychopharmacology, 33*, 56–72.

Quirk, G. J., Garcia, R., & Gonzalez-Lima, F. (2006). Prefrontal mechanisms in extinction of conditioned fear. *Biological Psychiatry, 60*, 337–343.

Qureshi, S. U., Long, M. E., Bradshaw, M. R., Pyne, J. M., Magruder, K. M., Kimbrell, T., … & Kunik, M. E. (2011). Does PTSD impair cognition beyond the effect of trauma? *Journal of Neuropsychiatry and Clinical Neuroscience, 23*, 16–28.

Rachman, S. (1977). The conditioning theory of fear-acquisition: A critical examination. *Behaviour Research and Therapy, 15*, 375–387.

Rao-Ruiz, P., Rotaru, D. C., van der Loo, R. J., Mansvelder, H. D., Stiedl, O., Smit, A. B., & Spijker, S. (2011). Retrieval-specific endocytosis of GluA2-AMPARs underlies adaptive reconsolidation of contextual fear. *Nature Neuroscience, 14*, 1302–1308.

Rapee, R. M., & Heimberg, R. G. (1997). A cognitive-behavioral model of anxiety in social phobia. *Behaviour Research and Therapy, 35*, 741–756.

Rauch, S. L., Shin, L. M., & Phelps, E. A. (2006). Neurocircuitry models of posttraumatic stress disorder and extinction: Human neuroimaging research—past, present, and future. *Biological Psychiatry, 60*, 376–382.

Rauch, S. L., Jenike, M. A., Alpert, N. M., Baer, L., Breiter, H. C., Savage, C. R., & Fischman, A. J. (1994). Regional cerebral blood flow measured during symptom provocation in obsessive-compulsive disorder using oxygen 15-labeled carbon dioxide and positron emission tomography. *Archives of General Psychiatry, 51*, 62–70.

Rauch, S. L., Shin, L. M., Segal, E., Pitman, R. K., Carson, M. A., McMullin, K., … & Makris, N. (2003). Selectively reduced regional cortical volumes in post-traumatic stress disorder. *Neuroreport, 14*, 913–916.

Rauch, S. L., van der Kolk, B. A., Fisler, R. E., Alpert, N. M., Orr, S. P., Savage, C. R., … & Pitman, R. K. (1996). A symptom provocation study of posttraumatic stress disorder using positron emission tomography and script-driven imagery. *Archives of General Psychiatry, 53*, 380–387.

Rauch, S. L., Wedig, M. M., Wright, C. I., Martis, B., McMullin, K. G., Shin, L. M., … & Wilhelm, S. (2007). Functional magnetic resonance imaging study of regional brain activation during implicit sequence learning in obsessive-compulsive disorder. *Biological Psychiatry, 61*(3), 330–336.

Rauch, S. L., Whalen, P. J., Shin, L. M., McInerney, S. C., Macklin, M. L., Lasko, N. B., … & Pitman, R. K. (2000). Exaggerated amygdala response to masked facial stimuli in posttraumatic stress disorder: A functional MRI study. *Biological Psychiatry, 47*, 769–776.

Ravindran, L. N., & Stein, M. B. (2010). The pharmacologic treatment of anxiety disorders: A review of progress. *Journal of Clinical Psychiatry, 71*, 839–854.

Reiss, S., Peterson, R. A., Gursky, D. M., & McNally, R. J. (1986). Anxiety sensitivity, anxiety frequency and the prediction of fearfulness. *Behaviour Research and Therapy, 24*, 1–8.

Ressler, K. J., Rothbaum, B. O., Tannenbaum, L., Anderson, P., Graap, K., Zimand, E., … & Davis, M. (2004). Cognitive enhancers as adjuncts to psychotherapy: Use of D-cycloserine in phobic individuals to facilitate extinction of fear. *Archives of General Psychiatry, 61*, 1136–1144.

Richardson, R., Ledgerwood, L., & Cranney, J. (2004). Facilitation of fear extinction by D-cycloserine: Theoretical and clinical implications. *Learning and Memory, 11*, 510–516.

Rinck, M., & Becker, E. S. (2007). Approach and avoidance in fear of spiders. *Journal of Behavior Therapy and Experimental Psychiatry, 38*, 105–120.

Roelofs, K., Putman, P., Schouten, S., Lange, W. G., Volman, I., & Rinck, M. (2010). Gaze direction differentially affects avoidance tendencies to happy and angry faces in socially anxious individuals. *Behaviour Research and Therapy, 48*, 290–294.

Sachinvala, N., Kling, A., Suffin, S., Lake, R., & Cohen, M. (2000). Increased regional cerebral perfusion by 99mTc hexamethyl propylene amine oxime single photon emission computed tomography in post-traumatic stress disorder. *Military Medicine, 165*, 473–479.

Sakai, Y., Kumano, H., Nishikawa, M., Sakano, Y., Kaiya, H., Imabayashi, E., … & Kuboki, T. (2006). Changes in cerebral glucose utilization in patients with panic disorder treated with cognitive-behavioral therapy. *NeuroImage, 33*, 218–226.

Sakai, Y., Kumano, H., Nishikawa, M., Sakano, Y., Kaiya, H., Imbayashi, E., Ohnishi, T., … & Kuboki, T. (2005). Cerebral glucose metabolism associated with a fear network in panic disorder. *Neuroreport, 16*, 927–931.

Sara, S. J. (2000). Retrieval and reconsolidation: Toward a neurobiology of remembering. *Learning and Memory, 7,* 73–84.

Saxena, S., & Rauch, S. L. (2000). Functional neuroimaging and the neuroanatomy of obsessive-compulsive disorder. *Psychiatric Clinics of North America, 23,* 563–586.

Schiller, D., & Phelps, E. A. (2011). Does reconsolidation occur in humans? *Frontiers Behavioral Neuroscience, 5,* 24.

Schiller, D., Monfils, M. H., Raio, C. M., Johnson, D. C., Ledoux, J. E., & Phelps, E. A. (2010). Preventing the return of fear in humans using reconsolidation update mechanisms. *Nature, 463,* 49–53.

Schmidt, N. B., Lerew, D. R., & Jackson, R. J. (1997). The role of anxiety sensitivity in the pathogenesis of panic: Prospective evaluation of spontaneous panic attacks during acute stress. *Journal of Abnormal Psychology, 106,* 355–364.

Schwartz, J. M., Stoessel, P. W., Baxter, L. R., Jr., Martin, K. M., & Phelps, M. E. (1996). Systematic changes in cerebral glucose metabolic rate after successful behavior modification treatment of obsessive-compulsive disorder. *Archives of General Psychiatry, 53,* 109–113.

See, J., MacLeod, C., & Bridle, R. (2009). The reduction of anxiety vulnerability through the modification of attentional bias: A real-world study using a home-based cognitive bias modification procedure. *Journal of Abnormal Psychology, 118,* 65–75.

Segal, Z. V., Williams, J. G., & Teasdale, J. D. (2002). Review of mindfulness-based cognitive therapy for depression. *Journal of Psychiatry & Law, 30,* 271–274.

Sehlmeyer, C., Schoning, S., Zwitserlood, P., Pfleiderer, B., Kircher, T., Arolt, V., & Konrad, C. (2009). Human fear conditioning and extinction in neuroimaging: A systematic review. *PLoS One, 4*(6), e5865.

Semple, W. E., Goyer, P. F., McCormick, R., Donovan, B., Muzic, R. F., Jr., Rugle, L., … & Schulz, S. C. (2000). Higher brain blood flow at amygdala and lower frontal cortex blood flow in PTSD patients with comorbid cocaine and alcohol abuse compared with normals. *Psychiatry, 63,* 65–74.

Shah, S. G., Klumpp, H., Angstadt, M., Nathan, P. J., & Phan, K. L. (2009). Amygdala and insula response to emotional images in patients with generalized social anxiety disorder. *Journal of Psychiatry and Neuroscience, 34,* 296–302.

Shin, L. M., Rauch, S. L., & Pitman, R. K. (2006). Amygdala, medial prefrontal cortex, and hippocampal function in PTSD. *Annals of the New York Academy of Science, 1071,* 67–79.

Shin, L. M., Orr, S. P., Carson, M. A., Rauch, S. L., Macklin, M. L., Lasko, N. B., … & Pitman, R. K. (2004). Regional cerebral blood flow in the amygdala and medial prefrontal cortex during traumatic imagery in male and female Vietnam veterans with PTSD. *Archives of General Psychiatry, 61,* 168–176.

Siegle, G. J., Ghinassi, F., & Thase, M. E. (2007). Neurobehavioral therapies in the 21st century: Summary of an emerging field and an extended example of cognitive control training for depression. *Cognitive Therapy and Research, 31,* 235–262.

Siegle, G. J., Price, R. B., Jones, N. P., Ghinassi, F., & Thase, M. E. (2014). You gotta work at it: Pupillary indices of task focus are prognostic for response to a neurocognitive intervention for depression. *Clinical Psychological Science, 2,* 455–471.

Siegmund, A., Golfels, F., Finck, C., Halisch, A., Rath, D., Plag, J., & Strohle, A. (2011). D-cycloserine does not improve but might slightly speed up the outcome of in-vivo exposure therapy in patients with severe agoraphobia and panic disorder in a randomized double blind clinical trial. *Journal of Psychiatric Research, 45,* 1042–1047.

Simon, D., Kaufmann, C., Musch, K., Kischkel, E., & Kathmann, N. (2010). Fronto-striato-limbic hyperactivation in obsessive-compulsive disorder during individually tailored symptom provocation. *Psychophysiology, 47,* 728–738.

Smits, J. A., Berry, A. C., Tart, C. D., & Powers, M. B. (2008). The efficacy of cognitive-behavioral interventions for reducing anxiety sensitivity: A meta-analytic review. *Behaviour Research and Therapy, 46,* 1047–1054.

Smits, J. A., Powers, M. B., Cho, Y., & Telch, M. J. (2004). Mechanism of change in cognitive-behavioral treatment of panic disorder: Evidence for the fear of fear mediational hypothesis. *Journal of Consulting and Clinical Psychology, 72,* 646–652.

Smits, J. A., Rosenfield, D., Davis, M. L., Julian, K., Handelsman, P. H., Otto, M. W., … & Powers, M. B. (2014). Yohimbine enhancement of exposure therapy for social anxiety disorder: A randomized controlled trial. *Biological Psychiatry, 75*(11) 840–846.

Smits, J. A., Rosenfield, D., Otto, M. W., Marques, L., Davis, M. L., Meuret, A. E., … & Hofmann, S. G. (2013). D-cycloserine enhancement of exposure therapy for social anxiety disorder depends on the success of exposure sessions. *Journal of Psychiatric Research, 47,* 1455–1461.

Smits, J. A., Rosenfield, D., Otto, M. W., Powers, M. B., Hofmann, S. G., Telch, M. J., … & Tart, C. D. (2013). D-cycloserine enhancement of fear extinction is specific to successful exposure sessions: Evidence from the treatment of height phobia. *Biological Psychiatry, 73,* 1054–1058.

Soeter, M., & Kindt, M. (2011). Disrupting reconsolidation: Pharmacological and behavioral manipulations. *Learning and Memory, 18,* 357–366.

Stein, D. J., Fineberg, N. A., Bienvenu, O. J., Denys, D., Lochner, C., Nestadt, G., … & Phillips, K. A. (2010). Should OCD be classified as an anxiety disorder in DSM-V? *Depression and Anxiety, 27,* 495–506.

Stein, M. B., Goldin, P. R., Sareen, J., Zorrilla, L. T., & Brown, G. G. (2002). Increased amygdala activation to angry and contemptuous faces in generalized social phobia. *Archives of General Psychiatry, 59,* 1027–1034.

Stein, M. B., Jang, K. L., Taylor, S., Vernon, P. A., & Livesley, W. J. (2002). Genetic and environmental influences on trauma exposure and posttraumatic stress disorder symptoms: A twin study. *American Journal of Psychiatry, 159,* 1675–1681.

Straube, T., Mentzel, H. J., & Miltner, W. H. (2005). Common and distinct brain activation to threat and safety signals in social phobia. *Neuropsychobiology, 52,* 163–168.

Straube, T., Glauer, M., Dilger, S., Mentzel, H. J., & Miltner, W. H. (2006). Effects of cognitive-behavioral therapy on brain activation in specific phobia. *NeuroImage, 29,* 125–135.

Sutterby, S. R., & Bedwell, J. S. (2012). Lack of neuropsychological deficits in generalized social phobia. *PLoS One, 7*(8), e42675.

Suzuki, A., Josselyn, S. A., Frankland, P. W., Masushige, S., Silva, A. J., & Kida, S. (2004). Memory reconsolidation and extinction have distinct temporal and biochemical signatures. *Journal of Neuroscience, 24,* 4787–4795.

Taylor, C. T., & Amir, N. (2012). Modifying automatic approach action tendencies in individuals with elevated social anxiety symptoms. *Behaviour Research and Therapy, 50,* 529–536.

Thomas, S. J., Gonsalvez, C. J., & Johnstone, S. J. (2014). How specific are inhibitory deficits to obsessive-compulsive disorder? A neuropsychological comparison with panic disorder. *Clinical Neurophysiology, 135*, 463–75..

Tolin, D. F. (2010). Is cognitive-behavioral therapy more effective than other therapies? A meta-analytic review. *Clinical Psychology Review, 30*, 710–720.

Tronson, N. C., & Taylor, J. R. (2007). Molecular mechanisms of memory reconsolidation. *Nature Reviews Neuroscience, 8*, 262–275.

True, W. R., Rice, J., Eisen, S. A., Heath, A. C., Goldberg, J., Lyons, M. J., & Nowak, J. (1993). A twin study of genetic and environmental contributions to liability for posttraumatic stress symptoms. *Archives of General Psychiatry, 50*, 257–264.

Tuescher, O., Protopopescu, X., Pan, H., Cloitre, M., Butler, T., Goldstein, M., … & Stern, E. (2011). Differential activity of subgenual cingulate and brainstem in panic disorder and PTSD. *Journal of Anxiety Disorders, 25*, 251–257.

van den Heuvel, O. A., Veltman, D. J., Groenewegen, H. J., Witter, M. P., Merkelbach, J., Cath, D. C., … & van Dyck, R. (2005). Disorder-specific neuroanatomical correlates of attentional bias in obsessive-compulsive disorder, panic disorder, and hypochondriasis. *Archives of General Psychiatry, 62*, 922–933.

Vasile, R. G., Bruce, S. E., Goisman, R. M., Pagano, M., & Keller, M. B. (2005). Results of a naturalistic longitudinal study of benzodiazepine and SSRI use in the treatment of generalized anxiety disorder and social phobia. *Depression and Anxiety, 22*, 59–67.

Walker, D. L., Ressler, K. J., Lu, K. T., & Davis, M. (2002). Facilitation of conditioned fear extinction by systemic administration or intra-amygdala infusions of D-cycloserine as assessed with fear-potentiated startle in rats. *Journal of Neuroscience, 22*, 2343–2351.

Warwick, J. M., Carey, P., Jordaan, G. P., Dupont, P., & Stein, D. J. (2008). Resting brain perfusion in social anxiety disorder: A voxel-wise whole brain comparison with healthy control subjects. *Progress in Neuro-Psychopharmacology and Biological Psychiatry, 32*, 1251–1256.

Wells, A. (2000). Treating pathological worry and generalized anxiety disorder. *Emotional Disorders and Metacognition: Innovative cognitive therapy* (pp. 155–178). Chichester: Wiley.

Wiedemann, G., Pauli, P., Dengler, W., Lutzenberger, W., Birbaumer, N., & Buchkremer, G. (1999). Frontal brain asymmetry as a biological substrate of emotions in patients with panic disorders. *Archives of General Psychiatry, 56*, 78–84.

Wilhelm, S., Buhlmann, U., Tolin, D. F., Meunier, S. A., Pearlson, G. D., Reese, H. E., … & Rauch, S. L. (2008). Augmentation of behavior therapy with D-cycloserine for obsessive-compulsive disorder. *American Journal of Psychiatry, 165*, 335–341.

Wolski, P., & Maj, S. (1998). Performance of clinical anxiety group on Sternberg memory scanning task: Possible cognitive and affective effects of worry. *Polish Psychological Bulletin, 29*, 47–56.

Woodward, S. H., Kaloupek, D. G., Streeter, C. C., Martinez, C., Schaer, M., & Eliez, S. (2006). Decreased anterior cingulate volume in combat-related PTSD. *Biological Psychiatry, 59*, 582–587.

Woon, F. L., Sood, S., & Hedges, D. W. (2010). Hippocampal volume deficits associated with exposure to psychological trauma and posttraumatic stress disorder in adults: A meta-analysis. *Progress in Neuro-Psychopharmacology and Biological Psychiatry, 34*, 1181–1188.

Wu, J. C., Buchsbaum, M. S., Hershey, T. G., Hazlett, E., Sicotte, N., & Johnson, J. C. (1991). PET in generalized anxiety disorder. *Biological Psychiatry, 29*, 1181–1199.

Xue, Y. X., Luo, Y. X., Wu, P., Shi, H. S., Xue, L. F., Chen, C., ... & Lu, L. (2012). A memory retrieval-extinction procedure to prevent drug craving and relapse. *Science, 336*, 241–245.

Yamanishi, T., Nakaaki, S., Omori, I. M., Hashimoto, N., Shinagawa, Y., Hongo, J., ... & Furukawa, T. A. (2009). Changes after behavior therapy among responsive and nonresponsive patients with obsessive-compulsive disorder. *Psychiatry Research, 172*, 242–250.

Yamasue, H., Kasai, K., Iwanami, A., Ohtani, T., Yamada, H., Abe, O., ... & Kato, N. (2003). Voxel-based analysis of MRI reveals anterior cingulate gray-matter volume reduction in posttraumatic stress disorder due to terrorism. *Proceedings of the National Academy of Sciences, 100*, 9039–9043.

Yoon, K. L., Fitzgerald, D. A., Angstadt, M., McCarron, R. A., & Phan, K. L. (2007). Amygdala reactivity to emotional faces at high and low intensity in generalized social phobia: A 4-Tesla functional MRI study. *Psychiatry Research, 154*, 93–98.

Zubieta, J. K., Chinitz, J. A., Lombardi, U., Fig, L. M., Cameron, O. G., & Liberzon, I. (1999). Medial frontal cortex involvement in PTSD symptoms: A SPECT study. *Journal of Psychiatric Research, 33*, 259–264.

5

NEUROCOGNITIVE ASPECTS OF ANXIETY IN COGNITIVELY INTACT OLDER ADULTS

Jan Mohlman, Sherry A. Beaudreau, and Rebecca B. Price

The past few decades have seen rapid development in three distinct but related areas of psychological research: late life anxiety, cognitive aging, and affective neuroscience. Clinical psychologists are now poised to integrate findings from these three areas. This interdisciplinary approach has the potential to enhance knowledge of anxiety and its treatment in the older population, which is a neglected area of study (Bryant, Jackson, & Ames, 2008). By taking into consideration cognitive aspects of anxiety disorders, aging, and their neural underpinnings, we can move toward the development of assessment strategies and interventions better tailored to the older individual. Given the global aging trend (Kalache, Baretto, & Keller, 2005), the widespread prevalence of anxiety in later life (Lenze, Mohlman, & Wetherell, 2014; Schutzer & Graves, 2004; Wolitzky-Taylor, Castriotta, Lenze, Stanley, & Craske, 2010), and the reduced therapeutic response rates in older as compared to younger adults (Ayers, Sorrell, Thorp, & Wetherell, 2007; Thorp et al., 2009), the neurocognitive perspective could be instrumental in taking the field in new directions.

Why a neurocognitive perspective on anxiety? Neurocognitive functioning associated with psychiatric symptoms and disorders is increasingly recognized as a critical aspect of interpreting late-life mental health research and developing empirically supported measures (Boddice, Pachana, & Byrne, 2008) and interventions (Butters et al., 2011; Mohlman, 2005; Wetherell et al., 2009; Rigler, Studenski, & Duncan, 1998). The domain of geriatric depression has been the source of much of this research (e.g., Butters et al., 2008), but the study of anxiety disorders is now gaining momentum (Beaudreau, MacKay-Brandt, & Reynolds, 2013; Mohlman, 2013a).

Anxiety as experienced by older adults may differ in meaningful ways than when it presents in young or middle-aged individuals (Bryant, 2010; Mohlman, Sirota et al., 2012; Wolitzky-Taylor et al., 2010). Early studies revealed basic characteristics of disorders and syndromes common to older individuals and emphasized the need for additional research (e.g., Salzman & Lebowitz, 1991). The most current conceptualization is that older adults experience anxiety states that are less intense and impairing than their younger counterparts (Basevitz, Pushkar, Chaikelson, Conway, & Dalton, 2008; Gould & Edelstein, 2010; Levenson, 2000; Skarborn & Nicki, 2000), though some have argued that this finding is partly an artifact of criteria listed in the *Diagnostic and Statistical Manual of Mental Disorders* (DSM; American Psychiatric Association [APA], 2013) or due to other measurement issues (Mohlman, Sirota et al., 2012; Kunzmann, Kupperbusch, & Levenson, 2005).

In the treatment domain, early clinical trials of psychotherapy for geriatric anxiety included relaxation, supportive therapy, and cognitive behavior therapy (CBT) and indicated that these interventions typically outperform wait list conditions (Ayers et al., 2007; Mohlman, 2004). Although recent meta-analyses suggest that both pharmacological and psychosocial treatments are moderately effective (Pinquart & Duberstein, 2007), older adults prefer psychotherapy to medications for the treatment of anxiety (Mohlman, 2012). Thus, although psychosocial interventions are preferred, there is room for improvement in terms of efficacy, given that response rates fall short of those seen in younger patients (Ayers et al., 2007; Gould, Coulson, & Howard, 2012; Mohlman, 2004).

To identify innovative strategies for optimizing assessment and outcome of interventions, clinical psychologists are increasingly turning to the literature on cognitive aging and affective neuroscience. These research domains, including studies of brain structure and function, have rapidly evolved over the past few decades (Salthouse, 2010a, 2010b). One particularly influential model first developed by West (1996) and elaborated by others (Braver & West, 2008; Raz, 2000) argues that executive skills governed by the prefrontal cortex (PFC) of the brain (particularly lateral and orbital PFC) are vulnerable to decline in normal aging (Raz, Rodrigue, Williamson, & Acker, 2004). Executive skills (ES) are complex mental abilities that allow for goal-driven modification of thoughts and behaviors (Baddeley, 1990; Norman & Shallice, 1986), such as dividing attention and self-monitoring. ES and the PFC are involved in the willful control of mood and emotion through processes such as inhibitory control (Beauregard, Levesque, & Bourgouin, 2000) or cognitive reappraisal (Gross & John, 2003; Urry, van Reekum, Johnstone, & Davidson, 2009).

A small body of research on anxiety and emotion regulation reveals age-associated behavioral divergence in neurocognitive performance despite similar neural activation patterns (e.g., Andreescu, Wu, et al., 2011; Urry et al., 2006, 2009). For instance, though older and younger adults show similar activation of neural circuitry in response to negatively valenced pictures, only among older adults was the ability to reappraise interpretations of the images related to memory and ES (Winecoff, LaBar, Madden, Cabeza, & Huettel, 2011). Findings such as these suggest that neurocognitive ability moderates the association between neural mechanisms and emotion regulation in older but not younger age groups. This neurocognitive moderation may result from the aging of the PFC.

Studies of cognitive and neurobiological factors as both dependent and independent variables (e.g., the effects of anxiety on cognitive abilities; neural and cognitive predictors of therapy outcome) continue to emerge (Butters et al., 2011; Johnco, Wuthrich, & Rapee, 2013; Mohlman, 2013b; Yochim, Mueller, & Segal, 2013). It is intuitive that symptoms of anxiety could interfere with cognitive abilities (ES in particular), even in older adults with otherwise normal cognition. For example, symptoms such as trouble concentrating, mind going blank, and obsessional thinking could "overtake" mental resources, leading to ES decrements. This interference could take place in a linear fashion, with increasingly severe anxiety associated with increasingly severe cognitive decrements. Alternatively, the Yerkes-Dodson Law (Yerkes & Dodson, 1908) forecasts a curvilinear relation of anxiety to ES, with those at the lower and higher range showing worse performance than those in the midrange, for whom anxious arousal would be facilitative. Alternatively, in older individuals who suffer from chronic anxiety, stress-related release of glucocorticoids could undermine a range of cognitive abilities that depend upon memory through toxic effects on hippocampal cells (Sapolsky, 2000). It is also possible that the neurobiology of anxiety interfaces with cognition, leading to facilitation or disruption of performance that is specific to cognitive tasks involving either the same (Bartolic, Basso, Schefft, Glauser, & Titanic-Shefft, 1999) or different areas of the brain (Schmeichel, 2007) as anxiety. Findings on this topic are limited, however, and have yet to provide compelling support for any one of these possible models.

To elucidate these issues, this chapter will review the literature on geriatric anxiety from a neurocognitive perspective. First, we will discuss neural and cognitive phenomena in anxious older adults such as anxiety neurobiology, basic cognitive skills (e.g., memory, simple attention), ES (e.g., inhibitory control, verbal fluency), and attentional bias (maladaptive preconscious and conscious focus on negative or threat cues). Subsequently, the association of cognitive abilities to treatment outcome in clinical samples with anxiety disorders will be reviewed. Discussion of anxiety and cognitive abilities in older adults with progressive disease such as dementia are beyond the scope of this chapter but can be found elsewhere (e.g., Beaudreau & O'Hara, 2008; Hynninen, Breitve, Rongve, Aarsland, & Nordhus, 2012; Potvin, Hudon, Dion, Grenier, & Préville, 2011).

Neurobiology of Anxiety in Older Adults

The existing literature on late-life anxiety neurobiology is extremely limited. Decreased structural connectivity in the fronto-limbic system provides a neurobiological basis for proposed functional deficits in the behavioral management of anxiety (Tromp et al., 2012). The major regions of interest in this system include the PFC and the anterior cingulate cortex (ACC). The PFC, particularly the dorsolateral region, appears most active during tasks involving ES used to manage conflict (Banich et al., 2000). The ACC plays an important role in dampening emotions, such as worry or anxiety, by inhibiting the amygdala. Patterns of functional connectivity in anxious older adults, relative to anxious young adults or older controls, suggest dysregulation of this system with age and anxiety. Specifically, the PFC is generally less active in older adults with clinical anxiety (Andreescu, Wu, et al., 2011; Price, Eldreth, & Mohlman, 2011), except in the process of worrying, in which PFC may be more active (Andreescu, Lenze, et al., 2011; Mohlman, Eldreth, Price, & Hanson, 2009). These findings contrast with what has been found in younger adults; namely, decreased ACC activity in generalized anxiety disorder (GAD) compared with controls (Paulesu et al., 2010).

Overall, this initial neurobiological evidence reveals both common and unique factors of anxiety across age groups. However, there is a critical need for continued investigations of neurobiological aspects of anxiety before the data implicate any particular brain area or circuit that can serve as a reliable assessment or treatment heuristic.

Studies of Neuropsychological Test Performance

The Relation of Anxiety and Cognition in Older Analog Samples

Analog samples are defined here as those groups of older adults deemed anxious (most often based on scores on self-report or clinician administered measures) but not formally diagnosed with any psychiatric disorders, or those with elevated anxiety symptoms that fall short of diagnostic criteria. Subsyndromal anxiety is pervasive in older community populations with estimates as high as 52.3 percent (Bryant et al., 2008). Results of a large-scale longitudinal study from the Netherlands, the Longitudinal Aging Study Amsterdam (Bierman, Comijs, Jonker, & Beekman, 2005), revealed a curvilinear relation of anxiety to cognitive skills as measured by raw scores on neuropsychological tests. After adjusting scores for the presence of depressive symptoms, those older adults with higher anxiety symptoms performed worse on verbal learning on the modified Dutch version of the Auditory Verbal Learning Test (AVLT) "learning" subscale

(Rey, 1964; Deelman, Brouwer, van Zomeren, & Saan, 1980) and two ES tasks, Digit Symbol Coding (Savage, 1984) and Raven's Progressive Matrices (Raven, 1995), than those with low scores on the Hospital Anxiety and Depression Scale (Zigmund & Snaith, 1983). Furthermore, a significant curvilinear relation was found within the anxious group whereby those with lowest and highest scores showed worse performance on AVLT learning, and those with midrange scores performed best. The authors, like others (e.g., Biringer et al., 2005), argue for the need to control for the presence of depression, which was differentially associated with cognitive abilities.

Beaudreau and O'Hara (2009) predicted lower ES in older adults with elevated somatic symptoms of anxiety based on attentional control theory, which posits that anxiety hinders control of attentional resources on ES tasks (Eysenck, Derakshan, Santos, & Calvo, 2007). The authors employed an observational methodology with no explicit manipulation of threat. Their rationale was that the pervasiveness of attentional bias toward threat in anxious individuals due to internal (e.g., worry about issues unrelated to testing) and external sources (e.g., the testing situation) would be sufficient to produce lower ES scores in anxious older adults. Results showed one distinctive negative relation of ES to anxiety on raw Stroop scores (Golden, 1978). Elevated scores on the Beck Anxiety Inventory (Beck & Steer, 1993) in both the presence and absence of elevated depressive symptoms predicted slower processing speed. Furthermore, the combination of elevated anxiety and depressive symptoms was negatively related to episodic and semantic memory. Inhibitory control was the only cognitive domain negatively related to anxiety symptoms in regression models that included depression. There were no decrements on verbal fluency in association with either anxiety or depressive symptoms. The authors posit that mildly anxious older adults, who comprised the majority of the sample reporting anxiety symptoms, have more difficulty with prepotent inhibition due to the chronically increased cognitive load brought about by age- and mood-related symptoms.

Okereke and Grodstein (2013) conducted a prospective study examining the relation of phobic anxiety on the Crown Crisp Index (Crown & Crisp, 1966) to cognition a decade later in 16,351 older women in the Nurses' Health Study (NHS). Using normed scores, the authors hypothesized that greater phobic anxiety would be associated with broad cognitive decrements due to its associations with vascular disease and inflammation, two factors implicated in cognitive impairment. Further, they reasoned that the characteristic early-life onset and unremitting course of phobic symptoms would occur before individuals develop other common mental health issues with a later onset or before they would be expected to show cognitive impairment. The NHS assessed phobic anxiety in 1988 when the participants averaged sixty-three years old. Participants completed three assessments of global cognition (Telephone

Interview for Cognitive Status; TICS; Brandt, Spencer, & Folstein, 1988), immediate and delayed verbal memory recall (East Boston Memory Test [Albert et al., 1991] and delayed word list recall on TICS), and ES (Animal Naming and Digit Span Backward) between 1995 and 2001 when participants were seventy or older. Raw scores were adjusted for education, depression, alcohol, and tobacco consumption, and major medical illness. Women with elevated self-reported phobic anxiety had weaker global cognition, verbal memory, and ES at the first cognitive assessment. Phobic anxiety did not predict hastened decline in any areas of cognition over subsequent assessments. Okereke and Grodstein (2013) proposed that phobic anxiety alters the absolute level of cognitive ability earlier in life, but it does not change the trajectory of cognitive decline. Nevertheless, this finding may not extend to other types of anxiety, given that older worriers have shown a steeper decline in learning and memory recall of visual and verbal information compared with non-worriers (Pietrzak et al., 2012).

Wetherell and colleagues tested hypotheses derived from Eysenck's processing efficiency model (1992), namely, that state anxiety would interfere with tasks that involve the phonological loop or central executive of working memory (Baddeley, 1990) and that neuroticism (a proxy for trait anxiety) would be associated with decrements on tests of memory and complex visuospatial skills on the Dureman–Sälde Battery (Dureman, Kebbon, & Osterberg, 1971) or subtests from other batteries (Names and Faces, DeFries, Plomin, Vandenberg, & Kuse, 1981; Analogies, Westrin, 1969; and Information, Jonsson & Molander, 1964). Although state anxiety was negatively related to percentage of correct items on tasks of visual learning (Names and Faces, Picture Memory), spatial reasoning (Block Design), and verbal reasoning (Synonyms, Analogies), no effect was found on tasks of nonverbal memory and reasoning or basic knowledge (Figure Identification, Figure Logic, or Symbol Digit Information). No effects were found in any regression models of neuroticism and cognitive performance. Measurement of state anxiety occurred in participants' homes on a different day from when cognitive testing took place, thus limiting any interpretation of scores on this variable as an index of participants' moods proximal to or during the testing period.

In a community sample using normed test scores, subsyndromal symptoms of anxiety and depression negatively predicted list learning on California Verbal Learning Test (CVLT; Delis, Kramer, Kaplan, & Ober, 2000) over five learning trials (Yochim et al., 2013). Semantic clustering of CVLT items in particular, a predominantly ES strategy that facilitates memory performance, explained the variance in lower memory performance in those with elevated affective anxiety symptoms. Anxiety also uniquely predicted categorization ability as measured by the Delis-Kaplan Executive Functioning System (DKEFS; Delis, Kaplan, & Kramer, 2001) 200 Questions initial abstraction score. Depression uniquely predicted DKEFS letter and category fluency. The authors argue that although some cases of cognitive deficits are intractable, anxiety can be effectively treated in older individuals. Thus, the effective treatment of anxiety could be a viable avenue for enhancing cognitive functions due to their bidirectional relation (Beaudreau & O'Hara, 2008; Yaffe et al., 2010). Like several others, Yochim and colleagues (2013) argue that anxiety could result in cognitive load, leading to reduced availability of task relevant resources, or that those with low ES are less able to manage anxiety. Based on this investigation, they posit that worry and somatic anxiety symptoms, for instance shortness of breath or heart racing, may be less demanding of cognitive resources and thus pose less interference with ES and memory than affective symptoms such as restlessness and irritability. These assertions are consistent with cross-sectional findings from Caudle et al. (2007), Price and Mohlman (2007), and Mohlman (2013b); however, in healthy older adults using normed data, Pietrzak et al. (2012) found that baseline worry predicted lower verbal memory two years later.

Notably, a subset of investigations report minimal-to-no relation of anxiety to ES but have identified alternative demographic, mood, and health-related predictors (e.g., depression, gender; Biringer et al., 2005; Booth, Schinka, Brown, Mortimer, & Borenstein, 2006). There is also some support for global reductions in cognitive function in geriatric anxiety. Older community-residing adults reporting more anxiety demonstrate lower general cognitive abilities according to normed scores from the Repeatable Battery for the Assessment of Neuropsychological Status (RBANS; Randolph, 1998). Moreover, Sinoff and Werner (2003) report that older memory clinic outpatients with no detectable cognitive impairment or depression also exhibit accelerated decline in general cognitive functioning on the Mini-Mental Status Exam (MMSE; Folstein, Folstein, & McHugh, 1975). These studies suggest that anxiety may have a broad negative influence on global cognitive functioning over time. Though faster decline in global memory ability on the Dementia Rating Scale (DRS; Mattis, 1988) has been predicted for individuals with major depressive disorder (MDD) and comorbid anxiety compared with MDD alone (DeLuca et al., 2005), no group differences were found for general cognition using the DRS total. Moreover, at least one large prospective study of nondemented community-dwelling elderly showed no risk posed by baseline anxiety symptoms or disorders for subsequent dementia (deBruijn et al., 2014).

Summary of Analog Studies

Taken together, studies of analog samples implicate problems with memory and ES. Specific neurocognitive abilities, such as learning and memory (Bierman et al., 2005; Booth et al., 2006; Pietrzak et al., 2012; Wetherell et al., 2002; Yochim et al., 2013), divided attention (Hogan, 2003), set shifting (Booth et al., 2006), and inhibitory control (Beaudreau & O'Hara, 2009), are poorer in anxious or worried community-dwelling older adults compared with those who are non-anxious. Elevated worry also predicts a steeper decline in visual learning and memory and poorer delayed verbal memory at two-year follow-up (Pietrzak et al., 2012), and elevated general anxiety and phobic fear predict lower verbal memory from mid-life to older age (Okereke & Grodstein, 2013). At least one study suggests that the affective symptoms of anxiety show stronger relationships with cognition than worry or somatic anxiety symptoms (Yochim et al., 2013). Empirical support in favor of weaker verbal memory and ES in analog samples with anxiety derives from studies using both raw scores and demographic corrected norms. Other variables, particularly depression and demographic characteristics, might be critical in these investigations. In few instances, health-related variables are covaried, which could also alter the relation of anxiety and cognition. This is potentially important given the overlap between medical problems and somatic anxiety.

Anxiety and Cognition in Older Clinical Samples

The estimated prevalence of the anxiety disorders in older adults ranges from 3.2 percent to 14.2 percent (Wolitzky-Taylor et al., 2010). The majority of studies with clinical samples have included older patients with GAD, which is one of the most common late-life psychological problems (Wolitzky-Taylor et al., 2010). Findings are somewhat mixed, indicating deficits in aspects of memory but not necessarily ES or other functions. Several studies reveal that older GAD patients have deficits in short- and longer-term memory for numeric and linguistic information. Mantella and colleagues (2007) compared older adults with GAD or major depression to age-matched controls on a battery of neuropsychological tests. Predictions were that those with GAD would be more prone to memory and attention problems compared to healthy controls and were also expected to differ from depressed participants, although no specific patterns were hypothesized. According to raw data, those in the GAD group showed weaker ability than controls but not depressed patients to learn word lists over five trials of the CVLT (Delis et al., 2000). They recalled fewer word lists after short and long delay periods. Rates of retention (i.e., remembering the same stimuli correctly over subsequent trials) were equivalent to the controls. The recognition test of CVLT word lists was not administered; thus it is not possible to identify whether the performance decrement was specific to the encoding or retrieval of information. Although attributable to medical rather than psychiatric burden, lower scores were also found on Trail Making B in the patient groups. The authors concluded that worrying in GAD might interfere with memory but not other cognitive abilities.

In one of the largest late-life GAD clinical trials conducted to date, Butters and colleagues (2011) compared the performance of 160 older GAD patients to thirty-nine controls on WAIS letter-numbering sequencing (Wechsler, 1997), DKEFS sorting (Delis et al., 2001), and seven neuropsychological tests from the RBANS (Randolph, 1998) before and after treatment with escitalopram. At baseline, the GAD group was expected to perform more poorly on tests of attention, processing speed, and ES due to divided attention brought about by worrying. There were no problems expected in the domains of visuospatial functioning or language. Scores on tests of ES were expected to show relations with self-reported disability scores. The authors found lower raw scores in the GAD patients on sorting (a problem solving, mental flexibility, and conceptual ability task) and memory recall tests, regardless of comorbid depression. There were no differences between the groups on the remaining tests. Memory (immediate and delayed), language, and several ES abilities (coding, sorting, working memory) predicted functional disability in the GAD group.

Also indicative of relatively weak short-term memory ability in late-life anxiety, Mohlman (2013b) found lower scores on Digits Forward (Wechsler, 1997) but on no other neuropsychological tests in sixty-nine older GAD patients compared to fifty-two age-matched controls. The author used normed scores for statistical analysis and covaried education, depression, and hypertension. There were no differences between the groups on any other tests in the battery, including those tapping ES. Similarly, Caudle et al. (2007) found no differences between patients and controls on ES domains of the MMSE (e.g., serial 7s; Folstein et al., 1975) although scores on the working memory subscale and symptom measures were negatively related to anxiety.

In addition to the lack of differences on ES tests between GAD patients and controls, Price and Mohlman (2007) and Mohlman (2013b) reported a *positive* relation of worry severity to ES (inhibitory control and a composite "Verbal ES" index, respectively). This counterintuitive effect was explained by the habitual and strategic use of worry to regulate emotion in the GAD group by inhibiting affect-laden mental imagery and the processing of physiological arousal cues (Borkovec, 1994). This relation was not detected among age- and gender-matched controls in either study, suggestive of a disorder-specific phenomenon.

The most recent revision of the DSM (American Psychiatric Association, 2013) created new sections for Trauma- and Stressor-Related Disorders and Obsessive-Compulsive and Related Disorders, which, unlike the specific disorders discussed so far, are no longer included under the rubric of "Anxiety Disorders." Nevertheless, the disorders in these new categories are marked by high levels of anxiety symptoms, share phenomenological overlap with the "Anxiety Disorders" proper, and may have relevance for understanding late-life anxiety from a neurocognitive perspective. For example, posttraumatic stress disorder (PTSD) and its symptoms appear to have broad influence on late-life cognitive functioning. Among older adults who were child indentured servants, elevated PTSD symptoms are associated with significantly lower general cognitive function (MMSE raw scores; Folstein et al., 1975; and the total score on the Structured Interview for Diagnosis of Dementia of Alzheimer Type, Multi-infarct Dementia and Dementia of other Etiology according to ICD-10 and DSM-III-R; SIDAM; Zaudig, Hiller, & Pauls, 1991), verbal knowledge, and construction ability (normed SIDAM subtests) compared with minimal PTSD symptoms (Burri, Maercker, Krammer, & Simmen-Janevska, 2013).

In addition, a recent meta-analysis reported weaker general cognitive functioning and performance across a range of cognitive abilities including premorbid intelligence, delayed memory recall, learning, attention and working memory language, processing speed, and visuospatial abilities in older adults with PTSD (PTSD+) versus those with a history of trauma but no PTSD (PTSD–) or healthy controls (Schuitevoerder et al., 2013). The largest effect sizes in the meta-analysis were observed for learning and memory recall between PTSD+ and the PTSD– or healthy. Reduced total verbal learning, in particular, appears to be specific to aging and PTSD at least in combat veterans, as this has not been found in younger veterans with PTSD (Yehuda, Golier, Tischler, Stavitsky, & Harvey, 2005).

With regard to hoarding, older adults disproportionately engage in hoarding behaviors compared with other age groups (Samuels et al., 2008), making this disorder a critical issue in geriatric mental health settings. ES deficits have long been theorized as central to the excessive inability to discard or give away useless objects in hoarding (Frost & Hartl, 1996), and more recent studies support this early claim. For instance, Mackin and colleagues (2011) found that seven older patients with MDD reporting severe compulsive hoarding behaviors (versus forty-five older patients with MDD only) performed worse in the ES of categorization and problem solving based on age-adjusted normed scores on the DKEFS card-sorting task. No other neuropsychological tasks were related to hoarding severity.

A recent investigation using raw scores demonstrated that older individuals meeting DSM-5 criteria for hoarding disorder with no other Axis I diagnoses ($n = 42$) exhibited worse performance than healthy older controls ($n = 25$) on multiple ES, namely attention and working memory (WAIS-IV Letter Number Sequencing and Digit Span) and abstract problem solving, organization, and inhibitory ability (WCST; Ayers, Wetherell, et al., 2013). Only the WCST, however, correlated with self-reported severity of hoarding.

Summary of Clinical Studies

Evidence for cognitive decrements in clinical samples is less consistent than what is seen in analog samples. Mantella and colleagues (2007), Mohlman (2013b), and Butters and colleagues (2011) found that older anxiety patients showed decreased short-term and delayed memory for linguistic and nonlinguistic information. Lower scores on working memory among older patients with GAD have also been reported (Caudle et al., 2007). Patients also exhibited weaker performance than controls on a sorting task that involved problem solving, mental flexibility, and conceptual ability (Butters et al., 2011) and on tests of learning (Mantella et al., 2007). Additionally, hoarding disorder, newly defined in the DSM, is associated with decrements on multiple tests of ES. Older PTSD patients have also shown weak test performance across a variety of cognitive domains including ES.

However, the majority of tests in Mohlman (2013b) as well as Price and Mohlman (2007) and Caudle and colleagues (2007), which were all studies of GAD, revealed no differences on any ES abilities between anxious and healthy older adult groups. Those patients who performed worse on the working memory section of the MMSE also showed elevated GAD severity, anxiety, and depression but not worry scores (Caudle et al., 2007). Thus, symptoms other than worry seem most strongly related to certain cognitive abilities in older adults with GAD.

Limitations of Analog and Clinical Studies

A range of limitations and unresolved issues are common to both analog and clinical studies. Scoring methodology (raw versus normed) is an issue in need of consensus in this research domain. Differences on raw scores may not be clinically meaningful, despite the fact that most of the studies reviewed herein used raw scores. On the other hand, normed scores are much less sensitive to change and run the risk of obscuring some degree of therapeutic gain. Because age, health status, education, and gender are important contributors to cognitive ability in later life, these variables could be controlled in statistical analyses. This can be achieved either with the use of norms or in the statistical models themselves, although this latter strategy precludes awareness of whether cognitive performance was within normal limits or impaired. Inclusion criteria for relevant studies (e.g., cognitive cutoffs) also need to be taken into account, as these could prevent those with very low scores on any test from being included.

Additional limitations are consistent across most of the studies discussed herein, including samples of predominantly higher functioning Caucasian elderly, exclusion of those older adults with progressive brain disease or other acute health problems, use of cross-sectional rather than longitudinal or sequential designs, and reliance on neuropsychological tests as indicators of general functioning. The next wave of research on late-life anxiety and neurocognitive factors might aim to improve upon these aspects.

Models and Theories of the Relation of Anxiety to Cognitive Performance in Older Adults

Explanations for reduced neuropsychological test performance in later life include the cognitive burden of anxiety on attention (Eysenck et al., 2007); age-associated cognitive decline, particularly in processing speed (Salthouse, 2010a, 2010b); or some combination of the two. As noted throughout, limited resource and divided attention models have often been used to formulate predictions about the relation of age, anxiety, and ES and other cognitive abilities. This view generally asserts that during testing, individuals become anxious and experience distracting symptoms (e.g., worrying, bodily arousal, attentional bias toward threat in the environment), which "hijack" attention or other essential operations, leaving inadequate mental resources available to solve the task at hand. This effect, driven by the transient elevation of state anxiety, would be more evident in older than younger adults, who may already have compromised cognitive resources at baseline due to aging (Braver & West, 2008; Raz, 2000; West, 1996). There are several variants of this model, each of which leads to a slightly different set of expectations.

Eysenck's processing efficiency theory (1992) predicts that state, rather than trait, anxiety would be the stronger predictor of task performance in anxious individuals. This is due to the fact that anxiety evokes internal processing of verbal information, specifically through the phonological loop and central executive components but not the visuospatial sketchpad component of working memory (Baddeley, 1986). This would lead to reduced focus and resources to apply toward complex tasks that require these same mental capabilities. A similar argument based on modality was made by Deptula and colleagues (1993). The authors posit that if anxiety is construed as having cognitive (i.e., worry) and emotional components (i.e., arousal), then it is specifically the worry component that would compete with cognitive functions. Moreover, even if an older adult attempts to compensate by increasing effort or focus on tasks, lowered reserve capacity would render attempts unsuccessful. Alternatively however, according to Esyenck, an increased expenditure of effort in anxiety may also equalize performance on some cognitive tasks between anxious and non-anxious individuals, leading to similar performance.

The models discussed above beg the question of whether anxious older patients are indeed actively worrying or focusing on threat cues during neurocognitive testing. This distinction seems necessary to either support or refute a limited resource conceptualization. However, to date, very few studies have assessed state anxiety during different phases of testing or taken the necessary steps to effectively disentangle state and trait anxiety. Furthermore, few alternatives to limited resource models have been hypothesized and tested. If an older adult was not worrying or focused on other threat cues during testing, what might lead to decreased performance? One possibility, illustrated by a conditioning model, is that the individual implicitly learns to exert only partial effort during challenging tasks such as cognitive testing, due to earlier experiences with anxiety-driven performance decrements. In other words, if an anxious older man worries whenever he tries to budget his finances and finds the overall experience aversive, then he might learn to allocate divided rather than full attention to similar numerical tasks. Over time, this might become a broadly applied strategy even when he is not actively engaged in worrying or anxious arousal.

Nonlinear models such as the Yerkes-Dodson law (1908) have also been proposed; for instance, that anxiety has facilitative effects on less complex and deleterious effects on more complex tasks (Humphreys & Revelle, 1984). A similar argument could be made based on task familiarity or automaticity, although we found no empirical data to support this contention. Hogan (2003) asserts that if negative feedback is given after task trials, performance under anxious conditions will suffer, whereas if positive feedback is provided, performance will improve. Humphreys and Revelle (1984) posit that an anxious individual's performance on tasks reliant on short-term memory will suffer compared to those reliant on longer-term memory tasks, for which no specific predictions are made. A cogent argument might also be made based on whether a task is timed or untimed, with timed tasks revealing the greatest deficits when attempted by anxious elderly (Salthouse, 1994). Yet another model states that it is the strength of the relation of anxiety and cognition that differs across age groups and determines performance, with a relatively diffuse relation among younger but a tighter connection in older adults (Deptula et al., 1993), leading to greatest interference in those who are both anxious and older.

Currently, our knowledge of the complex relation of age, anxiety, and cognition does not clearly implicate any one of several possible mechanisms of reduced performance on cognitive tests. Despite the intuitive appeal of limited resource models implicating state anxiety as a vulnerability to distraction or reduced resources during cognitive tasks, Hogan (2003) found that trait rather than state anxiety was actually the stronger predictor of cognitive performance.

Whereas anxiety leads to reduced functioning on some cognitive tasks, associations between worry (i.e., a critical subcomponent of anxiety) and cognitive outcomes yield less consistent findings. Caudle et al. (2007), Price and Mohlman (2007), Mohlman (2013b), and Yochim and colleagues (2013), failed to find support for worry scores (assumed to be the most likely type of impairing symptom) as compelling predictors of poor ES. Worry involving left frontal areas and the ability to mentally construct anticipated outcomes involves the executive system but does not appear to tax mental resources in a reliable manner. We, thus, recommend that alternatives to limited resource models be proposed and tested to better characterize the relation of worry to ES.

An intriguing new model identified the anxiety sensitivity trait and cognitive performance as precipitants of anxiety (Wilkes, Wilson, Woodard, & Calamari, 2013). The authors posit that worry about actual memory concerns in older, anxiety-sensitive individuals drives the development of anxiety in the future. Hence, multiple pathways, some not yet specified, could account for the inverse relationship between anxiety and neurocognitive performance. These emergent hypotheses await further empirical testing.

Attentional Bias: A Clinically Relevant Neurocognitive Phenomenon

In addition to problems with performance on neuropsychological tests, which typically assess cognitive abilities when neutral stimuli such as numbers are presented, anxious older adults show altered attentional patterns on cognitive tasks that present emotional stimuli. "Attentional bias" describes the tendency for anxious individuals to selectively allocate attention toward threatening or anxiety-related stimuli, such as words or pictures related to anxiety-provoking topics. Growing evidence suggests that attentional bias may play a key role in anxiety maintenance and etiology. Across a large number of studies using performance-based measures, a pattern of attentional bias toward threat has been documented across a range of anxious samples, including both clinically and subclinically anxious adults and youth (Bar-Haim, Lamy, Pergamin, Bakermans-Kranenburg, & van IJzendoorn, 2007). The clinical relevance of these findings is underscored by an emerging neurocognitive treatment literature. Treatment studies in younger adults and youth have now begun to establish empirically that anxiety in clinical samples can be ameliorated by computer-based paradigms that systematically train attention toward neutral stimuli (Attention Bias Modification, ABM; see Chapter 4 by Moshier, Calkins, Kredlow, and Otto in this volume for a comprehensive description and review of findings in younger adults). The research reviewed below highlights the potential relevance of this neurocognitive treatment approach for anxious older adults, although direct studies of ABM in older adults have not been published to date.

Effects of Normative Aging on Attention to Emotional Stimuli

As summarized above, research in anxious younger adults and youth suggests that selective attention toward negative stimuli (particularly threat cues) is a relatively robust phenomenon likely to contribute to anxiety maintenance and/ or etiology. However, with respect to older adults, a separate line of research within the normative cognitive aging literature suggests that, in samples not selected or assessed on anxiety, a distinct and potentially contradictory pattern of attention may emerge. Specifically, older adults have been shown to preferentially allocate attention toward *positive* emotional cues and *away* from negative cues. This pattern, known as the "positivity effect," has been documented in both reaction time (Mather & Carstensen, 2003) and eye tracking (Isaacowitz, Allard, Murphy, & Schlangel, 2009; Isaacowitz, Wadlinger, Goren, & Wilson, 2006) studies of attention. The positivity effect is assumed to reflect a shift in overt goals occurring in late life that causes older adults to preferentially allocate their attention toward the least negative or most positive stimuli available in the environment. For instance, older adults are posited to experience an increased desire to maintain a pleasant mood state, while previously prioritized long-term goals (e.g., career attainment) become less salient than they were earlier in life (Carstensen, Isaacowitz, & Charles, 1999), leading to the observed shift in attentional allocation.

Late-life anxiety, therefore, lies at the nexus of two potentially contradictory literatures: the "attentional bias" literature, which suggests that anxious individuals preferentially attend towards threat, and the positivity effect literature, which suggests that older adults preferentially attend toward positive stimuli and away from negative stimuli such as threats. Thus, with regard to attention toward emotional stimuli, do anxious older adults resemble anxious younger adult samples, normative older adult samples, or a combination of both? Several studies have been undertaken to directly address this question.

Studies of Attentional Bias in Late-life Anxiety

Fox and Knight (2005) selected two widely used reaction time tasks to assess attentional bias: the emotional Stroop task (e.g., Gotlib & McCann, 1984) and the modified dot-probe task. This study also examined the effects of trait anxiety, using a median split on the trait scale of the Spielberger State-Trait Anxiety Inventory (Spielberger, Gorsuch, Lushene, Vagg, & Jacobs, 1983), and state anxiety, manipulated by the experimenters in a between-subjects design by providing either an "anxious" reading task about "Biological Terrorism" (with the threat of a videotaped memory and comprehension test to be administered later) or a "neutral" reading task about "Renewable Energy Resources" (with no mention of memory testing).

The experimenters found that state and trait anxiety had differential effects on attentional bias depending on which task was used for assessment. Trait anxiety was associated with increased attentional bias on the emotional Stroop task, while state anxiety increased attentional bias on the dot-probe task. Experimentally induced state anxiety also yielded an unexpected interaction on the emotional Stroop whereby bias was *increased* in individuals with low trait anxiety and *decreased* in individuals with high trait anxiety. Taken together, these findings provided preliminary support for the existence of anxiety-related attentional bias toward threat in older adults but suggested that procedural variables, such as the paradigm used to assess attentional bias and the context in which a task is given (a high versus low anxiety state), can have a significant impact on the results obtained.

In a more recent study using the dot-probe task, emotional faces, pictures, and words were used as stimuli, and each stimulus type was presented in both masked format (50-ms presentation, followed immediately by a masking stimulus to preclude conscious awareness of the word) and unmasked format (1,500-ms presentation, allowing for conscious awareness; Lee & Knight, 2009). The design was selected to allow for detection of effects varying as a function of time course (i.e., duration of stimuli) and stimulus modality. Younger and older adults were included, and participants were divided into low, moderate, and high groups based on trait anxiety scores (Spielberger et al., 1983). Of the six total conditions used (masked and unmasked faces, pictures, and words), the typical bias toward negative items in the older adult high-anxiety group was seen only in the condition using unmasked words. Older adults with moderate levels of trait anxiety were the only group to show the expected pattern across masked and unmasked trials (i.e., vigilance on masked and avoidance on unmasked trials—a pattern seen in some studies of younger adults and labeled the "vigilance-avoidance" effect; Mogg, Bradley, Miles, & Dixon, 2004) and only when sad faces were used as stimuli. These mixed findings again suggest that attentional bias toward threat can be observed in anxious older adults, but the phenomenon occurs under circumscribed conditions and can be influenced by a wide range of procedural and participant variables.

Brown and colleagues (2011) used a dot-probe task to assess attentional bias toward fall-relevant stimuli in older adults with and without self-reported fear of falling. All older adults exhibited a larger bias toward words relevant to falling and balance than toward general threat-related words (presented for 500 ms). Older adults who endorsed fear of falling specifically showed elevated scores on a measure of difficulty disengaging from fall-related words. Together, the findings imply that all older adults exhibit attentional bias toward fall-relevant stimuli, possibly related to the salience of this threat in older age, but that those who chronically fear falling also have difficulty disengaging attention from these cues, which could perpetuate concerns over time and lead to decreased activity levels and quality of life.

Two studies by Price and colleagues used the emotional Stroop task to assess bias toward threatening words in the context of late-life GAD. In a behavioral study (Price, Siegle, & Mohlman, 2012), participants were divided into low, moderate, and high groups on the basis of Penn State Worry Questionnaire scores (Meyer, Miller, Metzger, & Borkovec, 1990). General threat-related, neutral, and positive words were included, and two variants of the emotional Stroop were used: a simpler two-color version and a more difficult four-color version. Older adults in the high-worry group exhibited the expected bias toward threat words as well as a bias *away* from positive words, in the four-color version of the task, while older adults with low and moderate levels of worry exhibited patterns consistent with the positivity effect literature (biases toward positive and away from threat-related words). None of these effects was significant in the simpler, two-color version of the task, suggesting that task difficulty is another parameter modulating the emergence of attentional bias effects in older adults.

Attentional bias toward negative words on the emotional Stroop was replicated by these authors in a functional magnetic resonance imaging (fMRI) study of late-life GAD (Price, Eldreth, & Mohlman, 2011). Treatment-seeking GAD patients showed the expected bias toward negative words in comparison to non-anxious older adults. This behavioral bias was accompanied by decreased activation to negative words in several PFC regions associated with top-down cognitive control and emotion regulation. In addition, the non-anxious control group showed *decreased* amygdalar activation to negative (as compared to neutral) words, potentially consistent with an age-normative bias away from negative emotional processing, while the GAD group failed to show this pattern of amygdalar down-regulation. Both amygdalar and PFC activations were correlated with behavioral attentional bias across all subjects, but the relationship between amygdalar responses and behavioral bias was mediated by decreased dorsolateral PFC activation, suggesting that amygdalar reactions led to attentional bias only in the context of deficient top-down cognitive control.

Most recently, Steiner and colleagues (2013) assessed biases in the processing of negative and positive words in relation to responses to escitalopram pharmacotherapy in late-life GAD. During an affective go/no go test, a performance pattern reflecting efficient engagement with positive words and/or success in inhibiting negative distracters (specifically, faster responses to positive than negative *go* words) was associated with better response to medication over the course of a twelve-week treatment protocol. Although no non-anxious comparison group was included, these findings suggest that biases in processing of negative and positive information may be useful as clinical prognostic indicators.

Summary of Attentional Bias Studies

Studies to date support the notion that anxiety in later life is characterized by attentional bias toward threat, similar to the effect seen in anxious younger adults. Thus the positivity effect reported in the cognitive aging literature appears to be modulated by anxiety, with anxiety-related effects trumping age-normative goals related to maintaining a pleasant mood state. However, task difficulty, stimulus duration (masked or unmasked), stimulus modality (pictures, faces, or words), participants' mood state (neutral or negative), the specific paradigm used (emotional Stroop or dot probe), and the severity of participant anxiety (moderate or high levels) have all been shown to influence the presence or absence of attentional bias in older adult studies to date. Interestingly, attentional bias effects have been most reliably observed when the emotional Stroop task has been used. While the emotional Stroop task has sometimes been described as a less pure measure of visual attention *per se* compared to other alternatives (e.g., the dot-probe task), a benefit of the task is that it allows for bias to be assessed on whatever time frame is suited to the participant's overall processing speed. By contrast, the dot-probe task, which has produced relatively mixed findings in older adult studies to date, provides a "snapshot" of bias assessed at a single point in time (the point at which the threat or neutral stimulus is first replaced by the probe). Given decreased overall processing speed and increased heterogeneity of processing speed in late life (Salthouse, 2000), it may be beneficial to assess attentional bias in older adults using tasks that flexibly accommodate a range of processing speeds rather than assessing attention at a fixed point in time.

Limitations of Attentional Bias Studies

Although the studies to date provide preliminary evidence for the relevance of attentional bias to late-life anxiety, further replication, particularly in larger samples, is clearly needed in light of the mixed findings reported across different paradigms and stimulus types. It is currently uncertain whether attentional bias varies as a function of time course in older adults. Given normative changes in overall processing speed across the life span (Salthouse, 2000), it is probable that the time course of attentional bias in anxious older adults will be distinct from that observed in other age groups, as suggested by the sole study exploring this issue. Future research in older adults may benefit from the use of methods capable of assessing attention continuously from the onset of a threat stimulus until its offset at a later point in time (e.g., eyetracking technology) in order to better delineate the potential influence of time on older adults' attention to threat.

Second, consistent with a neurocognitive perspective, attentional bias research in late-life anxiety would benefit from additional exploration of the neural mechanisms underlying this clinically relevant behavioral phenomenon. Explication of the pathway from brain activity to behavior could help point the way to novel treatment strategies and synergistic combinations of treatment approaches. For instance, perhaps in the future, attentional bias could be "repaired" in anxious older adults through a combination of behavioral strategies (such as attention retraining) and direct targeting of relevant brain structures through approaches such as neurofeedback (i.e., providing continuous operant feedback about the level of activation in target brain structures) or neurostimulation (e.g., transcranial magnetic stimulation, a technology that provides the ability to acutely modulate brain activity in a localized target area of the cerebral cortex). Furthermore, this line of research might provide the opportunity to personalize treatment by tailoring interventions to the specific brain mechanisms relevant to an individual patient's anxiety.

Finally, a critical and clinically relevant question that remains unanswered is whether attentional bias toward threat is malleable in anxious older adults as it appears to be in anxious younger adults, and if so, whether attentional bias modification (ABM) intervention strategies will be effective at decreasing anxiety in late-life samples. Given normative decreases across the adult life span in "fluid intelligence" abilities underlying acquisition of new skills and learning new tasks (Park et al., 2002), it is possible that attention retraining procedures will require modification before they can be used effectively to treat anxiety in late-life patients. For instance, learning to decrease attention to threat may require increased repetition, a slower pace of practice, or pharmacological enhancement of learning ability (e.g., through use of acute learning-enhancement agents with relevance to emotional learning, such as a D-cycloserine; Behar, McHugh, Peckham, & Otto, 2010) in order to help increase acquisition, retention, and generalization of the new attentional pattern. To our knowledge, no studies have yet tested ABM, either in its standard format or in an age-specific format, as an intervention for late-life anxiety.

Treatment Outcome in Clinical Groups

Treatment for anxiety with either pharmacological or psychosocial methods has been shown to improve cognitive performance. For example, Lenze and colleagues (2011) demonstrated that effective reduction of peak salivary cortisol in a subset of eight of twenty-eight older GAD patients over twelve weeks of treatment with escitalopram was associated with improvement in immediate and delayed memory scores. There was no such association in the placebo group or the remaining participants in the active treatment group, nor were significant relations found between cortisol change and ES task improvement in either group. The authors argue that regulation of HPA-axis function might be the mechanism of this observed relation.

Butters and colleagues (2011) hypothesized that older GAD patients would perform more poorly than controls on tests of attention, processing speed, memory, and ES; however, improvement after pharmacological treatment was expected. Sixty-six participants with low baseline scores on the RBANS (Randolph, 1998) completed a trial of escitalopram. The treated subgroup (n = thirty) showed significantly more improvement than controls on the RBANS sorting task. When results were analyzed using reduction in anxiety rather than treatment group as the independent variable, improvement was observed on RBANS immediate and delayed recall and Stroop (Trenerry, Crosson, DeBoe, & Leber, 1989) performance. This is evidence for the role of improvement in anxious mood (as opposed to a particular type of intervention) as one mechanism for increased cognitive abilities after treatment for anxiety.

In a trial of CBT for late-life GAD and ES, Mohlman (2013b) predicted a significant association of Verbal ES (average combined t-score of COWAT, VPA Total, Stroop Interference, Digit Span Backward) to clinical outcome measures due to the intervention's reliance on verbal processing. Verbal ES were related in a predictable manner to most outcome measures, specifically, homework compliance; dropout; evidence and effectiveness in cognitive restructuring. Although not expected, Nonverbal ES (average combined t-score of Traill Making B, Matrix Logic, Digit Symbol) were also related to dropout and the effectiveness of cognitive restructuring. Further, those with intact or improved ES had better therapeutic outcome than those with low overall ES.

A small but growing literature suggests a relation of ES and CBT in late life (Johnco et al., 2013; Mohlman, 2008, 2013b). Mohlman and Gorman (2005) tested thirty-two older GAD patients with intact versus borderline impaired to impaired ES treated with either CBT or assigned to a wait list condition. Results showed that seven with initially low scores showed meaningful ES increases after CBT for GAD, and five did not. In a small sample comparing CBT alone to CBT plus ES rehabilitation training for those with late-life GAD and low ES at baseline, both groups improved on ES; however, those in the combined treatment group showed far greater gains. Based on these investigations, the authors argue that CBT may involve ES; thus, those who enter treatment with weak abilities may show lower rates of response than those whose ES are intact. However, a subset will show ES improvement through the mechanism of improved mood, while others might show deficits that are more stable, even after the reduction of anxiety. Some may thus be in need of intentional cognitive enhancement prior to the start of CBT or other interventions to ensure optimal reduction of symptoms (Mohlman, 2008).

Similar findings have also been supported in older adults with hoarding disorder, where cognitive training targeting ES deficits plus CBT doubled the response rate as compared with standard CBT (Ayers, Wetherell, et al., 2013). Furthermore, a recent investigation of older analog participants demonstrated that lower ES on tests of cognitive flexibility predicts cognitive restructuring ability, a standard component of CBT for anxiety (Johnco et al., 2013).

Summary and Limitations of Treatment Outcome Studies

These results are promising in terms of guiding development of future interventions, although more research in this area is needed before cognitive measures can be recommended in the process of treatment planning or before interventions targeting anxious mood are indicated as first-line treatment for those with weak cognitive skills. The existing evidence suggests that these are possible outcomes. The mitigation of anxiety led to cognitive gains in studies by Butters and colleagues (2011), Mohlman and Gorman (2005), and Mohlman (2013b). In summary, there is a nascent body of evidence supporting the hypothesis that improving anxious mood can enhance ES and that improving ES can lead to enhanced therapy outcome. Nevertheless, the reliability of these findings could depend partly on methodology. Notably, in one study of late-life GAD, the ES domain of the MMSE (measured with one of two items) did not predict six-month treatment outcome in CBT, although baseline orientation errors did (Caudle et al., 2007). Additional studies should aim to specify which ES are most relevant to treatment response across a range of interventions.

Discussion

The first wave of literature on neurocognitive aspects of late-life anxiety has yielded several notable findings. First, anxiety, particularly when it presents subclinically, is associated with cognitive decrements in learning, memory, attentional control, and inhibition. More specifically, elevations on worry, general anxiety, and phobic fear predict problems with visual and verbal memory. However, affective symptoms of anxiety may show a stronger relation to cognition than either worry or somatic symptoms. Studies of older clinical patients focus mostly on GAD and reveal deficits in verbal and nonverbal short- and long-term memory. There is limited evidence for decrements on working memory, problem solving, mental flexibility, and conceptual reasoning in late-life GAD, and the majority of studies show no decrements on ES tasks in older adults with anxiety disorders relative to age-matched controls.

The attentional bias literature in older adults broadly suggests that anxious older adults resemble anxious younger adults in preferentially allocating attention toward threatening or negative information. Preferential attention toward *positive* information, sometimes shown to characterize older adults on the whole, therefore appears to be overridden in anxious older adults by a more tenacious bias toward negative stimuli. However, the number of studies examining this issue in older adults is vastly smaller compared to those in younger samples, and mixed findings are prevalent, suggesting the need for further research. Studies on attentional bias in late-life anxiety exemplify the manner in which a neurocognitive approach, utilizing cognitive science and neuroscience methodologies, can yield new insights into the substrates of a clinically relevant phenomenon.

Neurocognitive markers, identified through neuropsychological and attentional bias tasks, are especially in need of further study as predictors of clinical outcome. Baseline cognitive abilities such as memory and ES potentially identify subgroups of older patients who will and will not benefit from therapeutic interventions. A small number of treatment studies (also

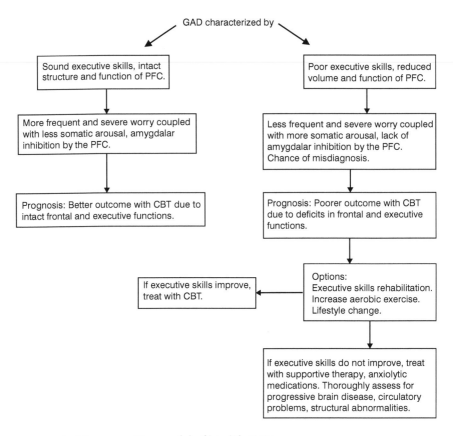

FIGURE 5.1   Neurocognitive model of late life GAD.

limited to GAD patients) suggest that anxiety reduction regardless of treatment type (i.e., pharmacological versus psychosocial) can lead to improved cognitive abilities; and enhancing cognitive abilities, such as ES, can enhance therapy outcome.

Studies by Mohlman (2008), Ayers and colleagues (Ayers, Saxena, et al., 2013; Ayers, Wetherell, et al., 2013), as well as Mohlman's nascent model (see Figure 5.1) illustrate how neurocognitive characteristics of anxious older patients could be translated into clinical research aimed at improving clinical response.

These early findings underscore the importance of assessing cognitive abilities and perhaps neural activity and connectivity before, during, and after treatment to effectively improve functioning. Clinicians working with anxious older adults may wish to bear in mind the potential impact that idiosyncratic neurocognitive patterns (e.g., attentional biases, ES deficits) may have on the course of treatment and consider integrating novel neurocognitive approaches (e.g., cognitive training/remediation) with conventional approaches (as suggested in Figure 5.1), in order to target symptoms in a given older adult most effectively. Future directions for research include pre- and posttreatment changes in brain circuitry or psychophysiology, a direction that might delineate biological models of geriatric anxiety and cognitive functioning. Preliminary behavioral and neurobiological findings discussed herein implicate new directions for clinical assessment and intervention approaches, which will certainly contribute to the evolution of our understanding of anxiety in later life.

References

Albert, M., Smith, L. A., Scherr, P. A., Taylor, J. O., Evans, D. A., & Funkenstein, H. H. (1991). Use of brief cognitive tests to identify individuals in the community with clinically diagnosed Alzheimer's disease. *International Journal of Neuroscience, 57*, 167–178.

American Psychiatric Association. (2013). *Diagnostic and statistical manual of mental disorders* (5th edn). Arlington, VA: American Psychiatric Publishing.

Andreescu, C. G., Lenze, J. J., Edelman, E., Snyder, K. D., Tanase, S., & Howard, C. A. (2011). Altered cerebral blood flow patterns associated with pathologic worry in the elderly. *Depression and Anxiety, 28*, 202–209.

Andreescu, C. G., Wu, M., Butters, M. A., Figurski, J., Reynolds, C. F. III, & Aizenstein, H. J. (2011). The default mode network in late-life anxious depression. *American Journal of Geriatric Psychiatry, 19*, 980–983.

Ayers, C. R., Sorrell, J. T., Thorp, S. R., & Wetherell, J. L. (2007). Evidence-based psychological treatments for late-life anxiety. *Psychology and Aging, 22*, 8–17.

Ayers, C. R., Saxena, S., Espejo, E., Twamley, E. W., Granholm, E., & Wetherell, J. L. (2013). Novel treatment for geriatric hoarding disorder: An open trial of cognitive rehabilitation paired with behavior therapy. *American Journal of Geriatric Psychiatry, 22*(3), 248–252.

Ayers, C. R., Wetherell, J. L., Schiehser, D., Almklov, E., Golshan, S., & Saxena, S. (2013). Executive functioning in older adults with hoarding disorder. *International Journal of Geriatric Psychiatry, 28*(11), 1175–1181.

Baddeley, A. (1990). *Human memory: Theory and practice.* Boston, MA: Allyn and Bacon.

Baddeley, A. D. (1986). *Working memory*. Oxford Psychology Series, No. 11. Oxford: Clarendon Press.

Banich, M. T., Milham, M. P., Atchley, R. A., Cohen, N. J., Webb, A., Wszalek, T., … & Brown, C. (2000). Prefrontal regions play a predominant role in imposing and attentional 'set': Evidence from fMRI. *Cognitive Brain Research, 10*, 1–9.

Bar-Haim, Y., Lamy, D., Pergamin, L., Bakermans-Kranenburg, M. J., & Van IJzendoorn, M. H. (2007). Threat-related attentional bias in anxious and nonanxious individuals: A meta-analytic study. *Psychological Bulletin, 133*, 1–24.

Bartolic, E. I., Basso, M. R., Schefft, B. K., Glauser, T., & Titanic-Schefft, M. (1999). Effects of experimentally-induced states on frontal love cognitive task performance. *Neuropsychologia, 37*, 677–683.

Basevitz, P., Pushkar, D., Chaikelson, J., Conway, M., & Dalton, C. (2008). Age-related differences in worry and related processes. *The International Journal of Aging & Human Development, 66*(4), 283–305.

Beaudreau, S. A., & O'Hara, R. (2008). Late-life anxiety and cognitive impairment: A review. *American Journal of Geriatric Psychiatry, 16*, 790–803.

Beaudreau, S. A., & O'Hara, R. (2009). The association of anxiety and depressive symptoms with cognitive performance in community-dwelling older adults. *Psychology of Aging, 24*, 507–512.

Beaudreau, S. A., MacKay-Brandt, A., & Reynolds, J. (2013). Application of a cognitive neuroscience perspective of cognitive control to late life anxiety. *Journal of Anxiety Disorders, 27*, 559–566.

Beauregard, M., Levesque, J., & Bourgouin, P. (2000). Neural correlates of conscious self-regulation of emotion. *Journal of Neuroscience, 21*, 1–6.

Beck A. T., & Steer, R. (1993). *Beck Anxiety Inventory manual* (2nd edn). San Antonio, TX: Psychological Corporation.

Behar, E., McHugh, R. K., Peckham, A., & Otto, M. W. (2010). D-cycloserine for the augmentation of an attentional training intervention for trait anxiety. *Journal of Anxiety Disorders, 24*, 440–445.

Bierman, E. J., Comijs, H. C., Jonker, C., & Beekman, A. T. (2005). Effects of anxiety versus depression on cognition in later life. *American Journal of Geriatric Psychiatry, 13*, 686–693.

Biringer, E., Mykletun, A., Dahl, A. A., Smith, A. D., Enegdal, K., Nygaard, H. A., & Lund, A. (2005). The association between depression, anxiety, and cognitive functions in the elderly general population—The Hordaland Health Study. *International Journal of Geriatric Psychiatry, 20*, 989–997.

Boddice, G., Pachana, N. A., & Byrne, G. J. (2008). This clinical utility of the geriatric anxiety inventory in older adults with cognitive impairment. *Nursing Older People, 20*, 36–39.

Booth, J. E., Schinka, J. A., Brown, L. M., Mortimer, J. A., & Borenstein, A. R. (2006). Five- factor personality dimensions, mood states, and cognitive performance in older adults. *Journal of Clinical and Experimental Neuropsychology, 28*, 676–683.

Borkovec, T. D. (1994). The nature, functions, and origins of worry. In G. Davey & F. Tallis (Eds.), *Worrying: Perspectives on theory, assessment and treatment* (pp. 5–33). Chichester: Wiley.

Brandt, J., Spencer, M., & Folstein, M. (1988). The telephone interview for cognitive status. *Neuropsychiatry, Neuropsychology, and Behavioral Neurology, 1*, 111–117.

Braver, T. S., & West, R. (2008). Working memory, executive control, and aging. In F. I. M. Craik & T. A. Salthouse (Eds.), *The handbook of aging and cognition* (pp. 311–372). New York, NY: Psychology Press.

Brown, L., White, P., Doan, J., & de Bruin, N. (2011). Selective attentional processing to fall-relevant stimuli among older adults who fear falling. *Experimental Aging Research, 37*, 330–345.

Bryant, C. (2010). Anxiety depression in old age: Challenges in recognition and diagnosis. *International Psychogeriatrics, 22*, 511–513.

Bryant, C., Jackson, H., & Ames, D. (2008). The prevalence of anxiety in older adults: Methodological issues and a review of the literature. *Journal of Affective Disorders, 109*, 233–250.

Burri, A., Maercker, A., Krammer, S., & Simmen-Janevska, K. (2013). Childhood trauma and PTSD symptoms increase the risk of cognitive impairment in a sample of former indentured child laborers in old age. *PLoS ONE, 8*, e57826.

Butters, M. A., Bhalla, R. K., Andreescu, C., Wetherell, J. L., Mantella, R., Begley, A. E., & Lenze, E. J. (2011). Changes in neuropsychological functioning following treatment for late-life generalized anxiety disorder. *British Journal of Psychiatry, 199*, 211–218.

Butters, M. A., Young, J. B., Lopez, O., Aizenstein, H. J., Mulsant, B. H., Reynolds, C. F., & Becker, J. T. (2008). Pathways linking late-life depression to persistent cognitive impairment and dementia. *Dialogues of Clinical Neuroscience, 10*, 343–357.

Carstensen, L. L., Isaacowitz, D. M., & Charles, S. T. (1999). Taking time seriously. A theory of socioemotional selectivity. *American Psychologist, 54*, 165–181.

Caudle, D. D., Senior, A. C., Wetherell, J. L., Rhoades, H. M., Beck, J. G., Kunik, M. E., … & Stanley, M. A. (2007). Cognitive errors, symptom severity, and response to cognitive behavior therapy in older adults with generalized anxiety disorder. *American Journal of Geriatric Psychiatry, 15*, 680–689.

Crown, S., & Crisp, A. H. (1966). A short clinical diagnostic self-rating scale for psychoneurotic patients. The Middlesex Hospital Questionnaire (M.H.Q.). *British Journal of Psychiatry, 112*, 917–923.

deBruijn, R. F. A. G., Direk, N., Mirza, S. S., Hofman, A., Koudstaal, P. J., Tiemeier, H., & Ikram, M. A. (2014). Anxiety is not associated with the risk of dementia or cognitive decline: The Rotterdam Study. *American Journal of Geriatric Psychiatry.* DOI: 10.1016/j.jagp.2014.03.001

Deelman, B. G., Brouwer, W. H., van Zomeren, A. H., & Saan, R. J. (1980). Functiestoornissen na trauma capitis [Cognitive impairment after trauma capitis]. In A. Jennekens-Schinkel, J. J. Diamant, H. B. A. Diesfeldt, & R. Haaxma (Eds), *Neuropsychologie in Nederland [Neuropsychology in the Netherland]* (pp. 253–281). Deventer: Van Loghum Slaterus.

DeFries, J. C., Plomin, R., Vandenberg, S. G., & Kuse, A. R. (1981). Parent–offspring resemblance for cognitive abilities in the Colorado Adoption Project: Biological, adoptive, and control parents and one-year-old children. *Intelligence, 5*, 245–277.

Delis, D. C., Kaplan, E., & Kramer, J. H. (2001). *Delis-Kaplan Executive Function System.* San Antonio, TX: Psychological Corporation.

Delis, D. C., Kramer, J. H., Kaplan, E., & Ober, B. A. (2000). *California Verbal Learning Test–Second Edition, Adult Version manual.* San Antonio, TX: The Psychological Corporation.

DeLuca, A. K., Lenze, E. J., Mulsant, B. H., Butters, M. A., Karp, J. F., Dew, M. A., & Reynolds, C. F., 3rd. (2005). Comorbid anxiety disorder in late life depression: Association with memory decline over four years. *International Journal of Geriatric Psychiatry, 20*, 848–854.

Deptula, D., Singh, R., & Pomara, N. (1993). Aging, emotional states, and memory. *American Journal of Psychiatry, 150*, 429–434.

Dureman, I., Kebbon, L., & Osterberg, E. (1971). *Manual till DS-Batteriet* [Manual of the DS-Battery]. Stockholm, Sweden: Psykologi Förlaget.

Eysenck, M. W. (1992). *Anxiety: The cognitive perspective.* Chichester: Erlbaum.

Eysenck, M. W., Derakshan, N., Santos, R., & Calvo, M. G. (2007). Anxiety and cognitive performance: Attentional control theory. *Emotion, 7*, 336–353.

Folstein, M. F., Folstein, S. E., & McHugh, P. R. (1975). Mini-mental state: A practical method for grading the cognitive state of patients for the clinician. *Journal of Psychiatric Research, 12*, 189–198.

Fox, L. S., & Knight, B. G. (2005). The effects of anxiety on attentional processes in older adults. *Aging and Mental Health, 9*, 585–593.

Frost, R. O., & Hartl, T. L. (1996). A cognitive-behavioral model of compulsive hoarding. *Behaviour Research and Therapy, 34,* 341–350.

Golden, C. J. (1978). *Stroop Color and Word Test.* Chicago, IL: Stoelting.

Gotlib, I. H., & McCann, C. D. (1984). Construct accessibility and depression: An examination of cognitive and affective factors. *Journal of Personality and Social Psychology, 47,* 427–439.

Gould, C. E., & Edelstein, B. A. (2010). Worry, emotion control, and anxiety control in old and young adults. *Journal of Anxiety Disorders, 24,* 759–766.

Gould, R. L., Coulson, M. C., & Howard, R. J. (2012). Efficacy of cognitive behavioral therapy for anxiety disorders in older people: A meta-analysis and meta-regression of randomized controlled trials. *Journal of the American Geriatrics Society, 60,* 218–229.

Gross, J. J., & John, O. P. (2003). Individual differences in two emotion regulation processes: Implications for affect, relationships, and well-being. *Journal of Personality and Social Psychology, 85,* 348–362.

Hogan, M. J. (2003). Divided attention in older but not younger adults is impaired by anxiety. *Experimental Aging Research, 29,* 111–136.

Humphreys, M. S., & Revelle, W. (1984). Personality, motivation, and performance: A theory of the relationship between individual differences and information processing. *Psychological Review, 91,* 153–184.

Hynninen, M. J., Breitve, M. H., Rongve, A., Aarsland, D., & Nordhus, I. H. (2012). The frequency and correlates of anxiety in patients with first-time diagnosed mild dementia. *International Psychogeriatrics, 24,* 1771–1778.

Isaacowitz, D. M., Allard, E. S., Murphy, N. A., & Schlangel, M. (2009). The time course of age-related preferences toward positive and negative stimuli. *The Journal of Gerontology. Series B, Psychological Sciences and Social Sciences, 64,* 188–192.

Isaacowitz, D. M., Wadlinger, H. A., Goren, D., & Wilson, H. R. (2006). Is there an age-related positivity effect in visual attention? A comparison of two methodologies. *Emotion, 6,* 511–516.

Johnco, C., Wuthrich, V. M., & Rapee, R. M. (2013). The role of cognitive flexibility in cognitive restructuring skill acquisition among older adults. *Journal of Anxiety Disorders, 27,* 576–584.

Jonsson, C-O., & Molander, L. (1964). *Manual till CVB-skalan [Manual of the CVB-Scales].* Stockholm: Psykologi Förlaget.

Kalache, A., Baretto, S., & Keller, I. (2005). Global ageing: The demographic revolution in all cultures and societies. In M. Johnson (Ed.), *The Cambridge handbook of age and ageing* (pp. 30–46). Cambridge, UK: Cambridge University Press.

Kunzmann, U., Kupperbusch, C. S., & Levenson, R. W. (2005). Behavioral inhibition and amplification during emotional arousal: A comparison of two age groups. *Psychology and Aging, 20,* 144–158.

Lee, L. O., & Knight, B. G. (2009). Attentional bias for threat in older adults: Moderation of the positivity bias by trait anxiety and stimulus modality. *Psychology and Aging, 24,* 741–747.

Lenze, E. J., Mohlman, J., & Wetherell, J. L. (2014). Anxiety disorders. In D. Blazer, D. Steffens, & M. Thakur (Eds.) *Textbook of geriatric psychiatry.* Washington, DC: American Psychiatric Association.

Lenze, E. J., Mantella, R. C., Shi, P., Goate, A. M., Nowotny, P., Butters, M. A., & Rollman, B. L. (2011). Elevated cortisol in older adults with generalized anxiety disorder is reduced by treatment: A placebo-controlled evaluation of escitalopram. *American Journal of Geriatric Psychiatry*, *19*, 482–490.

Levenson, R. W. (2000). Expressive, physiological, and subjective changes in emotion. In S. H. Qualls & N. Abeles (Eds.), *Psychology and the aging revolution: How we adapt to longer life* (pp. 123–140). Washington, DC: American Psychological Association.

Mackin, R. S., Areán, P. A., Delucchi, K. L., & Mathews, C. A. (2011). Cognitive functioning in individuals with severe compulsive hoarding behaviors and late life depression. *International Journal of Geriatric Psychiatry*, *26*, 314–321.

Mantella, R. C., Butters, M. A., Dew, M. A., Mulsant, B. H., Begley, A. E., Tracey, B., & Lenze, E. (2007). Cognitive impairment in late-life generalized anxiety disorder. *American Journal of Geriatric Psychiatry*, *15*, 673–679.

Mather, M., & Carstensen, L. L. (2003). Aging and attentional biases for emotional faces. *Psychological Science*, *14*, 409–415.

Mattis, S. (1988). *Dementia Rating Scale: Professional manual.* Odessa, FL: Psychological Assessment Resources, Inc.

Meyer, T. J., Miller, M. L., Metzger, R. L., & Borkovec, T. D. (1990). Development and validation of the Penn State Worry Questionnaire. *Behaviour Research and Therapy*, *28*, 487–495.

Mogg, K., Bradley, B. P., Miles, F., & Dixon, R. (2004). Time course of attentional bias for threat scenes: Testing the vigilance-avoidance hypothesis. *Cognition and Emotion*, *18*, 689–700.

Mohlman, J. (2004). Attention training as an intervention for anxiety: Review and rationale. *The Behavior Therapist*, *27*, 37–41.

Mohlman, J. (2005). Does executive dysfunction affect treatment outcome in late-life mood and anxiety disorders? *Journal of Geriatric Psychiatry and Neurology*, *18*, 97–108.

Mohlman, J. (2008). More power to the executive? A preliminary test of CBT plus executive skills training for treatment of late-life GAD. *Cognitive and Behavioral Practice*, *15*, 306–316.

Mohlman, J. (2013a). Late life anxiety and cognitive processes—We are rapidly gaining momentum; Introduction to the special issue. *Journal of Anxiety Disorders*, *27*, 547–549.

Mohlman, J. (2013b). Executive skills in older adults with GAD: Relations with clinical variables and CBT outcome. *Journal of Anxiety Disorders*, *27*, 131–139.

Mohlman, J., & Gorman, J. M. (2005). The role of executive functioning in CBT: A pilot study with anxious older adults. *Behaviour Research and Therapy*, *43*, 447–465.

Mohlman, J., Eldreth, D., Price, R. B., & Hanson, C. (2009) Shared neural pathways of worry and CBT in late life generalized anxiety disorder. Paper at 43rd Annual Conference of the Association for Behavioral and Cognitive Therapies, New York, November.

Mohlman, J., Price, D. A., Chazin, R. B., Glover, D., & Dorie, A. (2012). Predictors of unsuccessful magnetic resonance imaging scanning in older generalized anxiety disorder patients and controls. *Journal of Behavioral Medicine*, *35*, 19–26.

Mohlman, J., Sirota, K. G., Papp, L. A., Staples, A. M., King, A., & Gorenstein, E. E. (2012). Clinical interviewing with older adults. *Cognitive & Behavioral Practice*, *19*(1), 89–100.

Norman, D. A., & Shallice, T. (1986). Attention to action: Willed and automatic control of behavior. In R. J. Davidson, G. E. Schwarts, & D. Shapiro (Eds.), *Consciousness and self-regulation: Advances in research and therapy* (pp. 1–18). New York: Plenum Press.

Okereke, O. I., & Grodstein, F. (2013). Phobic anxiety and cognitive performance over 4 years among community-dwelling older women in the nurses' health study. *American Journal of Geriatric Psychiatry, 21*, 1125–1134.

Park, D., Lautenschlager, G., Hedden, T., Davidson, N., Smith, A., & Smith, P. (2002). Models of visuospatial and verbal memory across the adult life span. *Psychology and Aging, 17*, 299–320.

Paulesu, E., Sambugaro, E., Torti, T., Danelli, L., Ferri, F., Scialfa, G., ... & Sassaroli, S. (2010). Neural correlates of worry in generalized anxiety disorder and in normal controls: A functional MRI study. *Psychological Medicine, 40*, 117–124.

Pietrzak, R. H., Maruff, P., Woodward, M., Fredrickson, J., Fredrickson, A., Krystal, J. H., & Darby, D. (2012). Mild worry symptoms predict decline in learning and memory in healthy older adults: A 2-year prospective cohort study. *American Journal of Geriatric Psychiatry, 20*, 266–275. Erratum in: *American Journal of Geriatric Psychiatry, 20*, 634.

Pinquart, M., & Duberstein, P. R. (2007). Treatment of anxiety disorders in older adults: A meta-analytic comparison behavioral and pharmacological interventions. *The American Journal of Geriatric Psychiatry, 15*, 639–651.

Potvin, O., Hudon, C., Dion, M., Grenier, S., & Préville, M. (2011). Anxiety disorders, depressive episodes and cognitive impairment no dementia in community-dwelling older men and women. *International Journal of Geriatric Psychiatry, 26*, 1080–1088.

Price, R. B., & Mohlman, J. (2007). Inhibitory control and symptom severity in late life generalized anxiety disorder. *Behavior Research and Therapy, 45*, 2628–2639.

Price, R. B., Eldreth, D. A., & Mohlman, J. (2011). Deficient prefrontal attentional control in late-life generalized anxiety disorder: An fMRI investigation. *Translational Psychiatry, 1*, e46.

Price, R. B., Siegle, G., & Mohlman, J. (2012). Emotional Stroop performance in older adults: Effects of habitual worry. *American Journal of Geriatric Psychiatry, 20*, 798–805.

Randolph, C. (1998). *Repeatable Battery for the Assessment of Neuropsychological Status*. San Antonio, TX: The Psychological Corporation.

Raven, J. C. (1995). *Manual for the Coloured Progressive Matrices Test (Revised)*. Windsor: NFRE-Nelson.

Raz, N. (2000). Aging of the brain and its impact on cognitive performance: Integration of structural and functional findings. In F. I. M. Craik & T. A. Salthouse (Eds.), *The handbook of aging and cognition* (2nd edn) (pp. 1–90). Mahwah, NJ: Lawrence Erlbaum Associates.

Raz, N., Rodrigue, K. M., Williamson, A., & Acker, J. D. (2004). Aging, sexual dimorphism, and hemispheric asymmetry of the cerebral cortex: Replicability of regional differences in volume. *Neurobiology of Aging, 25*, 377–396.

Rey A. (1964). *L'Examen clinique en psychologie [Clinical examination in psychology]*. Paris: Presses Universitaires de France.

Rigler, S. K., Studenski, S., & Duncan, P. W. (1998). Pharmacologic treatment of geriatric depression: Key issues in interpreting the evidence. *Journal of the American Geriatrics Society, 46*, 106–110.

Salthouse, T. A. (1994). How many causes are there of aging-related decrements in cognitive functioning? *Developmental Review, 14*, 413–437.

Salthouse, T. A. (2000). Aging and measures of processing speed. *Biological Psychology, 54*, 35–54.

Salthouse, T. A. (2010a). *Major issues in cognitive aging*. New York: Oxford University Press.

Salthouse, T. A. (2010b). Selective review of cognitive aging. *Journal of the International Neuropsychological Society, 16*(05), 754–760.

Salzman, C., & Lebowitz, B. D. (1991) *Anxiety in the elderly: Treatment and research*. New York, NY: Springer Publishing.

Samuels, J. F., Bienvenu, O. J., Grados, M. A., Cullen, B., Riddle, M. A., Liang, K-Y., & Nestadt, G. (2008). Prevalence and correlates of hoarding behavior in a community-based sample. *Behaviour Research and Therapy, 46*, 836–844.

Sapolsky, R. M. (2000). Glucocorticoids and hippocampal atrophy in neuropsychiatric disorders. *Archives of General Psychiatry, 57*, 925–935.

Savage, R. D. (1984). *Alphabet Coding Task 15*. Western Australia: Murdoch University.

Schmeichel, B. J. (2007). Attention control, memory updating, and emotion regulation temporarily reduce the capacity for executive control. *Journal of Experimental Psychology: General, 136*, 241–255.

Schuitevoerder, S., Rosen, J. W., Twamley, E. W., Ayers, C. R., Sones, H., Lohr, J. B.,… & Thorp, S. R. (2013). A meta-analysis of cognitive functioning older adults with PTSD. *Journal of Anxiety Disorders, 27*(6), 550–558.

Schutzer, K. A., & Graves, B. S. (2004). Barriers and motivations to exercise in older adults. *An International Journal Devoted to Practice and Theory, 39*, 1056–1061.

Sinoff, G., & Werner, P. (2003). Anxiety disorder and accompanying subjective memory loss in the elderly as a predictor of future cognitive decline. *International Journal of Geriatric Psychiatry, 18*, 951–959.

Skarborn, M. & Nicki, R. (2000). Worry in pre- and post-retirement persons. *The International Journal of Aging & Human Development, 50*, 61–71.

Spielberger, C. D., Gorsuch, R. L., Lushene, R., Vagg, P. R., & Jacobs, G. A. (1983). *Manual for the State-Trait Anxiety Inventory (Form Y Self-evaluation Questionnaire)*. Palo Alto, CA: Consulting Psychologists Press.

Steiner, A., Petkus, A., Nguyen, H., & Wetherell, J. L. (2013). Information processing bias and pharmacotherapy outcome in older adults with generalized anxiety disorder. *Journal of Anxiety Disorders, 27*(6), 592–597.

Thorp, S. R., Ayers, C. R., Nuevo, R., Stoddard, J. A., Sorrell, J. T., & Wetherell, J. L. (2009). Meta-analysis comparing different behavioral treatments for late-life anxiety. *American Journal of Geriatric Psychiatry, 17*, 105–115.

Trenerry, M. R., Crosson, B., DeBoe, J., & Leber, W. R. (1989). *Stroop Neuropsychological Screening Test manual*. Odessa, FL: Psychological Assessment Resources, Inc.

Tromp, D. P. M., Grupe, D. W., Oathes, D. J., McFarlin, D. R., Hernandez, P. J., Kral, T. R. A., … & Nitschke, J. B. (2012). Reduced structural connectivity of a major frontolimbic pathway in generalized anxiety disorder. *JAMA Psychiatry, 69*, 925–934.

Urry, H. L., van Reekum, C. M., Johnstone, T., & Davidson, R. J. (2009). Individual differences in some (but not all) medial prefrontal regions reflect cognitive demand while regulating unpleasant emotion. *NeuroImage, 47*, 63S1–9.

Urry, H. L., van Reekum, C. M., Johnstone, T., Kalin, N. H., Thurow, M. E., Schaefer, H. S., … & Davidson, R. J. (2006). Amygdala and ventromedial prefrontal cortex are inversely coupled during regulation of negative affect and predict the diurnal pattern of cortisol secretion among older adults. *The Journal of Neuroscience, 26*, 4415–4425.

Wechsler, D. (1997). *Wechsler Adult Intelligence Scale* (3rd edn). San Antonio TX: Harcourt Assessment.

West, R. L. (1996). An application of prefrontal cortex function theory to cognitive aging. *Psychological Bulletin, 120*, 272–292.

Westrin, P. A. (1969). *WIT III manual*. Stockholm: Skandinaviska Test Förlaget.

Wetherell, J. L., Reynolds, C. A., Gatz, M., & Pedersen, N. L. (2002). Anxiety, cognitive performance, and cognitive decline in normal aging. *The Journals of Gerontology Series B, Psychological Sciences and Social Sciences, 57*, 246–255.

Wetherell, J. L., Ayers, C. R., Sorrell, J. T., Thorp, S. R., Nuevo, R., Belding, W., & Patterson, T. L. (2009). Modular psychotherapy for anxiety in older primary care patients. *The American Journal of Geriatric Psychiatry, 17*, 483–492.

Wilkes, C. M., Wilson, H. W., Woodard, J. L., & Calamari, J. E. (2013). Do negative affect characteristics and subjective memory concerns increase risk for late life anxiety? *Journal of Anxiety Disorders, 27*, 608–618.

Winecoff, A., LaBar, K. S., Madden, D. J., Cabeza, R., & Huettel, S. A. (2011). Cognitive and neural contributors to emotion regulation in aging. *Social Cognitive and Affective Neuroscience, 6*, 165–176.

Wolitzky-Taylor, K. B., Castriotta, N., Lenze, E. J., Stanley, M. A., & Craske, M. G. (2010). Anxiety disorders in older adults: A comprehensive review. *Depression and Anxiety, 27*, 190–211.

Yaffe, K., Vittinghoff, E., Lindquist, K., Barnes, D., Covinsky, K. E., Neylan, T., & Marmar, C. (2010). Posttraumatic stress disorder and risk of dementia among US veterans. *Archives of General Psychiatry, 67*, 608–613.

Yehuda, R., Golier, J. A., Tischler, L., Stavitsky, K., & Harvey, P. D. (2005). Learning and memory in aging combat veterans with PTSD. *Journal of Clinical and Experimental Neuropsychology, 27*, 504–515.

Yerkes, R. M., & Dodson, J. D. (1908). The relation of strength of stimulus of habit formation. *Journal of Comparative Neurology & Psychology, 18*, 459–482.

Yochim, B. P., Mueller, A. E., & Segal, D. L. (2013). Late life anxiety is associated with decreased memory and executive functioning in community dwelling older adults. *Journal of Anxiety Disorders, 27*, 567–575.

Zaudig, M. M., Hiller, J., & Pauls, W. (1991). SIDAM: A structured interview for the diagnosis of dementia of the Alzheimer type, multi-infarct dementia, and dementias of other aetiology according to ICD-10 and DSM-III-R. *Psychological Medicine, 21*, 225–236.

Zigmund, A. A., & Snaith, R. P. (1983). The Hospital Anxiety and Depression Scale. *Acta Psychiatrica Scandinavica, 67*, 361–370.

6

NEUROCOGNITIVE APPROACHES IN THE TREATMENT OF ADHD

Adam S. Weissman, Jocelyn Lichtin, and Allison P. Danzig

Attention-deficit/hyperactivity disorder (ADHD) is among the most common childhood neurodevelopmental disorders (Hale, Reddy, Weissman, Lukie, & Schneider, 2013). While it is natural for children to be energetic, exploratory, and distractible, ADHD is diagnosed in children for whom these qualities are extreme and impairing. Worldwide prevalence rates of ADHD approximate 5.3 percent (Polanczyk, de Lima, Horta, Beiderman, & Rohde, 2007), with current epidemiological reviews estimating rates ranging from 3 percent to 5 percent (American Psychiatric Association, 2013) to 17.8 percent, with boys constituting over 80 percent of all referrals (Rowland, Lesesne, & Abramowitz, 2002). ADHD symptom presentation is heterogeneous and includes inattention, impulsivity, and/or hyperactivity. These deficits are accompanied by poor executive functioning (EF), such as difficulty planning, organizing, self-monitoring, problem-solving, and shifting attention in a fluid and flexible manner (Hale et al., 2009). Symptoms present across multiple settings, contributing to impairment across social (e.g., problems with peer, family, and romantic relationships), behavioral (e.g., higher rates of car accidents, crime, unemployment, and substance abuse/dependence), and academic domains (e.g., school failure or dropout; Barkley, 1997; DuPaul & Stoner, 2003).

Despite decades of research on diagnostic assessment and both pharmacological and psychotherapeutic interventions for ADHD, many children with ADHD symptoms continue to be poorly identified and ineffectively treated (Molina et al., 2009). However, neuroscientifically informed assessment and intervention have the potential to augment and even transform the diagnosis and treatment of childhood disorders (Reddy, Weissman, & Hale, 2013; Richey et al., 2013). The goal of this chapter is to provide an integrated, clinical-neurocognitive perspective on ADHD and a review of empirically based, neuropsychologically informed methods, which may lead to a better understanding of how these alternative approaches can aid accurate diagnosis and safe, targeted, and effective treatment of children with ADHD. We begin with a review of ADHD symptom dimensions, neurocognitive/brain-based research and theory, and comorbidity patterns, with an emphasis on differential diagnosis of ADHD and other psychiatric disorders in children. We conclude with a comprehensive review of existing neurotherapeutic approaches for the treatment of ADHD that have received varying levels of empirical support.

Symptom Dimensions of ADHD

According to the *Diagnostic and Statistical Manual of Mental Disorders* (5th ed.), diagnosis of ADHD requires six symptoms of inattention and/or hyperactivity-impulsivity for a duration of at least six months, onset before the age of twelve, clinically significant impairment in two or more settings (e.g., home, school, work), and the occurrence of symptoms independent of the course of another disorder (American Psychiatric Association, 2013). Based on these criteria, the DSM-V identifies three subtypes of ADHD: predominantly inattentive type (IN), predominantly hyperactive-impulsive type (HI), and combined type (CO), the latter of which is most common and has received the most empirical attention (Gallagher & Rosenblatt, 2013).

Some researchers have posited that ADHD subtypes are associated with important differences, as the specific subtype may predict unique developmental trajectories. In particular, children who experience primarily IN symptoms are thought to represent a distinct subgroup from the CO group (Milich, Balentine, & Lynam, 2001). For example, children with ADHD who experience primarily IN symptoms tend to experience a later onset of symptoms relative to hyperactive children, usually between ages five to seven, with symptoms typically persisting throughout childhood before declining in adolescence (Drabick, Gadow, & Sprafkin, 2006). Additionally, the IN subtype primarily predicts academic problems, more so than comorbid externalizing symptoms. On the other hand, children with ADHD who present primarily with HI symptoms often experience earlier onset of the disorder (i.e., around ages three to four) and experience progressive symptom reduction into later childhood. Hyperactive children whose symptoms fail to significantly reduce in later childhood are at increased risk for developing conduct disorder. Finally, the CO subtype is the most severe and is associated with increased risk for future conduct problems.

Several noteworthy gender differences have been linked to specific ADHD subtypes. While males are more likely to experience HI symptoms, which are closely associated with social impairment, females are more likely to meet criteria for the IN subtype (Gershon, 2002), which is highly associated with shyness and comorbid internalizing symptoms (e.g., anxiety, depression; Drabick et al., 2006). These gender differences, paired with the distinct developmental trajectories associated with each subtype as described above, have led some to believe that ADHD IN and CO may constitute two distinct disorders (Milich et al., 2001), a theory supported by meta-analyses (Angold, Costello, & Erkanli, 1999).

Neurobiology of ADHD

Several neurobiological factors, including neurochemical regulation and brain structure, have been implicated in the etiology, development, and expression of ADHD (Durston, 2003). Catecholaminergic neurotransmitter systems are believed to play a central role in the pathophysiology of the disorder, with fronto-striatal dopaminergic pathways clearly implicated (Durston, 2003). Some have hypothesized that the hallmark cognitive and executive dysfunction associated with ADHD may arise from a hypodopaminergic state in the pre-frontal cortex (PFC), while hyperactivity may result secondarily from hyperdopaminergic states in the striatum (Durston, 2003). Research has also implicated the secondary involvement of the noradrenergic system in the pathophysiology of ADHD. However, these circuits may not be unique to ADHD, as individuals suffering from depression often exhibit low levels of dopamine, norepinephrine, and serotonin (Wagner & Ambrosini, 2001), which may account for overlapping deficits in attention and EF in depression (Mayberg, 2001). Therefore, differential diagnosis requires careful assessment of both attention and EF deficits specific to cortical-subcortical circuits and examination of behavioral manifestations of these disorders (Hale et al., 2013).

Studies examining brain structure via magnetic resonance imaging (MRI) have identified abnormalities in several fronto-striatal and frontal-subcortical networks in children with ADHD. Specifically, the dorsolateral structures of the prefrontal cortex, orbital frontal structures, basal ganglia (e.g., striatum, caudate nucleus, putamen), regions in the parietal lobe (e.g., somatosensory areas, attention-orienting areas), temporal lobes (e.g., hippocampus, amygdala), cerebellum (Cherkasova & Hechtman, 2009), anterior cingulate (Schulz et al., 2004), corpus callosum (Catherine, 1994), and white matter (Valera, Faraone, Murray, & Seidman, 2007) have all been identified as related to ADHD symptom expression. In addition, structural techniques have found that total brain volume in ADHD children may be upward of 5 percent smaller than matched controls, reporting marked reduction in prefrontal volume, predominantly in the right hemisphere (Castellanos et al., 2002). Functional MRI (fMRI) studies further highlight abnormalities in ADHD children, indicating decreased cerebral metabolism and hypoperfusion in frontal and striatal regions (Durston, 2003).

Although the clinical and pathogenetic implications of overall volume reduction remain unclear, abnormalities in the PFC have been associated with poor response inhibition, executive attention, and working memory, and deficits in the basal ganglia (e.g., caudate nucleus) have been linked to poor response inhibition, externalizing symptoms, and emotion dysregulation (Durston, 2003; Iversen & Dunnett, 1990). MRI results showing impairment in both specific and diffuse regions of the brain support the vastly heterogeneous clinical and neuropsychological presentation of ADHD across individuals (Durston, 2003).

In summary, compelling evidence suggests that ADHD may be associated with disruption of heterogeneous circuitry, most prominently involving fronto-striatal and cerebellar circuitry (Seidman, Valera, & Makris, 2005). More recently, findings of volumetric and functional differences have been augmented by developmentally sensitive imaging studies, exploring growth of brain regions over time. For instance, Shaw and colleagues (2007) have shown that while the brains of children with ADHD develop similarly to their neurotypical peers, significant maturational delays may be present within this trajectory. Specifically, the cortices of children with ADHD were markedly thinner than their same-aged peers' and comparable to neurotypical children two to three years their junior. Moreover, children with better outcomes demonstrated normalization within the right parietal cortex, whereas those with poorer outcomes showed "fixed" thinning of the left medial PFC.

Other researchers have similarly reported thinning, specifically within the dorsolateral prefrontal cortex, anterior cingulate, and inferior parietal lobe, to be linked to the persistence of ADHD symptoms into adulthood (Makris et al., 2007), whereas remission has been linked to thicker cortex in medial occipital, parahippocampal, insular, and prefrontal regions (Proal et al., 2011). Functionally speaking, growth of the anterior cingulate, striatum, and medial temporal cortex has elsewhere been associated with improved response inhibition in school-age children with ADHD (McAlonan et al., 2009), and more recently, improved neuropsychological test performance was associated with reductions in ADHD symptom severity among a sample of preschool children (Rajendran et al., 2013). Together, these studies indicate that normalization of brain anomalies or delays may be associated with disorder remission, whereas lack of normal maturation is predictive of persistence of ADHD throughout development (Halperin & Healey, 2011). It is thus conceivable that therapies targeting core neurodevelopmental processes via enrichment early in life could potentially alter the trajectory of brain development and, consequently, the course of ADHD (Halperin, Bedard, & Curchack-Lichtin, 2012).

Prevailing Neurocognitive Perspectives on ADHD

Prevailing neurocognitive theories of ADHD have highlighted the role of EF, attention, behavioral inhibition, working memory, and delay aversion in the neurocognitive and behavioral impairments associated with ADHD.

Executive Functioning

Executive functioning problems have been studied extensively in children with a variety of clinical disorders, but most of all, ADHD (Weyandt, 2005). Initially ascribed to the PFC, it is now recognized that the physiological substrates underlying EF include a complex network involving prefrontal, parietal, singular, insular, premotor cortices, and subcortical (e.g., basal ganglia) regions (Weyandt, 2005). However, only the PFC has been implicated consistently in neuroimaging studies using EF-related tasks. Associations between EF and other neurobiological structures have been task-specific and less consistent, which supports the elusive, multi-dimensional nature of this construct.

Despite the difficulty of operationalizing EF, a number of compelling, evidence-based models have been proposed in recent years. Many current conceptualizations break EF into several distinct cognitive factors, including behavioral inhibition, intentionality, and executive memory; volition, strategic planning, purposive action, and effective performance; and attention, interference control, working memory, and planning (Mohlman & Gorman, 2005). Factor analyses have also identified several key EF factors, including attention/set shifting, behavioral inhibition, and working memory (Seidman, 2006). Despite differences among models, it is generally agreed that EF comprises higher-order self-regulatory functions, including the ability to inhibit, plan, organize, problem-solve, use working memory, shift attentional set, and maintain attentional set for future goals (Seidman, 2006).

Attention

Evidence suggests that ADHD is associated with impairment in selective attention (the ability to ignore distracting information when performing a perceptual act on relevant information), sustained attention (the ability to sustain attention to relevant information over a relatively long period of time while withholding responses to irrelevant items), and the orienting of attention (the ability to benefit from a cue that automatically attracts attention to a specified location, or disengage and reorient to a different location; Tsal, Shalev, & Mevorach, 2005). Recent studies (e.g., Weissman, Chu, Reddy, & Mohlman, 2012) have demonstrated these distinct attentional deficits using a compendium of attentional paradigms to tap various attentional processes, including continuous performance tests (sustained attention; e.g., Conners Continuous Performance Test–II [CPT-II]; Conners, 2004), conjunctive visual search and Stroop tasks (selective attention; e.g., Stroop Color-Word Test [SCWT]; Stroop, 1935), and cost-benefit paradigms (orienting of attention). For example, the SCWT is commonly used with ADHD children age six years and older to assess selective attention, response inhibition, and controlled cognitive processing. In its standard format (Golden, 1978), the SCWT prompts the child to name (i.e., selectively attend to) the ink colors of a series of unmatched color words (e.g., the word, "red," printed in blue ink), while suppressing prepotent responding to the lexical feature of the words (i.e., reading the words). Each Stroop subtest comprises 100 items, and scoring is based on the number of items read or named correctly within a forty-five-second time interval. Neurophysiological and anatomical findings support the notion of multiple attentional deficits in ADHD, indicating abnormalities in the right frontal lobes (sustained attention), right parietal lobes (orienting of attention), and corpus callosum (orienting of attention; Tsal et al., 2005).

Behavioral Inhibition

It has simultaneously been proposed that deficits in behavioral inhibition or impulse control are central to ADHD (Barkley, 1997). Children with ADHD demonstrate impairment in three interrelated inhibitory processes: inhibition of the prepotent response to an event, stopping of an ongoing response, and interference control; these inhibitory deficits may independently characterize and explain the cognitive and attentional problems and impulsive behaviors associated with the disorder. Barkley's (1997) model of behavioral inhibition in ADHD proposed that impairment in this primary domain is linked to secondary impairment of four key EFs that rely heavily on inhibition for their successful execution: working memory, self-regulation of affect-motivation-arousal, internalization of speech, and reconstitution (behavioral analysis and synthesis).

Neuropsychological tests, including go-no-go, stop-signal, delayed response, Stroop (e.g., SCWT, Stroop, 1935; Golden, 1978), and CPT paradigms (e.g., Continuous Performance Test-II, Conners, 2004), have all been used to demonstrate inhibitory impairment in ADHD youth. For example, one of the most widely used tests of behavioral inhibition (and sustained attention) with ADHD youth is the CPT-II, which requires participants to press a specified key (i.e., spacebar) in response to any letter other than "X" but then suddenly not press when an "X" appears. Errors of *commission*—or how many times the child erroneously responds to a non-target (an "X")—is generally used as a measure of response inhibition or impulsivity, whereas errors of *omission*—how many times a child fails to respond to a target (a non-"X")—provide a measure of sustained attention and vigilance. Neurophysiological and anatomical studies of ADHD youth have ascribed these deficits in behavioral inhibition to the orbital-frontal regions of the PFC and its reciprocal interconnections with the ventromedial region of the striatum (Iversen & Dunnett, 1990).

Working Memory

Working memory is also frequently impacted in ADHD. Researchers generally agree that working memory is a more complex cognitive construct than short-term memory, involving the active manipulation of temporarily stored information in lieu of simple recall. Working memory affords a prolongation of reference, or the relation of recent past events to future actions, secondarily permitting both imagination and concept of time (Barkley, 1997). This specialized type of memory is highly correlated with performance on academic and language-related tasks, such as vocabulary, reading comprehension, mathematics, and problem solving (Tannock, Ickowicz, & Schachar, 1995). According to Barkley, children with ADHD may experience deficiencies in working memory and its subfunctions, including difficulty holding past information in mind (hindsight) for the formulation of future plans (forethought), temporal disorganization of retrospective recall, a compromised sense of time, and a tendency to be more influenced by temporally proximal events and consequences than those more distal in time. Working memory deficits have been documented in children with ADHD using tests of digit span, mental arithmetic (e.g., serial addition), and holding spatial arrays or sequences of information in memory to either locate stimuli or properly execute a task. For example, the Digit Span subtest of the Wechsler Intelligence Scale for Children (4th ed.; WISC-IV; Wechsler, 2003) is a measure of verbal working memory commonly administered to ADHD youth as part of a broader cognitive or psychoeducational assessment battery. The Digit Span subtest features two conditions: forward and backward serial recall. The aggregate score is the sum of the number of digits recalled correctly under each condition. It is argued by some that backward serial recall, alone, effectively assesses working memory, while forward recall is a more basic task of short-term memory requiring the simple reproduction of information in an untransformed manner (Tannock et al., 1995). At a neurobiological level, working memory has been ascribed to regions of the dorsolateral prefrontal cortex and its reciprocal connections to the central region of the striatum (Iversen & Dunnet, 1990)

Delay Aversion

In contrast to the dorsolateral-prefrontal cortical dopaminergic system associated with executive dysfunction in ADHD, dysregulation of the dopaminergic mesolimbic, ventral striatal pathway has been linked to deficits in reward processing or "Delay Aversion" (DA) in ADHD youth (Sagvolden, Aase, Zeiner, & Berger, 1998). DA refers to a difficulty delaying gratification and a tendency to "discount delay" by selecting immediate lesser rewards over delayed greater ones. In one of the most widely accepted theoretical models of ADHD to date, Sonuga-Barke (2003) proposes that two pathways exist that each contribute to the disorder, the first being executive dysfunction, as described above, and the second being deficits in reward processing or DA, making it difficult for ADHD children to put off a smaller immediate reward in favor of a larger reward later.

Differentiating Patterns of ADHD and Comorbid Conditions

Comorbidity between ADHD and other psychiatric diagnoses is common and complicates the clinical picture, particularly for those with severe symptomatology (Hale et al., 2013; Rowland et al., 2002). Thus, understanding and accurately detecting signs, symptoms, and risk factors of common co-occurring conditions associated with ADHD is an important precursor to timely and effective treatment of ADHD and related problems. The presence of comorbidity in individuals with ADHD may result from neurobiological underpinnings that heighten vulnerability to other disorders and/or associated elevations in social, behavioral, and academic impairments that often accompany ADHD. Regardless of the pathway, comorbid disorders vary across gender and age and may further exacerbate both clinical and neurocognitive functioning (Weissman & Bates, 2010), complicating clinical assessment and treatment planning. Therefore, integrating neuropsychological data with academic reports and behavioral assessment of symptoms may help practitioners better identify and differentiate unique underlying mechanisms and/or biomarkers of ADHD symptom phenotypes (e.g., inattention, impulsivity, excessive motor activity) that can present similarly in other childhood disorders (Weissman et al., 2012). The following section reviews differentiating patterns of behavioral and neurocognitive impairment across the disorders that most commonly co-occur with ADHD, including disruptive behavior disorders, learning disorders (LD), autism spectrum disorders (ASD), anxiety disorders, and mood disorders.

Disruptive Behavior Disorders

Oppositional defiant disorder (ODD) is the most prevalent co-occurring psychiatric condition with ADHD, with approximately half of children diagnosed with ADHD also meeting criteria for ODD (Willcutt et al., 2012). In addition, 22 percent of ADHD children also receive a diagnosis of conduct disorder (CD), a more severe form of behavior disruption that includes aggression toward people and/or animals, destruction of property, deceitfulness or theft, and serious violations of social norms (Willcutt et al., 2012). It can be challenging to differentiate attention problems in the context of a disruptive behavior disorder from ADHD. For example, children with early-onset ODD or CD often experience delayed cognitive and language skills (e.g., Lynam, Moffitt, & Stouthamer-Loeber, 1993), which are highly associated with decreased attentional capacity and may be misinterpreted as ADHD-like symptoms. Conversely, research also suggests that lower cognitive skills are highly associated with increased conduct problems over time, although it is not yet clear whether general intelligence (e.g., IQ) or a specific deficit (e.g., EF) is responsible for this association. In addition, meta-analytic findings have revealed that while ADHD symptoms and conduct problems co-occur at a higher-than-chance rate, children who demonstrate this comorbidity may be qualitatively different than children with pure ADHD or CD symptom presentations (Waschbusch, 2002), as the symptoms may compound one another. Additionally, social impairment is pervasive in ADHD, CD, and ODD, which is likely due to shared attentional deficits and similar displays of behavioral disruption (e.g., Fite, Evans, Cooley, & Rubens, 2014). Still, attentional impairment (e.g., selective, sustained, shifting attention) is a hallmark symptom of ADHD-IN and ADHD-CO and is more pronounced in these disorders than in pure CD or ODD.

Learning Disorders

Children with ADHD are often found to have one or more comorbid LD diagnoses, with prevalence rates approximating 31 percent (DuPaul & Stoner, 2003). In general, neuropsychological findings suggest that LD children have greater difficulty with the comprehension of instructions, whereas children with ADHD may understand instructions but not fully process them due to difficulties sustaining attention. A diagnosis of ADHD is likely when assessment data clearly indicate that a child has good cognitive functioning but poor executive control of attention, impulsivity, and hyperactivity, which leads to academic underachievement and behavior problems (Marzocchi et al., 2008). Additionally, early onset of disruptive behaviors (e.g., impulsivity, disinhibition, aggression) are commonly associated with ADHD but less frequently with LD. Children with ADHD display symptoms that are pervasive across social contexts (e.g., school, home, peers) and functional domains (e.g., silent reading, writing, participating in group sports, making and maintaining friends), whereas children with LD are more likely to have a specific academic area (or areas) of weakness. Furthermore, children with ADHD are likely to perform in the average range on standardized achievement tests (e.g., Woodcock-Johnson Tests of Achievement; Bradley-Johnson, Morgan, & Nutkins, 2004), while LD children are likely to perform in the below average to low range in specific domain areas (DuPaul & Stoner, 2003).

Autism Spectrum Disorders

Approximately 65 percent of children with high-functioning ASD demonstrate significant co-occurring attention problems that compound academic, behavioral, psychosocial, and neurocognitive impairment (Holtmann, Bolte, & Poustka, 2005; Weissman & Bates, 2010). Misdiagnosis of ADHD is common in children with high-functioning ASD, as poor attention to self and surroundings are common factors in both disorders (Hale et al., 2013). Common social and attentional impairments due to elevated activity level may also confound differential diagnosis between these disorders. However, increased energy in ADHD children is best explained by hyperactivity, whereas ASD children may become psychomotorically activated (e.g., flapping) in the face of undesired change (Tsujii et al., 2009). As such, ASD youth may be best differentiated by their repetitive, stereotypic behaviors and communication impairment (Sinzig, Walter, & Doepfner, 2009), with deficits in social communication and relatedness most useful in differentiating high-functioning ASD and ADHD groups (Hartley & Sikora, 2009). With regard to cognitive functioning, verbal working memory deficits are *more* common in ASD youth than children with ADHD (Willcutt & Pennington, 2000), whereas children with ADHD more often present with inhibitory problems (Pennington & Ozonoff, 1996). As such, response inhibition may be a key discriminating feature of the two disorders (Hale et al., 2009), and this deficit combined with impaired social judgment has been related to orbital-striatal-thalamic circuit function (Lichter & Cummings, 2001). Thus, the distinction between ASD and ADHD may be related to whether the problem involves the medial or lateral orbital dysfunction, respectively (Hale et al., 2009).

Mood Disorders

ADHD also co-occurs frequently with mood disorders, with approximately 14 percent of ADHD children experiencing major depressive disorder (MDD), 5 percent experiencing dysthymia, and 20 percent to 30 percent experiencing any type of comorbid mood condition (Kessler et al., 2005; Elia et al., 2009). Poor concentration is a core symptom of both depression and ADHD, complicating differential diagnosis (American Psychiatric Association, 2013). Other common symptoms of both disorders are boredom, weight loss, and self-harm behaviors; however, in ADHD, these symptoms typically do not stem from depressed mood but may instead result from core attentional issues, psychostimulant side effects, and/or low frustration tolerance.

Despite this symptom overlap, ADHD and depression are also phenotypically distinct in that depressed mood, fatigue, and psychomotor retardation are not seen in pure ADHD (Pliszka, Carlson, & Swanson, 1999). Additionally, there are neurobiological distinctions between depression and ADHD, with ADHD children typically experiencing hypoactivity in the right ventral and dorsal systems, with less impairment observed in the left hemisphere (Grimm et al., 2008). In depression, greater relative right hemisphere hyperactivity is observed in the orbital and ventral cingulate circuits, with hypoactivity evident in the left hemisphere dorsolateral and dorsal cingulate (Savitz & Drevets, 2009), suggesting differences in lateralization between these disorders.

Notwithstanding its controversial diagnosis, juvenile (or early-onset) bipolar disorder (BP) is also commonly associated with ADHD in youth, with comorbidity estimates ranging from 6 percent to 10 percent (Barkley, 2002). Common symptoms of ADHD and BP include inattention, impulsivity, hyperactivity, distractibility, irritability, pressured speech, and increased energy level (Wozniak, 2005). Hallmark symptoms of BP such as decreased need for sleep and mood elevation are what phenotypically differentiate the disorders (Luckenbaugh, Findling, Leverich, Pizzarello, & Post, 2009). Grandiosity and uncontrollable laughter for no apparent reason are also unique to BPD (Geller et al., 2003). However, individuals with ADHD and BP both suffer from attention and executive deficits (Shear, DelBello, Lee-Rosenberg, & Strakowski, 2002), such that symptoms must be carefully considered during the diagnostic process.

Anxiety Disorders

Anxiety is a highly prevalent condition composed of cognitive, physiological, and emotional distress (Weissman, Antinoro, & Chu, 2008). One-fourth to one-half of all children with ADHD also meet criteria for an anxiety disorder (Reynolds & Lane, 2009), and this comorbid pattern is associated with increased attention difficulties, academic deficits, and social impairment (Elia et al., 2009). It can be challenging to distinguish between anxiety and ADHD, especially in young children, as both disorders may feature attention problems, difficulty concentrating in class, and elevated motor activity (Weissman et al., 2012). Of the anxiety disorders, ADHD is most closely related to the neurophysiological symptoms of generalized anxiety disorder (GAD), including irritability, restlessness, and concentration difficulties. The major difference between the disorders is that anxious youth demonstrate these symptoms due to excessive and uncontrollable worry (American Psychiatric Association, 2013) and threat-related attentional biases (e.g., Weissman et al., 2012) rather than hyperactivity and deficits in selective and sustained attention and inhibitory control associated with ADHD (Pliszka & Olvera, 1999). Indeed, research has found that children with ADHD perform more poorly on neurocognitive tasks of general attention processes (selective, sustained, and shifting attention) relative to their anxious counterparts, who exhibit increased attentional biases toward threatening facial cues (Weissman et al., 2012). These findings lay the groundwork for the theory that distinct mechanisms or biomarkers of inattention may underlie anxiety and ADHD in youth and suggest that interventions should be differentially designed and implemented to target these distinct attention mechanisms (e.g., using executive training with ADHD children versus attentional bias modification with anxious youth).

In light of the widespread heterogeneity of ADHD symptoms, documented long-term functional impairment, and high rates of comorbidity and diagnostic/neurobiological overlap with other psychiatric disorders, effective assessment and treatment of ADHD require an understanding of both overlapping and differentiating symptoms as well as behavioral and brain-based patterns of many different disorders (Weissman et al., 2012). In addition, preliminary research suggests that children with comorbid conditions may represent a more severe population with respect to academic, behavioral, psychosocial, and neurocognitive impairment (Elia et al., 2009; Holtmann et al., 2005; Weissman & Bates, 2010). Thus, practitioners who adopt an integrated clinical-neurocognitive assessment and intervention framework may find improved efficiency, specificity, and efficacy in their work with ADHD youth with and without co-occurring symptoms and may choose to implement targeted "neurotherapeutic" interventions to enhance treatment outcomes and pinpoint core behavioral *and* neurocognitive mechanisms that may underlie ADHD and related disorders. The following section provides an overview of evidence-based treatments for ADHD, with an emphasis on novel "neurotherapeutic" approaches.

Empirically Supported Treatments for ADHD: Overview and Limitations

Two "empirically supported" treatments for ADHD currently exist (American Psychiatric Association, 2013): psychopharmacological treatment (methylphenidate, amphetamine, atomoxetine, or guanfacine) and behavioral therapy (specifically, a combination of parent training and school-based contingency management).

Pharmacotherapy

Stimulant and non-stimulant medications act upon the monoamine system, regulating availability of dopamine and/or norepinephrine (Minzenberg, 2012). These medications have been shown to be highly efficacious (supported by large effect sizes) in reducing the core symptoms of ADHD within the majority of cases across the life span (Greenhill, Halperin, & Abikoff, 1999; Minzenberg, 2012). However, medication is often not a first-resort treatment strategy for reasons related to side effects, patient and/or parent preferences or, in some cases, lack of response. Moreover, a fundamental limitation of medication is that its effects do not typically persist beyond the point of discontinuation (Molina et al., 2009). As such, there is a need for treatments that provide continued benefit throughout the lifespan.

Psychosocial Treatments

Behavioral treatments can be traced back to principles of operant conditioning in that behavior is shaped via provision of reinforcement contingencies (Pelham & Fabiano, 2008). As discussed earlier, ADHD has been posited as a disorder of the brain's reward circuitry, involving hypodopaminergic transmission in the mesolimbic-prefrontal cortical system. In much the same way that this has been related to reward sensitivity, the circuit is also likely involved in responsiveness to contingency management. Behavioral therapy is often highly effective at reducing off-task behavior and improving compliance and motivation in ADHD youth (with large effect sizes; Fabiano et al., 2009), although it is less apt to treat the core symptoms of inattention and hyperactivity/impulsivity (e.g., Abikoff, 2009). Examples of behavioral therapy approaches include *the Incredible Years* (Jones, Daley, Hutchings, Bywater, & Eames, 2008) and *Triple P* (Bor, Sanders, & Markie-Dadds, 2002), which are two parent-focused behavioral interventions for preschoolers that have demonstrated persisting effects at follow-up; however, their impact is more significant in reducing disruptive behaviors than core ADHD symptomatology. Additionally, with some exception (Hood & Eyberg, 2003), research has shown behavioral treatments to be similarly plagued by time, as medication, with problem behaviors recurring once treatment is discontinued (Molina et al., 2009).

Because of this, there is a need for treatments that offer longer-term remission for individuals suffering from ADHD. Unfortunately, alternative therapies are only newly emerging, and most have not received enough empirical support to be considered "well supported" or "probably efficacious" (Silverman & Hinshaw, 2008). However, an improved understanding of the neurodevelopmental etiology of the disorder, coupled with emerging research on neuroplasticity throughout development, provides an exciting forum for continued study and proliferation of experimental, "neurotherapeutic" approaches in the treatment of ADHD.

Neuropsychologically Informed ("Neurotherapeutic") Interventions

Within the past two decades, researchers have begun to explore the potential for ADHD treatments that more directly target the neurocognitive processes believed to underlie the disorder. Executive impairment and associated disinhibition, inattention, working memory impairment, disorganization, and/ or planning deficits, as described above, are prominent among virtually all individuals with ADHD. As such, a number of neuropsychologically informed or "neurotherapeutic" interventions have been developed to specifically target the neural and/or behavioral correlates of executive dysfunction. These include

(1) attention training, (2) working memory training, (3) developmentally sensitive cognitive enrichment, (4) organization and metacognitive/EF training, (5) neurofeedback, (6) exercise, and (7) reward sensitivity training.

Attention Training

Attention training paradigms are typically administered via computerized, game-like activities that target various aspects of attentional processing; as participants improve with practice, the level of difficulty is "scaffolded" up, akin to strength-building exercises that employ heavier and heavier weights. The principal of "scaffolding" refers to repeated practice of incrementally more challenging activities over time until each successive level of difficulty has been mastered, promoting both learning and development. Attention training exercises used with ADHD youth are often similar to those used in the assessment of attention and EF, such as Stroop or continuous performance tasks.

The first randomized controlled trial (RCT) of computerized attention training was conducted with a small sample of young children with ADHD (Kerns, Eso, & Thompson, 1999). After eight weeks of therapy (including exercises taxing selective, sustained, alternating, and divided attention), children completing the active treatment demonstrated significant improvements in non-trained tests of attention (i.e., tests other than those used in the treatment) and insignificant improvement in parent and teacher symptom ratings, the latter of which approached significance. A similar study conducted by Tamm and colleagues (2010) yielded more clinically promising results, reporting improvements in working memory, fluid reasoning, and core symptoms of hyperactivity-impulsivity in the ADHD group relative to the control group.

Shalev, Tsal, and Mevorach (2007) used the computerized progressive attentional training (CPAT) program with ADHD children, reporting improved parent-rated inattention and child reading comprehension among active-treatment children relative to controls. Another study of younger ADHD children (ages four to six) found improvements in event-related potential (ERP) functioning after attention-training tasks (Rueda, Rothbart, McCandliss, Saccomanno, & Posner, 2005). Finally, Steiner and colleagues (2011) found significant improvements in parent-rated attention and child EF post-attention training in a school setting.

In other studies, attention training was found to be superior at improving performance on tests of attention (e.g., compared to visual perception training; Tucha et al., 2011) relative to control interventions. However, this was not always the case (e.g., Rabiner, Murray, Skinner, & Malone, 2010). Unfortunately, where the training did lead to improvements on tests of attention, remission of symptoms as reported by parents and teachers did not always follow (e.g., Tucha et al., 2011).

Considered together, attention-training studies provide some initial evidence of improved attention and EF in children. However, more studies are needed. Importantly, while attention may be trainable, generalization of training effects to ADHD symptomatology must be addressed before these programs are to be recommended for commercial use.

Working Memory Training

Like computerized attention training, working memory training paradigms to date employ computerized activities that are scaffolded over the course of the training period. In general, research testing the efficacy of working memory training paradigms has yielded mixed results, and sample sizes have been small to moderate in all studies to date ($N < 100$). Cogmed Working Memory Training (Klingberg, Forssberg, & Westerberg, 2002) is the most well-studied working memory intervention to date. Cogmed is typically administered over five to six weeks, or until twenty-five sessions are completed, and involves the progressive scaffolding of difficulty of computerized visuospatial and spatial-verbal working memory exercises. Exercises are designed to tax working memory skills, for instance, requiring individuals to track and recreate sequences of visually presented stimuli (e.g., click on moving objects in the same order that they were presented). An exhaustive review of studies of Cogmed for ADHD is beyond the scope of this chapter, and the reader is referred to a recent review article for more detail (Chacko et al., 2013). Below, we briefly review the findings from the four studies deemed "acceptable" by Chacko and colleagues.

Klingberg and colleagues (2005) conducted an initial RCT for working memory training for ADHD in middle-childhood (ages seven to twelve). Children in the active group demonstrated increased performance on cognitive tests and reductions in parent-rated inattentive and hyperactive/impulsive symptoms that were maintained at three months. However, there was no significant change in teacher ratings of symptoms or on an objective measure of motor activity (Klingberg et al., 2002). Results of a similar RCT did not support improved ADHD symptomatology after treatment via parent-report (Green et al., 2012).

Beck and colleagues (2010) reported improved working memory and attention via parent report in a sample of ADHD youth, relative to a wait list control group, with gains persisting at three months; however, no changes were reported in the core symptoms of hyperactivity/ impulsivity. Finally, a study conducted with a more impaired sample of ADHD adolescents in a semi-residential school setting indicated improvement in trained but not untrained tests of working memory and no improvements in parent or teacher symptom ratings (Gray et al., 2012).

Considered together, none of the foregoing studies demonstrated consistent improvement as observed by multiple raters, and no studies to date have documented improvement on teacher rating scales. Chacko and colleagues (2013) concluded that, given existing research, Cogmed is best considered a "possibly efficacious treatment" for children with ADHD.

In summary, there is growing appeal for computerized executive skills training programs for a number of reasons, including but not limited to their grounding in neuropsychological principles, their portable and cost-effective technology (i.e., relative to psychotherapy or medication), and their virtual lack of side-effect profile. However, research has provided inconsistent evidence of effectiveness. Improvements have been noted in response inhibition, sustained attention, working memory, academic performance, and other measures of EF. Unfortunately, where treatments have yielded effects, they have not always extended to measures of the core symptoms of ADHD. As such, the extent to which training programs may reduce ADHD symptomatology is unclear, and questions remain as to whether gains can be considered generalizable.

Notably, although we have reviewed the literature on the use of these programs in children, the same programs are also being explored for their potential effectiveness among adults with ADHD. Nevertheless, these interventions are likely to have the greatest impact on children, whose brains are still developing and may be more capable of change.

Developmentally Sensitive Cognitive Enrichment

Because the brain is especially plastic and most susceptible to new learning during *early* childhood, early interventions have the potential for powerful and enduring change (Halperin et al., 2012). Beyond the attention training and working memory programs reviewed above, other programs emphasizing early cognitive enrichment for preschoolers with ADHD have provided some initial evidence of benefits that persist beyond active treatment. These "developmentally sensitive" cognitive enrichment programs share certain features, including the use of game-like intervention activities and the inclusion of parents as primary providers of treatment (i.e., by engaging in tasks with children at home). As with attention and working memory training, the principle of scaffolding is fundamental to these programs. However, in contrast, early cognitive enrichment programs employ "live," non-computerized tasks targeting attention and EF (for instance, attending to a moving cup with a candy beneath it or inhibiting a prepotent response, as in the game of "Simon Says") and, in some cases, other neuropsychological abilities as well.

Training executive attention and motor skills (TEAMS) is a program for preschool children with ADHD that employs various games designed to target inhibition, sustained attention, memory, planning, and visuospatial and motor skills, domains that are frequently impaired in ADHD youth (Halperin, Marks, et al., 2013). Open pilot results indicated medium-to-large effect size improvements on parent- and teacher-rated symptoms, both after treatment and at three-month follow-up. Enhancing neurocognitive growth with the aid of games and exercise (ENGAGE) is a similar program for preschoolers with difficulties in self-control that uses game-like activities to target behavior, cognition, and emotion. Open pilot results suggested improvements in working memory and parent-rated hyperactivity, with effects persisting twelve months after treatment (Healey & Halperin, 2014). Finally, executive training of attention and metacognition (ETAM) similarly uses games to target EF in young children with ADHD; here, metacognitive techniques are taught to children and their parents in order to develop a language for discussing attentional control (e.g., "eyes looking," "ears listening," "brain thinking"). In an open trial, ETAM demonstrated improvements in EF and parent-rated ADHD symptoms (Tamm, Nakonezny, & Hughes, 2012). Despite these promising findings with respect to symptom reduction, early cognitive enrichment programs are still in their infancy, and it remains to be seen whether they have the potential to truly alter the brain and thereby shift the disorder trajectory in young children with ADHD.

Neurofeedback

The rise of psychophysiological measures and techniques in psychological research suggests that children with ADHD experience altered electroencephalogram (EEG) activity. Studies conducted in ADHD youth reveal that this population has more theta activity (four to eight Hz), less beta activity (fifteen to twenty Hz), and a higher ratio of theta to beta waves relative to healthy controls (e.g., Arns, Gunkelman, Breteler, & Spronk, 2008). Moreover, whereas increased theta frequencies in conjunction with decreased beta waves are indicative of inattention, increased sensorimotor rhythm (SMR; twelve to fifteen Hz) is associated with hyperactivity (Fuchs, Birbaumer, Lutzenberger, Gruzelier, & Kaiser, 2003). Importantly, patterns of EEG activity in ADHD youth tend to normalize after psychostimulant treatment (Alexander et al., 2008).

Neurofeedback is a behaviorally based intervention that operates on the notion that changing an individual's pattern of EEG activity may reduce ADHD symptomatology. Neurofeedback trains individuals with ADHD to modulate neural activity while completing computer tasks, with the goal of increasing awareness of abnormal frequencies (Toplak, Connors, Shuster, Knezevic, & Parks, 2008). Participants are rewarded for reaching the target goal; typical aims are to decrease SMR and theta waves and to increase beta wave frequency. Parents often prefer neurofeedback to medication (Fuchs et al., 2003), particularly given that the time-of-day restrictions (e.g., psychostimulants effects wear off during the day; drug holidays) and physiological side effects that are seen in psychostimulants are not present (Strehl et al., 2006). While there are no current standard guidelines, thirty to thirty-six one-hour-long sessions over a six- to twelve-week period are usually recommended.

There are some data that suggest neurofeedback is efficacious in youth with ADHD (Moriyama et al., 2012). Positive findings demonstrate that youth treated with neurofeedback show significant improvements on cognitive and behavioral ratings relative to waitlist controls (Toplak et al., 2008). A review by Fox and colleagues (2005) summarizing seminal neurofeedback studies over the past two decades concluded that biofeedback helps patients modify brainwave activity to enhance attention, reduce impulsivity, and produce long-term change. However, a more recent review highlights differences in findings as a function of methodological rigor, with non-randomized clinical trials demonstrating greater efficacy than RCTs, which demonstrate less robust, albeit significant, effects (Moriyama et al., 2012). Neurofeedback may, therefore, have potential as an alternative intervention for individuals with ADHD, although more research is needed.

Training of Related Executive and Organizational Skills

Cognitive-behavioral therapy (CBT) with an emphasis on training organizational and executive skills has been studied and practiced for some time now, particularly with ADHD patients. These programs typically include training in planning, time management, and organization and are offered individually or in small groups. Differences between programs relate mostly to the length of the program and to the extent that emotion regulation and/or techniques for reducing comorbid anxiety and depression symptoms are incorporated alongside executive training skills. Such programs have received empirical support and are gaining popular use in clinical practice.

In the adult literature, Solanto and colleagues (2010) conducted an RCT to assess efficacy of a twelve-week, group treatment program for ADHD adults focusing on planning, time management, and organization. Relative to an active control group, ADHD participants showed greater reductions in ADHD symptoms among self-, coded-, and multi-informant reports. Safren and colleagues (2005) compared the effects of a similar program, in a sample of medicated adults with ADHD, to medication alone and to medication plus psychoeducation and relaxation techniques (Safren et al., 2010). Similar improvement in ADHD symptoms and impairment were reported in the executive skills group, as rated by participants and blinded staff members, which persisted one year after treatment.

Other programs have placed greater emphasis on issues like impulse control, anger management, and emotion regulation. Bramham and colleagues (2009) and Virta and colleagues (2010) incorporated these elements, in addition to EF skills, in CBT groups for adults with ADHD, comparing the active treatment group to wait list controls and to those receiving cognitive training, respectively. Both found evidence of symptom improvement relative to control participants. In addition, compared to those receiving treatment as usual, adults with ADHD receiving a CBT program targeting neurocognitive skills related to attention and impulse control showed significant improvements in ADHD symptoms after treatment (Emilsson et al., 2011). Finally, Weiss and colleagues (2012) reported that among ADHD adults receiving CBT, the degree of improvement did not differ between those simultaneously receiving medication and those receiving placebo, suggesting that CBT alone offers real benefit to adults with ADHD.

Only recently have researchers begun to assess the potential for similar treatment application with children and adolescents, and findings are promising to date. Abikoff and colleagues (2013) randomly enrolled 158 children with ADHD in grades three to five into either an organizational skills training (OST) program, a parent- and teacher-training program that implemented a contingency reinforcement system for completion of tasks (PATHKO), or a wait list control condition. Their treatment program included collaboration with parents and school personnel in training and practicing skills related to organization, time management, and planning. Findings showed that improvement in the OST and PATHKO groups was substantial relative to the wait list control group, with a remarkable 60 percent of the active conditions no longer meeting study entry criteria after treatment, compared to 3 percent of wait list controls. However, outcomes for OST and PATHKO differed minimally from each other. This begs the question of whether it is training of these executive skills that is most critical in children and to what extent motivational deficits, instead, drive impairment seen in untreated children (i.e., that the children have the skills but do not use them). A second study examined an integrated home-school behavioral treatment for children with ADHD IN by incorporating training in organizational as well as social skills and trained parents as "coaches" to assist children at home (Pfiffner et al., 2007). Reductions in parent- and teacher-reported inattention and increases in cognitive tempo were reported and maintained at three- to five-month follow-up. Finally, another group investigated the utility of a modified version of Safren and colleagues' (2005) CBT program, reporting that ADHD adolescents with comorbid anxiety and depression benefited most from the treatment relative to those with comorbid externalizing disorders (Antshel, Faraone, & Gordon, 2012).

Due to the different considerations when treating children and adolescents, programs training organizational and executive skills inevitably require a more collaborative treatment approach, which poses consideration under circumstances where such a team-based approach is less feasible (e.g., within low-income, low-SES populations). However, where possible, the training of such skills at an early age may have the potential to alter the trajectory of ADHD-related impairments, if not the core symptoms of the disorder. Further investigation is warranted and may benefit from more closely pinpointing which factors are predictive of outcome, such that these programs might become more widely available.

Physical Exercise and Reward Sensitivity Training

In addition to the targeted training of functions specifically linked to ADHD, other approaches have emerged to more broadly enrich the brain, among them physical exercise and reward sensitivity training.

PHYSICAL EXERCISE

An emerging body of research has examined the cognitive and emotional benefits of exercise. Exercise has widely been shown to increase levels of brain-derived neurotrophic factor as well as the availability of insulin-like growth factor, the number of glutamate receptors, and synaptic protein levels, all of which fundamentally contribute to cell proliferation and neural plasticity (e.g., Chaddock et al., 2012). In typically developing children, physical exercise leads to improvements in EF and activation within attention-related areas, as measured with ERP and fMRI techniques (Chaddock et al., 2012). However, only a limited number of published studies have examined the effect of exercise in ADHD children, with current data suggesting some improvement in symptomotology, varying motor changes (changes in eyeblink, or reduced motor response in boys; Tantillo, Kesick, Hynd, & Dishman, 2002), and blunted catecholamine response (Wigal et al., 2003). These results have generated significant interest in the therapeutic potential of exercise for children with ADHD (Archer & Kostrzewa, 2012).

REWARD SENSITIVITY TRAINING

Another form of cognitive enrichment with a strong theoretical basis for developing treatments for ADHD is reward sensitivity training, which directly targets deficits in reward circuitry and tolerance for delay (Schweitzer & McBurnett, 2012). However, only one published study to date has tested the efficacy of a reward sensitivity intervention (Schweitzer & Sulzer-Azaroff, 1988). Participants were six preschoolers (five active treatment, one control) whose teachers identified them as impulsive and whom researchers identified as consistently averse to delay in the laboratory. The delay task was repeated during intervention, and the duration of the delay gradually increased across sessions; by the end, children in the active treatment were more likely to choose the delayed reinforcer over the immediate one after treatment. As with cognitive training, the extent to which this type of intervention could generalize to functional improvement more broadly remains to be seen. However, the application of current neuropsychological understanding of ADHD toward informing treatment development and refinement will likely lead to further advances in the disorder's treatment.

In summary, a number of innovative "neurotherapeutic" approaches have demonstrated initial success in improving attention, EF, and related symptoms in children diagnosed with ADHD. With further research and dissemination, these treatment modalities may continue to show promise as effective alternatives or supplements to standard CBT or medication protocols, with the potential for providing more targeted treatment of the underlying neurocognitive mechanisms of ADHD.

Prognostic Implications and Adult ADHD

Although ADHD has historically been considered a childhood disorder, this assumption is changing. Recent evidence suggests that ADHD often persists into adulthood, with recovery less likely in individuals who had severe symptomatology as youth (Kessler et al., 2005). Indeed, as many as 60 percent of children with ADHD continue to experience clinically significant symptoms and associated impairments as adults (e.g., elevated rates of peer and family problems, academic difficulties, car accidents, substance use problems, divorce, crime, unemployment, and problems with adult social relationships; Barkley, 1997), and prognosis may be worse for youth with symptoms of both inattention and hyperactivity-impulsivity (Kessler et al., 2005). In a nationally representative survey of adults (NCS-R), Kessler and colleagues reported that 4.4 percent of eighteen- to forty-four-year-olds met criteria for ADHD (2006). Thus, early detection and accurate diagnosis are vital precursors to safe, timely, and effective intervention and functional improvement.

While treatments for ADHD adults notably lag behind, preliminary studies support the efficacy of neuroscientifically informed treatments with individuals who were diagnosed with ADHD later in life (e.g., executive skills training; Safren et al., 2010; Solanto et al., 2010), suggesting that similar neurocognitive mechanisms may underlie ADHD across the life span and may be targeted in treatment with the same "neurotherapeutic" principles. Nevertheless, early intervention programs are likely to have the greatest impact on the trajectory of ADHD symptoms, early in childhood when the developing brain is most susceptible to new learning, has heightened "neuroplasticity," and is ripe with the potential for powerful and enduring change.

Conclusions for Research, Policy, and Practice

ADHD is among the most prevalent neurodevelopmental disorders in childhood, encompassing a complex mix of neurocognitive deficits that contribute to developmentally inappropriate symptoms of inattention, impulsivity, and hyperactivity and deficits in EF, leading to impairments across multiple life domains. Despite promising initial evidence that neuroscientifically informed interventions may improve treatments for children with ADHD, bridging the science-practice gap continues to be a challenge. Children with symptoms of ADHD who present to mental health clinics are commonly diagnosed and treated based on subjective assessment data that lack scientific rigor. Potential explanations for the divide between better science and clinical application range from the lack of incentives for incorporating available technologies into treatment, to the dearth of sufficiently large and replicated RCTs (Richey et al., 2013).

Given the heterogeneous nature of attention problems found in children and adolescents, integrating academic, cognitive, and neurocognitive assessment data with the typical indirect informant reports of behavioral functioning may inform the ADHD diagnostic process and offer an evidence-based approach to pinpoint the unique and complex patterns of strengths and weaknesses found in children with ADHD (Hale et al., 2013). Although neuropsychological assessment is not required for a diagnosis of ADHD, a greater understanding of basic underlying processes may enhance our ability to target specific deficits in therapy. Moreover, an integrated clinical-neurocognitive approach is useful to better understand each child's underlying cognitive profile in order to optimally pace, structure, sequence, and synthesize treatments and may guide the appropriate use of targeted neurotherapeutic interventions (Reddy et al., 2013). For example, preliminary research suggests that assessment of executive-working memory and self-regulation impairments may inform differential diagnosis of ADHD subtypes as well as prediction of cognitive and academic response to treatment (Hale et al., 2009). Importantly, neuropsychological assessment may also be useful in determining the presence of common comorbid psychiatric and/or learning disorders as well as cognitive strengths or protective factors, including intact or superior verbal skills, visual-spatial abilities, or overall intellectual functioning, that may mitigate the impact of ADHD on the child's functioning in school, at home, or with peers (Hale et al., 2013).

Understanding and building on children's cognitive strengths, while identifying areas for growth, are critical to maximizing and individualizing treatment. Ultimately, with continued knowledge and research, practitioners adopting a combined, multimodal approach integrating neurocognitive, academic, and behavioral data are likely to achieve greater diagnostic specificity, a more ideographic case formulation, and a more thoughtful, integrative treatment plan; all of these factors may enhance treatment effectiveness and efficiency for children affected by ADHD. This chapter has highlighted that, as a field, we have much to learn from recent advances in both neuroscience and clinical research as well as the rapid development of new brain-based technologies. Further research and dissemination are needed to promote the utility of an integrated clinical-neurocognitive perspective in enhancing assessment and treatment of ADHD youth, including the experimental neurotherapeutic approaches reviewed in this chapter. It is encouraging that many new and innovative investigations are currently under way.

References

Abikoff, H. (2009). ADHD psychosocial treatments: Generalization reconsidered. *Journal of Attention Disorders, 13*(3), 207–210.

Abikoff, H., Gallagher, R., Wells, K. C., Murray, D. W., Huang, L., Lu, F., & Petkova, E. (2013). Remediating organizational functioning in children with ADHD: Immediate and long-term effects from a randomized controlled trial. *Journal of Consulting and Clinical Psychology, 81*(1), 113–128.

Alexander, D. M., Hermens, D. F., Keage, H. A., Clark, C. R., Williams, L. M., Kohn, M. R., ... & Gordon, E. (2008). Event-related wave activity in the EEG provides new marker of ADHD. *Clinical Neurophysiology, 119*(1), 163–179.

American Psychiatric Association. (2013). *Diagnostic and statistical manual of mental disorders* (5th edn). Washington, DC: American Psychiatric Association.

Angold, A., Costello, E. J., & Erkanli, A. (1999). Comorbidity. *Journal of Child Psychology and Psychiatry, and Allied Disciplines, 40*, 57–87.

Antshel, K. M., Faraone, S. V., & Gordon, M. (2012). Cognitive behavioral treatment outcomes in adolescent ADHD. *FOCUS: The Journal of Lifelong Learning in Psychiatry*, *10*(3), 334–345.

Archer, T. & Kostrzewa, R. M. (2012). Physical exercise alleviates ADHD symptoms: Regional deficits and development trajectory. *Neurotoxicity Research, 21*(2), 195–209.

Arns, M., Gunkelman, J., Breteler, M., & Spronk, D. (2008). EEG phenotypes predict treatment outcome to stimulants in children with ADHD. *Journal of Integrated Neuroscience, 7*(3), 421–438.

Barkley, R. A. (1997). Behavioral inhibition, sustained attention, and EFs: Constructing a unifying theory of ADHD. *Psychological Bulletin, 121*(1), 65.

Barkley, R. A. (2002). Major life activity and health outcomes associated with attention-deficit/hyperactivity disorder. *Journal of Clinical Psychiatry, 63*, 10–15.

Beck, S. J., Hanson, C. A., Puffenberger, S. S., Benninger, K. L., & Benninger, W. B. (2010). A controlled trial of working memory training for children and adolescents with ADHD. *Journal of Clinical Child & Adolescent Psychology, 39*(6), 825–836.

Bor, W., Sanders, M. R., & Markie-Dadds, C. (2002). The effects of the Triple P-Positive Parenting Program on preschool children with co-occurring disruptive behavior and attentional/hyperactive difficulties. *Journal of Abnormal Child Psychology, 30*(6), 571–587.

Bradley-Johnson, S., Morgan, S. K., & Nutkins, C. (2004). The Woodcock-Johnson Tests of Achievement. *Journal of Psychoeducational Assessment, 22*, 261–274.

Bramham, J., Young, S., Bickerdike, A., Spain, D., McCartan, D., & Xenitidis, K. (2009). Evaluation of group cognitive behavioral therapy for adults with ADHD. *Journal of Attention Disorders, 12*(5), 434–441.

Castellanos, F. X., Lee, P. P., Sharp, W., Jeffries, N. O., Greenstein, D. K., Clasen, L. S., … & Rapoport, J. L. (2002). Developmental trajectories of brain volume abnormalities in children and adolescents with attention-deficit/hyperactivity disorder. *JAMA: The Journal of the American Medical Association, 288*(14), 1740–1748.

Catherine, A. (1994). Quantitative morphology of the corpus callosum in attention deficit hyperactivity disorder. *American Journal of Psychiatry, 151*, 665–669.

Chacko, A., Feirsen, N., Bedard, A. C., Marks, D., Uderman, J.Z., & Chimiklis, A. (2013). Cogmed working memory training for youth with ADHD: A closer examination of efficacy utilizing evidence-based criteria. *Journal of Clinical Child & Adolescent Psychology, 42*(6), 769–783.

Chaddock, L., Erickson, K. I., Prakash, R. S., Voss, M. W., VanPatter, M., Pontifex, M. B., … & Kramer, A. F. (2012). A functional MRI investigation of the association between childhood aerobic fitness and neurocognitive control. *Biological Psychology, 89*(1), 260–268.

Cherkasova, M. V. & Hechtman, L. (2009). Neuroimaging in attention-deficit hyperactivity disorder: Beyond the frontostriatal circuitry. *The Canadian Journal of Psychiatry, 54*(10), 651–664.

Conners, C. K. (2004). *Conners' Continuous Performance Test II (CPT-II)*. Toronto, Canada: Multi-Health Systems Inc.

Drabick, D. A. G., Gadow, K. D., & Sprafkin, J. (2006). Co-occurence of conduct disorder and depression in a clinic-based sample of boys with ADHD. *Journal of Child Psychology and Psychiatry, 47*(8), 766–774.

DuPaul, G. J. & Stoner, G. (2003). *ADHD in the schools: Assessment and intervention strategies* (2nd edn). New York: Guilford Press.

Durston, S. (2003). A review of the biological bases of ADHD: What have we learned from imaging studies? *Mental Retardation and Developmental Disabilities Research Reviews, 9*, 184–195.

Elia, J., Gai, X., Xie, H. M., Perin, J. C., Geiger, E., Glessner, J. T., & D'arcy, M. (2009). Rare structural variants found in attention-deficit hyperactivity disorder are preferentially associated with neurodevelopmental genes. *Molecular Psychiatry, 15*(6), 637–646.

Emilsson, B., Gudjonsson, G., Sigurdsson, J. F., Baldursson, G., Einarsson, E., Olafsdottir, H., & Young, S. (2011). Cognitive behaviour therapy in medication-treated adults with ADHD and persistent symptoms: A randomized controlled trial. *BMC Psychiatry, 11*, 116.

Fabiano, G. A., Pelham, W. E. Jr., Coles, C. K., Gnagy, E. M., Chronis-Tuscano, A., & O'Connor, B. C. (2009). A meta-analysis of behavioral treatments for attention-deficit/hyperactivity disorder. *Clinical Psychology Review, 29*(2), 129–140.

Fite, P. J., Evans, S. C., Cooley, J. L., & Rubens, S. L. (2014). Further evaluation of associations between attention-deficit/hyperactivity and oppositional defiant disorder symptoms and bullying-victimization in adolescence. *Child Psychiatry & Human Development, 45*(1), 1–10.

Fox, D. J., Tharp, D. F., & Fox, L. C. (2005). Neurofeedback: An alternative and efficacious treatment for attention deficit hyperactivity disorder. *Applied Psychophysiology and Biofeedback*, *30*(4), 365–373.

Fuchs, T., Birbaumer, N., Lutzenberger, W., Gruzelier, J. H., & Kaiser, J. (2003). Neurofeedback treatment for attention-deficit/hyperactivity disorder in children: A comparison with methylphenidate. *Applied Psychophysiology and Biofeedback, 28*(1), 1–12.

Gallagher, R. & Rosenblatt, J. L. (2013). Attention-deficit/hyperactivity disorder predominantly inattentive type. In L. A. Reddy, A. S. Weissman, & J. B. Hale (Eds.), *Neuropsychological assessment and intervention for youth: An evidence-based approach to emotional and behavioral disorders* (pp. 155–176). Washington, DC: American Psychological Association.

Geller, B., Craney, J. L., Bolhofner, K., DelBello, M. P., Axelson, D., Luby, J., ... & Beringer, L. (2003). Phenomenology and longitudinal course of children with a prepubertal and early adolescent bipolar disorder phenotype. In B. Geller & M. P. DelBello (Eds.), *Bipolar disorder in childhood and early adolescence* (pp. 25–50). New York: Guilford Press.

Gershon, J. (2002). A meta-analytic review of gender differences in ADHD. *Journal of Attention Disorders, 5*(3), 143–154.

Golden, J. C. (1978). *Stroop Color and Word Test*. Chicago, IL: Stoelting Co.

Gray, S. A., Chaban, P., Martinussen, R., Goldberg, R., Gotlieb, H., Kronitz, R., ... & Tannock, R. (2012). Effects of a computerized working memory training program on working memory, attention, and academics in adolescents with severe LD and comorbid ADHD: A randomized controlled trial. *Journal of Child Psychology and Psychiatry, 53*(12), 1277–1284.

Green, C. T., Long, D. L., Green, D., Iosif, A. M., Dixon, J. F., Miller, M. R., ... & Schweitzer, J. B. (2012). Will working memory training generalize to improve off-task behavior in children with attention-deficit/hyperactivity disorder? *Neurotherapeutics, 9*(3), 639–648.

Greenhill, L. L., Halperin, J. M., & Abikoff, H. (1999). Stimulant medications. *Journal of the American Academy of Child & Adolescent Psychiatry, 38*(5), 503–512.

Grimm, S., Beck, J., Schuepbach, D., Hell, D., Boesiger, P., Bermpohl, F., ... & Northoff, G. (2008). Imbalance between left and right dorsolateral prefrontal cortex in major depression is linked to negative emotional judgment: An fMRI study in severe major depressive disorder. *Biological Psychiatry, 63*(4), 369–376.

Hale, J. B., Reddy, L. A., Weissman, A. S., Lukie, C., & Schneider, A. N. (2013). Integrated neuropsychological assessment and intervention for youth with attention-deficit/hyperactivity disorder. In L. A. Reddy, A. S. Weissman, & J. B. Hale (Eds.), *Neuropsychological assessment and intervention for youth: An evidence-based approach to emotional and behavioral disorders*. Washington, DC: APA Press.

Hale, J. B., Reddy, L. A., Decker, S. L., Thompson, R., Henzel, J., Teodori, A., ... & Denckla, M. B. (2009). Development and validation of a 15-minute EF and behavior rating screening battery for children with ADHD. *Journal of Clinical and Experimental Neuropsychology, 31*(8), 897–912.

Halperin, J. M. & Healey, D. M. (2011). The influences of environmental enrichment, cognitive enhancement, and physical exercise on brain development: Can we alter the developmental trajectory of ADHD? *Neuroscience & Biobehavioral Reviews, 35*(3), 621–634.

Halperin, J. M., Bedard, A. C., & Curchack-Lichtin, J. T. (2012). Preventive interventions for ADHD: A neurodevelopmental perspective. *Neurotherapeutics, 9*(3), 531–541.

Halperin, J. M., Marks, D. J., Bedard, A. C. V., Chacko, A., Curchack, J. T., Yoon, C. A., & Healey, D. M. (2013). Training executive, attention, and motor skills: A proof-of-concept study in preschool children with ADHD. *Journal of Attention Disorders, 17*(8), 711–721.

Hartley, S. L. & Sikora, D. M. (2009). Which DSM-IV-TR criteria best differentiate high-functioning autism spectrum disorder from ADHD and anxiety disorders in older children? *Autism, 13*(5), 485–509.

Healey, D. M. & Halperin, J. M. (2014). Enhancing neurobehavioral gains with the aid of games and exercise (ENGAGE): Initial open trial of a novel early intervention fostering the development of preschoolers' self-regulation. *Child Neuropsychology*, http://www.tandfonline.com/doi/abs/10.1080/.VBTjD1bhr-Q.

Holtmann, M., Bolte, S., & Poustka, F. (2005). ADHD, Asperger syndrome, and high functioning autism. *Journal of the American Academy of Child & Adolescent Psychiatry, 44*, 1101.

Hood, K. K. & Eyberg, S. M. (2003). Outcomes of parent-child interaction therapy: Mothers' reports of maintenance three to six years after treatment. *Journal of Clinical Child & Adolescent Psychology, 32*(3), 419–429.

Iversen, S. D. & Dunnett, S. B. (1990). Functional organization of striatum as studied with neural grafts. *Neuropsychologia, 28*, 601–626.

Jones, K., Daley, D., Hutchings, J., Bywater, T., & Eames, C. (2008). Efficacy of the Incredible Years Programme as an early intervention for children with conduct problems and ADHD: Long-term follow-up. *Child: Care, Health, and Development, 34*(3), 380–390.

Kerns, K. A., Eso, K., & Thompson, J. (1999). Investigation of a direct intervention for improving attention in young children with ADHD. *Developmental Neuropsychology, 16*, 273–295.

Kessler, R. C., Adler, L., Barkley, R., Biederman, J., Conners, C. K., Demler, O., … & Zaslavsky, A. M. (2006). The prevalence and correlates of adult ADHD in the United States: Results from the national comorbidity survey replication. *American Journal of Psychiatry, 163*(4), 716–723.

Kessler, R. C., Adler, L. A., Barkley, R., Biederman, J., Conners, C. K., Faraone, S. V., … & Zaslavsky, A. M. (2005). Patterns and predictors of attention-deficit/hyperactivity disorder persistence into adulthood: Results from the national comorbidity survey replication. *Biological Psychiatry, 57*, 1442–1451.

Klingberg, T., Forssberg, H., & Westerberg, H. (2002). Training of working memory in children with ADHD. *Journal of Clinical and Experimental Neuropsychology, 24*(6), 781–791.

Klingberg, T., Fernell, E., Olesen, P. J., Johnson, M., Gustafsson, P., Dahlstrom, K., … & Westerberg, H. (2005). Computerized training of working memory in children with ADHD: A randomized, controlled trial. *Journal of the American Academy of Child & Adolescent Psychiatry, 44*(2), 177–186.

Lichter, D. G. & Cummings, J. L. (Eds.) (2001). *Frontal-subcortical circuits in psychiatric and neurological disorders.* New York: Guilford Press.

Luckenbaugh, D. A., Findling, R. L., Leverich, G. S., Pizzarello, S. M., & Post, R. M. (2009). Earliest symptoms discriminating juvenile-onset bipolar illness from ADHD. *Bipolar Disorder, 11*(4), 441–451.

Lynam, D., Moffitt, T. E., & Stouthamer-Loeber, M. (1993). Explaining the relation between IQ and delinquency: Class, race, test motivation, school failure, or self-control? *Journal of Abnormal Psychology, 102*(2), 187.

Makris, N., Biederman, J., Valera, E. M., Bush, G., Kaiser, J., Kennedy, D. N., … & Seidman, L. J. (2007). Cortical thinning of the attention and EF networks in adults with attention-deficit/hyperactivity disorder. *Cerebral Cortex, 17*(6), 1364–1375.

Marzocchi, G. M., Oosterlaan, J., Zuddas, A., Cavolina, P., Geurts, H., Redigolo, D., … & Sergeant, J. A. (2008). Contrasting deficits on EFs between ADHD and reading disabled children. *Journal of Child Psychology and Psychiatry, 49*(5), 543–552.

Mayberg, H. (2001). Depression and frontal-subcortical circuits: Focus on prefrontal-limbic interactions. In D. G. Lichter & J. L. Cummings (Eds.), *Frontal-subcortical circuits in psychiatric and neurological disorders* (pp. 177–206). New York: Guilford Press.

McAlonan, G. M., Cheung, V., Chua, S. E., Oosterlaan, J., Hung, S. F., Tang, C. P., … & Leung, P. W. (2009). Age-related grey matter volume correlates of response inhibition and shifting in attention-deficit hyperactivity disorder. *The British Journal of Psychiatry, 194*(2), 123–129.

Milich, R., Balentine, A. C., & Lynam, D. R. (2001). ADHD combined type and ADHD predominantly inattentive type are distinct and unrelated disorders. *Clinical Psychology: Science and Practice, 8*(4), 463–488.

Minzenberg, M. J. (2012). Pharmacotherapy for attention-deficit/hyperactivity disorder: From cells to circuits. *Neurotherapeutics, 9*(3), 610–621.

Mohlman, J. & Gorman, J. M. (2005). The role of EF in CBT: A pilot study with anxious older adults. *Behaviour Research and Therapy, 43*, 447–465.

Molina, B. S., Hinshaw, S. P., Swanson, J. M., Arnold, L. E., Vitiello, B., Jensen, P. S., … & Houck, P. R. (2009). The MTA at 8 years: Prospective follow-up of children treated for combined-type ADHD in a multisite study. *Journal of the American Academy of Child & Adolescent Psychiatry, 48*(5), 484–500.

Moriyama, T. S., Polanczyk, G., Caye, A., Banaschewski, T., Brandeis, D., & Rohde, L. A. (2012). Evidence-based information on the clinical use of neurofeedback for ADHD. *Neurotherapeutics, 9*(3), 588–598.

Pelham, W. E., Jr. & Fabiano, G. A. (2008). Evidence-based psychosocial treatments for attention-deficit/hyperactivity disorder. *Journal of Clinical Child & Adolescent Psychology, 37*(1), 184–214.

Pennington, B. F. & Ozonoff, S. (1996). EFs and developmental psychopathology. *Journal of Child Psychology and Psychiatry, 37*(1), 51–87.

Pfiffner, L. J., Yee Mikami, A., Huang-Pollock, C., Easterlin, B., Zalecki, C., & McBurnett, K. (2007). A randomized, controlled trial of integrated home-school behavioral treatment for ADHD, predominantly inattentive type. *Journal of the American Academy of Child & Adolescent Psychiatry, 46*(8), 1041–1050.

Pliszka, S. R. & Olvera, R. L. (1999). Anxiety disorders. In S. Goldstein & C. R. Reynolds (Eds.), *Handbook of neurodevelopmental and genetic disorders in children* (pp. 216–246). New York: Guilford Press.

Pliszka, S. R., Carlson, C. L., & Swanson, J. M. (1999). *ADHD with comorbid disorders: Clinical assessment and management.* New York: Guilford Press.

Polanczyk, G., de Lima, M. S., Horta, B. L., Beiderman, J., & Rohde, L. A. (2007). The worldwide prevalence of ADHD: A systematic review and metaregression analysis. *American Journal of Psychiatry, 164,* 942–948.

Proal, E., Reiss, P. T., Klein, R. G., Mannuzza, S., Gotimer, K., Ramos-Olazagasti, M. A., ... & Castellanos, F. X. (2011). Brain gray matter deficits at 33-year follow-up in adults with attention-deficit/hyperactivity disorder established in childhood. *Archives of General Psychiatry, 68*(11), 1122–1134.

Rabiner, D. L., Murray, D. W., Skinner, A. T., & Malone, P. S. (2010). A randomized trial of two promising computer-based interventions for students with attention difficulties. *Journal of Abnormal Child Psychology, 38*(1), 131–142.

Rajendran, K., Trampush, J. W., Rindskopf, D., Marks, D. J., O'Neill, S., & Halperin, J. M. (2013). Association between variation in neuropsychological development and the trajectory of ADHD severity in early childhood. *American Journal of Psychiatry, 170*(10), 1205–1211.

Reddy, L. A., Weissman, A. S., & Hale, J. B. (2013). *Neuropsychological assessment and intervention for emotional and behavior disordered youth: An integrated step-by-step evidence-based approach.* Washington, DC: APA Press.

Reynolds, S. & Lane, S. J. (2009). Sensory overresponsivity and anxiety in children with ADHD. *American Journal of Occupational Therapy, 63*(4), 433–440.

Richey, J. A., Ellard, K. K., Siegle, G., Price, R., Mohlman, J., De Raedt, R., ... & Weissman, A. S. (2013). Closing the gap between science and practice: Report from the Neurocognitive Therapies/Translational Research (NT/TR) Special Interest Group. *The Behavior Therapist, 36,* 158–160.

Rowland, A. S., Lesesne, C. A., & Abramowitz, A. J. (2002). The epidemiology of attention-deficit/hyperactivity disorder (ADHD): A public health view. *Mental Retardation and Developmental Disabilities Research Reviews, 8,* 162–170.

Rueda, M. R., Rothbart, M. K., McCandliss, B. D., Saccomanno, L., & Posner, M. I. (2005). Training, maturation, and genetic influences on the development of executive attention. *Proceedings of the National Academy of Sciences, 102*(41), 14931–14936.

Safren, S. A., Otto, M. W., Sprich, S., Winett, C. L., Wilens, T. E., & Biederman, J. (2005). Cognitive-behavioral therapy for ADHD in medication-treated adults with continued symptoms. *Behavior Research and Therapy, 43*(7), 831–842.

Safren, S. A., Sprich, S., Mimiaga, M. J., Surman, C., Knouse, L., Groves, M., & Otto, M. W. (2010). Cognitive behavioral therapy vs relaxation with educational support for medication-treated adults with ADHD and persistent symptoms: A randomized controlled trial. *Journal of the American Medical Association, 304*(8), 875–880.

Sagvolden, T., Aase, H., Zeiner, P., & Berger, D. (1998). Altered reinforcement mechanisms in attention-deficit/hyperactivity disorder. *Behavioural Brain Research, 94*(1), 61–71.

Savitz, J. B. & Drevets, W. C. (2009). Imaging phenotypes of major depressive disorder: Genetic correlates. *Neuroscience, 164*(1), 300–330.

Schulz, K. P., Fan, J., Tang, C. Y., Newcorn, J. H., Buchsbaum, M. S., Cheung, A. M., & Halperin, J. M. (2004). Response inhibition in adolescents diagnosed with attention deficit hyperactivity disorder during childhood: An event-related fMRI study. *American Journal of Psychiatry, 161*(9), 1650–1657.

Schweitzer, J. B. & McBurnett, K. (2012). New directions for therapeutics in ADHD. *Neurotherapeutics, 9*(3), 487–489.

Schweitzer, J. B., & Sulzer-Azaroff, B. (1988). Self-control: Teaching tolerance for delay in impulsive children. *Journal of the Experimental Analysis of Behavior, 50*(2), 173–186.

Seidman, L. J. (2006). Neuropsychological functioning in people with ADHD across the lifespan. *Clinical Psychology Review, 26*, 466–485.

Seidman, L. J., Valera, E. M., & Makris, N. (2005). Structural brain imaging of attention-deficit/hyperactivity disorder. *Biological Psychiatry, 57*(11), 1263–1272.

Shalev, L., Tsal, Y., & Mevorach, C. (2007). Computerized progressive attentional training (CPAT) program: Effective direct intervention for children with ADHD. *Child Neuropsychology, 13*(4), 382–388.

Shaw, P., Eckstrand, K., Sharp, W., Blumenthal, J., Lerch, J. P., Greenstein, D., ... & Rapoport, J. L. (2007). Attention-deficit/hyperactivity disorder is characterized by a delay in cortical maturation. *Proceedings of the National Academy of Sciences, 104*(49), 19649–19654.

Shear, P. K., Delbello, M. P., Lee-Rosenberg, H., & Strakowski, S. M. (2002). Parental reports of executive dysfunction in adolescents with bipolar disorder. *Child Neuropsychology, 8*, 285–295.

Silverman, W. K. & Hinshaw, S. P. (2008). The second special issue on evidence-based psychosocial treatments for children and adolescents: A 10-year update. *Journal of Clinical Child & Adolescent Psychology, 37*(1), 1–7.

Sinzig, J., Walter, D., & Doepfner, M. (2009). Attention deficit/hyperactivity disorder in children and adolescents with autism spectrum disorder. *Journal of Attention Disorders, 13*(2), 117–126.

Solanto, M. V., Marks, D. J., Wasserstein, J., Mitchell, K., Abikoff, H., Alvir, J. M., & Kofman, M. D. (2010). Efficacy of meta-cognitive therapy for adult ADHD. *American Journal of Psychiatry, 167*(8), 958–968.

Sonuga-Barke, E. J. (2003). The dual pathway model of ADHD: An elaboration of neuro-developmental characteristics. *Neuroscience & Biobehavioral Reviews, 27*(7), 593–604.

Steiner, N. J., Sheldrick, R. C., Gotthelf, D., & Perrin, E. C. (2011). Computer-based attention training in the schools for children with attention deficit/hyperactivity disorder: A preliminary trial. *Clinical Pediatrics, 50*(7), 615–622.

Strehl, U., Leins, U., Goth, G., Klinger, C., Hinterberger, T., & Birbaumer, N. (2006). Self-regulation of slow cortical potentials: A new treatment for children with attention-deficit/hyperactivity disorder. *Pediatrics, 118*(5), 1530–1540.

Stroop, J. (1935). Studies of interference in serial verbal reactions. *Journal of Experimental Psychology, 28*, 643–662.

Tamm, L., Nakonezny, P. A., & Hughes, C. W. (2012). An open trial of a metacognitive EF training for young children with ADHD. *Journal of Attention Disorders, 18*(6), 551–9.

Tamm, L., Hughes, C., Ames, L., Pickering, J., Silver, C. H., Stavinoha, P., ... & Emslie, G. (2010). Attention training for school-aged children with ADHD: Results of an open trial. *Journal of Attention Disorders, 14*(1), 86–94.

Tannock, R., Ickowicz, A., & Schachar, R. (1995). Differential effects of methylphenidate on working memory in ADHD children with and without comorbid anxiety. *Journal of the American Academy of Child & Adolescent Psychiatry, 34*(7), 886–896.

Tantillo, M., Kesick, C. M., Hynd, G. W., & Dishman, R. K. (2002). The effects of exercise on children with attention-deficit hyperactivity disorder. *Medicine & Science in Sports & Exercise, 34*(2), 203–212.

Toplak, M. E., Connors, L., Shuster, J., Knezevic, B., & Parks, S. (2008). Review of cognitive, cognitive-behavioral, and neural-based interventions for attention-deficit/ hyperactivity disorder (ADHD). *Clinical Psychology Review, 28*(5), 801–823.

Tsal, Y., Shalev, L., & Mevorach, C. (2005). The diversity of attention deficits in ADHD: The prevalence of four cognitive factors in ADHD versus controls. *Journal of Learning Disabilities, 38*, 142–157.

Tsujii, N., Okada, A., Kaku, R., Kuriki, N., Hanada, K., & Shirakawa, O. (2009). Differentiation between attention-deficit/hyperactivity disorder and pervasive developmental disorders with hyperactivity on objective activity levels using actigraphs. *Psychiatry and Clinical Neurosciences, 63*(3), 336–343.

Tucha, O., Tucha, L., Kaumann, G., Konig, S., Lange, K. M., Stasik, D., ... & Lange, K. W. (2011). Training of attention functions in children with attention deficit hyperactivity disorder. *Attention Deficit and Hyperactivity Disorders, 3*(3), 271–283.

Valera, E. M., Faraone, S. V., Murray, K. E., & Seidman, L. J. (2007). Meta-analysis of structural imaging findings in attention-deficit/hyperactivity disorder. *Biological Psychiatry, 61*(12), 1361–1369.

Virta, M., Salakari, A., Antila, M., Chydenius, E., Partinen, M., Kaski, M., ... & Iivanainen, M. (2010). Short cognitive behavioral therapy and cognitive training for adults with ADHD: A randomized controlled pilot study. *Neuropsychiatric Disease and Treatment, 6*, 443–453.

Wagner, K. D. & Ambrosini, P. J. (2001). Childhood depression: Pharmacological therapy/treatment (pharmacology of childhood depression). *Journal of Clinical Child Psychology, 30*, 88–97.

Waschbusch, D. A. (2002). A meta-analytic examination of comorbid hyperactive-impulsive-attention problems and conduct problems. *Psychological Bulletin, 128*(1), 118.

Wechsler, D. (2003). *Wechsler Intelligence Scale for Children* (4th edn). New York: Psychological Corporation.

Weiss, M., Murray, C., Wasdell, M., Greenfield, B., Giles, L., & Hechtman, L. (2012). A randomized controlled trial of CBT therapy for adults with ADHD with and without medication. *BMC Psychiatry, 12*, 30.

Weissman, A. S. & Bates, M. E. (2010). Increased clinical and neurocognitive impairment in children with autism spectrum disorders and comorbid bipolar disorder. *Research in Autism Spectrum Disorders, 4*(4), 670–680.

Weissman, A. S., Antinoro, D., & Chu, B. C. (2008). Cognitive-behavioral therapy for anxiety in school settings: Advances and challenges. In M. Mayer, R. Van Acker, J. E. Lochman, & F. M. Gresham (Eds.), *Cognitive-behavioral interventions for students with emotional/behavioral disorders* (pp. 173–203). New York: Guilford Press.

Weissman, A. S., Chu, B. C., Reddy, L. R., & Mohlman, J. (2012). Attention mechanisms in children with anxiety disorders and in children with attention deficit hyperactivity disorder: Implications for research and practice. *Journal of Clinical Child & Adolescent Psychology, 41*(2), 117–126.

Weyandt, L. L. (2005). EF in children, adolescents, and adults with attention deficit hyperactivity disorder: Introduction to the special issue. *Developmental Neuropsychology, 27*, 1–10.

Wigal, S. B., Nemet, D., Swanson, J. M., Regino, R., Trampush, J., Ziegler, M. G., & Cooper, D. M. (2003). Catecholamine response to exercise in children with attention deficit hyperactivity disorder. *Pediatric Research, 53*(5), 756–761.

Willcutt, E. G. & Pennington, B. F. (2000). Comorbidity of reading disability and attention-deficit/hyperactivity disorder: Differences by gender and subtype. *Journal of Learning Disabilities, 33*, 179–191.

Willcutt, E. G., Nigg, J. T., Pennington, B. F., Solanto, M. V., Rohde, L. A., Tannock, R., … & Lahey, B. B. (2012). Validity of DSM–IV attention deficit/hyperactivity disorder symptom dimensions and subtypes. *Journal of Abnormal Psychology, 121*(4), 991.

Wozniak, J. (2005). Recognizing and managing bipolar disorder in children. *Journal of Clinical Psychiatry, 66 (suppl 1)*, 18–23.

7

NEUROCOGNITION IN SCHIZOPHRENIA

A Core Illness Feature and Novel Treatment Target

Matthew M. Kurtz

Deficits in neurocognition in schizophrenia such as attention deficits, while recognized in earliest descriptions of the disorder, remain a largely overlooked facet of the illness not captured in current diagnostic systems. Consequently, such deficits are frequently neglected in clinical care. The impact of this neglect is particularly profound given the independence of neurocognitive deficits from other psychiatric symptoms associated with the disorder, resistance of these deficits to routine pharmacotherapy and their close link to functional outcome. Thus, the goal of this chapter is to provide an overview to understanding schizophrenia as a disorder of neurocognition as well as a disorder affecting mood and insight. This goal is approached by defining the schizophrenia syndrome, summarizing the relevant research identifying neurocognitive impairment as a core feature of the illness and the many ways in which this impairment may manifest, and then providing a description of emerging work on contemporary interventions for cognitive impairment in schizophrenia. More specifically, the chapter begins by defining the disorder in terms of its DSM-5 categorization, briefly reviewing epidemiology and etiology, then focusing on what is known about neurocognitive impairment in schizophrenia as related to the clinical course of illness from the premorbid period to first episode to chronic illness and then in senescence. The chapter evaluates the literature on the relationship of neurocognition to structural and functional neuroimaging studies, symptoms, and functioning in the disorder. Last, this chapter will summarize the treatment implications of a neurocognitive approach to schizophrenia, discussing promising pharmacologic and behavioral approaches to treatment that have emerged from a neurocognitive perspective on the disorder.

Diagnosis

Just as the definition of schizophrenia has been somewhat incomplete, there is no reliable medical test for diagnosing the disorder. Instead, diagnosis is made by a mental health professional and relies on subjective symptoms reported by the individual and the observation of family members, other intimates of the individual, and the clinician. Definitions of the disorder have shifted substantially over time. Those found in DSM-I and II derived largely from psychoanalytic theory and bear only a modest resemblance to narrower standards developed for diagnosis in DSM-III, which was first published in 1980. Indeed, studies have shown only 41 percent of individuals assigned a DSM-II diagnosis schizophrenia would meet criteria by DSM-III standards (Harrow, Carone, & Westermeyer, 1985). The DSM-III criteria have been largely maintained in DSM-IV and DSM-5 and are derived more closely from Kraepelin's definition of the disorder, which was formulated at the turn of the twentieth century.

According to the DSM-IV TR (American Psychiatric Association [APA], 2001), the diagnosis of schizophrenia was made on the basis of three criteria: two or more of the following characteristic symptoms present for much of the time during a month (or less if effectively treated); *delusions, hallucinations, disorganized speech, grossly disorganized or catatonic behavior* and/or *negative symptoms* (blunted affect, alogia, or avolition); substantial decline in occupational, social, or self-care skills; and signs of the disturbance present for a six-month period of time with one month of symptoms (or fewer if successfully treated). DSM-5 has largely preserved the criteria of DSM-IV TR but has added dimensional 0 to 4 severity and frequency ratings of major elements of the disorder. Thus, in the first eighty years of the twentieth century in the United States, diagnostic conceptualizations of schizophrenia placed an emphasis on psychological mechanisms rather than symptomatic presentation and consequently were broad and ill-defined. From the time of the third to fifth editions of the DSM, that practice has changed and is now characterized by increased diagnostic reliability. This increase in reliability increases confidence in the consistency of findings on neurocognition and other aspects of the disorder that have emerged over the last thirty-five years of research and are discussed in the remainder of the chapter.

Epidemiology-etiology

Schizophrenia is a relatively common psychiatric disorder, with lifetime prevalence rates worldwide ranging from .5 percent to 1 percent. Schizophrenia is typically a chronic disorder, and thus incidence rates are lower at approximately 15.2 in 100,000 (McGrath et al., 2004). Incidence rates vary by season of birth (Kendall & Adams, 1991), urban versus rural location (Lewis, David,

Andreasson, & Allebeck, 1992) and immigrant status (e.g., Bhugra, 2000). It is among the most disabling of illnesses, with recent estimates suggesting that fewer than 20 percent of individuals with the disorder in the United States are able to hold full or even part-time competitive employment. Furthermore, only one-half of 1 percent who receive Social Security Insurance (SSI/SSDI) ever remove themselves from these entitlements (Salkever et al., 2007; Torrey, 1999). The World Health Organization lists schizophrenia as one of the top ten leading causes of disability among adults worldwide (World Health Organization [WHO], 1992). Consistent with this perspective, the majority of long-term psychiatric hospital beds are used for people diagnosed with schizophrenia (Pillay & Montcrief, 2011).

Although the exact etiological mechanisms of schizophrenia are unknown, there do appear to be clear genetic and environmental influences on the likelihood of emergence of the disorder. With respect to heredity, first-degree biological relatives of individuals with schizophrenia have a risk for developing the disorder that is ten times that of the general population. Concordance rates are higher in monozygotic than dizygotic twins. Biological relatives of adoptees who develop schizophrenia have increased risk for schizophrenia, whereas adoptive relatives do not (Tsuang, Stone, & Faraone, 1999). It has been known for many years that environmental stress (particularly early in development) also plays a role in the emergence of the disorder. For example, maternal starvation during pregnancy, evident in groups of women during specific historical epochs such as periods of World War II, has been linked to increased rates of incidence in children born in the months after these epochs (Susser & Lin, 1992). In a similar vein, numerous studies have indicated that a range of birth complications have also been linked to increased rates of schizophrenia (e.g., Clarke, Harley, & Cannon, 2006). Additionally, among one of the most salient recent findings is that one type of sustained environmental stress, the immigrant experience, can increase the likelihood of developing the disorder by as much as nine times as evidenced in recent studies of dark-skinned migrants of African-Caribbean and African origin living in northern Europe (Fearon et al., 2006).

Historical Perspectives on the Importance of Neurocognition

Early in the twentieth century, psychiatrists involved in first categorizing and naming schizophrenia recognized that there were cognitive deficits in individuals with schizophrenia. It is generally agreed that the contemporary definition of schizophrenia was most influenced by Emil Kraepelin's description of the disorder, as defined in the 1893 edition of his highly influential *Textbook of Psychiatry*, in which he grouped several previously distinct psychiatric entities— *hebephrenia*, *catatonia*, and *paranoia*—into a single disorder labeled *dementia praecox*, which was defined by its poor long-term outcome (Shorter, 1998). Bleuler (1950), whose work was subsequent to Kraepelin's, both expanded Kraepelin's initial definition of the disorder and placed a larger emphasis on cognition as one of four fundamental features of the disorder. Through his careful observation, Bleuler anticipated several of the substantive issues of contemporary neurocognitive research in schizophrenia: namely, that these deficits were common and heterogeneous, with some individuals suffering from extensive impairment and others not at all, and linked to functional outcome in the disorder.

> The schizophrenic is not generally demented but he is demented with regard to certain periods, to certain constellations, and to certain complexes. In mild cases, the defective functions are the exception. In most severe cases, those who sit around in our mental institutions taking no part in anything, the defective functions are the rule…The mildest case can commit as great a piece of folly as the most severe, but he commits it far more rarely.
>
> (Bleuler, 1951, pp. 73–74)

Domains of Neurocognitive Impairment

While many other defining features of schizophrenia such as delusions and auditory hallucinations are only evident in a subset of people with the diagnosis, deficits in neurocognition are ubiquitous, evident in virtually every instance of the disorder. For example, by some estimates, auditory hallucinations occur in an average of only 50 percent of people with the disorder (DeLeon, Cuesta, & Peralta, 1993). In contrast, while initial studies suggested that approximately 70 percent of people with the diagnosis would be considered "impaired" on a neuropsychological test battery (Palmer, Heaton, Kuck, & Braff, 1997), current research suggests that nearly 100 percent of individuals with the diagnosis demonstrate some decline in neurocognitive function when baseline IQ is accounted for (Kremen, Seidman, Faraone, & Tsuang, 2005; Wilk et al., 2000; Kurtz, Donato, & Rose, 2011).

A wealth of studies of neurocognitive function in schizophrenia have been conducted over the past twenty years (Harvey & Reichenberg, 2007; Kurtz & Marcopulos, 2012; Goldberg, David, & Gold, 2011) and can be grouped into two general categories: studies using standardized, clinical neuropsychological measures developed for settings in which the detection and localization of brain dysfunction was of central importance, or studies investigating experimental tools derived from cognitive psychological theory for parsing component cognitive mechanisms responsible for the production of mental activities, the experimental psychopathological or cognitive neuroscience approach. We approach this section of the chapter by reviewing findings for specific neurocognitive domains in schizophrenia as measured by standardized, clinical neuropsychological tests and experimental psychopathological neurocognitive tasks with an attempt to synthesize these literatures. To facilitate comparisons of findings across very different neurocognitive areas, for each domain we provide a standardized estimate of effect-size impairment in schizophrenia (Cohen's d) when available. We use the metric of small, $d = .2-.49$, medium $d = .5-.79$, and large effect-size ($d \geq .8$) impairment. Moderate-to-large effect-size deficits have been reported in nearly every area of neurocognition that has been measured in schizophrenia.

Full-scale IQ

Psychologists have made distinctions between cognitive capacity or "g" (Spearman, 1925) that represent skills evident in assessments of IQ presumed to be resistant to the effects of neural damage versus specific neurocognitive skills, such as attention, memory, and problem solving, that are more sensitive to neural damage. Despite this presumption, most studies of IQ in schizophrenia to date have shown effect-size impairment in the large range for full-scale IQ (e.g., Dickinson, Ramsey, & Gold, 2007; $d = .98$) with impairments in performance IQ that are 50 percent larger than verbal IQ (e.g., Heinrichs & Zakzanis, 1998). These findings suggest that deficits in specific neurocognitive functions in schizophrenia are commonly evident in concert with significant global IQ impairment.

Attention

Clinical neuropsychological approaches to the assessment of attention have most commonly focused on sustained visual vigilance, most frequently with several variants of the continuous performance test (CPT). CPT measures vary by placing differential demands on visual identification or by varying working memory (WM) demands. With respect to WM demands, in some CPT versions, participants respond to a single target (the "X" version of the CPT—low WM demands), while other versions ask the participant to respond as rapidly as possible when the participant see one stimulus but only when it is preceded by a second stimulus (the "A-X" version of the CPT—high WM demands). Other exemplars of the task increase perceptual demands on the participant by degrading the target (making the target blurred; the "degraded stimulus" version of the CPT). People with schizophrenia show deficits in the moderate–large (.66–1.16) range on these neurocognitive tasks (Dickinson et al., 2007; Heinrichs & Zakzanis, 1998) relative to matched healthy controls.

Experimental psychopathological approaches have viewed attention as a neurocognitive skill necessary for the support of other, more complex neurocognitive functions such as working memory and response selection, particularly under conditions of information overload (Goldberg et al., 2011). Attention in these studies has often been divided into the investigation of control processes that determine where attention is devoted among competing sensory inputs versus the study of the effects of focused attention on enhancement of other cognitive processes such as working memory. Measures of attention control processes reveal impairments largely consistent with those seen on standardized clinical instruments; people with a diagnosis of schizophrenia have difficulty shifting attention away from salient or prepotent environmental stimuli (e.g., Sereno & Holzman, 1996). In contrast, studies focusing on the effectiveness of attention processes for supporting other cognitive functions once attention has been successfully deployed to task-relevant environmental stimuli (labeled *attention implementation*) suggest intact attention implementation functions: for example, successfully encoding and storing of subgroups of stimuli from a broader stimulus array into working memory (Gold et al., 2006). Thus, in summary, studies of standardized clinical instruments for the assessment of attention have revealed moderate–large effect-size deficits. Finer-grained analysis of attention subcomponents in cognitive neuroscientific research have revealed a mixed picture, with attentional processes often impaired by overextension toward salient environmental stimuli but intact attentional processes when these skills are applied in the service of other neurocognitive skills, such as the necessary application of attention for successful encoding and rehearsal of memoranda in working memory. These elementary deficits in attention likely play a significant role in the neurocognitive domains we discuss in the following sections.

Episodic Memory

Clinical neuropsychological and experimental psychopathological measures of verbal episodic memory typically ask the participant to immediately recall items from a list of words after repeated list presentations (e.g., California Verbal Learning Test, Hopkins Verbal Learning Test, Rey Auditory Verbal Learning Test) or a passage of text (e.g., Logical Memory from the Wechsler Memory Scale). In these paradigms, delayed recall and recognition measures are administered as well. Meta-analyses have revealed that people with schizophrenia show severe levels of impairment on verbal memory measures (d = 1.20–1.22; Aleman, Hijman, deHaan, & Kahn, 1999). A clear message from the literature on schizophrenia is that episodic memory impairment lie largely at the levels of encoding and retrieval. Studies have suggested that these encoding deficits may be linked to the fact that people with schizophrenia are less likely to semantically encode to-be-remembered information. Strong support for this contention comes from studies indicating that when semantic relationships are highlighted during the study of to-be-remembered stimuli, recall is enhanced (Gold, Randolph, Carpenter, Goldberg, & Weinberger, 1992).

When verbal information is encoded successfully, retention is strong across a variety of different temporal intervals for most people with the diagnosis (e.g., Cirillo & Seidman, 2003). There is little evidence that increasing the retention interval for the same remembered material exacerbates performance deficits (Aleman et al., 1999). Studies of retrieval have been used to assess disruptions in the storage versus retrieval process for episodic memory. By this logic, if recognition performance, which is based on enhanced cueing of responses, is stronger than recall, this would suggest evidence of disruption in the retrieval of memories rather than disruptions in storage. One meta-analysis has revealed that recall is considerably more diminished than recognition memory in schizophrenia even when task difficulty is carefully titrated between the response formats (Aleman et al., 1999), arguing for retrieval deficits in the disorder. Clarity on this issue remains elusive, with other studies showing similar levels of recall and recognition impairment regardless of cue availability at retest (Paulsen et al., 1995).

Clinical neuropsychological studies of nonverbal memory often use difficult-to-verbalize figures that are in some cases complex (Rey Complex Figure Test) and in some cases simple (Visual Reproduction subtest of the WMS-III) and may be assessed by multiple stimulus presentations (Benton Visual Retention Test; BVRT). The magnitude of impairment in these studies is nearly identical to those for verbal memory measures, in the moderate–large range (d = .74–1.03; e.g., Heinrichs & Zakzanis, 1998; Aleman et al., 1999). Thus, there is no evidence for differential, material-specific memory impairment in schizophrenia.

Most recent experimental psychopathological work has attempted to identify illness factors critical for these well-documented impairments in verbal and nonverbal episodic memory paradigms. For example, Brebion, Bressan, Ohlsen, and David (2013) have investigated separate measurements of surface memory processing, processing stimuli by rote rehearsal versus deep memory processing (organizing to-be-learned items by semantic grouping) on recall of lists of words and pictures, and linked these measurements to other cognitive skills and diseases features. Results revealed that processing speed, along with working memory, was related to deep memory processing in both verbal and nonverbal domains and the processing of more difficult low-frequency words on verbal tasks.

In summary, moderate-to-large effect-size impairments in verbal and nonverbal episodic memory tasks are evident in schizophrenia using both clinical neuropsychological measurement instruments and cognitive neuroscientific approaches; these deficits have been linked most strongly to encoding processes and, in the case of deeper semantic encoding, may be influenced by processing speed and working memory skills. These cognitive skills are discussed in the next two sections of the chapter.

Working Memory

In WM tasks, a series of items are presented in one modality, and the participant has to store the items for later recall as well as perform mental manipulations on the memoranda. Memoranda in WM are also used to support other cognitive functions such as those underlying goal-directed behavior: for example, using working memory to actively represent three key ingredients for purchase at the supermarket in service of a goal of making a soup later in the day. Tasks to assess WM are often elements of a comprehensive clinical neuropsychological evaluation as well as an area of intensive study using experimental psychopathological cognitive tasks. Digits Backwards is a prototypical example of this type of task from the clinical neuropsychological literature, requiring the individual to both remember a set of items and then perform a manipulation (placing them in a reverse order). The *N-Back Task* from the experimental psychopathology literature would be another, requiring the participant to respond when a current stimulus (typically a letter or number) matches a previously presented stimulus with the number of intervening presentations of stimuli between target stimuli varying according to the difficulty level of the task (e.g., 2-back versus 3-back). Findings from this class of tasks are similar to those of episodic memory and are in the large (d = .8–1.1) range of impairment (Lee & Park, 2005; Aleman et al., 1999). Effects are evident across multiple modalities (Lee & Park, 2005) and are evident with loads of even a single item and very short delays (Fuller, Luck, McMahon, & Gold, 2005), supporting the contention that there is a fundamental deficit in working memory representations in the disorder rather than disruptions in working memory capacity or retention only.

Processing Speed

Processing speed has been putatively thought to serve as an underlying limiting factor in a variety of cognitive operations such as encoding, recall, mental manipulation, and decision making in schizophrenia. It is defined as the ability to complete a simple visual-motor task rapidly (Dickinson et al., 2007). Observations of processing speed deficits in the scientific literature are some of the earliest documented specific neurocognitive problems in schizophrenia. Indeed, David Wechsler in his original description of the WAIS noted that individuals with schizophrenia were most severely disrupted on these measures relative to other neurocognitive skills (Wechsler, 1955). Consistent with this observation, a meta-analysis of studies of neurocognitive function in schizophrenia (Dickinson et al., 2007) suggests that processing speed may be more impaired (d = 1.57) than other commonly studied neurocognitive functions such as verbal memory, executive function, or working memory in schizophrenia. Thus, these deficits may reflect a core dimension of all cognitive impairment in the disorder.

Two concerns have been raised about the interpretation of this work. First, more recent work has shown that impairment on processing speed measures is more closely linked to dosage of antipsychotic medications than other neurocognitive functions in schizophrenia and thus may reflect, at least partially, a treatment rather than illness variable (Knowles, David, & Reichenberg, 2010). Second, if processing speed measures truly reflected the core cognitive deficit in schizophrenia, they would likely show nearly complete separation between diagnosed individuals and matched healthy control groups. Instead, an obtained d-value of 1.57 indicates 27 percent overlap between patient and healthy samples on these types of tasks.

Executive Function

Executive functions (EF) have been most commonly studied in the clinical neuropsychological literature and include skills in formulating and representing a goal, implementing steps to attain that goal, and meta-cognitive skills to evaluate whether the goal was successfully attained. Schizophrenia consists of many clinical features that are suggestive of dysfunction in EF, such as reduced spontaneity, avolition, mental rigidity, and lack of social judgment. The most commonly used measure of EF is the Wisconsin Card Sorting Test (WCST), used to assess rule learning and cognitive flexibility; the Stroop Color Word Test for verbal inhibition; the Trail Making Test Part B, which measures set-shifting; and the Controlled Oral Word Association Test (COWAT), a test of word fluency. Mean effect-size impairments on these tasks have been in the large range for first-episode, chronic, and older individuals with the disorder. For example, individuals with chronic schizophrenia have WCST total score effect-size impairments of d = .88 (Heinrichs & Zakzanis, 1998; also see Mesholam-Gately, Giuliano, Goff, Faraone, & Seidman, 2009; Irani, Kalkstein, Moberg, & Moberg, 2011 for data from first-episode and older individuals, respectively) as well as large effect-size impairment on measures of category (d = 1.23) and phonemic (d = 1.01) word fluency (Bokat & Goldberg, 2003). Recent work on EF in schizophrenia has focused on factor analyses of the results of broad batteries of EF tests (i.e., Delis-Kaplan Executive Function Scale) from large samples of individuals with schizophrenia that include measures of set-switching, inhibition of prepotent responses, concept formation and conceptual flexibility, verbal and nonverbal fluency, and proverb interpretation and other skills. Results have revealed two underlying factors—cognitive flexibility (the ability to shift response sets) and abstraction (the ability to understand the underlying meaning of stimuli)—that account for much of the performance on these wide-ranging EF tests (Savla et al., 2012)

Sensory-motor Function

In the clinical neuropsychological literature, deficits of moderate size on measures of visual, auditory, and tactile sensory processing have typically been described, while most studies have suggested more profound moderate-to-severe deficits in motor speed (e.g., Dickinson et al., 2007). These effects are evident at first episode, in chronic samples, and in older samples of individuals with schizophrenia (d = .6–.8; Heinrichs & Zakzanis, 1998; Irani et al., 2011; Mesholam-Gately et al., 2009).

Experimental psychopathological studies have most often focused on detection of simple changes in the characteristics of auditory stimuli, such as frequency or duration of stimuli (e.g., Javitt, Zukin, Heresco-Levy, & Umbricht, 2012) or visual stimuli such as perception of contrast and integration of elementary visual features of an object (e.g., Butler et al., 2005). In some cases, these elementary sensory processing deficits have been linked to higher-order auditory emotion recognition and social cognition (Butler et al., 2009), and it has been hypothesized that deficits in elementary sensory processing in schizophrenia could serve as the source of the variegated deficits in higher level neurocognition reviewed in this chapter. For example, impaired free recall on a word list learning task could reflect altered auditory sensory processing and thus resultant low-fidelity mental representations of the word stimuli themselves, rather than a disruption in verbal memory per se.

Neurocognitive Subtypes

A key controversy in the study of neurocognition in schizophrenia is whether the pattern of neurocognitive decrements in schizophrenia is best characterized by a nonspecific or generalized deficit. It is possible that the pattern is characterized by poor performance on all neurocognitive tasks, which leads to highly inter-correlated task performance, and varies from individual to individual only by severity. An alternative model, the specific deficit model, suggests the pattern is instead representative of heterogeneous deficits. Consonant with this latter view, studies of attention shifting, attention for working memory storage, and some forms of implicit learning indicate intact functioning in schizophrenia, despite the legion of decrements in performance on neurocognitive tasks described in the previous section (e.g., Green, Horan, & Sugar, 2013). A corollary of this specific deficit view is that specific patterns of impairment differ across patients, but these patterns share sufficient variance across patients that they can guide the formation of specific neurocognitive subtypes.

Data in support of generalized neurocognitive deficits come from a number of sources. For example, a meta-analysis by Heinrichs and Zakzanis (1998) concluded that schizophrenia is characterized by a generalized neurocognitive impairment, based on the great degree of similarity of effect-sizes across highly varying neurocognitive domains. More recent studies have supported this contention (Dickinson, Ragland, Gold, & Gur, 2008) through the use of structural equation modeling. These authors grouped neurocognitive test data in a sample of 148 individuals with schizophrenia and 157 control participants into six common domains and linked these domains to a higher-order, general cognitive ability factor. A higher proportion (64 percent) of variance in test performance in diagnosed individuals was explained by this general factor than any specific neurocognitive function, and much smaller direct effects were evident only on two specific functions: processing speed and verbal memory. Thus, by this view, impaired performance across a variety of neurocognitive tasks in schizophrenia reflects a common impairment, possibly representing a core information processing skill or motivational system necessary for successful performance on most, if not all, neurocognitive tasks.

Factor-analytic Studies

Distinctive cognitive subtypes within schizophrenia have been investigated using broad-spectrum batteries of standardized neuropsychological instruments (Goldstein, Shemansky, & Allen, 2005; Heinrichs & Awad, 1993; Heinrichs, Ruttan, Zakzanis, & Case, 1997). Studies using cluster analytic studies applied to these test data have delineated three cognitive subtypes, including a high cognitive functioning, "neuropsychologically normal" group (Palmer et al., 1997; Silverstein & Zerwic, 1985), a very low cognitive functioning group (similar to dementia), and a group with motor impairment but relatively preserved verbal abilities (Seaton, Goldstein, & Allen, 2001). The "neuropsychologically normal" individuals were younger at the time of testing and had a relatively benign course characterized by a low number and short length of hospitalizations and lived stably in the community. They also had fewer negative symptoms and more positive symptoms. In contrast, the very low cognitive functioning group were older, less well-educated, and may have had a more severe prodrome with an earlier onset of the disorder. While the high-functioning group was normatively average on neuropsychological measures, it is not clear from these analyses whether their cognitive functioning would have been above average had they not become psychiatrically ill.

Memory-based Subtypes

Individuals with schizophrenia have also been grouped based on memory performance. Turetsky and colleagues (2002) delineated three subtypes based on the profile of memory deficits exhibited on the California Verbal Learning Test (CVLT), a sixteen-item measure of list learning. The "subcortical" subtype showed moderate to severely impaired free recall, normal retention across a delay interval, and disproportionate improvement on recognition testing. These individuals had a longer duration of illness and more severe psychiatric symptoms relative to the "unimpaired" subtype and evidenced ventricular enlargement relative to healthy, matched controls. The "cortical" group exhibited impaired learning, rapid forgetting of learned material, elevated cued-recall intrusions, and limited benefit from recognition testing on the CVLT. "Cortical" individuals were younger, on average, and had earlier illness onset, as compared to the "unimpaired" subtype, and they evidenced reduced temporal lobe gray matter and hypometabolism in temporal lobe structures linked to language and memory processes relative to healthy controls. The relatively unimpaired subtype had fewer negative symptoms and was less likely to be male than the other two subtypes. There was also evidence of increased neural activity in the dorsal medial prefrontal region in this group relative to healthy controls and other subtypes. Other studies have subtyped patients based on either near normality on both memory and attention tests (within .5 SD of healthy control performance) or impairment (greater than 1 SD impairment) and have reported similar reductions in gray matter in the two groups, suggesting neural compromise in individuals with ostensibly "normal" neurocognition but greater white matter loss and larger lateral ventricles in the neurocognitively impaired subgroup (Wexler et al., 2010). Thus, subtyping individuals with schizophrenia based on factor-analytic approaches to broad spectrum neurocognitive test batteries or on the basis of individual memory tests has revealed distinct intact and impaired neurocognitive subgroups. Emerging neuroimaging evidence suggests structural and functional neural abnormalities in all memory-defined groups but more profound abnormalities in impaired cognitive subgroups.

Neurocognitive Impairment in Different Phases of the Disorder

Neurocognitive Impairment Prior to Diagnosis

Neurocognitive impairment prior to diagnosis has been investigated in three ways: by studying people with elevated genetic risk for the disorder, in "follow-back" studies that track premorbid test performance in people already diagnosed with the illness, and by following individuals with attenuated symptoms of insufficient magnitude to reach diagnostic thresholds but consistent in quality with positive symptoms of full-blown schizophrenia. It is well established that cognitive deficits, primarily in attention, predate the onset of the illness in at-risk children (defined as those individuals with a first-degree relative with the disorder) followed longitudinally, even before the onset of first symptoms (Cornblatt & Erlenmeyer-Kimling, 1985). With respect to "follow-back" studies,

Woodberry, Giuliano, and Seidman (2008), in a meta-analysis of eighteen studies, found that many years prior to the onset of psychotic symptoms, individuals later diagnosed with schizophrenia score on average one-half a standard deviation below healthy controls on IQ tests. It is well known that low pre-morbid IQ is a risk factor for the development of schizophrenia (e.g., Aylward, Walker, & Bettes, 1984). Furthermore, epidemiological cohort studies have revealed that intellectual impairment is evident even during childhood in those destined to develop psychosis (e.g., Cannon et al., 2000), and a growing number of studies now also suggest that there are declines in estimated IQ in a substantial population of people with the illness between childhood and late adolescence (e.g., Reichenberg et al., 2005). Even for those who go on to develop schizophrenia and are within the normal range of IQ premorbidly, there is still a greater probability of significant intra-individual variability between IQ subtests relative to healthy controls (Reichenberg et al., 2006).

Individuals at clinical high risk (CHR) for schizophrenia are defined by the presence of attenuated positive symptoms in at least one of five categories: unusual thought content, suspicion/paranoia, grandiosity, perceptual anomalies, and/or disorganized communication. Neurocognitive evaluation of these patients has revealed deficits on a variety of neuropsychological measures that are intermediate in magnitude between healthy control performance and performance in full-blown illness. The most extensive study to date, funded by the National Institute of Mental Health (NIMH)—the multi-site North American Prodrome Longitudinal Study—has revealed that neuropsychological functioning is poorer in high-risk participants who go on to develop psychosis versus those who do not. Tests of processing speed and verbal learning and memory discriminated controls from high-risk participants most effectively, but the magnitude of impairment in these participants was still less than in those with full-blown psychosis. In these studies, performance on neurocognitive tests did not provide incremental validity for likelihood of conversion beyond clinical factors; however, there was evidence that poorer performance on verbal learning and memory tests predicted more rapid transition to psychosis (Seidman et al., 2010). Taken together, these studies support the idea that neurocognitive impairment represents a trait-like feature of the illness that is not secondary to psychiatric treatment and could represent an index of genetic risk for the disorder.

First-episode Studies

The profile and magnitude of deficits in first-episode (FE) schizophrenia are similar to deficits seen later during the course of the illness. The seminal study in this area was conducted by Saykin and colleagues (1994), in a sample of thirty-seven FE, never-treated individuals with schizophrenia compared to sixty-five previously treated diagnosed individuals off medication and 131 matched controls on a broad-spectrum battery of neurocognitive tests. Results revealed that the pattern of neurocognitive impairment in the FE group was identical to chronic patients even though first-episode individuals had no exposure to antipsychotic medication. In the largest study of its type, Sponheim and colleagues (2010) compared recent onset (mean length of illness, 2.6 years) and chronic (mean length of illness, 14 years) individuals with schizophrenia with matched controls. They found that recent-onset individuals with the diagnosis had similar deficits compared with chronic patients, except that timed motor tests and problem solving were worse in chronic patients. Motor deficits were associated with first-generation antipsychotic use in the chronic patients. Lower intellectual functioning, achievement scores, and planning were also seen in these patients. Episodic memory was modestly more impaired in individuals with longer duration of illness. Thus their findings also fit the model of fairly stable cognitive functioning across the life span in schizophrenia.

A recent comprehensive meta-analysis of forty-seven neurocognitive studies of first-episode psychosis has provided decided support for these individual study findings (Mesholam-Gately et al., 2009). Ten cognitive domains—memory, attention (divided into three subdomains of processing speed, working memory, and vigilance), nonverbal memory, general cognitive ability, language functions, visuospatial abilities, delayed verbal memory and learning strategies, executive functioning, social cognition, and motor skills—were studied. They compared their findings with those of Heinrichs and Zakzanis (1998), a meta-analysis that included patients throughout the course of the illness. These authors found medium-to-large effect-size impairments in all neurocognitive functions compared with controls, and deficits evidenced in the first episode in their study were comparable to findings from older, more chronic samples described in previous meta-analyses. Largest cognitive domain effect sizes were found in verbal learning and memory (d = 1.20) and attention/processing speed (d = 0.96). The largest individual test effect size was for digit symbol coding (d = 1.59). Their study shows that these neurocognitive deficits are widespread and generalized even at first episode but also heterogeneous even as compared to the generalized cognitive impairment, with greater deficits in memory relative to other neurocognitive domains.

Older Patients

Meta-analyses of older individuals (mean age, approximately sixty-five years) diagnosed with schizophrenia have shown large effect-size impairment across measures of global cognition and specific neurocognitive functions that are similar to those of younger individuals with the disorder (d = .8–1.3). Demographic (e.g., age, race, gender) and clinical factors (inpatient versus

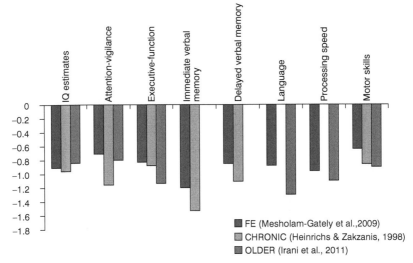

FIGURE 7.1   Mean effect-size impairment in a variety of np domains in first-episode (FE), chronic, and older samples of patients with schizophrenia.

outpatient status, positive and negative symptoms) played a role in the size of the effects (Irani et al., 2011).

Figure 7.1 compares levels of impairment on measures of IQ and specific neurocognitive domains across different age groups derived from the meta-analyses described in this section of the chapter. Effect sizes are in the moderate–large range (.6–1.00) for all areas of neurocognition, regardless of illness stage, with larger levels of impairment in immediate verbal memory for FE and chronic samples.

Longitudinal Course of Cognitive Deficits in Schizophrenia

Cross-sectional studies reviewed in this chapter suggest similar levels of cognitive impairment in different illness stages, but only longitudinal studies avoid cohort effects and increase power for detecting change in performance by studying the same individuals over time. For stable outpatients with schizophrenia, there is little evidence for a reduction in cognitive test performance over a one-and-a-half- to five-year test–retest interval. This observation is true whether patients are tested at first-episode (Censits, Ragland, Gur, & Gur, 1997; Hoff et al., 1999) or after many years of illness (Heaton et al., 2001) and whether raw scores are examined (Gold, Arndt, Nopoulos, O'Leary, & Andreasen, 1999) or test results are corrected for the effects of aging by comparing obtained scores to those of healthy matched controls (Hoff et al., 1999; Heaton et al., 2001). This stability was evident even when patients were neuroleptically naïve at initial testing but were retested on neuroleptic medication with decreased symptoms (Szöke et al., 2008).

Results from long-term hospitalized, highly impaired samples of patients, however, reveal a very different pattern of results. These studies suggest that for this sample of patients, high levels of cognitive impairment are evident at a relatively young age (e.g., at least by the second or third decade of life) but that these patients are at risk for even more profound levels of cognitive impairment as they age past sixty years (Kurtz, 2005). Studies have indicated that these patients show significant decreases in overall mental status in the sixth and seventh decade of life, and the probability of higher levels of impairment increases tremendously as the patient ages (e.g., Friedman et al., 2001; Harvey, 2001).

The Relationship between Symptoms and Neurocognition

One approach to understanding the relationship between symptoms and neurocognition in schizophrenia has been to study specific neurocognitive skills that could likely give rise to specific schizophrenia symptoms. One of the most important efforts in this regard has been to assess what has been labeled *source monitoring*: that is, tagging a memory for a specific event with the time and place in which it occurred. The ability to decide whether a voice or a thought is generated internally or externally is thus crucially dependent upon source monitoring (Johnson, Foley, & Leach, 1988). Consequently, these functions potentially have a large role in key features of the phenomenology in the disorder including the generation of both auditory hallucinations and the experience of thought control. Links between source monitoring difficulties for individuals with schizophrenia and specific positive symptoms of schizophrenia, however, have been only meagerly supported to date. For example, Keefe, Arnold, Bayen, and Harvey (1999) investigated source memory using a multinomial model and found that those with a schizophrenia diagnosis did in fact have difficulty distinguishing information coming from internal versus external sources, and there was a tendency for patients to over-attribute information to external, rather than internal sources, consistent with a source-monitoring model of schizophrenia symptoms. Crucially, however, correlations between the presence and frequency of auditory hallucinations and other positive symptoms and poorer source monitoring were not confirmed.

Another strategy in this line of research has been to analyze the relationship between factor-analyzed classes of symptoms of schizophrenia and neurocognitive functions without hypotheses regarding the relationship of specific cognitive skills and specific symptoms. Most studies indicate that individually rated symptoms in schizophrenia, regardless of the symptom-rating scale used, can be factor-analyzed into three groups: psychomotor poverty (consisting of reduced speech, lack of spontaneous movement, and blunting of affect), disorganization (inappropriate affect, poverty of content of speech, and disturbances in the form of thought), and reality distortion (delusions and hallucinations; Liddle, 1987). Meta-analyses (e.g., Dominguez, Viechtbauer, Simons, van Os, & Krabbendam, 2009; Ventura, Thames, Wood, Guzik, & Hellemann, 2010) have clarified the relationship between these symptom classes and neuropsychological test performance. They have evaluated a variety of neurocognitive constructs—IQ, reasoning and problem solving, processing speed, attention/vigilance, verbal fluency, executive functions, verbal working memory, verbal learning and memory, and visual learning and memory—derived from the NIMH-initiated Measurement and Treatment Research to Improve Cognition in Schizophrenia (MATRICS) test battery and linked these constructs to reality distortion, disorganization, and psychomotor poverty classes of symptoms along with less disorder-specific affective symptoms (including depression, hopelessness, self-depreciation, guilt, suicidal ideation, anxiety, and social avoidance). Results have revealed that negative symptoms frequently correlate with verbal fluency, verbal learning and memory, and IQ. Disorganized symptoms correlate with attention/vigilance, visual learning and memory, and IQ, while the only correlation between positive symptoms and neurocognitive function across meta-analyses was on measures of processing speed. In summary, studies reviewed in this section show small-to-moderate-size links between negative and disorganized symptoms and a variety of neurocognitive domains including IQ, attention, and learning and memory.

Neurocognition and Functioning in Schizophrenia

A key facet of schizophrenia is that neurocognitive deficits play an inordinately large role in contributing to the landscape of functional impairment that is a hallmark of the disorder. Estimates suggest that neurocognitive test performance explains from 20 percent to 60 percent of variance in outcome (Green, 1996; Green, Kern, Braff, & Mintz, 2000). These estimates are consistent when outcome is measured by other-rated indices of community function, clinic-administered role-play measures of social or self-care skills, or measured progress and participation in a variety of rehabilitation interventions including social skills training, cognitive remediation, work therapy and supported employment, cognitive-behavioral therapy, and comprehensive rehabilitation therapy programs consisting of several behavioral treatment elements offered simultaneously (Kurtz, 2011). Findings are consistent whether measured cross-sectionally or prospectively and whether prediction is based on change scores in function versus static indices. While more recent work has revealed that social cognitive deficits such as facial affect recognition and mentalizing may mediate some of these neurocognitive-function relationships (Schmidt, Mueller, & Roder, 2011), close ties between neurocognition and function in schizophrenia remain.

Neuroimaging Findings

Structural Neuroimaging

A potential explanation for the genesis of demonstrated neurocognitive deficits in schizophrenia are disruptions in the structural integrity of localized aspects of the brain. Since the publication of the first paper using structural magnetic resonance imaging (sMRI) in schizophrenia in 1984, there have been over 100 sMRI studies conducted (Lawrie & Pantelis, 2011). These studies have revealed several key replicated findings. First, mean reductions in brain volume of 5 percent in the frontal and temporal lobes of the brain and 5 percent to 10 percent in some of their component parts have been consistently reported in people with schizophrenia relative to matched, healthy control participants. Second, the lateral and third ventricles are, on average, 20 percent to 30 percent larger in people with schizophrenia compared to controls, and the body of the ventricles is 50 percent larger than those of controls. These reductions are highly disproportionate to reductions of 3 percent in total brain volume that have been reported. The stability of these findings is supported by their consistency with older CT neuroimaging technology results as well as by postmortem studies (Harrison, Lewis, & Kleinman, 2011). Third, parcellation techniques have also revealed that specifically the anterior cingulate, the superior temporal gyrus, and the medial temporal lobe structures, including amygdala, hippocampus, and parahippocampus, are all substantially reduced in volume (Fornito, Yucel, Patti, Wood, & Pantelis, 2009). Fourth, neuroimaging and postmortem studies have also revealed consistency around findings that the thalamus, particularly the medio-dorsal and pulvinar nuclei, are smaller than would be expected from overall tissue reductions (Konick & Freidman, 2001). While these neuroanatomical findings are consistent with many aspects of the cognitive landscape in schizophrenia, for example, deficits in executive-function and attention and reductions in frontal lobe volume, deficits in episodic memory, and reductions in temporal and hippocampal volume, very few studies to our knowledge have successfully linked specific aspects of neurocognition to the specific degree of volume loss in specific brain structures.

Functional Neuroimaging Studies

To date, over 300 functional neuroimaging studies using functional magnetic resonance imaging (fMRI) in schizophrenia have been conducted (Meyer-Lindenberg & Bullmore, 2011). The advantage of these studies in helping illuminate cognition-brain relationships relative to sMRI studies is they permit the evaluation of direct links between brain activity and cognitive operations and also reveal the degree to which cognitive dysfunction may be mediated by disruptions in connections between spatially distinct but highly interconnected brain regions. Three major domains of cognitive skills using fMRI have been studied to date: sustained attention and interference tasks, executive-function (EF) and working memory (WM) tasks, and episodic memory. Studies of sustained attention have revealed that tasks that require a response when a currently presented target item matches a previously presented stimulus (e.g., the commonly used A-X CPT task) show that individuals with schizophrenia show mean dorsolateral frontal lobe hypoactivation (e.g., MacDonald & Carter, 2003). This hypoactivation is evident in neuroleptic-naïve patients as well, suggesting these findings are not medication effects (Barch et al., 2001). Studies of interference tasks that involve responding to a target stimulus while ignoring pre-potent distracter stimuli have revealed reliable reductions in activation in the dorsal anterior cingulate in early positron emission tomography (PET) studies (Carter, Mintun, Nichols, & Cohen, 1997) that have been subsequently confirmed in multiple fMRI studies (e.g., Meyer-Lindenberg & Bullmore, 2011). These results map consistently onto studies of altered white matter connectivity of the cingulate bundle (e.g., Kubicki et al., 2003).

In terms of executive functions and working memory, a recent meta-analysis surveying forty-one fMRI studies using a variety of cognitive tasks and activation likelihood estimation procedures concluded that individuals with schizophrenia could not be distinguished from controls based on the topography of neural response to these EF and WM tasks, with both groups showing similar networks of activation including dorsolateral prefrontal cortex (DLPFC), ventro-lateral prefrontal cortex (VLPFC), anterior cingulate cortex (ACC) activation, and thalamic activation. People with schizophrenia showed quantitative reductions in the amount of activation in DLPFC, rostral ACC, the left medio-dorsal nucleus of the thalamus, as well as inferior parietal and occipital visual areas (Minzenberg, Laird, Thelen, Carter, & Glahn, 2009).

With respect to episodic memory, multiple fMRI studies indicate that reductions in activation in schizophrenia are centered in the prefrontal cortex rather than traditional medial temporal areas. Additionally, reductions in VLPFC activation during encoding and retrieval are associated with specific task performance, and reductions in DLPFC activation during task encoding and retrieval are non-specific with respect to task performance (Ragland et al., 2009).

Traditional Interventions for Schizophrenia

Management of positive symptoms (i.e., delusions and hallucinations) is accomplished through the administration of first- or second-generation antipsychotic medications that putatively attenuate symptoms by occupying striatal and limbic D_2 receptors (Sestito & Goldberg, 2012). These medications do not impact the cognitive deficits, negative symptoms, or severe social and functional disability associated with the disorder. Adjunctive, evidence-based psychosocial rehabilitation strategies for people with schizophrenia are typically focused on residual symptoms, managing relapse and addressing the disability and include social skills-training, cognitive-behavioral therapy, family therapy, and supported employment programs. Availability of these treatment modalities to individuals with schizophrenia, however, is often limited (Dixon et al., 2010).

Cognitive Remediation in Schizophrenia

Understanding schizophrenia as a disorder of neurocognition, consisting of moderate-level impairment across a variety of neurocognitive domains that link closely to functional outcome, provides a rationale for the development of novel training programs for the improvement of cognitive skill in the disorder that build on traditional interventions and might produce greater improvements in functioning. Over the past ten years, a growing number of randomized, controlled studies have supported the efficacy of a range of behavioral approaches to treatment of neurocognitive deficits in schizophrenia. These programs have differed according to training emphasis. Some train elementary sensory processing (e.g., tone frequency discrimination) as a method for increasing the fidelity of sensory representations in the mind (e.g., Fisher, Holland, Merzenich, & Vinogradov, 2009) as a first step to remediating cognition; others train discrete neuropsychological areas sequentially and hierarchically (attention, then memory, then problem solving; Bell, Bryson, Greig, Corcoran, & Wexler, 2001); while others place a focus on the acquisition of strategies to help organize learning of information (Wykes et al., 2007). These CR programs also vary widely in terms of duration, intensity, training stimuli used, and the degree to which generalization is explicitly targeted but can be summarized by a recent statement of the Experts in Cognitive Remediation Workshop (Florence, Italy, 2010): "A behavioral training based intervention that aims to improve cognitive processes (attention, memory, executive function, social cognition or metacognition) with the goal of durability and generalization." Indeed, a recent meta-analysis (Wykes, Huddy, Cellard, McGurk, & Czobor, 2011) of forty controlled studies and 2,104 participants revealed that cognitive training programs produced mild to moderate durable improvements across summary or global cognition measures as well as a range of neurocognitive areas including attention/vigilance, speed of processing, verbal working memory, verbal and visual learning and memory, reasoning and problem solving, and social cognition as well as function. The effect on global cognition was in the moderate range (d = .45). There was no effect of study quality, suggesting that the strength of these reported effects were not driven by more poorly designed studies. There was also clear evidence that the impact of these treatments on functioning was clearly boosted by participation in other rehabilitation interventions as compared to these interventions being offered as stand-alone treatments (d = .59 versus d = .28). The strength of findings is also supported by the fact that despite the broad range of therapies studied, varying widely in surface characteristics (e.g., computer-assisted or not) or substantive (specific training in generalization or not) in this analysis, findings were largely consistent. There was support in the meta-analysis for the contention that more strategy-focused CR training in the context of other rehabilitation treatments produced the largest effects on functioning measures.

These findings have been exemplified in a recent, large-scale study of 107 individuals with schizophrenia randomly assigned to twelve weeks of a functional adaptation skills–training intervention that consisted of acquisition of skills in social interaction, transportation, medication management, and community activities; a drill-and-practice CR intervention; or a combined treatment group (Bowie, McGurk, Mausbach, Patterson, & Harvey, 2012). Results revealed that CR training produced improvements in cognitive skills at an immediate post-training assessment and at a twelve-week follow-up but did not influence scores on a case manager-rated scale of function. Participants in the skills-training group improved on a performance-based measure of function and case-manager ratings of real world function but did not improve on cognitive measures. Participants in the combined treatment showed significant and more durable improvements on measures of community function, real-world work, and household behaviors than those treated with adaptive skills alone. This is the first study to show the independent effects of both skills training and cognitive remediation on such a wide array of outcome measures as well as the additive effects of combining interventions in the same sample of individuals with schizophrenia. Taken together, findings from this section suggest clearly that CR has its greatest future promise as a training strategy that can potentiate the effects of existing, more traditional forms of evidence-based psychosocial rehabilitation in schizophrenia.

Pharmacotherapy for Neurocognitive Deficits

With the growing number of studies indicating that second-generation atypical antipsychotic medications (like their first-generation predecessors) in the disorder are neutral with respect to cognitive deficits in schizophrenia (Sestito & Goldberg, 2012), there has been intensified interest in the development and assessment of novel add-on pharmaceutical compounds that influence the activity of brain neurotransmitter systems putatively linked to neurocognitive deficits in schizophrenia. The rationale for study of these medications, which have traditionally fallen into one of three receptor classes (i.e., cholinergic, glutamatergic, and serotenergic), is that the underlying neurotransmitter system has been implicated in genesis of the disorder (e.g., glutamate); the agent has been shown to improve cognitive function in animal models or, last, the medication has shown therapeutic benefit for cognition in other psychiatric disorders (Barch, Hill, & Goff, 2011).

In a recent meta-analysis (Choi, Wykes, & Kurtz, 2013), we investigated results from twenty-six placebo-controlled trials. Cognitive outcome measures were grouped into six MATRICS-defined domains of attention/vigilance, verbal learning and memory, spatial learning and memory, spatial working memory, reasoning and problem-solving, or speed of processing as well as summary scores of cognition when available. Cholinergic-enhancing medications produced an improvement in verbal learning and memory of borderline significance (d = .23, p = .06). Sub-analyses of the effects of cholinergic add-on medications on spatial learning and memory showed that the cholinergic-enhancing agent donepezil produced a moderate and significant effect on spatial learning and memory (d = .58) relative to a placebo control. No other classes of medication produced an effect on summary cognition scores or on specific neurocognitive domains. These findings suggest that neurocognitive deficits in schizophrenia may perhaps be reflective of nonspecific changes to gray and white matter or poor signal coordination across a variety of neural systems as opposed to more localized neural circuits defined by the presence of a specific neurotransmitter. These findings also suggest that pharmacologic agents focused on generalized neuroprotection, such as anti-inflammatory agents or agents targeted at enhanced neurogenesis, might be more likely to yield pro-cognitive effects.

Conclusion

Neurocognitive deficits in schizophrenia typically show effect sizes in the moderate-to-large range and are evident across a broad array of neurocognitive domains, as revealed by standardized clinical instruments and targeted experimental cognitive tasks. While some studies have indicated that impairment on neurocognitive measure is reflective of a common deficit across tests, many studies have subtyped patients according to patterns of memory impairment or other factors and linked these subtypes to differences in location and type of brain volume loss or patterns of neural activation. Studies of genetic and clinical high-risk individuals indicate that deficits are evident across a variety of neurocognitive measures at a level intermediate between patients with full-blown illness and controls, while "follow back" studies of people who have schizophrenia suggest that individuals who go on to develop the illness have a half-standard deviation impairment on IQ measures (e.g., Reichenberg et al., 2005).

There is no evidence that neurocognitive impairment serves as a predictor of who develops schizophrenia, although deficits in verbal learning have been linked to the more rapid onset of the disease. Once individuals are diagnosed, cross-sectional and longitudinal studies have shown that deficits on neurocognitive tests are similar in first-episode, never-treated individuals, middle-aged, and older people with schizophrenia, arguing strongly against a neurodegenerative model for the disorder. These findings also are at odds with explanation of deficits as an epiphenomenon of sustained psychiatric intervention. There is evidence of neurocognitive decline in a smaller subpopulation of patients with schizophrenia who are long-term hospitalized secondary to severe functional impairmen. This pattern of decline and impairment is not modal for the disorder and likely represents results from a distinct disorder subtype. To date, specific links between impaired neurocognitive skills with likely implications for symptom formation, such as source memory, and specific types of symptoms, such as auditory hallucinations, have not been identified. There is evidence for modest, less-specific relationships between negative and disorganization symptoms and neurocognitive impairment, with little evidence for relationships between positive symptoms and neurocognitive test performance (Dominguez et al., 2009).

In a highly promising area of research, behavioral treatment interventions focused on improving neurocognitive skills through repeated task practice and strategy training, labeled cognitive remediation, produce moderate improvements in neurocognition and functioning with stronger effects when remediation is offered as one element of a broader rehabilitation program. To date, controlled trials of novel, add-on pharmacotherapies targeted at glutamatergic, cholinergic, and serotenergic receptor classes have yielded, at best, only modest improvements in neurocognition, with effects linked to the use of cholinergic enhancing agents only.

In conclusion, while the origins of schizophrenia have long been characterized as, "…wrapped in impenetrable darkness" (Kraepelin, 1919), it is clear that 100 years of research on cognitive deficits and their treatment in schizophrenia has highlighted the outsized role of these illness features in the disorder's presentation. These findings have also provided the rationale for a new generation of rapidly developing, innovative therapies targeting these deficits directly and providing hope for improved outcome in this frequently disabling disorder in the not-too-distant future.

References

Aleman, A., Hijman, R., deHaan, E. H., & Kahn, R. S. (1999). Memory impairment in schizophrenia: A meta-analysis. *American Journal of Psychiatry, 156*(9), 1358–1366.

American Psychiatric Association. (2000). *Diagnostic and statistical manual of mental disorders* (4th edn, text rev.). Washington, DC: American Psychiatric Association.

Aylward, E., Walker, E., & Bettes, B. (1984). Intelligence in schizophrenia: Meta-analysis of the research. *Schizophrenia Bulletin, 10,* 430–459.

Barch, D. M., Hill, M., & Goff, D. C. (2011). The treatment of cognitive impairment in schizophrenia. *Pharmacology, Biochemistry and Behavior, 99,* 245–253.

Barch, D. M., Carter, C. S., Braver, T. S., Saab, F. W., MacDonald, A., Noll, D., & Cohen, J. D. (2001). Selective deficits in prefrontal cortex function in medication-naïve patients with schizophrenia. *Archives of General Psychiatry, 58,* 280–288.

Bell, M., Bryson, G., Greig, T., Corcoran, C., & Wexler, B. E. (2001). Neurocognitive enhancement therapy with work therapy: Effects on neuropsychological test performance. *Archives of General Psychiatry, 58,* 163–168.

Bhugra, D. (2000). Migration and schizophrenia. *Acta Psychiatric Scandinavica, 102,* 68–73.

Bleuler, E. (1950). *Dementia praecox or the group of schizophrenias.* J. Zinkin, trans. New York: International Universities Press.

Bleuler, E. (1951). The basic symptoms of schizophrenia. In D. Rapaport (Ed.), *Organization and pathology of thought: Selected sources* (pp. 581–649). New York: Columbia University Press.

Bokat, C. E., & Goldberg, T. E. (2003). Letter and category fluency in schizophrenia patients: A meta-analysis. *Schizophrenia Research, 64*(1), 73–78.

Bowie, C. R., McGurk, S. R., Mausbach, B., Patterson, T. L., & Harvey, P. D. (2012). Combined cognitive remediation and functional skills training for schizophrenia: Effects on cognition, functional competence and real-world behavior. *The American Journal of Psychiatry, 169,* 710–718.

Brebion, G., Bressan, R. A., Ohlsen, R. I., & David, A. S. (2013). A model of memory impairment in schizophrenia: Cognitive and clinical factors associated with memory efficiency and memory errors. *Schizophrenia Research, 151,* 70–77.

Butler, P., Abeles, I. Y., Weiskopf, N. G., Tambini, A., Jalbrzikowski, M., Legatt, M. E. … & Javitt, D. C. (2009). Sensory contributions to impaired emotion processing in schizophrenia. *Schizophrenia Bulletin, 35,* 1085–1094.

Butler, P. D., Zemon, V., Schechter, I., Saperstein, A. M., Hoptman, M. J., Lim, K. O., & Javitt, D. C. (2005). Early-stage visual processing and cortical amplification deficits in schizophrenia. *Archives of General Psychiatry, 62,* 495–504.

Cannon, T. D., Bearden, C. E., Hollister, J. M., Rosso, I. M., Sanchez, L. E., & Hadley, T. (2000). Childhood cognitive functioning in schizophrenia patients and their unaffected siblings: A prospective cohort study. *Schizophrenia Bulletin, 26,* 379–393.

Carter, C. S., Mintun, M., Nichols, T., & Cohen, J. D. (1997). Anterior cingulate dysfunction and selective attention deficits in schizophrenia: [15O] H2O PET study during single trial Stroop task performance. *American Journal of Psychiatry, 154,* 1670–1675.

Censits, D. M., Ragland, J. D., Gur, R. C., & Gur, R. E. (1997). Neuropsychological evidence supporting a neurodevelopmental model of schizophrenia: A longitudinal study. *Schizophrenia Research, 24,* 289–298.

Choi, K. H., Wykes, T., & Kurtz, M. M. (2013). Adjunctive pharmacotherapy for cognitive deficits in schizophrenia: A meta-analytic investigation. *The British Journal of Psychiatry, 203,* 172–178.

Cirillo, M. A., & Seidman, L. J. (2003). Verbal declarative memory dysfunction in schizophrenia: From clinical assessment to genetics and brain mechanisms. *Neuropsychology Review, 13*(2), 43–77.

Clarke, M. C., Harley, M., & Cannon, M. (2006). The role of obstetric events in schizophrenia. *Schizophrenia Bulletin, 32*(1), 3–8.

Cornblatt, B. A., & Erlenmeyer-Kimling, L. (1985). Global attentional deviance as a marker of risk for schizophrenia: Specificity and predictive validity. *Journal of Abnormal Psychology, 94*, 470–486.

DeLeon, J., Cuesta, M. J., & Peralta, V. (1993). Delusions and hallucinations in schizophrenic patients. *Psychopathology, 26*, 286–291.

Dickinson, D., Ramsey, M. E., & Gold, J. (2007). Overlooking the obvious: A meta-analytic comparison of digit symbol coding tasks and other cognitive measures in schizophrenia. *Archives of General Psychiatry, 64*(5), 532–542.

Dickinson, D., Ragland, J. D., Gold, J. M., & Gur, R. C. (2008). General and specific cognitive deficits in schizophrenia: Goliath defeats David? *Biological Psychiatry, 64*, 823–827.

Dixon, L. B., Dickerson, F., Bellack, A. S., Bennett, M., Dickinson, D., Goldberg, R. W. et al. (2010). The 2009 schizophrenia PORT psychosocial treatment recommendations and summary statements. *Schizophrenia Bulletin, 36*, 48–70.

Dominguez, M., Viechtbauer, W., Simons, C., van Os, J., & Krabbendam, L. (2009). Arepsychotic psychopathology and neurocognition orthogonal? A systematic review of their associations. *Psychological Bulletin, 135*, 157–171.

Fearon, P., Kirkbride, J. B., Morgan, V., Dazzan, P., Morgan, K., Lloyd, T., ... & Murray, R. M. (2006). Incidence of schizophrenia and other psychoses in ethnic minority groups: Results from the MRC AESOP Study. *Psychological Medicine, 36*, 1541–1550.

Fisher, M., Holland, C., Merzenich, M. M., & Vinogradov, S. (2009). Using neuroplasticity-based auditory training to improve verbal memory in schizophrenia. *American Journal of Psychiatry, 166*, 805–811.

Fornito, A., Yucel, M., Patti, J., Wood, S. J., & Pantelis, C. (2009). Mapping grey matter reductions in schizophrenia: An anatomical likelihood estimation analysis of voxel-based morphometry studies. *Schizophrenia Research, 108*, 104–113.

Friedman, J. I., Harvey, P. D., Coleman, T., Moriarty, P. J., Bowie, C., Parrella, M., ... & Davis, K. L. (2001). Six-year follow-up study of cognitive and functional status across the lifespan in schizophrenia: A comparison with Alzheimer's disease and normal aging. *American Journal of Psychiatry, 158*(9), 1441–1448.

Fuller, R. L., Luck, S. J., McMahon, R. P., & Gold, J. M. (2005). Working memory consolidation is abnormally slow in schizophrenia. *Journal of Abnormal Psychology, 114*, 279–290.

Gold, J. M., Randolph, C., Carpenter, C. J., Goldberg, T. E., & Weinberger, D. R. (1992). Forms of memory failure in in schizophrenia. *Journal of Abnormal Psychology, 101*, 487–494.

Gold, J. M., Fuller, R. L., Robinson, B. M., McMahon, R. P., Braun, E. L., & Luck, S. J. (2006). Intact attentional control of working memory encoding in schizophrenia. *Journal of Abnormal Psychology, 115*, 658–673.

Gold, S., Arndt, S., Nopoulos, P., O'Leary, D. S., & Andreasen, N. C. (1999). Longitudinal study of cognitive function in first-episode and recent-onset schizophrenia. *American Journal of Psychiatry, 156*, 1342–1348.

Goldberg, T. E., David, A. S., & Gold, J. M. (2011). Neurocognitive impairments in schizophrenia: Their character and role in symptom formation. In D. Weinberger & P. J. Harrison (Eds.), *Schizophrenia* (pp. 142–162). Chichester: Blackwell.

Goldstein, G., Shemansky, W. J., & Allen, D. N. (2005). Cognitive function in schizoaffective disorder and clinical subtypes of schizophrenia. *Archives of Clinical Neuropsychology, 20*, 153–159.

Green, M. F. (1996). What are the functional consequences of neurocognitive deficits in schizophrenia? *American Journal of Psychiatry, 153*(3), 321–330.

Green, M. F., Horan, W. P., & Sugar, C. A. (2013). Has the generalized deficit become the generalized criticism? *Schizophrenia Bulletin, 39,* 257–262.

Green, M. F., Kern, R. S., Braff, D. L., & Mintz, J. (2000). Neurocognitive deficits and functional outcome in schizophrenia: Are we measuring the "right stuff"? *Schizophrenia Bulletin, 26*(1), 119–136.

Harrison, P. J., Lewis, D. A., & Kleinman, J. E. (2011). Neuropathology of schizophrenia. In D. Weinberger & P. J. Harrison (Eds.), *Schizophrenia* (pp. 372–392). Chichester: Blackwell.

Harrow, M., Carone, B. J., & Westermeyer, J. F. (1985). The course of psychosis in early phase schizophrenia. *American Journal of Psychiatry, 147,* 702–707.

Harvey, P. D. (2001). Cognitive and functional impairments in elderly patients with schizophrenia: A review of the recent literature. *Harvard Review of Psychiatry, 9,* 59–68.

Harvey, P. D., & Reichenberg, A. (2007). Neuropsychological impairments in schizophrenia: Integration of performance-based and brain imaging findings. *Psychological Bulletin, 133*(5), 833–858.

Heaton, R. K., Gladsjo, J. A., Palmer, B. W., Kuck, J., Marcotte, T. D., & Jeste, D. V. (2001). Stability and course of neuropsychological deficits in schizophrenia. *Archives of General Psychiatry, 58,* 24–32.

Heinrichs, R. W., & Awad, A. G. (1993). Neurocognitive subtypes of chronic schizophrenia. *Schizophrenia Research, 9,* 49–58.

Heinrichs, R. W., & Zakzanis, K. K. (1998). Neurocognitive deficit in schizophrenia: A quantitative review of the evidence. *Neuropsychology, 12*(3), 426–445.

Heinrichs, R. W., Ruttan, L., Zakzanis, K. K., & Case, D. (1997). Parsing schizophrenia with neurocognitive tests: Evidence of stability and validity. *Brain & Cognition, 35*(2), 207–224.

Hoff, A. L., Sakuma, M., Wieneke, M., Horon, R., Kushner, M., & DeLisi, L. E. (1999). Longitudinal neuropsychological follow-up study of patients with first-episode schizophrenia. *American Journal of Psychiatry, 156*(9), 1336–1341.

Irani, F., Kalkstein, S., Moberg, E. A., & Moberg, P. J. (2011). Neuropsychological performance in older patients with schizophrenia: A meta-analysis of cross-sectional and longitudinal studies. *Schizophrenia Bulletin, 37,* 1318–1326.

Javitt, D. C., Zukin, S. R., Heresco-Levy, U., & Umbricht, D. (2012). Has an angel shown the way? Etiological and therapeutic implications of the PCP/NMDA model of schizophrenia. *Schizophrenia Bulletin, 38,* 958–966.

Johnson, M. K., Foley, M. A., & Leach, K. (1988). The consequence for memory of imagining in another person's voice. *Memory and Cognition, 16,* 337–342.

Keefe, R. S., Arnold, M. C., Bayen, U. J., & Harvey, P. D. (1999). Source monitoring deficits in patients with schizophrenia: A multinomial modelling analysis. *Psychological Medicine, 29,* 903–914.

Kendall, R. E., & Adams, W. (1991). Unexplained fluctuations in the risk for schizophrenia by the month and year of birth. *British Journal of Psychiatry, 158,* 758–763.

Knowles, E. E., David, A. S., & Reichenberg, A. (2010). Processing speed deficits in schizophrenia: Re-examining the evidence. *American Journal of Psychiatry, 167*(7), 828–835.

Konick, L. C., & Friedman, L. (2001). Meta-analysis of thalamic size in schizophrenia. *Biological Psychiatry, 49,* 28–38.

Kraepelin, E. (1919). *Dementia praecox and paraphrenia*, trans. R. M. Barclay, ed. G. M. Roberston. Edinburgh: Livingstone.

Kremen, W. S., Seidman, L. J., Faraone, S. V., & Tsuang, M. T. (2001). Intelligence quotient and neuropsychological profiles in patients with schizophrenia and in normal volunteers. *Biological Psychiatry, 50*, 453–462.

Kubicki, M., Westin, C. F., Nestor, P. G., Wible, C. G., Frumin, M., Maier, S., ... & Shenton, M. E. (2003). Cingulate fasciculus integrity disruption in schizophrenia: A magnetic resonance diffusion tensor imaging study. *Biological Psychiatry, 54*, 1171–1180.

Kurtz, M. M. (2005). Neurocognitive impairment across the lifespan: An update. *Schizophrenia Research, 74*(1), 15–26.

Kurtz, M. M. (2011). Neurocognition as a predictor of response to evidence-based psychosocial interventions in schizophrenia: What is the state of the evidence? *Clinical Psychology Review, 31*, 663–672.

Kurtz, M. M., & Marcopulos, B. (2012). Cognition in schizophrenia. In B. Marcopulos & M. Kurtz (Eds.), *Clinical neuropsychological foundations of schizophrenia*. New York: Psychology Press.

Kurtz, M. M., Donato, J., & Rose, J. (2011). Crystallized verbal skills: Relationship to neurocognition, symptoms and functioning in schizophrenia. *Neuropsychology, 25*, 784–791.

Lawrie, S. M., & Pantelis, C. (2011). Structural brain imaging in schizophrenia and related populations. In D. Weinberger & P. J. Harrison (Eds.), *Schizophrenia* (pp. 334–352). Chichester: Blackwell.

Lee, J., & Park, S. (2005). Working memory impairments in schizophrenia: A meta-analysis. *Journal of Abnormal Psychology, 114*(4), 599–611.

Lewis, G., David, A. S., Andreasson, S., & Allebeck, P. (1992). Schizophrenia and city life. *Lancet, 340*, 137–140.

Liddle, P. F. (1987). The symptoms of schizophrenia: A re-examination of the positive-negative dichotomy. *British Journal of Psychiatry, 151*, 145–151.

MacDonald, A. W. 3rd, & Carter, C. S. (2003). Event-related fMRI study of context processing in dorsolateral prefrontal cortex of patients with schizophrenia. *Journal of Abnormal Psychology, 112*, 689–697.

McGrath J., Saha, S., Welham, J., Saadi, O. E., MacCauley, C., & Chant, D. (2004). A systematic review of the incidence of schizophrenia: The distribution of rates and the influence of sex, urbanicity, migrant status and methodology. *BMC Medicine, 2*(13).

Mesholam-Gately, R. I., Giuliano, A. J., Goff, K. P., Faraone, S. V., & Seidman, L. J. (2009). Neurocognition in first-episode schizophrenia: A meta-analytic review. *Neuropsychology, 23*, 315–336.

Meyer-Lindenberg, A., & Bullmore, E. T. (2011). Functional brain imaging in schizophrenia. In D. Weinberger & P. J. Harrison (Eds.), *Schizophrenia* (pp. 353–371). New York, NY: Wiley-Blackwell.

Minzenberg, M. J., Laird, A. R., Thelen, S., Carter, C. S., & Glahn, D. C. (2009). Meta-analysis of 41 functional neuroimaging studies executive-function in schizophrenia. *Archives of General Psychiatry, 66*, 811–822.

Palmer, B., Heaton, R. K., Kuck, J., & Braff, D. (1997). Is it possible to be schizophrenic yet neuropsychologically normal? *Neuropsychology, 11*, 437–446.

Paulsen, J. S., Heaton, R. K., Sadek, J. R., Perry, W., Delis, D. C., Braff, D., … & Jeste, D. V. (1995). The nature of learning and memory impairments in schizophrenia. *Journal of the International Neuropsychological Society, 1*(01), 88–99.

Pillay, P., & Montcrieff, J. (2011). Contributions of psychiatric disorders to occupation of NHS beds: Analysis of hospital episode statistics. *The Psychiatrist, 35,* 56–59.

Ragland, J. D., Laird, A. R., Ranganath, C., Blumenfeld, R. S., Gonzalez, S. M., & Glahn, D. C. (2009). Prefrontal activation deficits during episodic memory in schizophrenia. *American Journal of Psychiatry, 166,* 863–874.

Reichenberg, A., Weiser, M., Rapp, M. A., Rabinowitz, J., Caspi, A., Schmeidler, J., … & Davidson, M. (2005). Elaboration on premorbid intellectual performance in schizophrenia. *Archives of General Psychiatry, 62,* 1297–1304.

Reichenberg, A., Weiser, M., Rapp, M. A., Rabinowitz, J., Caspi, A., Schmeidler, J., … & Davidson, M. (2006). Premorbid intra-individual variability in intellectual performance and risk for schizophrenia: A population-based study. *Schizophrenia Research, 85,* 49–57.

Salkever, D. S., Karakus, M. C., Slade, E. P., Harding, C. M., Hough, R. L., Rosenheck, R. A., … & Yamada, A. M. (2007). Measures and predictors of community-based employment and earnings of persons with schizophrenia in a multisite study. *Psychiatric Services, 58,* 315–324.

Savla, G. N., Twamley, E. W., Delis, D. C., Roesch, S. C., Jeste, D. V., & Palmer, B. W. (2012). Dimensions of executive functioning in schizophrenia and their relationship with processing speed. *Schizophrenia Bulletin, 38,* 760–768.

Saykin, A. J., Shtasel, D. L., Gur, R. E., Kester, D. B., Mosley, L. H., Stafiniak, P., & Gur, R. C. (1994). Neuropsychological deficits in neuroleptic naive patients with first-episode schizophrenia. *Archives of General Psychiatry, 51*(2), 124–131.

Schmidt, S., Mueller, D. R., & Roder, V. (2011). Social cognition as a mediator variable between neurocogniton and functional outcome in schizophrenia: Empirical review and new results from structural equation modeling. *Schizophrenia Bulletin, 37,* S41–54.

Seaton, B. E., Goldstein, G., & Allen, D. N. (2001). Sources of heterogeneity in schizophrenia: The role of neuropsychological functioning. *Neuropsychology Review, 11,* 45–67.

Seidman, L. J., Giuliano, A. J., Meyer, E. C., Addington, J., Cadenhead, K. S., Cannon, T. D., … & Cornblatt, B. A. (2010). Neuropsychology of the prodrome to psychosis in the NAPLS consortium. *Archives of General Psychiatry, 67,* 578–588.

Sereno, A. B., & Holzman, P. S. (1996). Spatial selective attention in schizophrenic, affective disorder, and normal subjects. *Schizophrenia Research, 20,* 33–50.

Sestito, N., & Goldberg T. (2012). Medication and cognition in schizophrenia. In B. Marcopulos & M. Kurtz (Eds.), *Clinical neuropsychological foundations of schizophrenia.* New York: Psychology Press.

Shorter, E. (1998). *A history of psychiatry.* New York: Wiley.

Silverstein, M. L., & Zerwic, M. J. (1985). Clinical psychopathologic symptoms in neuropsychologically impaired and intact schizophrenics. *Journal of Consulting and Clinical Psychology, 53,* 267–268.

Spearman, C. (1925). Some issues in the theory of "g" (including the law of diminishing returns). *Nature, 116*(2916), 436.

Sponheim, S. R., Jung, R. E., Seidman, L. J., Mesholam-Gately, R. I., Manoach, D. S., O'Leary, D. S., … & Schulz, S. C. (2010). Cognitive deficits in recent-onset and chronic schizophrenia. *Journal of Psychiatric Research, 44,* 421–428.

Susser, E. S., & Lin, S. P. (1992). Schizophrenia after prenatal exposure to the Dutch hunger winter of 1944–1945. *Archives of General Psychiatry, 49,* 983–988.

Szöke, A.,Trandafir, A., Dupont, M. E., Méary, A., Schürhoff, F., & LeBoyer, M. (2008). Longitudinal studies of cognition in schizophrenia: Meta-analysis. *British Journal of Psychiatry, 192,* 248–257.

Torrey, E. F. (1999). The cost of not treating serious mental illness. *Psychiatric Services, 50*(8), 1087–1088.

Tsuang, M. T., Stone, W. S., & Faraone, S. V. (1999). Schizophrenia: A review of genetic studies. *Harvard Review of Psychiatry, 7,* 185–207.

Turetsky, B. I., Moberg, P. J., Mozley, L. H., Moelter, S. T., Agrin, R. N., Gur, R. C., & Gur, R. E. (2002). Memory-delineated subtypes of schizophrenia: Relationship to clinical, neuroanatomical and neurophysiological measures. *Neuropsychology, 16,* 481–490.

Ventura, J., Thames, A. D., Wood, R. C., Guzik, L. H., & Hellemann, G. S. (2010). Disorganization and reality distortion in schizophrenia: A meta-analysis of the relationship between positive symptoms and neurocognitive deficits. *Schizophrenia Research, 121*(1–3), 1–14.

Wechsler, D. (1955). *The range of human capacities.* Baltimore, MD: Williams & Wilkins.

Wexler, B. E., Zhu, H., Bell, M. D., Nicholls, S. S., Fulbright, R. K., Gore, J. C., … & Peterson, B. S. (2009). Neuropsychological near normality and brain structure abnormality in schizophrenia. *American Journal of Psychiatry, 166*(2), 189–195.

Wilk, C. M., Gold, J. M., McMahon, R. P., Humber, K., Iaonnone, V. N., & Buchanan, R. W. (2000). No, it is not possible to be schizophrenic yet neuropsychologically normal. *Neuropsychology, 19,* 778–786.

Woodberry, K. A., Giuliano, A. J., & Seidman, L. J. (2008). Premorbid IQ in schizophrenia: A meta-analytic review. *American Journal of Psychiatry, 165*(5), 579–587.

World Health Organization (WHO). (1992). *International statistical classification of diseases and related health problems (ICD–10).* Geneva: WHO.

Wykes, T., Huddy, V., Cellard, C., McGurk, S. R., & Czobor, P. (2011). A meta-analysis of cognitive remediation for schizophrenia. *American Journal of Psychiatry, 23*(1), 41–46.

Wykes, T., Reeder, C., Landau, S., Everitt, B., Knapp, M., Patel, A., & Romeo, R. (2007). Cognitive remediation therapy in schizophrenia: Randomized controlled trial. *British Journal of Psychiatry, 190,* 421–427.

8

PEDIATRIC DEPRESSION

Neurocognitive Function and Treatment Implications

*Jennifer C. Britton, Sarah M. Kennedy, Ilana Seager,
Alexander H. Queen, Michael V. Hernandez,
Carolyn N. Spiro, and Jill Ehrenreich-May*

Introduction

Major depressive disorder (MDD) is common in children and adolescents, affecting up to 2 percent of children and 4 percent to 7 percent of adolescents in a given year (Costello et al., 2002). Pediatric depression negatively impacts mood, self-esteem, and daily functioning. For example, children may experience persistent sad mood, irritability, increased feelings of hopelessness, or disturbances in sleep and appetite (American Psychiatric Association, Association, 2013). The onset of MDD increases during adolescence, as compared to lower prevalence rates observed among younger children (Kessler, Avenevoli, & Ries Merikangas, 2001; Lewinsohn, Clarke, Seeley, & Rohde, 1994). Before reaching adulthood, approximately 20 percent of adolescents will have been diagnosed with MDD (Birmaher, Ryan, Williamson, Brent, & Kaufman, 1996; Birmaher, Ryan, Williamson, Brent, Kaufman, et al., 1996).

Neurocognitive functions shape how individuals think and feel through interactions between brain structure and function. Adolescence, in particular, is a developmental period of considerable physiological, social, and cognitive changes (Alexander-Bloch, Raznahan, Bullmore, & Giedd, 2013; Casey, Tottenham, Liston, & Durston, 2005; Mills, Lalonde, Clasen, Giedd, & Blakemore, 2012). These changes coincide with maturational changes in brain function (Gogtay et al., 2004). As pediatric depression predicts adulthood depression (Pine, Cohen, Gurley, Brook, & Ma, 1998; Rao et al., 1995; Weissman et al., 1999), an abnormal developmental trajectory of neurocognitive functions may lead to chronic mental health issues. Understanding the neurocognitive dysfunction of pediatric depression may provide insight into its onset, maintenance, treatment, and/or prevention.

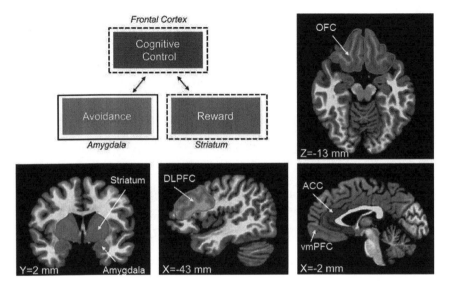

FIGURE 8.1 Neurocognitive domains and neural circuitry implicated in pediatric depression. The pathophysiology of pediatric depression may include perturbations in affective processing, reward processing, and cognitive control. Dysfunction may reflect imbalances in subcortical regions mediating avoidance (e.g., amygdala) and approach (e.g., striatum and cortical regions mediating regulation (e.g., dorsal lateral prefrontal cortex. ventromedial/orbitofrontal cortex, and anterior cingulate), whereby greater avoidance (solid lines), less approach, and cognitive control (dashed lines) may explain elevated negative mood and reduced pleasure and motivation in pediatric depression.

The pathophysiology underlying pediatric depression, which involves depressed or irritable mood and/or decreased interest, pleasure, and motivation, may include perturbations in affective processing, reward processing, and cognitive control (Ernst & Fudge, 2009; Forbes & Dahl, 2005). As seen in Figure 8.1, dysfunction in these cognitive domains may reflect imbalances between subcortical regions mediating avoidance (e.g., amygdala) and approach (e.g., striatum) and cortical regions mediating regulation of emotions and behavior (e.g., prefrontal cortex; Ernst & Fudge, 2009; Forbes & Dahl, 2005). These neural systems undergo major developmental changes during childhood and adolescence (Gogtay et al., 2004), and these changes may contribute to the onset and maintenance of depression. Additionally, treatment outcome may be influenced by neurocognitive function, and treatment outcome may be mediated by behavioral and neural functioning observed in pediatric MDD. Therefore, there is a critical need to understand the relationship between these dysfunctions and treatment approaches targeting these perturbations.

This review focuses on neurocognitive domains that are involved in the depressive symptomatology in pediatric MDD and may be targeted in standard psychosocial and pharmacological treatments. We illustrate how understanding neurocognitive dysfunction may aid in evaluating and refining current treatments (i.e., how targeting the underlying neurocognitive dysfunction may promote improved treatment outcome). The first section of this chapter summarizes the neurocognitive and neural dysfunctions in youth with MDD. As pediatric depression is more likely in children of depressed parents (Avenevoli & Merikangas, 2006), we also review studies examining at-risk populations. In addition, we focus our review on studies that attempt to measure cognitive function through experimental manipulation rather than subjective report. The second section of this chapter examines the effects of treatment on cognitive performance and neural functioning and highlights how the neurocognitive perspective can refine and generate novel treatments for pediatric depression.

Cognitive Domains Affected by Pediatric Depression

Individuals with depression have impairments in affective processing manifesting in aberrant emotion recognition (e.g., Bourke, Douglas, & Porter, 2010), emotion regulation (e.g., Silk et al., 2007), processing of self-relevant information (e.g., Zupan, Hammen, & Jaenicke, 1987), and reward processing and motivation (i.e., reduced responsiveness to reward; e.g., Forbes & Dahl, 2005). Dysfunction in affective and reward processing may arise from deficits in cognitive control (e.g., attention and executive control; Hankin, Gibb, Abela, & Flory, 2010; Ladouceur et al., 2006). These impairments are often accompanied by neural perturbations in brain circuitry associated with these affective and cognitive domains (e.g., Beesdo et al., 2009; Forbes et al., 2006, 2009; Halari et al., 2009; Monk et al., 2008; Perlman et al., 2012; Pine et al., 2004; Roberson-Nay et al., 2006; Yang et al., 2010).

Face Processing

The ability to interpret facial expressions is an important part of human behavior and social interaction; thus, biased processing of facial expressions may contribute to symptoms of MDD by reinforcing negative affect and withdrawal behavior. Past research has found that there are six basic emotions: happiness, surprise, fear, anger, disgust, and sadness (Ekman, Friesen, & Ellsworth, 1972). The basic emotions are reliably recognized through facial expressions and convey an important part of nonverbal communication. Emotion recognition abilities emerge throughout development. A child's ability to correctly interpret facial emotion follows a slow developmental course that evolves over a lifetime (Batty & Taylor, 2006). While behavioral data suggest that infants are able to categorize some emotions by seven to eight months (Caron, Caron, & Myers, 1982), a typically developing child's capacity to interpret emotional reactions does not emerge before the second year of life (Pons, Lawson, Harris, & De Rosnay, 2003). In addition, patterns of emotional processing are different in adolescents and adults, signifying continued development of emotion perception and interpretation (Batty & Taylor, 2006). Individuals who fail to discriminate emotions or understand facial expressions correctly may not interact appropriately due to misinterpreting social or emotional cues.

Indeed, individuals with MDD process facial expressions differently than individuals without MDD. A review of 40 studies on facial processing in adults with MDD consistently found a negative bias toward sadness, with adults with MDD interpreting neutral and ambiguous expressions as more intensely sad than healthy adults (Bourke et al., 2010). A negative bias toward sadness in facial expressions was related to higher depression scores and predicts persistence of depression in a sample of adults with MDD (Hale & William, 1998). Negative expectancies of depressed individuals may lead to decreased social support (Gotlib & Hammen, 1993). These findings suggest that negative facial expression biases, cognitions, and interpersonal behaviors in depressed patients may be strongly related. Facial processing impairments may result in inappropriate responses and may contribute to abnormal emotion regulation in mood disorders like MDD. However, few studies examine pediatric depression. The limited work has found biases toward sadness in samples of depressed youth (Ladouceur et al., 2005). In addition to sadness, the bias detected in pediatric depression extends to other negative emotions, such as fear (Pine et al., 2004).

Neuroimaging studies have often found amygdala dysfunction during facial processing and recognition tasks in children with and at risk for MDD compared to healthy controls; however, the directionality of amygdala dysfunction is mixed (Beesdo et al., 2009; Monk et al., 2008; Pine et al., 2004; Roberson-Nay et al., 2006; Yang et al., 2010). The amygdala responds most notably to fearful facial expressions (Adolphs, 2002; Phan, Wager, Taylor, & Liberzon, 2002) but also responds to a variety of other expressions (Britton, Taylor, Sudheimer, & Liberzon, 2006; Fitzgerald, Angstadt, Jelsone, Nathan, & Phan, 2006). Depressed adolescents appear to have greater amygdala and anterior cingulate cortex (ACC) activation than healthy controls when performing an emotion-matching task where participants completed emotion matching compared to a shape matching (Yang et al., 2010). A similar finding was detected in adolescents at high risk for MDD based on parental history, relative to low-risk adolescents when passively viewing fearful faces, but not when youth were required to make judgments of the face, such as, "How wide is the nose?" (Monk et al., 2008).

Exaggerated amygdala activation in response to facial expressions may be obscured with the addition of a cognitive task (Taylor, Phan, Decker, & Liberzon, 2003). When attention was directed to facial attributes (e.g., fearfulness or nose width), high-risk adolescents recruited the medial prefrontal cortex to a greater degree than in low-risk adolescents (Monk et al., 2008), possibly reflecting greater effort to successfully dampen the amygdala responses. Similarly, when judging the gender of emotional faces, a lack of group differences in amygdala activation was noted between children ages seven and eleven years with and without a history of preschool-onset depression. However, in this gender-discrimination task, greater amygdala activation to sad relative to neutral faces was associated with more severe depression. This positive correlation between depression and activation was noted in bilateral orbital frontal cortex, parahippocampal gyrus, and parietal regions as well (Barch, Gaffrey, Botteron, Belden, & Luby, 2012).

Contrary to these findings suggesting exaggerated or no group differences in amygdala activation, other studies report a blunted amygdala response to fearful faces (e.g., Thomas et al., 2001). Adolescents with MDD in relation to both healthy controls and adolescents with anxiety disorders demonstrated amygdala hypoactivation during passive viewing of fearful faces relative to happy faces (Beesdo et al., 2009). The inconsistencies regarding amygdala activation among studies may be due to the sample characteristics or task differences; therefore, further investigation is needed in youth with and at risk for depression.

Studies of face processing often reveal memory dysfunction in MDD. Individual differences in these deficits may signify emerging adolescent depression, suggesting that this dysfunction may be a vulnerability marker for depression (Guyer, Choate, Grimm, Pine, & Keenan, 2011). Girls ages nine to twelve with higher depressive symptom levels were less accurate in identifying previously viewed emotional faces, particularly happy and sad faces (Guyer et al., 2011). Extending this research to at-risk adolescents based on parental history of MDD, a specific deficit in memory for fearful faces was found in at-risk youth, but this face-memory deficit was not detected in the affected parent (Pine et al., 2004). Adolescents diagnosed with MDD had reduced memory for previously viewed emotional faces as compared to healthy controls, though the deficit was not restricted to specific face-emotion types. These memory deficits may correspond to amygdala dysfunction. Adolescents with MDD had greater left amygdala activation during successful (versus unsuccessful) encoding of evocative faces than healthy controls (Roberson-Nay et al., 2006).

Although memory deficits for previously seen facial expressions have been noted in pediatric MDD, the ability to recognize emotions was unaffected. This ability suggests that it is unlikely that there are broad perturbations in face emotion processing; rather, these deficits may highlight emotional memory deficits more specifically. Healthy and depressed adolescent participants completed an n-back task in which they viewed a letter superimposed on emotional pictures and judged whether the letter matched the letter in the nth preceding trial (Ladouceur et al., 2005). Adolescents with MDD had significantly longer reaction times than controls in the negative compared to neutral conditions (Ladouceur et al., 2005), suggesting that greater attentional resources were allocated to processing the irrelevant emotional stimulus than to the target letter.

While it is evident that symptoms of pediatric MDD may include deficits in facial emotion processing and memory of facial expressions, further research is needed to understand the differences between facial processing in pediatric and adult MDD as well as the impact that development has on facial processing in pediatric depression.

Emotion Regulation

Given the core features of pediatric depression (i.e., greater negative mood and irritability), impairments in emotion regulation are important to consider in the neurocognitive framework of this disorder. A broad construct, emotion regulation has been defined in numerous ways, ranging from a trait-like construct that prescribes a person's emotional life to a transitory state-change wherein emotion regulation is captured by moment-to-moment shifts in emotional experience (Bridges, Denham, & Ganiban, 2004; Cole, Martin, & Dennis, 2004; Eisenberg & Spinrad, 2004). The most widely accepted definition of this construct is Gross' process model of emotion (1998), which states that emotion regulation refers to the processes by which one consciously or subconsciously alters the experience of emotion and behavioral responses to such experiences. For example, conscious emotion regulation strategies such as cognitive reappraisal (i.e., formulating an alternative interpretation of a situation) or behavioral distraction (i.e., the redirection of attention and behavior to a different stimulus) may be invoked to decrease a negative mood. Similarly, automatic emotion regulation responses might occur in passive viewing tasks or in tasks that combine cognitive and emotional components. For instance, participants may subconsciously shift their attention away from upsetting stimuli in order to make cognitive judgments (Gross, 2013; Gyurak, Gross, & Etkin, 2011).

Emotion dysregulation in MDD may manifest in the form of rumination or suppression of negative emotion. Rumination can be conceptualized as having two main subtypes: reflection, which can be adaptive, and brooding, which is thought of as maladaptive. Reflection involves an active attempt to gain insight, whereas, brooding is defined as passive focus on symptoms with little effort to understand them (Burwell & Shirk, 2007). Maladaptive emotion regulation strategies may confer risk for or maintain depressive symptoms (Joormann, 2010; Nolen-Hoeksema, 1991). For instance, higher level of brooding rumination in children is associated with a greater likelihood of previous major depressive episodes, a higher likelihood of future episodes, and longer episode duration (Abela & Hankin, 2011). Adolescent girls aged eleven to fifteen are particularly inclined to co-ruminate or negatively self-disclose problems and emotions with their peers (Rose, 2002), suggesting co-rumination may have a stronger effect on depression onset, episode severity, and duration than rumination alone (Stone, Hankin, Gibb, & Abela, 2011). In addition to rumination, depressed youth may have difficulties suppressing emotion. Although initial reactions were similar, compared to healthy children and adolescents, depressed youth have less pupil dilation in late phases of processing emotional pictures, suggesting behavioral avoidance or diminished cognitive resources to regulate emotion (Silk et al., 2007).

Development may play a crucial role in the ability of a child to utilize certain emotion regulation strategies and thus alleviate or worsen the effects of depression. Although it seems that children use the same emotion regulation strategies (e.g., rumination, cognitive reappraisal, suppression) as adults, they may develop the ability to use unique strategies at different stages of development (Garber, Braafladt, & Weiss, 1995; Kuppens et al., 2012). During healthy development, the strategies children use shift over time from utilizing primarily external stimuli (e.g. feedback of a parental figure) to using more internal strategies (e.g., cognitive reappraisal) to regulate their emotions (Garnefski, Rieffe, Jellesma, Terwogt, & Kraaij, 2007). Children ages five to eight years use behavioral avoidance for regulating emotion significantly more than their peers ages nine to thirteen years (Garber et al., 1995). As young adolescents grow older, the rate at which various emotion regulation strategies are recruited begins to mirror that in adults (Garnefski & Kraaij, 2006). Young adolescents (twelve to fifteen years) used all the same strategies as older adolescents (sixteen to eighteen years) and adults (eighteen to sixty-five years), albeit at lower rates across all strategies (Garnefski & Kraaij, 2006). Delays in learning new emotion-regulation skills can have an important impact on a child's risk for developing depression. For example, children aged five to thirteen years old who reported using emotion regulation strategies (e.g., support-seeking, problem-solving) less frequently were more likely to report higher levels of depressive symptoms (Garber et al., 1995) and, in a sample of nine- to twelve-year-olds, high emotional inertia (emotional states' resistance to change) predicted the emergence of clinical depression five years later (Kuppens et al., 2012).

Although few studies compare depressed youth and depressed adults directly, the use of some emotion-regulation strategies in youth may be less effective in alleviating depressive symptoms than when employed by adults. For example, while the emotion-regulation strategies of problem solving and distraction are both associated with improved outcomes in the adult depression literature (Nolen-Hoeksema, 1991; Nolen-Hoeksema, Morrow, & Fredrickson, 1993), children with distraction and/or problem-solving–oriented response styles did not exhibit decreases in depressive symptoms at follow-up (Abela, Brozina, & Haigh, 2002). In addition, in a non-clinical sample of adolescents, reflection was not associated with the same positive, reparative effects seen in adults (Burwell & Shirk, 2007). The decreased efficacy of some emotion-regulation strategies in childhood and adolescence compared to adulthood may be related to adolescents' maturing executive functioning abilities (e.g., inhibitory control; Carlson & Wang, 2007) or to other developmental factors described above.

Neuroimaging data highlight aberrant activation during emotion regulation in depressed and at-risk youth. Compared to healthy adolescents, depressed adolescents aged thirteen to seventeen years showed greater amygdala and occipital cortex activation and less ventrolateral prefrontal cortex activation in response to negatively valenced images when maintaining versus regulating emotion (Perlman et al., 2012). Adolescents with depression exhibited less activity in circuits connecting amygdala, insula, and mPFC regions when asked to maintain either their emotional state and greater amygdala-subgenual ACC connectivity when asked to regulate their emotional state (Perlman et al., 2012). In another study, at-risk daughters aged nine to fourteen years of depressed mothers showed greater amygdala activation to negative mood induction compared to their low-risk peers. Unlike at-risk youth, when asked to recall positive autobiographical memories after a sad mood induction (i.e., automatic emotion regulation), healthy youth recruited greater activation in frontal areas, including the dorsolateral prefrontal cortex and dorsal ACC (Joormann, Cooney, Henry, & Gotlib, 2012). Together, these findings of exaggerated amygdala activation and deficient recruitment of frontal structures in youth at risk and suffering from depression further highlight the deficits in top-down emotion regulation. Additional research is needed to understand whether the neural correlates of emotion regulation change with age and predict onset of depression.

Self-referential Processing

Self-referential processing may play a key role in the development and maintenance of biased cognition among individuals suffering from MDD. Information pertaining to the self is processed preferentially compared to non-self-relevant stimuli. This preferential treatment of self-relevant information is supported by research spanning a number of domains, including attention (Cherry, 1953; Newman, 2005; Wood & Cowan, 1995) and memory (e.g., Rogers, Kuiper, & Kirker, 1977; Symons & Johnson, 1997). For example, a vast body of research literature has also explored what is referred to as the *self-reference effect* in memory, which posits that information processed in reference to the self (e.g., "Does this word describe you?) is better remembered than information that is not self-relevant (Rogers et al., 1977). A meta-analysis of research on the self-reference effect supports the robustness of the effect, noting self-relevant encoding is a deeper level of encoding compared to semantic encoding (i.e., making judgments about the meaning of words; Symons & Johnson, 1997). In addition, neuroimaging research highlights the importance of self-relevant information through investigations of resting state connectivity and default mode networks (Northoff et al., 2006; Schmitz, Kawahara-Baccus, & Johnson, 2004), which are engaged during self-reflective thoughts.

This preferential processing of self-related information can be attributed to the self-schema, a vast and highly organized repertoire of self-relevant data based on a lifetime of experiences that serves as the background to which new data may be related, compared with, or interpreted against (Rogers et al., 1977; Segal, 1988). Self-schemas are known to be negatively biased in depressed individuals (Segal, 1988), which when activated will disrupt information processing by directing attention to negative stimuli, distorting interpretations of the self and world (Beck, 2008). In adult samples, depressed individuals have shown better memory for depressive content versus non-depressive content when processed self-referentially (Denny & Hunt, 1992; Derry & Kuiper, 1981; Dozois & Dobson, 2001), reflecting both a negative self-schema and the role self-referential processing plays in depression. Numerous others have linked self-referential processing to depressive cognition in other domains, such as negative attribution styles or pervasive pessimism (Alloy & Ahrens, 1987; Garber & Hollon, 1980; Gladstone & Kaslow, 1995; Pyszczynski, Holt, & Greenberg, 1987; Schlenker & Britt, 1996; Sweeney, Shaeffer, & Golin, 1982).

Few studies have examined the relationship between self-referential processing and depressive symptoms in children. A self-reference effect for depression using a depth-of-processing incidental memory task was absent in healthy third to sixth graders (Hammen & Zupan, 1984). Development of higher levels of cognitive processing (commensurate with the middle school age range) may be necessary for children to have the ability to adequately process self-relevant information to a degree that results in biased cognitive processing (Cole & Jordan, 1995; Hammen & Zupan, 1984). Alternatively, the lack of findings could relate to the severity of depression symptoms in the sample. For example, children as young as five years old in non-clinical samples reporting high versus low levels of depressive symptoms demonstrated enhanced recall for negatively valenced information (Bishop, Dalgleish, & Yule, 2004). Consistent with adult research literature, self-reference effect was detected in a sample of clinically depressed youth, suggesting that the effects may be more likely observed in clinical populations (Zupan et al., 1987). In another study, better memory for negatively valenced trait adjectives was observed in clinically depressed youth compared to healthy controls (Neshat-Doost, Taghavi, Moradi, Yule, & Dalgleish, 1998).

More recent studies have investigated how self-referent processing interacts with other factors to contribute to pediatric depression. For example, youth reporting high ruminative brooding (e.g., Burwell & Shirk, 2007; Gonzalez, Nolen-Hoeksema, & Treynor, 2003) and self-referent processing, compared to youth reporting low levels, are more likely to develop depression six months later (Black & Pössel, 2012). Other research has investigated how self-referencing may be linked to psychosocial factors. Specifically, in a large school-based sample (grades four through eight), negative peer reviews significantly predicted recall of self-referent, negative adjectives (Cole & Jordan, 1995). Similarly, negatively biased, self-referent cognitions may be derived from ambiguous peer interactions, especially in children reporting high rates of peer-victimization (Prinstein, Cheah, & Guyer, 2005). Furthermore, covert peer victimization as opposed to overt or physical peer victimization plays a more maladaptive role in the development of valenced self-cognitions (Cole, Maxwell, Dukewich, & Yosick, 2010; Crick & Bigbee, 1998).

Regarding other risk factors, it is known that negative experiences in childhood (e.g., abuse or peer victimization) contribute to maladaptive attribution patterns, a risk factor strongly linked to the development of depression (Gladstone & Kaslow, 1995; Haines, Metalsky, Cardamone, & Joiner, 1999). Maladaptive attribution styles that characterize depressive cognition (e.g., "A negative event is more likely to happen to me than a stranger") often inherently involve self-referential processing. For example, negative, critical self-evaluations stemming from ambiguous peer interactions can interact with negative life events in predicting the emergence of depressive symptoms (Prinstein et al., 2005).

Neuroimaging studies in depressed adults suggest a more widespread activation of the self in the default-mode-network (DMN; Grimm et al., 2011). Specifically, adults with MDD were unable to disengage cortical midline structures (e.g., ventromedial prefrontal cortex (VMPFC) and rostral ACC) as well as the dorsolateral prefrontal cortex during a self-relatedness cognitive task (Grimm et al., 2011). Greater DMN activation independent of tasks suggests maintained focus on self-related processing (Grimm et al., 2011). This inability to down-regulate regions involved in self-referent processing in depressed adults is consistent with prior work (Greicius et al., 2007; Sheline et al., 2009). Additional research on self-referencing in pediatric depression should pursue downward extensions of neuroimaging studies with adults. While a number of studies note perturbed connectivity in pediatric samples with depression (for a review, see Hulvershorn, Cullen, & Anand, 2011), to date, it is unknown whether studies have specifically looked into brain activation patterns during self-referential processing.

Taken together, the role self-referencing plays in pediatric depression may be best understood as a byproduct of a negative self-schema, or a mediating factor, which may contribute to the development of MDD. Indeed, studies reflect that a negative self-schema may be a prerequisite for self-referencing to become negatively biased. To illustrate this concept, findings from the pediatric studies reviewed herein have found evidence of the self-reference effect only in samples diagnosed with clinical depression (e.g., Neshat-Doost et al., 1998; Zupan et al., 1987) while those using non-clinical samples have not (e.g., Hammen & Zupan, 1984). The only exception was a study that found evidence of the self-reference effect in a non-clinical sample but only among those reporting high levels of MDD symptoms (Bishop et al., 2004). Further investigation into the underlying neural circuitry of self-referential processing and DMN may help us understand these relationships.

Reward Processing

Due to positive reinforcing properties, rewards (e.g., positive facial expressions, money) typically activate approach behavior. Depressed individuals, however, experience decreased interest, pleasure, and motivation, which suggests that deficits in reward processing may also underlie the disorder (Forbes & Dahl, 2005). In most studies of reward processing, two phases—the anticipation of reward and the receipt of a reward—are examined. For example, during anticipation, a cue often signifies the type, amount, and/or probability of receiving a reward. After a delay, the receipt of reward may be passive, contingent upon performance (instrumental reward tasks), or by choice (decision-making tasks). The reward circuitry has been well delineated. The striatum and orbitofrontal cortex (OFC) have been implicated in both anticipation and outcome of positive rewards. Other regions, like the ACC, medial prefrontal cortex, and dorsolateral prefrontal cortex, may be involved in reward processing as well (for a review, see Richards, Plate, & Ernst, 2013). Abnormal behavioral responses to anticipating and receiving rewards and abnormal brain function within the reward circuitry may play a role in pediatric depression.

As with adults with MDD (Epstein et al., 2006; Lawrence et al., 2004), perturbations in reward-related brain regions have been detected in depressed adolescents. Most consistently, adolescents with major depression (Forbes et al., 2006, 2009) and adolescents at risk for depression (Gotlib et al., 2010) exhibit less striatal activation to both anticipation and monetary reward outcomes. Less striatal activation to reward is associated with less positive affect in the daily lives of depressed adolescents (Forbes et al., 2009) and predicts the development of depressive symptoms in healthy adolescents in mid-to-late pubertal stages two years later (Morgan, Olino, McMakin, Ryan, & Forbes, 2013). As such, the less striatal activation in pediatric depression may reflect a less positive value assigned to reward and/or a diminished ability to respond to reward.

Group differences between depressed and healthy adolescents have also been detected in frontal regions during reward anticipation. Less ACC and bilateral inferior OFC activation was found specifically when making decisions with regard to high rewards (Forbes et al., 2006; Shad, Bidesi, Chen, Ernst, &

Rao, 2011). Additionally, depressed adolescents, relative to healthy adolescents, exhibited greater medial frontal gyrus (BA10) and dorsolateral prefrontal cortex (DLPFC) activation when anticipating rewards during a guessing game (Forbes et al., 2009), possibly reflecting failed disengagement of self-related processing and enhanced regulation of reward, respectively. Consistent with enhanced regulation, greater ventrolateral OFC activation has been associated with a greater probability of receiving reward (Forbes et al., 2006; Shad et al., 2011). Although Shad and colleagues (2011) present the results in terms of risk rather than probability, lower risk yields higher probability of receiving reward. Seen from this viewpoint, ACC, OFC, and mPFC activation is positively correlated with probability of receiving reward (Shad et al., 2011). Unlike healthy adolescents, evidence suggests depressed boys (ten to eleven years) fail to choose high reward more often than low reward when probability of reward is high. This reduced reward-seeking behavior correlated with depressive symptoms one year later (Forbes, Shaw, & Dahl, 2007) and may reflect reward avoidance. Alternatively, it may reflect anhedonia, in which rewards tend to lose their value.

Differences in frontal activation are also evident when experiencing rewarding stimuli (e.g., pleasant sights and tastes). For instance, at-risk populations exhibit less OFC and ACC activation than healthy controls (McCabe, Woffindale, Harmer, & Cowen, 2012). Using electrophysiological evidence, it appears that less activation in response to reward may correspond to the absence of signals indicating favorable outcome. Approximately 300 ms after feedback, a fronto-central event-related potential component called the feedback negativity (FN) differentiates monetary gain versus loss, showing less negative deflection to gains. A blunted FN correlated with pediatric depression onset (Bress, Foti, Kotov, Klein, & Hajcak, 2013) and the extent of reduced FN positively correlated with depressive symptoms (Bress, Smith, Foti, Klein, & Hajcak, 2012). Depressed adolescents, relative to healthy controls, exhibited greater DLPFC (Forbes et al., 2009) and inferior OFC but less ACC activation to monetary gains, although differences in the inferior frontal cortex were specific to large wins (Forbes et al., 2006). In healthy boys, greater vmPFC activation to wins correlated with more depressive symptoms two years later (Morgan et al., 2013), suggesting inefficient regulation via frontal cortical regions.

Deficits in response to monetary rewards may extend to social rewards in youth with depression. Depressed adolescents exhibited greater amygdala activation to positive versus control peer evaluation (Davey, Allen, Harrison, & Yucel, 2011), and at-risk populations exhibited less nucleus accumbens activation to happy faces (Monk et al., 2008), suggesting positive social information is arousing or, alternatively, negatively valenced. Correlations between depressive symptoms and lower striatal and ACC activation in response to positive social behaviors (Whittle et al., 2012) may highlight a failure to experience positive affect in social situations. However, this deficit may not preclude sensitivities to social rejection. In fact, greater subgenual ACC activation during peer exclusion correlated with greater depressive symptoms one year later (Masten et al., 2011).

In summary, rewards appear to be processed differently in youth with MDD. Evidence suggests that the perceived positive value of rewards is distorted in youth with MDD such that rewards do not evoke the same approach behaviors as healthy controls. Underlying perturbations within the neural circuitry of reward pathways may explain this phenomenon.

Attention

Cognitive theories of depression posit that the manner in which an individual selectively attends to, processes, or interprets stimuli plays a role in the etiology and maintenance of depression (e.g., Clark, Beck, & Alford, 1999). Theories regarding the attentional biases in MDD hypothesize that depressed individuals selectively attend to stimuli conveying sadness, hopelessness, and loss. In addition, depressed individuals are believed to show reduced attention to and processing of positively valenced information. In a meta-analytic review of twenty-nine studies employing various methodologies to measure attentional biases using differential reaction times to incongruent and congruent stimuli (e.g., dot-probe task, Stroop task), depressed adults showed a greater attentional bias for negative information compared to healthy controls (Peckham, McHugh, & Otto, 2010). Similarly, a recent meta-analysis of thirty-three eye-tracking studies with adults found that compared to healthy controls, depressed adults showed longer gaze at dysphoric stimuli coupled with a reduced gaze toward positive stimuli (Armstrong & Olatunji, 2012).

Extending this cognitive model to children and adolescents has yielded mixed findings, possibly due to fewer studies conducted with youth compared to adults. While some have found an attentional bias for negative information among depressed youth (Hankin et al., 2010), others have found no differences between depressed youth and healthy controls (Neshat-Doost, Moradi, Taghavi, Yule, & Dalgleish, 2000; Neshat-Doost, Taghavi, Moradi, Yule, & Dalgleish, 1997; Taghavi, Neshat-Doost, Moradi, Yule, & Dalgleish, 1999). Although the reason for inconsistent findings is unclear, some (e.g., Joormann, Talbot, & Gotlib, 2007) have suggested that the type of stimuli used in dot-probe tasks may moderate findings in pediatric populations. For instance, studies using pictorial stimuli (e.g., faces) have found stronger evidence for an attentional bias in depression (Gibb, Benas, Grassia, & McGeary, 2009; Hankin et al., 2010; Joormann et al., 2007), whereas studies using textual stimuli (e.g., words) have generally produced null findings (Neshat-Doost et al., 1997, 2000; Taghavi et al., 1999).

Prior work has also found evidence for an attentional bias toward sad faces among youth at risk for depression. For instance, offspring of mothers with a history of MDD aged eight to fourteen years demonstrated an attentional bias for sad faces compared to children of healthy mothers (Gibb et al., 2009; Joormann et al., 2007). However, the direction of the attentional bias was mixed in these two studies. Consistent with clinically depressed youth (Hankin et al., 2010) as well as with prior theory, Joormann and colleagues (2007) found that at-risk youth attended toward sad faces; whereas, at-risk youth in the Gibb and colleagues' (2009) study avoided sad faces. Although reasons for the inconsistent findings are unclear, Joormann and colleagues (2007) utilized a negative mood induction exercise prior to the dot-probe task, whereas Gibb and colleagues (2009) did not, which the latter hypothesized could potentially explain the discrepant results.

At-risk girls may demonstrate this cognitive vulnerability for depression earlier in development, which may partially contribute to a greater risk for depression in later childhood and adolescence. Daughters of mothers with a history of MDD aged five to seven years old showed an attentional bias toward sad faces in a dot-probe task as compared to children of healthy mothers (Kujawa et al., 2011). Interestingly, sons of depressed mothers did not display an attentional bias. The higher rate of depression among girls is well observed, with girls approximately twice as likely to develop depression as boys in adolescence, a ratio that continues through adulthood (e.g., Hankin & Abramson, 2001).

Besides serving as a vulnerability factor for depression alone, prior (albeit limited) work has found that attentional bias may interact with genetic risk factors. Attentional avoidance of sad faces was stronger among children who were either homozygous or heterozygous for the short allele of the serotonin transporter gene 5-HTTLPR (Gibb et al., 2009), which has been shown to be a genetic vulnerability factor for depression (Caspi et al., 2003). Furthermore, mothers' and children's depressive symptoms were only predictive of one another longitudinally (up to six months) for children exhibiting both an attentional bias and genetic vulnerability. The influence of genetic risk factors on neurocognitive function should be further explored.

Youth at risk for depression may also focus less upon positive information compared to healthy controls. In a dot-probe task, girls at risk for depression selectively attended to sad faces but not happy faces, whereas healthy girls selectively attended to happy faces but not sad faces (Joormann et al., 2007). Thus, compared to healthy children, those at risk for depression may be less attentive toward positive or pleasant stimuli in their environment. These findings are consistent with eye-tracking studies in adults (Armstrong & Olatunji, 2012) and the tripartite model of anxiety and depression (Clark & Watson, 1991), which theorizes that depression is characterized by both high levels of negative affect and low levels of positive affect.

Adolescents with pediatric depression may also have deficits in selective and sustained attention, possibly relating to difficulties concentrating and lack of motivation. To study selective attention, adolescents with MDD who completed the Simon task exhibited less activation in DLPFC/ventrolateral PFC, precuneus, cuneus, and cerebellum in response to a target appearing in the less frequent, un-cued location compared to cued locations (Halari et al., 2009). While impaired sustained attention has been reported in depressed youth (Han et al., 2012), most studies do not find group differences between depressed and non-depressed youth (Calhoun & Mayes, 2005; Günther, Konrad, De Brito, Herpertz-Dahlmann, & Vloet, 2011; Mayes & Calhoun, 2007). Despite the lack of behavioral differences, compared to healthy controls, depressed adolescents exhibited less occipital activation during sustained attention task (e.g., continuous performance tasks). Moreover, unlike healthy adolescents who up-regulated frontal-striatal-thalamic circuitry and limbic areas when performance was rewarded, adolescents with MDD deactivated these regions (Chantiluke et al., 2011).

As reviewed, prior work on attention in at-risk and depressed youth has focused primarily on biases to negative information. At-risk and depressed youth attend to negative stimuli (e.g., sad faces) to a greater extent and may be less attentive toward positive stimuli. Despite the deficits of concentration and motivation in depression, selective and sustained attention have been understudied in pediatric depression. Finally, further efforts need to determine how genetic factors and underlying neural correlates (e.g., amygdala and vlPFC) of these attentional deficits influence onset, maintenance, and treatment of pediatric depression.

Executive Control

There is growing evidence to suggest that adults with a history of depression exhibit significant impairment on tasks of executive functioning (EF), including tasks of cognitive flexibility, response inhibition, processing speed, working memory, and fluency. Among depressed adults, the most robust deficits have been observed on tasks of cognitive flexibility, which require individuals to quickly shift attention to a new perceptual or cognitive set, and tests of semantic fluency, which require individuals to generate as many verbal utterances as possible within a given time frame (Beblo, Baumann, Bogerts, Wallesch, & Herrmann, 1999; Lee, Hermens, Porter, & Redoblado-Hodge, 2012). Although many studies have examined neurocognitive deficits in relatively homogenous samples of adults with histories of chronic depression, evidence is beginning to support the existence of neurocognitive deficits in depressed adults regardless of age of depression onset, depression chronicity, or depression type. Broad deficits in EF have been identified in adults experiencing a first episode of MDD (Lee et al., 2012) and in remitted patients currently experiencing low levels of depressive symptoms (Hasselbalch, Knorr, Hasselbalch, Gade, & Kessing,

2012). However, there is some evidence to suggest that past depression severity and chronicity may have a greater negative impact upon executive function than present symptom severity, with one study finding a trait-like association between lifetime depression severity and cognitive impairment (Sarapas, Shankman, Harrow, & Goldberg, 2012).

Evidence for EF deficits in adolescents is mixed, and very few studies have included children under the age of twelve. Existing studies have also been plagued by small sample sizes, with most studies including fewer than forty depressed youth in experimental groups. Although a lack of statistical power makes generalization of findings difficult, several consistent results are beginning to emerge from this literature. In general, most studies of EF in depressed children and adolescents have failed to find deficits in neuropsychological tasks of cognitive and attentional flexibility such as the Wisconsin Card Sorting Task, Trails Part B, or the Intra-Extra Dimensional set-shifting task on the CANTAB battery (Favre et al., 2008; Frost, Moffitt, & McGee, 1989; Klimkeit, Tonge, Bradshaw, Melvin, & Gould, 2011; Korhonen et al., 2002; Kyte, Goodyer, & Sahakian, 2005; Matthews, Coghill, & Rhodes, 2008). Results in at-risk adolescents based on parental psychopathology also do not find deficits in EF (Klimes-Dougan, Ronsaville, Wiggs, & Martinez, 2006). In fact, only one study to our knowledge has reported more total errors on the card sort task in depressed relative to healthy controls; however, this sample included both adolescents and adults between thirteen and twenty-five years old (Baune, Czira, Smith, Mitchell, & Sinnamon, 2012). Results have been more varied for tasks measuring response inhibition, such as the Stroop Color-Word task, with some studies finding no differences in performance between depressed youth and healthy controls (e.g., Favre et al., 2008; Klimkeit et al., 2011; Korhonen et al., 2002) and a few finding evidence of impaired performance and greater errors on the Stroop task (e.g., Brooks, Iverson, Sherman, & Roberge, 2010; Cataldo, Nobile, Lorusso, Battaglia, & Molteni, 2005). While findings have been either null or mixed for tests of cognitive flexibility and response inhibition, differences between depressed youth and controls are more consistent with respect to processing speed, reaction time, and response initiation. Youth with MDD may exhibit a more conservative response style, taking longer to initiate responses, execute movements, and process stimuli (Cataldo et al., 2005; Favre et al., 2008; Klimkeit et al., 2011; Matthews et al., 2008). In addition, several studies have found impairments on tasks of working memory (Gunther, Holtkamp, Jolles, Herpertz-Dahlmann, & Konrad, 2004; Klimkeit et al., 2011) and complex planning (Maalouf et al., 2011). Mixed samples of depressed adolescents and adults complicate these findings (Baune et al., 2012).

Given the relatively robust findings for deficits in executive control in depressed adult patients (e.g., Gualtieri, Johnson, & Benedict, 2006; Porter, Gallagher, Thompson, & Young, 2003), the lack of evidence for these deficits among children and adolescents is somewhat surprising. In addition to small sample size, these null findings may be a result of several limitations of existing research in this area. First, neuropsychological assessment batteries varied across studies, so discrepancies in findings among studies may be a function of differences in cognitive processes being assessed. Second, subjects in many of the studies were children and adolescents recently diagnosed with a first episode of MDD (e.g., Klimkeit et al., 2011; Kyte et al., 2005) or children and adolescents with single-episode MDD (e.g., Korhonen et al., 2002). Given that recent findings from the adult literature suggest that severity of EF deficits may correspond more to depression chronicity than current severity (e.g., Sarapas et al., 2012), it is possible that EF domains such as cognitive flexibility or response inhibition may indeed be impaired in children and adolescents with a more chronic course of depression. If this is indeed the case, it may be that initial episodes may degrade neurocognitive functions such as cognitive control and EF, predisposing individuals to further depressive episodes (De Raedt & Koster, 2010). There is also evidence that EF deficits may manifest in adolescents with acute but not remitted MDD, suggesting that the adolescent brain may be more plastic than the adult brain in its ability to recover from EF deficits associated with MDD (Maalouf et al., 2011). Another limitation is that all of these studies used non-emotional stimuli in examining deficits in cognitive flexibility and response inhibition, and a number of findings from the adult literature suggest that deficits in these areas of EF may be more pronounced for emotional than for non-emotional stimuli (e.g., Deveney & Deldin, 2006; Murphy et al., 2012). For example, adolescents with MDD were faster on an emotional go/no go task when sad faces were the target among neutral distractors (Ladouceur et al., 2006). Other studies in adolescents with and without MDD did not show group differences in performance; however, emotional no-go task performance in depressed youth was correlated with depressive symptoms (Han et al., 2012).

Despite the lack of significant differences in task performance in many domains of EF, some neuroimaging research suggests that youth with MDD may differ from healthy controls in patterns of brain activation during task performance. For example, even though adolescents recently diagnosed with a first episode of MDD performed similarly to healthy controls on tasks of attentional switching and response inhibition, they demonstrated less brain activation in areas of the lateral inferior frontal cortex, right DLPFC, ACC, and striatal brain regions (Halari et al., 2009). Using a modified version of the Eriksen-Flanker Task to assess response inhibition, participants attempt to suppress responding to irrelevant distractors flanking the target. In this response inhibition task, a reduced error-related negativity (ERN) amplitude in the dorsal region of the ACC was observed in children and adolescents with MDD as compared to healthy controls and a lack of normative age-related changes in ERN amplitudes (Ladouceur et al., 2012). These differences in

ERN amplitudes are thought to reflect differences in cognitive monitoring and error- and conflict-detection processes (Ladouceur et al., 2012). There is also evidence that children and adolescents with familial risk factors for MDD or a history of MDD may exhibit greater activation in brain regions associated with working memory during task performance, such as the subgenual ACC cortex (Yang et al., 2009), the lateral occipital cortex, the superior temporal gyrus, and the superior parietal/precuneus border (Mannie, Harmer, Cowen, & Norbury, 2010). Taken together, these findings suggest that familial risk factors for depression, depressive symptoms, or a combination of both may contribute to abnormalities in patterns of brain activation in depressed youth, but these perturbations may not necessarily result in differences in task performance until adulthood or when depression becomes more chronic.

Treatment Implications

Psychotherapeutic and pharmacological interventions, which are common and effective treatments for pediatric depression, are thought to target underlying neurocognitive dysfunction. Cognitive behavioral therapy (CBT) and interpersonal psychotherapy (IPT) are currently the psychotherapeutic treatments for depression with the most research support. Cognitive behavioral treatments for children and adolescents generally target depressive symptoms by facilitating emotional awareness through psychoeducation, identifying and correcting maladaptive cognitive biases, engaging in approach behaviors and mood-lifting activities, and utilizing problem-solving strategies. Throughout CBT, the connection between physical feelings, thoughts, and behaviors is emphasized, and the use of mood monitoring activities helps to reinforce this connection for youth. Like CBT, interpersonal psychotherapy for adolescents (IPT-A; Mufson et al., 1994) targets similar skills but does so in the context of interpersonal and communication skill development, linking the experience of depressive symptoms in adolescents to interpersonal disputes, role transitions, and skills deficits (Mufson et al., 1994). These interpersonal situations provide a platform to discuss emotions, coping strategies, and cognitive distortions. Both treatments have performed superior to control conditions in reducing depressive symptoms in youth (David-Ferdon & Kaslow, 2008), with a mean effect size of .34 across these different treatment modalities (Weisz, McCarty, & Valeri, 2006). According to a recent meta-analysis, CBT for both children and adolescents and IPT-A now appear to meet the Task Force on Promotion and Dissemination of Psychological Procedures criteria (Chambless et al., 1998; Chambless & Hollon, 1998) for well-established treatments (David-Ferdon & Kaslow, 2008). However, there is a significant amount of variability in effect sizes among studies, and there is some question about the sustainability of intervention effects. For example, one-year follow-up findings from the

Treatment for Adolescents with Depression Study (TADS) indicated that approximately 30 percent of adolescents who had been successfully treated with CBT alone had relapsed by the one-year follow-up point (Treatment for Adolescents With Depression Study et al., 2009).

Pharmacological interventions, which target perturbations in brain function via neurotransmitter systems (e.g., serotonin), have also been shown to be somewhat effective in treating youth depression alone and in combination with CBT. Randomized, controlled trials using selective-serotonin reuptake inhibitors (SSRIs) such as fluoxetine (Emslie et al., 1997), escitalopram (Yang & Scott, 2010) and paroxetine (Keller et al., 2001) have demonstrated clinical improvements in depressed youth following eight weeks of treatment, and findings from the TADS study indicate that combination therapy with fluoxetine and CBT resulted in a higher response rate (71.0 percent) than either treatment with fluoxetine alone (60.6 percent) or CBT alone (43.2 percent; March et al., 2004). Pharmacological or combination therapy may be particularly appropriate for more severe cases of depression, while youth with mild-to-moderate depression may respond well to psychotherapeutic treatment (March et al., 2004).

Despite these positive findings for a variety of treatment modalities, very few studies have examined their mechanisms of action (Weersing & Weisz, 2002). Furthermore, no known studies have examined whether the existence of neurocognitive impairments moderate treatment outcomes for depressed youth or whether changes in neurocognitive functioning mediate treatment outcome. Such studies might help to improve treatment response rates for depressed youth and aid in the development of more targeted intervention and prevention programs.

Theoretically, both CBT and IPT for youth depression may work in part by targeting and changing some of the neurocognitive deficits discussed in this chapter, such as perturbations in affective processing, reward processing, and cognitive control. For example, CBT attempts to teach children and adolescents emotion recognition strategies (e.g., recognizing their own and others' emotional experiences) and to identify and correct poor methods of regulating emotions (e.g., reduce rumination or avoidance behaviors, increase adaptive strategies). These treatment components attempt to improve deficiencies in facial processing and emotion regulation, respectively. CBT for depression also addresses maladaptive thinking styles and interpretation biases (e.g., the tendency to catastrophize or make global and stable inferences about the self, world, and future; Beck, 1979) through cognitive restructuring, a technique that might help increase cognitive flexibility and teach youth to redirect attention away from negative stimuli. CBT as well as more behaviorally based treatments for youth depression (e.g., Ritschel, Ramirez, Jones, & Craighead, 2011) also encourage reinforcing activities via behavioral activation, which may improve youth's access to rewarding experiences or alter reward processing. IPT-A is also effective in reducing depressive symptoms (Mufson, Moreau, Weissman, & Dorta, 2004), and these improvements may occur through mechanisms similar to those in CBT. Experimental designs and statistical techniques for examining treatment mechanisms, such as dismantling studies and mediation analyses, would help to elucidate whether and to what degree changes in neurocognitive functioning over the course of treatment might contribute to symptom improvement.

Few published studies have addressed the impact of treatment on neurocognitive deficits directly (Lenze, Pautsch, & Luby, 2011; Luby, Lenze, & Tillman, 2012; Tao et al., 2012). These studies suggest that neurocognitive dysfunction of emotion recognition, emotion regulation, and reward circuitry is minimized as targeted skills are learned during treatment. For example, prior to open-label fluoxetine treatment, adolescents with depression exhibited greater amygdala and OFC and less subgenual ACC activation in response to fearful versus neutral faces compared to a healthy comparison group; however, these differences were not present following eight-week fluoxetine treatment and symptom reduction. The lack of group differences after treatment reflects both decreased activation in the depression group and increased activations in the healthy comparison group (Tao et al., 2012). There is also some evidence that behavioral and cognitive-behavioral treatments for depression may improve emotion regulation skills, at least in younger children. For example, Parent–Child Interaction Therapy for depressed preschoolers, which aims to facilitate the development of emotion recognition and regulation, has been shown to decrease depression severity and increase emotion recognition skills (Lenze et al., 2011; Luby et al., 2012). Although no studies examining changes in emotion regulation have been conducted in adolescent depression, after mood induction, healthy youth randomized to either a distraction or mindfulness intervention, but not problem solving, experienced reduced rumination (Hilt & Pollak, 2012). Despite evidence that positive affect can be trained in healthy adolescents through cognitive bias modification (CBM) paradigms (Lothmann, Holmes, Chan, & Lau, 2011) and such CBM applications have been made to treat adults with depression (Hallion & Ruscio, 2011) and anxious children (Lau, Molyneaux, Telman, & Belli, 2011; Muris, Huijding, Mayer, & Hameetman, 2008; Salemink & Wiers, 2011), no known studies have been conducted in adolescents with depression.

Fewer treatment studies have investigated the treatment effects on reward processing and cognitive control. In a sample of adolescents with comorbid depression and anxiety disorders, neural activation in response to reward processing at baseline predicted reductions in post-CBT *anxiety* symptoms, but not *depressive* symptoms (Forbes et al., 2010); therefore, it is unclear whether treatment of depression alters reward circuitry. Furthermore, no known studies have reported the effects of treatment on attention or cognitive control processes. More research on these effects is clearly needed to determine what neurocognitive changes occur with treatment and what changes are predictive of outcome. Understanding these changes may inform us on how to target particular underlying deficits that would yield greater clinical effects.

In addition to examining whether neurocognitive changes occur with treatment and contribute to symptom improvement, knowledge of neurocognitive deficits associated with depression in youth may help to inform prevention efforts. As described earlier, high-risk adolescents without current depressive symptoms may show evidence of neurocognitive perturbations associated with depression (e.g., Joormann et al., 2012; Monk et al., 2008; Perlman et al., 2012), and many of the studies reviewed have also found neurocognitive deficits in youth with elevated but non-clinical depressive symptoms. Certain neurocognitive deficits may exist before the onset of depression in youth, and targeting these deficits might help prevent the emergence of depression.

Several depression prevention programs have been shown to be effective in reducing sub-clinical internalizing symptoms and preventing the development of later depressive symptoms. One cognitive-behavioral prevention program, the Penn Resiliency Program (PRP; Gillham, Jaycox, Reivich, Seligman, & Silver, 1990), teaches youth cognitive and social problem-solving skills and has been found to reduce depressive symptoms at post-intervention, six-month follow-up (Jaycox, Reivich, Gillham, & Seligman, 1994) and two-year follow-up (Gillham, Reivich, Jaycox, & Seligman, 1995). Programs such as the PRP teach youth interpretation bias or attribution retraining (i.e., identifying pessimistic explanatory styles and replacing them with more helpful ones). Additionally, interpersonal psychotherapy-adolescent skills training (IPT-AST; Young & Mufson, 2003) is a group-based adaptation of interpersonal psychotherapy designed for use in adolescents with subclinical depression. IPT-AST has been shown to be effective as an indicated prevention program for depression in subsyndromal adolescent populations (Young, Mufson, & Davies, 2006). IPT-AST targets many of the same skills as those targeted in interpersonal psychotherapy, such as negotiating relationship disputes or improving interpersonal deficits, by teaching adolescents to recognize the connection between mood and relationship issues and to increase their flexibility in approaching interpersonal situations. IPT-AST is more effective than control conditions in reducing depressive symptoms in adolescents (Horowitz, Garber, Ciesla, Young, & Mufson, 2007; Young, Mufson, & Gallop, 2010) and improves overall functioning and maintains these gains at three- and six-month follow-ups (Young, Mufson, & Davies, 2006). While there is a growing interest in understanding the mechanisms of action both for treatment and prevention, long-term effects still need to be investigated.

Although current research has supported the efficacy of psychotherapeutic and pharmacological interventions for treating pediatric depression, the development of novel approaches is imperative. One new direction is to augment psychotherapeutic interventions with behavioral treatments that target neurocognitive dysfunction more directly, such as cognitive bias modification interpretation (CBM-I), attention training, or executive function paradigms. Such paradigms may help to improve depressive symptoms by increasing prefrontal control over amygdala responses. For example, CBM-I paradigms that have been successfully used with healthy and socially anxious youth (Lau et al., 2011; Vassilopoulos, Banerjee, & Prantzalou, 2009) may be adapted to train depressed youth to interpret ambiguous scenarios in adaptive rather than depressogenic ways. Such paradigms could be investigated either as stand-alone treatments for depression or as adjunctive treatments to reinforce the cognitive restructuring component of CBT. Although typically investigated in anxious individuals (Eldar et al., 2012; Waters, Mogg, & Bradley, 2012), attention bias modification procedures may also be a promising stand-alone or adjunctive treatment for pediatric depression, in light of the evidence reviewed in this chapter that depressed youth may exhibit attentional biases toward negatively valenced content. Facilitating youth's ability to disengage from negatively valenced stimuli may decrease ruminative processes, facilitate reappraisal, and increase the ability to engage in more positively reinforcing activities.

Several neurobiological treatments for refractory depression in adolescents are currently being tested, including transcranial magnetic stimulation (TMS) and electroconvulsive therapy (ECT). TMS is a non-invasive neurostimulation technique that alters neural activity in targeted brain regions. Preliminary feasibility data indicate that TMS may be a generally acceptable treatment to most children and adolescents, with low discontinuation rates and limited adverse effects reported in child and adolescent samples (Croarkin, Wall, & Lee, 2011). Although there have been only a handful of small studies using TMS in adolescents with treatment-resistant depression, the existing literature suggests that stimulation of the left DLPFC using a pulse frequency of at least 1 Hz over a period of at least six weeks may lead to clinical improvement in between 50 percent to 100 percent of cases, though the small samples sizes used to date make generalization of treatment effects difficult (Croarkin et al., 2010; D'Agati, Bloch, Levkovitz, & Reti, 2010). ECT, which involves the electrical induction of seizures, is another treatment from refractory depression that has rarely been used in prepubertal children but has occasionally been used in adolescents. A review of the effectiveness of ECT in seventy-two adolescents who received the treatment within a ten-year time period indicated marked symptom improvement in over 50 percent of adolescents with chronic depression (Walter & Rey, 2003). However, in a study of sixteen treatment-resistant depressed adolescents receiving ECT, participants exhibited temporary decreased attention, concentration, and verbal fluency, though all cognitive function had returned to baseline levels eight months after treatment (Ghaziuddin, Laughrin, & Giordani, 2000). Although there seems to be improvement, there are relatively limited extant data regarding the effectiveness and safety of ECT in pediatric populations.

In addition to the development of novel treatments for pediatric depression, there is a need for studies examining how current psychotherapeutic and pharmacological treatments reviewed in this chapter impact neurocognitive functioning. Pharmacological treatment may alter facial processing biases in depressed adolescents (Tao et al., 2012), and psychosocial treatments for pediatric depression may result in some improvements in emotion dysregulation (Lenze et al., 2011; Luby et al., 2012). Future studies might utilize neurocognitive paradigms and neuroimaging to examine whether existing treatments result in improvements in neurocognitive functions such as attentional control or cognitive flexibility as well as changes in neuronal activity in related regions.

Summary

Research has shown impairments in several domains of neurocognitive dysfunction associated with pediatric depression, which may have treatment implications. Although we review domains of affective processing, reward processing, and cognitive control separately, these domains undoubtedly interact. In addition, the developmental trajectory of these processes and the maturation of neural correlates of these functions must be considered when refining treatments for pediatric depression. To have the greatest impact, future prevention and treatment strategies for pediatric depression should consider neurocognitive targets from a developmental perspective. Therefore, more research in pediatric depression is clearly needed to understand the relationship between neurocognitive function, development, and treatment.

References

Abela, J. R., & Hankin, B. L. (2011). Rumination as a vulnerability factor to depression during the transition from early to middle adolescence: a multiwave longitudinal study. *Journal of Abnormal Psychology, 120*(2), 259.

Abela, J. R., Brozina, K., & Haigh, E. P. (2002). An examination of the response styles theory of depression in third- and seventh-grade children: A short-term longitudinal study. *Journal of Abnormal Child Psychology, 30*(5), 515–527.

Adolphs, R. (2002). Neural systems for recognizing emotion. *Current Opinion in Neurobiology, 12*(2), 169–177.

Alexander-Bloch, A., Raznahan, A., Bullmore, E., & Giedd, J. (2013). The convergence of maturational change and structural covariance in human cortical networks. *The Journal of Neuroscience, 33*(7), 2889–2899. doi: 10.1523/jneurosci.3554–12.2013

Alloy, L. B., & Ahrens, A. H. (1987). Depression and pessimism for the future: Biased use of statistically relevant information in predictions for self versus others. *Journal of Personality and Social Psychology, 52*(2), 366–378. doi: 10.1037/0022–3514.52.2.366

American Psychiatric Association (2013). *Diagnostic and Statistical Manual of Mental Disorders, Fifth Edition (DSM-5)*. Washington, DC: American Psychiatric Association.

Armstrong, T., & Olatunji, B. O. (2012). Eye tracking of attention in the affective disorders: A meta-analytic review and synthesis. *Clinical Psychology Review, 32*, 704–723.

Avenevoli, S., & Merikangas, K. (2006). Implications of high-risk family studies for prevention of depression. *American Journal of Preventive Medicine, 31*(6), 126–135.

Barch, D. M., Gaffrey, M. S., Botteron, K. N., Belden, A. C., & Luby, J. L. (2012). Functional brain activation to emotionally valenced faces in school-aged children with a history of preschool-onset major depression. *Biological Psychiatry, 72*, 1035–1042.

Batty, M., & Taylor, M. J. (2006). The development of emotional face processing during childhood. *Dev Sci, 9*(2), 207–220. doi: 10.1111/j.1467-7687.2006.00480.x

Baune, B. T., Czira, M. E., Smith, A. L., Mitchell, D., & Sinnamon, G. (2012). Neuropsychological performance in a sample of 13–25 year olds with a history of non-psychotic major depressive disorder. *Journal of Affective Disorders, 141*(2–3), 441–448. doi: 10.1016/j.jad.2012.02.041

Beblo, T., Baumann, B., Bogerts, B., Wallesch, C., & Herrmann, M. (1999). Neuropsychological correlates of major depression: A short-term follow-up. *Cognitive Neuropsychiatry, 4*(4), 333–341.

Beck, A. T. (1979). *Cognitive therapy of depression*. New York: The Guilford Press.

Beck, A. T. (2008). The evolution of the cognitive model of depression and its neurobiological correlates. *American Journal of Psychiatry, 165*(8), 969–977. doi: 10.1176/appi.ajp.2008.08050721

Beesdo, K., Lau, J. F., Guyer, A. E., McClure-Tone, E. B., Monk, C. S., Nelson, E. E., Fromm, S., Goldwin, M. A., Wittchen, H.-U., Leibenluft, E., Ernst, E., & Pine, D. S. (2009). Common and distinct amygdala-function perturbations in depressed vs anxious adolescents. *Archives of General Psychiatry, 66*(3), 275–285. doi: 10.1001/archgenpsychiatry.2008.545

Birmaher, B., Ryan, N. D., Williamson, D. E., Brent, D. A., & Kaufman, J. (1996). Childhood and adolescent depression: A review of the past 10 years. Part II. *Journal of the American Academy of Child and Adolescent Psychiatry, 35*(12), 1575–1583. doi: 10.1097/00004583-199612000-00008

Birmaher, B., Ryan, N. D., Williamson, D. E., Brent, D. A., Kaufman, J., Dahl, R. E., Perel, J., & Nelson, B. (1996). Childhood and adolescent depression: A review of the past 10 years. Part I. *Journal of the American Academy of Child and Adolescent Psychiatry, 35*(11), 1427–1439. doi: 10.1097/00004583-199611000-00011

Bishop, S. J., Dalgleish, T., & Yule, W. (2004). Memory for emotional stories in high and low depressed children. *Memory, 12*(2), 214–230. doi: 10.1080/09658210244000667

Black, S. W., & Pössel, P. (2012). The combined effects of self-referent information processing and ruminative responses on adolescent depression. *Journal of Youth and Adolescence, 42*, 1145–1154.

Bourke, C., Douglas, K., & Porter, R. (2010). Processing of facial emotion expression in major depression: A review. *Australian and New Zealand Journal of Psychiatry, 44*(8), 681–696. doi: 10.3109/00048674.2010.496359

Bress, J. N., Foti, D., Kotov, R., Klein, D. N., & Hajcak, G. (2013). Blunted neural response to rewards prospectively predicts depression in adolescent girls. *Psychophysiology, 50*(1), 74–81.

Bress, J. N., Smith, E., Foti, D., Klein, D. N., & Hajcak, G. (2012). Neural response to reward and depressive symptoms in late childhood to early adolescence. *Biological Psychology, 89*(1), 156–162. doi: 10.1016/j.biopsycho.2011.10.004

Bridges, L. J., Denham, S. A., & Ganiban, J. M. (2004). Definitional issues in emotion regulation research. *Child Development, 75*(2), 340–345.

Britton, J. C., Taylor, S. F., Sudheimer, K. D., & Liberzon, I. (2006). Facial expressions and complex IAPS pictures: Common and differential networks. *Neuroimage, 31*(2), 906–919. doi: 10.1016/j.neuroimage.2005.12.050

Brooks, B. L., Iverson, G. L., Sherman, E. M., & Roberge, M. (2010). Identifying cognitive problems in children and adolescents with depression using computerized neuropsychological testing. *Applied Neuropsychology, 17*(1), 37–43.

Burwell, R. A., & Shirk, S. R. (2007). Subtypes of rumination in adolescence: Associations between brooding, reflection, depressive symptoms, and coping. *Journal of Clinical Child and Adolescent Psychology, 36*(1), 56–65.

Calhoun, S. L., & Mayes, S. D. (2005). Processing speed in children with clinical disorders. *Psychology in the Schools, 42*(4), 333–343.

Carlson, S. M., & Wang, T. S. (2007). Inhibitory control and emotion regulation in preschool children. *Cognitive Development, 22*(4), 489–510.

Caron, R. F., Caron, A. J., & Myers, R. S. (1982). Abstraction of invariant face expressions in infancy. *Child Development, 53*(4), 1008–1015.

Casey, B. J., Tottenham, N., Liston, C., & Durston, S. (2005). Imaging the developing brain: What have we learned about cognitive development? *Trends in Cognitive Science, 9*(3), 104–110. doi: 10.1016/j.tics.2005.01.011

Caspi, A., Sugden, K., Moffitt, T. E., Taylor, A., Craig, I. W., Harrington, H., McClay, J., Mill, J., Martin, J., & Braithwaite, A. (2003). Influence of life stress on depression: moderation by a polymorphism in the 5-HTT gene. *Science Signaling, 301*(5631), 386.

Cataldo, M. G., Nobile, M., Lorusso, M. L., Battaglia, M., & Molteni, M. (2005). Impulsivity in depressed children and adolescents: A comparison between behavioral and neuropsychological data. *Psychiatry Research, 136*(2), 123–133.

Chambless, D. L., & Hollon, S. D. (1998). Defining empirically supported therapies. *Journal of Consulting and Clinical Psychology, 66*(1), 7–18.

Chambless, D. L., Baker, M. J., Baucom, D. H., Beutler, L. E., Calhoun, K. S., Crits-Christoph, P., Daiuto, A., DeRubeis, R., Detweiler, J., & Haaga, D. A. (1998). Update on empirically validated therapies, II. *Clinical Psychologist, 51*(1), 3–16.

Chantiluke, K., Halari, R., Simic, M., Pariante, C. M., Papadopoulos, A., Giampietro, V., & Rubia, K. (2011). Fronto-striato-cerebellar dysregulation in adolescents with depression during motivated attention. *Biological Psychiatry, 71*, 59–67.

Cherry, E. C. (1953). Some experiments on the recognition of speech, with one and with two ears. *Journal of the Acoustical Society of America, 25*, 975–979. doi: 10.1121/1.1907229

Clark, D. A., Beck, A. T., & Alford, B. A. (1999). *Cognitive theory and therapy of depression*: New York: John Wiley & Sons.

Clark, L. A., & Watson, D. (1991). Tripartite model of anxiety and depression: Psychometric evidence and taxonomic implications. *Journal of Abnormal Psychology, 100*(3), 316.

Cole, D. A., & Jordan, A. E. (1995). Competence and memory: Integrating psychosocial and cognitive correlates of child depression. *Child Development, 66*(2), 459–473. doi: 10.1111/1467-8624.ep9505240345

Cole, D. A., Maxwell, M. A., Dukewich, T. L., & Yosick, R. (2010). Targeted peer victimization and the construction of positive and negative self-cognitions: Connections to depressive symptoms in children. *Journal of Clinical Child & Adolescent Psychology, 39*(3), 421–435.

Cole, P. M., Martin, S. E., & Dennis, T. A. (2004). Emotion regulation as a scientific construct: Methodological challenges and directions for child development research. *Child Development, 75*(2), 317–333.

Costello, E. J., Pine, D. S., Hammen, C., March, J. S., Plotsky, P. M., Weissman, M. M., Biederman, J., Goldsmith, H. H., Kaufman, J., Lewinsohn, P. M., Hellander, M., Hoagwood, K., Koretz, D. S., Nelson, C. A., & Leckman, J. F. (2002). Development and natural history of mood disorders. *Biological Psychiatry, 52*(6), 529–542.

Crick, N. R., & Bigbee, M. A. (1998). Relational and overt forms of peer victimization: A multiinformant approach. *Journal of Consulting and Clinical Psychology, 66*(2), 337.

Croarkin, P. E., Wall, C. A., & Lee, J. (2011). Applications of transcranial magnetic stimulation (TMS) in child and adolescent psychiatry. *International Review of Psychiatry, 23*(5), 445–453. doi: 10.3109/09540261.2011.623688

Croarkin, P. E., Wall, C. A., McClintock, S. M., Kozel, F. A., Husain, M. M., & Sampson, S. M. (2010). The emerging role for repetitive transcranial magnetic stimulation in optimizing the treatment of adolescent depression. *Journal of ECT, 26*(4), 323–329. doi: 10.1097/YCT.0b013e3181dd17eb

D'Agati, D., Bloch, Y., Levkovitz, Y., & Reti, I. (2010). rTMS for adolescents: Safety and efficacy considerations. *Psychiatry Research, 177*(3), 280–285. doi: 10.1016/j.psychres.2010.03.004

Davey, C. G., Allen, N. B., Harrison, B. J., & Yucel, M. (2011). Increased amygdala response to positive social feedback in young people with major depressive disorder. *Biological Psychiatry, 69*(8), 734–741. doi: 10.1016/j.biopsych.2010.12.004

David-Ferdon, C., & Kaslow, N. J. (2008). Evidence-based psychosocial treatments for child and adolescent depression. *Journal of Clinical Child & Adolescent Psychology, 37*(1), 62–104.

Denny, E. B., & Hunt, R. R. (1992). Affective valence and memory in depression: Dissociation of recall and fragment completion. *Journal of Abnormal Psychology, 101*(3), 575–580. doi: 10.1037/0021-843X.101.3.575

De Raedt, R., & Koster, E. H. (2010). Understanding vulnerability for depression from a cognitive neuroscience perspective: A reappraisal of attentional factors and a new conceptual framework. *Cognitive, Affective & Behavioral Neuroscience, 10*(1), 50–70. doi: 10.3758/CABN.10.1.50

Derry, P. A., & Kuiper, N. A. (1981). Schematic processing and self-reference in clinical depression. *Journal of Abnormal Psychology, 90*(4), 286–297.

Deveney, C. M., & Deldin, P. J. (2006). A preliminary investigation of cognitive flexibility for emotional information in major depressive disorder and non-psychiatric controls. *Emotion, 6*(3), 429.

Dozois, D. J. A., & Dobson, K. S. (2001). Information processing and cognitive organization in unipolar depression: Specificity and comorbidity issues. *Journal of Abnormal Psychology, 110*(2), 236–246. doi: 10.1037/0021-843X.110.2.236

Eisenberg, N., & Spinrad, T. L. (2004). Emotion-related regulation: Sharpening the definition. *Child Development, 75*(2), 334–339.

Ekman, P., Friesen, W. V., & Ellsworth, P. (1972). *Emotion in the human face: Guidelines for research and an integration of findings.* New York: Pergamon Press.

Eldar, S., Apter, A., Lotan, D., Edgar, K. P., Naim, R., Fox, N. A., Pine, D. S., & Bar-Haim, Y. (2012). Attention bias modification treatment for pediatric anxiety disorders: a randomized controlled trial. *American Journal of Psychiatry, 169*(2), 213–220.

Emslie, G. J., Rush, A. J., Weinberg, W. A., Kowatch, R. A., Hughes, C. W., Carmody, T., & Rintelmann, J. (1997). A double-blind, randomized, placebo-controlled trial of fluoxetine in children and adolescents with depression. *Archives of General Psychiatry, 54*(11), 1031–1037.

Epstein, J., Pan, H., Kocsis, J. H., Yang, Y., Butler, T., Chusid, J., Hochberg, H., Murrough, J., Strohmayer, E., Stern, E., & Silbersweig, D. A. (2006). Lack of ventral striatal response to positive stimuli in depressed versus normal subjects. *American Journal of Psychiatry, 163*(10), 1784–1790. doi: 10.1176/appi.ajp.163.10.1784

Ernst, M., & Fudge, J. L. (2009). A developmental neurobiological model of motivated behavior: anatomy, connectivity and ontogeny of the triadic nodes. *Neurosci Biobehav Rev, 33*(3), 367–382. doi: 10.1016/j.neubiorev.2008.10.009

Favre, T., Hughes, C., Emslie, G., Stavinoha, P., Kennard, B., & Carmody, T. (2008). Executive functioning in children and adolescents with major depressive disorder. *Child Neuropsychology, 15*(1), 85–98.

Fitzgerald, D. A., Angstadt, M., Jelsone, L. M., Nathan, P. J., & Phan, K. L. (2006). Beyond threat: Amygdala reactivity across multiple expressions of facial affect. *Neuroimage, 30*(4), 1441–1448. doi: 10.1016/j.neuroimage.2005.11.003

Forbes, E. E., & Dahl, R. E. (2005). Neural systems of positive affect: Relevance to understanding child and adolescent depression? *Development and Psychopathology, 17*(03), 827–850.

Forbes, E. E., Shaw, D. S., & Dahl, R. E. (2007). Alterations in reward-related decision making in boys with recent and future depression. *Biological Psychiatry, 61*(5), 633–639. doi: 10.1016/j.biopsych.2006.05.026

Forbes, E. E., Hariri, A. R., Martin, S. L., Silk, J. S., Moyles, D. L., Fisher, P. M., Brown, S. M., Ryan, N. D., Birmaher, B., Axelson, D. A., & Dahl, R. E. (2009). Altered striatal activation predicting real-world positive affect in adolescent major depressive disorder. *American Journal of Psychiatry, 166*(1), 64–73. doi: 10.1176/appi.ajp.2008.07081336

Forbes, E. E., Olino, T. M., Ryan, N. D., Birmaher, B., Axelson, D., Moyles, D. L., & Dahl, R. E. (2010). Reward-related brain function as a predictor of treatment response in adolescents with major depressive disorder. *Cognitive, Affective, & Behavioral Neuroscience, 10*(1), 107–118.

Forbes, E. E., Christopher May, J., Siegle, G. J., Ladouceur, C. D., Ryan, N. D., Carter, C. S., Birmaher, B., Axelson, D. A., & Dahl, R. E. (2006). Reward-related decision-making in pediatric major depressive disorder: An fMRI study. *Journal of Child Psychology & Psychiatry, 47*(10), 1031–1040. doi: 10.1111/j.1469–7610.2006.01673.x

Frost, L. A., Moffitt, T. E., & McGee, R. (1989). Neuropsychological correlates of psychopathology in an unselected cohort of young adolescents. *Journal of Abnormal Psychology, 98*(3), 307.

Garber, J., & Hollon, S. D. (1980). Universal versus personal helplessness in depression: Belief in uncontrollability or incompetence? *Journal of Abnormal Psychology, 89*(1), 56–66. doi: 10.1037/0021–843X.89.1.56

Garber, J., Braafladt, N., & Weiss, B. (1995). Affect regulation in depressed and nondepressed children and young adolescents. *Development and Psychopathology, 7*(01), 93–115.

Garnefski, N., & Kraaij, V. (2006). Relationships between cognitive emotion regulation strategies and depressive symptoms: A comparative study of five specific samples. *Personality and Individual Differences, 40*(8), 1659–1669.

Garnefski, N., Rieffe, C., Jellesma, F., Terwogt, M. M., & Kraaij, V. (2007). Cognitive emotion regulation strategies and emotional problems in 9–11-year-old children. *European Child & Adolescent Psychiatry, 16*(1), 1–9.

Ghaziuddin, N., Laughrin, D., & Giordani, B. (2000). Cognitive side effects of electroconvulsive therapy in adolescents. *Journal of Child and Adolescent Psychopharmacology, 10*(4), 269–276.

Gibb, B. E., Benas, J. S., Grassia, M., & McGeary, J. (2009). Children's attentional biases and 5-HTTLPR genotype: Potential mechanisms linking mother and child depression. *Journal of Clinical Child & Adolescent Psychology, 38*(3), 415–426.

Gillham, J. E., Reivich, K. J., Jaycox, L. H., & Seligman, M. E. (1995). Prevention of depressive symptoms in schoolchildren: Two-year follow-up. *Psychological Science*, 343–351.

Gillham, J. E., Jaycox, L. H., Reivich, K. J., Seligman, M. E. P., & Silver, T. (1990). *The Penn Resiliency Program*. Philadelphia, PA: University of Pennsylvania..

Gladstone, T. R. G., & Kaslow, N. J. (1995). Depression and attributions in children and adolescents: A meta-analytic review. *Journal of Abnormal Child Psychology, 23*(5), 597.

Gogtay, N., Giedd, J. N., Lusk, L., Hayashi, K. M., Greenstein, D., Vaituzis, A. C., Nugent, T. F., Herman, D. H., Clasen, L. S., & Toga, A. W. (2004). Dynamic mapping of human cortical development during childhood through early adulthood. *Proceedings of the National Academy of Sciences of the United States Of America, 101*(21), 8174–8179.

Gonzalez, R., Nolen-Hoeksema, S., & Treynor, W. (2003). Rumination reconsidered: A psychometric analysis. *Cognitive Therapy & Research, 27*(3), 247–259.

Gotlib, I. H., & Hammen, C. L. (1993). Psychological aspects of depression. Toward a cognitive-interpersonal integration. *Clinical Psychology & Psychotherapy, 1*(1), 61–61. doi: 10.1002/cpp.5640010109

Gotlib, I. H., Hamilton, J. P., Cooney, R. E., Singh, M. K., Henry, M. L., & Joormann, J. (2010). Neural processing of reward and loss in girls at risk for major depression. *Archives of General Psychiatry, 67*(4), 380.

Greicius, M. D., Flores, B. H., Menon, V., Glover, G. H., Solvason, H. B., Kenna, H., Reiss, A. L., & Schatzberg, A. F. (2007). Resting-state functional connectivity in major depression: Abnormally increased contributions from subgenual cingulate cortex and thalamus. *Biological Psychiatry, 62*(5), 429–437. doi: 10.1016/j.biopsych.2006.09.020

Grimm, S., Ernst, J., Boesiger, P., Schuepbach, D., Boeker, H., & Northoff, G. (2011). Reduced negative BOLD responses in the default-mode network and increased self-focus in depression. *The World Journal of Biological Psychiatry, 12*(8), 627–637. doi: 10.3109/15622975.2010.545145

Gross, J. J. (1998). The emerging field of emotion regulation: An integrative review. *Review of General Psychology, 2*(3), 271.

Gross, J. J. (2013). Emotion regulation: Taking stock and moving forward. *Emotion*. doi: 10.1037/a0032135

Gualtieri, C., Johnson, L., & Benedict, K. (2006). Neurocognition in depression: Patients on and off medication versus healthy comparison subjects. *The Journal of Neuropsychiatry and Clinical Neurosciences, 18*(2), 217–225.

Gunther, T., Holtkamp, K., Jolles, J., Herpertz-Dahlmann, B., & Konrad, K. (2004). Verbal memory and aspects of attentional control in children and adolescents with anxiety disorders or depressive disorders. *Journal of Affective Disorders, 82*(2), 265–269. doi: 10.1016/j.jad.2003.11.004

Günther, T., Konrad, K., De Brito, S. A., Herpertz-Dahlmann, B., & Vloet, T. D. (2011). Attentional functions in children and adolescents with ADHD, depressive disorders, and the comorbid condition. *Journal of Child Psychology and Psychiatry, 52*(3), 324–331.

Guyer, A. E., Choate, V. R., Grimm, K. J., Pine, D. S., & Keenan, K. (2011). Emerging depression is associated with face memory deficits in adolescent girls. *Journal of the American Academy of Child & Adolescent Psychiatry, 50*(2), 180–190.

Gyurak, A., Gross, J. J., & Etkin, A. (2011). Explicit and implicit emotion regulation: A dual-process framework. *Cognition and Emotion, 25*(3), 400–412.

Haines, B. A., Metalsky, G. I., Cardamone, A. L., & Joiner, T. (1999). Interpersonal and cognitive pathways into the origins of attributional style: A developmental perspective. In T. E. Joiner & J. C. Coyne (eds) *The Interactional Nature of Depression* (pp. 65–92). Washington, DC: American Psychological Association.

Halari, R., Simic, M., Pariante, C. M., Papadoulos, A., Cleare, A., Brammer, M., Fombonne, E., & Rubia, K. (2009). Reduced activation in lateral prefrontal cortex and anterior cingulate during attention and cognitive control functions in medication-naïve adolescents with depression compared to controls. *Journal of Child Psychology and Psychiatry, 50*(3), 307–316.

Hale, I., & William, W. (1998). Judgment of facial expressions and depression persistence. *Psychiatry Research, 80*(3), 265–274. doi: http://dx.doi.org/10.1016/S0165–1781(98)00070–5

Hallion, L. S., & Ruscio, A. M. (2011). A meta-analysis of the effect of cognitive bias modification on anxiety and depression. *Psychological Bulletin, 137*(6), 940.

Hammen, C., & Zupan, B. A. (1984). Self-schemas, depression, and the processing of personal information in children. *Journal of Experimental Child Psychology, 37*, 598–608. doi: 10.1016/0022–0965(84)90079–1

Han, G., Klimes-Dougan, B., Jepsen, S., Ballard, K., Nelson, M., Houri, A., Kumra, S., & Cullen, K. (2012). Selective neurocognitive impairments in adolescents with major depressive disorder. *Journal of Adolescence, 35*(1), 11–20.

Hankin, B. L., & Abramson, L. Y. (2001). Development of gender differences in depression: An elaborated cognitive vulnerability–transactional stress theory. *Psychological Bulletin, 127*(6), 773.

Hankin, B. L., Gibb, B. E., Abela, J. R., & Flory, K. (2010). Selective attention to affective stimuli and clinical depression among youths: Role of anxiety and specificity of emotion. *Journal of Abnormal Psychology, 119*(3), 491.

Hasselbalch, B. J., Knorr, U., Hasselbalch, S. G., Gade, A., & Kessing, L. V. (2012). Cognitive deficits in the remitted state of unipolar depressive disorder. *Neuropsychology, 26*, 642–651.

Hilt, L. M., & Pollak, S. D. (2012). Getting out of rumination: Comparison of three brief interventions in a sample of youth. *Journal of Abnormal Child Psychology, 40*(7), 1157–1165. doi: 10.1007/s10802–012–9638–3

Horowitz, J. L., Garber, J., Ciesla, J. A., Young, J. F., & Mufson, L. (2007). Prevention of depressive symptoms in adolescents: A randomized trial of cognitive-behavioral and interpersonal prevention programs. *Journal of Consulting and Clinical Psychology, 75*(5), 693.

Hulvershorn, L. A., Cullen, K., & Anand, A. (2011). Toward dysfunctional connectivity: A review of neuroimaging findings in pediatric major depressive disorder. *Brain Imaging and Behavior, 5*(4), 307–328. doi: 10.1007/s11682–011–9134–3

Jaycox, L. H., Reivich, K. J., Gillham, J., & Seligman, M. E. P. (1994). Prevention of depressive symptoms in school children. *Behaviour Research and Therapy, 32*(8), 801–816.

Joormann, J. (2010). Cognitive inhibition and emotion regulation in depression. *Current Directions in Psychological Science, 19*(3), 161–166.

Joormann, J., Talbot, L., & Gotlib, I. H. (2007). Biased processing of emotional information in girls at risk for depression. *Journal of Abnormal Psychology, 116*(1), 135.

Joormann, J., Cooney, R. E., Henry, M. L., & Gotlib, I. H. (2012). Neural correlates of automatic mood regulation in girls at high risk for depression. *Journal of Abnormal Psychology, 121*(1), 61.

Keller, M. B., Ryan, N. D., Strober, M., Klein, R. G., Kutcher, S. P., Birmaher, B., Hagino, O. R., Koplewicz, H., Carlson, G. A., Clarke, G. N., Emslie, G. J., Feinberg, D., Geller, B., Kusumakar, V., Papatheodorou, G., Sack, W. H., Sweeney, M., Wagner, K. D., Weller, E. B., Winters, N. C., Oakes, R., & McCafferty, J. P. (2001). Efficacy of paroxetine in the treatment of adolescent major depression: A randomized, controlled trial. *Journal of the American Academy of Child and Adolescent Psychiatry, 40*(7), 762–772. doi: 10.1097/00004583-200107000-00010

Kessler, R. C., Avenevoli, S., & Ries Merikangas, K. (2001). Mood disorders in children and adolescents: An epidemiologic perspective. *Biological Psychiatry, 49*(12), 1002–1014.

Klimes-Dougan, B., Ronsaville, D., Wiggs, E. A., & Martinez, P. E. (2006). Neuropsychological functioning in adolescent children of mothers with a history of bipolar or major depressive disorders. *Biological Psychiatry, 60*(9), 957–965. doi: 10.1016/j.biopsych.2006.03.031

Klimkeit, E. I., Tonge, B., Bradshaw, J. L., Melvin, G. A., & Gould, K. (2011). Neuropsychological deficits in adolescent unipolar depression. *Archives of Clinical Neuropsychology, 26*(7), 662–676.

Korhonen, V., Laukkanen, E., Antikainen, R., Peiponen, S., Lehtonen, J., & Viinamäki, H. (2002). Effect of major depression on cognitive performance among treatment-seeking adolescents. *Nordic Journal of Psychiatry, 56*(3), 187–193.

Kujawa, A. J., Torpey, D., Kim, J., Hajcak, G., Rose, S., Gotlib, I. H., & Klein, D. N. (2011). Attentional biases for emotional faces in young children of mothers with chronic or recurrent depression. *Journal of Abnormal Child Psychology, 39*(1), 125–135.

Kuppens, P., Sheeber, L. B., Yap, M. B., Whittle, S., Simmons, J. G., & Allen, N. B. (2012). Emotional inertia prospectively predicts the onset of depressive disorder in adolescence. *Emotion-APA, 12*(2), 283.

Kyte, Z. A., Goodyer, I. M., & Sahakian, B. J. (2005). Selected executive skills in adolescents with recent first episode major depression. *Journal of Child Psychology and Psychiatry, 46*(9), 995–1005.

Ladouceur, C. D., Dahl, R. E., Williamson, D. E., Birmaher, B., Ryan, N. D., & Casey, B. J. (2005). Altered emotional processing in pediatric anxiety, depression, and comorbid anxiety-depression. *Journal of Abnormal Child Psychology, 33*(2), 165–177.

Ladouceur, C. D., Slifka, J. S., Dahl, R. E., Birmaher, B., Axelson, D. A., & Ryan, N. D. (2012). Altered error-related brain activity in youth with major depression. *Developmental Cognitive Neuroscience, 2*(3), 351–362.

Ladouceur, C. D., Dahl, R. E., Williamson, D. E., Birmaher, B., Axelson, D. A., Ryan, N. D., & Casey, B. J. (2006). Processing emotional facial expressions influences performance on a Go/NoGo task in pediatric anxiety and depression. *Journal of Child Psychology & Psychiatry, 47*(11), 1107–1115. doi: 10.1111/j.1469-7610.2006.01640.x

Lau, J. Y., Molyneaux, E., Telman, M. D., & Belli, S. (2011). The plasticity of adolescent cognitions: Data from a novel cognitive bias modification training task. *Child Psychiatry & Human Development, 42*(6), 679–693.

Lawrence, N. S., Williams, A. M., Surguladze, S., Giampietro, V., Brammer, M. J., Andrew, C., Frangou, S., Ecker, C., & Phillips, M. L. (2004). Subcortical and ventral prefrontal cortical neural responses to facial expressions distinguish patients with bipolar disorder and major depression. *Biological Psychiatry, 55*(6), 578–587. doi: 10.1016/j.biopsych.2003.11.017

Lee, R. S., Hermens, D. F., Porter, M. A., & Redoblado-Hodge, M. A. (2012). A meta-analysis of cognitive deficits in first-episode major depressive disorder. *Journal of Affective Disorders, 140*(2), 113–124.

Lenze, S. N., Pautsch, J., & Luby, J. (2011). Parent–child interaction therapy emotion development: A novel treatment for depression in preschool children. *Depression and Anxiety, 28*(2), 153–159. doi: 10.1002/da.20770

Lewinsohn, P. M., Clarke, G. N., Seeley, J. R., & Rohde, P. (1994). Major depression in community adolescents: Age at onset, episode duration, and time to recurrence. *Journal of the American Academy of Child and Adolescent Psychiatry, 33*(6), 809–818. doi: 10.1097/00004583–199407000–00006

Lothmann, C., Holmes, E. A., Chan, S. W., & Lau, J. Y. (2011). Cognitive bias modification training in adolescents: Effects on interpretation biases and mood. *Journal of Child Psychology and Psychiatry, 52*(1), 24–32.

Luby, J., Lenze, S., & Tillman, R. (2012). A novel early intervention for preschool depression: Findings from a pilot randomized controlled trial. *Journal of Child Psychology & Psychiatry, 53*(3), 313–322. doi: 10.1111/j.1469–7610.2011.02483.x

Maalouf, F. T., Brent, D., Clark, L., Tavitian, L., McHugh, R. M., Sahakian, B. J., & Phillips, M. L. (2011). Neurocognitive impairment in adolescent major depressive disorder: State vs. trait illness markers. *Journal of Affective Disorders, 133*(3), 625–632.

Mannie, Z. N., Harmer, C. J., Cowen, P. J., & Norbury, R. (2010). A functional magnetic resonance imaging study of verbal working memory in young people at increased familial risk of depression. *Biological Psychiatry, 67*(5), 471–477.

March, J., Silva, S., Petrycki, S., Curry, J., Wells, K., Fairbank, J., Burns, B., Domino, M., McNulty, S., Vitiello, B., & Severe, J. (2004). Fluoxetine, cognitive-behavioral therapy, and their combination for adolescents with depression: Treatment for Adolescents With Depression Study (TADS) randomized controlled trial. *JAMA, 292*(7), 807–820. doi: 10.1001/jama.292.7.807

Masten, C. L., Eisenberger, N. I., Borofsky, L. A., McNealy, K., Pfeifer, J. H., & Dapretto, M. (2011). Subgenual anterior cingulate responses to peer rejection: A marker of adolescents' risk for depression. *Development and Psychopathology, 23*(1), 283.

Matthews, K., Coghill, D., & Rhodes, S. (2008). Neuropsychological functioning in depressed adolescent girls. *Journal of Affective Disorders, 111*(1), 113–118.

Mayes, S. D., & Calhoun, S. L. (2007). Learning, attention, writing, and processing speed in typical children and children with ADHD, autism, anxiety, depression, and oppositional-defiant disorder. *Child Neuropsychology, 13*(6), 469–493.

McCabe, C., Woffindale, C., Harmer, C. J., & Cowen, P. J. (2012). Neural processing of reward and punishment in young people at increased familial risk of depression. *Biological Psychiatry, 72*, 588–594.

Mills, K. L., Lalonde, F., Clasen, L. S., Giedd, J. N., & Blakemore, S. J. (2012). Developmental changes in the structure of the social brain in late childhood and adolescence. *Social Cognitive & Affective Neuroscience*. doi: 10.1093/scan/nss113

Monk, C. S., Klein, R. G., Telzer, E. H., Schroth, E. A., Mannuzza, S., Moulton, J. L., Guardino, M., Masten, C. L., McClure-Tone, E. B., Fromm, S., Blair, R. J., Pine, D. S., & Ernst, M. (2008). Amygdala and nucleus accumbens activation to emotional facial expressions in children and adolescents at risk for major depression. *American Journal of Psychiatry, 165*(1), 90–98. doi: 10.1176/appi.ajp.2007.06111917

Morgan, J. K., Olino, T. M., McMakin, D. L., Ryan, N. D., & Forbes, E. E. (2013). Neural response to reward as a predictor of increases in depressive symptoms in adolescence. *Neurobiological Disorders, 52*, 66–74. doi: 10.1016/j.nbd.2012.03.039

Mufson, L., Moreau, D., Weissman, M. M., & Dorta, K. P. (2004). *Interpersonal Psychotherapy for Depressed Adolescents*, 2nd edn. New York: Guilford Press.

Mufson, L., Moreau, D., Weissman, M. M., Wickramaratne, P., Martin, J., & Samoilov, A. (1994). Modification of interpersonal psychotherapy with depressed adolescents (IPT-A): Phase I and II studies. *Journal of the American Academy of Child & Adolescent Psychiatry, 33*(5), 695–705.

Muris, P., Huijding, J., Mayer, B., & Hameetman, M. (2008). A space odyssey: Experimental manipulation of threat perception and anxiety-related interpretation bias in children. *Child Psychiatry and Human Development, 39*(4), 469–480.

Murphy, F., Michael, A., Sahakian, B., Austin, M., Ross, M., Murray, C., O'Carroll, R., Ebmeier, K., Goodwin, G., & Beats, B. (2012). Emotion modulates cognitive flexibility in patients with major depression. *Psychological Medicine, 42*(7), 1373.

Neshat-Doost, H. T., Moradi, A. R., Taghavi, M. R., Yule, W., & Dalgleish, T. (2000). Lack of attentional bias for emotional information in clinically depressed children and adolescents on the dot probe task. *Journal of Child Psychology and Psychiatry, 41*(3), 363–368.

Neshat-Doost, H. T., Taghavi, M. R., Moradi, A. R., Yule, W., & Dalgleish, T. (1997). The performance of clinically depressed children and adolescents on the modified Stroop paradigm. *Personality and Individual Differences, 23*(5), 753–759.

Neshat-Doost, H. T., Taghavi, M. R., Moradi, A. R., Yule, W., & Dalgleish, T. (1998). Memory for emotional trait adjectives in clinically depressed youth. *Journal of Abnormal Psychology, 107*(4), 642–650. doi: 10.1037/0021-843X.107.4.642

Newman, R. S. (2005). The cocktail party effect in infants revisited: Listening to one's name in noise. *Developmental Psychology, 41*(2), 352–362. doi: 10.1037/0012–1649.41.2.352 10.1037/0012.1649.41.2.352.supp (Supplemental)

Nolen-Hoeksema, S. (1991). Responses to depression and their effects on the duration of depressive episodes. *Journal of Abnormal Psychology, 100*(4), 569.

Nolen-Hoeksema, S., Morrow, J., & Fredrickson, B. L. (1993). Response styles and the duration of episodes of depressed mood. *Journal of Abnormal Psychology, 102*(1), 20.

Northoff, G., Heinzel, A., de Greck, M., Bermpohl, F., Dobrowolny, H., & Panksepp, J. (2006). Self-referential processing in our brain—a meta-analysis of imaging studies on the self. *Neuroimage, 31*(1), 440–457.

Peckham, A. D., McHugh, R. K., & Otto, M. W. (2010). A meta-analysis of the magnitude of biased attention in depression. *Depression and Anxiety, 27*(12), 1135–1142.

Perlman, G., Simmons, A. N., Wu, J., Hahn, K. S., Tapert, S. F., Max, J. E., Paulus, M. P., Brown, G. G., Frank, G. K., & Campbell-Sills, L. (2012). Amygdala response and functional connectivity during emotion regulation: A study of 14 depressed adolescents. *Journal of Affective Disorders, 139*, 75–84.

Phan, K. L., Wager, T., Taylor, S. F., & Liberzon, I. (2002). Functional neuroanatomy of emotion: A meta-analysis of emotion activation studies in PET and fMRI. *Neuroimage, 16*(2), 331–348. doi: 10.1006/nimg.2002.1087

Pine, D. S., Cohen, P., Gurley, D., Brook, J., & Ma, Y. (1998). The risk for early-adulthood anxiety and depressive disorders in adolescents with anxiety and depressive disorders. *Archives of General Psychiatry, 55*(1), 56–64.

Pine, D. S., Lissek, S., Klein, R. G., Mannuzza, S., Moulton, J. L., 3rd, Guardino, M., & Woldehawariat, G. (2004). Face-memory and emotion: Associations with major depression in children and adolescents. *Journal of Child Psychology & Psychiatry, 45*(7), 1199–1208. doi: 10.1111/j.1469–7610.2004.00311.x

Pons, F., Lawson, J., Harris, P. L., & De Rosnay, M. (2003). Individual differences in children's emotion understanding: Effects of age and language. *Scandinavian Journal of Psychology, 44*(4), 347–353. doi: 10.1111/1467–9450.00354

Porter, R. J., Gallagher, P., Thompson, J. M., & Young, A. H. (2003). Neurocognitive impairment in drug-free patients with major depressive disorder. *The British Journal of Psychiatry, 182*(3), 214–220.

Prinstein, M. J., Cheah, C. S. L., & Guyer, A. E. (2005). Peer victimization, cue interpretation, and internalizing symptoms: Preliminary concurrent and longitudinal findings for children and adolescents. *Journal of Clinical Child & Adolescent Psychology, 34*(1), 11–24. doi: 10.1207/s15374424jccp3401_2

Pyszczynski, T., Holt, K., & Greenberg, J. (1987). Depression, self-focused attention, and expectancies for positive and negative future life events for self and others. *Journal of Personality and Social Psychology, 52*(5), 994–1001. doi: 10.1037/0022–3514.52.5.994

Rao, U., Ryan, N. D., Birmaher, B., Dahl, R. E., Williamson, D. E., Kaufman, J., Rao, R., & Nelson, B. (1995). Unipolar depression in adolescents: Clinical outcome in adulthood. *Journal of the American Academy of Child and Adolescent Psychiatry, 34*(5), 566–578. doi: 10.1097/00004583–199505000–00009

Richards, J. M., Plate, R. C., & Ernst, M. (2013). A systematic review of fMRI reward paradigms in adolescents vs. adults: The impact of task design and implications for understanding neurodevelopment. *Neuroscience Biobehavioral Review*. doi: 10.1016/j.neubiorev.2013.03.004

Ritschel, L. A., Ramirez, C. L., Jones, M., & Craighead, W. E. (2011). Behavioral activation for depressed teens: A pilot study. *Cognitive and Behavioral Practice, 18*(2), 281–299.

Roberson-Nay, R., McClure, E. B., Monk, C. S., Nelson, E. E., Guyer, A. E., Fromm, S. J., Charney, D. S., Leibenluft, E., Blair, J., Ernst, M., & Pine, D. S. (2006). Increased amygdala activity during successful memory encoding in adolescent major depressive disorder: An FMRI study. *Biological Psychiatry, 60*(9), 966–973. doi: 10.1016/j.biopsych.2006.02.018

Rogers, T. B., Kuiper, N. A., & Kirker, W. S. (1977). Self-reference and the encoding of personal information. *Journal of Personality and Social Psychology, 35*(9), 677–688. doi: 10.1037/0022–3514.35.9.677

Rose, A. J. (2002). Co–rumination in the friendships of girls and boys. *Child Development, 73*(6), 1830–1843.

Salemink, E., & Wiers, R. W. (2011). Modifying threat-related interpretive bias in adolescents. *Journal of Abnormal Child Psychology, 39*(7), 967–976.

Sarapas, C., Shankman, S. A., Harrow, M., & Goldberg, J. F. (2012). Parsing trait and state effects of depression severity on neurocognition: Evidence from a 26-year longitudinal study. Journal of Abnormal Psychology, 121, 830–837.

Schlenker, B. R., & Britt, T. W. (1996). Depression and the explanation of events that happen to self, close others, and strangers. *Journal of Personality and Social Psychology, 71*(1), 180–192. doi: 10.1037/0022–3514.71.1.180

Schmitz, T. W., Kawahara-Baccus, T. N., & Johnson, S. C. (2004). Metacognitive evaluation, self-relevance, and the right prefrontal cortex. *Neuroimage, 22*(2), 941–947.

Segal, Z. V. (1988). Appraisal of the self-schema construct in cognitive models of depression. *Psychological Bulletin, 103*(2), 147–162. doi: 10.1037/0033–2909.103.2.147

Shad, M. U., Bidesi, A. P., Chen, L. A., Ernst, M., & Rao, U. (2011). Neurobiology of decision making in depressed adolescents: A functional magnetic resonance imaging study. *Journal of the American Academy of Child and Adolescent Psychiatry, 50*(6), 612–621. e612. doi: 10.1016/j.jaac.2011.03.011

Sheline, Y. I., Barch, D. M., Price, J. L., Rundle, M. M., Vaishnavi, S. N., Snyder, A. Z., Mintun, M. A., Wang, S., Coalson, R. S., & Raichle, M. E. (2009). The default mode network and self-referential processes in depression. *Proceedings of the National Academy of Sciences of the United States of America, 106*(6), 1942–1947. doi: 10.1073/pnas.0812686106

Silk, J. S., Dahl, R. E., Ryan, N. D., Forbes, E. E., Axelson, D. A., Birmaher, B., & Siegle, G. J. (2007). Pupillary reactivity to emotional information in child and adolescent depression: Links to clinical and ecological measures. *The American Journal of Psychiatry, 164*(12), 1873.

Stone, L. B., Hankin, B. L., Gibb, B. E., & Abela, J. R. (2011). Co-rumination predicts the onset of depressive disorders during adolescence. *Journal of Abnormal Psychology, 120*(3), 752.

Sweeney, P. D., Shaeffer, D., & Golin, S. (1982). Attributions about self and others in depression. *Personality and Social Psychology Bulletin, 8*(1), 37–42. doi: 10.1177/014616728281006

Symons, C. S., & Johnson, B. T. (1997). The self-reference effect in memory: A meta-analysis. *Psychological Bulletin, 121*(3), 371–394. doi: 10.1037/0033–2909.121.3.371

Taghavi, M. R., Neshat-Doost, H. T., Moradi, A. R., Yule, W., & Dalgleish, T. (1999). Biases in visual attention in children and adolescents with clinical anxiety and mixed anxiety-depression. *Journal of Abnormal Child Psychology, 27*(3), 215–223.

Tao, R., Calley, C. S., Hart, J., Mayes, T. L., Nakonezny, P. A., Lu, H., Kennard, B. D., Tamminga, C. A., & Emslie, G. J. (2012). Brain activity in adolescent major depressive disorder before and after fluoxetine treatment. *American Journal of Psychiatry, 169*(4), 381–388.

Taylor, S. F., Phan, K. L., Decker, L. R., & Liberzon, I. (2003). Subjective rating of emotionally salient stimuli modulates neural activity. *Neuroimage, 18*(3), 650–659.

Thomas, K. M., Drevets, W. C., Dahl, R. E., Ryan, N. D., Birmaher, B., Eccard, C. H., Axelson, D., Whalen, P. J., & Casey, B. (2001). Amygdala response to fearful faces in anxious and depressed children. *Archives of General Psychiatry, 58*(11), 1057.

Treatment for Adolescents with Depression Study. March, J., Silva, S., Curry, J., Wells, K., Fairbank, J., Burns, B., Domino, M., Vitiello, B., Severe, J., Riedal, K., Goldman, M., Feeny, N., Findling, R., Stull, S., Baab, S., Weller, E. B., Robbins, M., Weller,

R. A., Jessani, N., Waslick, B., Sweeney, M., Dublin, R., Walkup, J., Ginsburg, G., Kastelic, E., Koo, H., Kratochvil, C., May, D., LaGrone, R., Vaughan, B., Albano, A. M., Hirsch, G. S., Podniesinki, E., Chu, A., Reincecke, M., Leventhal, B., Rogers, G., Jacobs, R., Pathak, S., Wells, J., Lavanier, S. A., Danielyan, A., Rohde, P., Simons, A., Grimm, J., Frank, S., Emslie, G., Kennard, B., Hughes, C., Mayes, T. L., Rosenberg, D., Benazon, N., Butkus, M., & Bartoi, M. (2009). The Treatment for Adolescents with Depression Study (TADS): outcomes over 1 year of naturalistic follow-up. *American Journal of Psychiatry, 166*(10), 1141–1149. doi: 10.1176/appi. ajp.2009.08111620

Vassilopoulos, S. P., Banerjee, R., & Prantzalou, C. (2009). Experimental modification of interpretation bias in socially anxious children: Changes in interpretation, anticipated interpersonal anxiety, and social anxiety symptoms. *Behaviour Research and Therapy, 47*(12), 1085–1089.

Walter, G., & Rey, J. M. (2003). Has the practice and outcome of ECT in adolescents changed? Findings from a whole-population study. *Journal of ECT, 19*(2), 84–87.

Waters, A. M., Mogg, K., & Bradley, B. P. (2012). Direction of threat attention bias predicts treatment outcome in anxious children receiving cognitive-behavioural therapy. *Behavior Research & Therapy, 50*(6), 428–434. doi: 10.1016/j.brat.2012.03.006

Weersing, V. R., & Weisz, J. R. (2002). Mechanisms of action in youth psychotherapy. *Journal of Child Psychology and Psychiatry, 43*(1), 3–29.

Weissman, M. M., Wolk, S., Goldstein, R. B., Moreau, D., Adams, P., Greenwald, S., Klier, C. M., Ryan, N. D., Dahl, R. E., & Wickramaratne, P. (1999). Depressed adolescents grown up. *JAMA, 281*(18), 1707–1713.

Weisz, J. R., McCarty, C. A., & Valeri, S. M. (2006). Effects of psychotherapy for depression in children and adolescents: A meta-analysis. *Psychological Bulletin, 132*(1), 132–149. doi: 10.1037/0033–2909.132.1.132

Whittle, S., Yucel, M., Forbes, E. E., Davey, C. G., Harding, I. H., Sheeber, L., Yap, M. B., & Allen, N. B. (2012). Adolescents' depressive symptoms moderate neural responses to their mothers' positive behavior. *Social Cognitive & Affective Neuroscience, 7*(1), 23–34. doi: 10.1093/scan/nsr049

Wood, N., & Cowan, N. (1995). The cocktail party phenomenon revisited: How frequent are attention shifts to one's name in an irrelevant auditory channel? *Journal of Experimental Psychology: Learning, Memory, and Cognition, 21*(1), 255–260. doi: 10.1037/0278–7393.21.1.255

Yang, T. T., Simmons, A. N., Matthews, S. C., Tapert, S. F., Frank, G. K., Bischoff-Grethe, A., Lansing, A. E., Wu, J., Brown, G. G., & Paulus, M. P. (2009). Depressed adolescents demonstrate greater subgenual anterior cingulate activity. *Neuroreport, 20*(4), 440.

Yang, L. P., & Scott, L. J. (2010). Escitalopram: In the treatment of major depressive disorder in adolescent patients. *Paediatric Drugs, 12*(3), 155–163. doi: 10.2165/11204340–000000000–00000

Yang, T. T., Simmons, A. N., Matthews, S. C., Tapert, S. F., Frank, G. K., Max, J. E., Bischoff-Grethe, A., Lansing, A. E., Brown, G., Strigo, I. A., Wu, J., & Paulus, M. P. (2010). Adolescents with major depression demonstrate increased amygdala activation. *Journal of the American Academy of Child and Adolescent Psychiatry, 49*(1), 42–51.

Young, J., & Mufson, L. (2003). Manual for interpersonal psychotherapy-adolescent skills training (IPT-AST). Unpublished manual, Columbia University, New York.

Young, J. F., Mufson, L., & Davies, M. (2006). Efficacy of interpersonal psychotherapy-adolescent skills training: An indicated preventive intervention for depression. *Journal of Child Psychology and Psychiatry, 47*(12), 1254–1262.

Young, J. F., Mufson, L., & Gallop, R. (2010). Preventing depression: A randomized trial of interpersonal psychotherapy-adolescent skills training. *Depression and Anxiety, 27*(5), 426–433. doi: 10.1002/da.20664

Zupan, B. A., Hammen, C., & Jaenicke, C. (1987). The effects of current mood and prior depressive history on self-schematic processing in children. *Journal of Experimental Child Psychology, 43*, 149–158. doi: 10.1016/0022–0965(87)90056–7

9

A NEUROCOGNITIVE APPROACH TO MAJOR DEPRESSIVE DISORDER

Combining Biological and Cognitive Interventions

Rudi De Raedt

The Clinical Problem

Major depressive disorder (MDD) is worldwide a prevalent and recurrent problem for many, with detrimental effects on family, work or school life, and general health (Richards, 2011). MDD is characterized by debilitating symptoms such as depressed mood, loss of interest or pleasure, appetite and sleep disturbance, loss of energy, feelings of worthlessness, guilt, and suicidal thoughts (American Psychiatric Association [APA], 2013).

Lifetime prevalence of this disorder in the United States has been estimated at 22.9 percent in females and 15.1 percent in males (Kessler et al., 2009), which is consistent with recent studies in the European Union (Wittchen et al., 2011). Age-of-onset distributions show that depression is prevalent over the entire life span, with a median onset at thirty years (Kessler et al., 2005), although the twelve-month prevalence rate tends to be lower in the oldest age cohorts, from 10.4 percent in the eighteen to thirty-four age group to 2.6 percent in the "over sixty-five" age group (Kessler et al., 2009). Moreover, depression is among the most important contributors to disease burden worldwide, accounting for 4.4 percent of total disability adjusted life years (Üstün, Ayuso-Mateos, Chatterji, Mathers, & Murray, 2004).

Current Treatment Approaches

Depression has been conceptualized both as a disorder of the mind and as a disorder of the brain, which has led to the development of different treatment strategies such as various forms of psychotherapy and pharmacotherapy

(Kriston, von Wolff, & Holzel, 2010). Based on a meta-analysis, Cuijpers and colleagues (2013) concluded that evidence-based therapies such as cognitive behavior therapy (CBT) are effective and that psychotherapy combined with pharmacotherapy is more effective than pharmacotherapy alone (Hedges's g of the difference = 0.49). However, a substantial number of patients (up to 15 percent) remain depressed in spite of the correct use of pharmacological and psychotherapeutic approaches (Burrows, Norman, & Judd, 1994). Furthermore, although many interventions such as CBT have been proven to be effective in the short term, relapse and recurrence rates remain high (Beshai, Dobson, Bockting, & Quigley, 2011). Indeed, the addition of CBT to treatment as usual (TAU; standard care including pharmacotherapy or no treatment) reduces cumulative recurrence rates from 72 percent to 46 percent in patients with five or more previous episodes (Bockting, Spinhoven, Koeter, Wouters, & Schene, 2006), but these rates are still elevated. This suggests that current treatment options are not entirely successful in targeting specific underlying vulnerability factors.

Therefore, there has recently been a shift in interest from general categorical diagnoses to the assessment of specific underlying processes (Insel et al., 2010). In contrast to a descriptive approach in which individuals are diagnosed with depression based on a constellation of symptoms and their duration (APA, 2013), a new approach is to assess each patient based on impaired neurocognitive processes. These neurocognitive processes refer to cognitive functions that can be linked to specific brain areas and/or neurocircuits.

The Neuropsychology and Neurocircuitry of Depression and its Treatment

Neuropsychological studies of depressed patients indicate deficits across a broad range of cognitive functions, including attention, verbal learning and fluency, working memory, episodic memory, processing speed, and executive functions. These effects are found regardless of age, age of depression onset, comorbidity, medication status, or type of depressive disorder (Andersson et al., 2010; Beaujean, Parker, & Qiu, 2013; Douglas & Porter, 2009; Dybedal et al., 2013; Porter et al. 2003). Furthermore, scores on tests of specific cognitive abilities have been shown to reliably predict treatment response (Alexopoulos, et al., 2005; Dunkin et al., 2000). Indeed, cognitive functioning and depression show a bidirectional relationship that is corroborated by brain imaging data (Fossati, Ergis, & Allilaire, 2002; Mayberg et al., 1999).

In this neuropsychological perspective, MDD has been conceptualized as a disorder of deregulated prefrontal-subcortical neuronal circuits and that decreased dorsal (prefrontal) neuronal activity is unable to control overactive limbic structures (Ray and Zald, 2012; Mayberg et al., 2005). This may explain why depressed patients suffer from cognitive as well as emotional disturbances, affecting adaptive responses to environmental stress (Disner, Beevers, Haigh, & Beck, 2011).

Neuropsychological studies of depression indicated deficits in neural systems that have consistently been found to be associated with MDD include subcortical regions involved in emotion processing (e.g., amygdala) and reward processing (e.g., ventral striatum) and cortical regions involved in automatic or implicit emotion processing (e.g., medioprefrontal and anterior cingulate cortex, ACC) and in cognitive control such as the ventrolateral (VLPFC) and dorsolateral prefrontal cortex (DLPFC; Kupfer, Frank, & Phillips, 2012). Although it remains uncertain exactly how these findings can help improve clinical outcome, it has been acknowledged that taking into account the interaction between biological, cognitive, and environmental factors can potentially increase our understanding of this complex disorder and its treatment (Ingram & Siegle, 2009).

A meta-analysis of neuroimaging studies on MDD revealed evidence for the involvement of two distinct neurocircuits in depression and its treatment. One circuit includes the DLPFC and dorsal regions of the ACC among other regions implicated in cognitive control. This network is characterized by reduced activity during resting state and returns to normal with pharmacotherapy (selective serotonin reuptake inhibitors: SSRI). The other circuit comprises the medial prefrontal cortex (mPFC) and subcortical regions such as the amygdala, is hyperactive to emotional stimuli during depressive episodes, and also returns to normal after pharmacotherapy (Fitzgerald, Laird, Maller, & Daskalakis, 2008). Robust evidence has demonstrated that treatment-sensitive regions are primarily lateral frontal regions, with support for both an increase and a decrease in activation of neighboring regions of the DLPFC (Graham et al., 2013).

It is in these prefrontal regions that CBT, in which MDD patients are taught behavioral and cognitive strategies to reduce negative thoughts and attitudes and corresponding reactivity, leads to changes in brain activity. This therapy requires patients to record their biased negative thinking using thought records and test their interpretations and beliefs via behavioral experiments. In a study using fluorodeoxyglucose positron emission tomography ([18]FDG PET, a neuroimaging technique that measures the uptake of glucose indicative of tissue metabolism), medication-free MDD outpatients were scanned before and after fifteen to twenty sessions of CBT. Significant clinical improvement was associated with increases in the hippocampus and the dorsal ACC and decreases in the DLPFC, the vPFC, and the mPFC. However, with pharmacotherapy, these effects were reversed, with increases in prefrontal areas and decreases in the hippocampal and cingulate regions (Goldapple et al., 2004). Because differences and inconsistencies in directional changes remain (see Graham et al., 2013), it has been acknowledged that measuring the neural correlates of therapeutic effects during cognitive tasks may be crucial (Frewen, Dozois, & Lanius, 2008).

Given that the abovementioned regions are associated with cognitive control and emotion processing, it has been proposed that techniques that aim at more directly influencing neurocircuits involved in these processes may hold potential for an overall improvement of the effectiveness of interventions (De Raedt, 2006; De Raedt, Koster, & Joormann, 2010).

A Neurocognitive Approach to Depression

Within the search for such techniques, an important discovery has been that the stress system plays a major role in the development of vulnerability. During the lifetime, depressive episodes are triggered by progressively milder stressors (Monroe & Harkness, 2005), which underscores the role of the stress system in the development of recurrent depression. Vulnerability can be conceptualized as a trait-like latent endogenous process reactive to the effects of stress, related to genetic, biological, and psychological variables (Ingram & Siegle, 2009).

From this perspective, depressive episodes have been suggested to leave a "scar," defined in terms of dysfunctional processes. Based on the integration of cognitive and neurobiological research, De Raedt and Koster (2010) developed a conceptual framework in which attentional processes are of crucial importance in understanding this scar. In this framework, attentional control is considered to be a central process, linked to neurobiological (e.g., prefrontal and subcortical functioning), cognitive (e.g., negative self-schemas and rumination), and affective (e.g., emotion regulation) processes, which are associated with the development of (recurrent) episodes of depression. This framework could lead to a new avenue in the treatment of MDD, targeting underlying processes such as rumination and emotion regulation by using interventions that aim at directly influencing the neurocircuitry underlying these processes.

The basic tenet of this process-oriented framework (De Raedt & Koster, 2010) is that an important aspect of increasing vulnerability is the consistently observed decreased activity in prefrontal areas, mediated by the serotonin metabolism that is controlled by the hypothalamic pituitary adrenal (HPA) axis. This HPA axis, which stimulates the release of corticosteroids, becomes increasingly impaired after periods of hypercortisolism during depressive episodes (van Praag, De Kloet, & van Os, 2004), meaning that it becomes more reactive to stressors. Consequently, reduced prefrontal activation with the accumulation of depressive episodes would cause reduced cognitive control and impaired attenuation of limbic activity, resulting in prolonged activation of the amygdala in response to stressors in the environment. This decreased prefrontal control is expressed in difficulties in disengaging attention from negative information in the environment and dysfunctional inhibitory control over negative elaborative self-referent thought processes triggered by stressors, leading to rumination and sustained negative affect.

Attentional Control and Depression

In the abovementioned framework, attentional processes are considered to be the crucial link between cognitive and biological characteristics of depression. When people cannot disengage from negative information in the environment, this maintained focus on negativity will continue to fuel negative thinking. A large body of literature using a variety of experimental paradigms has demonstrated that dysphoria and depression are characterized by an attentional bias for negative information at later stages of information processing (for a review, see De Raedt & Koster, 2010). This bias mainly reflects difficulties in inhibiting negative information (Goeleven, De Raedt, Baert, & Koster, 2006; Joormann, 2004) or disengaging attention from negative content (Leyman, De Raedt, Schacht, & Koster, 2007). Although most studies have used visual cueing paradigms indicating difficulties in disengaging from external negative information, a number of studies have also found evidence for cognitive control problems toward internal representations of negative thought in MDD (De Lissnyder, Koster, Everaert, et al., 2012).

In the remainder of this chapter, for reasons of clarity, we use the generic terms *cognitive control* to refer to internal executive functions (e.g., shifting away from negative internal thoughts) and *attentional control* to refer to visuospatial external attentional functions (e.g., disengaging from negative environmental information).

Cognitive Control and Rumination

Factor analysis of tasks measuring facets of cognitive control revealed three operations that are moderately correlated but to some extent also separable: (1) monitoring and updating of working memory representations; (2) inhibition; and (3) mental set shifting (Miyake et al., 2000). The functions most frequently associated with depression are inhibition and set shifting. Cognitive inhibition refers to the ability to effectively inhibit the processing of previously relevant, or irrelevant, distracting information. The set-shifting function concerns the ability to shift between multiple tasks, operations, or mental sets (Monsell, 1996).

Deficient cognitive control may be causally related to emotional reactivity and depressive symptoms. In addition, emerging research has linked cognitive control to depression-relevant cognitive processes such as rumination (Koster, De Lissnyder, Derakshan, & De Raedt, 2011). Rumination has been defined as "behaviors and thoughts that focus one's attention on one's depressive symptoms and on the implications of those symptoms" (Nolen-Hoeksema, 1991, p. 569), as a trait-like response style to distress. This process is considered to be a *style* of thinking rather than specified with regard to the *content* of thought (Nolen-

Hoeksema, Wisco, & Lyubomirsky, 2008). Research has consistently shown that rumination is associated with increased negative mood (Moberly & Watkins, 2008). In addition, numerous studies have demonstrated that rumination is related to depressive symptoms and is predictive of future depressive episodes as well as their duration (Nolen-Hoeksema, 2000) and severity (Just & Alloy, 1997; Kuehner & Weber, 1999). This evidence indicates that the tendency to ruminate in response to distress is a cognitive vulnerability factor for depression, and thus a potential target for interventions.

In studies using different experimental paradigms, rumination has been specifically related to inhibition impairments for negative emotional information (e.g., Joormann, 2006). Some studies have also found a relationship between cognitive control and rumination for both non-emotional (De Lissnyder, Derakshan, De Raedt, & Koster, 2011) and emotional information (De Lissnyder, Koster, Derakshan, & De Raedt, 2010), without a direct link to general depressive symptoms. This indicates that these dysfunctional processes may be particularly associated with perseverative thoughts and are not an epiphenomenon of depressive mood.

There is also a close relationship between inhibition and working memory processes, which are involved in rumination (Zetsche, D'Avanzato, & Joormann, 2012) and emotion regulation (Joormann, 2010). A variant of the internal shift task (IST) was developed to measure updating and shifting between specific emotional versus non-emotional internal representations in working memory (Koster, De Lissnyder, & De Raedt, 2013). The results of studies using this paradigm indicate that rumination is related to internal shifting impairments when negative information is held in working memory and, again, not to depressive symptoms in general (De Lissnyder, Koster, & De Raedt, 2012). Moreover, it could be demonstrated that impaired shifting—specifically for emotional information—at baseline predicts depressive symptoms one year later, a relationship that is fully mediated by rumination (Demeyer, De Lissnyder, Koster, & De Raedt, 2012). In another prospective IST study, larger switch costs when processing emotional material measured at baseline moderated the association between stress and increased rumination during a stressful life event six weeks later (De Lissnyder, Koster, Goubert, et al., 2012).

Joormann, Levens, and Gotlib (2011) used another paradigm to assess the ability to manipulate emotional information in working memory. Compared with healthy controls, MDD patients showed decreased performance, particularly when presented with negative words. Additionally, rumination scores predicted these deficits in cognitive control for negative information (and not neutral and positive), further indicating that rumination is associated with deficits in cognitive control for negative content.

To summarize, many data point to the link between repetitive thinking patters such as rumination, on the one hand, and inhibition impairments for negative emotional information and impaired set shifting when negative information is held in working memory, on the other. The identification of these underlying cognitive control processes is important because perseverative thinking is possibly caused by specific disabled neurocognitive functions, which could be the target of interventions.

The Neurocircuitry Underlying Cognitive and Attentional Control

Dysfunctional neural systems in MDD include circuits related not only to rumination and emotion processing but also to emotion regulation. From this perspective, depression has been conceptualized as a failure to recruit prefrontal, top-down cognitive control in order to regulate emotion-producing limbic activity, such as in the amygdala (Phillips, Ladouceur, & Drevets, 2008). Furthermore, sustained amygdala activity has been associated with self-reported rumination (Siegle, Steinhauer, Thase, Stenger, & Carter, 2002).

Several neuroimaging studies have underscored the idea that a functional balance between ventral (ventral ACC) and dorsal regions of the brain (dorsal ACC, DLPFC) is necessary to maintain homeostatic control over emotional information (for an overview, see Ochsner & Gross, 2005). The amygdala is automatically activated when people are confronted with negative, emotionally arousing events (Zald, 2003) and is tightly connected to the ventral ACC. In particular the subgenual cingulate region, which has direct bidirectional connections to the amygdala, can be implicated in inhibitory control over the amygdala and has been consistently related to depression (Hamani et al., 2011). The ACC acts as a bridge between subcortical emotion processing and prefrontal cognitive control, hence integrating signals from the ventral parts of the ACC and the dorsal ACC (Bush, Luu, & Posner, 2000). The dorsal ACC, which is implicated in conflict processing, sends signals to the DLPFC to enhance attentional control (Hopfinger, Buonocore, & Mangun, 2000; MacDonald, Cohen, Stenger, & Carter, 2000). Prefrontal regions such as the DLPFC can thus send feedback signals to the subcortical system to suppress emotional processing via connections with other brain regions such as the orbitofrontal cortex (OFC; Taylor & Fragopanagos, 2005).

Recently, this circuitry has been confirmed based on path analysis, guided by known anatomical connectivity in primates and applied to a large, human functional magnetic resonance imaging (fMRI) data set acquired during the processing of angry or fearful faces. The findings indicate that the OFC is reciprocally connected with the amygdala and with lateral and dorsal regions of the PFC, thus supporting the hypothesis that the OFC mediates connections between higher-order dorsolateral prefrontal regions and subcortical limbic regions such as the amygdala during emotion regulation (Stein et al., 2007).

The results of many studies have suggested that the DLPFC initiates cognitive or attentional control over emotions by causing inhibition of the amygdala (Siegle, Thompson, Carter, Steinhauer, & Thase, 2007). These findings are in line with the abovementioned functionally interactive network of cortical-limbic pathways that play a central role in emotion regulation. As mentioned earlier, difficulties to shift away from negative information have been linked to the tendency to ruminate, and the DLPFC has been revealed to be an important brain area implicated in the neurocircuitry of specific depression-related processes such as rumination. In a recent fMRI study in healthy, non-depressed individuals, brain activity was measured during the processing of emotional stimuli. Participants with high rumination scores showed higher DLPFC involvement when successfully disengaging from negative stimuli, which suggests that healthy individuals who tend to ruminate in daily life need to recruit more attentional control in order to successfully disengage from negative information (Vanderhasselt, Kuhn, & De Raedt, 2011). Given that the DLPFC has also been associated with emotion-regulation strategies, these findings may be indicative for enhanced emotion regulation.

The Neurocircuitry Underlying Emotion Regulation

Reappraisal is a well-studied emotion-regulation strategy and can be defined as a means of changing the way of thinking about an emotional situation in order to reduce its emotional impact (Gross, 1998). It can be considered as the opposite of rumination, the latter being defined as a focus of attention on one's depressive symptoms and on the implications of these symptoms (Nolen-Hoeksema, 1991). Rumination focuses on the upsetting situation and its consequences, whereas reappraisal reinterprets the meaning of an upsetting event (Ray, Wilhelm, & Gross, 2008). High reappraisers are behaviorally faster and exert more DLPFC and dACC activity when inhibiting a response to negative information (compared to inhibiting a positive response; Vanderhasselt, De Raedt, et al., 2013). This clearly suggests the involvement of cognitive control in reappraisal. Other studies have underscored the role of the OFC in reappraisal (Kanske, Heissler, Schonfelder, Bongers, & Wessa, 2011; Wager, Davidson, Hughes, Lindquist, & Ochsner, 2008). Ochsner and Gross (2005) proposed a hypothetical continuum regarding sub-processes involved in cognitive control over emotions. At one end of the continuum is the exclusive use of attentional or cognitive control, including engagement and disengagement to emotional stimuli, and at the other end is the exclusive use of cognitive change, including appraisal and reappraisal processes. In a recent study, indications have been found that both the DLPFC and the lateral OFC contribute to emotion regulation through reappraisal (Golkar et al., 2012). DLPFC activity was found to be related to reappraisal independently of whether negative or neutral stimuli were reappraised by the participants, whereas the lateral OFC was linked only to reappraisal of negative material. These results provide evidence for contributions of specific parts of the circuitry to mood repair through specific emotion-regulation strategies and suggest that prefrontal dysfunction makes it harder to reappraise. Consistent with the model discussed earlier, these data provide a further indication that the inability to exert DLPFC-related effortful control over depressive cognition leads to rumination.

In brief, cognitive and attentional control are considered to be the crucial link between cognitive and biological characteristics of depression, mediating the occurrence of maladaptive responses to stress. Neurocircuits that are dysfunctional in major depressive disorder include those related to inhibition, disengagement, rumination, and emotion regulation. This suggests that strengthening DLPFC-related cognitive control processes increases the ability to use emotion regulation.

Attentional and Cognitive Training

The process-oriented approach to depression and encouraging results in the domain of anxiety have stimulated researchers to investigate whether it would be possible to influence attentional control processes that have been associated with depression. MacLeod and colleagues (2002) developed an attentional bias modification (ABM) procedure to influence engagement or disengagement from emotional stimuli. In this procedure, specific contingencies between the location of a threat or non-threat cue and the location of a following target are imposed during a spatial cueing task. In anxiety disorders, although not all studies have yielded consistent results, training anxious individuals to attend away from threat to non-threat cues has been found to reduce attentional bias, which, in turn, reduces anxiety (for a meta-analysis, see Beard, Sawyer, & Hofmann, 2012). In addition, in a study by Browning and colleagues (2010), it could be demonstrated that attention bias retraining (ABM) altered DLPFC activation to emotional stimuli, which supports the hypothesis that this intervention influences attention via an effect on the prefrontal cortex.

Studies in non-clinically dysphoric individuals have reported promising results. In the first published study using ABM, mildly-to-moderately depressed undergraduates were randomly assigned to four sessions of either attention training or no training during a two-week period. Participants in the training condition showed a significantly larger decrease in depressive symptoms from baseline to follow-up as compared to the participants in the control condition. The group difference was mediated by the change in attentional bias, suggesting that the change of attention was the causal factor in the decrease of depressive symptoms (Wells & Beevers, 2010). In another study using only one session, ABM training had no effect on attentional bias or on mood states (Kruijt, Putman, & Van der Does, 2013).

To further investigate the effects of multiple sessions on dysphoric individuals and MDD patients, Baert, De Raedt, Schacht, and Koster (2010) used an intensive, Internet-delivered ABM procedure. In two experiments, the effects of ten daily sessions of ABM on attentional bias, mood, and depressive symptoms were analyzed. In both experiments, attention bias was not differentially changed compared to a control procedure. In the first experiment, the effect of ABM was investigated in a sample of dysphoric undergraduates with mild-to-severe levels of depressive symptoms. Despite the absence of differential changes in attentional bias as compared to the control procedure, there were improvements on symptom severity in students showing mild depressive symptoms in the active ABM condition. However, depressive symptoms increased after the training in students showing moderate-to-severe depressive symptoms. In the second experiment, the same ABM procedure was used for MDD patients; however, no beneficial effects were found beyond those of psychotherapy or pharmacotherapy. These results suggest that the therapeutic effects of ABM depend on depression severity and that depressed patients may, therefore, not benefit from attentional training procedures. Moreover, a comprehensive review by Hallion and Ruscio (2011) indicated that there is currently no evidence of positive effects of ABM training in MDD patients.

However, ABM has been demonstrated to be effective in recovered MDD patients (Browning, Holmes, Charles, Cowen, & Harmer, 2012). Remitted euthymic, previously depressed patients with at least two previous episodes were randomly assigned to receive either an active (positive) or a placebo (neutral) ABM training with faces or words, spread over two weeks. The positive, face-based ABM procedure reduced two measures of recurrence risk (Beck Depression Inventory and cortisol awakening response) during the month after completion of bias modification. The fact that this training has beneficial effects in formerly euthymic depressed patients suggests that ABM offers a useful strategy in the secondary prevention of the illness. Intriguingly, mindfulness-based cognitive therapy, which can be considered as a generic attentional and cognitive control training with favorable effects on relapse when applied in recovered depressed patients (Chiesa & Serretti, 2010), also influences emotion-specific inhibitory processes (De Raedt et al., 2012). However, the question remains whether there is a neurocognitive strategy that can be used *during* the depressive episode.

None of these training procedures was specifically developed to target the neurocircuits underlying depression-related symptoms such as rumination. All abovementioned studies used a similar ABM procedure based on training visuospatial attentional disengagement and engagement toward emotional faces. Although Browning and colleagues (2010) observed that the effect of these face-based ABM retraining procedures is related to changes in the DLPFC and another group showed that stimulation of the DLPFC influences emotion-specific spatial cueing (using face stimuli; De Raedt, Leyman, et al., 2010), other training procedures may induce even more DLPFC activation. Siegle and colleagues (2014) adopted an approach using a more generic DLPFC-related executive-function training procedure. These researchers started from the abovementioned observations: Disruptions of executive control, associated with a decreased DLPFC function, are related to ruminative processes as observed in depression (Israel, Seibert, Black, & Brewer, 2010); conventional therapies have been hypothesized to act by increasing emotion regulation; and beneficial therapeutic effects have been associated with an increased prefrontal activity during cognitive tasks (DeRubeis, Siegle, & Hollon, 2008). They suggested that neurocognitive interventions should specifically target prefrontal function, using tasks that activate the prefrontal cortex. To this end, they developed a cognitive control training (CCT) procedure to correct limbic dysregulation by repeatedly exposing depressed individuals to different tasks that require prefrontal activity. These tasks include a computer-based version of attention-training exercises that have been associated with decreased rumination (Papageorgiou & Wells, 2000), and an adaptive version of the Paced Auditory Serial Attention Task (PASAT; Gronwall, 1977) which has been shown to activate the DLPFC (Lazeron, Rombouts, de Sonneville, Barkhof, & Scheltens, 2003) and which is deficient in depression (Landro, Stiles, & Sletvold, 2001).

In a pilot study, Siegle and colleagues demonstrated that this six-session intervention was associated with increased reductions in symptoms and rumination as well as increases in behavioral performance and normalization of brain reactivity, above and beyond treatment as usual (TAU; pharmacotherapy and psychotherapy; Siegle, Ghinassi, & Thase, 2007). Recently, the sample has been extended to investigate changes in depressive symptoms and rumination as well as long-term symptom improvement. Compared to TAU, the group receiving the cognitive exercises in addition to medication and psychotherapy showed decreases in rumination, early reduction in depressive symptomatology and a decreased use of intensive outpatient services during the following year. Moreover, these responses were moderated by cognitive engagement during the first exercise day, as measured by pupillary responses as an index of task-related resource allocation (Siegle et al., 2014). The usefulness of pupillary responses to index task-related resource allocation has been underscored in a study where pupil and fMRI assessment were combined (Siegle, Steinhauer, Friedman, Thompson, & Thase, 2011). Compared to healthy controls, MDD patients were found to display decreased pupillary responses following the frequency of task stimuli, and increased pupillary variation diverging from the task frequency. This could reflect a lack of task-related resource allocation in combination with non–task-related processing such as rumination (Jones, Siegle, Muelly, Haggerty, & Ghinassi, 2010). Furthermore, pupil motility varied with DLPFC activity on the cognitive task. Given that rumination has been linked to DLPFC activity (Vanderhasselt et al., 2011) and that abnormalities in DLPFC activity related to cognitive control over emotional information have been consistently observed in depression (De Raedt & Koster, 2010), the finding that patients who are not able to exert cognitive engagement benefit less from cognitive training may be attributable to deficiencies in activation of the DLPFC. These deficiencies may also be the reason why ABM seems to work in dysphoric (Wells & Beevers, 2010), mildly depressed individuals (Baert et al., 2010), and depressed patients in remission (Browning et al., 2012) but not in currently depressed individuals (Baert et al., 2010). Note that all abovementioned studies used procedures that have been linked to changes in the DLPFC.

In short, Siegle et al. (2014) employed a generic non-emotional DLPFC-related attentional paradigm in MDD patients and showed that the positive outcome was related to a DLPFC-related measure (pupillary motion), whereas other studies have used emotion-specific visuospatial attentional training tasks that have also been associated with DLPFC activity. Cognitive or attentional control training procedures may be useful in the treatment of depression, but deficient DLPFC functioning in currently depressed patients may limit the generalizability of the effects. Therefore, neurostimulation techniques aimed at directly influencing DLPFC activity possibly provide a valuable alternative.

Neurostimulation in Major Depressive Disorder

Transcranial magnetic stimulation (TMS) is a non-invasive neurostimulation technique performed by placing an electromagnetic coil of wire above the scalp. A high-intensity current is rapidly turned on and off in this coil, which produces a time-varying magnetic field. This magnetic field passes through the skin, muscle, and skull to the surface of the brain, where it encounters neurons and induces weak electric currents to flow. If stimulation is provided above a certain threshold, these neurons will be induced to fire. Repetitive TMS (rTMS) has been shown to alter cortical excitability. High-frequency (HF) stimulation produces an increase in local cortical excitability after stimulation (not during), whereas low-frequency (LF) stimulation (0.1–1.0 Hz) has the opposite effect (Fitzgerald, Fountain, & Daskalakis, 2006). This technique has been tested as a treatment tool for various psychiatric disorders. Treatment protocols for depression typically include five to twenty-five sessions of HF-rTMS (10–20 Hz) to the left DLPFC, but several studies have applied LF-rTMS to the right DLPFC with similar results. A meta-analysis of thirty-four studies comparing rTMS to sham treatment (left- and right-sided) for the acute treatment of depression showed a moderate effect size (Slotema, Blom, Hoek, & Sommer, 2010). The largest effect size was obtained by HF-rTMS to the left DLPFC, and most studies in this meta-analysis used ten sessions of HF-rTMS (10–20 Hz). These figures are comparable to effect sizes of pharmacological and CBT interventions for depression, which are commonly around .50 (Roshanaei-Moghaddam et al., 2011).

However, it remains unknown whether full remission can be achieved using HF-rTMS. This hypothesis was tested in a large-scale ($N = 190$), prospective, multi-site, randomized, active sham-controlled, duration-adaptive, intention-to-treat study with three weeks of daily weekday treatment (left DLPFC, 10 Hz) followed by continued blinded treatment for up to another three weeks in improvers (who did not achieve full remission but a 30 percent reduction on the HAM-D score; George et al., 2010). The primary efficacy analysis revealed statistically significant effects of treatment on the proportion of remitters, which were a modest 14.1 percent in the active HF-rTMS and 5.1 percent in the sham condition. In addition, most remitters had had low antidepressant treatment resistance in the past, which is to some extent problematic because rTMS is often used as an alternative strategy in treatment-resistant depression. In an open-label follow-up phase in non-improvers, 30 percent of the patients remitted (nearly half of them were originally in the sham condition). The researchers concluded that, although the treatment produced a statistically significant effect on remission, the overall number of remitters and responders was lower than one would like with a treatment that requires a daily intervention for three weeks or more. The long-term durability of the effect is also limited.

In a retrospective, naturalistic study with 204 patients by Cohen and colleagues (2009), a group of patients who remitted after HF-rTMS treatment were then followed up for up to six months. Remission was 75.3 percent at two months, 60.0 percent at three months, 42.7 percent at four months, and 22.6 percent at six months. Mantovani et al. (2012) reported on the three-month follow-up effects of the antidepressant response in the abovementioned trial (George, Taylor, and Short, 2013). Of the fifty patients who eventually remitted and agreed to participate in this follow-up, twenty-nine were classified as in remission at three months, but of these twenty-nine, eleven remitters (37.9 percent) were also receiving pharmacotherapy.

In brief, although HF-rTMS produces beneficial effects on depression, these effects are modest. Moreover, there is a problem with long-term durability, and treatment resistance appears to be a contraindication. Neurostimulation seems capable of temporarily decreasing depressive symptoms but fails to produce long-lasting effects. A better understanding of the underlying mechanisms of HF-rTMS at the biological and cognitive level is needed to increase its effectiveness as an antidepressant treatment. A crucial question is whether HF-rTMS acts through its influence on the neurocircuitry underlying cognitive control and emotion regulation.

The influence of HF-rTMS on top-down cognitive control has been investigated using basic interference paradigms, such as regular Stroop tasks (Vanderhasselt, De Raedt, Baeken, Leyman, & D'Haenen, 2006a), modified versions with high versus low expectancy conditions to manipulate the degree of conflict (Vanderhasselt et al., 2007) and intentional switching paradigms (Vanderhasselt, De Raedt, Baeken, Leyman, & D'Haenen, 2006b). These studies demonstrated that HF-rTMS of the left DLPFC is capable of influencing cognitive control in healthy populations. Furthermore, one session of HF-rTMS was revealed to have a temporary, positive effect on cognitive control in MDD patients (Vanderhasselt, De Raedt, Baeken, Leyman, & D'Haenen, 2009), and this acute effect was predictive for antidepressant outcome after ten sessions (Vanderhasselt, De Raedt, Leyman, & Baeken, 2009).

Other studies have also explored whether these effects are emotion specific. Using a negative affective priming paradigm (NAP) with negative versus positive and neutral faces to measure inhibitory control toward emotional information in healthy individuals, these studies showed that HF-rTMS to the DLPFC increases inhibitory control for sad and not for happy faces (Leyman, De Raedt, Vanderhasselt, & Baeken, 2009). In another HF-rTMS study, activity within the right and left DLPFC of healthy participants was experimentally manipulated, and changes in the attentional processing of emotional information were measured using an emotional modification of a spatial cueing task during event-related fMRI (De Raedt, Leyman et al., 2010). Right-sided prefrontal HF-rTMS was first applied in order to experimentally mimic the asymmetry observed in depressed patients. This right-sided prefrontal stimulation resulted in an impaired disengagement from angry faces, associated with a decreased activation in the right DLPFC, the dorsal anterior cingulate cortex (dACC) and the left superior parietal gyrus, combined with an increased activity in the right amygdala during disengagement efforts. Left prefrontal HF-rTMS caused diminished attentional engagement for angry faces and was associated with an increased activity in the right DLPFC, the dACC, the right superior parietal gyrus, and the left orbitofrontal cortex during engagement, all regions that are implicated in the neurocircuitry involved in emotion regulation. In treatment-resistant depressed (TRD) patients who were tapered off their medication, successful clinical outcome after ten sessions of HF-rTMS to the left DLPFC was related to an increased inhibition for sad faces (NAP paradigm; Leyman, De Raedt, Vanderhasselt, & Baeken, 2011). These results show that HF-rTMS is capable of influencing emotion-specific control processes that are linked to depression.

The primary action mechanisms of antidepressant drugs have been hypothesized to remediate attentional biases for negative information, providing a more positive social environment in which the patient can relearn emotional associations, thus leading to a later improvement in mood (Pringle, Browning, Cowen, & Harmer, 2011). These authors provide evidence from behavioral and fMRI studies to support this hypothesis. The fact that HF-rTMS also seems capable of temporarily influencing these attentional processes suggests that

HF-rTMS acts in a similar manner as pharmacotherapy and, indeed, George and colleagues (2013) suggested that TMS acts as a "focal pharmacotherapy."

The link between neurostimulation and traditional pharmacological interventions (e.g., SSRIs) commonly used in the treatment of depression is illustrated by a recent study that used radioligands to investigate the influence of HF-rTMS on modulation of the serotonin system (Baeken et al., 2011). The impact of ten daily HF-rTMS sessions applied to the left DLPFC on postsynaptic serotonin (5-HT 2A) receptor-binding indices was measured with single-photon emission computed tomography ((1)(2)(3)I-5-I-R91150 SPECT) in antidepressant-free, treatment-resistant TRD patients. Compared with controls, these patients displayed significantly less bilateral DLPFC and a significantly higher left hippocampal baseline serotonin (5-HT 2A) receptor binding. Successful HF-rTMS treatment was related to increased 5-HT(2A) receptor binding in the DLPFC bilaterally and decreased right hippocampal 5-HT2A receptor uptake values. In another study, successful HF-rTMS treatment in TRD patients was found to relate to metabolic changes (glucose metabolism measured with [18]FDG-PET) in dorsal subdivisions of the ACC after treatment (Baeken et al., 2009). The fact that this biological effect after treatment is also observed in remote brain areas is indicative of the importance of connectivity. It has also been reported that limbic-cortical connections (DLPFC-subgenual cingulate-OFC) differentiated drug treatment responders from non-responders (Seminowicz et al., 2004).

Several studies have shown that the influence of rTMS is observed not only in the area under the stimulation coil but in synaptically connected ipsi- and contralateral areas (Paus, Castro-Alamancos, & Petrides, 2001; Paus & Barrett, 2004). In a recent study in TRD patients, the effects of rTMS on functional connectivity were assessed using functional connectivity (fc) fMRI. At baseline, HF-rTMS responders showed a stronger fc anti-correlation between the subgenual (sg) ACC and parts of the prefrontal cortex compared to non-responders, similar to what has been observed with other treatment modalities. This finding suggests that fc measurement could be used as a diagnostic tool to select a subgroup of patients who would benefit from this therapeutic approach. Moreover, clinical response to HF-rTMS of the left DLPFC was related to a stronger fc between sgACC and areas in the prefrontal cortex (Baeken, Marinazzo, et al., 2014). The subgenual anterior cingulate cortex, which is part of distributed corticolimbic neurocircuits implicated in modulating affect such as sadness activation and ruminative thought patterns (Disner, Beevers, Haigh, & Beck, 2011; Smith et al., 2011), has consistently been shown to be hyperactive during depressive episodes (Drevets, Savitz, & Trimble, 2008; Mayberg et al., 2005).

Fox and colleagues (2012) proposed that TMS shows promise as a method to manipulate brain connectivity. They discussed clinical applications using resting-state fcMRI to guide target selection for TMS and using TMS to modulate pathological network interactions identified with resting-state fcMRI. Furthermore, they argued that the combination of TMS and resting-state fcMRI might be translated into clinical applications as a new approach to diagnosis and treatment of psychiatric diseases.

In short, there are indications that HF-rTMS influences attentional and cognitive control processes and neurocircuits related to emotion regulation and rumination. Nevertheless, there are also other techniques that can be used to alter brain activity.

For example, transcranial direct current stimulation (tDCS) is a neurostimulation technique that can be easily combined with cognitive training. It is an easy-to-use, safe, low-cost procedure, with reliable sham (placebo) methodology. It differs from TMS in that it can manipulate the membrane potential of neurons but is not capable of activating the neuron itself (Paulus, 2011). Because of this distinction, tDCS is often referred to as neuromodulation and rTMS as a neurostimulation technique. However, for reasons of clarity, we refer to both techniques as *neurostimulation*. tDCS uses a constant low current (1–2 mA) delivered directly to the brain area of interest via electrodes positioned on the scalp (on saline-soaked patches of 25/35 cm^2), inducing intracerebral current flow. The device has an anodal electrode (the positively charged electrode) and a cathodal electrode (the negatively charged electrode). One electrode (the anode) is placed over the region of interest, and the other electrode, the reference electrode (cathode), is placed in another location to create a circuit. In many studies, the anode is placed over the DLPFC, and the cathode over the contralateral DLPFC or supraorbital region. The current flows from the anode through the skull and brain to the cathode. Anodal tDCS enhances excitability, whereas cathodal tDCS reduces it (Nitsche & Paulus, 2000; Nitsche et al., 2005). tDCS, usually applied for five to twenty minutes, causes changes in cortical excitability that can persist up to ninety minutes after stimulation has ceased (Nitsche & Paulus, 2001).

tDCS has been proposed as a possible treatment for major depression, and some clinical trials have yielded encouraging results. However, based on several meta-analyses, its clinical utility remains unclear when response and remission rates are considered (Brunoni, Ferrucci, Fregni, Boggio, & Priori, 2012; Kalu, Sexton, Loo, & Ebmeier, 2012). New clinical studies with larger and more representative samples and optimized protocols are needed to further evaluate the efficacy of tDCS in the treatment of depression. However, tDCS can produce substantial effects on cognition (for a review, see Kuo & Nitsche, 2012). Several studies have demonstrated that tDCS can cause similar effects on behavioral and physiological aspects of emotion processing as compared to rTMS. Additionally, Brunoni et al. (2013) investigated the effects of tDCS on salivary cortisol and heart rate variability as proxies of the HPA and the sympathetic adrenal medullary system (SAM) in healthy individuals. Participants were shown negative or neutral pictures. Left anodal tDCS induced a decrease in stress hormone (cortisol) levels, an effect that was more pronounced during the processing of negative stimuli. Moreover, heart rate variability was higher (indicating an adaptive reaction to stress) during left anodal tDCS and emotional, negative stimuli, as compared to sham stimulation and neutral images. In HF-rTMS studies, a similar decreased stress response to a stressor has been observed, as measured by cortisol reactivity (Baeken, Vanderhasselt, et al., 2014). These findings indicate that both tDCS and TMS induce transient top-down effects, leading to a down-regulation of HPA and SAM systems, which highlights the potential of neurostimulation for increasing stress resilience.

Other studies have found cognitive effects on the processing of emotional information similar to the abovementioned effects of HF-rTMS. For instance, a sham-controlled, within-subjects study in healthy participants, using behavioral measures and event-related potentials as indexes, examined the effects of one session of anodal tDCS of the left DLPFC on cognitive control for positive or negative valenced stimuli. In line with the valence theory of side-lateralized activity, neurostimulation of the left prefrontal cortex resulted in an augmented cognitive control, specifically for positive relative to negative stimuli (Vanderhasselt, De Raedt, et al., 2013).

Stimulation of the DLPFC by tDCS also influences functional connectivity. Pena-Gomez and coworkers (2012) analyzed the influence of tDCS during rest on the default-mode network (DMN), combining tDCS with fMRI. The DMN is consistently deactivated during task performance and is linked with a variety of functions related to cognitive reactivity, rumination, and attentional control (Marchetti, Koster, Sonuga-Barke, & De Raedt, 2012). The results of this analysis revealed a reconfiguration of intrinsic brain activity networks after active tDCS, in line with improvements in cognitive functions that have been observed after anodal tDCS. In addition, increasing cortical excitability in areas related to attentional and cognitive control may have facilitated the reconfiguration of functional brain networks in order to address cognitive task demands. These data indicate that tDCS may have similar effects on cognitive and emotional control and on related neurocircuits than HF-rTMS.

Combining Neurostimulation and Training

HF-rTMS and tDCS alter brain activity and fc in areas related to the neurocircuits underlying cognitive and attentional control and emotion processing, and consequently, just as pharmacotherapy, can influence cognitive and attentional control. However, until now, neither pharmacotherapy nor HF-rTMS or tDCS alone seems to be able to produce long-lasting benefits in MDD patients. Possibly, the patient has to acquire new learning during or after biological interventions, which suggests that a combination of neurostimulation and cognitive or attentional control training holds potential as a new neurocognitive intervention. Training may be necessary to yield long-term benefits from enhancing DLPFC activity in emotion-regulation circuits. Given that the effects of both HF-rTMS and tDCS last between thirty and ninety minutes after stimulation, control training could be implemented after stimulation of the DLPFC. The positive effects of HF-rTMS only start after stimulation (during stimulation, HF-rTMS disrupts brain functioning), which supports why the training should start after TMS. However, tDCS does not induce neuronal firing by suprathreshold neuronal membrane depolarization but modulates spontaneous neuronal activity in a network (Nitsche et al., 2008), which makes it suitable to enhance the effects of task-related brain processing. Because cognitive and attentional control training has been associated with DLPFC activity, tDCS of the DLPFC may be particularly useful to apply during training for enhancement of its effects. Therefore, if we know that a specific cognitive task is related to activity in the DLPFC, modulating the excitability of this region may boost performance during this task, hence increasing learning benefits. Ultimately, this may lead to increases of cognitive or attentional control, which may facilitate emotion regulation.

The abovementioned CCT (Siegle et al., 2014) was recently co-administered with tDCS of the left DLPFC during five consecutive daily sessions (Segrave, Arnold, Hoy, & Fitzgerald, 2014). Twenty-seven adult participants with MDD were randomized into a three-arm, sham-controlled, between-groups pilot study that compared the efficacy of tDCS combined with CCT, sham tDCS combined with CCT, and sham CCT. Reduction in depression severity at the end of treatment was observed in all three treatment conditions. However, only the tDCS + CCT condition resulted in a sustained antidepressant response at follow-up, the magnitude of which was greater than that observed immediately after the treatment procedure. This preliminary result provides a "proof of principle" for the use of concurrent CCT and tDCS.

In another study with a larger sample ($N = 37$) and more sessions (ten), CCT and tDCS of the left prefrontal cortex versus sham were also combined with CCT (Brunoni et al., 2014). CCT ameliorated depressive symptoms after the acute treatment period and at follow-up, without a difference between tDCS and sham. However, older patients and those who performed better in the task throughout the trial (which may be indicative of greater engagement and activation of the DLPFC) showed more depression improvement in the combined treatment group. In order to test the hypothesis that increasing left DLPFC activity using cognitive training and tDCS (versus sham) reduces rumination, depressive rumination (brooding) was measured after the ten sessions (Vanderhasselt et al., in press). The more patients improved on CCT performance over the ten days of CCT, the greater the reduction in rumination after versus before treatment. However, neurostimulation of the left prefrontal cortex versus sham did not influence this relation between CCT and rumination. These findings suggest not only that prefrontal cognitive control is indeed a key mechanism underlying the occurrence of ruminative thoughts but that more research is needed to corroborate the potential of combining tDCS with CCT in order to reduce depressogenic thought processes such as rumination.

Effects of Increased Cognitive and Attentional Control on Depressive Symptoms

Although the importance of maladaptive information processing is acknowledged in the cognitive theory of depression, the adjustment of schema content is the main target of CBT. Nonetheless, Beck (1967) has consistently emphasized that encouraging behavioral activation in CBT is essential to foster new real-world experiences in order to facilitate the development of more adaptive schema content. There is robust evidence for the importance of the behavioral component of CBT, which even outperforms the effect of the cognitive component (Dimidjian et al., 2006). However, as already mentioned, the relapse rate after CBT remains high. When stressors are perceived in the environment by those vulnerable to depression, dysfunctional schemas and self-reflective negative thoughts become activated, leading to sustained negative affect and new depressive episodes.

In order to provoke long-term change, it may be crucial to create new experiences by influencing the way in which patients perceive their environment and to expose them to schema-incompatible information, thus disengaging from negative environmental information. Because behavioral activation alone is probably insufficient to achieve this, we suggest that ABM may influence this essential attentional focus. As already mentioned, in anxiety, ABM has been demonstrated to be able to change biased attention toward threatening information (for a meta-analysis, see Beard et al., 2012). In keeping with the difference between attentional and cognitive control, we have distinguished two different control processes that can be trained: (1) attentional control training using visuospatial cueing tasks to train attention away from negative toward positive information and to influence the way individuals perceive their environment, which would eventually lead to new corrective experiences; and (2) cognitive control training to increase the ability to shift away from negative internal presentations in working memory and to decrease rumination and facilitate reappraisal (De Raedt, Vanderhasselt, & Baeken, in press). These enhanced emotion-regulation abilities might ultimately foster the development of more adaptive schemas of the self and the environment, decreased self-reflective rumination and increased resilience for future depressive episodes. These procedures can be applied in a repetitive schedule in order to facilitate new adaptive habit learning. We suggest that

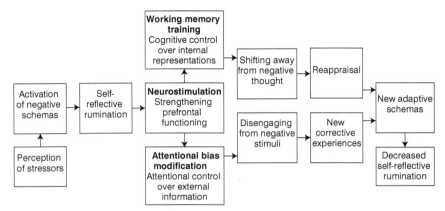

FIGURE 9.1 The working mechanisms of cognitive and attentional control training combined with neurostimulation.

these training procedures could be combined with neurostimulation in order to enhance the effects (Figure 9.1).

In a placebo-controlled, within-subjects study, anodal tDCS was applied to the left DLPFC (cathode over the right supraorbital region) in healthy participants during performance of the abovementioned IST (cognitive control task in which participants shift and update emotional information in working memory) as a proof to test the usefulness of the combination of tDCS and a cognitive control task. During an unguided rest period, approximately twenty minutes after neurostimulation, the occurrence of momentary self-referent ruminative thought was assessed. The influence of tDCS (but not placebo) on ruminative thought was mediated by an increased shifting ability away from negative to neutral information (Vanderhasselt, Brunoni, Loeys, Boggio, & De Raedt, 2013). Although the paradigm was not a training task, these findings suggest that enhancing cognitive control by training the ability to update and shift away from negative representations in working memory combined with tDCS may help patients to manage and regulate unintentional streams of rumination.

With regard to attentional control for external information, Clarke and colleagues (in press) provided evidence that increasing activity in the left DLPFC increases the effects of ABM in healthy participants. During an ABM procedure to induce an AB either toward or away from a threat (words), participants received either anodal or a sham (no stimulation) tDCS. Participants receiving anodal tDCS showed more evidence of AB change in the targeted direction (toward or away from threat) as compared to those receiving sham stimulation.

It can be hypothesized that modulating neurocircuits and increasing cognitive control automatically leads to increased abilities to inhibit preservative thought processes and that increasing attentional control possibly results in exposure to more positive information in depressed patients, fostering the development of more adaptive schemas. However, there is also evidence for differences in neurobiological pathways for subtypes of depression (Sharpley & Bitsika, 2013). For example, subtypes mainly characterized by somatic symptoms such as psychomotor retardation, fatigue, and sleep disturbances may be less responsive to this kind of treatment. A particular diagnostic procedure based on deficient processes and neurocircuits may be used to tailor specific interventions to the cognitive, behavioral, and biological characteristics of patients.

Avenues for Future Research and Practice

Although the neurocognitive approach is very promising as a framework for diagnosis and treatment, further research is necessary to confirm the circumstances under which it may be most useful. There are five major avenues for further research: (1) analyzing the effects of general executive training programs on the neurocircuits associated with emotion regulation and specific aspects of attentional and cognitive control over internal and external emotional information; (2) creating more potent emotion-specific training procedures, targeting both internal and external information; (3) investigating whether the effect of one type of training may influence attentional and cognitive control, which is plausible given that both processes are linked to the DLPFC and related neurocircuits; (4) further studying the potential of new protocols for tDCS (e.g., high-definition tDCS) or TMS (e.g., theta burst stimulation) to increase the effects on cognition and stress resilience; and (5) exploring the potential of combining the different abovementioned cognitive and attentional control training strategies with TMS and tDCS. In addition, it would be useful to establish the necessary number of training sessions and predictors of successful outcome for each intervention. Given that there is some evidence that CBT also causes changes in prefrontal subcortical circuitries (Goldapple et al., 2004), combining CBT with neurostimulation may be a potential avenue for future research as well.

Directly assessing dysfunctional neurocircuits may also be valuable, although this is admittedly challenging in clinical practice settings. It seems more feasible to focus on dysfunctional information processing as measured with behavioral tasks, but an important obstacle is the low reliability of current cognitive and attentional control measurements (Schmukle, 2005). When treatment strategies are being tailored to individual characteristics such as a decreased cognitive control over negative perseverative thoughts or an attentional bias for negative information, it is crucial to be able to assess these processes in a reliable way, which should also be an important focus for future research.

Conclusion

Although current treatment options for depression are effective in the short term, relapse rates are high, which suggests that they are inadequate in identifying and diminishing underlying vulnerability factors. Given that evidence points toward the involvement of a hypoactive network centerd on the dorsal PFC and a hyperactive network centerd on the mPFC and the amygdala in vulnerability for depression (neurocircuits related to attentional control, cognitive control, and emotion regulation), research efforts should be focused on the further development of strategies to influence these dysfunctional networks. The neurocognitive approach is promising, but more systematic research is required to firmly establish guidelines for clinical practice.

References

Alexopoulos, G. S., Kiosses, D. N., Heo, M., Murphy, C. F., Shanmugham, B., & Gunning-Dixon, F. (2005). Executive dysfunction and the course of geriatric depression. *Biological Psychiatry, 58*(3), 204–210.

American Psychiatric Association (APA) (2013). *Diagnostic and statistical manual of mental disorders* (5th edn). Washington, DC: American Psychiatric Association.

Andersson, S., Lovdahl, H., & Malt, U. F. (2010). Neuropsychological function in unmedicated recurrent brief depression. *Journal of Affective Disorders, 125*, 155–164.

Baeken, C., De Raedt, R., Van Hove, C., Clerinx, P., De Mey, J., & Bossuyt, A. (2009). HF-rT MS treatment in medication-resistant melancholic depression: Results from 18FDG-PET brain imaging. *CNS Spectrums, 14*, 439–448.

Baeken, C., De Raedt, R., Bossuyt, A., Van Hove, C., Mertens, J., Dobbeleir, A., … & Goethals, I. (2011). The impact of HF-rTMS treatment on serotonin(2A) receptors in unipolar melancholic depression. *Brain Stimulation, 4*(2), 104–111.

Baeken, C., Marinazzo, D., Wu, G. R., Van Schuerbeek, P., De Mey, J., Marchetti, I., … & De Raedt, R. (2014). Accelerated HF-rTMS in treatment-resistant unipolar depression: Insights from subgenual anterior cingulate functional connectivity. *World Journal of Biological Psychiatry, 15*(2), 286–297.

Baeken, C., Vanderhasselt, M. A., Remue, J., Rossi, V., Schiettecatte, J., Anckaert E., & De Raedt, R. (2014). A single session of left dorsolateral prefrontal cortical HF-rTMS attenuates HPA-system sensitivity to induced stress in healthy females. *Neuropsychologia, 57*, 112–121.

Baert, S., De Raedt, R., Schacht, R., & Koster, E. H. W. (2010). Attentional bias training in depression: Therapeutic effects depend on depression severity. *Journal of Behavior Therapy and Experimental Psychiatry, 41*(3), 265–274.

Beard, C., Sawyer, A. T., & Hofmann, S. G. (2012). Efficacy of attention bias modification using threat and appetitive stimuli: A meta-analytic review. *Behavior Therapy, 43*(4), 724–740.

Beaujean, A. A., Parker, S., & Qiu, X. (2013). The relationship between cognitive ability and depression: A longitudinal data analysis. *Social Psychiatry and Psychiatric Epidemiology, 48*, 1983–1992.

Beck, A.T. (1967). *Depression: Clinical, experimental, and theoretical aspects*. New York: Hoeber.

Beshai, S., Dobson, K. S., Bockting, C. L. H., & Quigley, L. (2011). Relapse and recurrence prevention in depression: Current research and future prospects. *Clinical Psychology Review, 31*(8), 1349–1360.

Bockting, C. L. H., Spinhoven, P., Koeter, M. W. J., Wouters, L. F., & Schene, A. H. (2006). Prediction of recurrence in recurrent depression and the influence of consecutive episodes on vulnerability for depression: A 2-year prospective study. *Journal of Clinical Psychiatry, 67*(5), 747–755.

Browning, M., Holmes, E. A., Charles, M., Cowen, P. J., & Harmer, C. J. (2012). Using attentional bias modification as a cognitive vaccine against depression. *Biological Psychiatry, 72*(7), 572–579.

Browning, M., Holmes, E. A., Murphy, S. E., Goodwin, G. M., & Harmer, C. J. (2010). Lateral prefrontal cortex mediates the cognitive modification of attentional bias. *Biological Psychiatry, 67*(10), 919–925.

Brunoni, A. R., Ferrucci, R., Fregni, F., Boggio, P. S., & Priori, A. (2012). Transcranial direct current stimulation for the treatment of major depressive disorder: A summary of preclinical, clinical and translational findings. *Progress in Neuro-Psychopharmacology & Biological Psychiatry, 39*(1), 9–16.

Brunoni, A. R., Boggio, P. S., De Raedt, R., Benseñor, I. M., Lotufo, P. A., Namur, V., … & Vanderhasselt, M. A. (2014). Cognitive control therapy and transcranial direct current stimulation for depression: A randomized, double-blinded, controlled trial. *Journal of Affective Disorders, 162,* 43–49.

Brunoni, A. R., Vanderhasselt, M. A., Boggio, P. S., Fregni, F., Dantas, E. M., Mill, J. G., … & Bensenor, I. M. (2013). Polarity- and valence-dependent effects of prefrontal transcranial direct current stimulation on heart rate variability and salivary cortisol. *Psychoneuroendocrinology, 38*(1), 58–66.

Burrows, G. D., Norman, T. R., & Judd, F. K. (1994). Definition and differential diagnosis of treatment resistant depression. *International Clinical Psychopharmacology, 9,* 5–10.

Bush, G., Luu, P., & Posner, M. I. (2000). Cognitive and emotional influences in anterior cingulate cortex. *Trends in Cognitive Sciences, 4*(6), 215–222.

Chiesa, A., & Serretti, A. (2010). A systematic review of neurobiological and clinical features of mindfulness meditations. *Psychological Medicine, 40*(8), 1239–1252.

Clarke, P. J. F., Browning, M., Hammond, G., Notebaert, L., & MacLeod, C. (in press). The causal role of the dorsolateral prefrontal cortex in the modification of attentional bias: Evidence from transcranial direct current stimulation. *Biological Psychiatry, 76,* 946–952.

Cohen, R. B., Boggio, P. S., & Fregni, F. (2009). Risk factors for relapse after remission with repetitive transcranial magnetic stimulation for the treatment of depression. *Depression and Anxiety, 26*(7), 682–688.

Cuijpers, P., Berking, M., Andersson, G., Quigley, L., Kleiboer, A., & Dobson, K. S. (2013). A meta-analysis of cognitive-behavioural therapy for adult depression, alone and in comparison with other treatments. *Canadian Journal of Psychiatry – Revue Canadienne de Psychiatrie, 58*(7), 376–385.

De Lissnyder, E., Koster, E. H. W., & De Raedt, R. (2012). Emotional interference in working memory is related to rumination. *Cognitive Therapy and Research, 36*(4), 348–357.

De Lissnyder, E., Derakshan, N., De Raedt, R., & Koster, E. H. W. (2011). Depressive symptoms and cognitive control in a mixed antisaccade task: Specific effects of depressive rumination. *Cognition & Emotion, 25*(5), 886–897.

De Lissnyder, E., Koster, E. H. W., Derakshan, N., & De Raedt, R. (2010). The association between depressive symptoms and executive control impairments in response to emotional and non-emotional information. *Cognition & Emotion, 24*(2), 264–280.

De Lissnyder, E., Koster, E. H. W., Everaert, J., Schacht, R., Van den Abbeele, D., & De Raedt, R. (2012). Internal cognitive control in clinical depression: General but no emotion-specific impairments. *Psychiatry Research, 199*(2), 124–130.

De Lissnyder, E., Koster, E. H. W., Goubert, L., Onraedt, T., Vanderhasselt, M. A., & De Raedt, R. (2012). Cognitive control moderates the association between stress and rumination. *Journal of Behavior Therapy and Experimental Psychiatry, 43*(1), 519–525.

Demeyer, I., De Lissnyder, E., Koster, E. H. W., & De Raedt, R. (2012). Rumination mediates the relationship between impaired cognitive control for emotional information and depressive symptoms: A prospective study in remitted depressed adults. *Behaviour Research and Therapy, 50*(5), 292–297.

De Raedt, R. (2006). Does neuroscience hold promise for the further development of behavior therapy? The case of emotional change after exposure in anxiety and depression. *Scandinavian Journal of Psychology, 47*(3), 225–236.

De Raedt, R., & Koster, E. H. W. (2010). Understanding vulnerability for depression from a cognitive neuroscience perspective: A reappraisal of attentional factors and a new conceptual framework. *Cognitive Affective & Behavioral Neuroscience, 10*(1), 50–70.

De Raedt, R., Koster, E. H. W., & Joormann, J. (2010). Attentional control in depression: A translational affective neuroscience approach. *Cognitive, Affective, and Behavioral Neuroscience, 10*(01), 1–7.

De Raedt, R., Vanderhasselt, M. A., & Baeken, C. (in press). Neurostimulation as an intervention for treatment resistant depression: From research on mechanisms towards targeted neurocognitive strategies. *Clinical Psychology Review.*

De Raedt, R., Baert, S., Demeyer, I., Goeleven, E., Raes, A., Visser, A., ... & Speckens, A. (2012). Changes in attentional processing of emotional information following mindfulness-based cognitive therapy in people with a history of depression: Towards an open attention for all emotional experiences. *Cognitive Therapy and Research, 36*, 612–620.

De Raedt, R., Leyman, L., Baeken, C., Van Schuerbeek, P., Luypaert, R., Vanderhasselt, M. A., & Dannlowski, U. (2010). Neurocognitive effects of HF-rTMS over the dorsolateral prefrontal cortex on the attentional processing of emotional information in healthy women: An event-related fMRI study. *Biological Psychology, 85*(3), 487–495.

DeRubeis, R. J., Siegle, G. J., & Hollon, S. D. (2008). Opinion—Cognitive therapy versus medication for depression: Treatment outcomes and neural mechanisms. *Nature Reviews Neuroscience, 9*(10), 788–796.

Dimidjian, S., Hollon, S. D., Dobson, K. S., Schmaling, K. B., Kohlenberg, R. J., Addis, M. E., ... & Jacobson, N. S. (2006). Randomized trial of behavioral activation, cognitive therapy, and antidepressant medication in the acute treatment of adults with major depression. *Journal of Consulting and Clinical Psychology, 74*(4), 658–670.

Disner, S. G., Beevers, C. G., Haigh, E. A. P., & Beck, A. T. (2011). Neural mechanisms of the cognitive model of depression. *Nature Reviews Neuroscience, 12*(8), 467–477.

Douglas, K. M., & Porter, R. J. (2009). Longitudinal assessment of neurpsychological funciton in major depression. *Australian and New Zealand Journal of Psychiatry, 43*, 1105–1117.

Drevets, W. C., Savitz, J., & Trimble, M. (2008). The subgenual anterior cingulate cortex in mood disorders. *CNS Spectrums, 13*(8), 663–681.

Dunkin, J., Leuchter, A. F., Cook, I. A., Kasl-Godley, J. E., Abrams, M., & Rosenberg-Thompson, S. (2000). Executive dysfunction predicts nonresponse to fluoxetine in major depression. *Journal of Affective Disorders, 60,* 13–23.

Dybedal, G. S., Tanum, L., Sundet, K., Gaarden, T. L., & Bjolseth, T. M. (2013). Neuropsychological functioning in late life depression. *Frontiers in Psychology, 4,* 381.

Fitzgerald, P. B., Fountain, S., & Daskalakis, Z. J. (2006). A comprehensive review of the effects of rTMS on motor cortical excitability and inhibition. *Clinical Neurophysiology, 117,* 2584–2596.

Fitzgerald, P. B., Laird, A. R., Maller, J., & Daskalakis, Z. J. (2008). A meta-analytic study of changes in brain activation in depression. *Human Brain Mapping, 29,* 683–695.

Fossati, P., Ergis, A. M., & Allilaire, J. F. (2002). Executive functioning in unipolar depression: A review. *Encephale, 28,* 97–107.

Fox, M. D., Halko, M. A., Eldaief, M. C., & Pascual-Leone, A. (2012). Measuring and manipulating brain connectivity with resting state functional connectivity magnetic resonance imaging (fcMRI) and transcranial magnetic stimulation (TMS). *Neuroimage, 62*(4), 2232–2243.

Frewen, P. A., Dozois, D. J. A., & Lanius, R. A. (2008). Neuroimaging studies of psychological interventions for mood and anxiety disorders: Empirical and methodological review. *Clinical Psychology Review, 28*(2), 228–246.

George, M. S., Taylor, J. J., & Short, E. B. (2013). The expanding evidence base for rTMS treatment of depression. *Current Opinion in Psychiatry, 26*(1), 13–18.

George, M. S., Lisanby, S. H., Avery, D., McDonald, W. M., Durkalski, V., Pavlicova, M., ... & Sackeim, H. A. (2010). Daily left prefrontal transcranial magnetic stimulation therapy for major depressive disorder: A sham-controlled randomized trial. *Archives of General Psychiatry, 67*(5), 507–516.

Goeleven, E., De Raedt, R., Baert, S., & Koster, E. H. W. (2006). Deficient inhibition of emotional information in depression. *Journal of Affective Disorders, 93*(1–3), 149–157.

Goldapple, K., Segal, Z., Garson, C., Lau, M., Bieling, P., Kennedy, S., & Mayberg, H. (2004). Modulation of cortical-limbic pathways in major depression – Treatment-specific effects of cognitive behavior therapy. *Archives of General Psychiatry, 61*(1), 34–41.

Golkar, A., Lonsdorf, T. B., Olsson, A., Lindstrom, K. M., Berrebi, J., Fransson, P., ... & Ohman, A. (2012). Distinct contributions of the dorsolateral prefrontal and orbitofrontal cortex during emotion regulation. *Plos One, 7*(11), e48107.

Graham, J., Salimi-Khorshidi, G., Hagan, C., Walsh, N., Goodyer, I., Lennox, B., & Suckling, J. (2013). Meta-analytic evidence for neuroimaging models of depression: State or trait? *Journal of Affective Disorders, 151*(2), 423–431.

Gronwall, D. M. A. (1977). Paced auditory serial-addition task: A measure of recovery from concussion. *Perceptual and Motor Skills, 44*(2), 367–373.

Gross, J. J. (1998). Antecedent- and response-focused emotion regulation: Divergent consequences for experience, expression, and physiology. *Journal of Personality and Social Psychology, 74*(1), 224–237.

Hallion, L. S., & Ruscio, A. M. (2011). A meta-analysis of the effect of cognitive bias modification on anxiety and depression. *Psychological Bulletin, 137*(6), 940–958.

Hamani, C., Mayberg, H., Stone, S., Laxton, A., Haber, S., & Lozano, A. M. (2011). The subcallosal cingulate gyrus in the context of major depression. *Biological Psychiatry, 69*(4), 301–308.

Hopfinger, J. B., Buonocore, M. H., & Mangun, G. R. (2000). The neural mechanisms of top-down attentional control. *Nature Neuroscience, 3*(3), 284–291.

Ingram, R. E., & Siegle, G. J. (2009). Methodological issues in the study of depression. In I. H. Gotlib & C. L. Hammen (Eds.), *Handbook of depression* 2nd edn (pp. 69–92). New York: Guilford.

Insel, T., Cuthbert, B., Garvey, M., Heinssen, R., Pine, D. S., Quinn, K., … & Wang, P. (2010). Research Domain Criteria (RDoC): Toward a new classification framework for research on mental disorders. *American Journal of Psychiatry, 167*(7), 748–751.

Israel, S. L., Seibert, T. M., Black, M. L., & Brewer, J. B. (2010). Going their separate ways: Dissociation of hippocampal and dorsolateral prefrontal activation during episodic retrieval and post-retrieval processing. *Journal of Cognitive Neuroscience, 22*(3), 513–525.

Jones, N. P., Siegle, G. J., Muelly, E. R., Haggerty, A., & Ghinassi, F. (2010). Poor performance on cognitive tasks in depression: Doing too much or not enough? *Cognitive Affective & Behavioral Neuroscience, 10*(1), 129–140.

Joormann, J. (2004). Attentional bias in dysphoria: The role of inhibitory processes. *Cognition & Emotion, 18*(1), 125–147.

Joormann, J. (2006). Differential effects of rumination and dysphoria on the inhibition of irrelevant emotional material: Evidence from a negative priming task. *Cognitive Therapy and Research, 30*(2), 149–160.

Joormann, J. (2010). Cognitive inhibition and emotion regulation in depression. *Current Directions in Psychological Science, 19*(3), 161–166.

Joormann, J., Levens, S. M., & Gotlib, I. H. (2011). Sticky thoughts: Depression and rumination are associated with difficulties manipulating emotional material in working memory. *Psychological Science, 22*(8), 979–983.

Just, N., & Alloy, L. B. (1997). The response styles theory of depression: Tests and an extension of the theory. *Journal of Abnormal Psychology, 106*(2), 221–229.

Kalu, U. G., Sexton, C. E., Loo, C. K., & Ebmeier, K. P. (2012). Transcranial direct current stimulation in the treatment of major depression: A meta-analysis. *Psychological Medicine, 42*(9), 1791–1800.

Kanske, P., Heissler, J., Schonfelder, S., Bongers, A., & Wessa, M. (2011). How to regulate emotion? Neural networks for reappraisal and distraction. *Cerebral Cortex, 21*(6), 1379–1388.

Kessler, R. C., Birnbaum, H., Bromet, E., Hwang, I., Sampson, N., & Shahly, V. (2009). Age differences in major depression: Results from the National Comorbidity Survey Replication (NCS-R). *Psychological Medicine, 40*(2), 225–237.

Kessler, R. C., Berglund, P., Demler, O., Jin, R., Merikangas, K. R., & Walters, E. E. (2005). Lifetime prevalence and age-of-onset distributions of DSM-IV disorders in the National Comorbidity Survey Replication. *Archives of General Psychiatry, 62*(6), 593–602.

Koster, E. H. W., De Lissnyder, E., & De Raedt, R. (2013). Rumination is characterized by valence-specific impairments in switching of attention. *Acta Psychologica, 144*(3), 563–570.

Koster, E. H. W., De Lissnyder, E., Derakshan, N., & De Raedt, R. (2011). Understanding depressive rumination from a cognitive science perspective: The impaired disengagement hypothesis. *Clinical Psychology Review, 31*(1), 138–145.

Kriston, L., von Wolff, A., & Holzel, L. (2010). Effectiveness of psychotherapeutic, pharmacological, and combined treatments for chronic depression: A systematic review (METACHRON). *BMC Psychiatry, 10*, 95.

Kruijt, A. W., Putman, P., & Van der Does, W. (2013). The effects of a visual search attentional bias modification paradigm on attentional bias in dysphoric individuals. *Journal of Behavior Therapy and Experimental Psychiatry, 44*(2), 248–254.

Kuehner, C., & Weber, I. (1999). Responses to depression in unipolar depressed patients: An investigation of Nolen-Hoeksema's response styles theory. *Psychological Medicine, 29*(6), 1323–1333.

Kuo, M. F., & Nitsche, M. A. (2012). Effects of transcranial electrical stimulation on cognition. *Clinical EEG and Neuroscience, 43*(3), 192–199.

Kupfer, D. J., Frank, E., & Phillips, M. L. (2012). Major depressive disorder: New clinical, neurobiological, and treatment perspectives. *Lancet, 379*(9820), 1045–1055.

Landro, N. I., Stiles, T. C., & Sletvold, H. (2001). Neuropsychological function in nonpsychotic unipolar major depression. *Neuropsychiatry, Neuropsychology, and Behavioral Neurology, 14*(4), 233–240.

Lazeron, R. H. C., Rombouts, S., de Sonneville, L., Barkhof, F., & Scheltens, P. (2003). A paced visual serial addition test for fMRI. *Journal of the Neurological Sciences, 213*(1–2), 29–34.

Leyman, L., De Raedt, R., Schacht, R., & Koster, E. H. W. (2007). Attentional biases for angry faces in unipolar depression. *Psychological Medicine, 37*(3), 393–402.

Leyman, L., De Raedt, R., Vanderhasselt, M. A., & Baeken, C. (2009). Influence of high-frequency repetitive transcranial magnetic stimulation over the dorsolateral prefrontal cortex on the inhibition of emotional information in healthy volunteers. *Psychological Medicine, 39*(6), 1019–1028.

Leyman, L., De Raedt, R., Vanderhasselt, M. A., & Baeken, C. (2011). Effects of repetitive transcranial magnetic stimulation of the dorsolateral prefrontal cortex on the attentional processing of emotional information in major depression: A pilot study. *Psychiatry Research, 185*(1–2), 102–107.

MacDonald, A. W., Cohen, J. D., Stenger, V. A., & Carter, C. S. (2000). Dissociating the role of the dorsolateral prefrontal and anterior cingulate cortex in cognitive control. *Science, 288*(5472), 1835–1838.

MacLeod, C., Rutherford, E., Campbell, L., Ebsworthy, G., & Holker, L. (2002). Selective attention and emotional vulnerability: Assessing the causal basis of their association through the experimental manipulation of attentional bias. *Journal of Abnormal Psychology, 111*(1), 107–123.

Mantovani, A., Pavlicova, M., Avery, D., Nahas, Z., McDonald, W. M., Wajdik, C. D., ... & Lisanby, S. H. (2012). Long-term effciacy of repeated daily prefrontal transcranial magnetic stimulation (TMS) in treatment-resistant depression. *Depression and Anxiety, 29*(10), 883–890.

Marchetti, I., Koster, E. H. W., Sonuga-Barke, E. J., & De Raedt, R. (2012). The default mode network and recurrent depression: A neurobiological model of cognitive risk factors. *Neuropsychology Review, 22*(3), 229–251.

Mayberg, H. S., Liotti, M., Brannan, S. K., McGinnis, S., Mahurin, R. K., Jerabek, P. A., ... & Fox, P. T. (1999). Reciprocal limbic-cortical function and negative mood: Converging PET findings in depression and normal sadness. *American Journal of Psychiatry, 156*, 675–682.

Mayberg, H. S., Lozano, A. M., Voon, V., McNeely, H. E., Seminowicz, D., Hamani, C., ... & Kennedy, S. H. (2005). Deep brain stimulation for treatment-resistant depression. *Neuron, 45*(5), 651–660.

Miyake, A., Friedman, N. P., Emerson, M. J., Witzki, A. H., Howerter, A., & Wager, T. D. (2000). The unity and diversity of executive functions and their contributions to complex "frontal lobe" tasks: A latent variable analysis. *Cognitive Psychology, 41*(1), 49–100.

Moberly, N. J., & Watkins, E. R. (2008). Ruminative self-focus and negative affect: An experience sampling study. *Journal of Abnormal Psychology, 117*(2), 314–323.

Monroe, S. M., & Harkness, K. L. (2005). Life stress, the "kindling" hypothesis, and the recurrence of depression: Considerations from a life stress perspective. *Psychological Review, 112*(2), 417–445.

Monsell, S. (1996). Control of mental processes. In V. Bruce (Ed.), *Unsolved mysteries of the mind: Tutorial essays in cognition* (pp. 93–148). Hove: Erlbaum.

Nitsche, M. A., & Paulus, W. (2000). Excitability changes induced in the human motor cortex by weak transcranial direct current stimulation. *Journal of Physiology-London, 527*(3), 633–639.

Nitsche, M. A., & Paulus, W. (2001). Sustained excitability elevations induced by transcranial DC motor cortex stimulation in humans. *Neurology, 57*(10), 1899–1901.

Nitsche, M. A., Cohen, L. G., Wassermann, E. M., Priori, A., Lang, N., Antal, A., ... & Pascual-Leone, A. (2008). Transcranial direct current stimulation: State of the art 2008. *Brain Stimulation, 1*(3), 206–223.

Nitsche, M. A., Seeber, A., Frommann, K., Mein, C. C., Rochford, C., Nitsche, M. S., ... & Tergau, F. (2005). Modulating parameters of excitability during and after transcranial direct current stimulation of the human motor cortex. *Journal of Physiology – London, 568*(1), 291–303.

Nolen-Hoeksema, S. (1991). Responses to depression and their effects on the duration of depressive episodes. *Journal of Abnormal Psychology, 100*(4), 569–582.

Nolen-Hoeksema, S. (2000). The role of rumination in depressive disorders and mixed anxiety/depressive symptoms. *Journal of Abnormal Psychology, 109*(3), 504–511.

Nolen-Hoeksema, S., Wisco, B. E., & Lyubomirsky, S. (2008). Rethinking rumination. *Perspectives on Psychological Science, 3*(5), 400–424.

Ochsner, K. N., & Gross, J. J. (2005). The cognitive control of emotion. *Trends in Cognitive Sciences, 9*(5), 242–249.

Papageorgiou, C., & Wells, A. (2000). Treatment of recurrent major depression with attention training. *Cognitive and Behavioral Practice, 7*(4), 407–413.

Paulus, W. (2011). Transcranial electrical stimulation (tES – tDCS; tRNS, tACS) methods. *Neuropsychological Rehabilitation, 21*(5), 602–617.

Paus, T., & Barrett, J. (2004). Transcranial magnetic stimulation (TMS) of the human frontal cortex: Implications for repetitive TMS treatment of depression. *Journal of Psychiatry & Neuroscience, 29*(4), 268–279.

Paus, T., Castro-Alamancos, M. A., & Petrides, M. (2001). Cortico-cortical connectivity of the human mid-dorsolateral frontal cortex and its modulation by repetitive transcranial magnetic stimulation. *European Journal of Neuroscience, 14*(8), 1405–1411.

Pena-Gomez, C., Sala-Lonch, R., Junque, C., Clemente, I. C., Vidal, D., Bargallo, N., … & Bartres-Faz, D. (2012). Modulation of large-scale brain networks by transcranial direct current stimulation evidenced by resting-state functional MRI. *Brain Stimulation, 5*(3), 252–263.

Phillips, M., Ladouceur, C., & Drevets, W. (2008). A neural model of voluntary and automatic emotion regulation: Implications for understanding the pathophysiology and neurodevelopment of bipolar disorder. *Molecular Psychiatry, 13*, 833–857.

Porter, R. J., Gallagher, P., Thompson, J. M., & Young, A. H. (2003). Neurocognitive impairment in drug-free patients with major depressive disorder. *British Journal of Psychiatry, 82*, 214–220.

Pringle, A., Browning, M., Cowen, P. J., & Harmer, C. J. (2011). A cognitive neuropsychological model of antidepressant drug action. *Progress in Neuro-Psychopharmacology & Biological Psychiatry, 35*(7), 1586–1592.

Ray, R. D., & Zald, D. H. (2012). Anatomical insights into the interaction of emotion and cognition in the prefrontal cortex. *Neuroscience and Biobehavioral Reviews, 36*(1).

Ray, R. D., Wilhelm, F. H., & Gross, J. J. (2008). All in the mind's eye? Anger rumination and reappraisal. *Journal of Personality and Social Psychology, 94*(1), 133–145.

Richards, D. (2011). Prevalence and clinical course of depression: A review. *Clinical Psychology Review, 31*(7), 1117–1125.

Roshanaei-Moghaddam, B., Pauly, M. C., Atkins, D. C., Baldwin, S. A., Stein, M. B., & Roy-Byrne, P. (2011). Relative effects of CBT and pharmacotherapy in depression versus anxiety: Is medication somewhat better for depression, and CBT somewhat better for anxiety? *Depression and Anxiety, 28*(7), 560–567.

Schmukle, S. C. (2005). Unreliability of the dot probe task. *European Journal of Personality, 19*(7), 595–605.

Segrave, R. A., Arnold, S., Hoy, K., & Fitzgerald, P. B. (2014). Concurrent cognitive control training augments the antidepressant efficacy of tDCS: A pilot study. *Brain Stimulation, 7*(2), 325–331.

Seminowicz, D. A., Mayberg, H. S., McIntosh, A. R., Goldapple, K., Kennedy, S., Segal, Z., & Rafi-Tari, S. (2004). Limbic-frontal circuitry in major depression: A path modeling metanalysis. *Neuroimage, 22*(1), 409–418.

Sharpley, C. F., & Bitsika, V. (2013). Differences in neurobiological pathways of four "clinical content" subtypes of depression. *Behavioural Brain Research, 256*, 368–376.

Siegle, G. J., Ghinassi, F., & Thase, M. E. (2007). Neurobehavioral therapies in the 21st century: Summary of an emerging field and an extended example of cognitive control training for depression. *Cognitive Therapy and Research, 31*(2), 235–262.

Siegle, G. J., Steinhauer, S. R., Friedman, E. S., Thompson, W. S., & Thase, M. E. (2011). Remission prognosis for cognitive therapy for recurrent depression using the pupil: Utility and neural correlates. *Biological Psychiatry, 69*(8), 726–733.

Siegle, G. J., Steinhauer, S. R., Thase, M. E., Stenger, V. A., & Carter, C. S. (2002). Can't shake that feeling: Assessment of sustained event-related fMRI amygdala activity in response to emotional information in depressed individuals. *Biological Psychiatry, 51*(9), 693–707.

Siegle, G. J., Thompson, W., Carter, C. S., Steinhauer, S. R., & Thase, M. E. (2007). Increased amygdala and decreased dorsolateral prefrontal BOLD responses in unipolar depression: Related and independent features. *Biological Psychiatry, 61*(2), 198–209.

Siegle, G. J., Price, R. B., Jones, N. P., Ghinassi, F., Painter, T., & Thase, M. A. (2014). You gotta work at it: Pupillary indices of task focus are prognostic for response to a neurocognitive intervention for rumination in depression. *Clinical Psychological Science, 2*(4), 455–471.

Slotema, C. W., Blom, J. D., Hoek, H. W., & Sommer, I. E. C. (2010). Should we expand the toolbox of psychiatric treatment methods to include repetitive transcranial magnetic stimulation (rTMS)? A meta-analysis of the efficacy of rTMS in psychiatric disorders. *Journal of Clinical Psychiatry, 71*(7), 873–884.

Smith, R., Fadok, R. A., Purcell, M., Liu, S., Stonnington, C., Spetzler, R. F., & Baxter, L. C. (2011). Localizing sadness activation within the subgenual cingulate in individuals: A novel functional MRI paradigm for detecting individual differences in the neural circuitry underlying depression. *Brain Imaging and Behavior, 5*(3), 229–239.

Stein, J. L., Wiedholz, L. M., Bassett, D. S., Weinberger, D. R., Zink, C. F., Mattay, V. S., & Meyer-Lindenberg, A. (2007). A validated network of effective amygdalla connectivity. *Neuroimage, 36*(3), 736–745.

Taylor, J. G., & Fragopanagos, N. F. (2005). The interaction of attention and emotion. *Neural Networks, 18*(4), 353–369.

Üstün, T. B., Ayuso-Mateos, J. L., Chatterji, S., Mathers, C., & Murray, C. J. L. (2004). Global burden of depressive disorders in the year 2000. *British Journal of Psychiatry, 184*, 386–392.

Vanderhasselt, M. A., Kuhn, S., & De Raedt, R. (2011). Healthy brooders employ more attentional resources when disengaging from the negative: An event-related fMRI study. *Cognitive Affective & Behavioral Neuroscience, 11*(2), 207–216.

Vanderhasselt, M. A., De Raedt, R., Leyman, L., & Baeken, C. (2009). Acute effects of repetitive transcranial magnetic stimulation on attentional control are related to antidepressant outcomes. *Journal of Psychiatry & Neuroscience, 34*(2), 119–126.

Vanderhasselt, M. A., De Raedt, R., Baeken, C., Leyman, L., & D'Haenen, H. (2006a). The influence of rTMS over the left dorsolateral prefrontal cortex on Stroop task performance. *Experimental Brain Research, 169*(2), 279–282.

Vanderhasselt, M. A., De Raedt, R., Baeken, C., Leyman, L., & D'Haenen, H. (2006b). The influence of rTMS over the right dorsolateral prefrontal cortex on intentional set switching. *Experimental Brain Research, 172*(4), 561–565.

Vanderhasselt, M. A., De Raedt, R., Baeken, C., Leyman, L., & D'Haenen, H. (2009). A single session of rTMS over the left dorsolateral prefrontal cortex influences attentional control in depressed patients. *World Journal of Biological Psychiatry, 10*(1), 34–42.

Vanderhasselt, M. A., Brunoni, A. R., Loeys, T., Boggio, P. S., & De Raedt, R. (2013). Nosce te ipsum –Socrates revisited? An experiment using transcranial direct current stimulation to modulate working memory and self-referent thoughts. *Neuropsychologia, 51*, 2581–2589.

Vanderhasselt, M. A., De Raedt, R., Baeken, C., Leyman, L., Clerinx, P., & D'Haenen, H. (2007). The influence of rTMS over the right dorsolateral prefrontal cortex on top-down attentional processes. *Brain Research, 1137*(1), 111–116.

Vanderhasselt, M. A., De Raedt, R., Boggio, P. S., Lotufo, P.A., Bensenor, I. M., & Brunoni, A. R. (in press). Transcranial electric stimulation does not influence the effect of cognitive training on rumination. *Progress in Neuro-Pyschopharmacology & Biological Psychiatry*.

Vanderhasselt, M. A., De Raedt, R., Brunoni, A. R., Campanha, C., Baeken, C., Remue, J., & Boggio, P. S. (2013). tDCS over the left prefrontal cortex enhances cognitive control for positive affective stimuli. *PloS One, 8*(5), e62219.

Van Praag, H. M., de Kloet, E. R., van Os, J. (2004). *Stress, the brain, and depression.* Cambridge: Cambridge University Press.

Wager, T. D., Davidson, M. L., Hughes, B. L., Lindquist, M. A., & Ochsner, K. N. (2008). Prefrontal-subcortical pathways mediating successful emotion regulation. *Neuron, 59*(6), 1037–1050.

Wells, T. T., & Beevers, C. G. (2010). Biased attention and dysphoria: Manipulating selective attention reduces subsequent depressive symptoms. *Cognition & Emotion, 24*(4), 719–728.

Wittchen, H. U., Jacobi, F., Rehm, J., Gustavsson, A., Svensson, M., Jonsson, B., … & Steinhausen, H. C. (2011). The size and burden of mental disorders and other disorders of the brain in Europe 2010. *European Neuropsychopharmacology, 21*(9), 655–679.

Zald, D. H. (2003). The human amygdala and the emotional evaluation of sensory stimuli. *Brain Research Reviews, 41*(1), 88–123.

Zetsche, U., D'Avanzato, C., & Joormann, J. (2012). Depression and rumination: Relation to components of inhibition. *Cognition & Emotion, 26*(4), 758–767.

10

BIPOLAR DISORDER

A Neurocognitive Perspective

*Thilo Deckersbach, Navneet Kaur, and
Natasha S. Hansen*

Bipolar disorder is characterized by recurrent manic and/or depressive episodes. It affects approximately 5.7 million (2.6%) American adults and causes severe impairments in functioning (Kessler, Chiu, Demler, Merikangas, & Walters, 2005; US Census Bureau, 2005). Hypomania/mania refers to a period of elevated, expansive, or irritable mood associated with inflated self-esteem, decreased need for sleep, being more talkative, flight of ideas or racing thoughts, increased distractibility, and increased goal directed behaviors often involving risky activities (e.g., excessive spending of money; American Psychiatric Association, 2013). Mania is diagnosed when the period of mood elevation lasts at least a week and is associated with functional impairment, whereas hypomanic episodes can be shorter (at least four days) and do not necessarily cause functional impairment (American Psychiatric Association, 2013). The traditional and widely accepted view of bipolar disorder is that of an illness that is characterized by time-limited acute episodes of hypomania, mania, and most often major depression interspersed with periods of symptomatic recovery associated with favorable functional outcomes (Trede et al., 2005). Mood-stabilizing medications are considered the first line of treatment for patients with bipolar disorder, although these treatments fail to bring many patients to sustained symptomatic and functional remission (Judd et al., 1998a, 1998b; Judd, Akiskal, et al., 2003; Judd et al., 2002; Judd, Schettler, et al., 2003; Perlis et al., 2006). In recent years, it has become increasingly clear that bipolar disorder, similar to schizophrenia, is a condition that for many patients is severely debilitating and worsens with the duration of the illness (Kessing, Andersen, & Mortensen, 1998; Rosa et al., 2012; Roy-Byrne, Post, Uhde, Porcu, & Davis, 1985). Neuroimaging studies in bipolar disorder have revealed functional abnormalities in brain regions involved in emotional and cognitive functioning.

Neuropsychological studies in bipolar disorder not only have documented cognitive disturbances during mood episodes but show performance decrements in attention, memory, and executive functioning when patients are euthymic (i.e., neither depressed nor manic).

These cognitive decrements are associated with difficulties in daily functioning, such as remembering tasks and appointments and time management (Altshuler et al., 2007; Bonnin et al., 2010, 2013; Dickerson et al., 2004; Dittmann et al., 2007; Jaeger, Berns, Loftus, Gonzalez, & Czobor, 2007; Martinez-Aran, Vieta, Colom, et al., 2004; Martinez-Aran, Vieta, Reinares, et al., 2004; Zubieta, Huguelet, O'Neil, & Giordani, 2001). To alleviate the impact of the illness, several psychosocial interventions have been developed to treat bipolar disorder adjunctive to mood-stabilizing medication. These include cognitive-behavioral therapies (CBTs), family-focused therapy (FFT), and interpersonal and social rhythm therapy (IPSRT). Overall, these treatments have received empirical support for their efficacy in increasing medication adherence, preventing relapse, and treating acute depressive mood symptoms.

In this chapter, we briefly review functional neuroimaging findings in bipolar disorder as well as the presence and nature of cognitive problems found in individuals with bipolar disorder and their relationship to daily functioning. After a review of the established psychosocial treatments for bipolar disorder, we discuss recently developed cognitive remediation approaches to bipolar disorder and their effects on symptoms and functioning.

Neuroimaging in Bipolar Disorder

Functional neuroimaging studies in bipolar disorder using positron emission tomography (PET) and functional magnetic resonance imaging (fMRI) have found abnormalities in the prefrontal cortex (e.g., ventrolateral [vlPFC] ventromedial [vmPFC], and dorsolateral]dlPFC] prefrontal cortex and anterior cingulate), in the basal ganglia, and in the medial temporal lobe (e.g. amygdala, hippocampus, and parahippocampal gyrus; for reviews see Phillips, Ladouceur, & Drevets, 2008; Chen et al., 2011). These brain regions subserve emotional processing (emotion generation and emotion regulation) as well as cognitive functions such as working memory and various forms of long-term memory (e.g., declarative or episodic memory).

In terms of emotional processing, studies suggest exaggerated limbic activations in emotion-generating areas (e.g., amygdala) coupled with impaired abilities to down-regulate exaggerated activations by ventral prefrontal areas (e.g., vlPFC and vmPFC). For example, a frequently used fMRI paradigm involves showing emotional facial expressions to participants during MRI scans (e.g., fearful, sad, or angry faces) and comparing them with neutral facial expressions. In bipolar disorder, most studies have found exaggerated amygdala responses in individuals with bipolar disorder compared to healthy control participants while viewing (processing) emotional facial expressions compared to neutral faces (Van der Schot, Kahn, Ramsey, Nolen, & Vink, 2010; Hassel et al., 2008). Conversely, many studies using a variety of emotional stimuli have found decreased frontal activation in the vmPFC and vlPFC in bipolar disorder (Malhi, Lagopoulos, Sachdev, Ivanovski, & Shnier, 2005; Lagopoulos & Malhi, 2011), brain regions involved in providing top-down regulation of exaggerated emotional responses. For example, Lagopoulos and Malhi (2007) found that patients with bipolar disorder exhibited attenuated vmPFC and vlPFC activity relative to healthy controls during performance of the emotional Stroop task. Recent studies have shown amygdala and vlPFC activation to be further differentiated in bipolar disorder relative to unipolar depression. For example, Diler and colleagues (2013) found significantly greater amygdala activation in patients with bipolar disorder relative to patients with unipolar depression in response to both positive and negative emotional stimuli. Similarly, it was found that elevated left amygdala activation in response to mild, sad, and neutral faces differentiated bipolar depression from unipolar depression, suggesting a depression-specific marker in bipolar disorder (Almeida, Versace, Hassel, Kupfer, & Phillips, 2010). The degree to which these abnormal activations are mood state-dependent (depressed, manic, euthymic) is not clear (Chen et al., 2011).

Cognitive functioning difficulties in individuals with bipolar disorder (see below) appear to be associated with abnormal activations (or hypoactivations) in regions involved in attention, memory, and executive functioning (organization of information, planning, and problem solving; Adler, Holland, Schmithorst, Tuchfarber, & Strakowski, 2004; Dupont et al., 1990). fMRI studies of working memory in euthymic patient have found abnormalities in the dlPFC although the directionality of the abnormalities (i.e., hyper- or hypoactivation) varies across studies (Chang et al., 2004; Deckersbach et al., 2006; Lagopoulos, Ivanovski, & Malhi, 2007; Monks et al., 2004). For example, both (Monks et al., 2004; Lagopoulos et al., 2007), using n-back and Sternberg working memory tasks, reported reduced activations in the middle frontal gyrus, the inferior frontal gyrus, and the dorsal anterior cingulate in bipolar disorder compared to normal control participants. Chang and colleagues (2004), on the other hand, found increased activation in the left dlPFC (Brodmann areas 9/46) and dorsal anterior cingulate in a two-back working memory paradigm in a cohort of pediatric patients with bipolar disorder. Glahn and colleagues (2010) and Deckersbach and colleagues (2008) found abnormal activations in the dlPFC and/or hippocampus in explicit long-term memory tasks. More specifically, increased dlPFC activation was observed during a face–name association encoding task (Glahn et al., 2010) whereas decreased dlPFC and decreased hippocampal activation were observed in euthymic patients with bipolar disorder during a word list-learning task (Deckersbach et al., 2008). Although the directionality of the abnormalities is inconsistent, there are clear abnormal activations in regions associated with cognitive functioning difficulties in attention, memory, and executive functioning.

Cognitive Problems

Neuropsychological studies have consistently documented cognitive problems in individuals with bipolar disorder (Arts, Jabben, Krabbendam, & van Os, 2008; Bora, Yucel, & Pantelis, 2009; Robinson et al., 2006; Torrent et al., 2013; Torres, Boudreau, & Yatham, 2007). Once thought of as present only during periods of depression or mania, neuropsychological studies have shown that approximately 30% to 60% of individuals with bipolar disorder exhibit cognitive difficulties when they are euthymic (Arts et al., 2008; Bora et al., 2009; Robinson et al., 2006; Torrent et al., 2013; Torres et al., 2007). These deficits cannot be attributed to a lower IQ or differences in education between patients with bipolar disorder and controls (Robinson et al., 2006; Torres et al., 2007). On average, cognitive functioning in euthymic bipolar patients ranges between a half and one standard deviation below that of normal control participants (Arts et al., 2008; Bora et al., 2009; Robinson et al., 2006; Torres et al., 2007). Three cognitive domains appear to be consistently affected: attention/processing speed, memory, and executive functioning (Arts et al., 2008; Bora et al., 2009; Robinson et al., 2006; Torres et al., 2007).

Attention/processing Speed

Attention and processing speed in bipolar disorder have been commonly assessed with tests such as the Trailmaking Test Part A (Reitan, 1958), which requires subjects to connect letters that are randomly distributed on a page in ascending alphabetic order. Other tests commonly used in this domain include the Digit Symbol Substitution Test (DSST; Wechsler, 1997), where numbers have to be assigned to symbols in a predetermined fashion, and the Continuous Performance Test (CPT; Beck, Bransome, Mirsky, Rosvold, & Sarason, 1956), in which the presence of a target letter (e.g., X) is to be indicated if it directly follows another pre-specified letter (e.g., A). Overall, individuals with bipolar disorder score about half a standard deviation below that of normal control participants in these measures (Arts et al., 2008; Bora et al., 2009; Robinson et al., 2006; Torres et al., 2007).

Memory

Individuals with bipolar disorder have consistently been found to have difficulties in measures of explicit memory, whereas implicit memory appears to be preserved (Altshuler et al., 2004; van Gorp, Altshuler, Theberge, Wilkins, & Dixon, 1998). Explicit memory refers to a type of memory for which contents can be declared (or brought) to mind, whereas implicit (or procedural) memory largely refers to non-conscious learning processes that take place outside an individual's awareness (Graf & Schacter, 1985). In the domain of explicit memory, one of the most consistently reported findings in euthymic individuals with bipolar disorder is a decrement in episodic memory, the ability to recollect information encountered in a previous study episode (Graf & Schacter, 1985). For an event to be remembered, it must be encoded, stored, and consolidated over time and then retrieved from storage (Kapur et al., 1996). Encoding refers to the processes that convert a perceived event into an enduring cognitive representation. Retrieval is the process that reactivates a stored representation leading to the experience of explicit recollection of the past event (Kapur et al., 1996). In bipolar disorder, learning and memory have been investigated using word list-learning tasks, in which patients study a word list over repeated study test trials followed by short- and long-delayed recall and recognition trials (Arts et al., 2008; Bora et al., 2009; Cavanagh, Van Beck, Muir, & Blackwood, 2002; Clark, Iversen, & Goodwin, 2002; Deckersbach, Savage, et al., 2004; Martinez-Aran, Vieta, Colom, et al., 2004; Martinez-Aran, Vieta, Reinares, et al., 2004; Robinson et al., 2006; Torres et al., 2007). This has shown that individuals with bipolar disorder have difficulties learning the word list over repeated study test trials but seem to be able to retain what they have learned over short and long delays (short delay/long delay recall).

These findings suggest that it is primarily the ability to learn (encode) and retrieve new episodes that is affected. Storage and retrieval difficulties can be disentangled by comparing an individual's free recall and recognition performance. In recognition tests, a subject is asked to discriminate between the original items and distractors. If an item has not been stored, the ability to discriminate between the original item and a distractor item should be near chance. While considerably smaller than difficulties in learning, individuals with bipolar disorder have been shown to also exhibit difficulties with recognition corresponding to a medium effect size (Bora et al., 2009).

Executive Functioning

The term *executive function* typically refers to a set of higher-order control processes that serve to control, regulate, and guide lower-level processes in the service of planning and problem solving. Performance decrements have been found in a variety of tests of executive functioning including the Trailmaking Test Part B (Reitan, 1958); the Wisconsin Card Sorting Test (WCST; Heaton, Chelune, Talley, Kay, & Curtiss, 1993; Heaton, 1981); the Stroop test (Golden & Freshwater, 2002; Golden, 1978); Digits Backwards (Wechsler, 1995); and strategic memory measures of the Rey Osterrieth Complex Figure Test (Lu, Boone, Cozolino, & Mitchell, 2003; Meyers & Meyers, 1995); and the California Verbal Learning Test (CVLT; Arts et al., 2008; Bora et al., 2009; Delis, Kramer, Kaplan, & Ober, 2000; Robinson et al., 2006; Torres et al., 2007). Overall, these measures tap into various aspects of executive functioning, such as the ability to plan and implement strategic action, monitor and flexibly shift behavior when it is no longer appropriate, and withhold pre-potent automatic response in favor of or initiating an intentionally executed response. For example, in the WCST, participants sort cards with symbols according to attributes such the number of symbols, the shape, or the color on the card. From time to time, the sorting rule changes, and subjects need to incorporate the feedback about their sorting behavior ("right" or "wrong") to adjust their sorting behavior. Continued sorting based on an outdated rule despite corrective feedback is regarded as a difficulty to shift mental sets. In the Stroop test, subjects are asked to name the color a word is written in. When the content of the word (e.g., "blue") conflicts with the color it is displayed in (e.g., green ink), individuals need to inhibit their pre-potent response to name the word ("blue") instead of stating the color it is written in (correct response: "green"). In the Digit Span Backwards, individuals are asked to repeat back a sequence of numbers read by an examiner in reverse order. Longer digit sequences draw heavily upon an individual's ability to reorganize information in working memory in order to reverse the sequence. Difficulties organizing information also appear to affect verbal and nonverbal learning and memory in bipolar disorder (Deckersbach, McMurrich, et al., 2004; Deckersbach, Savage, et al., 2004; Deckersbach et al., 2005). For example, if the task involves learning a word list and words in this list stem from different categories (e.g., tools, clothing), then mentally grouping the words into their categories during list presentation typically enhances subsequent recall from memory. Similarly free recall of geometric information is typically better when it was encoded as meaningful units (e.g., a large square, diagonals; Deckersbach, McMurrich, et al., 2004). As shown by Deckersbach and colleagues (Deckersbach, McMurrich, et al., 2004; Deckersbach, Savage, et al., 2004), individuals with bipolar disorder have been shown to exhibit difficulties organizing words and geometric information during encoding.

Moderators of Cognitive Difficulties

Medication and subclinical mood symptoms are two factors that may influence the degree of cognitive problems in euthymic individuals with bipolar disorder. Many medications have the potential for cognitive side effects. For example, lithium carbonate (a mood stabilizer) appears to have some effect on processing speed and verbal memory (Pachet & Wisniewski, 2003). Likewise topiramate (an anticonvulsant) may have less favorable cognitive effects compared to other anticonvulsants such as lamotrigine (Dunner, 2005; Goldberg & Burdick, 2001; Macqueen & Young, 2003). Overall, most studies have not found an association between medication dose and cognitive problems in euthymic patients with bipolar disorder. With respect to subclinical symptoms, to date most studies have shown that despite co-varying subclinical mood symptoms, cognitive difficulties in attention and processing speed, memory, and executive functioning persist (Deckersbach, Savage, et al., 2004; Martinez-Aran, Vieta, Colom, et al., 2004; Martinez-Aran, Vieta, Reinares, et al., 2004).

Another question that has been raised is whether cognitive difficulties in euthymic patients are relatively stable or whether they emerge as a consequence of illness progression. Studies that compared first-degree relatives of individuals with bipolar disorder with normal controls revealed lower performance of first-degree relatives mostly in the domains of verbal memory and executive functioning (Arts et al., 2008). Overall, however, the effects in first-degree relative were considerably smaller than those found in euthymic individuals with bipolar disorder, suggesting that cognitive functions may be a marker for the genetic liability for bipolar disorder (Arts et al., 2008). On the other hand, it remains unclear whether neuropsychological difficulties are present before the onset of bipolar disorder. Studies that analyzed cognitive performance of children or young adults who later developed bipolar disorder or schizophrenia did not find evidence for severe cognitive problems prior to onset of bipolar disorder, whereas there appears to be one for schizophrenia (Reichenberg et al., 2002; Zammit et al., 2004). However, the neuropsychological tests used in these studies only insufficiently capture those cognitive domains for which difficulties in euthymic individuals with bipolar disorder have been reported. With respect to cognitive functioning and illness progression, although inconsistently, studies have shown associations between self-reported duration of bipolar illness, the number of depressive and/or manic mood episodes, and cognitive problems such that longer duration of illness and more mood episodes were associated with more cognitive difficulties in the domains of attention, memory, and executive functioning (Cavanagh et al., 2002; Clark et al., 2002; Deckersbach, Savage, et al., 2004; Martinez-Aran, Vieta, Colom, et al., 2004; Martinez-Aran, Vieta, Reinares, et al., 2004). As described below, individuals with bipolar disorder exhibit psychosocial and functioning impairments even after symptomatic remission or recovery (MacQueen, Young, & Joffe, 2001), and these functioning difficulties are associated with cognitive problems (Altshuler et al., 2007; Bonnin et al., 2010, 2013; Dickerson et al., 2004; Dittmann et al., 2007; Jaeger et al., 2007; Martinez-Aran, Vieta, Colom, et al., 2004; Martinez-Aran, Vieta, Reinares, et al., 2004; Zubieta et al., 2001).

Traditional Treatments for Bipolar Disorder

Pharmacotherapy

Mood-stabilizing medication remains the first-line treatment for bipolar disorder. The challenge for mood-stabilizing medication involves treating the different phases of the disorder such as acute mood episodes (i.e., mania or hypomania, acute depression) as well as maintenance treatment for relapse prevention and the management of ongoing subsyndromal symptoms (Bersudsky & Belmaker, 2009). Medications effective for hypomanic or manic episodes include the classic "mood stabilizers" (e.g., lithium, valproate, carbamazepine, and antipsychotic medication) either alone or in combination. FDA-approved treatments for bipolar depression include the combination of olanzapine and fluoxetine and quetiapine monotherapy. Lamotrigine, an anticonvulsant, appears to have unique preventive antidepressant properties but weaker acute antidepressant effectiveness and maintenance antimanic effects (Geddes, Calabrese, & Goodwin, 2009). Typically, patients with bipolar disorder are treated with multiple medications to relieve their symptoms (Ghaemi et al., 2006).

Despite pharmacotherapy, most patients will experience recurrent mood episodes (Gitlin, Swendsen, Heller, & Hammen, 1995). A major complication for pharmacotherapy is that many patients with bipolar disorder are either not adherent to their medication regimens (Colom, Veita, Tacchi, SanchezMoreno, & Scott, 2005) and/or discontinue medications soon after it was started (Keck et al., 1998). Not taking the prescribed medications, or only taking them irregularly, substantially increases the risk for relapse and re-hospitalization (Keck et al., 1998; Scott & Pope, 2002). Reasons for discontinuing medications are multifaceted. They include severe side effects (Morselli & Elgie, 2003), lack of insight into the chronic nature of bipolar disorder and the need for medication treatment (Peralta & Cuesta, 1998), denial of the severity of the disorder, fear of dependence (Morselli & Elgie, 2003), and the belief that if one just tries hard, one can control mood without medications (Scott & Tacchi, 2002). Discontinuing medication can also be a prodromal sign of mania (i.e., overconfidence that one can manage without medication; Keck et al., 1998).

Psychosocial Treatments for Bipolar Disorder

Thoughts and beliefs related to medication non-adherence were targeted in an early cognitive-behavior treatment study conducted by Cochran (1984). At the end of CBT (as well at the six-month follow-up), patients were taking their medication (lithium) more regularly, and had fewer mood episodes caused by non-adherence than patients who had received regular clinical care (Cochran, 1984). More recent treatments for bipolar disorder have broadened the focus to include treatments and treatment strategies designed to prevent relapse (e.g., psychoeducation, mood monitoring, early detection of prodromal signs, adjusting social rhythms, changing behaviors that increase the risk of mood episode recurrence, family therapy) and to treat acute depression (e.g., behavioral activation, cognitive restructuring, interpersonal and family therapy; Colom et al., 2009; Frank et al., 2005; Lam, Hayward, Watkins, Wright, & Sham, 2005; Lam et al., 2003; Meyer & Hautzinger, 2012; Miklowitz, George, Richards, Simoneau, & Suddath, 2003; Perry, Tarrier, Morriss, McCarthy, & Limb, 1999; Rea et al., 2003; Scott et al., 2006). Overall, most psychosocial treatment approaches rest on the assumption that if people with bipolar disorder learn more about their illness, monitor their symptoms, become more adherent to medication, and adjust their behavior and their environment in ways that minimize risk for relapse (e.g., irregular medication adherence, lack of sleep, alcohol and substance abuse, family criticism, stress), this may have beneficial effects on the course of the illness and ultimately improve people's quality of life (Miklowitz & Johnson, 2006).

Free-standing psychoeducation programs for remitted, stable patients with bipolar disorder in conjunction with medication have been shown to lower the rate of manic recurrences (Perry et al., 1999) or both manic and depressive recurrences (Colom et al., 2009). It had been recognized that despite pharmacotherapy, patients with bipolar disorder often do not achieve remission. Many patients continue to experience residual mood symptoms between episodes, particularly symptoms of depression (Judd, Schettler, Akiskal, et al., 2008). Residual depressive and manic symptoms predict the recurrence of mood episodes (Perlis et al., 2006). However, full-blown mania and depression typically do not appear suddenly. Usually, there is a ramping up in symptom severity (called "prodromal signs") that foreshadow the onset or worsening of hypomanic or depressive symptoms (Carlson & Goodwin, 1973). Therefore, mood monitoring and early detection of prodromal signs have become a cornerstone of most, if not all, relapse prevention programs.

Lam and colleagues (2003, 2005) compared treatment as usual with a cognitive-behavioral therapy consisting of treatment elements such as psychoeducation, mood monitoring (early detection of mood symptoms), cognitive restructuring, and modification of behaviors that increase the risk for mood episodes. They found that patients who received CBT had fewer mood episodes within the first year. Although there was no difference in the number of mood episodes between CBT and treatment as usual at the two-year follow-up, patients with bipolar disorder who had received CBT had shorter mood episodes, fewer overall mood symptoms, and fewer admissions to the hospital (Lam et al., 2003, 2005). A similar "decay" of the effects of CBT was reported by Meyer and Hautzinger (2012). They found that patients receiving CBT had lower relapse rates than patients receiving supportive psychotherapy while in active treatment for nine months, although there were no differences in overall relapse rates at the two-year follow-up (Meyer & Hautzinger, 2012). Scott et al. (2006) also did not find a difference in the overall relapse rates between patients who received CBT or treatment as usual (TAU). However, for patients with fewer than twelve lifetime mood episodes, CBT was more effective than treatment as usual, whereas for patients with more than twelve lifetime mood episodes, TAU was the better option (Scott et al., 2006). This effect became more pronounced for patients with 20 or 30 lifetime mood episodes, suggesting that CBT may work less well for individuals with particularly severe and recurrent bipolar disorder or those who are early in their course of illness (i.e. fewer episodes yet). In family focused therapy (FFT), patients with bipolar disorder and their family members can learn about the elements of the disorder and practice a variety of skills, including more effective communication (e.g., reducing criticism and hostility), and problem-solving about stress-inducing issues related to the disorder. Miklowitz and colleagues (2003) showed that FFT participants had fewer relapses than patients who received psychoeducation alone (Miklowitz et al., 2003; Rea et al., 2003). As shown by Frank and colleagues (2005), psychotherapy can help to prevent relapse if it is started even when patients are acutely ill. They randomized acutely ill patients with bipolar disorder to interpersonal and social rhythm therapy (IPSRT) or intensive clinical management. IPSRT combines interpersonal psychotherapy with strategies to maintain regular routines (Frank, Hlastala, Ritenour, & Houck, 1997; Frank et al., 2005). The interpersonal component focuses on unresolved grief, interpersonal disputes, role transitions, and interpersonal deficits (Frank, Swartz, & Kupfer, 2000). During the acute phase, there was no difference in the time between the two treatment strategies until patients were stabilized. However, after stabilization, patients who had received IPSRT when they were acutely ill survived longer without a mood episode compared to patients who had received intensive clinical management (Frank et al., 2005).

When depressed, patients with bipolar disorder, similar to patients with unipolar major depression, exhibit high levels of negative thinking and dysfunctional attitudes. These aspects as well as activity management, problem solving abilities, improving family communication, interpersonal factors and social rhythms (among others), were the focus of treatment elements employed in a recent large randomized controlled trial that was embedded in the Systematic Treatment Enhancement Program for Bipolar Disorder (STEP-BD) (Miklowitz, Otto, Frank, Reilly-Harrington, Wisniewski et al., 2007). STEP-BD is the largest naturalistic study of bipolar disorder to date. The trial compared the efficacy of CBT, FFT, and IPSRT with a low-level treatment condition called "Collaborative Care" that provided depressed patients with bipolar disorder with a workbook with information about bipolar disorder and the opportunity to meet with a professional up to three times (Miklowitz, Otto, Frank, Reilly-Harrington, Wisniewski et al., 2007). All three treatments were successful in decreasing the length of the depressive episodes over the course of a year and increased recovery rates compared to Collaborative Care (intensive psychotherapy 64.4% recovery rate vs. collaborative care 51.5% recovery rate). The three active treatments also led to more days of wellness over the study year and improved relationship functioning and life-satisfaction.

Despite its success, the STEP-BD study added to a growing realization that persistent depressive symptoms and depressive episodes and impairments in functioning are the most difficult aspects to treat in patients with bipolar disorder (Belmaker, 2007; Miklowitz, Otto, Frank, Reilly-Harrington, Wisniewski, et al., 2007). For example, two large-scale studies besides STEP-BD failed to find beneficial effects of cognitive-behavioral strategies for decreasing depressive symptoms. Bauer and colleagues (2006a, 2006b) and Simon and colleagues (2006) combined group psychoeducation (recognition of triggers for episodes, monitoring warning signs, developing relapse prevention strategies, and increasing medication adherence) with sessions that focused on increasing functioning through achieving goals in life (Bauer et al., 2006a, 2006b; Simon et al., 2006). A nurse care coordinator was available to reach out to patients when things were not going well. Both studies observed beneficial effects in terms of shortening manic episodes (Bauer et al., 2006a; Simon et al., 2006) and lowering the risk of manic episodes (Simon et al., 2006). However, there were no effects on depression severity, number of weeks depressed, or depressive recurrences (Simon et al., 2006). With respect to functioning, in STEP-BD, although intensive psychotherapy was more effective than collaborative care in decreasing depression, the impact on patients' functioning was mixed. While relationship functioning and life-satisfaction with intensive psychotherapy improved more than in Collaborative Care, there was no difference between the treatments with respect to work or role functioning (Miklowitz, Otto, Frank, Reilly-Harrington, Wisniewski et al., 2007). Other studies showed that work functioning and social functioning does not improve much during psychosocial maintenance treatment (Frank et al., 2008; Lam et al., 2003, 2005), raising concern about the ability of established psychosocial treatments to sufficiently impact psychosocial functioning above and beyond improvements in clinical symptoms.

Functioning and Cognitive Difficulties

Large clinical and epidemiological studies have revealed a chronic and often disabling course of bipolar disorder (Kessler et al., 2006; Kogan et al., 2004; Morris et al., 2005; Tohen et al., 2003). Two-thirds of patients with bipolar disorder experience a moderate-to-severe impact of the illness on occupational functioning (Suppes et al., 2001). After treatment for a mood episode, many patients remain functionally impaired during follow-up periods despite syndromal and/or symptomatic recovery (Fagiolini et al., 2005; Keck et al., 1998;

Tohen et al., 2003). The Collaborative Depression Study, a study that followed up patients with unipolar and bipolar disorder over a thirteen-year period, found that patients with bipolar disorder experienced severe work impairment 20% to 30% of the time. This was more than in any other domain of functioning (Judd, Schettler, Solomon, et al., 2008). Although functioning was improved when patients were not symptomatic, functioning remained impaired relative to healthy controls even when patients were asymptomatic (Judd et al., 2005). The National Comorbidity Survey Replication (NCS-R) study (Kessler et al., 2005, 2006), a large epidemiological study in the United States, found that on average individuals with bipolar disorder miss the equivalent of sixty-five days at work per year. This corresponds to the equivalent of 5.4 missed days at work per month. More than half of this was due to impaired performance at work (2.9 lost workdays due to impaired work performance) rather than days missed at work, equating to a full week of lost productivity every month (Kessler et al., 2006). Not surprisingly, rates of unemployment of individuals with bipolar disorder are substantially higher than in the normal population (Kogan et al., 2004), and bipolar disorder is among the top ten causes for disability in the world (Kogan et al., 2004; Murray & Lopez, 1997; Sanderson & Andrews, 2006). Studies that assessed cognitive, role, and work functioning have found associations between cognitive difficulties and functioning, most consistently with the domains of memory and executive functioning (Altshuler et al., 2007; Bonnin et al., 2010, 2013; Dickerson et al., 2004; Dittmann et al., 2007; Jaeger et al., 2007; Martinez-Aran, Vieta, Colom, et al., 2004; Martinez-Aran, Vieta, Reinares, et al., 2004; Zubieta et al., 2001).

Memory and Functional Impairment

Several studies have reported associations between verbal learning and memory and impaired global functioning (Bonnin et al., 2010; Dickerson et al., 2004; Martinez-Aran, Vieta, Colom, et al., 2004; Martinez-Aran, Vieta, Reinares, et al., 2004; Zubieta et al., 2001). In multiple publications, Martinez-Aran and colleagues (Martinez-Aran, Vieta, Colom, et al., 2004; Martinez-Aran, Vieta, Reinares, et al., 2004) compared euthymic bipolar patients with healthy control participants and found that performance decrements in CVLT verbal learning and memory were significantly correlated with functioning as assessed by the Global Assessment of Functioning Scale of the DSM (American Psychiatric Association, 2000). Bonnin and colleagues (2010) followed patients with bipolar disorder longitudinally for four years after patients had completed a neuropsychological assessment when they were euthymic (neither depressed nor manic). She found that better delayed-recall performance at the baseline assessment independent from subthreshold depressive symptoms predicted occupational functioning at the four-year follow-up (Bonnin et al., 2010). Dickerson and colleagues (2004) evaluated cognitive functioning of 117 individuals with bipolar disorder using the Repeatable Battery for the Assessment of Neuropsychological Status (Randolph, Tierney, Mohr, & Chase, 1998), the information and letter-number sequencing subtests of the Wechsler Adult Intelligence Scale III, and Trailmaking Test Part A, and also assessed their current employment status. Current employment status was significantly associated with cognitive performance, especially verbal memory (Dickerson et al., 2004).

Executive Function and Functional Impairment

Associations between difficulties in executive functioning and global and occupational functioning have been reported using both executive functioning rating scales and objective measures of aspects of executive functioning (Bonnin et al., 2013; Martinez-Aran, Vieta, Colom, et al., 2004; Martinez-Aran, Vieta, Reinares, et al., 2004; Torrent et al., 2006; Zubieta et al., 2001). For example, both Zubieta and colleagues (2001) and Martinez-Aran and colleagues (Martinez-Aran, Vieta, Reinares, et al., 2004) found that performance on the Stroop Test correlated negatively with measures of social and occupational outcomes (Zubieta et al., 2001) or global functioning (Martinez-Aran, Vieta, Reinares, et al., 2004).

Several studies have reported that difficulties in the ability to shift mental sets and cognitive flexibility (as assessed by the Trailmaking Test Part B or preservative errors in the WCST) correlated with global functioning and work adjustment (Bonnin et al., 2013; Martinez-Aran, Vieta, Colom, et al., 2004; Martinez-Aran, Vieta, Reinares, et al., 2004; Torrent et al., 2006). In addition, both Dittmann and colleagues (2007) and Martinez and colleagues (Martinez-Aran, Vieta, Reinares, et al., 2004) found that more difficulties with reordering information in working memory (as assessed by digits backward and letter-number sequencing) were associated with lower social and global functioning. Jaeger and colleagues (2007) found that neurocognitive status after stabilization following an initial hospitalization predicted the ability to live independently at the twelve-month follow-up. Attention, processing speed, and fluency (e.g., word fluency) were most predictive of functioning even when mood and medication status at follow-up (depression and mania) were controlled. Finally, as shown by Altshuler and colleagues (2007), ratings of executive functioning discriminate between employed and unemployed veterans with bipolar disorder. Using an executive functioning interview they found that unemployed veterans with bipolar disorder had greater executive difficulties. Although lifetime psychiatric hospitalizations and the number of psychotropic medications prescribed had significant associations with employment status, the relationship between employment status and executive functioning remained significant when these variables were controlled. Overall, these findings support the view that cognitive problems in bipolar disorder, especially verbal memory and executive functioning, are associated with corresponding difficulties in occupational and social functioning, even when clinical variables are controlled. This raises the intriguing hypothesis of whether treating cognitive difficulties could improve functional outcome in patients with bipolar disorder.

Cognitive Remediation

Established psychosocial treatments such as CBT, FFT, or IPSRT draw upon a patient's intact cognitive functioning. For example, for education about bipolar disorder to have a meaningful impact, patients not only need to understand the information that is provided but remember it at times when it is critical. Mood monitoring requires the ability to pay and sustain attention. The ability to change thinking patterns and consider alternative views or problem solutions draw upon an individual's ability to shift mental sets. Therefore, cognitive or functional remediation approaches are increasingly explored as alternative or adjunctive treatment options.

Cognitive remediation refers to a treatment approach that seeks to improve or rehabilitate cognitive functioning with the goal of alleviating symptoms and improving functioning. Cognitive remediation approaches have been extensively studied in patients with schizophrenia (for a review, see McGurk, Mueser, DeRosa, & Wolfe, 2009). Following a neuropsychological assessment, cognitive remediation often involves systematic training in paper-and-pencil or computer-based exercises that target specific cognitive functions (e.g., attention). After the training, improvements in these domains as well as overall functioning are then assessed.

To date, there are only four studies that either included a sufficiently large subgroup of patients with bipolar disorder (Choi & Medalia, 2005; Meusel, Hall, Fougere, McKinnon, & Macqueen, 2013) or were specifically focused on patients with bipolar disorder (Deckersbach et al., 2010; Torrent et al., 2013). Choi and Medalia (2005) investigated the effect of unspecified computer-assisted exercise in a sample of forty-eight psychiatric outpatients, 19% of which had a diagnosis of bipolar disorder. They observed improvements in attention and supervisor-rated work functioning but did not specify whether this effect was also present in patients with bipolar disorder. The effect of a ten-week computer-assisted cognitive remediation program focused on attention, processing speed, verbal memory, and executive functioning in patients with unipolar depression (n = twenty-five) and bipolar disorder (n = thirteen) but did not report subgroup results (Meusel et al., 2013). Overall, after training, participants showed improved performance on Digits Backward (Wechsler, 1997) but no improvements in verbal memory (Meusel et al., 2013). Participants also completed an N-Back working memory task (Meusel et al., 2013) and a recollection memory task concurrent with fMRI scanning before and after cognitive remediation. After cognitive remediation, activation increased in lateral and medial prefrontal, superior temporal, and lateral parietal regions (N-Back task) bilaterally in the hippocampus (recollection task) (Meusel et al., 2013).

Two studies have specifically focused on patients with bipolar disorder (Deckersbach et al., 2010; Torrent et al., 2013). The design of these studies was influenced by advances in the field of cognitive remediation in schizophrenia. Specifically, a meta-analysis of remediation studies in schizophrenia reveals a moderate effect of cognitive remediation for improved cognitive functioning and somewhat lower for psychosocial functioning and symptoms. The impact of cognitive remediation was moderated by presence of adjunctive psychiatric rehabilitation (McGurk, Twamley, Sitzer, McHugo, & Mueser, 2007). That is, studies that evaluated the effects of adding cognitive remediation to a specific psychiatric rehabilitation program reported significant improvements in psychosocial functioning, whereas studies that compared cognitive remediation alone to usual services did not (McGurk et al., 2007). Both studies in bipolar disorder combined training of cognitive functioning in the domains of attention, memory, and executive functioning but also combined it with bridging the effects of training to daily life by providing strategies to manage cognitive deficiencies in daily life (Martinez-Aran et al., 2011). Therefore, because of the focus on cognitive and psychiatric rehabilitation taken in these two studies, the approach is perhaps best described as "functional rehabilitation" (Martinez-Aran et al., 2011).

The first study to apply functional rehabilitation to bipolar disorder was conducted by Deckersbach and colleagues (2010). In this open-label study, eighteen employed stable adult outpatients with bipolar disorder who experienced difficulties functioning at work completed a fourteen-session remediation program focusing on preventing relapse, as well as improving cognitive and work functioning. Treatment consisted of three modules: mood monitoring and treatment of residual depressive symptoms; organization, planning, and time management; and attention and memory. In the first module, patients were introduced to daily mood monitoring, activity management (e.g., increasing pleasurable and mastery-based activities), problem solving, increasing awareness of negative automatic thoughts, and cognitive restructuring thereof. As needed, emergency control techniques were implemented to prevent job loss if a patient was at risk of losing his or her current job. Functional remediation treatment techniques used in the second and third module were in part adapted from Safren and colleagues (2005) and Sohlberg and Mateer (2001). In the organization, planning, and time management module, patients learned to systematically use schedule and notebooks, keep daily task lists, and practice prioritizing activities, as well as breaking down complex tasks into simpler tasks and making more realistic time estimations for activities and projects. In the attention and memory module, patients learned to structure tasks around their concentration abilities, deal with both neutral as well as affective distractions, and use external and internal reminder cues as well as encoding strategies to improve memory. Results indicated that at the end of treatment, as well as at the three-months follow-up, patients showed lower residual depressive symptoms and increased occupational, as well as overall psychosocial functioning. More specifically, while there was no change in the days patients missed at work, they significantly improved their performance while at work. In addition, patients improved significantly in executive functioning as assessed by the Frontal Systems Behavior Rating Scale (FrSbe; Grace & Malloy, 2001). Improvements in occupational functioning, overall functioning, and executive functioning remained significant when residual depression scores were included as a covariate (Deckersbach et al., 2010).

The largest functional remediation study to date conducted by Torrent and colleagues (2013) was conducted at ten sites. Euthymic patients with bipolar disorder who had at least a moderate to severe degree of functional impairment were randomized to twenty-one weekly ninety-minute sessions of either functional remediation (n = seventy-seven), psychoeducation (n = eighty-two), or treatment as usual (n = eighty). Functional remediation focused on the domains of attention, memory, and executive function and involved enhancing functioning in daily routine. Patients were trained with ecologic (resembling real-life tasks) exercises for memory, attention, problem solving and reasoning, multitasking, and organization in order to improve their functional outcome. Psychoeducation aimed at preventing relapse by improving illness awareness, treatment adherence, early detection of prodromal symptoms of relapse, and lifestyle regularity. In TAU, patients received pharmacological treatment

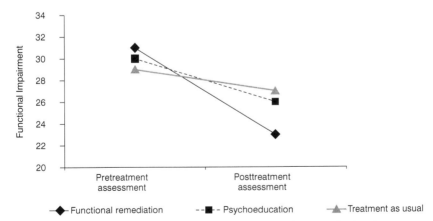

FIGURE 10.1 Functional impairment as measured with the Functioning Assessment Short Test.

without any adjunctive psychosocial therapy (Torrent et al., 2013). At the end of treatment, patients in functional remediation showed significantly more functional improvement than patients receiving TAU, and there was a statistical trend toward more functional improvement in the functional remediation group compared to the psychoeducation group. Effect sizes within the groups confirmed these findings, showing a large effect for functional remediation (d: = 0.93), followed by a small medium effect for psychoeducation (d: = 0.41) and a small effect for TAU (d: = 0.22; Torrent et al., 2013).

A more detailed analysis revealed that functional remediation improved functioning in two particular domains, interpersonal and occupational functioning. No differences in clinical or neurocognitive functioning (assessed by a comprehensive neuropsychological battery) were observed, although there were improvements in neuropsychological testing performance across all groups (Torrent et al., 2013).

Summary and Future Directions

Once thought of as an illness with an episodic course and favorable symptomatic and functional outcomes between episodes, the view on bipolar disorder has changed to that of a chronic and progressively disabling illness that leaves many patients with bipolar disorder unemployed or disabled. Compared to the rich set of data that have been accumulated in other areas (e.g., schizophrenia), research on cognitive or functional remediation in bipolar is in its infancy. However, the initial results of the two functional remediation studies conducted in bipolar disorder are encouraging. Many other aspects of where progress has been made in other disorders have not yet been addressed in bipolar disorders (e.g., attentional bias modification training for depressed patients). Future studies should also investigate whether the combination of brain function-enhancing techniques (e.g., repetitive transcranial magnetic stimulation of the dlPFC) can be used to augment the effect of functional rehabilitation in bipolar disorder.

References

Adler, C. M., Holland, S. K., Schmithorst, V., Tuchfarber, M. J., & Strakowski, S. M. (2004). Changes in neuronal activation in patients with bipolar disorder during performance of a working memory task. *Bipolar Disorder, 6*(6), 540–549.

Almeida, J. R., Versace, A., Hassel, S., Kupfer, D. J., & Phillips, M. L. (2010). Elevated amygdala activity to sad facial expressions: A state marker of bipolar but not unipolar depression. *Biological Psychiatry, 67*(5), 414–421.

Altshuler, L., Tekell, J., Biswas, K., Kilbourne, A. M., Evans, D., Tang, D., & Bauer, M. S. (2007). Executive function and employment status among veterans with bipolar disorder. *Psychiatric Services, 58*(11), 1441–1447.

Altshuler, L. L., Ventura, J., van Gorp, W. G., Green, M. F., Theberge, D. C., & Mintz, J. (2004). Neurocognitive function in clinically stable men with bipolar I disorder or schizophrenia and normal control subjects. *Biological Psychiatry, 56*(8), 560–569.

American Psychiatric Association (2000). *Diagnostic and statistical manual of mental disorders—text revision* (4th edn). Washington, DC: American Psychiatric Publishing.

American Psychiatric Association. (2013). *Diagnostic and statistical manual of mental disorders* (5th edn). Washington, DC: American Psychiatric Association.

Arts, B., Jabben, N., Krabbendam, L., & van Os, J. (2008). Meta-analyses of cognitive functioning in euthymic bipolar patients and their first-degree relatives. *Psychological Medicine, 38*(6), 771–785.

Bauer, M. S., McBride, L., Williford, W. O., Glick, H., Kinosian, B., Altshuler, L., … & Sajatovic, M. (2006a). Collaborative care for bipolar disorder: Part I. Intervention and implementation in a randomized effectiveness trial. *Psychiatric Services, 57*(7), 927–936.

Bauer, M. S., McBride, L., Williford, W. O., Glick, H., Kinosian, B., Altshuler, L., … & Sajatovic, M. (2006b). Collaborative care for bipolar disorder: Part II. Impact on clinical outcome, function, and costs. *Psychiatric Services, 57*(7), 937–945.

Beck, L. H., Bransome, E. D., Jr., Mirsky, A. F., Rosvold, H. E., & Sarason, I. (1956). A continuous performance test of brain damage. *Journal of Consulting Psychology, 20*(5), 343–350.

Belmaker, R. H. (2007). Treatment of bipolar depression. *New England Journal of Medicine, 356*(17), 1771–1773.

Bersudsky, Y., & Belmaker, R. H. (2009). 'Treatment of bipolar disorder: A systematic review of available data and clinical perspectives' by Fountoulakis & Vieta (2008). *International Journal of Neuropsychopharmacology, 12*(2), 285–286.

Bonnin, C. M., Martinez-Aran, A., Torrent, C., Pacchiarotti, I., Rosa, A. R., Franco, C., … & Vieta, E. (2010). Clinical and neurocognitive predictors of functional outcome in bipolar euthymic patients: A long-term, follow-up study. *Journal of Affective Disorders, 121*(1–2), 156–160.

Bonnin, C. M., Torrent, C., Goikolea, J. M., Reinares, M., Sole, B., Valenti, M., … & Vieta, E. (2013). The impact of repeated manic episodes and executive dysfunction on work adjustment in bipolar disorder. *European Archives of Psychiatry and Clinical Neuroscience, 264*(3), 247–54.

Bora, E., Yucel, M., & Pantelis, C. (2009). Cognitive endophenotypes of bipolar disorder: A meta-analysis of neuropsychological deficits in euthymic patients and their first-degree relatives. *Journal of Affective Disorders, 113*(1–2), 1–20.

Carlson, G. A., & Goodwin, E. K. (1973). The stages of mania: A longitudinal analysis of the manic episode. *Archives of General Psychiatry, 28*, 221–228.

Cavanagh, J. T., Van Beck, M., Muir, W., & Blackwood, D. H. (2002). Case-control study of neurocognitive function in euthymic patients with bipolar disorder: An association with mania. *British Journal of Psychiatry, 180*, 320–326.

Chang, K., Adleman, N. E., Dienes, K., Simeonova, D. I., Menon, V., & Reiss, A. (2004). Anomalous prefrontal-subcortical activation in familial pediatric bipolar disorder: A functional magnetic resonance imaging investigation. *Archives of General Psychiatry, 61*(8), 781–792.

Chen, C.-H., Suckling, J., Lennox, B. R., Ooi, C., & Bullmore, E. T. (2011). A quantitative meta-analysis of MRI studies in bipolar disorder. *Bipolar Disorder, 13*(1), 1–15.

Choi, J., & Medalia, A. (2005). Factors associated with a positive response to cognitive remediation in a community psychiatric sample. *Psychiatric Services, 56*(5), 602–604.

Clark, L., Iversen, S. D., & Goodwin, G. M. (2002). Sustained attention deficit in bipolar disorder. *British Journal of Psychiatry, 180,* 313–319.

Cochran, S. D. (1984). Preventing medical noncompliance in the outpatient treatment of bipolar affective disorders. *Journal of Consulting and Clinical Psychology, 52*(5), 873–878.

Colom, F., Veita, E., Tacchi, M. J., SanchezMoreno, J., & Scott, J. (2005). Identifying and improving non-adherence in bipolar disorders. *Bipolar Disorder,* 7(Suppl5), 24–31.

Colom, F., Vieta, E., Sanchez-Moreno, J., Palomino-Otiniano, R., Reinares, M., Goikolea, J. M., ... & Martinez-Aran, A. (2009). Group psychoeducation for stabilised bipolar disorders: 5-year outcome of a randomised clinical trial. *British Journal of Psychiatry, 194*(3), 260–265.

Deckersbach, T., McMurrich, S., Ogutha, J., Savage, C. R., Sachs, G., & Rauch, S. L. (2004). Characteristics of non-verbal memory impairment in bipolar disorder: The role of encoding strategies. *Psychological Medicine, 34*(5), 823–832.

Deckersbach, T., Savage, C., Reilly-Harrington, N., Clark, L., Sachs, G., & Rauch, S. L. (2004). Episodic memory impairment in bipolar disorder and obsessive-compulsive disorder: The role of memory strategies. *Bipolar Disorder, 6*(3), 233–244.

Deckersbach, T., Dougherty, D. D., Savage, C., McMurrich, S., Fischman, A. J., Nierenberg, A., ... & Rauch, S. L. (2006). Impaired recruitment of the dorsolateral prefrontal cortex and hippocampus during encoding in bipolar disorder. *Biological Psychiatry, 59*(2), 138–146.

Deckersbach, T., Nierenberg, A. A., Kessler, R., Lund, H. G., Ametrano, R. M., Sachs, G., ... & Dougherty, D. (2010). Cognitive rehabilitation for bipolar disorder: An open trial for employed patients with residual depressive symptoms. *CNS Neuroscience & Therapeutics, 16*(5), 298–307.

Deckersbach, T., Rauch, S. L., Buhlmann, U., Ostacher, M. J., Beucke, J. C., Nierenberg, A. A., ... & Dougherty, D. D. (2008). An fMRI investigation of working memory and sadness in females with bipolar disorder: A brief report. *Bipolar Disorder, 10*(8), 928–942.

Deckersbach, T., Savage, C. R., Dougherty, D. D., Bohne, A., Loh, R., Nierenberg, A., ... & Rauch, S. L. (2005). Spontaneous and directed application of verbal learning strategies in bipolar disorder and obsessive-compulsive disorder. *Bipolar Disorder,* 7(2), 166–175.

Delis, D. C., Kramer, J. H., Kaplan, E., & Ober, B. A. (2000). *California Verbal Learning Test, Adult Version.* 2nd edn. San Antonio, TX: The Psychological Corporation.

Dickerson, F. B., Boronow, J. J., Stallings, C. R., Origoni, A. E., Cole, S., & Yolken, R. H. (2004). Association between cognitive functioning and employment status of persons with bipolar disorder. *Psychiatric Services, 55*(1), 54–58.

Diler, R. S., de Almeida, J. R., Ladouceur, C., Birmaher, B., Axelson, D., & Phillips, M. (2013). Neural activity to intense positive versus negative stimuli can help differentiate bipolar disorder from unipolar major depressive disorder in depressed adolescents: A pilot fMRI study. *Psychiatry Research, 214*(3), 277–284.

Dittmann, S., Seemuller, F., Schwarz, M. J., Kleindienst, N., Stampfer, R., Zach, J., ... & Severus, E. (2007). Association of cognitive deficits with elevated homocysteine levels in euthymic bipolar patients and its impact on psychosocial functioning: Preliminary results. *Bipolar Disorder, 9*(1–2), 63–70.

Dunner, D. L. (2005). Atypical antipsychotics: Efficacy across bipolar disorder subpopulations. *Journal of Clinical Psychiatry, 66*(Suppl 3), 20–27.

Dupont, R. M., Jernigan, T. L., Butters, N., Delis, D., Hesselink, J. R., Heindel, W., & Gillin, J. C. (1990). Subcortical abnormalities detected in bipolar affective disorder using magnetic resonance imaging. Clinical and neuropsychological significance. *Archives of General Psychiatry, 47*(1), 55–59.

Fagiolini, A., Kupfer, D. J., Masalehdan, A., Scott, J. A., Houck, P. R., & Frank, E. (2005). Functional impairment in the remission phase of bipolar disorder. *Bipolar Disorder, 7*(3), 281–285.

Frank, E., Swartz, H. A., & Kupfer, D. J. (2000). Interpersonal and social rhythm therapy: Managing the chaos of bipolar disorder. *Biological Psychiatry, 48*(6), 593–604.

Frank, E., Hlastala, S., Ritenour, A., & Houck, P. (1997). Inducing lifestyle regularity in recovering bipolar disorder patients: Results from the maintenance therapies in bipolar disorder protocol. *Biological Psychiatry, 41*(12), 1165–1173.

Frank, E., Kupfer, D. J., Thase, M. E., Mallinger, A. G., Swartz, H. A., Fagiolini, A. M., … & Monk, T. (2005). Two-year outcomes for interpersonal and social rhythm therapy in individuals with bipolar I disorder. *Archives of General Psychiatry, 62*(9), 996–1004.

Frank, E., Soreca, I., Swartz, H. A., Fagiolini, A. M., Mallinger, A. G., Thase, M. E., … & Kupfer, D. J. (2008). The role of interpersonal and social rhythm therapy in improving occupational functioning in patients with bipolar I disorder. *American Journal of Psychiatry, 165*(12), 1559–1565.

Geddes, J. R., Calabrese, J. R., & Goodwin, G. M. (2009). Lamotrigine for treatment of bipolar depression: Independent meta-analysis and meta-regression of individual patient data from five randomised trials. *British Journal of Psychiatry, 194*(1), 4–9.

Ghaemi, S. N., Hsu, D. J., Thase, M. E., Wisniewski, S. R., Nierenberg, A. A., Miyahara, S., & Sachs, G. (2006). Pharmacological treatment patterns at study entry for the first 500 STEP-BD participants. *Psychiatric Services, 57*(5), 660–665.

Gitlin, M. J., Swendsen, J., Heller, T. L., & Hammen, C. (1995). Relapse and impairment in bipolar disorder. *American Journal of Psychiatry, 152*(11), 1635–1640.

Glahn, D. C., Robinson, J. L., Tordesillas-Gutierrez, D., Monkul, E. S., Holmes, M. K., Green, M. J., & Bearden, C. E. (2010). Fronto-temporal dysregulation in asymptomatic bipolar I patients: A paired associate functional MRI study. *Human Brain Mapping, 31*(7), 1041–1051.

Goldberg, J. F., & Burdick, K. E. (2001). Cognitive side effects of anticonvulsants. *Journal of Clinical Psychiatry, 62*(Suppl 14), 27–33.

Golden, C. J. (1978). *Stroop Colour and Word Test*. Chicago, IL: Stoelting.

Golden, C. J., & Freshwater, S. M. (2002). *Stroop Color and Word Test. A manual for clinical and experimental uses*. Wood Dale, IL: Stoelting Co.

Grace, J., & Malloy, P. F. (2001). *Frontal systems behavior rating scale (FrSBe) professional manual*. Lutz, FL: Psychological Assessment Resources.

Graf, P., & Schacter, D. L. (1985). Implicit and explicit memory for new associations in normal and amnesic subjects. *Journal of Experimental Psychology: Learning, Memory, and Cognition, 11*(3), 501–518.

Hassel, S., Almeida, J. R., Kerr, N., Nau, S., Ladouceur, C. D., Fissell, K., … & Phillips, M. L. (2008). Elevated striatal and decreased dorsolateral prefrontal cortical activity in response to emotional stimuli in euthymic bipolar disorder: No associations with psychotropic medication load. *Bipolar Disorder, 10*(8), 916–927.

Heaton, R. K. (1981). *Wisconsin Card Sorting Test manual*. Odessa, FL: Psychological Assessment Resources.

Heaton, R. K., Chelune, G. J., Talley, J. L., Kay, G. G., & Curtiss, G. (1993). *Wisconsin Card Sorting Test manual. Revised and expanded*. Odessa, FL: Psychological Assessment Resources.

Jaeger, J., Berns, S., Loftus, S., Gonzalez, C., & Czobor, P. (2007). Neurocognitive test performance predicts functional recovery from acute exacerbation leading to hospitalization in bipolar disorder. *Bipolar Disorder, 9*(1–2), 93–102.

Judd, L. L., Akiskal, H. S., Maser, J. D., Zeller, P. J., Endicott, J., Coryell, W., ... & Keller, M. B. (1998a). Major depressive disorder: A prospective study of residual subthreshold depressive symptoms as predictor of rapid relapse. *Journal of Affective Disorders, 50*(2–3), 97–108.

Judd, L. L., Akiskal, H. S., Maser, J. D., Zeller, P. J., Endicott, J., Coryell, W., ... Keller, M. B. (1998b). A prospective 12-year study of subsyndromal and syndromal depressive symptoms in unipolar major depressive disorders. *Archives of General Psychiatry, 55*(8), 694–700.

Judd, L. L., Akiskal, H. S., Schettler, P. J., Coryell, W., Endicott, J., Maser, J. D., ... & Keller, M. B. (2003). A prospective investigation of the natural history of the long-term weekly symptomatic status of bipolar II disorder. *Archives of General Psychiatry, 60*(3), 261–269.

Judd, L. L., Akiskal, H. S., Schettler, P. J., Endicott, J., Leon, A. C., Solomon, D. A., ... & Keller, M. B. (2005). Psychosocial disability in the course of bipolar I and II disorders: A prospective, comparative, longitudinal study. *Archives of General Psychiatry, 62*(12), 1322–1330.

Judd, L. L., Akiskal, H. S., Schettler, P. J., Endicott, J., Maser, J., Solomon, D. A., ... & Keller, M. B. (2002). The long-term natural history of the weekly symptomatic status of bipolar I disorder. *Archives of General Psychiatry, 59*(6), 530–537.

Judd, L. L., Schettler, P. J., Akiskal, H. S., Coryell, W., Leon, A. C., Maser, J. D., & Solomon, D. A. (2008). Residual symptom recovery from major affective episodes in bipolar disorders and rapid episode relapse/recurrence. *Archives of General Psychiatry, 65*(4), 386–394.

Judd, L. L., Schettler, P. J., Akiskal, H. S., Maser, J., Coryell, W., Solomon, D., ... & Keller, M. (2003). Long-term symptomatic status of bipolar I vs. bipolar II disorders. *International Journal of Neuropsychopharmacology, 6*(2), 127–137.

Judd, L. L., Schettler, P. J., Solomon, D. A., Maser, J. D., Coryell, W., Endicott, J., & Akiskal, H. S. (2008). Psychosocial disability and work role function compared across the long-term course of bipolar I, bipolar II and unipolar major depressive disorders. *Journal of Affective Disorder, 108*(1–2), 49–58.

Kapur, S., Tulving, E., Cabeza, R., McIntosh, A. R., Houle, S., & Craik, F. I. (1996). The neural correlates of intentional learning of verbal materials: A PET study in humans. *Cognitive Brain Research, 4*(4), 243–249.

Keck, P. E., Jr., McElroy, S. L., Strakowski, S. M., West, S. A., Sax, K. W., Hawkins, J. M., ... & Haggard, P. (1998). 12-month outcome of patients with bipolar disorder following hospitalization for a manic or mixed episode. *American Journal of Psychiatry, 155*(5), 646–652.

Kessing, L. V., Andersen, P. K., & Mortensen, P. B. (1998). Predictors of recurrence in affective disorder. A case register study. *Journal of Affective Disorders, 49*(2), 101–108.

Kessler, R. C., Chiu, W. T., Demler, O., Merikangas, K. R., & Walters, E. E. (2005). Prevalence, severity, and comorbidity of 12-month DSM-IV disorders in the National Comorbidity Survey Replication. *Archives of General Psychiatry, 62*(6), 617–627.

Kessler, R. C., Akiskal, H. S., Ames, M., Birnbaum, H., Greenberg, P., Hirschfeld, R. M., … & Wang, P. S. (2006). Prevalence and effects of mood disorders on work performance in a nationally representative sample of U.S. workers. *American Journal of Psychiatry, 163*(9), 1561–1568.

Kogan, J. N., Otto, M. W., Bauer, M. S., Dennehy, E. B., Miklowitz, D. J., Zhang, H. W., … & Sachs, G. S. (2004). Demographic and diagnostic characteristics of the first 1000 patients enrolled in the Systematic Treatment Enhancement Program for Bipolar Disorder (STEP-BD). *Bipolar Disorder, 6*(6), 460–469.

Lagopoulos, J., & Malhi, G. (2011). Impairments in "top-down" processing in bipolar disorder: A simultaneous fMRI-GSR study. *Psychiatry Research, 192*(2), 100–108.

Lagopoulos, J., & Malhi, G. S. (2007). A functional magnetic resonance imaging study of emotional Stroop in euthymic bipolar disorder. *Neuroreport, 18*(15), 1583–1587.

Lagopoulos, J., Ivanovski, B., & Malhi, G. S. (2007). An event-related functional MRI study of working memory in euthymic bipolar disorder. *Journal of Psychiatry & Neuroscience, 32*(3), 174–184.

Lam, D. H., Hayward, P., Watkins, E. R., Wright, K., & Sham, P. (2005). Relapse prevention in patients with bipolar disorder: Cognitive therapy outcome after 2 years. *American Journal of Psychiatry, 162*(2), 324–329.

Lam, D. H., Watkins, E. R., Hayward, P., Bright, J., Wright, K., Kerr, N., … & Sham, P. (2003). A randomized controlled study of cognitive therapy for relapse prevention for bipolar affective disorder: Outcome of the first year. *Archives of General Psychiatry, 60*(2), 145–152.

Lu, P. H., Boone, K. B., Cozolino, L., & Mitchell, C. (2003). Effectiveness of the Rey-Osterrieth Complex Figure Test and the Meyers and Meyers recognition trial in the detection of suspect effort. *Clinical Neuropsychology, 17*(3), 426–440.

Macqueen, G., & Young, T. (2003). Cognitive effects of atypical antipsychotics: Focus on bipolar spectrum disorders. *Bipolar Disorder, 5*(Suppl 2), 53–61.

MacQueen, G. M., Young, L. T., & Joffe, R. T. (2001). A review of psychosocial outcome in patients with bipolar disorder. *Acta Psychiatrica Scandinavica, 103*(3), 163–170.

Malhi, G. S., Lagopoulos, J., Sachdev, P. S., Ivanovski, B., & Shnier, R. (2005). An emotional Stroop functional MRI study of euthymic bipolar disorder. *Bipolar Disorder, 7*(Suppl 5), 58–69.

Martinez-Aran, A., Torrent, C., Sole, B., Bonnin, C. M., Rosa, A. R., Sanchez-Moreno, J., & Vieta, E. (2011). Functional remediation for bipolar disorder. *Clinical Practice and Epidemiology in Mental Health, 7*, 112–116.

Martinez-Aran, A., Vieta, E., Colom, F., Torrent, C., Sanchez-Moreno, J., Reinares, M., … & Salamero, M. (2004). Cognitive impairment in euthymic bipolar patients: Implications for clinical and functional outcome. *Bipolar Disorder, 6*(3), 224–232.

Martinez-Aran, A., Vieta, E., Reinares, M., Colom, F., Torrent, C., Sanchez-Moreno, J., … & Salamero, M. (2004). Cognitive function across manic or hypomanic, depressed, and euthymic states in bipolar disorder. *American Journal of Psychiatry, 161*(2), 262–270.

McGurk, S. R., Mueser, K. T., DeRosa, T. J., & Wolfe, R. (2009). Work, recovery, and comorbidity in schizophrenia: A randomized controlled trial of cognitive remediation. *Schizophrenia Bulletin, 35*(2), 319–335.

McGurk, S. R., Twamley, E. W., Sitzer, D. I., McHugo, G. J., & Mueser, K. T. (2007). A meta-analysis of cognitive remediation in schizophrenia. *American Journal of Psychiatry, 164*(12), 1791–1802.

Meusel, L. A., Hall, G. B., Fougere, P., McKinnon, M. C., & Macqueen, G. M. (2013). Neural correlates of cognitive remediation in patients with mood disorders. *Psychiatry Research: Neuroimaging, 214*(2), 142–152.

Meyer, T. D., & Hautzinger, M. (2012). Cognitive behaviour therapy and supportive therapy for bipolar disorders: Relapse rates for treatment period and 2-year follow-up. *Psychological Medicine, 42*(7), 1429–1439.

Meyers, J., & Meyers, K. (1995). *Rey Complex Figure and Recognition Trial: Professional manual.* Odessa, FL: Ann Arbor Publishers.

Miklowitz, D. J., & Johnson, S. L. (2006). The psychopathology and treatment of bipolar disorder. *Annual Review of Clinical Psychology, 2*, 199–235.

Miklowitz, D. J., George, E. L., Richards, J. A., Simoneau, T. L., & Suddath, R. L. (2003). A randomized study of family-focused psychoeducation and pharmacotherapy in the outpatient management of bipolar disorder. *Archives of General Psychiatry, 60*(9), 904–912.

Miklowitz, D. J., Otto, M. W., Frank, E., Reilly-Harrington, N. A., Wisniewski, S. R., Kogan, J. N., … & Sachs, G. S. (2007). Psychosocial treatments for bipolar depression: A 1-year randomized trial from the Systematic Treatment Enhancement Program. *Archives of General Psychiatry, 64*(4), 419–427.

Monks, P. J., Thompson, J. M., Bullmore, E. T., Suckling, J., Brammer, M. J., Williams, S. C., …& Curtis, V. A. (2004). A functional MRI study of working memory task in euthymic bipolar disorder: Evidence for task-specific dysfunction. *Bipolar Disorder, 6*(6), 550–564.

Morris, C. D., Miklowitz, D. J., Wisniewski, S. R., Giese, A. A., Thomas, M. R., & Allen, M. H. (2005). Care satisfaction, hope, and life functioning among adults with bipolar disorder: Data from the first 1000 participants in the Systematic Treatment Enhancement Program. *Comprehensive Psychiatry, 46*(2), 98–104.

Morselli, P. L., & Elgie, R. (2003). GAMIAN-Europe/BEAM survey I–Global analysis of a patient questionnaire circulated to 3450 members of 12 European advocacy groups operating in the field of mood disorders. *Bipolar Disorder, 5*(4), 265–278.

Murray, C. J., & Lopez, A. D. (1997). Global mortality, disability, and the contribution of risk factors: Global Burden of Disease Study. *Lancet, 349*(9063), 1436–1442.

Pachet, A. K., & Wisniewski, A. M. (2003). The effects of lithium on cognition: An updated review. *Psychopharmacology (Berl), 170*(3), 225–234.

Peralta, V., & Cuesta, M. J. (1998). Lack of insight in mood disorders. *Journal of Affective Disorders, 49*(1), 55–58.

Perlis, R. H., Ostacher, M. J., Patel, J. K., Marangell, L. B., Zhang, H., Wisniewski, S. R., … & Thase, M. E. (2006). Predictors of recurrence in bipolar disorder: Primary outcomes from the Systematic Treatment Enhancement Program for Bipolar Disorder (STEP-BD). *American Journal of Psychiatry, 163*(2), 217–224.

Perry, A., Tarrier, N., Morriss, R., McCarthy, E., & Limb, K. (1999). Randomised controlled trial of efficacy of teaching patients with bipolar disorder to identify early symptoms of relapse and obtain treatment. *British Medical Journal, 318*(7177), 149–153.

Phillips, M. L., Ladouceur, C. D., & Drevets, W. C. (2008). A neural model of voluntary and automatic emotion regulation: Implications for understanding the pathophysiology and neurodevelopment of bipolar disorder. *Molecular Psychiatry, 13*(9), 829, 833–857.

Randolph, C., Tierney, M. C., Mohr, E., & Chase, T. N. (1998). The Repeatable Battery for the Assessment of Neuropsychological Status (RBANS): Preliminary clinical validity. *Journal of Clinical Experimental Neuropsychology, 20*(3), 310–319.

Rea, M. M., Tompson, M. C., Miklowitz, D. J., Goldstein, M. J., Hwang, S., & Mintz, J. (2003). Family-focused treatment versus individual treatment for bipolar disorder: Results of a randomized clinical trial. *Journal of Consulting and Clinical Psychology, 71*(3), 482–492.

Reichenberg, A., Weiser, M., Rabinowitz, J., Caspi, A., Schmeidler, J., Mark, M., ... & Davidson, M. (2002). A population-based cohort study of premorbid intellectual, language, and behavioral functioning in patients with schizophrenia, schizoaffective disorder, and nonpsychotic bipolar disorder. *American Journal of Psychiatry, 159*(12), 2027–2035.

Reitan, R.M. (1958). Validity of the trailmaking test as an indication of organic brain damage. *Perceptual & Motor Skills, 8*, 271–276.

Robinson, L. J., Thompson, J. M., Gallagher, P., Goswami, U., Young, A. H., Ferrier, I. N., & Moore, P. B. (2006). A meta-analysis of cognitive deficits in euthymic patients with bipolar disorder. *Journal of Affective Disorders, 93*(1–3), 105–115.

Rosa, A. R., Gonzalez-Ortega, I., Gonzalez-Pinto, A., Echeburua, E., Comes, M., Martinez-Aran, A., ... & Vieta, E. (2012). One-year psychosocial functioning in patients in the early vs. late stage of bipolar disorder. *Acta Psychiatrica Scandinavica, 125*(4), 335–341.

Roy-Byrne, P., Post, R. M., Uhde, T. W., Porcu, T., & Davis, D. (1985). The longitudinal course of recurrent affective illness: Life chart data from research patients at the NIMH. *Acta Psychiatrica Scandinavica Supplementum, 317*, 1–34.

Safren, S.A., Perlman, C. A., Sprich, S., & Otto, M. W. (2005). *Mastering your adult ADHD. A cognitive behavioral treatment program*. New York: Oxford University Press.

Sanderson, K., & Andrews, G. (2006). Common mental disorders in the workforce: Recent findings from descriptive and social epidemiology. *Canadian Journal of Psychiatry, 51*(2), 63–75.

Scott, J., & Pope, M. (2002). Self-reported adherence to treatment with mood stabilizers, plasma levels, and psychiatric hospitalization. *American Journal of Psychiatry, 159*(11), 1927–1929.

Scott, J., & Tacchi, M. J. (2002). A pilot study of concordance therapy for individuals with bipolar disorders who are non-adherent with lithium prophylaxis. *Bipolar Disorder, 4*(6), 386–392.

Scott, J., Paykel, E., Morriss, R., Bentall, R., Kinderman, P., Johnson, T., ... & Hayhurst, H. (2006). Cognitive-behavioural therapy for bipolar disorder. *British Journal of Psychiatry, 188*, 488–489.

Simon, G. E., Ludman, E. J., Bauer, M. S., Unutzer, J., & Operskalski, B. (2006). Long-term effectiveness and cost of a systematic care program for bipolar disorder. *Archives of General Psychiatry, 63*(5), 500–508.

Sohlberg, M. M., & Mateer, C. A. (2001). *Cognitive rehabilitation. An integrative neuropsychological approach*. New York: The Guilford Press.

Suppes, T., Leverich, G. S., Keck, P. E., Nolen, W. A., Denicoff, K. D., Altshuler, L. L., ... & Post, R. M. (2001). The Stanley Foundation Bipolar Treatment Outcome Network. II. Demographics and illness characteristics of the first 261 patients. *Journal of Affective Disorders, 67*(1–3), 45–59.

Tohen, M., Zarate, C. A., Jr., Hennen, J., Khalsa, H. M., Strakowski, S. M., Gebre-Medhin, P., ... & Baldessarini, R. J. (2003). The McLean-Harvard First-Episode Mania Study: Prediction of recovery and first recurrence. *American Journal of Psychiatry, 160*(12), 2099–2107.

Torrent, C., Bonnin, C. D. M., Martinez-Aran, A., Valle, J., Amann, B. L., Gonzalez-Pinto, A., ... & Vieta, E. (2013). Efficacy of functional remediation in bipolar disorder: A multicenter randomized controlled study. *American Journal of Psychiatry, 170*(8), 852–859.

Torrent, C., Martinez-Aran, A., Daban, C., Sanchez-Moreno, J., Comes, M., Goikolea, J. M., ... & Vieta, E. (2006). Cognitive impairment in bipolar II disorder. *British Journal of Psychiatry, 189*, 254–259.

Torres, I. J., Boudreau, V. G., & Yatham, L. N. (2007). Neuropsychological functioning in euthymic bipolar disorder: A meta-analysis. *Acta Psychiatrica Scandinavica Supplementum,* (434), 17–26.

Trede, K., Salvatore, P., Baethge, C., Gerhard, A., Maggini, C., & Baldessarini, R. J. (2005). Manic-depressive illness: Evolution in Kraepelin's Textbook, 1883–1926. *Harvard Review of Psychiatry, 13*(3), 155–178.

US Census Bureau (2005). Population estimates by demographic characteristics. Table 2: Annual estimates of the population by selected age groups and sex for the United States: April 1, 2000 to July 1, 2004 (NC-EST2004–02). Source: Population Division, U.S. Census Bureau. Release Date: June 9, 2005. http://www.census.gov/popest/national/asrh/.

Van der Schot, A., Kahn, R., Ramsey, N., Nolen, W., & Vink, M. (2010). Trait and state dependent functional impairments in bipolar disorder. *Psychiatry Research, 184*(3), 135–142.

van Gorp, W. G., Altshuler, L., Theberge, D. C., Wilkins, J., & Dixon, W. (1998). Cognitive impairment in euthymic bipolar patients with and without prior alcohol dependence. A preliminary study. *Archives of General Psychiatry, 55*(1), 41–46.

Wechsler, D. (1995). *Wechsler Adult Intelligence Scale.* New York Pschological Corporation.

Wechsler, D. (1997). *Wechsler Adult Intelligence Scale.* San Antonio, TX: Harcour Assessment.

Zammit, S., Allebeck, P., David, A. S., Dalman, C., Hemmingsson, T., Lundberg, I., & Lewis, G. (2004). A longitudinal study of premorbid IQ Score and risk of developing schizophrenia, bipolar disorder, severe depression, and other nonaffective psychoses. *Archives of General Psychiatry, 61*(4), 354–360.

Zubieta, J. K., Huguelet, P., O'Neil, R. L., & Giordani, B. J. (2001). Cognitive function in euthymic bipolar I disorder. *Psychiatry Research, 102*(1), 9–20.

11

TREATMENT OF PHANTOM LIMB PAIN

Application of Neuroscience to a Disorder of Neuroplasticity

John R. McQuaid

While the primary focus of this book is the application of advances in cognitive neuroscience to understanding and treating psychopathology, science is leading to profound changes in our understanding of the etiology and treatment of all disorders associated with the central nervous system (CNS). Key exemplars that have served as a model for understanding neuroplasticity include phantom limb sensation (PLS) and, in particular, phantom limb pain (PLP). These sensations that map to a missing limb after amputation or other loss of innervation are common and frequently impairing. For example, 76 percent of combat veterans from the most recent conflicts, Operation Enduring Freedom and Operation Iraqi Freedom, reported experiencing PLP (Reiber et al., 2010).

While there are descriptions of PLS in the medical literature dating back to the sixteenth century (Wade & Finger, 2003), the understanding of its biological basis has been transformed within the last twenty years by the combination of behavioral observation, psychophysiology, and neuroimaging. The understanding of the etiology of PLS from a neurocognitive perspective has led to a model for understanding neuroplasticity. However, the neurocognitive view of PLS also has important clinical application for developing innovative treatments.

The current chapter provides an overview and description of PLS and PLP and then reviews proposed etiological models. The literature supporting the maladaptive neural plasticity model of PLP is then discussed. The final sections of the chapter describe treatment interventions developed based on the neural plasticity hypothesis, the research literature regarding their efficacy, and proposed future directions for intervention.

Overview of Phantom Limb

PLS is the perception of sensory response from a limb or body part that has been amputated or otherwise deafferentated. Some studies find PLS occurs in over 80 percent of amputees (e.g., Dijkstra, Geertzen, Stewart, & van der Schans, 2002). Within the definition of PLS, there is a great deal of variability, including the experience of sensations that are not at all impairing and some that are even welcomed by the individual. However, up to 80 percent of amputees with PLS report PLP (Kooljman, Dijkstra, Geertzen, Elzinga, & van der Schans, 2000; Richardson, Glenn, Nurmikko, & Horgan, 2006). In one study, 83.6 percent of amputees with PLS experienced PLP (Dijkstra et al., 2002). The intensity of PLP varied from mild to severe, as did the level of associated disability. Of those with PLP, 23 percent reported it caused high disability. In a sample of thirty combat veterans with amputations within the past five years, 78 percent reported PLP at some time (Ketz, 2008). Patients reported descriptors of sensation that included sharp pain, cramping, itchiness, sensitivity, and burning. The site of pain within the limb also varied. In addition, the presence of residual limb pain (that is, pain in the remaining stump) and PLP were positively correlated.

In addition to distress due to the pain itself, PLP can lead to impairments in functioning and quality of life above and beyond the impairment due to loss of limb. Lower-limb amputees with PLP reported poorer functioning in general, reduced quality of life, and greater psychological distress than amputees without PLP (Kashani, 1983; van der Schans, Geertzen, Tanneke Schoppen, & Dijkstra, 2002). Older patients with a lower-limb amputation and PLP were significantly less likely to use a prosthesis than those without PLP, greatly reducing their mobility (Spruit-van Eijk et al., 2012).

PLSs vary dramatically not only in frequency, duration, and intensity but in subjective quality. General PLS can include the perception of the fully intact limb. A subset of limbs are distorted relative to the actual structure of the lost limb. For example, telescoping (the perceived retraction of a portion of the phantom into the stump, creating the perception that the limb is shorter than the actual limb was) is a common experience (Schmalzl et al., 2011). Some individuals perceive the ability to move and control the limb while others have limbs frozen in place. This range of experience in both the sensory map of the limb and level of motor control reflects the role of both the somatosensory and motor cortices in the experience of PLS.

Painful sensations include the full range of pain descriptors, such as cramping, burning, stabbing, and shocking sensations (Katz, 2000; Sherman, 1997). Frequency, as noted, can vary from intermittent to continuous, and for those with intermittent PLP, duration of sensation can vary from brief seconds to prolonged hours of sensation (Ketz, 2008).

The literature examining mediators and moderators of PLP has generated mixed findings. Several authors report that prevalence or severity of PLP is not related to the nature of amputation (e.g., vascular versus traumatic amputations; Sherman, 1997; Ephraim, Wegener, MacKenzie, Dillingham, & Pezzin, 2005; Houghton, Nicholls, Houghton, Saadah, & McColl, 1994), age (Ephraim et al., 2005), level of amputation (Ephraim et al., 2005), or military versus civilian populations (Sherman, 1997). One study of PLS and PLP found they are more common in lower-limb amputees than upper-limb amputees, and PLP was more common in proximal versus distal amputations, bilateral amputations, and when stump pain was present (Dijkstra et al., 2002). In contrast, lower rates of PLP in lower-limb amputees have also been reported and, in this study, females had higher rates of PLP than males (Bosmans, Geertzen, Post, van der Schans, & Dijkstra, 2010). The differences in findings may reflect differences in definitions of pain and demonstrate the complexity of fully understanding PLP. In general, there is extensive variability in the experience in PLP that current models cannot completely explain.

Despite the variability in PLS and PLP, there are some aspects that are generally consistent. There is a much lower rate of PLP in patients missing limbs at birth, with frequency ranging from 8 percent to 18 percent (Melzak, Israel, Lacroix, & Schultz, 1997; Montoya et al., 1998; Wilkins, McGrath, Finley, & Katz, 1998) as is discussed later in this chapter. Although there is some evidence that severity of PLP decreases over time (Bosmans et al., 2010; Dijkstra et al., 2002; Sherman, 1997), the majority of patients continue to experience symptoms for decades. Sherman (1997) found that patients had experienced PLP for an average of twenty-nine years, whereas Katz (2000) found that between 78 percent and 85 percent of amputee patients continued to experience significant amounts of PLP more than twenty-five years after amputation. In a prospective study, the proportion of amputees experiencing PLP reduced from 72 percent eight days after surgery to 59 percent two years after surgery, which is lower than rates reported in other studies (Jensen, Krebs, Nielsen, & Rasmussen, 1985). However, even in this case, more than half of amputees continue to experience PLP over time.

These findings indicate that PLS and PLP are the consequence of cortical remapping that occurs after limb loss rather than the result of a preexisting cognitive structure in place from birth. The fact that symptoms tend to reduce initially and yet, for most patients, are persistent over time suggests that the neural basis for PLS and PLP is at least initially malleable. What is unclear from these findings is what factors facilitate those initial changes and what differentiates between individuals with improvement and those without.

Consideration of PLS Historically

References of phantom limb date back to the sixteenth century. An eighteenth-century physician, William Porterfield, provided a detailed description of his own phantom limb (Wade & Finger, 2003). Porterfield, an expert in optometry, concluded from his experience with PLS that there must be a representation of all that is perceived in the brain and reflected on the conclusion that although the pain was perceived as actually being in a limb, he realized the perception could only be occurring in his mind. He compared this to the perception of color, which he as a vision specialist understood as achieved in the mind but perceived as external. These early observations anticipate the role that the observation of PLS would later play in helping to elucidate how the brain represents perceptual experiences. Similarly, after the Civil War, neurologist Silas Mitchell speculated that phantom limb was the result of sensory input from the remaining nerves in the stump to the cortex (Bourke, 2009). These conceptualizations provided an early template for later recognition of the CNS basis for phantom limb.

The Neural Underpinnings of Phantom Limb

The nature of PLS provides an opportunity to develop and test hypotheses of the relationship among neural input, external stimulation, and cortical organization. In particular, converging lines of evidence related to PLS and PLP support the conclusion that these experiences arise from what has been called "maladaptive neuroplasticity" (Flor, Nikolajsen, & Jensen, 2006). Modern understanding of PLP emphasizes the role of reorganization of the somatosensory and motor cortices after amputation. Functional reorganization of the somatosensory cortex in animals has been demonstrated since the 1970s (see Nardone et al., 2013 for a review). Evidence in rats shows that new connections are established after incomplete deafferentation. Additional studies found evidence that forelimb area activation increases in rats within three days after transection with expansion to the hind limb area deprived of input. Similar patterns were found in both owl and macaque monkeys, with face inputs expanding into the hand areas after hand deafferentation, although some studies that did not completely sever neural input did not find evidence of reorganization.

In humans, it appears that (1) the experience of PLS is associated with the motor and somatosensory cortices associated with the missing limb; (2) PLS and PLP are associated with referred sensation in other body areas in a manner that is predictable based on the organization of the somatosensory and motor cortices and that suggests a reorganization of these structures; and (3) a variety of stimuli can both modify the experience of PLS and PLP as well as modify or even reverse the associated reorganization.

Initial Evidence of the Cortical Basis of PLP

There is strong evidence that the initial establishment of cortical representations of the body requires sensory input (Reilly & Sirigu, 2011). The vast majority of individuals born without a limb do not experience phantom sensation, suggesting that some level of input or experience is needed to establish the organization of these cortical structures and implying neuroplasticity at least at an early period of development (Reilly & Sirigu, 2011). There are rare individuals who do report phantom limb experience with congenitally missing limbs. These examples may represent phantom limb that is acquired through observation and provide more evidence of the power of visual input to facilitate cortical reorganization (Montoya et al., 1998).

Phantom limb perception can be modified by external stimuli, and the patterns with which this occurs provide insight into the relationship of PLS and cortical organization. A series of case studies examining the effect of visual feedback using a mirror device on the reported perception of PLS demonstrated that the perceptual experience could be dramatically modified (Ramachandran & Rogers-Ramachandran, 1996, 2000). Participants who had experienced an amputation and experienced phantom sensation placed their existing limb in position relative to a mirror to create a reflection that aligned with their body in such a manner that the image appeared to be the missing limb. The investigators instructed the participants to move the existing limb and imagine that they were moving the missing limb in parallel. Participants reported significant changes in their perception. In several cases, phantom limbs that were perceived as frozen in place came under voluntary control. In three cases, the participants reported a reduction of pain when moving a limb previously frozen in a cramped position. This evidence that visual input modified the experience of phantom limb implied a neural basis for the experience that was reactive to input and that was modifiable with a relatively brief exposure. Initial studies with the mirror box reported perceptual changes often occurring immediately (Ramachandran & Rogers-Ramachandran, 1996). These findings were consistent with early research that demonstrated that visual input that was in conflict with tactile input would dominate the perception of an object, with recall being more consistent with the visual information (Rock & Victor, 1964). Ramachandran and Rogers-Ramachandran (2000) concluded that PLS was likely a consequence of cortical functioning, and the visual input affected the cortical functioning.

Another key finding was the relationship of PLS to referred sensation (RS), that is, the perception of tactile stimulation in the phantom when another body part is touched. The PLS can be activated or modified by stimulation applied to other body areas, and the relationship of those areas to the organization of somatosensory and motor cortices suggests a predictable relationship based on the organization of the cortex. In the brain, the somatosensory and motor cortex maps of the body are arranged in a manner that is generally consistent with the form of the body. However, in both areas, the hand is mapped adjacent to the face. In a classic example, an individual with an amputated arm reported sensation in the fingers and hand of that limb when a stimulus was applied to the face (Ramachandran, 1998). Other cases showed individuals experiencing stimulation in their phantom when areas of their residual limb (which are also mapped adjacent to the missing limb in the somatosensory cortex) are touched, and this response could be mapped on the residual limb (i.e., literally drawing the shape of the phantom and its response on the stump or face). The relationship was suggestive of a remapping of the cortex in a predictable manner. In a later study, perceived intentional movement of the phantom led to change in the location of the area of the face that when stimulated led to sensation in the phantom (Ramachandran, Brang, & McGeoch, 2010). It is unclear what the neural mechanism would be for this rapid change.

Psychophysiology and Imaging Studies of PLS

Advances in psychophysiology and neuroimaging have provided critical tools to better understand the cortical activity associated with PLS and PLP, and there is a growing body of research that provides evidence in support of cortical reorganization after nerve damage (Nardone et al., 2013). In one of the earliest psychophysiology studies with PLS, investigators compared responses to transcranial magnetic stimulation (TMS) among patients who had lost limbs to amputations, a patient who was missing a limb since birth, and normal controls (Cohen, Bandinelli, Findley, & Hallett, 1991). They found that while TMS elicited phantom movements in those who had amputations, it did not in the participant who was born missing a hand. This suggests that cortical mapping developed in response to experience with the limb and was at least somewhat intact after loss of the limb. This finding was replicated by Mercier and colleagues (2006). They found that TMS applied to the area of the motor cortex associated with the missing limb could generate movement perception in the phantom. This occurred even when the participant had no voluntary control, suggesting that hand representation is maintained in the reorganized motor cortex.

Cohen and colleagues (1991) also found evidence of cortical reorganization in their study. The authors examined the size of the area of the motor cortex that, when stimulated, activated the muscles in the stump on the amputation side or the matching muscles in the intact limb. They found that stimulation of a larger area of the cortex led to muscle activation in the stump muscles than in the intact muscle, indicating that the cortical area associated with stump muscles had expanded. The cortical area associated with stump muscle activation was also larger in the participants with amputations than in the control participants.

Flor and colleagues (1995) tested the hypothesis that phantom limb resulted from cortical reorganization after amputation by providing mild stimulation to a series of positions on the intact hand and face. They recorded magnetic fields associated with the stimulation and superimposed them on a map of the participant's brain previously generated using magnetic resonance imaging (MRI). The investigators found that the amount of cortical reorganization was positively correlated with the PLP. They proposed that PLS and PLP are the consequence of maladaptive neural plasticity, with areas of the brain that are adjacent to that where the missing limb is mapped "invading" that area. Additional findings indicate the severity of PLP was associated with the extent of the remapping experienced as assessed with fMRI (Lotz, Flor, Grodd, Larbig, & Birbaumer, 2001).

An imaging study examining RS found results consistent with this model (Bjorkman et al., 2012). In a sample of forearm amputees, stimulation of those areas of the residual limb now mapped to the phantom led to activation in the hand area of the somatosensory cortex (e.g., touching the finger map on the limb activated the associated cortex area; Bjorkman et al., 2012). The investigators first provided stimulation to the stump of six hand amputees and mapped where on the stump stimulation elicited phantom perception (e.g., the point on the stump where a phantom finger perceived being touched). They then stimulated those points while conducting fMRI and found that stimulation of the phantom map on the stump was associated with activation of a greater area of the somatosensory cortex than stimulation of the stump outside the area of the hand map. As with previous studies, the authors conclude that the data support a remapping of the cortex.

Results in normal controls have demonstrated that remapping can be elicited with even fairly brief interventions. In a study designed to examine the influence of discrepancies between visual perception and tactile stimulation, the investigators used high-density 128-channel electroencephalography (EEG) to examine whether the mirror illusion led to changes in the location of cortical generation in response to tactile stimulation (Egsgaard, Petrini, Christoffersen, & Arendt-Nielsen, 2011). They found that a brief illusion (using a mirror image to create the illusion that both thumbs were being stimulated when only one was, or conversely that neither was being stimulated when one was) produced a significant change in EEG location relative to a control condition (directly observing the stimulation). In particular, for men, N70 dipole localization shifted between the two illusions towards the midline, suggesting cortical reorganization in the course of the illusion. Interestingly, the authors did not find the same results in women and suggest that differences between gender on lateralization and visuospatial tasks may contribute to these findings. Such differences may imply different responsivity to visually based interventions for PLP between men and women. More important, however, it appears that visual feedback can significantly influence brain localization even in a very brief period.

Another relevant finding is that the nature of the influence of visual feedback on the brain appears to depend on the presence of PLP. Diers and colleagues (2010) compared amputees with or without PLP and controls with intact limbs. For mirrored movement, both amputees without PLP and controls showed activation in the primary motor and somatosensory cortices associated with the limb in the mirror (i.e., contralateral to the mirror image) while the PLP group did not.

Giraux and Sirigu (2003) examined the level of activation in the motor cortex among three individuals who experienced paralysis in an upper limb. While being scanned using an fMRI procedure, participants were instructed to purse their lips. The area of the somatosensory cortex associated with the mouth was bilaterally activated in both controls and the patient without PLP. However, the patient with PLP experienced additional unilateral activation in the somatosensory area associated with the missing limb that was adjacent to the area mapping the mouth. They found that using an illusory motor task, participants had a perception of limb control. In addition, areas of the brain associated with movement of the damaged limb were activated by the illusory information. Of note, for one participant who did not experience change in perception, there was no evidence of increased activation. This supports the hypothesis that cortical reorganization had led to a remapping of the brain and that this remapping was associated with the likelihood of PLP.

In a series of case studies using electromyography (EMG) measuring input from muscles on the intact arm and the same muscles on the stump, phantom limb movements produced distinct patterns of response (Gagné, Reilly, Hétu, & Mercier, 2009). Participants were instructed to produce parallel movements with their existing hand/arm and their phantom. The EMG patterns associated with the phantom limb movement were different between subjects, although the pattern within subjects was the same for any particular phantom movement. The most activated muscle was always that immediately above the amputation level. While the participants could produce phantom movement that led to detectable EMG, they reported the movement in the phantom they achieved was on average 41 percent of the intact limb's range of motion, and they showed delay in time to conduct the exercise, both of which suggest reduced control over phantom movement. A positive relationship between PLP severity and EMG modulation in stump muscles during phantom movements was found, with higher PLP associated with greater variation in the movement cycle (i.e., more activity being associated with more pain). These results were surprising because intensive use of a prosthetic hand is thought to decrease PLP and would be expected to increase EMG, although these hypotheses have not been directly tested.

It is clear that the cortex is involved with the perception of the phantom limb and that cortical reorganization is associated with the experience of PLS and

PLP. There is also evidence that this reorganization can be corrected. Probably the most dramatic evidence of the ability to reverse changes after amputation arises from the cortical changes associated with upper-limb transplantations. In a study of referred sensation in a bilateral hand amputee after bilateral transplantation, the respondent demonstrated significant overlap between referred sensation (touch to the face being perceived in the hand) five months after surgery, but this significantly reduced by eleven months after surgery. In another study, the representation of transplanted hand muscles as well as intact upper-limb muscles was examined using motor evoked potentials (MEPs) and EMG techniques (Vargas et al., 2009). Over time, the transplanted hand acquired representation in the motor cortex, with simultaneous reduction in the representation of the upper-limb muscle of the participants.

The preponderance of evidence suggests that limb loss can lead to reorganization of cortical areas, that this reorganization can lead to symptomatology in a predictable manner, and that external stimuli can reverse or at least modify this reorganization, leading to changes in the perceptual consequences (Flor et al., 1995). There is some evidence of structural changes in gray-matter volume associated with cortical reorganization and some suggestion that this is associated with intensity of PLP (Makin et al., 2013), although these findings have not been consistent (Preissler et al., 2013). Makin and colleagues (2013) have suggested that the neural plasticity hypothesis needs modification to explain phantom experiences. They examined the motor cortex of three groups of participants (traumatic amputees, patients with a congenitally missing limb, and controls with both limbs) using fMRI while engaging in a movement (phantom movement in the traumatic amputees, physical movement in the controls, and imagined movement in those with a congenitally missing limb). The authors concluded that PLP was associated with preserved representation of the missing limb in the motor cortex, not the degradation of this representation. They noted both greater activation with more PLP and greater gray-matter volume associated with higher levels of PLP. They concluded that "cortical changes following limb amputation are most likely due to a combination of loss of sensory inputs and phantom pain experience." Whereas loss of sensory input can result in disrupted representations, they argue that PLP, emerging from either nociceptive input or input from other pain-related brain regions, can actually maintain local cortical representations while disrupting inter-regional connectivity. However, given that other studies have found contradictory results (Preissler et al., 2013), there is need for replication of these findings.

Summary of Literature

Based on the literature to date, it appears that PLP is a commonly occurring result of cortical reorganization after amputation or other loss of afferent input.

It appears that the level of reorganization determines the level and severity of pain. In addition, it appears that cortical reorganization may be mitigated or reversed using a number of techniques. Based on these findings, a number of interventions have been developed and tested for reducing PLP, which are reviewed below.

Treatment of PLP

While the directional effects of neural plasticity and amputation and the relationship to PLP are still not clear, a number of models of intervention have been developed, based on the evidence that visual or other stimuli can modify the experience of PLP. The range of effective treatment options for PLP is limited. A broad range of pharmacological approaches have been tested, including local anesthesia in the stump, analgesics, opioids, muscle relaxants, antidepressants, antipsychotics, anticonvulsants, antihypertensive medications, ketamine, calcitonin, and capsaicin. Most pharmacotherapy approaches have only partial benefit (Guimmarra & Moseley, 2011). A systematic review (McCormick, Chang-Chien, Marshall, Huang, & Harden, 2014) examined pharmacological treatment of PLP targeting different proposed mechanisms. Interventions targeting peripheral afferent mechanisms (e.g., epidural morphine, topical capsaicin) are based on the assumption that PLP arises from the influence of neuromas at the cut end of the nerves, generating pain and providing feedback to the CNS that contribute to cortical reorganization associated with PLP. Interventions targeting CNS mechanisms (e.g., oral (PO) or intravenous (IV) morphine, PO gabapentin, IV and epidural ketamine, methadone) directly target the CNS areas associated with pain. Interventions targeting efferent sympathetic mechanisms of PLP (e.g., beta-blockers) are based on evidence that PLP may be maintained by sympathetic dysregulation in the residual limb. The best evidence is for CNS targeted interventions. The reviewers found that IV ketamine and IV morphine provided perioperatively was effective for short-term (30–120 minutes) treatment of PLP but were not associated with prolonged relief. Sustained-release morphine administered orally provided some relief for intermediate to long-term treatment, with 53 percent pain relief compared to 19 percent for placebo and five of twelve participants experiencing greater than 50 percent pain relief for up to one year after treatment. Most other medications showed either mixed results or had insufficient trials to determine efficacy, and even in the studies showing efficacy, a large portion of the sample did not benefit.

Even individuals with good access to health care often do not receive adequate care. Among one group of combat veterans with PLP, 82 percent talked to a provider about the symptoms; however, only 68 percent received treatment (Ketz, 2008). Most of those treated (53 percent) received pharmacotherapy, while others used distraction and relaxation techniques with limited benefit. One participant found relief with transcutaneous electrical nerve stimulation, an approach that involves directing low voltage electrical stimulation to the skin near the source of pain (in the case of PLP, at the stump).

The range of options reported in this survey reflects the state of PLP treatment. There are limited options that have been appropriately evaluated. However, the evidence of visual and input-modifying PLP has led to a number of proposed treatments based on the neuroplasticity model of PLP. The primary interventions include visual feedback (including mirrors, video, models, and virtual reality); imagery; and TMS. Each will be reviewed in turn.

Visual Input as a Treatment for PLP

Ramachandran and Rogers-Ramachandran (1996, 2000) conducted a series of case studies with the goal of exploring the impact of visual input on the perception of the phantom limb. Theorizing that visual input can have an influence on the cortical organizations, they developed a simple device that uses a mirror to create the illusion of the missing limb. By orienting the mirror in a particular way, the reflection of the existing limb aligns with where the missing limb would be and provides the perception that the missing limb is present.

Participants observe the image and are instructed to move the existing limb while imagining they are moving both limbs in parallel. Initial case reports found that patients using a mirror in this manner experienced amelioration in PLP (Ramachandran & Rogers-Ramachandran, 1996, 2000). Since the initial case studies, there have been several attempts to replicate and expand on these findings. In the largest treatment study to date, eighty participants with amputation were randomly assigned to either mirror treatment or a control condition (placing their limb in a mirror box with the mirror obscured; Brodie, Whyte, & Niven, 2007). They found that the mirror produced significantly more phantom limb movements but did not lead to reductions in PLP relative to the control. However, this study was limited in that 15 percent reported no PLP at baseline.

In contrast, a study of eighteen combat veterans assigned to one of three conditions (mirror, sham mirror, or imaginal practice) found significant reduction in pain (Chan et al., 2007). The active condition consisted of fifteen-minute sessions daily for four weeks of either mirror treatment or the sham condition. Participants in the active condition had significantly greater reduction of PLP at the end of treatment relative to the sham condition. The investigators then conducted a crossover with sham or imaginal treatment participants receiving the active condition and demonstrating significant improvement as well.

One of the key advantages of the mirror intervention, if effective, is its relative simplicity. Forty participants with unilateral amputations received

FIGURE 11.1 Use of a mirror to create the perception of a missing limb; the participant positions the mirror so that from their perspective, the reflection of the intact limb is aligned with where the phantom limb would be, giving visual feedback that the missing limb is present (McQuaid, J. R., Peterzell, D., & Cone, R., 2008).

mirror in home with only an explanation of the intervention, and reported significant improvement in symptom at one and two months after treatment (Darnall & Li, 2012). Unfortunately, the lack of randomization or any control condition limited overall conclusions from that study, but the ability to deliver an affordable intervention with potentially little or no staffing requirement could dramatically increase the feasibility of treatment for a large portion of those with PLP.

Another study examined whether preoperative mirror therapy could prevent or reduce the severity of postoperative PLP (Hanling, Wallace, Hollenbeck, Belnap, & Tulis, 2010). Four patients received mirror preoperatively. After amputation, one individual reported no phantom pain, two reported mild pain, and the fourth reported moderate pain. While the authors suggest this may reflect a reduction in incidence, lack of control conditions limits potential interpretation.

In a more technologically complex approach, eight male participants with phantom pain received treatment using a virtual image of the arm (Mercier & Sirigu, 2009). The investigator initially filmed the intact limb conducting a series of movements, flipped the image, and then presented the image via a mirror above the missing limb. Participants were instructed to follow movements as much as possible with their phantom limb. After sixteen sessions, five of eight participants reported reduction of pain (on average 38 percent) and four of five

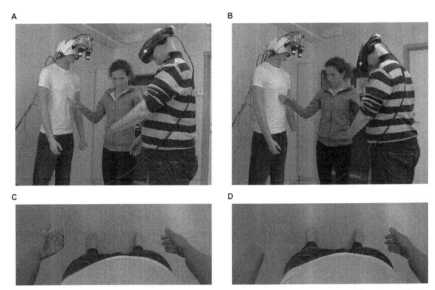

FIGURE 11.2 Use of a mannequin and virtual reality to create an illusion of the missing limb and a control condition (from Schmalzl et al., 2011). The camera on the mannequin projects an image to the virtual reality visor that provides a first-person view of the mannequin body. Image A shows the equipment using an intact mannequin, and image B shows the equipment with a mannequin missing the left arm below the elbow. Images C and D show the view seen by the participant in conditions A and B, respectively. In the procedure, the researcher touches the body of the participant as well as the mannequin. When touching the mannequin's hand in the experimental condition, the researcher also touches the area of the stump associated with referred sensation of the phantom hand, to create combined visual and tactile experience of the hand being touched. This is associated both perceiving the mannequin hand as "owned" by the participant, and changes in perception of the phantom (e.g., perceiving it to be located below rather than in the stump) (used with permission of Dr. Schmalzl).

maintained improvement at four weeks after treatment. While the design did not allow comparison with a control or traditional mirror approach, results are consistent with other findings suggesting visual feedback reduces PLP.

Another approach to visual input is the use of mannequins or prostheses to mimic the missing limb. In one study, amputees viewed a "first-person" virtual reality image of a mannequin. A camera is placed where the mannequin's eyes would be and aimed down, so that the virtual reality goggles worn by the participant show an image as if the mannequin body was in the place of the participant's own body (Schmalzl et al., 2011).

Participants reported RS when observing the image of the mannequin being touched from this perspective, and perception of "ownership" of the mannequin limbs. Some participants also reported reduction in phantom pain. Again, this was not a randomized controlled trial, and implications for treatment are unclear.

The results of these studies suggest visual feedback may be effective in reducing PLP, but clearly additional studies are needed to clarify findings, with larger samples and better control conditions. The current literature precludes confident statements of the efficacy of visual feedback.

Imagery

Several studies have examined mental imagery alone or as a comparison. These approaches involve using general relaxation strategies to prepare and then imagining comfortable and non-painful movement and sensation in the limb (for example, imagining stretching out the phantom arm, then allowing it to rest gently in one's lap). As noted above, Chan and colleagues (2007) found that imagery alone was not effective in reducing PLP. However, some cases studies have suggested that imagery may be beneficial. In a study of thirteen upper-limb amputees, imagery alone led to reduction of PLP, with average pain intensity on a 0-to-10 scale reducing from 7.5 to 4 (MacIver, Lloyd, Kelly, Roberts, & Nurmikko, 2008). The authors conducted pre- and post-treatment fMRI and found evidence of cortical reorganization in both motor and somatosensory hand areas of the cortex after visual imagery of the phantom limb moving. In contrast, two other studies found mixed results. A study of six individuals that combined observation of movement (i.e., watching a video of movements of a limb matching the phantom limb) with imaginal practice of moving the limb found reduction in pain for four of seven participants after eight weeks of practice (Beaumont, Mercier, Michon, Malouin, & Jackson, 2011). However, symptoms returned to baseline at six months after treatment. A study of four individuals found mixed results, with two patients experiencing some improvement, one reporting no improvement, and one reporting emergence of PLP (McAvinue & Robertson, 2011). The differences in such results may reflect frequency and intensity of practice and variability in the interventions. In the MacIver et al. (2008) study, participants received six hour-long imagery therapy sessions plus conducted forty minutes of daily practice. They also strongly emphasized a relaxation technique known as a body scan, where the individual shifts concentration throughout the body in an organized approach. Beaumont and colleagues (2011) had biweekly thirty-minute sessions for four weeks followed by four weeks in which the patients were asked to practice the same intervention five days a week and initial observation of videos, as mentioned. McAvinue and Robertson (2011) had four weekly sessions (the length of which was not specified) and ten minutes of daily practice. None of these studies included a control group, which is a limitation.

Another study examining imagery used a standardized approach (imaginative resonance therapy or IRT) that has been applied to a variety of other disorders (Meyer, Matthes, Kusche, & Maurer, 2011). The intervention involves a series of imaginal exercises that include perceiving not only the limb but also the limb in relation to or in contact with tactile stimulation, in motion or effort, perceiving sensory input, and in both relaxed and tensed states. The authors note there are a number of studies for a variety of disorders in addition to PLP. In their study, they describe one individual who had an above-knee amputation and significant PLP. Using fMRI imaging techniques and comparing to an aggregated sample of sixteen pain-free controls without an amputation, the authors report that the patient had a representation of the foot and thigh in the motor cortex that was distinctly smaller than those of controls. After treatment, the authors report that the participant reported no PLP. In addition, the representations of the imagined limbs both increased in volume and shifted nearly fourteen millimeters in the axial plane. While the case study design prevents any definitive conclusion that the changes observed were due to the intervention, this is consistent with the body of evidence that visual and possibly even imaginal interventions can lead to remapping of the body representations. It is less clear whether this strategy can consistently lead to pain reduction.

Repetitive Transcranial Magnetic Stimulation

A number of case studies have investigated repetitive transcranial magnetic stimulation (rTMS) for reducing PLP. In a study of two patients, stimulation of the contralateral parietal cortex led to reduction in pain lasting up to ten minutes, but the benefits were not maintained with pain returning to baseline levels (Töpper, Foltys, Meister, Sparing, & Boroojerdi, 2003). In contrast, a single case study using rTMS produced 33 percent reduction in PLP during the course of treatment, and a 17 percent reduction from baseline was maintained at three weeks after treatment (Di Rollo & Pallanti, 2011). These are clearly very preliminary findings, and further work is necessary to establish the efficacy of this intervention.

Summary

The current state of the science around PLP holds promise both for effective intervention around the disorder and continued improvement of our understanding of neuroplasticity. However, this promise has not yet been fulfilled. As reviewed, interventions for PLP based on neuroplasticity have been mixed, with some (but not all) studies across a range of approaches showing efficacy. In addition, the sample sizes have been small and designs limited, as is common in an early area of research. Future directions need to include larger sample sizes and better controlled trials. In addition, few of the studies reviewed above have taken advantage of neuroimaging techniques to explore the underlying mechanisms of change. Optimally, treatment studies would use fMRI to establish a baseline cortical map associated with the PLS and PLP sensations, and follow-up imaging would examine changes that occur both during and after treatment. This is a clear next step in developing these treatments. Understanding the role of feedback and phantom sensation is not only important for pain treatment but can have implications for prosthesis use. As new myoelectric devices become more widely available, understanding the representation of the missing limb in the brain and incorporating it into design of a prosthesis can potentially lead to better acceptance and control.

Another key issue is the identification of predictors of treatment response. This has implications both for clinical care and for improved understanding of neuroplasticity. Current anecdotal findings suggest some qualitative aspects of PLP may relate both to the likelihood of treatment response and underlying neural activity. Imaging studies give evidence of the relationship between PLP and cortical reorganization, but understanding more subtle variation in response can be critical in developing an improved knowledge of the processes involved in cortical reorganization. Future studies need to explore treatment non-responders and the changes (or lack thereof) in cortical organization and also explore variations in intervention (length, intensity, and immersiveness, i.e., how much the virtual reality is experienced as real) that may moderate the effect on cortical organization. This area of research is growing quickly and promises significant benefit in the near future.

Implications of PLP for a Neurocognitive Approach to Treatment

The developing research on the neurocognitive basis of PLP holds important promise for the treatment of this disorder as well as other disorders that may have a basis in these same mechanisms. There is a broad recognition of the importance of a psychological perspective for the management and treatment of a range of behavioral health problems, and progress in PLP may suggest a new pathway for treatment of a number of more common health problems. Other pain disorders are an obvious example. Understanding the role of neuroplasticity in pain perception may provide implications for the application of techniques like TMS and DBS and potentially even mirror therapy for treating disorders like neuropathic pain (pain stemming from peripheral nerve damage) or other pain disorders with poorly elucidated mechanisms such as fibromyalgia. Another key example is tinnitus. Tinnitus is a common consequence of exposure to extreme noise and is now recognized to involve similar processes of cortical reorganization as phantom pain (Herraiz, Diges,

Cobo, & Aparicio, 2009). It may, therefore, also be responsive to interventions targeting this reorganization, such as providing compensatory auditory inputs that can facilitate neural reorganization.

Key to making progress in exploring these possibilities is the increased availability of advanced imaging technologies that can allow researchers to establish how behavioral health problems like pain and tinnitus are related to cortical reorganization and then test the influence of noninvasive interventions, such as visual feedback or auditory masking, on those neurological bases for the disorders. The neurocognitive science of PLP illustrates the potential of a new dimension of effective, noninvasive interventions that are based in the understanding of how the brain remakes itself. The opportunity to combine cognitive neuroscience with behavioral health interventions promises the chance both to advance our treatment of previously untreatable disorders and simultaneously to develop a more profound understanding of the organization and malleability of the brain.

References

Beaumont, G., Mercier, C., Michon, P., Malouin, F., & Jackson, P. L. (2011). Decreasing phantom limb pain through observation of action and imagery: A case series. *Pain Medicine, 12*, 289–299.

Bjorkman, A., Weibull, A., Olsrud, J., Ehrsson, H. H., Rosén, B., & Bjorkman-Burtscher, I. M. (2012). Phantom digit somatotopy: A functional magnetic resonance study in forearm amputees. *European Journal of Neuroscience, 36*, 2098–2106.

Bosmans, J. C., Geertzen, J. H. B., Post, W. J., van der Schans, C. P., & Dijkstra, P. U. (2010). Factors associated with phantom limb pain: A 3½-year prospective study. *Clinical Rehabilitation, 24*, 444–453.

Bourke, J. (2009). Silas Weir Mitchell's "The Case of George Dedlow." *The Lancet, 373*, 1331–1333.

Brodie, E. E., Whyte, A., & Niven, C. A. (2007). Analgesia through the looking-glass? A randomized controlled trial investigating the effect of viewing a 'virtual' limb upon phantom limb pain, sensation and movement. *European Journal of Pain, 11*, 428–436.

Chan, B. L., Wit, R., Charrow, A. P., Magee, A., Howard, R., Pasquina, P. F., ... & Tsao, J. W. (2007). Mirror therapy for phantom limb pain. *New England Journal of Medicine, 357*, 2206–2207.

Cohen, L. G., Bandinelli, S., Findley, T. W., & Hallett, M. (1991). Motor reorganization after upper limb amputation in man. *Brain, 114*, 615–627.

Darnall, B. D., & Li, H. (2012). Home-based self-delivered mirror therapy for phantom pain: A pilot study. *Journal of Rehabilitation Medicine, 44*, 254–260.

Diers, M., Christmann, C., Koeppe, C., Ruf, M., & Flor, H. (2010). Mirrored, imagined and executed movements differentially activate sensorimotor cortex in amputees with and without phantom limb pain. *Pain, 149*, 296–304.

Dijkstra, P. U., Geertzen, J. H. B., Stewart, R., & van der Schans, C. P. (2002). Phantom pain and risk factors: A multivariate analysis. *Journal of Pain and Symptom Management, 24*, 578–585.

Di Rollo, A., & Pallanti, S. (2011). Phantom limb pain: Low frequency repetitive transcranial magnetic stimulation in unaffected hemisphere. *Case Reports in Medicine,* Article ID 130751, 1–4.

Egsgaard, L. L., Petrini, L., Christoffersen, G., & Arendt-Nielsen, L. (2011). Cortical responses to the mirror box illusion: A high resolution EEG study. *Experimental Brain Research, 215,* 345–357.

Ephraim, P. L., Wegener, S. T., MacKenzie, E. J., Dillingham, T. R., & Pezzin, L. E. (2005). Phantom pain, residual limb pain, and back pain in amputees: Results of a national survey. *Archives of Physical Medicine and Rehabilitation, 86,* 1910–1919.

Flor, H., Nikolajsen, L., & Jensen, T. S. (2006). Phantom limb pain: A case of maladaptive CNS plasticity? *Nature Reviews Neuroscience, 7,* 873–881.

Flor, H., Elbert, T., Knecht, S., & Wienbruch, C. (1995). Phantom-limb pain as a perceptual correlate of cortical reorganization following arm amputation. *Nature, 375,* 482–484.

Gagné, M., Reilly, K. T., Hétu, S., & Mercier, C. (2009). Motor control over the phantom limb in above-elbow amputees and its relationship with phantom limb pain. *Neuroscience, 162,* 78–86.

Giraux, P., & Sirigu, A. (2003). Illusory movement of the paralyzed limb restore motor cortex activity. *Neuroimage, 20,* S107–S111.

Guimmarra, M. J., & Moseley, G. L. (2011). Phantom limb pain and bodily awareness: Current concepts and future directions. *Current Opinions in Anesthesiology, 24,* 524–531.

Hanling, S. R., Wallace, S. C., Hollenbeck, K. J., Belnap, B. D., & Tulis, M. R. (2010). Preamputation mirror therapy may prevent development of phantom limb pain: A case series. *Anesthesia and Analgesia, 110,* 611–614.

Herraiz, C., Diges, I., Cobo, P., & Aparicio, J. M. (2009). Cortical reorganisation and tinnitus: Principles of auditory discrimination training for tinnitus management. *European Archives of Otorhinolaryngology, 266,* 9–16.

Houghton, A. D., Nicholls, G., Houghton, A. L., Saadah, E., & McColl, L. (1994). Phantom pain: Natural history and association with rehabilitation. *Annals of the Royal College of Surgeons of England, 76,* 22–25.

Jensen, T. S., Krebs, B., Nielsen, J., & Rasmussen, P. (1985). Immediate and long-term phantom limb pain in amputees: Incidence, clinical characteristics and relationship to pre-amputation limb pain. *Pain, 21,* 267–278.

Kashani, J. H. (1983). Depression among amputees. *Journal of Clinical Psychiatry, 44,* 256–258.

Katz, J. (2000). Individual differences in the consciousness of phantom limbs. In R. G. Kunzendorf & B. Wallace (Eds.), *Individual Differences in Conscious Experience* (45–97). Amsterdam: John Benjamins Publishing Company.

Ketz, A. K. (2008). The experience of phantom limb pain in patients with combat-related traumatic amputations. *Archives of Physical Medicine and Rehabilitation, 89,* 1127–1132.

Kooljman, C. M., Dijkstra, P. U., Geertzen, J. H. B., Elzinga, A., & van der Schans, C. P. (2000). Phantom pain and phantom sensations in upper limb amputees: An epidemiology study. *Pain, 87,* 33–41.

Lotz, M., Flor, H., Grodd, W., Larbig, W., & Birbaumer, N. (2001). Phantom movements and pain: An fMRI study in upper limb amputees. *Brain, 124,* 2268–2277.

MacIver, K., Lloyd, D. M., Kelly, S., Roberts, N., & Nurmikko, T. (2008). Phantom limb pain, cortical reorganization and the therapeutic effect of mental imagery. *Brain, 131,* 2181–2191.

Makin, T. R., Scholz, J., Filippini, N., Slater, D. H., Tracey, I., & Johansen-Berg, H. (2013). Phantom pain is associated with preserved structure and function in the former hand area. *Nature Communications, 4*, 1–8.

McAvinue, L. P., & Robertson, I. H. (2011). Individual differences in response to phantom limb movement therapy. *Disability and Rehabilitation, 33*, 2186–2195.

McCormick, Z., Chang-Chien, G., Marshall, B., Huang, M., & Harden, R. N. (2014). Phantom limb pain: A systematic neuroanatomical-based review of pharmacologic treatment. *Pain Medicine, 15*, 292–305.

McQuaid, J. R., Peterzell, D., & Cone, R. (2008). Phantom limb pain: From observation to intervention. Paper presented to the Neurocognitive Therapies/Translational Research Special Interest Group at the 42nd Annual Convention of the Association for Behavioral and Cognitive Therapies, Orlando, FL.

Melzak, R., Israel, R., Lacroix, R., & Schultz, G. (1997). Phantom limbs in people with congenital limb deficiency or amputation in early childhood. *Brain, 120*, 1603–1620.

Mercier, C., & Sirigu, A. (2009). Training with virtual visual feedback to alleviate phantom limb pain. *Neurorehabilitation and Neural Repair, 23*, 587–594.

Mercier, C., Reilly, K. T., Vargas, C. D., Aballea, A., & Sirigu, A. (2006). Mapping phantom movement representations in the motor cortex of amputees. *Brain, 129*, 2202–2210.

Meyer, P., Matthes, C., Kusche, K. E., & Maurer, K. (2011). Imaginative resonance therapy (IRT) achieves elimination of amputees' phantom pain (PLP) coupled with a spontaneous in-depth proprioception of a restored limb as a marker for permanence and supported by pre-post functional magnetic resonance imaging (fMRI). *Psychiatry Research: Neuroimaging, 202*, 175–179.

Montoya, P., Ritter, K., Huse, E., Larbig, W., Braun, C., Topfner, S., ... & Birbaumer, N. (1998). The cortical somatotopic map and phantom phenomena in subjects with congenital limb atrophy and traumatic amputees with phantom limb pain. *European Journal of Neuroscience, 10*, 1095–1102.

Nardone, R., Hller, Y., Brigo, F., Seidl, M., Christova, M., Bergmann, J., ... & Trinka, E. (2013). Functional brain reorganization after spinal cord injury: Systematic review of animal and human studies. *Brain Research, 1504*, 58–73.

Preissler, S., Feiler, J., Dietrich, C., Hofmann, G. O., Miltner, W. H. R., & Weiss, T. (2013). Gray matter changes following limb amputation with high and low intensities of phantom limb pain. *Cerebral Cortex, 23*, 1038–1048.

Ramachandran, V. S. (1998). Consciousness and body image: Lessons from phantom limbs, Capgras syndrome and pain asymbolia. *Philosophical Transactions of the Royal Society: Biological Sciences, 353*, 1851–1859.

Ramachandran, V. S., & Rogers-Ramachandran, D. (1996). Synaesthesia in phantom limbs induced with mirrors. *Proceedings: Biological Sciences, 263*, 377–386.

Ramachandran, V. S., & Rogers-Ramachandran, D. (2000). Phantom limbs and neural plasticity. *Archives of Neurology, 57*, 317–320.

Ramachandran, V. S., Brang, D., & McGeoch, P. D. (2010). Dynamic reorganization of referred sensations by movements of phantom limb. *NeuroReport, 21*, 727–730.

Reiber, G. E., McFarland, L. V., Hubbard, S., Maynard, C., Blough, D. K., Gambel, J. M., & Smith, D. G. (2010). Servicemembers and veterans with major traumatic limb loss from Vietnam war and OIF/OEF conflicts: Survey methods, participants, and summary findings. *Journal of Rehabilitation Research & Development, 47*, 275–298.

Reilly, K. T., & Sirigu, A. (2011). Motor cortex representation of the upper-limb in individuals born without a hand. *PLOS One, 6*, 1–8.

Richardson, C., Glenn, S., Nurmikko, T., & Horgan, M. (2006). Incidence of phantom phenomena including phantom limb pain 6 months after major lower limb amputation in patients with peripheral vascular disease. *Clinical Journal of Pain, 22*, 353–358.

Rock, I., & Victor, J. (1964) Vision and touch: An experimentally created conflict between the two senses. *Science, 143*, 594–596.

Schmalzl, L., Thomke, E., Ragnö, C., Nilseryd, M., Stockselius, A., & Ehrsson, H. H. (2011). "Pulling telescoped phantoms out of the stump": Manipulating the perceived position of phantom limbs using a full-body illusion. *Frontiers in Human Neuroscience, 5*, 1–12.

Sherman, R. A. (1997). *Phantom pain*. The Plenum Series in Behavioral Psychophysiology and Medicine. New York, NY: Plenum Press.

Spruit-van Eijk, M., van der Linde, H., Buijck, B., Geurts, A., Zuidema, S., & Koopmans, R. (2012). Predicting prosthetic use in elderly patients after major lower limb amputation. *Prosthetics and Orthotics International, 36*, 45–52.

Töpper, R., Foltys, H., Meister, I. G., Sparing, R., & Boroojerdi, B. (2003). Repetitive transcranial magnetic stimulation of the parietal cortex transiently ameliorates phantom limb pain-like syndrome. *Clinical Neurophysiology, 114*, 1521–1530.

van der Schans, C. P., Geertzen, J. H. B., Tanneke Schoppen, T., & Dijkstra, P. U. (2002). Phantom pain and health-related quality of life in lower limb amputees. *Journal of Pain and Symptom Management, 24*, 429–436.

Vargas, C. D., Aballéa, A., Rodrigues, E. C., Reilly, K. T., Mercier, C., Petruzzo, P., …& Sirigu, A. (2009). Re-emergence of hand-muscle representation in human motor cortex after hand allograft. *PNAS, 106*, 7197–7202.

Wade, N. J., & Finger, S. (2003). William Porter (ca. 1696–1771) and his phantom limb: An overlooked first self-report by a man of medicine. *Neurosurgery, 52*, 1196–1199.

Wilkins, K. L., McGrath, P. J., Finley, G. A., & Katz, J. (1998) Phantom limb sensations and phantom limb pain in child and adolescent amputees. *Pain, 78*, 7–12.

12

THE NEUROCOGNITIVE VIEW OF SUBSTANCE USE DISORDERS

Stephanie M. Gorka, Yun Chen, and Stacey B. Daughters

Prevalence and Impact of Substance Use Disorders

Substance use disorders (SUDs) are common and associated with pervasive adverse social and economic consequences. Within the past year, an estimated 22.2 million persons aged twelve years or older were classified with substance abuse or dependence (Substance Abuse and Mental Health Services Administration [SAMHSA], 2013), a rate that has remained relatively stable for the past ten years. Individuals with SUDs evidence increased rates of unemployment, accidents, injuries, suicide, psychiatric illness, and chronic disease (Jacobs & Gill, 2002; Khalsa, Treisman, McCance-Katz, & Tedaldi, 2008; Movig et al., 2004; SAMHSA, 2013). In addition to the personal costs of these outcomes, the estimated annual financial burden of SUDs in the United States is over $450 *billion*. Notably, although substantial prevention and intervention efforts have been developed to address these issues, only 33 percent of individuals with self-identified drug and alcohol problems seek treatment (SAMHSA, 201). Moreover, of those who seek treatment, a small minority remain abstinent for more than twelve months (Darke et al., 2005; Prochaska, Delucchi, & Hall, 2004). Given these statistics, SUDs are a major public health concern, and there is a critical need to apply our growing understanding of addiction to the development of more targeted treatment interventions.

Clinical Picture

SUDs are chronically relapsing disorders characterized by compulsive drug consumption, impaired self-control, and high levels of negative affect during withdrawal. Addiction is considered clinically distinct from controlled, occasional substance use, as individuals with SUDs continuously cycle between drug intoxication, withdrawal, and preoccupation/anticipation. Data indicate that substance use is initiated for a variety of reasons (e.g., peer pressure, desires to modify affective states; Simons-Morton & Chen, 2006; Wills, 1986) but that, over time, there is a shift from impulsive to compulsive drug-taking behavior (Koob, 2004, 2009). This shift parallels the progression of substance use that is predominately motivated by positive reinforcement to negative reinforcement processes. That is, individuals typically begin using substances for their reinforcing, hedonic effects but ultimately lose control of these behaviors to the point where drug use becomes habitual and focused on the avoidance of withdrawal symptoms.

In addition to compulsive drug taking, individuals with SUDs exhibit decreased sensitivity to reward, enhanced salience attribution to drugs and drug cues, and impaired cognitive and emotional control (Al-Zahrani & Elsayed, 2009; Childress et al., 1993; Fox, Hong, & Sinha, 2008; Goldstein & Volkow, 2011; Koob & Nestler, 1997; Volkow et al., 2010). These features understandably contribute to the retractable nature of SUDs and are important clinical and research targets. Although not fully understood, a large body of evidence suggests that the prototypical features of SUDs are mediated by pharmacological neuroadaptations within specific circuits (Clapp, Bhave, & Hoffman, 2008; Volkow, Wang, Tomasi, & Baler, 2013). Broadly, in the early stages of addiction, the primitive areas of the brain that process reward (e.g., nucleus accumbens) are affected. Over time, impairment spreads to higher-order circuits responsible for complex cognitive functions (e.g., dorsolateral prefrontal cortex) including inhibitory control, decision making, and emotion regulation. Given these proposed brain-based mechanisms, a neurocognitive approach to understanding SUDs is critical. Therefore, the present chapter first reviews the existing literature on the neurobiology of SUDs. Instead of discussing each drug class individually (e.g., cannabis, alcohol, cocaine), we present information that is common across all substances and make note of potential discrepancies between drug classes. A summary of the neuropsychological consequences of substance use is highlighted in Table 12.1. Next, we discuss the implications of this information on current and future treatment approaches.

Substance Use Disorder Neurobiology

Mesocorticolimbic Dopamine System

The mesocorticolimbic dopamine system (i.e., the reward system) is one of the most heavily implicated neural circuits in addiction. It originates in the ventral tegmental area (VTA) and projects to the nucleus accumbens (NAc) of

TABLE 12.1 Summary of neuropsychological findings associated with substance use disorders

Neuropsychological Domain	Citations	Findings	Possible Mechanisms
Memory	Baldacchino, Balfour, Passetti, Humphris, & Matthews, 2012; Canales, 2010; Lundqvist, 2005; Mintzer, 2007; Solowij et al., 2011	Impaired verbal, working, spatial, episodic, visual, and semantic memory, as well as impaired acquisition, storage, retention and retrieval of information.	Related to alterations in the hippocampus, prefrontal cortex, frontal-temporal regions, striatum, and subcortical brain.
Executive Functioning	Ersche, Clark, London, Robbins, & Sahakian, 2006; Houston et al., 2013; Paulus et al., 2002; Verdejo-García, López-Torrecillas, Aguilar de Arcos, & Pérez-García, 2005	Poor executive functioning and problem solving capabilities.	Deficits in orbitofrontal and dorsolateral prefrontal cortex, medial prefrontal cortex, anterior cingulate cortex, inferior frontal gyrus, and middle frontal gyrus.
Attention	Abdullaev, Posner, Nunnally, & Dishion, 2010; Fu et al., 2008; McKinney, Coyle, Penning, & Verster, 2012	Impaired sustained and selective attention for alcohol, stimulants, and opiates; mixed findings for cannabis.	Default mode network dysfunction. Altered anterior cingulate cortex functioning. Hypoactive medial prefrontal cortex and anterior cingulate cortex.
Processing Speed	Hekmat, Mehrjerdi, Moradi, Ekhtiari, & Bakhshi, 2011; Kelleher, Stough, Sergejew, & Rolfe, 2004; Schweizer, & Vogel-Sprott, 2008	Declined speed of cognitive performance.	Specific brain regions and networks that contribute to such impairment are not well-understood.

continued …

Table 12.1 continued

Neuropsychological Domain	Citations	Findings	Possible Mechanisms
Visuospatial Ability	Gruber, Silveri, & Yurgelun-Todd, 2007; Martin, Singleton, & Hiller-Sturmhofel, 2003; Stavro et al., 2013	Impaired visuospatial and constructional abilities for alcohol, stimulants, and opiates; relatively intact abilities for cannabis though research on the topic is scarce.	Hippocampal dysfunction and decreased prefrontal and temporal gray matter density. Alcohol-related impairments linked to effects of thiamine deficiency.
Psychomotor Functioning	King et al., 2011; Konrad et al., 2012; Toomey et al., 2003	Impaired psychomotor functioning for alcohol, cannabis, and stimulants; mixed findings on psychomotor functioning for opiates.	White matter tissue abnormalities in the corpus callosum and alternation in dopamine system. Mechanisms not well-understood for opiates.

the ventral striatum as well as the dorsal striatum, amygdala, hippocampus, and medial prefrontal cortex (mPFC; Morales & Pickel, 2012). Dopamine (Da) is the major neurotransmitter used by the system to relay information and plays a critical role in the rewarding aspects of drug consumption, learning, and memory. Importantly, all drugs (either directly or indirectly) produce a brief surge of dopaminergic transmission in the NAc upon ingestion (Di Chiara et al., 2004; Drevets et al., 2001; Volkow et al., 1999). This surge has been shown to be greater than that of natural reinforcers (e.g., food, sex) and does not undergo the typical habituation process with repeated exposure (Di Chiara, 1999; Self & Tamminga, 2004). These properties understandably promote a preference for drug use over natural rewards.

Paradoxically, chronic substance use dampens dopaminergic transmission in the reward system. Evidence indicates that there is a decrease in the amount of high-affinity Da receptors in the reward pathway, and the amount of Da that is released during cell firing is attenuated (Volkow et al., 1996). This creates a hypodopaminergic state during abstinence that exacerbates withdrawal symptoms. More specifically, decreased dopaminergic functioning is thought to contribute to the high levels of negative affect experienced by the drug user due to over-activation of the opponent human stress response system (Koob,

2008, 2010, 2013; Koob & Le Moal, 2008). It has been postulated that in order to compensate for these pharmacological and affective deficits, individuals continue and/or escalate their drug use. Therefore, over time, drug use predominantly serves to alleviate aversive withdrawal symptoms rather than produce euphoria.

It is important to highlight that the mesocorticolimbic system is implicated in several other aspects of SUDs. For instance, research indicates that increases in Da in the reward system enhance learning of associations between drugs and stimuli that predict their availability (Everitt, Dickinson, & Robbins, 2001; Wheeler et al., 2011). In other words, drug-induced activation of the reward system facilitates the "stamping-in" of response-reward and stimulus-reward associations (Hyman, 2005; Wise, 2004). Some studies have suggested the strength of these stamped-in associations is abnormally strong, causing habits to be quickly formed (Berke, 2003; Nelson & Killcross, 2006). Relatedly, recent research and theory has emphasized the role of the reward system in drug "craving." It is posited that via activation of the reward system, excessive salience is attributed to drug-related associations, resulting in powerful conditioned motivational responses to consume the drug (Berridge, 2007). Taken together, acute activations and long-term neuroadapative changes in the mesocorticolimbic system underlie many features of SUDs including reduced reward sensitivity, enhanced salience attribution to drugs and drug cues, and compulsive drug taking.

Prefrontal Cortex

Although the reward circuit is undoubtedly implicated in SUDs, it does not sufficiently account for the complex deficits seen in addicted individuals. Indeed, accumulating evidence suggests that the prefrontal cortex (PFC) also plays a key role in drug addiction (Goldstein & Volkow, 2002; Li & Sinha, 2008; Volkow et al., 2013). The PFC is a neocortical region of interconnected areas that project to sensory, motor, and subcortical structures. It is involved in almost all higher-order cognitive functions, including the hallmark features of addiction—loss of inhibitory control and impaired emotion regulation (Barber, Caffo, Pekar, & Mostofsky, 2013; Krueger, Osterweil, Chen, Tye, & Bear, 2011). Review of human and animal imaging studies suggests that specific sub-regions of the PFC contribute to pathophysiology of addiction in unique ways. For example, the dorsolateral prefrontal cortex (DLPFC) is predominantly implicated in top-down inhibitory control; the ventromedial PFC is responsible for emotion regulation; and the ventrolateral PFC and lateral orbitofrontal cortex (OFC) in impulsive automatic responding (Goldstein & Volkow, 2011). Despite these different roles, research broadly suggests that, over time, acute PFC activation in response to drug consumption and presentation of drug cues is replaced by widespread PFC hypoactivation—especially during emotional and cognitive challenge (Crego et al., 2010; Crowley et al., 2010; Morein-Zamir, Jones, Bullmore, Robbins, & Ersche, 2013).

Several converging lines of evidence support the role of the PFC in addiction. First, dependent individuals, across a range of substances, exhibit PFC volume loss (Matochik, London, Eldreth, Cadet, & Bolla, 2003). Second, individuals with SUDs typically show enhanced PFC activation in response to drug-related cues and drug anticipation (Myrick et al., 2004; Goldstein & Volkow, 2002) and diminished PFC activation to non-drug rewards (Goldstein, & Volkow, 2011). Third, the cognitive control regions of the PFC have been shown to mediate effective regulation of emotion and drug craving (Kober et al., 2010; Sutherland, Carroll, Salmeron, Ross, & Stein, 2013) and, recently, stimulating the PFC in drug-addicted animals has been shown to prevent compulsive drug-seeking behaviors (Chen et al., 2013).

Dysfunctional Neural Interactions

It is necessary to point out that aberrant functional interactions between the mesocorticolimbic system and PFC are proposed to ultimately contribute to the onset and maintenance of SUDs (Volkow et al., 2013; Ma et al., 2010). It is not an additive effect of impairment in both circuits but rather an imbalance in the way the circuits interact with one another. Although not well understood, it has been postulated that neuroplastic changes in any of the nodes mentioned above can alter neurotransmission and tip the balance (Moussawi & Kalivas, 2010). Once the circuits no longer effectively communicate, the hyperactive motivation to consume drugs is essentially unregulated, as the weakened prefrontal circuit is unable to exhibit top-down inhibitory control. This loss of voluntary control over drug taking facilitates relapse and, consequently, should be a fundamental target for SUD interventions. Notably, however, not all existing treatments take a neurocognitive perspective and conceptualize SUDs as a compulsive disorder, but those that do will be highlighted below.

Established Treatments and How Well They Work

Several psychological and pharmacological treatments have been shown to be moderately effective for SUDs (Carroll & Onken, 2005; Chambless & Ollendick, 2001; Dutra et al., 2008). According to the American Psychological Association (APA), psychosocial therapies including motivational interviewing (MI), motivational enhancement therapy (MET), MET plus cognitive-behavior therapy (CBT), and contingency management (CM) have demonstrated enough research support to be considered "empirically supported treatments." Comprehensive meta-analyses and literature reviews also indicate that pharmacological strategies can significantly improve SUD outcomes, particularly during detoxification (Kosten & O'Connor, 2003; Maisel, Blodgett, Wilbourne, Humphreys, & Finney, 2013; Marsch, 1998). Although existing treatments vary in their theory and approach, all aim to disrupt the positive-feedback loop of addiction. Psychological interventions typically aim to enhance motivation to remain abstinent, develop strategies to tolerate cravings, and create new patterns of behavior so that drug use becomes replaced by alternative, natural rewards. Pharmacological interventions target similar process via modulation of neurotransmitter systems instead of cognitive and behavioral strategies. Research on the active ingredients of efficacious SUD treatments continues to be a prolific area of investigation, and new therapies and treatment targets are continuously being developed.

Despite these promising findings, recovery from SUDs has proven to be incredibly difficult. A large percentage of individuals drop out of treatment prematurely or relapse shortly after termination (Heinz, Beck, Grüsser, Grace, & Wrase, 2009; Ravndal & Vaglum, 2002; Stark, 1992). Indeed, studies suggest that 10 percent to 30 percent of individuals terminate SUD treatment early (De Leon, 1991; Mertens & Weisner, 2000; Rabinowitz & Marjefsky, 1998). This is a significant clinical issue given that length of treatment is a consistent predictor of long-term SUD outcomes including relapse, unemployment, homelessness, and poverty (Hubbard, Craddock, & Anderson, 2003; Simpson, Joe, & Brown, 1997). In addition to high attrition rates, research indicates that as many as 90 percent of individuals relapse to substance use within four years of treatment (e.g., Morgenstern, Blanchard, Morgan, Labouvie, & Hayaki, 2001; Office of Applied Studies, 2009). Thus, although a sizable percentage of individuals are able to achieve initial SUD recovery, it is difficult to sustain abstinence, resulting in reentry into SUD treatment or return to prior functioning.

A large body of evidence indicates that multiple factors contribute to poor SUD outcomes. For example, younger age (Maglione, Chao, & Anglin, 2000), psychiatric comorbidity (Hättenschwiler, Rueesch, & Modestin, 2001), cognitive deficits (Aharonovich et al., 2006), drug use severity (Ravndal & Vaglum, 1991), low social support (Myers, Pasche, & Adam, 2010), and motivation to change (Ball, Carroll, Canning-Ball, & Rounsaville, 2006) have all been shown to impact treatment dropout and relapse. This literature highlights that there is no single treatment that has been shown to be effective for everyone and that outcomes can vary widely depending on characteristics of the individual (Dutra et al., 2008).

There are other factors that also contribute to low rates of SUD remission. First, although we know that certain treatments are effective, we know relatively little about how these treatments work. Broad hypotheses have been put forth such that cognitive and behavioral therapies directly and indirectly enhance PFC functioning, which improves self-control, but these proposed mechanisms are imprecise and have led to many unanswered questions. Relatedly, the field has made limited progress in adopting a neurocognitive approach to treatment and applying our knowledge of SUD neurobiology to the development of novel and effective interventions. It is likely that this difficulty in translating basic neurobiological science into efficacious treatments is due in part to lack of interdisciplinary collaboration. Fortunately, these issues are being increasingly recognized in the literature, and substantial progress has been made as of late. Therefore, in the sections below, we review existing SUD treatments that have demonstrated favorable outcomes. Although limited research has examined the neurobiological targets of these intervention approaches, we discuss their hypothesized mechanisms.

Motivational Interviewing

MI is a client-centered psychological treatment that aims to enhance intrinsic motivation to change using a non-judgmental interviewing style (Hettema, Steele, & Miller, 2005; Miller & Rollnick, 1991). The treatment is based on the beliefs of Carl Rogers (1951) and includes four main principles: (1) express empathy, (2) support self-efficacy, (3) roll with resistance, and (4) develop discrepancy. These principles broadly translate into acknowledging and validating the client's perspective while openly discussing the consequences of changing versus staying the same. At no point does the clinician attempt to persuade the client to change. Instead, discrepancies between the client's goals and their current behavior are repeatedly highlighted by the clinician. It is theorized that when clients perceive their drug use as inconsistent with their self-identified goals, they become motivated to change and pursue alternative rewards. The fact that this motivation is generated by the client, rather than the clinician, is a key piece of the MI framework.

A brief, manualized version of MI, called motivational enhancement therapy (MET), was developed by Project MATCH (Allen et al., 1997)—an extensive randomized control trial (RCT) of psychological interventions for alcohol dependence. Notably, results from Project MATCH indicated that four sessions of MET (spread out over the course of twelve weeks) were as effective at reducing alcohol use as twelve sessions of CBT or twelve-step facilitation. This study, as well as several others, suggests that MI techniques can have rapid effects (Burke, Arkowitz, & Menchola, 2003; Miller & Rollnick, 2002), although maintaining long-term abstinence after treatment continues to be a challenge.

As was noted above, the neural mechanisms mediating these effects are still unclear. However, it is assumed that by working through the principles of MI and implementing actual behavior change (e.g., abstaining from drug use), motivational neurocircuitry involved in risk-reward decision making and cognitive control is modified (Potenza, Sofuglu, Carroll, & Rousanville, 2011). In order to successfully inhibit compulsive drug-seeking behaviors and execute behavior changes, it has also been speculated that the DLPFC may be indirectly affected, given its role in planning and executive functioning (Bush et al., 2002; Dalley, Everitt, & Robbins, 2011). Interestingly, a recent study attempted to investigate the neural mechanisms of MI by providing community volunteers with alcohol dependence a single, hour-long session of MI (Feldstein Ewing, Filbey, Sabbineni, Chandler, & Hutchison, 2011). Approximately one week later, participants completed a functional magnetic resonance imaging scan during which they were exposed to their own "change talk" (e.g., I want to quit) and "counter-change talk" (e.g., I don't have a problem) statements, followed by presentation of alcohol cues. Results indicated that after counter-change talk statements, reward regions of the brain were significantly activated in response to alcohol cues (e.g., NAc, caudate, putamen). In contrast, there was no significant brain activation during alcohol cues after change talk. This suggests that MI-based dialogue may facilitate inhibition of reward-related brain activation to drug and alcohol-related cues. This would likely lead to beneficial outcomes as enhanced neural inhibition may translate into improved affect and behavior regulation capabilities in high risk for relapse situations (i.e., during exposure to drug cues).

Cognitive-behavior Therapy

CBT interventions are used to treat a wide range of psychiatric disorders and target causal relationships between dysfunctional thoughts, behaviors, and emotions (Beck, 2011). Consistent with the guidelines published by the National Institute on Drug Abuse, CBT for addiction focuses on modifying behaviors and cognitions that maintain substance use while improving skills to cope with negative affect and drug craving. More specifically, techniques such as weighing the pros and cons of continued use, self-monitoring thoughts and behaviors, identifying natural rewards that compete with drug use, and employing emotion regulation skills are often included in a comprehensive CBT treatment package. Many of these approaches are based on theories of classical and operant conditioning (Kaplan, Heinrichs, & Carey, 2011; Petry, Martin, Cooney, & Kranzler, 2000), in that by enhancing awareness of internal and external stimuli that increase the likelihood of drug use, individuals will be able to break these associations and develop new cognitive and behavioral patterns. These interventions have been shown to be effective at facilitating short-term abstinence and typically include twelve weekly sessions; although shorter protocols have also become common.

Because CBT addresses several cognitive and behavioral processes, the neural mechanisms of these interventions are likely multifaceted. The use of cognitive strategies to attenuate drug cravings is thought to alter functioning of the medial PFC and ACC—regions implicated in cue-induced drug craving

(Wexler et al., 2001). Increasing focus on the long-term adverse consequences of drug use has been empirically demonstrated to strengthen the inhibitory influence of the DLPFC on reward regions (i.e., the ventral striatum; Kober et al., 2010). Similarly, there is evidence to suggest that repeatedly practicing emotion regulation strategies within the context of CBT may increase functional connectivity between PFC and limbic circuits (Potenza et al., 2011). Although much of the literature on the neural consequences of CBT has been done in patients with depression and anxiety, it has also been demonstrated that completion of CBT is associated with metabolic changes in the hippocampus, dorsal ACC, DLPFC, and VMPFC (Goldapple et al., 2004). Taken together, this emerging literature suggests that CBT may help restore the functional balance between PFC circuits and reward pathways.

Contingency Management

CM is a technique that uses external incentives to achieve therapy goals (Petry et al., 2006; Higgins et al., 1991). Most often, prizes or vouchers are systematically provided upon objective evidence of drug abstinence (e.g., negative urine screen). Although CM can be a stand-alone treatment, it is frequently incorporated into larger programs and may be used to promote treatment retention, attendance at therapy sessions, or medication adherence. CM is based on basic science that conceptualizes drug use as a form of operant behavior (Higgins, 1997; Higgins, Heil, & Lussier, 2004) and posits that in order to decrease drug use, salient non-drug reinforcers must be immediately available. These theories are supported by extensive work demonstrating that substance users place more value on proximal—relative to distal—rewards (Johnson et al., 2010; Petry, 2001). Notably, a meta-analysis of existing psychological interventions for SUDs indicated that CM has the highest effect size estimates (Dutra et al., 2008). However, CM can be costly to implement, as patients can typically earn up to $1,000 worth of vouchers (Higgins, Wong, Badger, Ogden, & Dantona, 2000). There is also some concern that CM does not facilitate long-lasting behavior change and that once external contingencies are removed, patients are susceptible to relapse.

CM approaches are designed to target reward processes. Alternative, non-drug rewards are offered to compete, and override, the desire to engage in substance use. In other words, CM approaches utilize the delay-discounting deficits of chronic substance users. It is suggested that these processes engage neural regions associated with determining the salience of immediate rewards such as the ventral striatum and VMPFC (Stanger et al., 2013; Wittmann, Lovero, Lane, & Paulus, 2010). In addition, although the neurobiological consequences of CM are still unclear, neural circuits implicated in reward-related decision making, such as the medial PFC, ACC, and OFC (Hampton & O'Doherty, 2007), may be strengthened given that patients must repeatedly decide whether treatment contingences outweigh the benefits of drug use. In line with this hypothesis, during tasks where non-treatment-seeking substance users are asked to choose between competing rewards, they typically exhibit decreased activation in brain regions such as the ACC, DLPFC, and caudate (e.g., Hoffman et al., 2008). Of note, in addition to further delineating the neural processes that underlie CM, it will be important to assess the durability of these changes, given the aforementioned concerns about whether CM can lead to long-lasting benefits.

Pharmacological Interventions

Traditional pharmacological treatments for SUDs can be broadly classified into two categories: receptor agonists and antagonists. Receptor agonists include medications that have similar, albeit weaker, psychophysiological effects as abused substances. The rationale is that substituting a safer, controlled substance for a riskier, uncontrolled substance will lead to an overall reduction in harm. Indeed, these approaches have been shown to reduce the risk of criminal activity, disease transmission, and drug overdose (Bruce, 2010; Davstad, Stenbacka, Leifman, & Romelsjö, 2009; Seal et al, 2001). Over time, the goal is to taper individuals off the agonist so that they can safely achieve abstinence. The most common example of a receptor agonist approach is methadone maintenance. Methadone is a synthetic μ-opioid agonist (e.g., having similar pharmacological properties as heroin and other opiates). Opioid-addicted individuals are typically prescribed one oral dose of methadone daily, which serves to prevent withdrawal symptoms without producing intense euphoria. As such, receptor agonists target the negative reinforcement processes of SUDs. The substituted drug allows the individual to remain in a state of homeostasis whereby they can engage in other rehabilitative activities. Currently, methadone maintenance is considered one of the most effective treatments for dependence. Similar approaches are now being used to treat nicotine, methamphetamine, and cocaine addiction (Devroye, Filip, Przegaliński, McCreary, & Spampinato, 2013; Herin, Rush, & Grabowski, 2010; Levin et al., 2010; Longo et al., 2010; McDaid et al., 2007).

In contrast to the mechanisms described above, drug antagonists block or dampen the psychophysiological effects of abused substances. This is achieved by occupying the same receptor sites as drugs of abuse or modifying receptor activity so that illicit drugs do not produce their hedonic effects. The rationale for this approach is drawn from literature noting that chronic substance use is compulsive, and addicted individuals have limited self-control. Because of these characteristics, antagonists remove the positive reinforcing aspects of intoxication in an attempt to break conditioned drug associations and reduce motivation to engage in substance use. In other words, once addicted individuals learn that they are no longer able to physically get "high," their desire to consume drugs will decline and eventually taper off. A classic example of this approach is the μ-opioid antagonist naltrexone. Naltrexone is used to treat opioid and alcohol addiction and can be administered orally or as a monthly injection. It does not produce any hedonic or rewarding effects but does minimize withdrawal symptoms. Most important, once naltrexone has been ingested, alcohol and opioids no longer produce the same psychopharmacological effects. Prior research indicates that this approach is moderately effective at reducing substance use and retaining patients in treatment (e.g., Johansson, Berglund, & Lindgren, 2006).

In summary, pharmacological treatments directly target neurotransmitter systems. Given that changes in neurotransmission have down-stream effects, it is likely that pharmacological treatments have pervasive neurocognitive consequences. Simply speaking, however, current cognitive and behavioral therapies tend to take a top-down approach to treatment by targeting higher-order cognitive functions, whereas SUD medications take a bottom-down approach by targeting subcortical processes that mediate reinforcement. Both strategies have been shown to be moderately effective, but the literature on the mechanisms underlying these treatments is scarce. Improving our understanding of these processes will be important as we look toward the future of SUD treatment.

Novel Approaches to SUD Treatment

As was mentioned earlier, a large percentage of individuals with SUDs do not seek treatment or evidence poor treatment outcomes. In a way, this is not surprising given the literature on the complex and interrelated neuroadaptive changes associated with chronic drug use. SUDs have been said to hijack many of the brain's natural functions, and when this is coupled with an incomplete understanding of SUD pathophysiology, treatment development is understandably difficult. Nevertheless, due to significant advancements in technology and more recent cross-disciplinary neurocognitive approaches to SUD research, the emerging treatment literature is promising. Several novel treatment approaches have had encouraging preliminary data, which are reviewed below.

Cognitive Remediation

A large body of evidence indicates that chronic substance users have neurocognitive deficits in decision making, response inhibition, planning, working memory, and attention (Fernández-Serrano, Perales, Moreno-López, Pérez-García, & Verdejo-García, 2012; Scott et al., 2007; Stavro, Pelletier, & Potvin, 2013). These deficits are due, in large part, to PFC dysfunction, and have several important clinical implications. First and foremost, cognitive impairment contributes to the maintenance of SUD symptoms, as weakened response inhibition and decision-making capabilities facilitate compulsive drug use. Second, existing cognitive and behavioral therapies require patients to pay attention, encode new information, and organize and initiate behavioral plans. As these are relatively complex neuropsychological tasks, individuals with SUDs have difficulty engaging in treatment and executing therapy goals. In fact, cognitive impairment is associated with poor treatment adherence (Bates, Pawlak, Tonigan, & Buckman, 2006), inefficient skill acquisition (Smith & McCrady, 1991), and lower levels of treatment engagement (Katz et al., 2005).

Given these clinical correlates, researchers have speculated that improving overall executive functioning may lead to better SUD treatment outcomes. Therefore, recent work has taken a cognitive remediation approach whereby computer tasks designed to strengthen working memory, attention, and executive functioning are repeatedly administered to individuals with SUDs. Early findings from this literature suggest that computerized cognitive rehabilitation does translate into measurable improvements (e.g., Rupp, Kemmler, Kurz, Hinterhuber, & Fleischhacker, 2012) and can enhance treatment retention among individuals in long-term residential programs (Grohman & Fals-Stewart, 2003). Moreover, in a recent, well-designed treatment outcome study, Fals-Stewart and Lam (2010) randomly assigned patients with SUDs to treatment-as-usual (i.e., long-term residential care) plus cognitive remediation or treatment-as-usual plus a non-cognitive, typing tutorial. Their results indicated that patients who received cognitive remediation were significantly more engaged in treatment and had less dropout and a higher percentage of days abstinent after treatment. Therefore, the cognitive remediation approach is promising, and initial work suggests that it may be especially beneficial as an adjunct to existing treatments.

Worth noting, cognitive enhancing medications are also being tested as possible supplements to SUD treatment. For example, data suggest that cholinesterase inhibitors like donepezil and tacrine, which have been used to treat cognitive impairment in other disorders like dementia, may be beneficial for the treatment of cocaine addiction (see Potenza et al., 2011). Another emerging candidate is atomoxetine—a selective norepinephrine transporter inhibitor used to treat attention deficit–hyperactivity disorder. Studies have found that atomoxetine improves attention and response inhibition capabilities (Chamberlain et al., 2009), which makes it an attractive potential treatment for SUDs.

Mindfulness and Acceptance-based Therapies

Mindfulness and acceptance-based treatments have existed for years and are effective for several psychopathologies including mood, anxiety, and personality disorders (e.g., Hayes, Strosahl, & Wilson, 1999; Linehan, 1993). However, accumulating research suggests that these therapies may also be useful for the treatment of SUDs. The main focus of mindfulness approaches is keeping one's attention on the present and adopting an open, non-judgmental attitude toward one's experiences. Theoretically, it has been argued that mindfulness and acceptance-based treatments simultaneously improve executive control functions and reduce stress reactivity (Brewer, Bowen, Smith, Marlatt, & Potenza, 2010). Thus, they may help restore functional balance between reward, stress, and PFC neural circuits. Indeed, a recent study found that mindfulness training strengthened white matter-tracts that connect affective and cognitive control regions (Tang et al., 2010). In addition, mindfulness-based treatments for SUDs have been shown to cause greater reductions in self-reported and physiological indices of stress reactivity relative to standard addiction treatments (Brewer et al., 2009). This suggests that mindfulness-based treatments may be particularly salient for relapse prevention. Future work, however, is needed to determine whether it holds promise as a stand-alone intervention or should be combined with other approaches. Consistent with the larger field of psychotherapy, there is also a need to better understand the neural mechanisms of change.

Behavioral Activation

Research indicates that mood disorders, and depression in particular, are highly prevalent among individuals with SUDs. In fact, over 50 percent of treatment-seeking drug users exhibit significant depressive symptoms (Johnson, Neal, Brems, & Fisher, 2006). These rates are especially salient given that depressed substance users evidence worse treatment outcomes than non-depressed substance users (Tate, Brown, Unrod, & Ramo, 2004). As such, addressing the role of depressive symptoms within a context of existing SUD treatments has recently been recognized as an important clinical target.

In line with this initiative, a brief treatment based on behavioral activation (BA) has been developed, the Life Enhancement Treatment for Substance Use (LETS ACT; Daughters et al., 2008). In line with BA, LETS ACT is focused on increasing individualized, goal-driven, substance-free forms of positive reinforcement to alleviate depressive symptoms and facilitate long-lasting behavior change. To date, there have been two RCTs examining the efficacy of LETS ACT. The first study compared LETS ACT to treatment-as-usual at a large, urban residential substance abuse treatment center (Daughters et al., 2008). Results indicated that patients who received LETS ACT reported significantly higher rates of environmental reward and lower rates of depression after treatment. A second study compared LETS ACT to a contact-time-matched control condition (i.e., Supportive Counseling [SC]) at the same residential treatment center (Magidson et al., 2011). Whereas both groups evidenced a decline in depressive symptoms after treatment, patients in LETS

ACT had significantly higher rates of treatment retention and greater increases in behavioral activation relative to patients in SC. Overall, these findings suggest that LETS ACT may be a useful adjunct to traditional SUD treatment programs.

Although no study has examined the neural targets of LETS ACT, theory indicates that the treatment has an effect on reward-related decision making. Similar to CM, non-drug-related rewards are offered to compete against drug use. Unlike CM, however, the rewards are internally generated, as patients identify and engage in rewarding behaviors that are consistent with their internal values. This process of identifying and choosing new behavior patterns has the potential to engage mesolimbic incentive-motivational neurocircuitry.

Anti-addiction Vaccines

Anti-addiction vaccines are increasingly being considered for the treatment of SUDs. These vaccines work by triggering the immune system to produce antibodies that bind to the illicit substance when it is ingested and limit the amount that can pass through the blood-brain barrier. Because lower amounts of the drug enter the brain, the psychophysiological effects are weakened (Laurenzana et al., 2009; Pentel et al., 2000). Although the initial goals of this approach were to facilitate abstinence within addicted individuals, it is also possible that anti-addiction vaccines will be useful tools for preventing the onset of addiction in high-risk populations. To date, vaccines for nicotine, heroin, cocaine, and methamphetamine are all in various stages of development and clinical testing. One vaccine that has accumulated considerable research support is NicVAX, which was developed for smoking cessation. It is currently in Phase III clinical trials and has been shown to significantly decrease smoking rates with little or no adverse side effects. An important caveat to these findings, however, is that anti-addiction vaccines are effective only if sufficient levels of antibodies are achieved and maintained. This has been a major issue for all anti-addiction vaccines as, in some studies, as little as 25 percent of patients achieved sufficiently high antibody levels. There are several potential explanations for this phenomenon including the design of the vaccine, the dosing, and the frequency of vaccinations. Genetic variations among individuals and the development of immunological tolerance have also been identified as contributing factors. Moving forward, gaining a better understanding of these issues so that vaccines can be appropriately tailored will be an essential area of investigation.

Glutamatergic Medications

With the exception of drug substitution strategies, traditional pharmacological approaches to SUDs have targeted monoamines or the endogenous opioid system. However, a growing body of literature suggests that glutamatergic neurotransmission is implicated in the pathophysiology of SUDs and, therefore, may be a promising novel treatment target (Olive, 2010; Reissner & Kalivas, 2010). Several medications that act on glutamate neurotransmission are currently being investigated for their utility in the treatment of SUDs, and early results have been promising. For example, gabapentin, an anticonvulsant medication that inhibits the release of glutamate (Coderre, Kumar, Lefebvre, & Yu, 2007), has been shown to alleviate alcohol withdrawal symptoms (Bozikas, Petrikis, Gamvrula, Savvidou, & Karavatos, 2002), reduce cravings (Mason, Light, Williams, & Drobes, 2009), and facilitate abstinence among alcohol-dependent patients (Bowers et al., 2008). Notably, however, not all studies have found gabapentin to be efficacious, especially for substances other than alcohol. Modafinil, the central nervous system stimulant used to treat narcolepsy, is another medication that has recently received much empirical attention. The pharmacological effects of modafinil are still unclear; however, it has been shown to increase extracellular glutamate levels in the brain (Ferraro et al., 1999). Moreover, research suggests that modafinil may block the hedonic effects of cocaine (Malcolm et al., 2006) and reduce daily cocaine use (Dackis, 2005). It has also shown promise as a possible treatment for methamphetamine addiction and pathological gambling (Shearer et al., 2009; Zack & Poulos, 2009) but not smoking cessation (Schnoll et al., 2008). Initial hypotheses about modafinil's effectiveness are that it works as a cognitive enhancer, potentially by strengthening neural circuits involved in learning and inhibitory control.

Summary and Conclusions

Taken together, SUDs are devastating, difficult-to-treat disorders that are characterized by compulsive drug-taking behaviors and a loss of self-control. Although several treatments have been shown to be moderately effective, rates of recovery are low, and there continues to be a critical need to improve treatment outcomes. Toward this end, the field of addiction has made notable progress in identifying the active ingredients of existing treatments and the neural correlates of treatment success. There have also been substantial improvements in our understanding of SUD neurobiology, though translation of this knowledge into novel treatments has been sluggish.

To continue to move forward, it is essential that researchers continue to adopt collaborative, interdisciplinary, neurocognitive approaches to the study of addiction. For example, incorporating pre- and post-multi-modal assessment batteries into RCTs will significantly improve our understanding of how treatments work. It could also lead to the discovery of reliable treatment predictors, such that individuals vulnerable to relapse or dropout could be identified. Along these same lines, continued assessment and investigation on how individual difference factors interact with types of treatment (e.g., CBT, glutamatergic medications) will be important. It is the hope that one day, we will be able to successfully match specific types of individuals to specific types of treatment. Last, it is necessary that researchers address the way genetics, neurobiology, environment, and behavior interact to influence the pathophysiology of SUDs. Neurobiological factors are not the sole contributors to SUDs, and studying neural processes in isolation will hinder progress. As new tools, methods, and techniques become available, we will be able to answer a wider range of clinical research questions and, consequently, increase our success and efficiency in applying the neurocognitive perspective to the treatment of SUDs.

References

Abdullaev, Y., Posner, M. I., Nunnally, R., & Dishion, T. J. (2010) Functional MRI evidence for inefficient attentional control in adolescent chronic cannabis abuse. *Behavioural Brain Research, 215*(1), 45–57.

Aharonovich, E., Hasin, D. S., Brooks, A. C., Liu, X., Bisaga, A., & Nunes, E. V. (2006). Cognitive deficits predict low treatment retention in cocaine dependent patients. *Drug and Alcohol Dependence, 81*(3), 313–322.

Allen, J. P., Mattson, M. E., Miller, W. R., Tonigan, J. S., Connors, G. J., Rychtarik, R. G., … & Townsend, M. (1997). Matching alcoholism treatments to client heterogeneity: Project MATCH posttreatment drinking outcomes. *Journal of Studies on Alcohol, 58*(1), 7–29.

Al-Zahrani, M., & Elsayed, Y. (2009). The impacts of substance abuse and dependence on neuropsychological functions in a sample of patients from Saudi Arabia. *Behavioral and Brain Functions, 5*(1), 5–48.

Baldacchino, A., Balfour, D. J. K., Passetti, F., Humphris, G., & Matthews, K. (2012). Neuropsychological consequences of chronic opioid use: A quantitative review and meta-analysis. *Neuroscience & Biobehavioral Reviews, 36*(9), 2056–2068.

Ball, S. A., Carroll, K. M., Canning-Ball, M., & Rounsaville, B. J. (2006). Reasons for dropout from drug abuse treatment: Symptoms, personality, and motivation. *Addictive Behaviors, 31*(2), 320–330.

Barber, A. D., Caffo, B. S., Pekar, J. J., & Mostofsky, S. H. (2013). Developmental changes in within- and between-network connectivity between late childhood and adulthood. *Neuropsychologia, 51*(1), 156–167.

Bates, M. E., Pawlak, A. P., Tonigan, J. S., & Buckman, J. F. (2006). Cognitive impairment influences drinking outcome by altering therapeutic mechanisms of change. *Psychology of Addictive Behaviors, 20*(3), 241–253.

Beck, J. S. (2011). *Cognitive behavior therapy: Basics and beyond* (2nd edn). New York: Guilford Press.

Berke, J. D. (2003). Learning and memory mechanisms involved in compulsive drug use and relapse. In J. Q. Wang (Ed.), *Drugs of Abuse* (pp. 75–101). Totowa, NJ: Humana Press.

Berridge, K. C. (2007). The debate over dopamine's role in reward: The case for incentive salience. *Psychopharmacology, 191*(3), 391–431.

Bowers, M. S., Hopf, F. W., Chou, J. K., Guillory, A. M., Chang, S. J., Janak, P. H., ... & Diamond, I. (2008). Nucleus accumbens AGS3 expression drives ethanol seeking through Gβγ. *Proceedings of the National Academy of Sciences*, *105*(34), 12533–12538.

Bozikas, V., Petrikis, P., Gamvrula, K., Savvidou, I., & Karavatos, A. (2002). Treatment of alcohol withdrawal with gabapentin. *Progress in Neuropsychopharmacology and Biological Psychiatry*, *26*(1), 197–199.

Brewer, J. A., Bowen, S., Smith, J. T., Marlatt, G. A., & Potenza, M. N. (2010). Mindfulness-based treatments for co-occurring depression and substance use disorders: What can we learn from the brain? *Addiction*, *105*(10), 1698–1706.

Brewer, J. A., Sinha, R., Chen, J. A., Michalsen, R. N., Babuscio, T. A., Nich, C., ... & Rounsaville, B. J. (2009). Mindfulness training reduces stress reactivity and relapse in substance abuse: Results from a randomized, controlled pilot study. *Substance Abuse, 30*(4), 306–317.

Bruce, R. (2010). Methadone as HIV prevention: High volume methadone sites to decrease HIV incidence rates in resource limited settings. *International Journal of Drug Policy, 21*(2), 122–124.

Burke, B. L., Arkowitz, H., & Menchola, M. (2003). The efficacy of motivational interviewing: A meta-analysis of controlled clinical trials. *Journal of Consulting and Clinical Psychology*, *71*(5), 843–861.

Bush, G., Vogt, B. A., Holmes, J., Dale, A. M., Greve, D., Jenike, M. A., & Rosen, B. R. (2002). Dorsal anterior cingulate cortex: A role in reward-based decision making. *Proceedings of the National Academy of Sciences*, *99*(1), 523–528.

Canales, J. J. (2010). Comparative neuroscience of stimulant-induced memory dysfunction: Role for neurogenesis in the adult hippocampus. *Behavioural Pharmacology, 21*(5–6), 379–398.

Carroll, K. M., & Onken, L. S. (2005). Behavioral therapies for drug abuse. *The American Journal of Psychiatry*, *162*(8), 1452–1460.

Chamberlain, S. R., Hampshire, A., Müller, U., Rubia, K., Del Campo, N., Craig, K., ... & Sahakian, B. J. (2009). Atomoxetine modulates right inferior frontal activation during inhibitory control: A pharmacological functional magnetic resonance imaging study. *Biological Psychiatry*, *65*(7), 550–555.

Chambless, D. L., & Ollendick, T. H. (2001). Empirically supported psychological interventions: Controversies and evidence. *Annual Review of Psychology*, *52*(1), 685–716.

Chen, B. T., Yau, H. J., Hatch, C., Kusumoto-Yoshida, I., Cho, S. L., Hopf, F. W., & Bonci, A. (2013). Rescuing cocaine-induced prefrontal cortex hypoactivity prevents compulsive cocaine seeking. *Nature*, *496*(7445), 359–362.

Childress, A. R., Hole, A. V., Ehrman, R. N., Robbins, S. J., McLellan, A. T., & O'Brien, C. P. (1993). Cue reactivity and cue reactivity interventions in drug dependence. *NIDA Research Monographs, 137*, 73–95.

Clapp, P., Bhave, S. V., & Hoffman, P. L. (2008). How adaptation of the brain to alcohol leads to dependence: A pharmacological perspective. *Alcohol Research & Health, 31*(4), 310–339.

Coderre, T. J., Kumar, N., Lefebvre, C. D., & Yu, J. S. C. (2007). A comparison of the glutamate release inhibition and anti-allodynic effects of gabapentin, lamotrigine, and riluzole in a model of neuropathic pain. *Journal of Neurochemistry*, *100*(5), 1289–1299.

Crego, A., Rodriguez-Holguín, S., Parada, M., Mota, N., Corral, M., & Cadaveira, F. (2010). Reduced anterior prefrontal cortex activation in young binge drinkers during a visual working memory task. *Drug and Alcohol Dependence*, *109*(1–3), 45–56.

Crowley, T. J., Dalwani, M. S., Mikulich-Gilbertson, S. K., Du, Y. P., Lejuez, C. W., Raymond, K. M., & Banich, M. T. (2010). Risky decisions and their consequences: Neural processing by boys with antisocial substance disorder. *Plos ONE*, *5*(9), e12835.

Dackis, C. A. (2005). New treatments for cocaine abuse. *Drug Discovery Today: Therapeutic Strategies*, *2*(1), 79–86.

Dalley, J. W., Everitt, B. J., & Robbins, T. W. (2011). Impulsivity, compulsivity, and top-down cognitive control. *Neuron*, *69*(4), 680–694.

Darke, S., Ross, J., Teesson, M., Ali, R., Cooke, R., Ritter, A., & Lynskey, M. (2005). Factors associated with 12 months continuous heroin abstinence: Findings from the Australian Treatment Outcome Study (ATOS). *Journal of Substance Abuse Treatment*, *28*(3), 255–263.

Daughters, S. B., Braun, A. R., Sargeant, M. N., Reynolds, E. K., Hopko, D. R., Blanco, C., & Lejuez, C. W. (2008). Effectiveness of a brief behavioral treatment for inner-city illicit drug users with elevated depressive symptoms: The Life Enhancement Treatment for Substance Use (LETS ACT). *Journal of Clinical Psychiatry*, *69*(1), 122–129.

Davstad, I., Stenbacka, M., Leifman, A., & Romelsjö, A. (2009). An 18-year follow-up of patients admitted to methadone treatment for the first time. *Journal of Addictive Diseases*, *28*(1), 39–52.

De Leon, G. (1991). Retention in drug-free therapeutic communities. *Improving Drug Abuse Treatment*, *106*, 91–1754.

Devroye, C., Filip, M., Przegaliński, E., McCreary, A. C., & Spampinato, U. (2013). Serotonin$_{2C}$ receptors and drug addiction: Focus on cocaine. *Experimental Brain Research*, *230*(4), 537–545.

Di Chiara, G. (1999). Drug addiction as dopamine-dependent associative learning disorder. *European Journal of Pharmacology*, *375*(1), 13–30.

Di Chiara, G., Bassareo, V., Fenu, S., De Luca, M. A., Spina, L., Cadoni, C., ... & Lecca, D. (2004). Dopamine and drug addiction: The nucleus accumbens shell connection. *Neuropharmacology*, *47*, 227–241.

Drevets, W. C., Gautier, C., Price, J. C., Kupfer, D. J., Kinahan, P. E., Grace, A. A., ... & Mathis, C. A. (2001). Amphetamine-induced dopamine release in human ventral striatum correlates with euphoria. *Biological Psychiatry*, *49*(2), 81–96.

Dutra, L., Stathopoulou, G., Basden, S., Leyro, T., Powers, M., & Otto, M. (2008). A meta-analytic review of psychosocial interventions for substance use disorders. *American Journal of Psychiatry*, *165*(2), 179–187.

Ersche, K. D., Clark, L., London, M., Robbins, T. W., & Sahakian, B. J. (2006). Profile of executive and memory function associated with amphetamine and opiate dependence. *Neuropsychopharmacology*, *31*(5), 1036–1047.

Everitt, B. J., Dickinson, A., & Robbins, T. W. (2001). The neuropsychological basis of addictive behaviour. *Brain Research Reviews*, *36*(2), 129–138.

Fals-Stewart, W., & Lam, W. K. (2010). Computer-assisted cognitive rehabilitation for the treatment of patients with substance use disorders: A randomized clinical trial. *Experimental and Clinical Psychopharmacology*, *18*(1), 87–98.

Feldstein Ewing, S. W., Filbey, F. M., Sabbineni, A., Chandler, L. D., & Hutchison, K. E. (2011). How psychosocial alcohol interventions work: A preliminary look at what fMRI can tell us. *Alcoholism: Clinical and Experimental Research, 35*(4), 643–651.

Fernández-Serrano, M. J., Perales, J. C., Moreno-López, L., Pérez-García, M., & Verdejo-García, A. (2012). Neuropsychological profiling of impulsivity and compulsivity in cocaine dependent individuals. *Psychopharmacology, 219*(2), 673–683.

Ferraro, L., Antonelli, T., Tanganelli, S., O'Connor, W. T., de la Mora, M. P., Mendez-Franco, J., ... & Fuxe, K. (1999). The vigilance promoting drug modafinil increases extracellular glutamate levels in the medial preoptic area and the posterior hypothalamus of the conscious rat: Prevention by local GABAA receptor blockade. *Neuropsychopharmacology, 20*(4), 346–356.

Fox, H. C., Hong, K. A., & Sinha, R. R. (2008). Difficulties in emotion regulation and impulse control in recently abstinent alcoholics compared with social drinkers. *Addictive Behaviors, 33*(2), 388–394.

Fu, L. P., Bi, G. H., Zou, Z. T., Wang, Y., Ye, E. M., Ma, L., & Yang, Z. (2008). Impaired response inhibition function in abstinent heroin dependents: An fMRI study. *Neuroscience Letters, 438*(3), 322–326.

Goldapple, K., Segal, Z., Garson, C., Lau, M., Bieling, P., Kennedy, S., & Mayberg, H. (2004). Modulation of cortical-limbic pathways in major depression: Treatment-specific effects of cognitive behavior therapy. *Archives of General Psychiatry, 61*(1), 34–41.

Goldstein, R. Z., & Volkow, N. D. (2002). Drug addiction and its underlying neurobiological basis: Neuroimaging evidence for the involvement of the frontal cortex. *The American Journal of Psychiatry, 159*(10), 1642–1652.

Goldstein, R. Z., & Volkow, N. D. (2011). Dysfunction of the prefrontal cortex in addiction: Neuroimaging findings and clinical implications. *Nature Reviews Neuroscience, 12*(11), 652–669.

Grohman, K., & Fals-Stewart, W. (2003). Computer-assisted cognitive rehabilitation with substance-abusing patients: Effects on treatment response. *Journal of Cognitive Rehabilitation, 21*(4), 10–17.

Gruber, S. A., Silveri, M. M., & Yurgelun-Todd, D. A. (2007). Neuropsychological consequences of opiate use. *Neuropsychology Review, 17*(3), 299–315.

Hampton, A. N., & O'Doherty, J. P. (2007). Decoding the neural substrates of reward-related decision making with functional MRI. *Proceedings of the National Academy of Sciences, 104*(4), 1377–1382.

Hättenschwiler, J., Rueesch, P., & Modestin, J. (2001). Comparison of four groups of substance-abusing in-patients with different psychiatric comorbidity. *Acta Psychiatrica Scandinavica, 104*(1), 59–65.

Hayes, S. C., Strosahl, K., & Wilson, K. G. (1999). *Acceptance and commitment therapy: An experiential approach to behavior change*. New York: Guilford Press.

Heinz, A., Beck, A., Grüsser, S. M., Grace, A. A., & Wrase, J. (2009). Identifying the neural circuitry of alcohol craving and relapse vulnerability. *Addiction Biology, 14*(1), 108–118.

Hekmat, S., Mehrjerdi, Z., Moradi, A., Ekhtiari, H., & Bakhshi, S. (2011). Cognitive flexibility, attention and speed of mental processing in opioid and methamphetamine addicts in comparison with non-addicts. *Basic and Clinical Neuroscience, 2*(2), 12–19.

Herin, D. V., Rush, C., & Grabowski, J. (2010). Agonist-like pharmacotherapy for stimulant dependence: Preclinical, human laboratory, and clinical studies. *Annals of the New York Academy of Sciences, 1187*(1), 76–100.

Hettema, J., Steele, J., & Miller, W. R. (2005). Motivational interviewing. *Annual Review of Clinical Psychology*, *1*, 91–111.

Higgins, S. T. (1997). The influence of alternative reinforcers on cocaine use and abuse: A brief review. *Pharmacology Biochemistry and Behavior*, *57*(3), 419–427.

Higgins, S. T., Heil, S. H., & Lussier, J. P. (2004). Clinical implications of reinforcement as a determinant of substance use disorders. *Annual Review of Psychology*, *55*, 431–461.

Higgins, S. T., Wong, C. J., Badger, G. J., Ogden, D., & Dantona, R. L. (2000). Contingent reinforcement increases cocaine abstinence during outpatient treatment and one year of follow-up. *Journal of Consulting and Clinical Psychology*, *68*, 64–72.

Higgins, S. T., Delaney, D. D., Budney, A. J., Bickel, W. K., Hughes, J. R., Foerg, F., & Fenwick, J. W. (1991). A behavioral approach to achieving initial cocaine abstinence. *American Journal of Psychiatry*, *148*(9), 1218–1224.

Hoffman, W. F., Schwartz, D. L., Huckans, M. S., McFarland, B. H., Meiri, G., Stevens, A. A., & Mitchell, S. H. (2008). Cortical activation during delay discounting in abstinent methamphetamine dependent individuals. *Psychopharmacology*, *201*(2), 183–193.

Houston, R. J., Derrick, J. L., Leonard, K. E., Testa, M., Quigley, B. M., & Kubiak, A. (2013). Effects of heavy drinking on executive cognitive functioning in a community sample. *Addictive Behaviors*, *39*(1), 345–349.

Hubbard, R. L., Craddock, S. G., & Anderson, J. (2003). Overview of 5-year follow-up outcomes in the drug abuse treatment outcome studies (DATOS). *Journal of Substance Abuse Treatment*, *25*(3), 125–134.

Hyman, S. E. (2005). Addiction: A disease of learning and memory. *American Journal of Psychiatry*, *162*(8), 1414–1422.

Jacobs, K., & Gill, K. (2002). Substance abuse in an urban aboriginal population: Social, legal and psychological consequences. *Journal of Ethnicity in Substance Abuse*, *1*(1), 7–25.

Johansson, B. A., Berglund, M., & Lindgren, A. (2006). Efficacy of maintenance treatment with naltrexone for opioid dependence: A meta-analytical review. *Addiction*, *101*(4), 491–503.

Johnson, M. E., Neal, D. B., Brems, C., & Fisher, D. G. (2006). Depression as measured by the Beck Depression Inventory-II among injecting drug users. *Assessment*, *13*(2), 168–177.

Johnson, M. W., Bickel, W. K., Baker, F., Moore, B. A., Badger, G. J., & Budney, A. J. (2010). Delay discounting in current and former marijuana-dependent individuals. *Experimental and Clinical Psychopharmacology*, *18*(1), 99–107.

Kaplan, G. B., Heinrichs, S. C., & Carey, R. J. (2011). Treatment of addiction and anxiety using extinction approaches: Neural mechanisms and their treatment implications. *Pharmacology, Biochemistry and Behavior*, *97*(3), 619–625.

Katz, E. C., King, S. D., Schwartz, R. P., Weintraub, E., Barksdale, W., Robinson, R., & Brown, B. S. (2005). Cognitive ability as a factor in engagement in drug abuse treatment. *The American Journal of Drug and Alcohol Abuse*, *31*(3), 359–369.

Kelleher, L. M., Stough, C., Sergejew, A. A., & Rolfe, T. (2004). The effects of cannabis on information-processing speed. *Addictive Behaviors*, *29*(6), 1213–1219.

Khalsa, J. H., Treisman, G., McCance-Katz, E., & Tedaldi, E. (2008). Medical consequences of drug abuse and co-occurring infections: Research at the National Institute on Drug Abuse. *Substance Abuse*, *29*(3), 5–16.

King, G. R., Ernst, T., Deng, W., Stenger, A., Gonzales, R. M., Nakama, H., & Chang, L. (2011). Altered brain activation during visuomotor integration in chronic active cannabis users: Relationship to cortisol levels. *The Journal of Neuroscience, 31*(49), 17923–17931

Kober, H., Mende-Siedlecki, P., Kross, E. F., Weber, J., Mischel, W., Hart, C. L., & Ochsner, K. N. (2010). Prefrontal–striatal pathway underlies cognitive regulation of craving. *Proceedings of the National Academy of Sciences of the United States of America, 107*(33), 14811–14816.

Konrad, A., Vucurevic, G., Lorscheider, M., Bernow, N., Thümmel, M., Chai, C., … & Fehr, C. (2012). Broad disruption of brain white matter microstructure and relationship with neuropsychological performance in male patients with severe alcohol dependence. *Alcohol and Alcoholism, 47*(2), 118–126.

Koob, G. F. (2004). A role for GABA mechanisms in the motivational effects of alcohol. *Biochemical Pharmacology, 68*(8), 1515–1525.

Koob, G. F. (2008). A role for brain stress systems in addiction. *Neuron, 59*(1), 11–34.

Koob, G. F. (2009). Neurobiological substrates for the dark side of compulsivity in addiction. *Neuropharmacology, 56*, 18–31.

Koob, G. F. (2010). The role of CRF and CRF-related peptides in the dark side of addiction. *Brain Research, 1314*, 3–14.

Koob, G. F. (2013). Negative reinforcement in drug addiction: The darkness within. *Current Opinion in Neurobiology, 23*(4), 559–563.

Koob, G. F., & Le Moal, M. (2008). Addiction and the brain antireward system. *Annual Review of Psychology, 59*, 29–53.

Koob, G. F., & Nestler, E. J. (1997). The neurobiology of drug addiction. *Journal of Neuropsychiatry and Clinical Neurosciences, 9*(3), 482–497.

Kosten, T. R., & O'Connor, P. G. (2003). Management of drug and alcohol withdrawal. *New England Journal of Medicine, 348*(18), 1786–1795.

Krueger, D. D., Osterweil, E. K., Chen, S. P., Tye, L. D., & Bear, M. F. (2011). Cognitive dysfunction and prefrontal synaptic abnormalities in a mouse model of fragile X syndrome. *Proceedings of the National Academy of Sciences of the United States of America, 108*(6), 2587–2592.

Laurenzana, E. M., Hendrickson, H. P., Carpenter, D., Peterson, E. C., Gentry, W. B., West, M., … & Owens, S. M. (2009). Functional and biological determinants affecting the duration of action and efficacy of anti-(+)-methamphetamine monoclonal antibodies in rats. *Vaccine, 27*(50), 7011–7020.

Levin, E. D., Rezvani, A. H., Xiao, Y., Slade, S., Cauley, M., Wells, C., … & Kellar, K. J. (2010). Sazetidine-A, a selective α4β2 nicotinic receptor desensitizing agent and partial agonist, reduces nicotine self-administration in rats. *The Journal of Pharmacology and Experimental Therapeutics, 332*(3), 933–939.

Li, C. S. R., & Sinha, R. (2008). Inhibitory control and emotional stress regulation: Neuroimaging evidence for frontal–limbic dysfunction in psycho-stimulant addiction. *Neuroscience & Biobehavioral Reviews, 32*(3), 581–597.

Linehan, M. M. (1993). *Cognitive-behavioral treatment of borderline personality disorder.* New York: Guilford Press.

Longo, M., Wickes, W., Smout, M., Harrison, S., Cahill, S., & White, J. M. (2010). Randomized controlled trial of dexamphetamine maintenance for the treatment of methamphetamine dependence. *Addiction, 105*(1), 146–154.

Lundqvist, T. (2005). Cognitive consequences of cannabis use: Comparison with abuse of stimulants and heroin with regard to attention, memory and executive functions. *Pharmacology, Biochemistry and Behavior, 81*(2), 319–330.

Ma, N., Liu, Y., Li, N., Wang, C. X., Zhang, H., Jiang, X. F., … & Zhang, D. R. (2010). Addiction related alteration in resting-state brain connectivity. *Neuroimage, 49*(1), 738–744.

Magidson, J. F., Gorka, S. M., MacPherson, L., Hopko, D. R., Blanco, C., Lejuez, C. W., & Daughters, S. B. (2011). Examining the effect of the Life Enhancement Treatment for Substance Use (LETS ACT) on residential substance abuse treatment retention. *Addictive Behaviors, 36*(6), 615–623.

Maglione, M., Chao, B., & Anglin, M. D. (2000). Correlates of outpatient drug treatment drop-out among methamphetamine users. *Journal of Psychoactive Drugs, 32*(2), 221–228.

Maisel, N. C., Blodgett, J. C., Wilbourne, P. L., Humphreys, K., & Finney, J. W. (2013). Meta-analysis of naltrexone and acamprosate for treating alcohol use disorders: When are these medications most helpful? *Addiction, 108*(2), 275–293.

Malcolm, R., Swayngim, K., Donovan, J. L., DeVane, C. L., Elkashef, A., Chiang, N., … & Woolson, R. F. (2006). Modafinil and cocaine interactions. *The American Journal of Drug and Alcohol Abuse, 32*(4), 577–587.

Marsch, L. A. (1998). The efficacy of methadone maintenance interventions in reducing illicit opiate use, HIV risk behavior and criminality: A meta-analysis. *Addiction, 93*(4), 515–532.

Martin, P. R., Singleton, C. K., & Hiller-Sturmhofel, S. (2003). The role of thiamine deficiency in alcoholic brain disease. *Alcohol Research and Health, 27*(2), 134–142.

Mason, B. J., Light, J. M., Williams, L. D., & Drobes, D. J. (2009). Proof-of-concept human laboratory study for protracted abstinence in alcohol dependence: Effects of gabapentin. *Addiction Biology, 14*(1), 73–83.

Matochik, J. A., London, E. D., Eldreth, D. A., Cadet, J. L., & Bolla, K. I. (2003). Frontal cortical tissue composition in abstinent cocaine abusers: A magnetic resonance imaging study. *Neuroimage, 19*(3), 1095–1102.

McDaid, J. J., Tedford, C. E., Mackie, A. R., Dallimore, J. E., Mickiewicz, A. L., Shen, F. F., … & Napier, T. C. (2007). Nullifying drug-induced sensitization: Behavioral and electrophysiological evaluations of dopaminergic and serotonergic ligands in methamphetamine-sensitized rats. *Drug and Alcohol Dependence, 86*(1), 55–66.

McKinney, A., Coyle, K., Penning, R., & Verster, J. C. (2012). Next day effects of naturalistic alcohol consumption on tasks of attention. *Human Psychopharmacology: Clinical and Experimental, 27*(6), 587–594.

Mertens, J. R., & Weisner, C. M. (2000). Predictors of substance abuse treatment retention among women and men in an HMO. *Alcoholism: Clinical and Experimental Research, 24*(10), 1525–1533.

Miller, W. R., & Rollnick, S. (1991). *Motivational interviewing: Preparing people to change addictive behavior.* New York: Guilford Press.

Miller, W. R., & Rollnick, S. (2002). *Motivational interviewing: Preparing people for change.* New York: Guilford Press.

Mintzer, M. Z. (2007). The acute effects of alcohol on memory: A review of laboratory studies in healthy adults. *International Journal On Disability And Human Development, 6*(4), 397–403.

Morales, M., & Pickel, V. M. (2012). Insights to drug addiction derived from ultrastructural views of the mesocorticolimbic system. *Annals of the New York Academy of Sciences*, *1248*(1), 71–88.

Morein-Zamir, S., Jones, P., Bullmore, E. T., Robbins, T. W., & Ersche, K. D. (2013). Prefrontal hypoactivity associated with impaired inhibition in stimulant-dependent individuals but evidence for hyperactivation in their unaffected siblings. *Neuropsychopharmacology*, *38*(10), 1945–1953.

Morgenstern, J., Blanchard, K. A., Morgan, T. J., Labouvie, E., & Hayaki, J. (2001). Testing the effectiveness of cognitive-behavioral treatment for substance abuse in a community setting: Within treatment and posttreatment findings. *Journal of Consulting and Clinical Psychology*, *69*(6), 1007–1017.

Moussawi, K., & Kalivas, P. W. (2010). Group II metabotropic glutamate receptors in drug addiction. *European Journal of Pharmacology*, *639*(1), 115–122.

Movig, K. L. L., Mathijssen, M. P. M., Nagel, P. H. A., Van Egmond, T., De Gier, J. J., Leufkens, H. G. M., & Egberts, A. C. (2004). Psychoactive substance use and the risk of motor vehicle accidents. *Accident Analysis & Prevention*, *36*(4), 631–636.

Myers, B., Pasche, S., & Adam, M. (2010). Correlates of substance abuse treatment completion among disadvantaged communities in Cape Town, South Africa. *Substance Abuse Treatment, Prevention, and Policy*, *5*(1), 3.

Myrick, H., Anton, R. F., Li, X., Henderson, S., Drobes, D., Voronin, K., & George, M. S. (2004). Differential brain activity in alcoholics and social drinkers to alcohol cues: Relationship to craving. *Neuropsychopharmacology*, *29*(2), 393–402.

Nelson, A., & Killcross, S. (2006). Amphetamine exposure enhances habit formation. *The Journal of Neuroscience*, *26*(14), 3805–3812.

Office of Applied Studies (2009). *Results from the 2008 Survey on Drug Use and Health: National Findings*. Rockville, MD: Substance Abuse and Mental Health Services Administration, Department of Health and Human Services.

Olive, M. F. (2010). Cognitive effects of group I metabotropic glutamate receptor ligands in the context of drug addiction. *European Journal of Pharmacology*, *639*(1), 47–58.

Paulus, M. P., Hozack, N. E., Zauscher, B. E., Frank, L., Brown, G. G., Braff, D. L., & Schuckit, M. A. (2002). Behavioral and functional neuroimaging evidence for prefrontal dysfunction in methamphetamine-dependent subjects. *Neuropsychopharmacology*, *26*, 53–63.

Pentel, P. R., Malin, D. H., Ennifar, S., Hieda, Y., Keyler, D. E., Lake, J. R., ... & Fattom, A. (2000). A nicotine conjugate vaccine reduces nicotine distribution to brain and attenuates its behavioral and cardiovascular effects in rats. *Pharmacology Biochemistry and Behavior*, *65*(1), 191–198.

Petry, N. M. (2001). Delay discounting of money and alcohol in actively using alcoholics, currently abstinent alcoholics, and controls. *Psychopharmacology*, *154*(3), 243–250.

Petry, N. M., Martin, B., Cooney, J. L., & Kranzler, H. R. (2000). Give them prizes and they will come: Contingency management for treatment of alcohol dependence. *Journal of Consulting and Clinical Psychology*, *68*(2), 250–257.

Petry, N. M., Alessi, S. M., Carroll, K. M., Hanson, T., MacKinnon, S., Rounsaville, B., & Sierra, S. (2006). Contingency management treatments: Reinforcing abstinence versus adherence with goal-related activities. *Journal of Consulting and Clinical Psychology*, *74*(3), 592–601.

Potenza, M. N., Sofuoglu, M., Carroll, K. M., & Rounsaville, B. J. (2011). Neuroscience of behavioral and pharmacological treatments for addictions. *Neuron*, *69*(4), 695–712.

Prochaska, J. J., Delucchi, K., & Hall, S. M. (2004). A meta-analysis of smoking cessation interventions with individuals in substance abuse treatment or recovery. *Journal of Consulting and Clinical Psychology*, *72*(6), 1144–1156.

Rabinowitz, J., & Marjefsky, S. (1998). Alcohol & drug abuse: Predictors of being expelled from and dropping out of alcohol treatment. *Psychiatric Services*, *49*(2), 187–189.

Ravndal, E., & Vaglum, P. (1991). Psychopathology and substance abuse as predictors of program completion in a therapeutic community for drug abusers: A prospective study. *Acta Psychiatrica Scandinavica*, *83*(3), 217–222.

Ravndal, E., & Vaglum, P. (2002). Psychopathology, treatment completion, and 5 years outcome: A prospective study of drug abusers. *Journal of Substance Abuse Treatment*, *15*, 135–142.

Reissner, K. J., & Kalivas, P. W. (2010). Using glutamate homeostasis as a target for treating addictive disorders. *Behavioural Pharmacology*, *21*(5–6), 514.

Rogers, C. R. (1951). *Client-centered therapy: Its current practice, implications and theory*. Boston, MA: Houghton Mifflin.

Rupp, C. I., Kemmler, G., Kurz, M., Hinterhuber, H., & Fleischhacker, W. W. (2012). Cognitive remediation therapy during treatment for alcohol dependence. *Journal of Studies on Alcohol and Drugs*, *73*(4), 625–634.

Schnoll, R. A., Wileyto, E. P., Pinto, A., Leone, F., Gariti, P., Siegel, S., … & Lerman, C. (2008). A placebo-controlled trial of modafinil for nicotine dependence. *Drug and Alcohol Dependence*, *98*(1), 86–93.

Schweizer, T. A., & Vogel-Sprott, M. (2008). Alcohol-impaired speed and accuracy of cognitive functions: A review of acute tolerance and recovery of cognitive performance. *Experimental and Clinical Psychopharmacology*, *16*(3), 240–250.

Scott, J. C., Woods, S. P., Matt, G. E., Meyer, R. A., Heaton, R. K., Atkinson, J. H., & Grant, I. (2007). Neurocognitive effects of methamphetamine: A critical review and meta-analysis. *Neuropsychology Review*, *17*(3), 275–297.

Seal, K. H., Kral, A. H., Gee, L., Moore, L. D., Bluthenthal, R. N., Lorvick, J., & Edlin, B. R. (2001). Predictors and prevention of nonfatal overdose among street-recruited injection heroin users in the San Francisco Bay Area, 1998–1999. *American Journal of Public Health*, *91*(11), 1842–1846.

Self, D., & Tamminga, C. A. (2004). Drug dependence and addiction. *The American Journal of Psychiatry*, *161*(2), 223–223.

Shearer, J., Darke, S., Rodgers, C., Slade, T., Van Beek, I., Lewis, J., … & Wodak, A. (2009). A double-blind, placebo-controlled trial of modafinil (200 mg/day) for methamphetamine dependence. *Addiction*, *104*(2), 224–233.

Simons-Morton, B., & Chen, R. S. (2006). Over time relationships between early adolescent and peer substance use. *Addictive Behaviors*, *31*(7), 1211–1223.

Simpson, D. D., Joe, G. W., & Brown, B. S. (1997). Treatment retention and follow-up outcomes in the Drug Abuse Treatment Outcome Study (DATOS). *Psychology of Addictive Behaviors*, *11*(4), 294–307.

Smith, D. E., & McCrady, B. S. (1991). Cognitive impairment among alcoholics: Impact on drink refusal skill acquisition and treatment outcome. *Addictive Behaviors*, *16*(5), 265–274.

348 Stephanie M. Gorka, Yun Chen, and Stacey B. Daughters

Solowij, N., Jones, K. A., Rozman, M. E., Davis, S. M., Ciarrochi, J., Heaven, P. L., ... & Yücel, M. (2011). Verbal learning and memory in adolescent cannabis users, alcohol users and non-users. *Psychopharmacology, 216*(1), 131–144.

Stanger, C., Elton, A., Ryan, S. R., James, G., Budney, A. J., & Kilts, C. D. (2013). Neuroeconomics and adolescent substance abuse: Individual differences in neural networks and delay discounting. *Journal of the American Academy of Child & Adolescent Psychiatry, 52*(7), 747–755.

Stark, M. J. (1992). Dropping out of substance abuse treatment: A clinically oriented review. *Clinical Psychology Review, 12*(1), 93–116.

Stavro, K., Pelletier, J., & Potvin, S. (2013). Widespread and sustained cognitive deficits in alcoholism: A meta-analysis. *Addiction Biology, 18*(2), 203–213.

Substance Abuse and Mental Health Services Administration (SAMHSA) (2013). *Results from the 2012 National Survey on Drug Use and Health: Mental health findings and detailed tables*. NSDUH Series H-47, HHS Publication No. (SMA) 13–4805. Rockville, MD: SAMHSA.

Sutherland, M. T., Carroll, A. J., Salmeron, B., Ross, T. J., & Stein, E. A. (2013). Insula's functional connectivity with ventromedial prefrontal cortex mediates the impact of trait alexithymia on state tobacco craving. *Psychopharmacology, 228*(1), 143–155.

Tang, Y. Y., Lu, Q., Geng, X., Stein, E. A., Yang, Y., & Posner, M. I. (2010). Short-term meditation induces white matter changes in the anterior cingulate. *Proceedings of the National Academy of Sciences, 107*(35), 15649–15652.

Tate, S. R., Brown, S. A., Unrod, M., & Ramo, D. E. (2004). Context of relapse for substance-dependent adults with and without comorbid psychiatric disorders. *Addictive Behaviors, 29*(9), 1707–1724.

Toomey, R., Lyons, M. J., Eisen, S. A., Xian, H., Chantarujikapong, S., Seidman, L. J., ... & Tsuang, M. T. (2003). A twin study of the neuropsychological consequences of stimulant abuse. *Archives Of General Psychiatry, 60*(3), 303–310.

Verdejo-García, A., López-Torrecillas, F., Aguilar de Arcos, F., & Pérez-García, M. (2005). Differential effects of MDMA, cocaine, and cannabis use severity on distinctive components of the executive functions in polysubstance users: A multiple regression analysis. *Addictive Behaviors, 30*(1), 89–101.

Volkow, N. D., Wang, G. J., Tomasi, D., & Baler, R. D. (2013). Unbalanced neuronal circuits in addiction. *Current Opinion in Neurobiology,* 23(4), 639–648.

Volkow, N. D., Wang, G. J., Fowler, J. S., Tomasi, D., Telang, F., & Baler, R. (2010). Addiction: Decreased reward sensitivity and increased expectation sensitivity conspire to overwhelm the brain's control circuit. *Bioessays, 32*(9), 748–755.

Volkow, N. D., Wang, G. J., Fowler, J. S., Logan, J., Gatley, S. J., Wong, C., ... & Pappas, N. R. (1999). Reinforcing effects of psychostimulants in humans are associated with increases in brain dopamine and occupancy of D2Receptors. *Journal of Pharmacology and Experimental Therapeutics, 291*(1), 409–415.

Volkow, N. D., Wang, G. J., Fowler, J. S., Logan, J., Hitzemann, R., Gatley, S. J., ... & Wolf, A. P. (1996). Cocaine uptake is decreased in the brain of detoxified cocaine abusers. *Neuropsychopharmacology, 14*(3), 159–168.

Wexler, B. E., Gottschalk, C. H., Fulbright, R. K., Prohovnik, I., Lacadie, C. M., Rounsaville, B. J., & Gore, J. C. (2001). Functional magnetic resonance imaging of cocaine craving. *American Journal of Psychiatry, 158*(1), 86–95.

Wheeler, R. A., Aragona, B. J., Fuhrmann, K. A., Jones, J. L., Day, J. J., Cacciapaglia, F., … & Carelli, R. M. (2011). Cocaine cues drive opposing context-dependent shifts in reward processing and emotional state. *Biological Psychiatry, 69*(11), 1067–1074.

Wills, T. A. (1986). Stress and coping in early adolescence: Relationships to substance use in urban school samples. *Health Psychology, 5*(6), 503–529.

Wise, R. A. (2004). Dopamine, learning and motivation. *Nature Reviews Neuroscience, 5*(6), 483–494.

Wittmann, M., Lovero, K. L., Lane, S. D., & Paulus, M. P. (2010). Now or later? Striatum and insula activation to immediate versus delayed rewards. *Journal of Neuroscience, Psychology, and Economics, 3*(1), 15–26.

Zack, M., & Poulos, C. X. (2009). Effects of the atypical stimulant modafinil on a brief gambling episode in pathological gamblers with high vs. low impulsivity. *Journal of Psychopharmacology, 23*(6), 660–671.

13

PAVING THE ROAD TO THE NEUROCOGNITIVE CLINIC OF TOMORROW

Appealing to Standards

Natasha S. Hansen and Greg Siegle

The treatment of psychiatric symptoms is rapidly moving toward an era of personalized, precision medicine in which a focus on *disorders* is replaced by a focus on *mechanisms*. The promise is that assessments of mechanisms will be used to guide treatment decisions, and specialized treatments will address mechanisms specifically (Forgeard et al., 2011; Insel et al., 2010; Siegle, Ghinassi, & Thase, 2007). The neurocognitive clinic of the future may thus bear little resemblance to the treatment settings of today. For example, a clinic employing neurocognitive methods may rely more strongly on automated exercises than therapist expertise-dependent conversation, with the advantages of reduced cost in time and suffering.

Here, we address standards useful for transforming today's psychiatry clinic intake procedures, which rarely include assessments suitable for prescribing an intervention specific to the patient's condition. We also discuss standards to assist in the transformation of interventions that today rely primarily on mechanistically non-specific medications and talk therapies into tomorrow's mechanistically targeted treatments and associated assessments. This transformation will involve making sure each neurocognitive assessment and treatment is held to ideals deemed acceptable for use in the clinic by scientists, the legal system, insurance companies, and clinicians alike. As many of the exciting new neurocognitive methods described in this book are still in their infancy, we are at an ideal place to lay strong foundational standards so that emerging neurocognitive technologies, assessments, and treatments will be held to the same specifications of quality currently being applied in other areas of medicine. Thus, this chapter specifically concentrates on standards for tomorrow's neurocognitive clinic.

Because traditionally defined disorders may be too heterogeneous to treat with mechanistic specificity, we reference "tomorrow's" mechanistic formulations via a guiding framework recently advanced by the National Institute of Mental Health (NIMH) entitled the Research Diagnostic Criteria (RDoC; Insel et al., 2010). Rather than rely on traditional disorder categories, this framework divides psychiatric symptoms into domains that are supported by basic research and have clear underlying mechanisms. The framework includes five transdiagnostic domains in which aspects of psychological dysfunction may occur: negative valence systems, positive valence systems, cognitive systems, systems for social processes, and arousal/regulatory systems. Disturbances in these systems are described across multiple levels of analysis including self-report, psychophysiology, neural circuits, and molecules.

Why Standards?

To illustrate the utility of appealing to standards, consider the alternative—the approach of today. A person presenting to a psychiatry clinic is assessed by reporting on his or her symptoms. Some clinics use unstandardized interviews. Others use self-report measures, some of which are validated and others are not. The only "standard" is that a licensed professional must sign off on the diagnosis. Psychometric properties of this process, such as reliability, are not assessed. The diagnostic system—*Diagnostic and Statistical Manual of Mental Disorders* (DSM-5; American Psychiatric Association, 2013)—is not strongly linked to treatment outcome, so prescription is not based on assessment. There are no standardized assessments that lead to specific prescriptions, though empirically supported treatment recommendations are on the rise. While other medical specialties are quickly adopting standards-based assessments and prescriptions to where drug store–based clinics can be entirely manual-driven, mental health care is far from having such an ability. In part, this is due to the fact that at present, diagnoses are not mechanistic: Individuals presenting with vastly different symptom clusters can be given the same diagnosis. In contrast, the promise of a standards-based future orientation is that mechanistic assessments can be linked to mechanistically specific treatments yielding precision medicine for mental health.

As an example, consider a single father whose child has left for college, leaving him feeling empty. His mood is sad, he experiences little pleasure from his life, has little appetite, does not get out of bed, and is hopeless about this situation changing. Given six of nine symptoms of DSM-defined depression, he can be diagnosed as depressed using the standards of today, but there is no unique treatment recommendation and little guidance for how to choose among empirically supported treatments for depression that generally work for 40 percent to 60 percent of individuals who receive this diagnosis

(Thase & Rush, 1997). In contrast, an RDoC-informed standards-based approach might identify this person as having a confluence of features of "loss," for which both cognitive correlates (e.g., rumination), biological mechanisms (e.g., sustained amygdala reactivity), and molecular features (e.g., down-regulation of glucocorticoid receptors) are well characterized (NIMH, 2011). The clinic of the future could thus address such symptoms at multiple levels (e.g., using cognitive training suited to remediating rumination; Calkins, McMorran, Siegle, & Otto, in press; Siegle et al., 2007; Siegle, Price, Jones, Ghinassi, & Thase, in press), neurofeedback on amygdala reactivity (Bruhl et al., 2014; Young et al., 2014; Zotev, Phillips, Young, Drevets, & Bodurka, 2013), and medications that affect glucocorticoid receptor activity (Baes, Martins, Tofoli, & Juruena, 2014; Zalachoras et al., 2013).

To recommend one or more of these rigorously, we would need significant developments on both the assessment and mechanistic sides. For example, neurocognitive training studies are still characterized by small samples, and randomized trials need replication with clinical populations. Norms on mechanistic assessments of amygdala activity are not yet available. In assessing glucocorticoid reactivity, the dexamethasone suppression test (DST) has a strong history. While the DST is not diagnostically specific (Madakasira & Taylor, 1986), the foundations have long been laid for its use in a post-diagnostic era (Carroll, 1985), in particular for identifying mechanistically unique subtypes (Zimmerman, Coryell, & Black, 1990). That said, it is not reliably administered (Meltzer & Fang, 1983), yielding failure to change prescribing patterns by clinicians (McGee, 1984) and suggesting increased utility for standards in administration.

Gathering Standards

Before next-generation neurocognitive technologies and associated procedures pervade tomorrow's clinics, a number of standards may be useful. Such standards would help ensure neurocognitive methods are safe for use in the lab and clinic, that their assessments are reliable and valid, that their treatments are specific and effective, and that such methods will be reimbursed by insurance companies. Other fields have established standards that may be useful to reference for this purpose.

For psychological assessments, we will appeal to standards for evaluation of neuropsychological tests, as described in testing and measurement textbooks (e.g., Friedenberg, 1995). In particular, basic psychometric features of reliability and validity are emphasized. For specific types of assessments, we recommend that the prospective intervention developers look for standards in their domain, often developed outside the context of neurobehavioral interventions. For example, for psychophysiological assessments, there are strong guidelines papers published by the Society for Psychophysiological Research (Society for Psychophysiological Research [SPR], 2012) for heart rate (Jennings et al., 1981); electrodermal measurements (Fowles et al., 1981); electromyography (Fridlund & Cacioppo, 1986); and a host of other measures. These would be appropriate guidelines for the increasingly pervasive, if disparate, bio- and neuro-feedback genres.

For novel assessments and technologies, standards outlined by the American Society for Testing and Materials (ASTM; www.astm.org) may be particularly useful. The ASTM is globally recognized as a leader in providing standards of quality and safety for new products and technologies. ASTM standards are developed through the contribution and consensus of its more than 30,000 technical expert members and are today applied in 150 countries worldwide. The Institute of Electrical and Electronics Engineers (IEEE) Standards Association (standards.ieee.org) also presents valuable standards for evaluating emerging technologies in the engineering world. The IEEE is an internationally respected organization, including leaders in technological innovation from 160 countries, dedicated to the development and advancement of new technologies and the standards that ensure their quality, safety, and utility.

Some neurocognitive technologies have already developed initial standards of use. For functional magnetic resonance imagining (fMRI), in particular, there are increasingly strongly developed standards. The Functional Imaging Research of Schizophrenia Testbed Biomedical Informatics Research Network (fBIRN) was created to provide an experimental platform that allows multisite imaging in clinical research practice. The fBIRN has begun to publish relevant information in this regard (Magnotta & Friedman, 2006) that has translated to a set of uniformly characterized publications (Potkin & Ford, 2009). Their task specifications, scan parameters, quality assurance procedures, and analytic procedures are available for use as models (fBIRN, 2013a). The fBIRN has specifically created a best-practices document for multi-site studies that can serve as a useful research model (fBIRN, 2013b). In addition, the Human Connectome project (Van Essen et al., 2013) has described specific procedures used for a widely distributed collaborative fMRI initiative (National Institute of Health [NIH], 2013). Their task battery and reasons for its selection are specifically described (Barch et al., 2013) along with their quality control procedures (Marcus et al., 2013) and preprocessing decisions (Glasser et al., 2013).

For interventions, we recommend standards applied to understanding drug mechanisms and efficacy. There is a standards paper for neurofeedback focused primarily on training and clinical administration procedures (Hammond et al., 2011) that would be useful in establishing standards for future neurocognitive assessments.

Standards for Assessments

We suggest initial consideration of standards described in Table 13.1 when proposing and considering disseminating neurocognitive assessments and treatments. Most of the remainder of this chapter describes the rationale, process for selection, and content associated with this table.

Neurocognitive therapies generally target brain processes. As such, a critical element of evaluating outcome for these interventions is testing whether these brain processes change. Clinically significant change must be detectable on an individual level. Many promising neurocognitive assessment techniques used in research have not been examined for such clinical utility, which is our focus, to promote translation to real-world clinics. As a popular method for understanding brain targets in the research world that is currently being considered for clinical utility, we consider the running example of fMRI. This method is chosen because it is a relatively novel technology for which standards are just now emerging (e.g., via the fBIRN and Human Connectome projects). Here, we specifically comment on standards useful for making sure fMRI assessments inform (1) the choice of specific conventional treatments, (2) mechanisms that may be useful to address with targeted treatments, and (3) whether relevant brain mechanisms are being targeted in treatment.

Utility

Demonstrating utility involves showing that a test has practical value in assessing some construct of interest. Novel psychological assessments are usually used for forward inference at the level of groups, for example, showing that groups differ on some measure. To be used clinically, it would be important for such findings to be valid for reverse inference. That is, it would be useful to show that a specific pattern of results (e.g., an fMRI-derived estimate of brain activity) uniquely represents some clinically meaningful feature (e.g., reactivity to potential threat). Moreover, the test results would have to be interpretable at the level of single subjects (e.g., to say whether a specific patient's brain was abnormal or predictive of response). If a dimensional formulation such as the RDoC is used, making the dimension interpretable by clinicians is essential. For example, using fMRI, it could be useful to report on reactivity in brain systems subserving threat response after a threat stimulus compared to a baseline condition. The stimulus would be presented on a specific experimental paradigm with well-characterized psychometric properties and validated to vary with clinical characteristics of interest in large samples, with values specified across multiple scanners in different age, gender, and ethnicity categories. Ideally, standard software for presenting stimuli and processing the data in a standard way and deriving relevant scores

TABLE 13.1 Proposed standards for neurocognitive assessments and interventions

Area	Standard	Description
Theory	Utility	The method should measure or affect a clearly defined construct that has demonstrated clinical significance. Ideally this will come from multiple publications at the level of reverse inference.
Psychometrics	Standard administration	The method's administration should be well documented and repeatable.
	Reliability	The method should get the same results when repeated (standard psychometrics, e.g., test-retest reliability).
	Validity	The method should measure what it claims to measure (standard psychometrics, e.g., convergent, construct, and external validity).
	Available Norms	Measures from comparison groups of healthy subjects are made available. Ideally, patient groups of interest will also be represented for comparison of individual patients.
Practical implementation & dissemination	Safety	Ideally, the method should cause no harm. In cases in which methods could be harmful or have side effects, these should be well characterized and clearly specified.
	Affordability	Method should come at a cost likely to be effectively borne by those who need the procedure or their insurance.
	Accessibility	The method should be widely available. This involves both ability to access the method as well as ability to be trained in its proper use.
	Usability	The method should be easy to use, quick enough to undergo that patients are willing to tolerate it (repeatedly if necessary), and for measures, the ability for results to easily be translated such that a clinician who is not a specialist can interpret them.

would be provided so that clinicians would end up with a single number, such as a Z-score that is easily interpreted.

Standardized Administration

The goal of standardized administration is that if two sites were to administer the same test to the same individual, they would use similar procedures that would yield similar results. Standardized administration can refer to any elements from requiring that the same scanning or therapeutic administration hardware is used, to making sure the technologist uses the same color accessories (earplugs, sheets for fMRI) for each patient. For fMRI, to date, relevant variables for standardization have been considered for specific test batteries (Barch et al., 2013). Procedural standardization is likely important given well-known performance differences associated with variability in demand characteristics (Hancock, Williams, Manning, & Miyake, 1995). Toward that end, establishing standardized instructions and stimuli for tasks will be increasingly important, along with standards for task administration orders. If a new assessment technology such as fMRI is to represent a comprehensive psychiatric assessment, it would be useful for a clinician to be able to order a canonical battery of tests, like the Heaton Battery (Heaton & Psychological Assessment Resources Inc., 2004). The fBIRN and Human Connectome batteries (for example, standardized tasks, structural, and functional MRI scanning protocols) are also diagnostic test candidates; both include tasks chosen to identify mechanisms of healthy functioning or a specific disease. Such tests could be chosen for either their predictive validity or their ability to identify specific mechanisms and would ideally have canonical, accessible versions.

There are not yet standards for assessments of constructs in typical or neurocognitive interventions. For example, many neurocognitive interventions nominally address emotional information processing. Yet, there is little agreement regarding the tasks or stimuli that should be used in assessing whether the interventions work. Common tasks involving presentation of fearful faces or standardized affective pictures using the International Affective Pictures System (IAPS; Lang, Bradley, & Cuthbert, 2005), on which hundreds of studies have been published, use different stimuli, stimulus durations, and tasks involving these stimuli. Variables, from task instructions to how tasks should be administered, screen size or degrees of visual angle for stimuli, administration hardware (e.g. button box, keyboard, mouse), and stimulus sets, have all been shown to be critical to results. For example, small changes to the stimulus presentation duration on the "dot probe" task common in attentional bias modification appears to strongly affect results in some clinical populations, such that the longer the stimulus was presented, the more likely it would be that depressed patients displayed a significant negative attention bias

(Donaldson, Lam, & Mathews, 2007). Agreement on stimulus characteristics, either for standard administration or how they should be varied to test specific mechanisms, would be useful. Canonical administration hardware, quality control procedures, data pre-processing, and analyses would also be useful. For fMRI, considerations of scan parameters, quality assurance, and region and network selection and how the time-course of brain activity is handled will likely be particularly important; the fBIRN and Human Connectome project guidelines represent excellent models for initial test-beds and decision processes.

Reliability

Multiple types of reliability are typically evaluated for psychological tests. Of particular utility for physiological testing, test-retest reliability regards the extent to which data acquired within one subject is replicable over time. Test-retest reliability is difficult to estimate for neurocognitive interventions given that the signal is expected to change as patients improve at the intervention, and neurocognitive tasks often depend on repeating similar events many times to estimate effects from small signals; thus, practice and habituation effects are inevitable. This is particularly true for fMRI in brain areas, most commonly the focus of scientific research such as the amygdala (Wright et al., 2001), and for physiological proxies such as decreases in startle reflex over time (Lee, Shackman, Jackson, & Davidson, 2009). For psychophysiological methods such as fMRI and EEG, time-series are acquired, which are often highly auto-correlated. Thus, test-retest reliability may be overestimated due to the nature of the acquired signal. Various approaches have been advanced for estimating test-retest reliability in psychophysiological assessment, such as explicitly parcellating variance into time and condition-related components using "G-theory" (e.g., Hinz, Hueber, Schreinicke, & Seibt, 2002; Nocera, Ferlazzo, & Borghi, 2001). As we move toward an era in which neurocognitive assessments are headed for the clinic, it may be useful to select measures, modalities, and paradigms with regard to properties such as test-retest reliability rather than to evaluate their psychometric properties post hoc (Milanesi, Romano, Castellani, Remondini, & Lio, 2009) as is often done for fMRI.

Test-retest reliability regards the extent to which an assessment would produce consistent results if the same subject were assessed at different time points. Being able to evaluate this type of reliability would mean regularly testing the same participants on the same task on multiple occasions. For clinical procedures, there is historical debate regarding whether test-retest reliability should be calculated on healthy individuals (in which case they may not show the effects of interest for the test and thus unstable noise is being correlated over time) or patients who are subject to recovery effects and variations in severity and in whom no-treatment waiting periods to calculate reliability may be unethical; both have been reported (Heaton et al., 2001). Of note, test-retest reliability is rarely evaluated for expensive assessment modalities such as fMRI, and when it is done, it is generally in healthy individuals, which may significantly underestimate relevant effects in the groups of choice.

Consistent with psychological testing in other domains, our recommendation is that neurocognitive assessments be evaluated (and regularly *re*evaluated) for all of these types of reliability. This may take expanding budgets for trials involving neurocognitive therapies but, without such data, it will be difficult to evaluate their utility.

For research purposes, in modalities where many measurements are taken simultaneously (e.g., throughout the brain for fMRI or EEG), assessment could regard stability over all the measurements over time (e.g., Keil, Stolarova, Heim, Gruber, & Muller, 2003). Clinically, it is expected that this would not be the norm but, rather, one or a few specific indices would be extracted per patient. There is also a strong consideration regarding variability across assessment hardware, which has been explored in the fBIRN's guidelines for best practices for multi-site studies (fBIRN, 2013a). Considerations such as whether to require standard assessment hardware (e.g., scanners from a single vendor at a single field strength, with a single head coil) or to create tasks that generalize to multiple types of hardware will need to be resolved eventually. Test-retest reliability has been shown to be relatively high within a scanner (Friedman et al., 2008), but between-scanner reliability is low (Brown et al., 2011; Friedman et al., 2008). For fMRI, specific corrections have been suggested to improve reliability across scanner brands. For example, one suggestion is to hold protocols (e.g., smoothness) consistent. Another suggested correction is to increase the size of the regions of interest (Friedman, Glover, Krenz, & Magnotta, 2006). We recommend attending to issues of generalization to modality when creating an assessment measure or designing an intervention (i.e., who will use the technique, and what would it take to make it generalize to this audience, and planning trials with these considerations in mind). For fMRI, this may require increased multi-site trials.

Validity

Validity regards the extent to which an index represents what it is said to represent. Again, there are many standard checks for validity to which psychological tests are regularly subjected (Friedenberg, 1995). The value and methods for attending to these considerations in fMRI of clinical interventions, specifically, have been laid out neatly along with a strong summary of how far the field is from meeting them (Frewen, Dozois, & Lanius, 2008). Examples include "face validity"—whether the derived index could intuitively be plausible. For fMRI, it is on this basis that predictive regions in the white matter, where no signal could reasonably be expected, are rejected despite strong statistical properties.

Convergent validity regards the extent to which indices are consistent with indices derived from other methods. To assess this type of validity, it is important to administer other instruments thought to correlate with the signal of interest, for example, to correlate more standard and accepted self-report measures with novel (e.g., fMRI) assessments.

Construct validity represents whether the measures can assess a construct of theoretical interest. Here, studies of group differences could help to support the use of an index, even though it will eventually be used on an individual basis. That said, the types of group difference studies popular in the literature are not entirely useful. As previously noted, studies with groups of patients with like diagnoses (e.g., generalized anxiety disorder) may reveal differences between healthy controls and patients but, often, abnormalities revealed for one disorder overlap across diagnoses, (e.g., startle reactivity; McTeague & Lang, 2012). This could be because constructs of interest reflect transdiagnostic processes, in which case those phenomena should be referenced as the classification performed by the administered assessment. Alternately, if a more specific classification is desired, designs that afford reverse inference may be preferable.

In addition to these concerns, Type I and Type II error control is a critical issue for studies contributing to validation of standard measures. Methods that yield many outcome variables (e.g., exploratory fMRI analyses that yield thousands of measurements throughout the brain, and orders of magnitude more information regarding connections between brain regions) are particularly subject to these considerations as indices are frequently derived from the "best" outcomes of thousands of tests (Bennet, Baird, Miller, & Wolford, 2010). Many controls for such inferences have been suggested (e.g., requiring large spatially contiguous regions to be detected; Forman et al., 1995) or analogously for other psychophysiological, large temporally contiguous regions (Guthrie & Buchwald, 1991). However, it is expected that by the time such indices are proposed for clinical use, basic studies will have yielded one or several derived aggregate indices of interest. Ideally, these indices will be replicated relevant predictions or individual difference assessments on these singular indices, and both methods manuals and relevant software will be easily accessible. It is important that such indices not be derived from a single exploratory study, as for each study, only the strongest effects from many evaluated are examined (Vul, Harris, Winkielman, & Pashler, 2009). Initial forays in this area have thus used replication approaches in which a region is identified in an exploratory study (Siegle, Carter, & Thase, 2006), and then a replication study uses the identified area to predict the same outcomes in a new sample (Siegle et al., 2012). Attention to such issues will be increasingly critical as neurocognitive measures are more widely adopted and clinicians grow used to asking about the strength of relevant effect sizes. Having strong assessments that are not psychometrically compromised from the outset could help to promote the translation of fMRI, and similar neurocognitive methods, to the clinic.

Norms

It is critical to recognize those test scores that are clinically meaningful. Toward that end, psychological tests generally either (1) publish norms such as means and standard deviations, ideally stratified by common variables that affect individual difference measures such as age and ethnicity, or (2) provide scoring algorithms that can be accessed from any clinic that calculates these measures. As it is not expected that clinicians will regularly have the computational ability to process the complex genetic, psychophysiological, and neuroimaging data on which treatment decisions will be made, examples of best practices for transfer of raw data to cloud-based services (i.e., uploading raw data to a Web-based cloud) that provide scores are already underway (Goscinski and Gureyev, 2011; Muehlboeck, Westman, & Simmons, 2014).

Though norming is the most common standard and often required for psychological assessment methods, it has rarely been met for neurocognitive measures such as fMRI. For fMRI in particular, there are no norms for any proposed group difference or predictive measure. Difficulties equating data across sites is one contributing factor. Another is that norms are generally calculated with respect to a "healthy" population, and most clinical studies have only run small samples of healthy individuals. Large cohorts of healthy individuals would ideally be scanned to determine the distribution of activations of each brain region within healthy populations, just as was done to establish the range "healthy" for other medical indexes such as heart rate or body mass index (BMI). Once established, such norms would need to be collected in a published database, with each entry based on peer-reviewed studies, and then translated into standardized scales.

As neurocognitive interventions more clearly target mechanisms, it would be essential to measure change in those mechanisms. Yet, such a strategy is extraordinarily far from the clinic. No norms for change have yet been established for most neurocognitive assessments. Ideally, efforts moving toward the clinic must identify thresholds for the degree of change that can be expected over time with and without treatment.

Safety

The safe implementation of neurocognitive assessments and interventions is a primary concern, particularly where considerations such as Food and Drug Administration (FDA) approval and insurance reimbursement may become issues. Including safety as a consideration in developing lab protocols is thus recommended. For fMRI, safety has long been addressed (Kanal et al., 2004) as clinical MRI exists at many hospitals and has long been subjected to scrutiny for safety and deemed safe when specific conditions are met (e.g., the absence of subcutaneous metal). That said, as the field evolves, so do safety considerations (de Vocht & Kromhout, 2008).

A note on FDA approval: Although acceptable levels of safety are often assumed with FDA approval, they are not equivalent. Rather, FDA approval suggests that a device does what it says it does. FDA approval is generally only pursued for devices used clinically, so the lack of FDA approval does not mean a device is not safe. FDA approvals have three levels: Class I being needing no prior approval—it is likely to be effective; Class II, having some restrictions—generally needing to conform to performance standards; and Class III, needing specific approval before marketing. Those interested in neurocognitive assessments and treatments may particularly benefit from consideration of the Code of Federal Regulations (CFR; Government Printing Office, 2014) 21 part 882, which regards Neurological Diagnostic Devices. Devices for Transcranial Magnetic Stimulation (TMS) and Transcranial Direct Current Stimulation (TDCS) (CFR 21 part 882.1870) and EEG (882.1400) are all considered Class II devices subject to demonstrated performance standards, which is also true of any "aversive conditioning" (e.g., shock) device (882.5235). In contrast, skull punches (makes holes in the skull; 882.4750) and spiky pinwheels used to test pain perception are class I (no approval required; 882.1750). Of specific note, though MRI is approved by the FDA (CFR 21, 892.1000), they are just now evaluating fMRI as a clinical tool (i.e., examining its likely reliability, validity, and other features of clinical assessments; Soltystik & Rajan, 2014). Thus, we recommend considering FDA approval as part of a long-term strategy to helping novel assessments on their journey to the clinic; whether it is critical for initial trials is less clear and may be worth postponing until it is necessary.

Affordability

One consideration regarding affordability is how much the assessment actually costs. There are few assessments in psychiatry with which to gauge affordability. Clinical MRI assessments, which are common in neurological exams, are approximately $500 per hour. In contrast, self-report questionnaires usually cost under $5 and thyroid tests under $50 to administer. The cost of an intervention such as an antidepressant for several weeks is also negligible ($10 for a month of a generic medication). It is estimated that a single treatment course, including doctor visits, costs approximately $2,000 (Crogan, Obenchain, & Crown, 1998), and the cost savings associated with an assessment compared to the personal or societal cost of incorrect treatment (potentially involving patient death) are certainly preferable. However, convincing insurance companies of this will be a job that the proponents of pre-treatment assessment need to take on; potential money saved is not generally part of the calculation in how much to spend on an assessment. To the extent that an untrained assistant can administer an assessment or a patient can complete the assessment at home, expensive clinician time will be saved. This is undoubtedly one major advantage of the neurocognitive approach.

A second, and potentially more poignant, concern is who will pay for the assessment. That is, for both assessments and treatments, to adopt an assessment, clinicians must be able to bill for their time to order, possibly administer, and interpret a test or to administer a therapy. If insurance is not involved, clinician-administered procedures may be affordable; externally administered procedures such as MRIs may not be. Finding ways to bill insurance providers for neurocognitive procedures will be a challenge for the field. Of note, there are existing continuous performance tests (CPT) codes for MRI administered by a psychologist (Hart, Rao, & Nuwer, 2007), for primary use in pre-epilepsy surgery evaluation, but use of these codes for other purposes is likely to not be covered by insurance companies. The question of affordability may thus prove a strong initial impediment to the advance of the most expensive neurocognitive clinical methods, as many patients may be unwilling or unable to pay for expensive assessments like fMRI out of pocket, and insurance companies may be equally reluctant to cover such procedures until they gain wider clinical acceptance. Consideration of such factors, such as recommending the use of fMRI for some versus all patients with a given presentation, may thus be important in promoting the clinical viability of these technologies.

Accessibility

If a given procedure is accessible, it is readily available to all clinicians who want to use the technique. If the assessment technology costs a great deal of money, it will likely not be used, even if individual assessments are inexpensive.

Initial informal discussions with real-world clinicians have suggested some unanticipated barriers. At the most basic level, many neurocognitive assessments and interventions require the use of a computer or smart phone. However, clinicians in some more rural areas of the United States have reported that at this time, many of their patients still do not have access to personal computers or smart phones, and clinics have no computer that patients could use. If technology-based interventions are to be widely accessible, they must be able to be accessed over the Web, by patients, outside a clinician's office (e.g., at their home or a library).

Accessibility is a major obstacle for the clinical use of fMRI in particular. Many locations do not have access to MRI and, though MRI is possible at many hospitals, the necessary hardware and software for fMRI are not available (e.g., head coils, pulse sequences, projection and stimulus presentation systems). The research standard for fMRI magnet strength is currently 3 or 7 tesla. Hospital MRI systems are generally 1.5 tesla. As such, clinical translation of fMRI will take a strong infrastructure investment. For this reason, many have suggested that fMRI may best be thought of as a method for identifying candidate brain systems in neuroscience laboratories, with the ultimate goal being to identify proxy procedures that do not require fMRI for use in the clinic. For example, a less costly, more easily accessible measure such as pupil dilation or a well-established neuropsychological test might be used as a proxy for prefrontal lobe brain activity (Siegle, Steinhauer, Friedman, Thompson, & Thase, 2011). As neurocognitive clinical science advances, it may be useful to rely, when possible, on technologies that can be reasonably accessible for use in even less-resource-rich environments.

Usability

With relevant hardware and software in place, collection of neurocognitive data is often possible by novice users. Its analysis and extraction of relevant indices is generally more difficult. This is a problem the field has not yet addressed. Automated systems for other complicated imaging procedures such as 3-D reconstruction of CT scans have been created. Alternately, in other fields, complex analytics are generally performed by outside labs. For example, genetic material is often easily collected at sites with no local expertise and then sent out for analysis. Such may become the standard for fMRI. In the meantime, there are hosts of technologies, from self-report and behavioral assessments/ treatments that have well-characterized neural features, as have been used for the past century in neurology clinics, to cognitive training software that is available over the Web. Physiological assessment technologies such as wearable heart-rate, skin conductance, and temperature monitors are increasingly available. Consumer-grade EEG systems are also available with increasingly simple smart phone-based interfaces. So, the future for useable novel technologies is bright. Keeping in mind that smart phone-accessible assessments and interventions are fast becoming the de facto standard for the consumer may help orient future technologies in this arena.

Standards for Therapeutic Techniques and Technologies

Most of the considerations for interventions are the same as for assessments, as described above, but some are unique. For example, consider a neurocognitive training devoted to remediating panic attacks. With regard to utility, symptoms are not necessarily the outcome of interest. Rather, the basis of neurocognitive interventions is to target a mechanism of interest. So it may be important to first establish that the mechanism to be targeted (e.g., amygdala activation) is abnormal, in the expected direction in a given patient before using the intervention. An intervention could be shown to target that abnormality by normalizing the mechanism (e.g., decreasing amygdala activity). Alternately, it could be demonstrated that the intervention targets a different brain mechanism to compensate for the abnormal activity (e.g., increasing prefrontal control), as in neurorehabilitation for stroke, where the lesioned area is not remediated but other areas are brought online to compensate for the lesion. Standard psychometric considerations for evaluating interventions could be employed (e.g., per-visit outlier control, sophisticated handling of missing data, placebo control, comparison to existing interventions, adequate sample sizes to assure generalization).

A key difference between neurocognitive and standard interventions regards targeting a mechanism. Selection of patients to validate the intervention may profitably involve choosing only those who have abnormalities in the mechanism to begin with as the intervention is not expected to help those who do not have abnormalities. If it does help individuals without the abnormalities, then the targeted mechanism may be incorrect. For example, it has consistently been shown that attention biases need not be present for attention bias training to help an individual. From this, we may conclude that attention bias training does not specifically target attentional biases: other factors such as mastery, exposure, and increasing prefrontal control (Bar-Haim, 2010) may be at play.

Winning Trust

A further and essential step in the dissemination of neurocognitive clinical methods will be winning the acceptance and ultimately the trust of clinicians and patients. Clinicians must believe in a new method before they will employ it, and patients will not use the tools they are offered if they sense their doctors do not trust the tools to be effective.

Researchers

Researchers need standards that are reliable and trustworthy. Currently, there is no widely acknowledged standards body for neurocognitive assessments or clear organization to whom the field would appeal for the development of such standards. There are beginnings such as the Neurocognitive Therapies/Translational Research Special Interest Group within the Association for Behavioral and Cognitive Therapies; the Entertainment Software and Cognitive Neurotherapeutics Society; and the American Society for NeuroRehabilitation, the International Society for Neurofeedback and Research, which has published initial standards for clinical administration of neurofeedback (Hammond et al., 2011). When these groups or others should step up to formally suggest detailed procedural standards, that is, when procedures have been well-enough explored but when the field has not become so fragmented that it is thought of as untenable, is unclear. Ideally, however, that time is coming soon.

Clinicians, Employers, and Insurance Companies

A potentially equally important step will involve getting clinicians' acceptance for their use. Though initial data suggest that clinicians are enthusiastic about bringing mechanistic measures to the clinic (Illes, Lombera, Rosenberg, & Arnow, 2008), this practice has largely gone untested in real-world clinics that are not specifically devoted to adjunctive mechanistic assessment. A primary issue in this regard involves achieving commitment from insurance companies and employers for reimbursement for this work, for instance, clinician and technician time engaged in assessments and interventions and, possibly, scanner time. Public relations campaigns highlighting the excellent science and results from this discipline could be key in this regard. Being able to tout conformity to strong standards for employing neurocognitive interventions could bring numerous benefits to the neurocognitive perspective. Such guidelines could help this burgeoning field over other psychiatric assessments and interventions that may have some studies suggesting empirical validation but, due to lack of standards, are hard to interpret and implement faithfully elsewhere and replicate associated results. Standards such as affordability and accessibility make translation of these types of interventions to real-world clinics particularly feasible.

Conclusions

In summary, the neurocognitive strategies described in this book introduce promising, innovative methods for assessing and treating psychopathology. The potential is to address symptoms not in terms of broadly constructed DSM disorder categories but based on the precise empirical evidence of the mechanisms that underlie those symptoms. This mechanism-based evidence could be applied to allow clinicians to rapidly assess and tailor treatments to an individual's unique dimensional symptom profile, cutting costs in finances, time, and most important, prolonged patient suffering. Before any such ideal can be achieved, however, the road to the neurocognitive clinic of the future must be paved with dependable standards of scientific investigation—the same standards we would expect of any other field entrusted with human care. This chapter has detailed these standards and illustrated paths the neurocognitive field may take toward meeting these goals. Standards could undoubtedly help with multiple roadblocks, including helping to achieve not only patient but clinician, clinician-employer, and insurance-company buy-in for their use. Our hope is that recognizing and opening discussion on these issues is the first step to resolving them. Progress toward the neurocognitive clinic of the future has already begun.

References

American Psychiatric Association. (2013). *Diagnostic and statistical manual of mental disorders* (5th edn). Washington, DC: American Psychiatric Association.
American Society for Testing and Material. (2014). *Standards & Publications*. Retrieved from http://www.astm.org/Standard/standards-and-publications.html
Baes, C., Martins, C. M., Tofoli, S. M., & Juruena, M. F. (2014). Early life stress in depressive patients: HPA axis response to GR and MR agonist. *Frontiers in Psychiatry, 5*(2). doi: 10.3389/fpsyt.2014.00002.
Barch, D. M., Burgess, G. C., Harms, M. P., Petersen, S. E., Schlaggar, B. L., Corbetta, M., … & Van Essen, D. C. (2013). Function in the human connectome: Task-fMRI and individual differences in behavior. *NeuroImage, 80*, 169–189.
Bar-Haim, Y. (2010). Research review: Attention bias modification (ABM): A novel treatment for anxiety disorders. *Journal of Child Psychololgy and Psychiatry, 51*(8), 859–870.
Bennet, C., Baird, A. A., Miller, M. B., & Wolford, G. L. (2010). Neural correlates of interspecies perspective taking in the post-mortem Atlantic salmon: An argument for proper multiple comparisons correction. *Journal of Serendipitous and Unexpected Results, 1*(1), 1–5.
Brown, G. G., Mathalon, D. H., Stern, H., Ford, J., Mueller, B., Greve, D. N., … & Potkin, S. G. (2011). Multisite reliability of cognitive BOLD data. *NeuroImage, 54*(3), 2163–2175.
Bruhl, A. B., Scherpiet, S., Sulzer, J., Stampfli, P., Seifritz, E., & Herwig, U. (2014). Real-time neurofeedback using functional MRI could improve down-regulation of amygdala activity during emotional stimulation: A proof-of-concept study. *Brain Topography, 27*(1), 138–148.
Calkins, A. W., McMorran, C. G., Siegle, G. J., & Otto, M. W. (in press). The effects of computerized cognitive control training on community adults with depressed mood. *Behavioural and Cognitive Psychotherapy*.
Carroll, B. J. (1985). Dexamethasone suppression test: A review of contemporary confusion. *Journal of Clinical Psychiatry, 46*(2 Pt 2), 13–24.
Crogan, T. W., Obenchain, R. L., & Crown, W. E. (1998). What does treatment of depression really cost? *DataWatch, 17*(4), 199–208.
de Vocht, F., & Kromhout, H. (2008). Human MRI above the FDA 8 T guideline: Can we conclude that it is safe? *Journal of Magnetic Resonance Imaging, 27*(4), 938–939.
Donaldson, C., Lam, D., & Mathews, A. (2007). Rumination and attention in major depression. *Behavioral Research and Therapy, 45*(11), 2664–2678.
fBIRN (2013a). *FBIRN Recommendations for multi-center fMRI studies: Supplemental material (JMRI cite)*. Retrieved 9/20/2014 from http://www.birncommunity.org/resources/supplements/fbirn-recommendations-for-multi-center-fmri-studies/
fBIRN (2013b). *FBIRN best practices for multi-site fMRI studies*. Retrieved 9/20/2013from https://xwiki.nbirn.org:8443/bin/view/Function-BIRN/FBIRN_Best_Practices

Forgeard, M. J. C., Haigh, E. A. P., Beck, A. T., Davidson, R. J., Henn, F. A., Maier, S. F., ... & Seligman, M. E. P. (2011). Beyond depression: Towards a process-based approach to research, diagnosis, and treatment. *Clinical Psychology: Science & Practice, 18*(4), 275–299.

Forman, S. D., Cohen, J. D., Fitzgerald, M., Eddy, W. F., Mintun, M. A., & Noll, D. C. (1995). Improved assessment of significant activation in functional magnetic resonance imaging (fMRI): Use of a cluster-size threshold. *Magnetic Resonance in Medicine, 33*(5), 636–647.

Fowles, D. C., Christie, M. J., Edelberg, R., Grings, W. W., Lykken, D. T., & Venables, P. H. (1981). Publication recommendations for electrodermal measurements. *Psychophysiology, 18*(3), 232–239.

Frewen, P. A., Dozois, D. J., & Lanius, R. A. (2008). Neuroimaging studies of psychological interventions for mood and anxiety disorders: Empirical and methodological review. *Clinical Psychology Review, 28*(2), 228–246.

Fridlund, A. J., & Cacioppo, J. T. (1986). Guidelines for human electromyographic research. *Psychophysiology, 23*(5), 567–589.

Friedenberg, L. (1995). *Psychological testing: Design, analysis, and use.* Boston, MA: Allyn and Bacon.

Friedman, L., Glover, G. H., Krenz, D., & Magnotta, V. (2006). Reducing inter-scanner variability of activation in a multicenter fMRI study: Role of smoothness equalization. *NeuroImage, 32*(4), 1656–1668.

Friedman, L., Stern, H., Brown, G. G., Mathalon, D. H., Turner, J., Glover, G. H., ... & Potkin, S. G. (2008). Test-retest and between-site reliability in a multicenter fMRI study. *Human Brain Mapping, 29*(8), 958–972.

Glasser, M. F., Sotiropoulos, S. N., Wilson, J. A., Coalson, T. S., Fischl, B., Andersson, J. L., ... & Jenkinson, M. (2013). The minimal preprocessing pipelines for the Human Connectome Project. *NeuroImage, 80*, 105–124.

Goscinski, W., & Gureyev, T. (2011). The multi-modal Australian sciences imaging and visualisation environment (MASSIVE) for near realtime CT reconstruction using XLI. Paper given at the eResearch Australasia Conference, Melbourne, 6–10 November.

Government Printing Office. (2014). *Code of federal regulations.* Washington, DC. Retrieved 9/20/2014 from http://www.gpo.gov/fdsys/browse/collectionCfr. action?collectionCode=CFR

Guthrie, D., & Buchwald, J. S. (1991). Significance testing of difference potentials. *Psychophysiology, 28*(2), 240–244.

Hammond, D. C., Bodenheimer-Davis, G., Gluck, G., Stokes, D., Harper, S. H., Trudeau, D., ... & Kirk, L. (2011). Standards of practice for neurofeedback and neurotherapy: A position paper of the international society for neurofeedback and research. *Journal of Neurotherapy, 15*(1), 54–64.

Hancock, P. A., Williams, G., Manning, C. M., & Miyake, S. (1995). Influence of task demand characteristics on workload and performance. *International Journal of Aviation Psychology, 5*(1), 63–86.

Hart, J., Jr., Rao, S. M., & Nuwer, M. (2007). Clinical functional magnetic resonance imaging. *Cognitive and Behavioral Neurology, 20*(3), 141–144.

Heaton, R. K., & Psychological Assessment Resources Inc. (2004). *Revised comprehensive norms for an expanded Halstead-Reitan battery: Demographically adjusted neuropsychological norms for African American and Caucasian adults, professional manual* (Updated edn). Lutz, FL: Psychological Assessment Resources.

Heaton, R. K., Gladsjo, J. A., Palmer, B. W., Kuck, J., Marcotte, T. D., & Jeste, D. V. (2001). Stability and course of neuropsychological deficits in schizophrenia. *Archives of General Psychiatry, 58*(1), 24–32.

Hinz, A., Hueber, B., Schreinicke, G., & Seibt, R. (2002). Temporal stability of psychophysiological response patterns: Concepts and statistical tools. *International Journal of Psychophysiololgy, 44*(1), 57–65.

Illes, J., Lombera, S., Rosenberg, J., & Arnow, B. (2008). In the mind's eye: Provider and patient attitudes on functional brain imaging. *Journal of Psychiatric Research, 43*(2), 107–114.

Insel, T., Cuthbert, B., Garvey, M., Heinssen, R., Pine, D. S., Quinn, K., ... & Wang, P. (2010). Research domain criteria (RDoC): Toward a new classification framework for research on mental disorders. *American Journal of Psychiatry, 167*(7), 748–751.

Institute of Electrical and Electronics Engineers Standards Association. (2014). *Standards & Publications*. Retrieved from http://www.ieee.org/index.html

Jennings, J. R., Berg, W. K., Hutcheson, J. S., Obrist, P., Porges, S., & Turpin, G. (1981). Publication guidelines for heart rate studies in man. *Psychophysiology, 18*(3), 226–231.

Kanal, E., Borgstede, J. P., Barkovich, A. J., Bell, C., Bradley, W. G., Etheridge, S., ... & Zinninger, M. D. (2004). American College of Radiology white paper on MR safety: 2004 update and revisions. *AJR American Journal of Roentgenology, 182*(5), 1111–1114.

Keil, A., Stolarova, M., Heim, S., Gruber, T., & Muller, M. M. (2003). Temporal stability of high-frequency brain oscillations in the human EEG. *Brain Topography, 16*(2), 101–110.

Lang, P. J., Bradley, M. M., & Cuthbert, B. N. (2005). *International affective picture system (IAPS): Digitized photographs, instruction manual and affective ratings*. Gainesvill, FL: NIMH, Center for the Study of Emotion & Attention.

Lee, H., Shackman, A. J., Jackson, D. C., & Davidson, R. J. (2009). Test-retest reliability of voluntary emotion regulation. *Psychophysiology, 46*(4), 874–879.

Madakasira, S., & Taylor, T. K. (1986). Misuse of the dexamethasone suppression test as a diagnostic tool. *International Journal of Psychiatry Medicine, 16*(1), 77–84.

Magnotta, V. A., & Friedman, L. (2006). Measurement of signal-to-noise and contrast-to-noise in the fBIRN multicenter imaging study. *Journal of Digital Imaging, 19*(2), 140–147.

Marcus, D. S., Harms, M. P., Snyder, A. Z., Jenkinson, M., Wilson, J. A., Glasser, M. F., ... & Van Essen, D. C. (2013). Human Connectome Project informatics: Quality control, database services, and data visualization. *NeuroImage, 80*, 202–219.

McGee, J. P. (1984). The dexamethasone suppression test and clinical decision making. *Journal of Nervous and Mental Disease, 172*(6), 361–363.

McTeague, L. M., & Lang, P. J. (2012). The anxiety spectrum and the reflex physiology of defense: From circumscribed fear to broad distress. *Depression and Anxiety, 29*(4), 264–281.

Meltzer, H. Y., & Fang, V. S. (1983). Cortisol determination and the dexamethasone suppression test: A review. *Archives of General Psychiatry, 40*(5), 501–505.

Milanesi, L., Romano, P., Castellani, G., Remondini, D., & Lio, P. (2009). Trends in modeling biomedical complex systems. *BMC Bioinformatics, 10*(Suppl 12), I1.

Muehlboeck, J. S., Westman, E., & Simmons, A. (2014). TheHiveDB image data management and analysis framework. *Frontiers in Neuroinformatics, 7*, 49.

National Institute of Health (NIH). (2013). Human connectome projects. Retrieved 9/20/2014 from http://www.humanconnectome.org/about/publications.html

National Institute of Mental Health (NIMH). (2011). NIMH Research Domain Criteria (RDoC). Retrieved 9/20/2014 from http://www.nimh.nih.gov/research-priorities/rdoc/nimh-research-domain-criteria-rdoc.shtml

Nocera, F. D., Ferlazzo, F., & Borghi, V. (2001). G theory and the reliability of psychophysiological measures: A tutorial. *Psychophysiology, 38*(5), 796–806.

Potkin, S. G., & Ford, J. M. (2009). Widespread cortical dysfunction in schizophrenia: The fBIRN imaging consortium. *Schizophrenica Bulletin, 35*(1), 15–18.

Siegle, G. J., Carter, C. S., & Thase, M. E. (2006). Use of fMRI to predict recovery from unipolar depression with cognitive behavior therapy. *American Journal of Psychiatry, 163*, 735–738.

Siegle, G. J., Ghinassi, F., & Thase, M. E. (2007). Neurobehavioral therapies in the 21st century: Summary of an emerging field and an extended example of cognitive control training for depression. *Cognitive Therapy & Research, 31*, 235–262.

Siegle, G. J., Price, R. B., Jones, N. P., Ghinassi, F., & Thase, M. E. (in press). You gotta work at it: Pupillary indices of task focus are prognostic for response to a neurocognitive intervention for depression. *Clinical Psychological Science, 2*(4) 455–471.

Siegle, G. J., Steinhauer, S. R., Friedman, E. S., Thompson, W. S., & Thase, M. E. (2011). Remission prognosis for cognitive therapy for recurrent depression using the pupil: Utility and neural correlates. *Biological Psychiatry, 69*(8), 726–733.

Siegle, G. J., Thompson, W. K., Collier, A., Berman, S. R., Feldmiller, J., Thase, M. E., & Friedman, E. S. (2012). Toward clinically useful neuroimaging in depression treatment: Prognostic utility of subgenual cingulate activity for determining depression outcome in cognitive therapy across studies, scanners, and patient characteristics. *Archives of General Psychiatry, 69*(9), 913–924.

Society for Psychophysiological Research (SPR). (2012). Society for Psychophysiological Research guidelines papers. Retrieved 9/20/2014 from https://www.sprweb.org/journal/index.cfm

Soltystik, D., & Rajan, S. (2014). Research project: Functional magnetic resonance imaging. Retrieved 9/20/2014 from http://www.fda.gov/AboutFDA/CentersOffices/OfficeofMedicalProductsandTobacco/CDRH/CDRHOffices/ucm300723.htm

Thase, M. E., & Rush, A. J. (1997). When at first you don't succeed: Sequential strategies for antidepressant nonresponders. *Journal of Clinical Psychiatry, 58*(Suppl 13), 23–29.

Van Essen, D. C., Smith, S. M., Barch, D. M., Behrens, T. E., Yacoub, E., & Ugurbil, K. (2013). The WU-Minn Human connectoe project: An overview. *NeuroImage, 80*, 62–79.

Vul, E., Harris, C., Winkielman, P., & Pashler, H. (2009). Puzzlingly high correlations in fMRI studies of emotion, personality, and social cognition. *Perspectives on Psychological Science, 4*(3), 274–290.

Wright, C. I., Fischer, H., Whalen, P. J., McInerney, S. C., Shin, L. M., & Rauch, S. L. (2001). Differential prefrontal cortex and amygdala habituation to repeatedly presented emotional stimuli. *Neuroreport, 12*(2), 379–383.

Young, K. D., Zotev, V., Phillips, R., Misaki, M., Yuan, H., Drevets, W. C., & Bodurka, J. (2014). Real-time fMRI neurofeedback training of amygdala activity in patients with major depressive disorder. *PLoS ONE, 9*(2), e88785.

Zalachoras, I., Houtman, R., Atucha, E., Devos, R., Tijssen, A. M., Hu, P., ... & Meijer, O. C. (2013). Differential targeting of brain stress circuits with a selective glucocorticoid receptor modulator. *Procedings of the National Academy of Sciences USA, 110*(19), 7910–7915.

Zimmerman, M., Coryell, W. H., & Black, D. W. (1990). Variability in the application of contemporary diagnostic criteria: Endogenous depression as an example. *American Journal of Psychiatry, 147*(9), 1173–1179.

Zotev, V., Phillips, R., Young, K. D., Drevets, W. C., & Bodurka, J. (2013). Prefrontal control of the amygdala during real-time fMRI neurofeedback training of emotion regulation. *PLoS ONE, 8*(11), e79184.

INDEX

Printed by PGSTL